Poverty and Politics

POVERTY and POLITICS
The Urban Poor in Brazil, 1870-1920

June E. Hahner

University of New Mexico Press
Albuquerque

Florida Gulf Coast University

Library of Congress Cataloging-in-Publication Data

Hahner, June Edith, 1940–
  Poverty and politics.

  Bibliography: p.
  Includes index.
    1. Urban poor—Brazil—History.   2. Urbanization—
Brazil—History.   3. Laboring and laboring classes—
Brazil—Political activity—History.   4. Brazil—Social
conditions.   5. Brazil—Politics and government—
1822–   I. Title.
HC190.P6H34   1986   305.5′69′0981   86-1258
ISBN 0-8263-0878-3

For those who care

Contents

TABLES

Illustrations

Maps

Preface

For years, historians of Latin America neglected the impoverished sectors of society. At best, general histories of countries such as Brazil treated poor people as undifferentiated masses of population, ignoring the specificity of their lives.[1] Before the 1960s, most Latin American history dealt predominantly with elites and with the transmission and exercise of power. Only a few, relatively isolated individuals such as Robert Alexander devoted their attention to organized labor.[2] But by the early 1980s, following a series of military coups d'etat which frequently inflicted brutal repression on organized labor, scholarly interest in the Latin American urban working class was apparent.[3] Latin Americanists in the United States moved away from liberal developmentalist assumptions, demonstrating a greater variety of ideological positions. Like the "new" social history, the resurgence of Marxist thought in the United States fostered interest in the history of the working class in general. Western European specialists on Latin America emphasized class analysis as the key to understanding the region, as did the majority of social scientists trained within Latin America in recent decades. Latin America labor history, however, remained far less broadly conceived than that of the United States or Europe, and was still largely limited to organized labor.

In the United States, the "new" social history and the "new" labor history display a multiplicity of aims and methods.[4] Some social historians have embraced the analytic approaches of contemporary social theorists while others favor quantitative methods or practice critical democratic scholarship. They benefitted from the methodologies and concerns of English labor historians, especially E. P. Thompson, and the approach of the *Annalistes*, who stressed the prime structural features of social, technological, and cultural life within a specific geographic environment.[5]

Under the guiding influence of the English labor historians and the new social history, labor history in the United States became a history of workers, not just of their institutions. For over half a century the followers of John R. Commons and the so-called Wisconsin school of labor history had defined their field as the study of trade unionism and collective bargaining. Only after World War II, when more people with working-class and immigrant backgrounds entered the historical profession in the United States, did labor history concentrate on working-class culture. Historians such as Herbert Gutman drew attention away from unions and strikes to the communities where workers lived and fought.[6] Generally employing a pragmatic, empiricist approach, they tended to focus on the details of existence and people's perceptions of them. Close, local study of workers came to characterize much of the research in U. S. labor history. However, this narrow research focus, together with an acute sense of the complexity and variety of the working-class experience, militated against the construction of a new framework or obvious synthesis to replace that of institutional history.

Given the general underdevelopment of both monographic and synthetic studies of Latin American workers, we cannot expect the same type of full-scale revisionist reaction to the concentration on trade unions and labor leadership as occurred in U. S. labor history. We lack sufficient research on unions and legal structures, not just on workers' lives. Many sources of information on unionized workers, such as syndicate or party archives, labor newspapers, or personal documents, have been lost or destroyed; others never existed. Unlike the French police, whose detailed records of strikes proved invaluable for researchers such as Charles Tilly and Edward Shorter, police in Latin American countries rarely kept any systematic accounts in the nineteenth or early twentieth centuries.[7] Sources on the large majority of the labor force, those who never joined unions, are even harder to locate. Scholars seeking to write a history of the inarticulate in Latin America lack materials available elsewhere. Census schedules, the central statistical resource for research on workers in nineteenth-century United States, simply do not exist for much of Latin America. Then there is the further difficulty of finding satisfactory analytical concepts for the "new" labor history. Different modes of comprehension—quantitative, conceptual, or narrative—always have different strengths and weaknesses. Quantification, for example, achieves incontestable interpretive conclusions only in restricted areas of research, those dealing with established institutional systems, clearly defined rules of behavior, or a small number of discrete variables, as in the case of legislative voting. And such institutions can be difficult to find amid the complex reality of Latin America.

No single approach to the study of Latin America workers currently predominates. In fact, a sharp debate over competing conceptual frameworks and historical methodologies is underway, as seen in the spirited exchange in the *Latin American Research Review* between Eugene F. Sofer, on the one hand, and Kenneth Paul Erickson, Patrick V. Peppe, and Hobart A. Spalding, Jr., on the other.[8] Sofer advocates the study of working people from the bottom up while the others focus on the larger economic and political constructs in which that history occurs. Historians like Thomas E. Skidmore seek not only to situate Latin American labor history in a comparative regional context, but also to place it in the broad flow of economic, political, and institutional history.[9]

Since so much must be done, a pluralistic approach to the study of Latin America's working people is in order. This includes the use of narratives, presenting identifiable actors in a distinct spatial-temporal setting and telling the story from the perspective of those historical actors. But it is questionable whether history "with the politics left out," as social history was once defined, is valid for Latin America. We all know that theoretical interpretations can be very fragile when they lack the underpinnings of evidence and solid research and that a too-precipitious rush to grand generalizations must be avoided when investigating this complex, diverse, deeply stratified region.

This study examines the urban laboring poor in Brazil and their struggle to survive during a period of rapid economic change. It focuses on workers' lives and activities and on their exploitation and manipulation by others during a crucial period extending from the 1870s, when the imperial cities were at their peak, until 1920, when the incipient labor movement was severely repressed, following a wave of strikes and outbreaks.

Rather than merely investigate syndicalist organization, sectarian debate, or labor leadership, it is necessary to examine the concrete and complex realities of Brazilian workers' lives: the precise dimensions of their poverty, the specific abuses which most concerned them, and the ways in which they demonstrated their distress. The eight chapters of this book assess the differential treatment and position of male and female workers, the gap between skilled and unskilled labor, the preoccupations of the lower classes, the impact of immigration and internal migration on labor supply, the quality of urban housing, and the character and significance of urban radicalism, urban upheavals, and other forms of social protest during this crucial period.

This study concentrates on the urban laboring poor in Rio de Janeiro, the nation's capital and largest city from the late eighteenth until the midtwentieth century, and the center of Brazil's cultural, economic, and intellectual life. Rio provided the nation with its prime political arena and the matrix for major attempts at social and political change in the empire and early republic. Yet, unlike São Paulo, the most active center of social science research in Brazil, Rio remains one of the least studied among major Brazilian cities.

No analysis of the neglected impoverished elements in Brazil and their struggle for survival can ignore the relationship between elites and workers. This book examines the nature of the imperial and early republican political systems, the exclusion of the lower classes from the decision-making process, the impact of trends in the economy, particularly inflation, prevailing elite conceptions of labor relations, and, especially, the reaction of ruling elites to any challenge to their power and position. In late nineteenth-century Brazil, a variety of radical movements and radical groups emerged in the urban areas. Nationalists and nativists, as well as anarchists and socialists, challenged existing political and economic structures. Shrewd politicians sought to co-opt a fledgling labor movement, while the dominant elites attempted to supress lower-class unrest. Yet Brazil's urban poor were not mere passive recipients of elite or employer decisions, victims of the politics of repression and manipulation. They participated actively in shaping their own destinies.

The force and continuity of Brazilian conservatism has given that country's history an undramatic, even monotonous appearance. While the history of some Latin American nations, such as Mexico, is often depicted as a series of violent upheavals against entrenched conservatism, Brazil's past is not written in terms of such wars and revolutions, ideological conflicts, or mass movements. Many scholars view Brazil's dominant elites as more flexible and restrained than those of other countries, knowing when and where to yield to pressure for change. However, beneath the surface of Brazilian governmental continuity, we find confused and tangled sets of frustrated aspirations and hidden conflicts. Patterns prove more complex and events less peaceful than they first appear. Popular protests, like individual and unstructured violence, erupted in the cities, not just in the backlands of Brazil. When these struggles are carefully examined, the results of such investigations enable us to question the traditional view of much of Brazilian history.

Changes in Brazilian orthography can cause confusion. Throughout this book, names or words in Portuguese in the text will be given in the modern spelling, but in the footnotes and bibliography authors' names and titles of works will be cited in the original orthography.

Prices and wages are given in Brazilian *milreis* unless otherwise stated. The *milreis*, the standard currency in Brazil until 1942, was divided into a thousand *reis*. The "$" sign separated the *milreis* and the *reis* so that, for example, two *milreis* and 500 *reis* would be written 2$500.

The research on which this book is based was conducted in Brazil during several periods in the 1970s ranging in length from two months to a year. I am profoundly grateful for the financial support given by the National Endowment for the Humanities, the American Philosophical Society, the Research Foundation of the State University of New York, and the Organization of American States.

A work of history, dependent on written materials, derives from archives, libraries, and private collections. I wish to express special thanks to the directors and staff of the Arquivo Nacional, the Instituto Histórico e Geográfico Brasileiro, the Arquivo Geral da Cidade do Rio de Janeiro, the Casa de Rui Barbosa, the Museu Imperial, the Arquivo do Estado de São Paulo, the Arquivo Histórico do Ministério das Relações Exteriores, and the Arquivo do Ministério dos Negócios Estrangeiros in Lisbon, and in particular to Américo Jacobina Lacombe, José Gabriel da Costa Pinto, Isabel Morais, Maria Luiza Fernandez de Carvalho, Marta Gonçalves, José Luiz Werneck da Silva, and Zilda Galhardo de Araujo. I am most appreciative to Afonso Arinos de Melo Franco, the late Ranulfo Bocaiúva Cunha, Roberto Piragibe da Fonseca, the late Rudolfo de Freitas, the late Francisco Glycério Neto, Antônio de Freitas, Clovis Glycério de Freitas, General Humberto Peregrino, and José Leite Cordeiro, for facilitating access to or making available private papers.

Dauril Alden gave generously of his time and talents, focusing his unparalleled critical intelligence on this manuscript and greatly improving it. Roderick J. Barman kindly read much of the manuscript and offered valuable suggestions. The patience and generosity of my mother, Edith Hahner, during the writing of this manuscript, deserve special recognition.

The support and understanding shown by one's colleagues and associates extend beyond specific acts of kindness or generosity and can be crucial during all stages of any research project but especially one so long in progress. In Brazil I have been very fortunate, and my appreciation and gratitude to all who aided me go far beyond words and far beyond this project. I am particularly indebted to Helena Lewin, Eulália Maria Lahmeyer Lobo, Nícia Villela Luz, Myriam Ellis, Suely Robles Reis de Queiroz, Edgard Carone, Azis Simão, José Honório Rodrigues, and José Sebastião Witter. To them and all the others I owe much, and this book is but a token repayment of such an immense debt.

Albany, New York   June E. Hahner
October 1984

1 / The Evolving Cities of Imperial Brazil

In 1872, the date of Brazil's first national census, the nation's leading cities lay scattered along the coast, each with its separate hinterland, as in the days of Portuguese rule. Far larger in size and population than in the colonial period, even before mass European immigration began in the 1880s, the cities of imperial Brazil impressed foreign travelers with their colorful street life, massive public buildings, and increasing public services. Although some travelers complained of dirty streets and noxious odors, they rarely heeded the living conditions of the poor, the vast majority of the urban populace, even in their observations of Rio de Janeiro, the national capital and largest city of all. The urban changes and improvements visitors described proceeded for the benefit of the elite, who dominated the cities as they did the nation.

The Portuguese had founded all but two of their major settlements along the extensive coastline, based on the need to defend its broad expanse and the desire to exploit the land. Even the location of Piratininga, the future São Paulo, the only major inland center until the eighteenth century, seems to have been guided in part by concern for defense and by the desire to find a place insulated against outside influence. The commercial and military functions of the early coastal cities, little more than small fortified towns on hills, were paramount.[1]

Portugal did not begin permanent colonization of the Brazilian coast

1

until after 1530, due largely to concentration on the East Indian spice trade. But with the rise and spread of sugarcane cultivation and its complementary industries on the northeastern coast in the midsixteenth century, the young colony found its basis of wealth; Salvador, established as the capital in 1549, and Pernambuco became the richest centers of the Portuguese empire in the Americas. During the period of Dutch control of Pernambuco from 1630 to 1654, Brazilian sugar gained easier, more direct access to the markets of northern Europe and to needed credit facilities. In the 1640s, thanks largely to the presence and activity of Prince Mauritz of Nassau, Recife was transformed into the active and elegant urban hub of the United Provinces' richest, but temporary colony. At the time of the expulsion of the Dutch in 1654, Recife had some 8,000 inhabitants and 2,000 houses.[2]

While Caribbean colonies of northern European countries replaced Brazil as the world's major sugar supplier by the end of the seventeenth century, sugar, raised mainly on large plantations worked by African slaves, continued to be the major export of Brazil's Northeast. Urban centers such as Salvador and Recife, recipients of increased numbers of Portuguese immigrants in the late seventeenth century, provided the sugar planters with needed credit, and conflicts between merchants and planters frequently arose. Though nominally the capital of the colony, Salvador exercised no effective control over the other major urban centers of Brazil, each of which maintained independent maritime communications with the metropolis.

Only São Paulo de Piratininga, a collection of thatched, mostly wattle-and-daub structures sheltering some one hundred and fifty white and mixed-blood households in 1600[3] and located on the plateau of the center south, looked inland, not to the Atlantic and to trade with Europe, for possible sources of wealth. The other cities clung to the coast. Roads rather than shipping routes formed the *Paulistas'* line of advance westward. São Paulo remained a small, poor city, although its people founded various other towns, often without planning or official sanction, and set in motion the eighteenth-century gold boom which in turn led to a relative expansion of urban life.

New cities appeared in inland Minas Gerais, and the eighteenth century, the century of gold, witnessed an artistic and literary outpouring in this previously empty region of central Brazil. Vila Rica de Ouro Prêto served as the headquarters of the mineowners as well as the seat of administration. With its gold-embellished churches, solid government buildings, graceful fountains, and two-story tile-roofed houses set on steep streets winding up and down hill and some 30,000 inhabitants in the mideighteenth century, Vila Rica may have rivaled Salvador in afflu-

MAP 1   Principal Cities of Brazil

3

ence, though not in population. Not only did Minas attract the largest migrations of the whole colonial period, but the area's demand for labor and supplies also led to the establishment of the first important set of internal transportation routes among the colony's regions. Mule trains from Salvador to the north and São Paulo to the south, and later from Rio de Janeiro to the east, climbed over the mountains into Minas. The mining zone then moved into Brazil's far west, Mato Grosso, and Goiás, leading to the establishment of additional cities, while settlements in the far south expanded, due to Portuguese fears of increasing Spanish activities in the Río de la Plata region as well as to the trade in mules and cattle for Minas Gerais. The population growth of the coastal cities failed to keep pace with the overall expansion of the colony at this time.

During the gold boom in Minas Gerais, Rio de Janeiro became the major center exporting this mineral wealth, and the city facilitated communications and the exchange of goods between the mines and the outside world, thereby extending its own influence over a larger region. The vast expansion in wealth and population of southern Brazil during the eighteenth century, combined with the Spanish threat in the far south, led to the transference of the capital of the Portuguese empire in the Americas from Salvador to Rio in 1763.

In the late eighteenth century both Salvador and Rio de Janeiro could boast of imposing civil and religious architecture. Likewise, both reflected the physical constraints of their majestic settings. Situated on the ample Bay of All the Saints, Salvador stood on two levels. The commercial lower city, pressed between the bay and a sharp escarpment, contained warehouses, docks, and business houses, as well as the dwellings of merchants and the lower classes; the upper city, spread along the bluff overlooking the bay, displayed government buildings, the homes of the wealthy, and sumptuous religious edifices. Steep, ill-paved paths connected the two parts of this venerable city of narrow, winding streets and buildings crowded one upon the other. The city's population numbered some fifty thousand at the time the seat of royal government passed from Salvador to its economic rival, Rio de Janeiro.[4] Located on the spectacular Bay of Guanabara and locked between bay and mountains, Rio also had imposing government and religious buildings, some set on small hills overlooking the bay, as well as two- and three-story homes for the wealthy. Where the land was flat, streets intersected each other at right angles, but the terrain frequently permitted only narrow, crooked passageways. Rio's population would not reach fifty thousand until the turn of the nineteenth century.

With the decline in the late eighteenth century of the gold production which had provided the basis for the expansion of urban life during that century, Brazil's economy became depressed and more heavily agricultural. For several decades São Luís de Maranhão served as a major cotton exporter, as did Recife, and Belém exported cacao, while Salvador traded tobacco and hides as well as sugar. In the southern-most captaincy of Rio Grande do Sul, Pôrto Alegre concentrated on wheat, and the town of Rio Grande developed a dried beef (*charque*) industry. Through the first half of the nineteenth century, most of the towns of this large but sparsely populated nation remained small, sleepy places, with muddy streets frequented by pack mules, pigs, and chickens, although they also served as social, religious, and market centers for surrounding areas.

The arrival of the royal Portuguese family in Rio de Janeiro in 1808, retreating before the Napoleonic invasion of the metropolis, and the opening of the port to foreign commerce accelerated the development of the city and increased ties with Europe. João VI not only installed the royal court in Rio, but he also created the royal press, a public library, medical and military schools, and a botanical garden, introduced European cultural missions, and oversaw urban improvements such as the paving of additional streets, the filling in of more land for construction, and the melioration of the water supply, all of which contributed to an intensification of the urban life of the city. The capital evolved far more rapidly than the countryside, and the differences and disparities between the two increased, for the changes wrought directly and indirectly by the arrival of the royal court were overwhelmingly concentrated in the urban areas, primarily Rio. For thirteen years this city served as the seat of an empire extending far beyond the Americas. Rio's population, over sixty thousand in 1808, doubled by 1822, surpassing that of Salvador, with Recife in third place.[5]

Independence from Portugal in 1822 only confirmed Brazil's export dependency as well as the predominance of Rio de Janeiro as the nation's leading commercial center and principal city of export. By 1830, coffee earned more foreign exchange than any other export, and it continued to lengthen its lead. The production and exportation of coffee, a luxury item millions of people in the United States and Europe could afford, would dominate Brazil's economic life for decades.

By the 1850s and 1860s, the rising coffee exports of south-central Brazil overshadowed the relatively inefficient sugar cultivation and processing in the Northeast struggling to meet the competition of European beet sugar. The balance of income and population shifted more decisively to the south. The principal coffee growing provinces of Rio de Janeiro, São Paulo, and Minas Gerais drained slaves from the Northeast following the end of the international slave trade in 1850 and attracted increasing quantities of European immigrants and capital after 1880. The cities of Rio de Janeiro and then São Paulo served as centers of coffee exportation and benefitted financially and politically, as well as in size and population, from the growing coffee economy.[6]

Railroad construction began in the 1850s, largely to aid the export trade. Until then, Brazil's inland transportation basically consisted of mule trains and oxcarts, with horse-drawn vehicles and paved roads mostly limited to urban areas and their surroundings. The new railroads, infused with foreign capital, quickly extended into the coffee regions, first the Paraíba Valley, then reaching its peak productivity, and soon afterwards São Paulo. Railroads stretched out from Rio de Janeiro and from São Paulo; fan-shaped networks of railroad lines brought coffee into São Paulo and down to its port of Santos. Short lines from Recife and Salvador penetrated the sugar districts. The growth of railway lines intensified the process of concentration of activities in major cities at the expense of minor ones and fostered dependence on exports. By the end of the nineteenth century, Rio and São Paulo controlled the commercial activity of a vast surrounding area through the railroads.[7]

Exports provided funds for beautification and for improvement of municipal services in Brazil's major cities. Planters and their families increasingly deserted the somnolent rural towns for the greater excitement and amenities of urban life. Due to improvements in communication and transportation, many landless rural workers and townsmen living hard lives in weakly organized communities in the interior also became aware of the attractions of city life and migrated to the cities. Urban centers likewise provided shelter for some runaway and former slaves. During the late empire, as throughout the colonial period, the Brazilian economy depended on a slave labor system which, however, was coming under increasing criticism, especially in the cities, following the end of the Paraguayan War in 1870.

The enhancement of the cities, and seats of power, proceeded rapidly in the third quarter of the nineteenth century. By the 1870s, Brazil's major cities had shed many of their colonial airs and could boast improvements in public transportation, lighting, and water supply, as well as numerous paved streets, more elegant public buildings, and ever-increasing populations.

Belém, the only northern Brazilian city of consequence during the empire, lay at the mouth of the immense Amazon basin, some ninety miles up the Pará River from the Atlantic, in the most underdeveloped region of Brazil. Yet in 1872, Belém claimed a population of 62,000 (Table 1). Approached from the river, Belém presented the visitor with a row of white and yellow washed warehouses along the water front, a large stone, twin towered custom house, formerly a convent, and the square

Table 1. Population of Brazil and Its Principal Cities, 1872–1920

	Brazil	Rio de Janeiro	São Paulo	Salvador	Recife	Belém	Pôrto Alegre
	(Percentages, given in parentheses, are relative to the 1872 populations.)						
1872	10,112,061	274,972	31,385	129,109	116,671	61,997	43,998
	(100)	(100)	(100)	(100)	(100)	(100)	(100)
1890	14,333,915	522,651	64,934	174,412	111,556[a]	50,064[a]	52,421
	(142)	(190)	(207)	(135)	(96)	(81)	(119)
1900	17,318,556	811,443[b]	239,820	205,813	113,106	96,560	73,674
	(171)	(295)	(764)	(159)	(97)	(156)	(167)
1920	30,635,605	1,157,873	579,093	283,422	238,843	236,402	179,263
	(303)	(419)	(1,845)	(216)	(205)	(381)	(407)

Adapted from: Brazil, Directoria Geral de Estatística, *Recenseamento do Brazil realizado em 1 de setembro de 1920*, *iv*, 1[a], x. All data are for *municípios*. Rio's population is that of the former Município Neutro, then the Federal District.
[a]The 1890 results for Recife and Belém are generally considered erroneous and extremely low.
[b]The 1900 census results for Rio were set aside and another census conducted in 1906, with the results given here.

towers of several churches—the whole city hemmed in by tropical vege-
tation and bathed in blazing sunshine. Its main streets, especially the
Rua da Imperatriz, home of the largest wholesale houses and lined with
two- and three-story buildings, were broad and paved. In the 1870s, the
city had gas lights and mule-drawn street cars, but wells served as the
only source of water, which cartmen still hawked about the city. Belém
served as outlet for the Amazonian rubber trade, a role it would continue to play well into the twentieth century.[8]

To the south, on the hump of Brazil, Recife dominated the Northeast and a network of smaller cities. Founded in the 1530s as a seaport
for the neighboring administrative center of Olinda, Recife had evolved
principally as a commercial center, exporting sugar to Europe. By 1872,
its population officially stood at 117,000 (Table 1), and it could claim
some of Brazil's tallest buildings, up to four and five stories, increasing
numbers of paved streets, gas lamps, and water pipes, and one of the
country's first animal-drawn streetcar services, inaugurated in September 1870. By March 1872, the British-owned Pernambuco Street Railway Company, with its twenty closed and five open cars, employed two
hundred and fifty mules and an equal number of men.[9]

Recife had spread out from a low sandy peninsula onto several is-
lands and then across to the mainland. Bridges connected the older portion of Recife, the commercial center with its narrow, crooked streets
and high buildings, to the new city with wide, straight streets and more
modern houses. Recife grew steadily throughout the nineteenth century
as migrants arrived from the interior as well as from overseas. Not only
did the industrialization of sugar hasten the exodus of rural workers to
the cities, but in the Northeast natural catastrophies temporarily swelled
urban populations and sometimes left permanent residue. The intense
suffering from the terrible drought of 1877–1880 in Ceará and adjacent
portions of the *sertão* drove most of the survivors to the coastal cities,
from which many people eventually were dispatched to the Amazon region or returned home to the interior.[10]

Like Recife to its north, Salvador remained dependent on sugar.
Brazil's first capital, Salvador had ranked first in size and commercial
wealth until just before independence. In 1872, with its 129,000 inhabitants (Table 1), it stood second only to Rio de Janeiro. Seen from the
immense Bay of All the Saints, Salvador displayed a crowded skyline of
white houses, forts, churches, hospitals, and government buildings gleam-
ing in the fierce sun. Visitors found it the most picturesque of Brazilian
cities, exuding an air of antiquity and repose, with its colonial buildings
lining narrow, winding streets filled with gaily costumed blacks. However, in the 1870s, not only did Salvador acquire animal traction street-

cars and additional paved streets connecting sections of the city, but the provincial government also granted concessions for the construction of hydraulic elevators linking the lower and upper cities. Soon the sedan chairs used by foreign travelers and the local elite alike to make that steep climb would begin to disappear. [11]

In contrast to the cities of northern and northeastern Brazil, those of the south demonstrated greater dynamism and growth in the late nineteenth century. In 1872, the population of Pôrto Alegre, at the country's southern extremity, numbered scarcely 44,000 (Table 1), but the city's location at the confluence of river and maritime navigation and the intersection of diverse economic regions promised future growth. Before the close of the century, Pôrto Alegre would consolidate its regional dominance, outdistancing Rio Grande, port of the southern cattle zone of the province of Rio Grande do Sul. Founded in 1740 during the wars between Spain and Portugal for domination of the Río de la Plata area, Pôrto Alegre became the commercial center for the agricultural regions of the central and northern parts of the province. Throughout the nineteenth century, this area, settled by German and then Italian colonists, remained distinct and separate from the pastoral society in the south served by Rio Grande. From 1820 to 1860, Pôrto Alegre vegetated, while *charque*, dried meat, replaced wheat as the province's chief export, and economic leadership passed to Rio Grande. Then Pôrto Alegre recuperated, with increases in European colonization and exports of food products for the national market, while the southern cattle industry stagnated, and economic hegemony of the province passed from south to north. Like larger Brazilian cities, Pôrto Alegre received such urban improvements as animal drawn streetcars and gas illumination in the early 1870s. Foreigners found the city, with its attractive public buildings, substantial homes, and numerous squares, one of the most agreeable in Brazil. Pôrto Alegre's most rapid expansion came after 1889 and the end of the empire, when the city also surpassed Rio Grande in industry. [12]

The rise to prominence and power of São Paulo, well situated on the central plateau near the crest of the steep Serra do Mar at the intersection of road and river communications, was the most rapid of all. Smaller than Pôrto Alegre in 1872, the population of São Paulo grew from 31,000 to 240,000 by the end of the century, when it outnumbered all Brazilian cities except Rio de Janeiro (Table 1). For three centuries São Paulo had served as a point of passage for products coming from the interior and imports arriving from Santos on the coast. Although the Brazilian economy was comprised of a big subsistence sector and only a small external market sector, São Paulo's geographic location permitted its conversion into a crossroads of the small existing currents of trade. Then came coffee, and coffee fueled São Paulo's growth. The deepening penetration of coffee into the province of São Paulo in the 1850s and 1860s was reflected in the city's expansion of the 1870s, as railroads based in the city reached into new coffee regions of the province.

In both appearance and substance, São Paulo changed. Animaldrawn streetcars and gas lamps arrived in 1872. Piped water replaced public fountains. Commercial life quickened. No longer would observers see the life of the city as focused on the Law School, created in 1828. Nor would the city be confined to a "triangle" of some dozen streets bounded by the Carmelite, Benedictine, and Franciscan monasteries set between two small streams on an elevation and encircled by a plain covered with woods, fields, and country estates. In the nineteenth century the city broke forth from its old center and expanded in all directions, though unevenly, following the contours of the land, and swallowing many of the former country estates. By the end of the empire, the city formed an irregular rectangle, two miles or less on each side, with several attached districts and outlying nuclei of population. Austere colonial homes turned into copies of elegant European dwellings, as coffee *fazendeiros* erected impressive urban residences. The city would become theirs, not the students'. João Teodoro Xavier, president of the province of São Paulo from 1872 to 1875, spent an amount equal to nearly half the annual provincial budget beautifying and embellishing the capital. São Paulo was being transformed long before coffee planting started attracting heavy European immigration in the mid-1880s, an influx which in turn would contribute to a more spectacular population growth, and also provide the market and labor for industrialization.[13]

Like São Paulo, the imperial capital of Rio de Janeiro served as a commercial, financial, administrative, and transportation center based on the cultivation and exportation of coffee and the importation and distribution of both necessities and luxury items, including the latest European fads and notions. The seat of national power and the country's economic, cultural, and intellectual leader, Rio had well over a quarter of a million inhabitants by 1872, making it the largest city in South America.[14]

Strong trade ties linked the capital to its hinterland in the province of Rio de Janeiro and the southern part of Minas Gerais. Portugal provided the capital with salt, wine, olive oil, and dried cod, and Brazil's southern-most province of Rio Grande do Sul together with the Río de la Plata region supplied dried beef. However, such basic foodstuffs as beans, manioc flour, corn, bacon, meat, and sugar arrived by ship from the small ports along the coast of Rio de Janeiro Province or by mule caravan from southern Minas Gerais. In the eighteenth century, southern Minas Gerais supplied the gold mining region with cattle, mules, and foodstuffs, but the mining crisis forced the area to seek markets elsewhere. During the early nineteenth century, the regional economy was reorganized and directed toward the slowly growing Rio market. New or repaired roads linking the capital with southern Minas served as effective agents of population for the area as well as fostering land concentration. The roads also facilitated migration to the capital from the old mining zones. As their commercial activities expanded, landowners from southern Minas increased their political influence within the province and, more slowly, at the imperial court.[15]

Rio's hinterland in southern Minas Gerais and Rio de Janeiro Province not only supplied the capital with most of the foodstuffs needed for local consumption and with migrants from all social classes, but also produced the nation's principal export, coffee. During the nineteenth century, Brazilian financial prosperity depended primarily upon the export of that cash commodity, and Rio de Janeiro served as the center for the sale, export, and financing of coffee in Brazil. Coffee spread into the Paraíba River Valley, nestled between the mountains of southern Minas Gerais and the long, rolling coastal escarpment, in the 1830s. Climatic and topological conditions in that upland river valley stretching from eastern São Paulo across the entire length of Rio de Janeiro Province and the southern section of Minas Gerais to the edge of Espírito Santo permitted the temperamental trees to flourish. By mule train and then by railroad, coffee flowed into the port of Rio de Janeiro, following paths traced by gold exports from Minas Gerais in the eighteenth century and foodstuffs in the early nineteenth century. A vigorous import and export trade brought growth to Rio, and solidified its position as the nation's economic and political capital. As coffee production in the Paraíba Valley reached its peak in the midnineteenth century, planters, merchants, and bankers tended to coalesce into a regional elite committed to the continued prosperity of the export economy. Rio de Janeiro served as their political, social, economic, and cultural center, and became the prime recipient of the costly urban improvements that the Brazilian elite adored and foreign visitors admired.[16]

After first exclaiming over the natural beauties of "glorious," "splendid" Guanabara Bay, foreign travelers then inspected downtown Rio de Janeiro, the old colonial central city, where only the red-tiled roofs struck them as "essentially tropical."[17] In the 1870s, the Primeiro de Março (First of March) was the city's principal artery. Once called the Rua Direita (Straight Street), running the length of the colonial city, from the Morro do Castelo, site of the oldest settlement, to São Bento hill, it paralleled the waterfront where the visitors had landed. Approximately midway along this wide street, filled with a "noisy multitude"[18] and lined with wholesale merchants' establishments, banks, warehouses, offices, three- and four-story houses, and various public buildings, such as the Customshouse, Exchange, and Post Office, the visitor came to the Largo do Paço, with the government palace and the church and convent of Carmo. One of the major public fountains functioned in this square since colonial times.

Many foreigners preferred to stroll along fashionable Ouvidor Street, one of the transversals of the Primeiro de Março, lined with the city's best shops, including numerous jewelry stores. But even here some visitors experienced dirt and discomfort. In this older section of Rio they found the sidewalks "scarcely wide enough for two to go abreast" and they fled from coffee and ships' cargos being drawn through the streets "at reckless speed" on mule-drawn wagons "with the yelling of excited drivers." During a heavy shower Ouvidor Street became impassible for pedestrians, unless a street porter fixed "a temporary foot-bridge." Otherwise, "a too confident jumper" could "land in the water, much to the amusement of the bystanders."[19] While foreigners acquainted with the city a decade or two earlier noted improvements in drainage, sewerage, and lighting, others associated faulty sanitation with feared diseases.[20]

Despite some visitors' complaints, Rio's boosters could cite a series of municipal improvements in the third quarter of the nineteenth century. Public gas lighting first appeared in Rio in 1854, replacing fish oil on a few downtown streets. By the 1870s even the most critical foreigners agreed that the city was well lighted and its main thoroughfares well paved, although their appraisals of the sewer system, begun in 1862, differed. The 1860s also witnessed the planting of trees on city streets and the improvement of public gardens and squares. Communications and transportation advanced. The telegraph arrived in 1854, and submarine cable services linked north to south in 1873 and Brazil to Europe the following year. In 1856 the omnibus, a large carriage driven over fixed routes on a rough schedule, made its appearance, followed in 1868 by the *bondes*, mule-drawn cars on rails. New railroads edged northward from Rio, beginning with the Estrada de Ferro Dom Pedro Segundo, later called the Central do Brasil, whose first section was completed in 1858. These improvements in urban transportation accelerated Rio's growth, both in physical area and in population size.[21]

In 1763, when Rio de Janeiro became Brazil's capital, the compact city resembled a rough rectangle, three miles in compass and some dozen blocks long and half a dozen wide. The presence of buildings along the principal roads running south and west indicated the direction of future city growth. Strands of streets soon stretched out from the colonial nu-

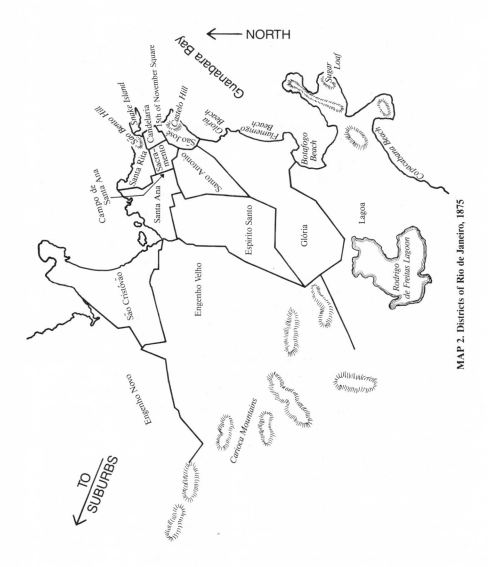

MAP 2. Districts of Rio de Janeiro, 1875

← NORTH

Guanabara Bay

Sugar Loaf

Snake Island
São Bento Hill
Santa Rita
Candelaria
5th of November Square
Castelo Hill
São José
Glória Beach
Flamengo Beach
Campo de Santa Ana
Sacra-mento
Santa Ana
Santo Antonio
Botafogo Beach
Copacabana Beach

Espírito Santo

Glória

Lagoa

São Cristóvão
Engenho Velho
Rodrigo de Freitas Lagoon

Carioca Mountains

Engenho Novo

TO SUBURBS

13

cleus. Late eighteenth-century maps show the city had reached the Campo de Santa Ana to the west and Glória Beach to the south. While buildings also spread along the thin tract to the north between the hills and the sea, the major thrusts of urban growth would continue through the flat area to the west between the hills and along the narrow southern beaches next to the mountains. Landfills and drainage laid the basis for much of the expansion from colonial times onward. By the early nineteenth century the city grew past the Campo de Santa Ana and in the south soon reached Catete. As the century progressed, growth became far more rapid, and Rio sprawled outward, largely due to the mobility offered by collective transportation. The city continued westward, avoiding the hills; an 1850 map shows the districts of Tijuca and São Cristóvão, site of the imperial family's residence. At the same time, streets spread southward through Flamengo and up toward Cosme Velho; a string of buildings encircled Botafogo Bay and then advanced inland along one main road, followed by the construction of a network of streets and cross streets. By the 1870s, streets existed in Copacabana in the south and in Vila Isabel far to the west, leaving unoccupied areas in between. In 1808, Rio contained seventy-five streets, alleys, and squares; by 1870, these totaled 563.[22] By 1872, the city extended over four miles to the west and as far to the south, while more distant suburban nuclei of population followed railroad expansion further westward.[23]

Although rich and poor often lived in closer physical proximity in Brazil and other Latin American countries than in the United States, the new residential districts made possible by the improvements in urban mass transportation during the second half of the nineteenth century were more stratified by income and social level than the colonial and early nineteenth-century cities.[24] The new neighborhoods south of the old city center attracted wealthier Brazilians while the far more populous areas to the west housed a larger population of the urban poor. Residents of less desirable districts were more likely to suffer the disadvantages of urban development and early industrialization. The growing population of the port district of Saúde directly west of downtown Rio was subjected to noxious odors emitted by soap, candle, and tobacco factories. In a petition to the municipal government requesting removal of these factories to less crowded areas, residents complained that the rancid tallow used by the soap and candle factories made the "air so pestilent and unbearable that many times the neighborhood residents could not endure it even with their windows and doors closed."[25]

Rio's wealthier inhabitants were able to escape congested or unpleasant older districts. By the 1860s, perceptive American Protestant missionaries observed Rio's merchants abandoning residences above their downtown business establishments for "picturesque suburbs" and evening rush hours.[26] Rather than continue to live in the closely packed buildings edging the streets of Rio's old, restricted, mixed commercial and residential center, the wealthy constructed impressive, separate houses "standing in delightful grounds" with "avenues of royal palms, and gorgeous flowering shrubs, and dark-tinted trees" in distant, newer neighborhoods. This "crown of gardens," as two visitors from the United States agreed, formed the "glory" of the "prettiest" districts, such as Botafogo.[27] According to a Portuguese political exile at the end of the century, the best and newest streetcars served these "aristocratic districts," running punctually along their wider streets with second-class cars "for Colored, barefoot people."[28] The well-to-do commuted comfortably "over very smoothly laid street rails" in ample "seats of polished Brazil wood or mahogany." By the early 1880s, a foreign traveler walking through the Ouvidor around ten o'clock in the morning would encounter "squads of businessmen, brokers, and clerks, who left from half an hour to an hour before on the street-cars," hurrying "with umbrella in hand, to their several places of business."[29]

Whether businessmen or French-oriented heirs to agricultural fortunes, wealthy Brazilians felt themselves far removed from the rest of society. Their housing, occupations, incomes, and even dress differed markedly from those of the poor. Despite the infusion of new ideas concerning progress, industry, and science in the second half of the nineteenth century, the traditional disdain for manual labor continued, as did the gulf between those who worked with their hands and those who did not.[30] Visitors from the United States and England who noted the pervasiveness of French fashions, literature, and philosophy among the elite found the strong class distinctions even more striking. An English newspaperman observing the "great regard" Brazilians paid "to distinction and rank," claimed that "perhaps in no other language are these so precisely determined."[31] As an American zoologist reported, the upper classes would "not soil their hands with tools" and "looked down upon" even skilled craftsmen as members "of an inferior class."[32]

Wealth brought privileges. The elite, with their family connections, controlled access to status and political power in Brazil. Distinctions between planter and urban merchant faded as commerce and agriculture coalesced during the late empire.[33] Education remained largely the prerogative of those entitled to its benefits by birth or position. According to the census of 1872, Brazil had a total population of 10,112,061, but only 1,012,097 free men, 550,981 free women, and 958 slave men and 445 slave women were able to read and write.[34] Social mobility proved difficult, perhaps in part as there was no established middle ground between the wealthy and the mass of the population.

Members of the civil and military bureaucracies, commercial workers, store and workshop owners, and professionals such as pharmacists comprised the principal components of the poorly defined, diverse Brazilian middle sectors.[35] Rio de Janeiro, the nation's commercial and governmental center, contained the largest collection of these urban elements in Brazil. There they played important roles in the abolitionist movement in the 1880s and in nativist agitation in the following decade, as we shall see in later chapters. But they only emerged as a politically significant group after 1920.

Rather than forming a distinct group which could claim the attention of nineteenth-century foreign travelers, the urban middle sectors proved heterogenous socially, culturally, ideologically, and economically. In fact, one of the most perspicacious foreign visitors, an American zoologist who traveled widely in Brazil in the 1870s, grouped together as the " 'society' stratum" what would later be termed the urban upper and middle classes. Those were the "people who, by birth, or education, or wealth, are able to retain a certain standing, which separates them from the mass of their countrymen." Far below them came the three other principal sectors of society: "the mechanics and small shop-keepers, the laborers and peasants, and the slaves."[36]

In a country like Brazil with a largely bifurcated class structure, the middle sectors occupied an uncertain position, with each sector divided from those below and above it.[37] Those members of the most prestigious liberal professions, medicine and law, who depended upon fixed wages or fees as a principal source of income, might be considered upper-middle class. But they were frequently the sons or impoverished relatives of large landowners, and they preferred to avoid social intimacy with petty bureaucrats, poorly paid primary-school teachers, bookkeepers, and shop clerks, who comprised what might be termed the lower-middle classes. These lower-middle class elements, in turn, felt superior to skilled workers, not to mention the large pool of menial workers.

Whether salaried or self-employed, the middle sectors aspired to gentility. The lower level of the middle sectors lacked the upper level's kinship ties and family connections which facilitated access to government employment, but they still attempted to emulate the upper classes, their life-style and appearance, whenever possible. Dressed in coat and tie, not workers' frayed or casual clothing, the men spent their shorter workdays in offices rather than in workshops, soiling neither their hands nor their clothing. Their economic and professional dependence on the governing elites reinforced the social and ideological bonds tying them to the upper classes. The middle classes did not really constitute the median in Brazilian society. A wide gap separated the urban poor, even skilled workers who in Europe might be considered an aristocracy of labor, from members of the Brazilian middle sectors, who had escaped the stigma of manual labor in a slavocrat society. The difference between physical and mental labor could not be overcome.

Unlike the elite, the urban poor of the 1870s possessed little class consciousness or solidarity. They formed no coherent or homogeneous whole. Occupations best differentiated elements of the lower strata of this basically preindustrial society and gave some more status than others, at least in their own eyes. Among these people, the principal division was that separating petty shopkeepers and skilled craftsmen from laborers dependent on their physical toil alone. As the American zoologist noted, the skilled laborers "work hard to keep themselves above the common laborers, whom they look down on; they never aspire to the magnificence of the privileged class, the educated ones, who look down on them, or rather ignore them, except as they must make use of their services."[38] Owning a cheap restaurant for workers or a kiosk selling coffee, liquor, cigarettes, and lottery tickets generally provided more security and income than peddling a small supply of fruit or brushes along the streets. Artisans and skilled craftsmen such as typographers not only displayed a sense of pride in their work, but were also more likely to be literate than were unskilled workers like cartmen, porters, dock workers, ambulatory vendors, domestic servants, laundresses, and day laborers. These occupations involved a more dependent employee status and such people had little training and owned few tools or equipment. Many lacked steady employment and, like porters, often just waited on street corners for jobs. Ranged below the unskilled workers with more or less steady employment were the underemployed and marginal people, such as shoeshine boys, beggars, and criminals, who lived in want and constant insecurity.

Legally separate from other urban workers yet performing many of the same jobs were the slaves. In 1872, slaves formed fifteen percent of Brazil's total population, comprising eighteen percent of the inhabitants of Rio de Janeiro, twelve percent of the city of São Paulo, thirteen percent in both Salvador and Recife, fourteen percent in Belém in the far north, and nineteen percent of the inhabitants of Pôrto Alegre in the far south.[39] Urban slaves ranged in employment from skilled craftsmen to day laborers, domestic servants, and prostitutes. While many domestic slaves performed only menial tasks, such as cleaning, carrying water, or kitchen work, others, better trained and more specialized, served as cooks, seamstresses, laundresses, nursemaids, or even housekeepers and virtual ladies-in-waiting to wealthy women. Among poorer free families, female slaves performed all household duties and often worked outside the home as well. Street vendors sometimes sold their wares during only part of the day, when not engaged in household work. Female slaves seemed to monopolize the marketing of fruits and vegetables and prepared foods like confectioneries, while male slaves sold meat and fish.[40] In Rio de Janeiro, thirty-five percent of the male slaves served as domestic servants, twenty percent as day laborers, and eleven percent as skilled workers; another thirteen percent toiled in agriculture. Domestic service remained the major occupation for female slaves, with females outnumbering males 14,184 to 8,658. Agriculture (2,488) trailed well behind, followed by dressmaking (1,384), a profession no male slaves followed (Table 3).

Whether slave or free, the majority of female urban workers in 1872 were domestic servants. In Rio they outnumbered seamstresses, the next most common occupation, 38,462 to 11,592. Domestic service, an overwhelming female field—seventy percent of all domestics were women—employed sixty-three percent of the city's total female labor force. Little change would occur in the next half century, so that in 1920, when eighty-two percent of all domestic servants were women, fifty percent of Rio's female labor force would be employed in domestic service (Tables 3 and 4).

By the 1870s the declining numbers of slaves in Rio de Janeiro no longer dominated the skilled trades to the same degree as they had a few decades earlier. As slaves were in shorter supply following the suppression of the slave trade in the midnineteenth century, more were shifted into the countryside. In Brazil slaves did not maintain their numbers through natural reproduction. Foreign immigrants came to dominate certain skilled urban occupations in Rio de Janeiro. The 1872 census indicated that the majority of Rio's workers in such areas as shoemaking or carpentry were foreign-born. Altogether, forty-two percent of the skilled workers and artisans were Brazilian born and free, forty-nine percent foreign born, and ten percent were slaves (Table 3). Foreigners comprised a greater percentage of the total urban population of Rio, as well as of its laboring classes, than of São Paulo, which experienced the beginnings of mass foreign immigration only in the 1880s. In 1872, thirty percent of Rio's inhabitants were foreign born, as compared to eight percent for São Paulo.[41]

Unfortunately, the 1872 census did not correlate occupations with color or specific nationality, so some questions concerning the ethnic composition of different occupational groups cannot be answered precisely. But the census does indicate a heavy concentration of foreign-born in commerce nation-wide and a predominance in Rio de Janeiro

Table 2. Occupations in Brazil, 1872

| | Free Population | | | | Slave Population | | |
| | Men | | Women | | | | |
Occupations	Brazilian Born	Foreign Born	Brazilian Born	Foreign Born	Men	Women	Total
Jurists	6,886	72	—	—	—	—	6,958
Doctors and Surgeons	1,763	204	—	—	—	—	1,967
Pharmacists	1,150	242	—	—	—	—	1,392
Religious	2,087	245	226	60	—	—	2,618
Capitalists and Proprietors	21,527	1,613	8,362	361	—	—	31,863
Professors and Men of Letters	771	536	2,045	173	—	—	3,525
Midwives	47	3	1,021	126	—	—	1,197
Public Functionaries	10,680	30	—	—	—	—	10,710
Commerce (including bookkeepers)	63,347	30,230	7,330	1,226	—	—	102,133
Manufacturers	12,204	2,292	4,653	217	—	—	19,366
SKILLED WORKERS AND ARTISANS							
Artists-Artisans	29,480	5,909	3,425	531	1,517	341	41,203
Miners and Quarrymen	2,553	1,010	—	—	769	—	4,332
Metal Workers	15,504	2,882	—	—	1,075	—	19,461
Carpenters	28,987	4,906	—	—	5,599	—	39,492
Textile Workers	4,305	1,166	119,532	1,143	842	12,354	139,342
Construction Workers	14,966	1,981	—	—	4,013	—	20,960
Leather Workers	4,488	564	9	3	560	3	5,627

Table 2. (continued)

Occupations	Free Population				Slave Population		Total
	Men		Women				
	Brazilian Born	Foreign Born	Brazilian Born	Foreign Born	Men	Women	
Dyers	314	68	117	6	40	4	549
Clothing Workers	7,574	2,289	—	—	1,379	—	11,242
Hat Makers	1,020	475	166	3	216	50	1,930
Shoemakers	15,715	2,123	—	—	2,163	—	20,001
SUBTOTAL: SKILLED WORKERS AND ARTISANS	124,906	23,373	123,249	1,686	18,173	12,752	304,139
Seamstresses	—	—	458,009	7,675	—	40,766	506,450
Domestic Servants	144,712	6,511	703,458	15,552	45,561	129,816	1,045,615
Day Laborers and Servants	199,594	25,428	86,991	3,171	49,195	45,293	409,672
Military	27,410	306	—	—	—	—	27,716
Sailors	16,804	3,111	—	—	1,788	—	21,703
Fishermen	15,746	734	—	—	1,262	—	17,742
Agriculturists	1,706,776	68,753	642,174	17,494	503,744	304,657	3,243,598
Without Professions[a]	1,782,952	15,654	1,999,311	16,398	185,447	172,352	4,172,114

Adapted from: Brazil, Directoria Geral de Estatistica, *Recenseamento da população do Império do Brazil a que se procedeu no dia 1º de agosto de 1872*, XIX (Quadros Gerais), 5.

[a]Includes those who did not declare a profession and those under age.

Does not include 181,583 people whose professions are not listed in the table.

Table 3. Occupations in Rio de Janeiro, 1872

| Occupations | Free Population | | | | Slave Population | | Total |
| | Men | | Women | | | | |
	Brazilian Born	Foreign Born	Brazilian Born	Foreign Born	Men	Women	
Jurists	561	64	—	—	—	—	625
Doctors and Surgeons	375	63	—	—	—	—	438
Pharmacists	257	112	—	—	—	—	369
Religious	148	66	—	50	—	—	264
Capitalists and Proprietors	580	404	912	111	—	—	2,007
Professors and Men of Letters	396	188	269	44	—	—	897
Midwives	—	—	24	30	—	—	54
Public Functionaries	2,328	23	—	—	—	—	2,351
Commerce (including bookkeepers)	6,007	17,038	116	320	—	—	23,481
Manufacturers	233	589	—	—	—	—	822
SKILLED WORKERS AND ARTISANS							
Artists-Artisans	4,782	3,930	130	88	494	4	9,428
Miners and Quarrymen	243	620	—	—	65	—	928
Metal Workers	1,112	1,599	—	—	276	—	2,987
Carpenters	2,276	2,954	—	—	690	—	5,920
Textile Workers	4	10	—	—	—	—	14
Construction Workers	1,062	1,080	—	—	596	—	2,738

21

Table 3. (continued)

Occupations	Free Population				Slave Population		Total
	Men		Women				
	Brazilian Born	Foreign Born	Brazilian Born	Foreign Born	Men	Women	
Leather Workers	228	197	—	—	54	—	479
Dyers	1	7	—	—	—	—	8
Clothing Workers	864	1,414	1	8	232	—	2,519
Hat Makers	144	318	—	2	34	—	498
Shoemakers	563	1,249	—	—	188	—	2,000
SUBTOTAL: SKILLED WORKERS AND ARTISANS	11,279	13,378	131	98	2,629	4	27,519
Seamstresses	—	—	7,785	2,423	—	1,384	11,592
Domestic Servants	4,118	3,773	16,683	7,595	8,658	14,184	55,011
Day Laborers and Servants	5,348	13,351	522	680	4,997	788	25,686
Military	5,313	161	—	—	—	—	5,474
Sailors	6,188	1,324	—	—	527	—	8,039
Fishermen	831	211	—	—	174	—	1,216
Agriculturists	4,889	1,094	5,104	239	3,207	2,488	17,021
Without Professions[a]	29,025	4,165	43,305	5,712	4,674	5,205	92,106

Adapted from: Brazil, Recenseamento da população . . . 1872, XXI (Município Neutro), 61.
[a]Includes those who did not declare a profession and those under age.

Table 4.   Domestic Service, Rio de Janeiro, 1872–1920

	Total Number of Women in Labor Force	Male Domestic Servants	Female Domestic Servants	Total Domestic Servants	Female domestic servants as a percentage of total	Percentage of total female labor force employed in domestic service
1872	60,961	16,549	38,462	55,011	70.0	63.1
1906	124,181	23,174	94,730	117,904[a]	80.3	76.3
1920	117,327	12,852	58,895	71,752	82.1	50.2

Adapted from: *Recenseamento da População* . . . 1872, *xxi* (Município Neutro), 61; Brazil, Directoria Geral de Estatistica, I, 100,104; *Recenseamento do Rio de Janeiro* (Districto Federal) realizado em 20 de setembro de 1906, *Recenseamento do Brasil* . . . 1920, II, 1ª parte, 514.
[a] According to the 1920 Census, the 1906 figures on domestic servants are far too high, as many women doing housework without remuneration were inadvertently included in this category.

(Tables 2 and 3). There foreigners dominated both petty retail commerce and the major import trade. As visitors to Rio observed, most small shopkeepers were Portuguese—the case throughout the nineteenth century—and Portuguese could also be found among the porters, cartmen, and boatmen of the capital, along with free blacks. However, market women and fruit and food sellers were generally black.[42]

Census data, with all their faults, remain the only comprehensive source on the number of working people and their occupations in Brazil during the nineteenth century. The 1872 census, the nation's first national census, was one of the most accurate ever carried out in Brazil. But occupational classifications derived from this census cannot precisely define the country's social structure. They oversimplify a complex and stratified situation, and provide only a rough measure. The same census category could encompass different groups better separated. In the case of textiles, not only may the enumeration be incorrect, but also different means of production employed by different types of workers—home looms and mill machinery—must have been combined to give a remarkably high figure for textile workers nationwide (139,342) and a surprisingly low one for Rio de Janeiro (14).[43] The census designation "capitalists and proprietors" presents a different problem, as this category could include the owners of everything from cheap boardinghouses to large estates. "Manufacturers" also differed widely in income and status. The 1872 census lumped together merchants, both petty shopkeepers and large importers, with bookkeepers and clerks. The category of "professors and men of letters" consisted mostly of poorly paid and regarded women elementary-school teachers. Although the census classified them, as well as public functionaries and midwives, and even artists and artisans—some of whom were slaves—as part of the liberal professions, they cannot be considered part of the elite, but rather of the nebulous middle sectors. They enjoyed far less prestige, respect, and income than jurists and doctors, or even pharmacists and clergy. Those high status professionals, together with some capitalist-proprietors, manufacturers, and merchants, more truly comprised Brazil's elite, although lower clergy must be excluded, as well as the handful of Protestants and foreign missionaries.

In the upper strata of Brazilian society male occupations, not female, served as indicators of position. The male generally established the family's status. Male members of the elite expected lower-class women, but never their own female relatives, to enter the work force. Few "proper" women engaged in any moneymaking activities, let alone work for wages. Only schoolteaching provided a genteel means of earning a living. The replacement of men by lower paid women in the nation's primary school classrooms was well underway by the end of the nineteenth century. In Rio de Janeiro in 1872, women already comprised approximately a third of the city's teachers. By the early twentieth century, over two-thirds were women, and by 1920, over eighty percent.[44]

While occupations served as major determinants of status and social position, other indicators proved more striking to anyone strolling the streets of Brazil's cities. Dress sharply set off the elite from the urban poor. Like Americans and Europeans in far cooler climates, a gentleman in Rio de Janeiro or Recife wore a "stiff silk hat" and a "double-breasted frock coat of black cloth, closely buttoned even in the warmest weather." Some donned gloves as well as garments of English wool. Europeans commented on the "oddity" of such attire "in a climate where lightweight and colored clothing and straw hats were naturally advisable." Only in the far north of Brazil, in a city like Belém, would upper-class men dress in white linen, with ladies wearing flowers in their hair instead of French bonnets.[45] In contrast, the poor wore lightweight cotton clothing, "often much faded and patched." A pair of pants and a shirt sufficed the men year round. Women wore just a blouse and skirt. Some men sported black felt hats, and skilled workers such as typographers might take pride in their caps. Not only slaves, but also many free laborers went barefoot. The unshod could find themselves barred from some streetcars, and men without coats were not supposed to enter public buildings.[46] Dress reflected class position and indicated the type of treatment due each person.

Housing strongly differentiated Brazil's urban poor from the nation's elite, and unsanitary, congested dwellings remained the mark of the lower classes' way of life. In the second half of the nineteenth century, the crowded, disease-ridden collective habitations known as *cortiços* (literally beehives) provided the most visible manifestation of lower-class housing. With their "innumerable narrow and dark cubicles packed with people," Brazilian *cortiços* shared characteristics of high-density, low-income housing elsewhere.[47] Some *cortiços* began as a series of small buildings owned by different individuals and built over a period of years. Units might be grouped about an interior patio, containing latrines and water spigots as well as tubs and drying space for women tenants toiling as laundresses. In time the patio might be almost completely filled in with added rooms, further reducing available light, air, and space. Better quarters might consist of a living room, bedroom, and kitchen, while the worst would be nothing but a small, suffocating room housing perhaps a dozen persons. *Cortiços* formed a prominent part of the urban landscape in such cities as Rio de Janeiro and São Paulo.

Beginning in the 1850s, when yellow fever epidemics became a major danger in Rio de Janeiro, the imperial government demonstrated concern about *cortiços*. Imperial officials acknowledged that the "extremely high price of homes in this capital gave rise" to *cortiços* sheltering a very large poor population; these dwellings became "permanent havens for contagions endangering public health."[48] "Due to excessive rents," only the "middle class" could earn enough "to afford more or less comfortable homes."[49] As a police official lamented in 1860, rents in Rio continued "so exaggerated that the class of people least favored by fortune" could only afford *cortiço* housing, where they suffered from "excessive mortality" in buildings which were "carelessly constructed in violation of all rules of hygiene, just to have as many rooms as possible in order to produce more revenue for their owners."[50]

Cortiço rents strained the budgets of the poor while affording handsome profits for the owners. According to one foreign observer, workers paid one-fourth of their wages for their congested, unsanitary quarters.[51] But for the owners, the annual rents of these collective habitations might amount to as much as fifty percent of their original cost.[52] The urban poor could be profitably crammed into small spaces for the benefit of the well-to-do.

During the 1860s and 1870s, Rio's *cortiço* population increased at a more rapid rate than did the city's total population (Table 5). Some of the Brazilians torn loose from their traditional moorings by the Paraguayan War (1865–1870) drifted toward the cities, where they encountered the old problems of scarce housing and high rents, now exacerbated

Table 5.   Rio de Janeiro's *Cortiço* Population, 1867–1888

	Number of Cortiços	Total Number of Rooms	Number of Inhabitants in Cortiços	Number of Brazilians	Number of Foreignors
1867	502	7,255	15,054	5,257	9,797
1869	642	9,769	21,929	9,630[a]	12,299[b]
1875	876	—	33,255	13,863	19,392
1888	1,331	18,866	46,680	—	—

Sources: Brazil, Ministério da Justiça, *Relatórios*, 1867, p. 69; 1870, p. 58; 1875 p. 214; Antonio Martins de Azevedo Pimental, *Subsidios para o estudo de hygiene do Rio de Janeiro*, 1890, p. 188.
[a]4,735 men and 4,895 women.   [b]8,820 men and 3,479 women.

by the war, and took up residence in *cortiços*. Imperial government officials voiced great concern over the rapid increase in the numbers of *cortiço* dwellers, who, they claimed, included army deserters. The police long considered the *cortiços* "an evil which most directly affects public order" and the "scene of constant commotions and crimes, the sanctuary of criminals, runaways, fugitive slaves."[53]

While the heaviest concentrations of *cortiços* in Rio de Janeiro were in the older downtown districts, these tenements were not located exclusively in the city's commercial center. In fact, the main business district of Rio contained relatively few *cortiços* as compared to adjacent commercial areas. In the mid-1870s Candelária, the oldest and choicest commercial district in Rio, had one-third the population of adjoining Santa Rita, but only six percent as many *cortiço* dwellers. Some two percent of Candelária's inhabitants lived in *cortiços*, as opposed to almost ten percent for Santa Rita. Approximately one-fourth of the residents of Santa Ana, a less centrally located downtown district encompassing the Campo de Santa Ana, later called the Praça da República, and its surroundings inhabited these dank structures (Tables 6 and 7).

In Rio's *cortiços*, the foreign-born predominated. Only in several outlying districts did the numbers of Brazilians living in *cortiços* equal or surpass that of European immigrants (Tables 5 and 7). In the mid-1870s, *cortiços* sheltered approximately one-fourth of Rio's foreign-born population, but less than one-tenth of Brazilian born (Tables 7 and 9). The recently arrived immigrants who congregated in *cortiços* could acquire a familiarity with the city and adapt to Brazilian ways while living close to their work. In the downtown *cortiços*—some of the worst—adults and

Table 6.   Rio de Janeiro, Population By District, 1872

Districts	Brazilians Male	Female	Foreign Born Male	Female	Total
URBAN					
Candelária	2,822	1,386	5,309	488	10,005
São José	6,228	5,831	6,229	1,994	20,282
Santa Rita	15,737	7,188	9,691	2,219	34,835
Sacramento	7,135	7,981	9,236	2,725	27,077
Santa Ana	12,608	13,984	9,098	3,213	38,903
Santo Antonio	5,629	8,144	4,227	2,693	20,693
Glória	7,050	8,338	4,874	2,223	22,485
Lagoa	4,973	5,188	2,393	1,062	13,616
Espírito Santo	4,600	5,252	3,017	1,261	14,130
São Cristóvão	3,881	4,669	1,697	714	10,961
Engenho Velho	5,269	6,247	2,950	1,290	15,756
RURAL-SUBURBAN					
Irajá	2,512	2,418	730	250	5,910
Jacarépaguá	3,588	3,697	657	276	8,218
Inhaúma	2,854	2,807	1,340	443	7,444
Guaratiba	3,560	3,638	267	162	7,627
Campo Grande	4,445	4,701	389	212	9,747
Santa Cruz	1,283	1,632	59	44	3,018
Ilha do Governador	1,208	1,163	428	57	2,856
Ilha do Paquetá	499	543	294	543	1,879
TOTALS	95,881	94,807	62,885	21,869	275,442

Source: Brazil, Directoria geral de Estatistica, *Recenseamento geral de República dos Estados Unidos do Brazil em 31 de dezembro de 1890. Districto Federal (Cidade do Rio de Janeiro)*, xiii.

males predominated, reflecting the nature of European immigration. Only among the Brazilian inhabitants of Rio's *cortiços* did the sex ratio remain in rough balance and marriage and children become more common. During the 1870s and 1880s, the more heavily Brazilian and sexually balanced *cortiço* population of an "aristocratic district" like Glória increased less rapidly than that of downtown areas, although it still exceeded the general population growth rate.[54]

In São Paulo too, *cortiços* remained concentrated in the downtown area, where the foreign-born predominated. The largest proportion of single male immigrants was located in the city's central commercial district, Sé. Urban workers living in the congested, damp, poorly lit and

Table 7.   *Cortiços* and Their Populations in Rio de Janeiro
By District: 1867–1875

District	Number of *Cortiços*	Number of Inhabitants	Brazilian	Foreign Born
Candelária				
1867	—a	—	—	—
1875	7	180	62	118
São José				
1867	12	529	168	361
1875	48	2,888	816	2,072
Santa Rita				
1867	44	1,752	312	1,371
1875	59	2,997	840	2,150
Sacramento				
1867	35	602	144	458
1875	48	1,209	316	893
Santa Ana				
1867	140	4,954	2,048	2,906
1875	231	9,850	4,458	5,302
Santo Antonio				
1867	46	2,179	804	1,375
1875	86	4,434	1,738	2,696
Glória				
1867	95	2,174	759	1,415
1875	136	3,736	1,694	2,042
Lagoa				
1867	—	—	—	—
1875	54	1,344	648	696
Espírito Santo				
1867	57	1,685	476	1,209
1875	108	4,285	2,218	2,067
São Cristóvão				
1867	29	503	280	223
1875	31	733	384	349
Engenho Velho				
1867	44	676	197	479
1875	62	1,532	631	901
Engenho Novo				
1867	—	—	—	—
1875	5	74	58	16
TOTALS				
1867	502	15,054	5,188	9,797
1875	875	33,262	13,863	19,302

Sources: Brazil, Ministério da Justiça, *Relatórios*, 1867, p. 69; 1875, p. 214.
aBlanks in Brazilian archival sources seem to indicate "zero," but may in fact
simply reflect lost or unknown data.

ventilated tenements fell victim to epidemic disease more frequently than those who could afford better housing.[55]

By the end of the nineteenth century, some of Brazil's *cortiços* would evolve into larger, more elaborate structures. In the 1860s and 1870s only the term *cortiço* was in general use in Rio de Janeiro. By the 1880s the term *estalagem* also appeared frequently in government inspection reports, and was used virtually interchangeably with *cortiço*, even though *estalagens* might be newer and larger. A foreign observer in Rio in the early 1880s attempting to distinguish between these two types of housing claimed the term *estalagem* was "given to a number of small houses, built together and forming a square." Accommodations in *cortiços* were "almost always limited to one room each, and have to be reached by a common staircase and veranda."[56]

Over the years, a small, haphazardly constructed *cortiço* might evolve into a larger, more complex structure housing less poverty-stricken segments of the urban lower classes, as in the fictional *cortiço* of the 1880s depicted by Aluísio Azevedo in his novel O *Cortiço*.[57] In keeping with the common stereotype of Portuguese immigrants as hardworking but greedy and crude, Azevedo portrayed his *cortiço* owner as a money-hungry, unscrupulous Portuguese shopkeeper. First this coarse social climber built three small houses behind his store and restaurant and then, acquiring more land, he erected some ninety units set about an internal patio where the laundresses worked. The *cortiço's* inhabitants, a mélange of Brazilians of all ethnic types and colors and of foreigners, especially Portuguese and Italians, were eventually obliged to pay higher rents for their quarters. Instead of peddlers, washerwomen, quarrymen, blacksmiths, policemen, and day laborers, now artisans, watchmakers, tailors, cigar makers, small merchants, clerks, and students began to live there. Finally, the enterprising businessman rebuilt the *cortiço*, quadrupling the number of rooms by adding a second story and expanding into the garden and courtyard areas until the garden disappeared and the courtyard measured only the width of a street, and he owned the impressive *estalagem* of his dreams.

Not only *cortiços* sheltered Brazil's urban poor. Somewhat better as well as even more wretched accommodations could also be found in a city such as Rio de Janeiro. While families or acquaintances might band together to lease quarters in *cortiços* by the month, some of the poverty-stricken slept in beds rented by the night, crammed into the rooms and corridors of fetid, malodorous old buildings.[58] Others lived a short distance from the city center in small, damp houses set on narrow streets. According to a professor of medicine in Rio de Janeiro, most of the poor lived in such dwellings, "generally cramped, low, built directly on the ground, with only a tiny number of windows; often they lack a wooden floor and have as ceiling just the tile roof." Nevertheless, he considered these accommodations superior to *cortiços*.[59]

As the nineteenth century advanced, more workers moved further from the city center. Improved mass transportation speeded this outward movement, enabling some of the urban poor to find less crowded housing in distant suburbs generally built along the railroad lines. Skilled workers such as typographers or employees of the marine arsenal, whose ranks included fewer recent immigrants, seemed best able to take advantage of this possibility. Members of the elite concerned with urban sanitation and "promiscuity," as well as real estate promotors, advocated the construction of worker housing in the suburbs. By the early twentieth century, ever more urban laborers would spend hours commuting to small houses lining the dirt streets of districts lacking most municipal services, instead of living in expensive, congested, unpleasant but conveniently located *cortiços*. Yet these more visible downtown tenements continued to attract the most attention.[60]

Food absorbed a far larger proportion of workers' income than housing, although this food was limited in variety and often spoiled or adulterated. In the early nineteenth century, beans and manioc flour were the principal staple foods of the slave population as well as much of the free lower classes. Most foodstuffs were locally produced and locally consumed. Regional variations in diet could be found, with fresh meat in Rio Grande do Sul and corn in Minas Gerais and São Paulo. While the owner of a *fazenda* in Minas might supplement his beans and corn with pork, bacon, greens, stewed fowl, coffee, milk, and bread, slaves might find their cornmeal mush and boiled beans only occasionally flavored with fat or a bit of pork. By the midnineteenth century, bread, bacon, and dried beef and fish formed part of the diet of some of the urban lower classes in major cities like Rio de Janeiro and Recife. The wheat flour and dried meat consumed in Rio came largely from the Rio Grande do Sul and the Platine nations, and the bacon from Minas Gerais and the interior of Rio de Janeiro. The vicissitudes of commerce and communications subjected these food products to price fluctuations. Unskilled urban workers in Rio consumed mostly manioc flour and black beans, sometimes with a little dried meat or codfish. Skilled workers might eat bread, oranges and bananas, even fresh beef, and drink coffee. In fact, some such workers claimed bread to be their "principal food." But fresh produce was commonly reserved for better-off sectors of urban society, although even on their tables many green vegetables appeared more rarely than chicken, rice, fruit, wine, or sweets. Beans were generally the common element in the diets of both rich and poor. Even if members of the lower classes could obtain adequate quantities of foodstuffs, serious questions should be raised as to the nutritional balance and caloric value of their monotonous, limited diets, deficient in animal proteins, fresh produce, and essential vitamins. Malnutrition was far from unknown.[61]

Food prices in Rio de Janeiro astonished foreigners, who found it "hard to understand why oranges and pineapples should cost three times as much as in New York, or why onions and sweet potatoes should be very much higher than they are at home." When they compared food prices with local wage levels, the disparities increased. In the 1870s, an American zoologist advised any workers thinking of emigrating from the United States to "keep away from Brazil." Not only would they find living expenses "very high" and payment for their work "not very secure," but also "in nine cases out of ten, a poor mechanic will make more money in the United States than in Brazil."[62]

During the second half of the nineteenth century, prices tended both to rise more rapidly than during earlier decades of the century and to fluctuate sharply over short periods. The expansion of commercial agriculture helped raise food costs. In south-central Brazil, many slaves were shifted from domestic food production to growing coffee for export. While colonial regulations had required manioc be grown on sugar plantations, no such laws existed in the nineteenth century. With major cities such as Rio de Janeiro and Bahia dependent on distant food producers, transportation problems added to high costs, as did periodic crop failures and shortages. Such severe food crises as that which caused the Brazilian government concern in the mid-1850s lowered workers' standard of living as food prices rose precipitously. The budget deficits and emission of paper money during the Paraguayan War (1865–1870) contributed to inflation and to a decline in buying power. By the end of the 1870s, matters began to improve. However, the disparity in wage levels between northern and southern Brazil remained; workers in Rio de Janeiro and São Paulo earned slightly more than their counterparts in the north or Northeast. Throughout the nation, women and children employed in such industries as textiles continued to receive far lower wages than men. Family survival depended on their pitiful contributions. Food and rent costs remained the overriding problem for the lower classes, as articulated by skilled workers in early labor newspapers.[63]

Inadequate diet, housing, and clothing, and the long hours of exhausting labor needed to sustain their low standard of living left urban workers more susceptible than the elite to the ravages of disease in nineteenth century Brazil. Lack of adequate sanitation in Brazilian cities and especially in congested, dirty, poorly ventilated *cortiços* facilitated the rapid spread of various contagions. Not uncommon was the experience of a Rio police official in 1875 who investigated the death of an Italian from yellow fever and found two other people in the same *cortiço* room with that disease, together with a woman who had just given birth. Yellow fever, like tuberculosis, smallpox, measles, syphilis, and scurvy, could be clearly recognized. But many of the diseases urban dwellers suffered, including certain parasitic infections, could not be properly diagnosed in the nineteenth century. Contemporary medical reports referred vaguely to fevers, liver disturbances, dysentery, indigestions, and skin infections. Smallpox, one of the earliest epidemics to visit Brazil, was intimately linked with the African slave trade, and ports such as Rio de Janeiro suffered frequent attacks, especially in the first half of the nineteenth century, before the suppression of the slave traffic. In 1849, a major yellow fever epidemic struck Brazil, devastating first Bahia and then Pernambuco and Rio. Throughout the second half of the nineteenth century, the disease claimed its largest number of victims in the coastal cities, for the mosquitos that carry yellow fever prefer an urban environment and shun higher altitudes. The sickness rarely appeared on the *planalto* of São Paulo. Cholera epidemics also first appeared in Brazil in the mid-nineteenth century, and like yellow fever proved more destructive during the hot summer months. Together with tuberculosis, they ranked as the major known killers of adults in Brazil's cities. In the hospital maintained by the Sociedade Portuguesa de Beneficência of Rio de Janeiro, a mutual benefit society whose membership included skilled workers and bookkeepers, tuberculosis claimed the largest number of fatalities; their records listed one-third of the deaths in 1878–1879, for example, as stemming from that "fatal sickness." Lethal childhood diseases were less clearly recognized, and infant mortality remained very high, especially among slaves. Those malnourished children who survived sometimes suffered retardation of mind and body.[64]

Medical specialists blamed much of the severity and spread of diseases on faulty water supply and sewerage. Neither homes nor city streets could be kept properly clean. In the midnineteenth century, Rio de Janeiro not only suffered annual summer water shortages in different districts, but also periodic droughts. One doctor calculated the declining water supply per capita at fifty liters per day in 1851, twenty in 1860, thirty-one in 1864, and fifteen to eighteen liters in 1866, but with marked improvements in the 1870s. Moreover, available water was inadequately distributed. In the early 1870s, only 4,566 of the 21,665 buildings in the urbanized sections of Rio had expensive individual water service. The others depended on 711 public water spigots. By 1880, almost one-fourth of the city's houses received water, and the number continued to increase. Other Brazilian cities experienced similar or worse water supply problems. In the mid-1870s, public fountains—not necessarily free or flowing—still supplied the vast majority of urban dwellers, with one public spigot for roughly every 2,000 inhabitants of Bahia and Recife and every 700 residents of Pôrto Alegre and São Paulo, as compared to one spigot per 400 people in Rio de Janeiro.[65]

The recreational escapes from dreary living conditions open to the urban poor were simple and not always healthy. Although associations of skilled workers sponsored festivities and night classes, less organized forms of diversion such as card playing, visiting friends and relatives, singing, and playing accordians and guitars proved more common. As in colonial times, church festivals afforded free public displays. While Carnaval served as a source of amusement for foreign visitors and for the Brazilian elite, it provided a temporary escape for the poor. So did gambling and drinking.[66] Foreign travelers noted the pervasiveness of cheap sugarcane brandy (*cachaça*) and of lotteries, in which laborers "invest their savings . . . very often."[67] Brazilian doctors inveighed against the "abuse of alcoholic beverages," which constituted a "true calamity . . . particularly among the lower classes."[68] Pursuit of such individual releases was unlikely to hasten change in the political or social system of Brazil.

Although the urban poor remained sharply marked off from the elite, in everything from income, occupations, and education to dress, food, and housing, they remained divided among themselves. Not only did they lack the power to alter existing relationships, but the diversity within the lower classes also lessened any possibility of their directly challenging the tight rule of the elite. The poor, however, could react to elite pressures against them. On specific occasions, they manifested their dissatisfactions, frightening the upper class with violent outbursts and protests. Dissident political elements, especially abolitionists and republicans, at times attempted to utilize lower class discontent in their own challenges to the existing order, and in the process would help raise political aspirations among some skilled workers.

2 / Challenges and Popular Outbursts in the Late Empire

National politics in imperial Brazil centered on the cities, especially the capital, Rio de Janeiro. Although the rural areas provided power bases for most of the elite, as well as furnishing the exports that made the empire appear prosperous, the capital offered high-level prestigious government positions and authority. Rivals for national control, as well as those challenging certain elite policies, met and maneuvered in the urban arena. Moreover, in crowded urban areas, the relative facility of contacts and the lessened constraints of a patriarchal society permitted highly visible popular demonstrations of anger and dissatisfaction with existing conditions. Although such violent urban manifestations of discontent troubled the elites, violating the myth of a peaceful empire, they posed no serious threat to their position.

The political culture, formulated by the elites since colonial times, stressed conciliation, class harmony, and respect for hierarchy. Violence should not be manifested in the political realm. The powerful Brazilian institution of patronage pervaded society, extending to the diffuse and divided majority of the population, rather than functioning only within the upper strata. Through paternalism and clientelism, urban as well as rural, strong vertical ties linking the classes were established, conflicts muted, and horizontal solidarities and the formation of autonomous lower-class organizations inhibited.[1] Continued contact between rich and poor reinforced the power of authority of the dominant elites. Members of the upper classes could provide employment, charity, and protection. The beneficent societies organized by immigrant groups in the cities and sustained largely by their wealthy members linked rich and poor members. In addition to such formal institutions, individual charity such as the gift of used objects and old clothing given to maids and retainers cemented vertical ties between the elite and the diffuse lower classes. Within the households of the dominant elites, the personal and proximate relationships of masters and servants played out in daily repetitions bound them together. Masters strengthened those bonds by rewarding devoted service, providing care during illness, and structuring the small rituals which reinforced authority and obedience.

Since they lacked the resources provided by property and family connections, the poor and vulnerable had to seek alliances with those possessing the power to protect or to grant favors. Members of the urban poor tried to ally themselves with individuals from the upper classes who could protect them from police persecution or from forced recruitment into the armed forces. In exchange for political protection and favors, some bands of *capoeiras* skilled in African martial arts served as political shock troops who disrupted meetings, created disorders, and intimidated voters during the late empire. By incorporating these black and mulatto *capoeiras* into the lowest levels of the political system and giving them an interest in it, politicians stifled whatever potential threat they may have posed to the existing political and social order. Through their systems of patronage and clientelism, the dominant elites also controlled the channels for upward mobility. A small number of outsiders did rise, and remain, within the system. Such social co-optation provided another effective method of social control.

Although sectors of the national elites competed among themselves for political and economic advantage, during the last four decades of the monarchy they preferred to resolve their disputes peacefully, through compromise. Even major political changes like the fall of the empire and establishment of a republic in 1889 did not involve bloodshed, or mark a sharp break in Brazilian history. The use of force was generally limited to dealings with the poor. And threats usually proved sufficient. Segmented and divided by ethnicity, nationality, occupation, and workplace, the poor and powerless had little means of articulating their common interests. They could not act as one, as the dominant elites well knew.

Even though paternalistic methods of social control generally proved sufficient, the elites' control of the state provided the means to repress when necessary. Should common elite goals be endangered, force would be employed. The dominant elites would act to preserve their status, access to wealth, and exercise of political power. The elite response to popular challenges was firm and uncompromising. The failure of virtually all movements of social protest in Brazil since the colonial period attests to the resilience and effectiveness of the political order. In addition to violence and police repression, recruitment into the armed forces served as another method of social control and punishment. On the whole no major disagreements arose within the governing elites concerning the treatment of the urban poor and the need to "keep them in their place." Formal politics remained an elite activity, not a form of class conflict.

During the late empire, politics proved highly personal in nature, marked by shifting coalitions of factions and individuals within the upper classes. Personalism and clientelism marked relations among members of the upper strata of society just as it did their dealings with the lower orders. Within the small political community, personal relationships, distinctions, and interests rather than ideologies guided decision making. The parties lacked national organization and popularity as well as political philosophies. Their major concern remained the control of local patronage and power so as to secure their places in the central government. The vast authority of Emperor Pedro II further personalized imperial politics. He appointed ministers of state and presidents of the provinces, as well as naming ambassadors, magistrates, and bishops. He could veto legislation, dissolve the Chamber of Deputies at will, and make war or peace. Because of D. Pedro's authority to intervene in all important matters of policy and personnel, the imperial political system resembled absolute as well as constitutional monarchy.[2]

The extensive powers of the monarch placed great responsibility for the fate of the regime in his hands. Generally conservative and lacking in imagination, during his early reign Pedro II had provided the elite with efficient government reflective of their needs. While D. Pedro retained great personal prestige and authority in his later years, he proved less active as a ruler. His decreasing energies and powers of concentration contributed to the decline in efficiency and effectiveness of the imperial government in the 1880s.[3]

The central government could never impose its authority evenly throughout the vast territorial expanse of Brazil. The cities, rather than the interior, felt its control, while also benefitting from its largess. As the Portuguese minister in Rio de Janeiro, beset with problems of protecting his country's nationals, complained in the late 1880s, "The central government's acts are almost always annulled by local authorities and electoral influences. Any criminal can ensure his freedom from punishment if he obtains the patronage of a powerful personage."[4] However, such local challenges posed no serious threat to the central government or to the national elite. Although rural oligarchies maintained their relative autonomy, their diversity and factionalism ensured over-all dominance by the national elite, which controlled the national government, the urban areas, and the customshouse.

During the empire, national power lay in the hands of those who gained entrance to the ministries, the Council of State, the Senate, and the Chamber of Deputies, or who held high military and judicial appointments or provincial presidencies.[5] They comprised the national elite, based in Rio de Janeiro but linked to different local elites. A post-secondary degree was a major prerequisite for entrance into this elite. Law graduates comprised the largest number of *letrados*, or degree holders, dominating political life in Brazil during the empire and into the republic. While some practiced law or entered business, many considered public office the only proper employment for their talents. Few other high status occupations existed. As the number of law graduates increased in the late 1870s and 1880s, exceeding the supply of available positions, the ranks of the discontented grew. Accusations of nepotism multiplied. Disappointment and disillusionment could lead to political opposition.

In the 1880s, challenges to the existing political and economic structures mounted, with the ebbing of the monarchy, the decline of coffee cultivation in the Paraíba Valley, the successful campaign for the abolition of slavery, and the beginnings of mass European immigration to south-central Brazil. The republican movement provided one of the earliest, if long ineffective, visible sources of opposition.

Republican sentiment in Brazil dates back at least as far as the late eighteenth century to the conspiracy in Minas Gerais known as the *Inconfidência*. However, this republicanism remained largely quiescent until the ministerial crisis of 1868 during the Paraguayan War and the formation of a Republican Club in 1870. That same year the club issued the manifesto regarded as the official beginning of the Republican Party, a declaration signed by many discontented young law graduates.

Although slower to take the form of republicanism than the frustrations of the *letrados*, *Paulista* dissatisfaction with imperial policies also fueled the anti-monarchist movement. With the crumbling of the coffee economy in the Paraíba Valley of Rio de Janeiro by the 1870s and the expansion of production in the province of São Paulo, *Paulista* planters had assumed a position of economic importance. But they did not exercise commensurate political power. The sugar barons of the Northeast and the coffee planters of the Paraíba Valley retained the ear of the imperial court and remained principal pillars of support for the existing political structure. The central government showed little concern about administrative and other reforms required by the social and economic transformations occurring in southern Brazil. *Paulistas* complained of neglect by the central government, unfair revenue allocations to their province, and underrepresentation in Parliament. A federal regime with great local autonomy, whether monarchical or republican, would best serve their expanding export economy.

The Republican Party of São Paulo, founded in 1873 and the best organized republican group under the empire, advocated a federal regime. Alberto Sales, their chief theoretician, was the brother of Manuel Ferraz de Campos Sales, a leading politician and coffee planter. In Alberto Sales's writings, the benefits of this form of government are extolled almost to the point of separatism. Under a federal regime, each local center would "employ its own resources as best it thought," and "the elements of wealth which exist in the different localities, instead of all being drained off to the general treasury" of the imperial government, would remain to benefit each locality.[6] São Paulo was "incontestably the only one giving to the imperial government without receiving." Even under the "regime of despotic centralization of the empire," São Paulo had advanced to the forefront of the nation, and Alberto Sales dwelt on the vast increase in agriculture, immigration, commerce, industry, railroads, and general prosperity which would result when the overwhelming proportion of the province's revenues ceased to enter the imperial treasury.[7]

Although separatism served the *Paulistas* as a tactical weapon to frighten the central government, rather than providing a practical or popular political program, Alberto Sales's arguments reflected the discontent and desires of many of his contemporaries and predecessors in the province. The coffee planters had learned the importance of government as an instrument of economic action, and they were aware that with state autonomy São Paulo would progress more rapidly and less of its wealth would flow into the coffers of the central government. Decentralization remained one of the few issues on which the Republican Party of São Paulo never compromised. On the most important political question of the late empire, the abolition of slavery, party leaders long pursued an opportunistic policy of deliberate ambiguity.[8]

The gradual elimination of slavery elsewhere in the Western Hemisphere left Brazil as the institution's largest and last bastion, to the chagrin of many foreign-oriented members of the elite.[9] Pressure from abroad had helped lead to the suppression of the African slave trade in the mid-nineteenth century. Within Brazil, slavery declined in importance in the impoverished Northeast while intensifying within the prosperous southern coffee provinces (Table 8). In 1864, one-fifth of the inhabitants of the northeastern sugar province of Pernambuco were slaves, while cap-

Table 8.   Slave Population in Brazil and Selected Provinces, 1819–1887

	1819	1864	1874	1884	1887
Brazil	1,107,391	1,715,000	1,540,829	1,240,806	723,419
Ceará	55,439	36,000	31,975	—	108
Pernambuco	97,633	260,000	106,236	72,709	41,122
Bahia	147,263	300,000	165,403	132,822	76,838
Minas Gerais	168,543	250,000	311,304	301,125	191,952
Rio de Janeiro	146,060[a]	300,000	301,352	258,238	162,421
São Paulo	77,667	80,000	174,622	167,493	107,329
Paraná	10,191	20,000	11,249	7,768	3,513
Rio Grande do Sul	28,253	40,000	98,450	60,136	8,442
Município Neutro (city of Rio)	146,060[b]	100,000	47,084	32,103	7,488

Adapted from: Brazil, Ministério da Agricultura, *Relatórios*, May 10, 1883, p. 10; April 30, 1885, p. 372; May 14, 1888, p. 24; Perdigão Malheiro, A *escravidão no Brasil* 3rd ed. II, 150–51; Herbert Klein, "The Internal Slave Trade in Nineteenth-Century Brazil," p. 584.
[a] Includes the city of Rio de Janeiro.
[b] Includes the province of Rio de Janeiro.

tives comprised only one-tenth of the population of São Paulo. In the early 1870s, approximately one-fifth of the inhabitants of that prosperous coffee exporting province were enslaved, as compared to one-tenth of the people of Pernambuco. During this period, the proportion of slave to free within the nation as a whole declined only slightly, to approximately fifteen percent.[10] Abolitionist sentiment proved strongest in those regions of Brazil with the fewest slaves, and in the cities. A year before final abolition, the city of Rio de Janeiro, an abolitionist stronghold with a total population of approximately half a million, contained fewer than 7,500 slaves, while the province of São Paulo, with well over a million inhabitants, had 107,329 slaves.[11]

As the abolitionist campaign gathered strength in the 1880s, the handful of active, urban-based abolitionists skillfully mounted their verbal attacks on the institution of slavery. Military officers, engineers, bureaucrats, journalists, and businessmen all participated. Some abolitionist societies also sent agents into the countryside to provoke slave flights, as well as aiding the escapees arriving in the cities. However, many slaves needed no persuasion to abandon the plantations, especially by the late 1880s. Defenders of slavery, such as the powerful Conservative Party leader and Bahian sugar planter, João Maurício Wanderly, Baron of Cotegipe, nevertheless blamed "the abandonment of the *fazendas* and the increasing audacity of the slaves" on the provocations of "anarchists," and voiced fears of slave insurrections as well.[12]

Although the emancipation movement gained increasing popularity in the cities, final abolition of slavery in Brazil would be postponed as long as the landowning elite considered slavery economically and socially indispensable. The emperor personally disliked slavery, but he took no decisive action. Nor did the Roman Catholic Church. But the mass slave flights of 1886 and 1887 in south-central Brazil frightened some masters into giving immediate freedom to their slaves in hopes of stemming social disruption and the exodus from the plantations. Abolition offered the possibility of regularizing a potentially chaotic situation for those planters still dependent on slave labor.

By the time the Princess Regent Isabel signed the "golden law" abolishing slavery in Brazil without compensation on 13 May 1888, *Paulista* planters had accepted the inevitability of abolition. Their expanding coffee economy suffered from labor scarcities, for the interprovincial slave trade had proved unable to meet the demand. By the late 1880s, European immigration had demonstrated its worth as an acceptable alternative source of labor supply for the coffee plantations, especially those on São Paulo's western plateau. Those planters, unlike the sugar and cotton producers in the north, could afford the initial costs of importing immigrants as slave substitutes.[13]

Slavery had long discouraged large scale European immigration to Brazil. Many potential immigrants were reluctant to compete with servile labor. But by the late 1880s the institution's imminent demise encouraged an upsurge in immigration (Table 9), largely directed toward southern Brazil.

Although many planters, particularly in São Paulo, considered European workers the best solution to a perceived labor shortage, other alternatives existed. Freedmen provided another source of agricultural labor in Brazil, but some planters feared the former slaves would prove insubordinate and unwilling to submit once again to plantation discipline. However, other landowners succeeded in making contractual arrangements with ex-slaves. Even though many freedmen left for the cities, large numbers stayed or returned to work their ex-masters' land following abolition, as they lacked alternative employment opportunities elsewhere. Native Brazilians living largely outside the plantation economy could also be used as plantation laborers, but they often proved reluctant to submit to the harsh regime of the plantations without adequate compensation or incentives. Instead of subjecting themselves to additional obligations, many pursued their percarious and marginal rural existence, and continued to be viewed by the elite as undisciplined, lazy, unde-

Table 9. Immigrants (Selected Nationalities) Entering Brazil, 1884–1923

	1884	1885	1886	1887	1888	1889	1890	1891	1892	1893
Argentine[a]	185	108	156	173	145	139	75	174	—	70
Austrian	651	524	728	274	1,156	550	2,246	4,244	574	2,737
English	100	90	93	72	129	76	193	1,950	67	100
French	243	233	218	241	478	608	2,844	1,921	575	616
German	1,719	2,848	2,114	1,147	782	1,903	4,812	5,285	800	1,368
Italian	10,502	21,765	20,430	40,157	104,353	36,124	31,275	132,326	55,049	58,552
Portuguese	8,683	7,611	6,287	10,205	18,289	15,240	25,174	32,349	17,797	28,986
Russian[b]	457	275	146	197	259	—	27,125	11,817	158	155
Spanish[c]	710	952	1,617	1,766	4,736	9,712	12,008	22,146	10,471	38,998
"Turks"[d]	—	—	—	—	—	—	—	3	—	—
U.S.A.	31	37	43	59	87	76	44	59	14	199
Total Number of Immigrants	23,574	34,724	32,650	54,932	132,070	65,165	106,819	215,239	85,906	132,589

	1894	1895	1896	1897	1898	1899	1900	1901	1902	1903
Argentine	51	288	175	225	189	131	359	421	379	305
Austrian	789	10,108	11,365	3,665	924	1,826	2,089	696	511	474
English	91	28	63	106	103	101	166	47	35	85
French	309	286	327	225	255	217	233	—	151	302
German	790	973	1,070	930	535	521	217	166	265	1,231
Italian	34,872	97,344	96,505	104,510	49,086	30,846	19,671	59,869	32,111	12,970
Portuguese	17,041	36,055	22,299	13,558	15,105	10,989	8,250	11,261	11,606	11,378

(continued)

Table 9. Immigrants (Selected Nationalities) Entering Brazil, 1884–1923   (continued)

	1894	1895	1896	1897	1898	1899	1900	1901	1902	1903
Russian	57	275	592	567	258	412	147	99	108	371
Spanish	5,986	17,641	24,154	19,466	8,024	5,399	4,834	212	3,588	4,466
"Turks"	—	146	19	646	978	1,823	874	781	772	481
U.S.A.	32	226	124	257	369	343	375	358	301	279
Total Number of Immigrants	60,182	164,831	157,423	144,866	76,862	53,610	37,807	83,116	50,472	32,941

	1904	1905	1906	1907	1908	1909	1910	1911	1912	1913
Argentine	407	513	278	356	329	176	477	624	500	353
Austrian	387	427	1,012	522	5,317	4,008	2,636	3,352	3,045	2,255
English	362	123	73	119	1,109	778	1,087	1,157	1,077	825
French	228	224	109	202	992	1,241	1,134	1,397	1,513	1,432
German	797	650	1,333	845	2,931	5,413	3,902	4,251	5,733	8,004
Italian	12,857	17,360	20,777	18,873	13,873	13,668	14,163	22,914	31,785	30,886
Japanese[e]	—	—	—	—	18	—	13	—	—	—
Portuguese	17,318	20,181	21,706	25,681	37,628	30,577	30,857	47,493	76,530	76,701
Russian	287	996	751	703	5,781	5,663	2,462	14,013	9,193	8,251
Spanish	10,046	25,329	24,441	9,235	14,862	16,219	20,843	27,141	35,492	41,064
"Turks"	1,097	1,446	1,193	1,480	3,170	4,027	5,257	6,319	7,302	10,886
U.S.A.	258	364	265	198	338	272	344	275	370	265
Total Number of Immigrants	44,706	68,488	72,332	57,919	90,536	84,090	86,751	33,575	177,887	190,333

Table 9. *(continued)*

	1914	1915	1916	1917	1918	1919	1920	1921	1922	1923
Argentine	362	178	388	680	141	177	191	196	404	419
Austrian	971	104	155	18	1	548	757	760	808	2,163
English	462	311	244	243	69	369	658	492	532	584
French	696	410	292	273	226	690	838	633	725	609
German	2,811	169	364	201	1	466	4,120	7,915	5,038	8,254
Italian	15,542	5,779	5,340	5,478	1,050	5,231	10,005	10,779	11,277	15,839
Japanese	3,675	65	165	3,899	5,599	3,022	1,013	840	1,225	895
Portuguese	27,935	15,118	11,981	6,817	7,98¹ₛ	17,068	33,883	19,981	28,622	31,866
Russian	2,958	640	616	644	181	330	245	1,526	279	777
Spanish	18,945	5,895	10,306	11,113	4,225	6,627	9,136	9,523	8,869	10,140
"Turks"	3,456	514	603	259	93	504	4,854	1,865	2,278	4,829
U.S.A.	173	113	164	126	48	138	295	338	270	223
Total Number of Immigrants	79,232	30,333	31,245	30,277	19,793	36,027	69,042	58,476	65,007	84,549

Source: *Revista de Imigração e Colonização*, I (Oct. 1940), 617-30.

[a] The total number of Argentines, like other Spanish American immigrants, should be higher, as many went unrecorded.

[b] Many of those listed as Russian, and as Austrian, immigrants before World War I were Polish.

[c] Many of those listed as Spanish probably came from northern Portugal.

[d] Includes Syrians and other Levantine and Arabic groups.

[e] These figures for Japanese immigrants are probably too low, as many illegal immigrants entered Brazil also. Japanese immigration was overwhelmingly confined to São Paulo State.

pendable, and even degenerate. Only in poorer regions with few slaves and large numbers of free agricultural laborers would many landowners consider free Brazilian workers an acceptable alternative. In Pernambuco, for example, free labor had become dominant by the 1870s. Among the planters, even the importation of Chinese coolies had its advocates, but European immigrants were deemed superior in every way. Those *fazendeiros* with the resources to bring in foreign workers generally preferred Europeans.[14]

While the imperial government had periodically pursued a policy aimed at creating independent agricultural nuclei of European settlers— to "civilize" and modernize Brazil—these colonies suffered from the difficulties of acquiring land near transportation and markets and from competition with slave labor. Those which succeeded, despite the frequent difficulties and high costs, involved only a small percentage of the total number of immigrants to Brazil. Planters preferred immigrant workers committed by contract to labor on their estates to independent agriculturalists.[15] But only the *Paulistas* succeeded in organizing a mass movement of Europeans onto their *fazendas* during the last years of slavery.

Planters in São Paulo actively promoted European immigration through government subsidies, various organizations, missions to Europe, and propaganda, and developed a program of recruitment, transport, and distribution of free labor to the coffee *fazendas*. Coffee profits not only provided the incentive for this extensive immigration program, but also much of the government revenue to finance it. After 1884, the provincial assembly furnished free passage for immigrants entering agriculture, but limited the subsidy to families in order to reduce the incidence of re-emigration, which, however, remained high. The planters preferred to sponsor poor peasants whom they hoped would not protest abuses, harsh working conditions, and minimal wages on coffee *fazendas*, and who would be unable to buy land or establish small businesses.[16]

Italy proved the best source of cheap replacements for black plantation hands. The severe agricultural crises of the 1880s facing this recently united nation, compounded by the competition of cheap American grain in Italian markets, facilitated large-scale recruitment of Italian peasants by Brazilian labor contractors. Difficulties stemming from credit shortages, low productivity, and absentee land ownership in the Po Valley combined with a price decline in the local silk industry to provide Brazil with a major source of willing immigrants.[17]

Tens of thousands of Italians left for Brazil annually during the 1880s and 1890s, along with sizeable migrations to the United States and Argentina. Only Brazil consistently provided paid passage, thus helping to ensure a constant flow of immigrants despite reports of dismal working conditions. During the 1890s, some 690,000 Italians arrived in Brazil, surpassing the total of all other nationalities combined (Table 9). The number who did not stay is less certain, but apparently quite large. Perhaps over one-third of the Italian immigrants to Brazil re-emigrated elsewhere.[18] The overwhelming majority of the Italians came directly to São Paulo state, generally bound for the coffee plantations to serve as wage laborers. However, some never reached the *fazendas*, managing to stay in the cities, and others left the countryside for the urban areas, becoming day laborers, factory workers, and vendors, or sought odd jobs.[19] *Colonos* on the coffee *fazendas* apparently had little opportunity to acquire significant amounts of land, which remained concentrated in large estates, but they could sell any surplus from their subsistence plots. Those who managed to work off their obligations to the *fazendeiros* and perhaps accumulate some savings could migrate to urban areas in search of more remunerative employment.[20]

Few alternatives traditionally existed for poor immigrants or native-born lower-class Brazilians. Ever since colonial times, a powerful minority had controlled land near towns, as in the Spanish colonies in the New World. With the cities encircled by private holdings, new arrivals and individual farmers found little opportunity to become freeholders in settled areas. Nineteenth-century Brazilian law and government policies helped prevent small-scale squatters from becoming proprietors. Only the wealthy and powerful bought land easily or secured title to disputed property.[21] Aside from contract laborers, few among the vast majority of immigrants to Brazil had strong reasons to go into the countryside. Whatever alternative employment existed tended to be found in the urban areas.

By the end of the nineteenth century the ethnic composition of the city of São Paulo had been drastically altered through immigration. While foreigners comprised less than eight percent of the city's inhabitants in 1872, they formed a majority only two decades later, making São Paulo a far less typically Brazilian city than Rio de Janeiro. Italians predominated among São Paulo's foreign-born, outnumbering the Portuguese, the second largest group, by more than three to one (Table 10). The proportion of Italians (though not the absolute number) in São Paulo's population at this time (34.8% in 1893) even surpassed that in the far larger city of Buenos Aires (27.4% in 1895), let alone contemporary New York City (2.6% in 1890).[22]

Unlike the Italians, Portuguese immigrants to Brazil settled largely in the cities. And more chose Rio de Janeiro, the best known place within Brazil, than any other city. Portuguese comprised the second largest immigrant contingent to Brazil during the 1880s and 1890s (Table 9) and

Table 10. Foreigners By Nationality in Rio de Janeiro and São Paulo, 1872–1920

	Total City Population	Total Foreign (percentage of total city population)	Portuguese	Italian	Spanish	French
Rio de Janeiro						
1872	274,972	84,279 (30.7)	55,933 (20.3)	1,738 (.6)	1,451 (.5)	2,884 (1.0)
1890	522,651	155,202 (29.7)	106,461 (20.4)	17,789 (3.4)	10,750 (2.1)	3,962 (.8)
1906	811,443	210,515 (25.9)	133,393 (16.4)	25,557 (3.1)	20,699 (2.6)	3,474 (.4)
1920	1,157,873	240,392 (20.8)	172,338 (14.9)	21,929 (1.9)	18,221 (1.6)	3,538 (.3)
São Paulo						
1872	31,385	2,459 (7.8)	999 (3.2)	167 (.5)	44 (.1)	133 (.4)
1893	130,775	71,468 (54.7)	14,437 (11.0)	45,457 (34.8)	4,818 (3.7)	1,110 (.8)
1920	579,093	205,245 (35.4)	64,687 (11.2)	91,544 (15.8)	24,903 (4.3)	1,859 (.3)

Adapted from: *Recenseamento da população . . . 1872*, XXI (Município Neutro), 61; XIX (São Paulo), 2–26; Brazil, *Recenseamento geral . . . do Brazil . . . 1890. Districto Federal*, xxii, xxiii, xxvii; São Paulo [State], Repartição de Estatística e Arquivo, *Relátorio*, 1894, unpaged; Brazil, *Recenseamento do Rio de Janeiro . . . 1906*, I, 126–129; *Recenseamento do Brazil . . . 1920*, II, 1° parte, lix; IV, 1° parte, 545, 861.

the most important for the nation over the course of its long history.[23] As they themselves stated, Portuguese immigrants received no government subsidies, coming "at their own expense, or that of their relations,"[24] unlike most of the Italians, or the Japanese in the twentieth century.

In Portugal, as in many areas of Europe, nineteenth century population growth and local political and economic problems joined with general improvements in communication and transportation to foster emigration to the New World. Northern Portugal, a densely populated·region of small landholdings, traditionally exported people as well as wine. In the early 1890s, an epidemic of *phyloxera* devastated the vineyards, reducing the demand for laborers. A major bank crisis, the growing British threat to Portuguese-claimed territories in Africa, and the government's difficulties in meeting foreign debt payments further demonstrated Portugal's weakness and poverty. As the District Commissioner of Statistics in Angra do Heroismo, in the Azores, another major center of Portuguese emigration, recognized, "Emigration is fostered by ambition, stimulated by the example of those who return home wealthy, by the hatred of military service and by poverty; it is also furthered by the low level of salaries, which are almost always out of line with the prices of basic necessities."[25] Hardly a village in northern Portugal could not boast of a native son living in Brazil who steadfastly sent remittances to his relatives or provided sufficient funds to construct a church, hospital or school in his home village. This proved perhaps the best propaganda for immigraton to Brazil, as Portuguese government officials who encouraged such remittances well knew.[26]

Portuguese emigration was predominantly composed of young single males who, like the Portuguese population in general, were very often illiterate. An observant Portuguese visitor to Brazil in the 1890s, voicing concern over the population drain at home and the emigrants' hard lives abroad, claimed that the Portuguese emigrants were no longer "seeking to enrich themselves, but simply to eat"; moreover, "once emigration was almost exclusively rural; today the cities are also emigrating, since the woes of the countryside have invaded them too, and Lisbon like Oporto is now sending forth a powerful contingent of emigrants."[27] In contrast with Portugal and its stagnant economy and low wages, Brazil seemed a land of opportunities.

In the late nineteenth century, those opportunities appeared greatest in Rio de Janeiro. The Portuguese scattered to cities along the coast from the Amazon to Rio Grande do Sul, and could be found in sections of the north where other foreigners were rarely seen, as travelers reported.[28] But they preferred Rio, with its long-established Portuguese colony, by far the largest in Brazil. Although the percentage of foreign-born in Rio de Janeiro at the end of the nineteenth century never rose to São Paulo's level, the Portuguese predominated among that sector of the city's population even more heavily than did the Italians among São Paulo's immigrant population (Table 10).

Whether foreign or Brazilian-born, the lower classes were looked upon as "inferior" by the elite. The nation's rulers remained preoccupied with their own world, largely ignoring that of the urban poor. They cared about the appearance of the cities, not the living conditions of the lower classes, except when contagious diseases threatened to spread from the *cortiços* to their own homes. A midnineteenth century popular quatrain which appeared when Rio de Janeiro's streetlamps burned ever less brightly reflects this divergence:

> When dried meat is expensive
> When the poor are afflicted
> The press doesn't protest; it only says
> That the gas lamps have turned into night-lights. [29]

For many members of the elite, the poor served mainly as cannon fodder and as foci of infection. Brazil's poor did not always acquiesce passively to the governing elite's programs; at times they attempted to block official activities they considered detrimental to their vital interests. Popular violence and unplanned uprisings occurred in both rual and urban areas in the nineteenth century. [30] Crowds smashed the symbols of despised government policies, demonstrated hostility toward public officials and police, refused to pay taxes, and destroyed judicial and tax records. Perhaps the structure of politics in imperial Brazil encouraged groups on the margin of the formal political process to bring such extrainstitutional pressures to bear, as few realistic alternatives existed. A riot or display of violence could achieve an immediate objective, such as the temporary end of forced army recruitment in a specific town or the rescinding of trolley fare increases in the capital. Popular uprisings might serve as a warning to the government to moderate its demands upon the lower classes. Even individual acts of violence—freeing a relative from the press-gang—could secure quick relief and incline officials to caution.

Throughout the nineteenth century, forced recruitment into the armed forces generated great popular resentment and resistance. Brazil's lower classes alone were forced to fill the harshly treated, poorly paid ranks. As government officials publicly admitted, only the "poor and unprotected" had to pay the "blood tax." [31] Very few enlisted men ever rose into the officer corps. The common soldiers were separated from the commissioned officers by an immense social, educational, economic, and even racial gap. A midnineteenth-century foreign traveler in Brazil, who quickly learned how recruits were "caught and made to serve," described a group of one hundred such captives sent to Rio de Janeiro from a northern province as "nearly all colored; one-third were Indians."[32]

The Brazilian poor shunned military service. A soldier's life seemed little better than a slave's.[33] Not even in peacetime did sufficient numbers of men volunteer. Officers complained that Brazilians lacked a military "vocation" and contended that they needed discipline. But few lower-class men wished to face death or severe physical hardships, suffer loss of livelihood, or abandon unprotected families without adequate return. The press gang recruitment used to fill the ranks rendered military service even less appealing. Laws and regulations which exempted married men, only sons of widows, and those in certain occupations were far more frequently honored for the rich than for the poor.[34] Individuals and groups continually sought to protect themselves if possible. The more articulate elements of the lower classes, such as the typographers, sought legal exemption from military service, but they lacked the power to win concessions.[35] In contrast, major concerns like a Rio de Janeiro trolley company might secure freedom from recruitment for their employees, thereby providing themselves with a more stable work force.[36] But unprotected, unsuspecting, or slow-footed Amazon Indians, *nordestino* peasants, artisans, factory workers, retail clerks, and marginally employed men all fell into the hands of the press-gangs.[37] Even unprotected foreigners could be forcibly recruited. As one group of Portuguese retail clerks in Rio de Janeiro complained to their monarch, foreigners and Brazilians alike were "seized in broad daylight and sent along under guard, their arms or shoulders tied as if they were thieves or murderers; they are taken to the barracks and from there sent to the forts or to the remote province of Mato Grosso, while the boys are handed over to the navy."[38]

During the Paraguayan War (1865–1870), the imperial government expanded its press-gang activity, citing the increase in "the natural repugnance of sedentary peoples for military service."[39] The patriotically titled National Guard battalions of "Volunteers of the Nation," backbone of the Brazilian campaign, were popularly called "Club and Rope Volunteers."[40] Skilled workers protested that "the Paraguayan War was waged exclusively by workers, either as army troops or as Volunteers of the Nation."[41] Decades after the war, centenarian mothers lamented never having learned the fate of sons sent off to Paraguay.[42]

Besides providing bodies for the Brazilian armed forces, recruitment served as a method of social control and punishment. Both government officials and their opponents linked enlistment with imprisonment as weapons with which to threaten people.[43] Not only "vagabonds," "disorderly fellows," or unruly slaves could be sent into the army, but also those who offended the local "potentates."[44] High government officials recognized that recruitment became an "instrument of persecution and vengeance."[45] Publicly as well as privately they admitted abuses, for some individuals were protected from military service "for electoral ends" and others persecuted "to satisfy party hatreds."[46]

"Respectable" Brazilians and men of property found a refuge in the officer corps of the National Guard, which conferred authority and prestige, especially in the rural areas, reinforcing the power of the local chiefs or "colonels."[47] But the poor and unprotected—those least missed by the landowners or business concerns—and the supposedly unemployed were caught in the periodic "sweeps" and "manhunts."

To escape military service some Brazilians resorted to violence, while others resisted passively. They hid or fled, upon hearing that press-gangs were in the area, or employed evasive tactics. Since recruiters sought out free blacks, often recognizable by their shoes, "the badge of freedom," those freedmen "aware of the danger go barefoot and sometimes throw the recruiting officers off their guard."[48] During the Paraguayan War other Brazilians resisted actively. Sporatic violence occurred across the nation, as individual recruits shot their captors, or fathers and brothers raided jails where impressed relatives were held. Armed friends and relations, occasionally including wives and daughters, repulsed the authorities and freed recruits.[49]

Additional incidents occurred shortly after the Paraguayan War when the imperial government attempted to revise the recruitment system. As part of its modernization and reform program, the ministry of the Viscount of Rio Branco, José Maria da Silva Paranhos, proposed replacing the existing practice of forced recruitment into the armed forces with a national system of registration and enlistment based on European models.[50] Such a system, the war minister asserted, would "comply much more with the norms of civilization and increase the efficiency of the army."[51] While the imperial government claimed that under the new law the burden of military service would now be shared equally by rich and poor alike, the poor could but draw on past experience without any return benefits. They might well suspect that a better organized system of recruitment would make them more likely to be seized for military service.

When the imperial government attempted to enroll men eligible for the new military draft, opposition spread across much of Brazil. The continuation of forced recruitment during the registration period no doubt did nothing to ease popular suspicions of government motives and actions.[52] In areas like the Northeast and Minas Gerais angry crowds invaded government offices in different towns and destroyed registration records. These acts, designed to damage the authorities' capacity for future recruitment and harassment, resembled behavior during the Quebra-Quilo revolt, the most famous uprising of the period, more than they did the action of "mobs" rescuing individual imprisoned recruits.[53] Even during the Quebra-Quilo revolt, rioters expressed their hostility to the new recruitment law, which they termed the "law of captivity," as well as to the installation of the metric system and the payment of taxes.[54]

During the next several years, provincial efforts to comply with the new national military service regulations and register eligible Brazilians males met with open hostility. Groups of men, and sometimes women also, invaded the enlistment commissions' meeting places, interrupting their work or destroying enlistment records.[55] In Ponte Nova, Minas Gerais, over sixty women, "armed with clubs, invaded the church" where the parochial junta met, "managed to seize all the papers and books, ripping them," and then throwing them "into the fountain in the town square and into the holy water font."[56] Sometimes threats sufficed to keep local enlistment juntas from gathering and executing the law.[57] Provincial authorities reported "delays and difficulties" in executing recruitment laws and requested additional military forces to control these "seditious movements."[58]

Unlike the large-scale opposition to the introduction of the metric system, largely confined to small towns in the interior of the Northeast, the popular animosity toward the enlistment procedures raged across much of the nation and into large cities like Salvador. In July 1875 the capital of Bahia endured three days of strife. Provincial authorities had not succeeded in complying with confidential orders from Rio de Janeiro to avoid "seditious movements" over enlistment.[59]

As recruitment efforts declined, so did disturbances. Draft registrations never were completed and the "lottery" system never put into effect. Although some districts drew up enrollment lists and forwarded them to provincial capitals, others did not. Throughout the remainder of the empire, successive provincial presidents, as in Pernambuco, publicly bemoaned the "extreme slowness and manifest repugnance" with which those local officials worked.[60] Despite some official denials, the law had proved unenforceable, although it was never formally repealed.

Protests by the poor remained part of nineteenth-century Brazilian experience. Although the central government preferred officially to ignore demonstrations of distress, which belied its image of peaceful empire, this proved easier in areas of peripheral concern, such as the backlands, than in major cities. Movements originating in distant rural areas did not pose a direct threat to Brazil's urban centers or to the political elite.

The precarious economic status of the largest part of Brazil's urban population made it vulnerable to fluctuations in the prices of basic commodities. Immediate resentments might prompt violent disturbances without plan or program. In some ways, these protests resembled colonial Spanish American riots, such as the tumults of 1624 and 1692 in Mexico City, or the late eighteenth- and early nineteenth-century European urban riots which also served as vehicles of political and social unrest.[61] Rioters in midnineteenth-century Brazil did not attempt to overthrow the government, but rather directed their hostility toward local officials or individuals contributing to their distress. Through direct action they might extract immediate concessions from the authorities.

Due to the nature of the Brazilian political system, with its emphasis on conciliation and the avoidance of political manifestations of violence, the urban poor could not look for allies among warring political factions, as occurred in Mexico in the early nineteenth century following a long, bloody independence struggle.[62] Not only had Brazil secured political independence peacefully from Portugal, without social upheaval, but in Brazil, unlike Mexico in the first decades after independence, political power was not widely distributed. Politics in Brazil was marked by shifting coalitions of factions and individuals within a small upper class. While some dissident politicians attempted to use popular demands and resentments to harrass opponents, they fled before any possibility of political upheaval or mass violence in the cities. In Brazil, sporatic popular explosions and riots subsidized without much loss of life or any damage to the political structure.

Economic distress, social tensions, police action, specific resentments, and, at times, political disputes all played a part in urban upheavals and disorders in imperial Brazil, such as the 1858 "carne sem osso" (meat without bones) uprising in Salvador.[63] During the 1850s, both epidemics and food crises flagellated Salvador's populace. The provincial capital suffered from its first major yellow fever outbreak in 1849, followed by cholera epidemics in 1855 and 1856. Heavy rains in 1851 and 1852 not only destroyed export crops but also subsistence foodstuffs such as manioc. Then came several years of drought. With production down and supply disorganized, food prices rose relentlessly. By the end of the decade, the prices of locally produced and consumed products, manioc flour, dried and fresh beef, beans, rice, chicken, and salt, all reached new highs.[64] This led to conflict between the Municipal Council of Salvador and João Lins Vieira Cansansão de Sinimbú, president of the province. When the council voted to limit the sale of manioc flour entering Salvador to the municipal granaries, Sinimbú suspended the execution of this act for six months, until the Provincial Assembly would meet and resolve the issue. But the assembly vacillated, reaching no decision, so the council reenacted its earlier measure. According to the British consul in Bahia, this "met with *universal* satisfaction" and led to an immediate decline in the price of manioc flour, the "primary necessity of life, . . . the bread of the people."[65] But Sinimbú ordered the Municipal Council to revoke the edict, and when it refused, he suspended the council members—a legally questionable action.

Several days later matters came to a head. Placards appeared at night in the streets threatening the life of President Sinimbú, a Conservative Party leader with numerous opponents. On 28 February 1858, crowds of unarmed lower-class Bahians gathered outside public buildings, converging on the government palace. Protesting the rise in food prices and calling for cheaper manioc flour, they forced their way into the town hall, crying "we want meat without bones and flour without stones." The crowd also demanded that the dismissed municipal councilors be reinstated and that the troops be withdrawn from the area. Only after the cavalry charged them did they retreat. Similar scenes occurred the following morning.[66]

In dealing with such popular disturbances, Brazilian authorities generally employed force and violence, no matter what the circumstances. During all the events of 28 February and 1 March 1858 in Salvador, the crowds remained unarmed, as the police chief himself confirmed, yet they were still charged by infantry and cavalry.[67] Both Sinimbú and his police chief praised the army, national guard, and police forces for their nobility and restraint, but the British consul told a different story. Four national guard battalions known to sympathize with the demonstrators were not issued cartridges or called on to act. The battalion from São Pedro parish, "seeing the cavalry ill-treating some persons in the square, actually lowered their bayonets and advanced to charge the troops on the line! All this is suppressed by the Government authorities, but it is true that its Lieutenant Colonel threw himself in front of the battalion and begged and prayed his men not to cause his ruin. Had a shot been fired, this city would have been a scene of bloodshed."[68]

No doubt the authorities felt freer to employ force when the lower classes alone demonstrated against them. Both the police chief and the British consul testified that the Bahian crowds were "composed exclusively of the lower order," without "a single man of importance."[69] The frustrated police chief found no "head" or a "single voice" with whom he could speak, for the crowds lacked all "direction."[70] During this outbreak, no "middle-class" agitators or dissidents guided lower-class resentments for their own ends. Nor did slaves participate—they only observed the excitement.[71]

In cities, government forces could quickly suppress outbreaks by elements of the unorganized lower classes. The Sinimbú regime arrested large numbers of men and sent them into the army. Military service again served both as a punishment and as a control mechanism, an attempt to "guarantee this city the nonrepetition of such scenes."[72] Although the central government sustained Sinimbú's dismissal of the Salvador city council, the month after the uprising he handed the provincial presidency over to the first vice-president and left for Rio de Janeiro admist demonstrations of popular hostility. Later that year manioc flour and dried beef again began to fall in price, as did fresh beef the following year, beans two years later, and then rice.[73]

Popular outbursts continued to puncture the official calm of the empire, even in the nation's capital. The imposition of the metric system in 1874 led to several days of attacks on businesses, especially meat markets, in Rio de Janeiro.[74] In 1882 an increase in gas prices triggered three days of disorder in the capital. On 9 November some of Rio's merchants met and resolved not to consume gas. That night groups of men forced those stores remaining lit to extinguish their lamps or to close down; apparently some of these men also turned off streetlamps. Then other groups, unconnected with Rio's commerce, broke streetlamps, stoned buildings, including a police station, and, aided by the darkness, sacked some stores. As the police could not handle matters—they kept off the streets the first evening—the government sent in the cavalry, whose horses indiscriminately trampled rioters and bystanders alike. The government also pressured the Rio de Janeiro Gas Company to rescind its price increase.[75]

Noneconomic events could also precipitate upheavals. Late on the afternoon of 25 October 1883, several disguised army officers murdered Apulcro de Castro, a mulatto journalist and editor of O Corsário, a newspaper noted for vicious personal attacks and charges. Only an hour before, a fearful Castro had requested official protection, and the assassination occurred immediately after he left the police station in the protective company of an army captain. The following day, according to a visiting prominent member of the German colony in Rio Grande do Sul, groups of young men and boys, including bootblacks, newspaper vendors, and other street sellers, rolled two large barrels down the main shopping street, the Ouvidor, shouting and attempting to force commerce to close. These precariously employed individuals, who often helped precipitate urban disturbances, were then joined by more lawless elements.

Together they stoned the city police, until police cavalry with drawn swords cleared the streets. Shots, stones, and sabers wounded both demonstrators and passersby. Unlike protestors in some other urban disturbances, they voiced no specific demands or complaints. At dusk on 29 November large numbers of *capoeiras*, street fighters known for their distinctive African-derived combatative skills, broke gas lamps along the Ouvidor, and later that night some men unsuccessfully attempted to burn the Casino Fluminense, mistaking it for the Ministry of Justice next door. This time the police arrived quickly, arresting the arsonists as well as numerous others.[76]

A complicated web, impossible to untangle completely, surrounds the assassination of Apulcro de Castro. No mere muckracking journalist, he had risen from typographer to elegantly dressed, luxuriously living newspaper owner, rumored to have contacts and paid informants in high circles.[77] No doubt some of Apulcro de Castro's attacks on individuals profited their political opponents who might protect him. But his assaults on officers of the first cavalry regiment during the "military question," the series of incidents between the imperial government and sectors of the armed forces during the 1880s, roused these quick-tempered officers to bloodshed. While the government did not hesitate to send police cavalry galloping through the streets against rioters, it handled the actual assassination more gingerly, and merely dismissed the chief of police. Several days later, the emperor "ostentatiously visited" the barracks of the first cavalry regiment, who served as his body guards. Both Brazilians and foreign diplomats reported rumors that this regiment refused to obey orders to leave the capital for Rio Grande do Sul. However, the presumed assassins were transferred to far-off Mato Grosso.[78]

Not only army officers proved insubordinate. The indiscipline and unruliness of both army troops and urban police intensified, and sometimes even provoked, popular disorders, as well as causing frequent incidents between members of both bodies. Able citizens remained almost as reluctant to join the poorly paid and treated urban police force as to enter army ranks. Portuguese diplomats in Brazil agreed that police ranks included too many vagabonds and "bad elements," and that "many times they were the ones provoking disorders, until matters reached the point where they had to be kept in their quarters on holidays, in the interest of public order."[79]

Police behavior earned them unending lower-class resentment and hostility. They were the ones who captured recruits for the army and national guard for both war and peace time service.[80] Police authorities were directed to conduct frequent searches of the *cortiços* for vagabonds, escaped slaves, and "turbulent elements."[81] To punish gambling and

drunkenness, police charged into individual rooms, smashing and breaking the belongings of slum dwellers such as those depicted in Aluísio
Azevedo's novel *O Cortiço*; these people saw the police as their feared
and sworn enemies, and responded to police guns and sabers with clubs,
stones, empty bottles, and iron rods. In their newspapers, skilled workers
castigated the police for "beatings and all kinds of assaults on personal
security and public order."[82] Both police and workers attributed most of
the riots to a small group. But the police blamed a criminal element
among the lower classes, while workers held the police responsible.

Although economic distress underlay most nineteenth-century urban outbreaks in Brazil, both police excesses and destructive acts by marginal groups of society helped turn protests into riots. Agitation and action
by other elements, both in and out of power, also contributed, as officials sometimes acknowledged. One Rio police chief privately advised
his superior that "among the masses suffering great hardships, passions
easily rise which even more easily can be misguided"; "if important persons rouse the masses, I do not know to what lengths they will go."[83]
During such outbursts as the "carne sem osso" upheaval, antienlistment
disturbances, and the Quebra-Quilo revolt, provincial authorities blamed
the opposition party for stirring up the "mobs"—always an easy charge
to levy. Although these and other outbreaks show no signs of careful
advanced planning, crowds might be stimulated by opposition leaders
and even mobilize behind them. But upper-class individuals fostering
disturbances with an eye to gaining or maintaining power could not control the outcome of their efforts.

Some politicians also maintained ties with marginal elements living on the edge of the law. The parties could not depend on unpredict-
able protesting crowds to intimidate their opponents. In the countryside,
local leaders and landowners long employed *capangas*, henchmen who
could punish opposition, control elections, and secure general obedience. Provincial authorities acknowledged the importance of "bands of
criminals shielded by influential figures of one or the other party."[84] In
the cities, other marginal elements, protected by and even related to members of the elite, performed similar services. Although some imperial statesmen such as Joaquim Nabuco opposed "machine" politics and henchmen
who made a "profession out of parochial influence," nothing came of
their proposed reforms.[85]

One of the most vivid descriptions of urban electoral *capangas*, who
often employed *capoeiras*, skilled in African martial arts, came from the
pen of Joaquim Serra. This journalist from Maranhão published a long
satirical poem on imperial politics which should not remain forgotten.[86]
Bitterly attacking the ministry of the Vicount of Rio Branco, in power

from 1871 to 1875, Serra portrayed Rio Branco calling in *capangas* when he saw "the elections almost lost." The local political boss of the Glória district of Rio de Jáneiro, ambitious for a Senate seat and quite willing to accept cash, promised to "fix things there in Glória" with his *capoeiras*. On the "great day" of the election, the "ministry seeks the vote of—the police." Using knives and razors or brandishing bayonets and swords, both *capoeiras* and police attacked and intimidated voters and produced the desired electoral results.[87] While the events in Glória that Joaquim Serra described surpassed the usual level of municipal violence, few elections passed without violence or coercion. As foreign diplomats reported, it was "the custom" for "the party in power" to win, with bloodshed and fatalities even in the capital.[88]

The *capoeiras* used in political disputes of the late empire have a long, complex history in Brazil, weaving across race and class lines. Beginning as a distinct form of defense and diversion among African slaves in Brazil, *capoeira* became an organized, deadly form of fighting in the major nineteenth-century urban centers, especially Rio de Janeiro, Salvador, and Recife. In the twentieth century it evolved into an all-male ballet-like sport and expression of folklore.[89] African slaves forbidden the use of firearms and swords, their masters' weapons, agilely employed head, hands, and feet in butting, tripping, and kicking their adversaries. Excluded from all decision-making bodies in the masters' political system, slaves developed their own institutions and organizations in which they could hold positions of authority. *Capoeiras* may well have represented political leadership among the slaves, forming brotherhoods to protect the slaves in their territories. Their masters' recognition of the potential power *capoeiras* held over slave loyalties may have combined with fears of this deadly method of fighting to lead the government to order restrictions on its use.

In the early nineteenth century, Rio de Janeiro's police moved against *capoeiras* as they did against *quilombos* of escaped slaves and African religious ceremonies. But *capoeira* continued. Nineteenth-century police officials considered *capoeiras* to be dangerous criminal elements of society, perhaps in part because they dealt with numerous assaults by lone *capoeiras* against other blacks on city streets, especially at night. Whites were rarely attacked, no doubt as this would bring surer punishment.[90]

By the 1870s, *capoeira* activity in Rio de Janeiro, its major center, became more intense. Although many individual *capoeiras* used their skills just to entertain and protect themselves, observers reported others now organized into relatively autonomous gangs, or *maltas*, of from twenty to one hundred men, with their own chiefs, territories, signals, and slang. With ever fewer Africans in the population following the end of the slave trade in 1850, feuds founded on tribal divisions declined, but the *maltas* fought rival gangs based in other neighborhoods. According to police records, the ranks of the *capoeiras* contained increasing numbers of freedmen and mulattoes. Of the 237 *capoeiras* imprisoned in Rio de Janeiro during the first two months of 1877, 191 were free and 46 slave. Distinctively dressed in unbuttoned jackets, colored shirts, broad-brimmed felt hats, and neckerchiefs, *capoeiras* employed razors and clubs in their attacks, although these were less honorable weapons by their own standards. Not only isolated individuals but also merrymakers during popular festivities met with unprovoked assaults. Both police reports and newspapers detailed the destruction of stores and the beating and slashing of customers and passersby.[91]

No doubt the political protection enjoyed by certain *capoeiras* permitted their intense activity. Although the police locked up some *capoeiras* guilty of individual attacks, they could not incarcerate those with political connections. For example, Manduca da Praia, a carefully dressed tall mulatto with a fish stand at the Rio market and the possessor of an impressive gold watch chain, was arrested dozens of times. But this participant in electoral affairs in the São José district was always acquitted, due to his friends' influence.[92] The *capoeiras* had become known for their ability to create disorders almost instantly, without getting hurt themselves. Such skills proved useful to politicians not only at election time but also during their opponents' public meetings. *Capoeiras* functioned as political shock troops and body guards, and heads of *maltas* were rumored to receive public funds for their services. In this way, politicians stifled whatever potential threat *capoeiras* may have posed to that system. Co-optation continued to function as an effective method of social control. What was once a parallel political institution of a segmented society became partially incorporated into the elite political system.

During the late empire, new elements had entered *capoeira* ranks, intensifying the political connections. In nineteenth-century Rio de Janeiro, more than elsewhere, *capoeira* spread beyond Afro-Brazilian circles and even touched high levels of society. Some Europeans became *capoeiras,* such as the Frenchman cited in an 1871 Rio newspaper. José Elísio Reis, better known as Juca Reis, one of the most famous *capoeiras,* was the son of a leading Portuguese businessman, the first Count São Salvador de Matosinhos, and brother of the second count, owner of *O País,* one of Rio's leading newspapers. With a few wealthy whites heading *capoeira* bands, police crackdowns during the empire became even less likely, despite calls for laws against the *capoeiras.*[93]

Only after the declaration of the republic did the government move decisively against the *capoeiras* in Rio de Janeiro, Salvador, Recife, Santos, and São Paulo. With new men in power, leading *capoeiras* no longer enjoyed the same political protection. Nor did a military-dominated government lacking competing parties need their services. Even Juca Reis, recently returned from Lisbon, was included with other *capoeiras* ordered to the island prison of Fernando de Noronha by Rio's new police chief, João Batista Sampaio Ferraz. This led to a cabinet crisis. Quintino Bocaiúva, Minister of Foreign Relations and editor of *O País*, protested police "excesses" and threatened to resign. But both Bocaiúva and Sampaio Ferraz remained in their posts. Juca Reis's brother, the Count of Matosinhos, sold *O País* and moved to Europe, and Juca Reis went to Fernando de Noronha before being permitted to leave the country.[94]

The new penal code of 1890 prohibited the public "exercise of agility and corporal dexterity known by the designation of *capoeiragem*." Not just the individuals but the "art" itself was to be suppressed, as part of a broader move against customs of African origins, such as celebration of the religious rites of *candomblé*. By the early twentieth century the press again reported attacks on holiday merrymakers by *capoeiras* armed with clubs and razors, although in a few more decades *capoeira* would be commonly considered merely an acrobatic expression of Brazilian culture.[95]

The attempted suppression of *capoeira* during the first years of the republic also reflects hostilities engendered during the republican campaign. The monarchical parties not only set *capoeiras* against their long-time electoral opponents, but also employed them against dissident elements such as republicans and abolitionists. *Capoeiras* and other police agents disrupted public meetings and damaged the buildings and presses of radical newspapers in Rio de Janeiro, Recife, Campos and other cities.[96] While occasional bonds might be formed between individual republicans and *capoeiras*, such as José Lopes da Silva Trovão, a popular and fiery republican orator and journalist, and the *capoeira* who saved him from an assassination attempt, the republicans did not use *capoeiras* in their struggle against the monarchy. Even if they wished to do so, republicans held virtually no public offices and could not provide protection in exchange for the *capoeiras*' services.

A small minority, republicans sought support among various segments of the population. In São Paulo, they appealed to local economic interests, attracting some prosperous planters into their fold. Other republicans attempted to make converts among the armed forces, championing demands of army officers during the "military question." Although few republicans could be termed radical in their thinking or behavior, some sought to assure urban workers of their support. In 1872, three leading republicans and signers of the 1870 Republican Manifesto, Joaquim Saldanha Marinho, Aristides Lobo, and Salvador de Mendonça,

offered their services to Rio's newly formed Liga Operária, a mutual benefit society composed of skilled workers from various trades. However,
the league refused to elect them honorary members, preferring to have
only regular members.[97] In Recife, republican newspapers of the 1870s
portrayed artisans as victims of unemployment, low salaries and high
taxes and prices, who could expect no improvement in their difficult
lives as long as Brazil remained a monarchy.[98] During the waning years
of the monarchy, *O Grito dos Pobres* in São Paulo solicited the support
of skilled urban workers as well as students and army officers by arguing
that "The poor will only have the vote and guarantees, they will only be
respected and heeded, they will only be independent and free citizens"
when the republic is proclaimed, "because the republic equals social
justice."[99]

A few republicans actively sought to stimulate lower-class resentments, rather than merely to offer general expressions of sympathy, com-
miserate over high food prices and rents, or occasionally protest forced
recruitment into the armed forces. In Rio de Janeiro, José Lopes da Silva
Trovão drew large crowds with his fiery and florid speeches against the
monarchy. Not all republican leaders approved of his activities. This tall,
thin figure, who frequently sported a top hat and monocle, played a major role in sparking the *vintém* upheaval—the most serious urban uprising of the empire and the most upsetting to the elite—which convulsed
Rio de Janeiro during the opening days of 1880.

Late in 1879 the imperial government decreed a tax of twenty *reis*,
or one *vintém*, on all streetcar rides in Rio de Janeiro. This tax, imposed
just in the capital, would not be paid by the streetcar companies, but by
the passengers, with coins—which were always in short supply, or with
paper cards liable, according to a local newspaper, to be "lost," "torn,"
or "easily counterfeited." Part of a series of new or higher taxes designed
to help the government cope with a growing budgetary deficit, the *vintém* levy was to take effect on 1 January 1880.[100]

People of every class rode Rio's mule-drawn streetcars. For members of the lower classes living in outlying suburbs, the trolleys provided
essential transportation to their places of employment, while consuming
perhaps ten percent of their daily wages. The new nongraduated tax fell
heaviest on these second class passengers, raising their fares by some twenty
percent.[101] Militant opponents of the tax could whip widespread hostility and anger into open rebellion.

During the weeks between the announcement of the tax and its sched-
uled enforcement, republicans as well as abolitionists and opposition Con-
servatives protested the tax and attacked the Liberal ministry. Lopes Trovão,
director of *A Gazeta da Noite*, and other journalists organized a series of

public meetings, marches, and demonstrations in Rio. Parades wound from one newspaper office to another, with speeches by journalists at each stop. On 28 December 1879, Lopes Trovão addressed a mass meeting near the emperor's palace in São Cristóvão which attracted some five thousand people. Followed by large crowds, he attemped to deliver a petition to the emperor requesting repeal of the tax. Despite secret police provocations, order prevailed. These activities by opposition journalists alerted more of Rio's inhabitants to the tax issue, and helped to create a climate of conflict and crisis.[102]

At noon on 1 January 1880, the day streetcar conductors first attempted to collect the *vintém*, Lopes Trovão addressed a meeting of some three thousand people and counseled them not to pay this tax. Earlier that hot summer day, in different parts of the city, men began overturning and destroying streetcars and beating drivers and conductors. Pedro II later privately maintained that "from the hour at which the disorders broke out one can see that they are created by day laborers," that is, by people personally hurt by the tax; the emperor believed that "the disorders have no political character."[103] The vast majority of the people milling about Rio's streets were "curious spectators," not participants. Nor was the destruction on the first day of the riots indiscriminate. The Vila Isabel streetcar line, considered the most hostile toward passengers, felt the brunt of popular ire. In contrast, cars of the Botantical Garden line, whose American owners had offered to pay the *vintém* themselves and refused to expel passengers for nonpayment, continued to run when all others were forced to stop.[104]

An anxious government, fearful that Rio's police could not control matters, had posted army troops at key points throughout the city, as well as on some streetcars. Before the first day of riots ended, these troops fired on the milling crowds. But who provoked whom? Not only opposition newspapers blamed secret police agents for violent acts which could be used to justify further repressive action. One of the least partial observers, the editor of the English-language *Rio News*, was "unable to discover either pistol or knife in the hands of the rioters. It was purely and plainly an unarmed mob."[105] Yet a leading arms store had unexpectedly sold 150 revolvers in December, guns which the very poor could not afford.[106] It is not hard to believe that police agents used knives and guns and threw paving stones at troops and demonstrators. The troops responded and fired on the crowds, killing several bystanders.[107]

During the next two days destruction and disturbances continued, with fewer rioters and more armed marginal elements now in evidence. The government declared a state of seige, sent in additional forces, carried out numerous arrests, including that of Lopes Trovão, and suspended the *Gazeta de Notícias*, one of the most vocal opposition journals. Heavy rain on 4 January helped dampen the revolt, although sporatic incidents continued throughout the month.[108]

Journalists who had previously advised resistance to payment of the *vintém*, as well as more cautious newspapermen, had all appealed to the people to disperse and return to their labors.[109] They might have helped precipitate the uprising, but they could not control a movement too violent for their liking. Several months later, the popular poet João de Santa Ana de Maria, a mulatto from the north who earned coins with his songs in Rio's major squares, composed one of his most popular pieces, the "*Vintém* Tax." In this song, he described Lopes Trovão's rapid retreat:

> When the fracas began,
> And the common people were rounded up,
> Dr. Lopes Trovão
> Ran off on his thin legs,
> He was careful on Grand Beach
> But he still got his boots wet.[110]

This major uprising, occurring in the nation's capital under the eyes of the central government and of representatives of foreign countries, upset the elite. They feared disorder and disliked admitting that such urban riots could take place. Pedro II privately expressed his unhappiness over this disgrace, lamenting the need to "employ more force against the people than has been required for almost forty years."[111] No doubt the comments directed at him as he passed through the city also proved upsetting.

The *vintém* outburst undermined confidence in the ability of the ministry of João Lins Vieira Cansansão de Sinimbú to handle the nation's affairs. Opposition congressmen denounced both the tax and government's execution of it.[112] Members of the urban populace, egged on by dissident politicians, had successfully brought pressure on the political process. The government ceased attempting to collect the *vintém*. On 28 March 1880 the Sinimbú ministry was replaced by that of José Antonio Saraiva, which officially abolished this tax, although others were kept or even increased.

Lopes Trovão continued to write and speak out in favor of a republic, remaining a popular figure in Rio de Janeiro. But he never became a major republican leader. Sent by friends to Europe the year after the *vintém* uprising, he returned to promote more demonstrations over sensitive issues troubling the urban lower classes. However, none of those meetings, despite police intervention, generated as much emotion as those leading to the *vintém* upheaval, and Lopes Trovão himself exercised more moderation. In March 1889, when Rio de Janeiro suffered from a severe water shortage, Lopes Trovão held a large public protest meeting which the government attempted to dissolve. The opposition press lambasted the administration for not constructing new waterworks, so that the public was reduced to buying barrels of water at "fabulous prices." Tensions generated by the progressive water shortage probably prompted the government to engage a young engineer, Paulo de Frontin, who promised to complete the necessary construction and supply the city with sufficient supplementary water within six days, at a small fraction of the cost and in a fraction of the time estimated by a well-known firm. When water actually flowed from Rio's public fountains on the sixth day, Paulo de Frontin became the city's hero—eight thousand people massed to greet him at the start of the victory parade.[113]

Less than two years before the fall of the empire, another fiery orator, Antônio da Silva Jardim, began his career as the greatest and supposedly the most radical republican propagandist in Brazil. Born in the province of Rio de Janeiro in 1860, he converted to positivism in 1881, while still a student at the São Paulo law school. His attempts to propagate the doctrines of August Comte foreshadowed the long speaking tours later dedicated to the republican cause. In 1887 Silva Jardim joined the Republican Club in Santos. Early in 1888, after his break with the orthodox positivists, he initiated his strident republican propaganda. Silva Jardim's views reflected Comtian ideas of a republican dictatorship; he led a group of young men wishing to replace the pacific program of the moderate Republican Party leaders with one of direct action.[114]

During propaganda excursions to cities across Brazil, this slight figure, always dressed in black, galvanized large audiences with his fervent oratory. Rather than direct his energies toward established politicians, merchants, or planters, Silva Jardim sought to attract students, retail clerks, small businessmen, and some urban workers to the republican cause. He mixed patriotic praise for Brazil's accomplishments with denunciations of a retrograde monarchy inhibiting greater progress. Silva Jardim condemned the ruling dynasty as "a house of adventurers and rich men, without exception, meanspirited and power hungry."[115] Pedro II was incompetent and his son-in-law, the French-born Count d'Eu, tyrannical, militaristic, and corrupt. Under a republic, Brazil would become a progressive, industrialized nation with an expanded educational system.

Considered a "radical Republican" by both contemporaries and later observers, Silva Jardim did favor the forcible establishment of a republic, but never a radical transformation of society. He voiced sympathy for the hungry but also praised hard work and harmonious class relations, a reflection of his paternalistic positivist approach to social questions. Rather than "leveling or merging classes," he favored "conciliating all of them, and allowing each one self-determination." Large estates should not be divided; their proprietors "have rendered services to humanity."[116] When Silva Jardim addressed retail clerks, one of his major constituencies, in support of their campaign for Sunday store closings, he based his defense of a weekly day of rest on the hard work clerks perform and on the intelligent use they would make of their free time; he opposed government intervention in this matter.[117]

At the May 1889 congress of the Republican Party, the conflict between Silva Jardim and followers and more cautious, orderly elements came to a head. The election of Quintino Bocaiúva as party chief signified continued control by the long-dominant conservative groups. This victory over those favoring an armed movement of the people precipitated the final break between the two men. Silva Jardim refused to recognize Quintino Bocaiúva's leadership, attacking him bitterly. Quintino excluded Silva Jardim from the military conspiracy which culminated in the overthrow of the empire and the establishment of a republic on 15 November 1889. Sent to Europe shortly afterwards, Silva Jardim met a spectacular death in Vesuvius' crater on 1 July 1891 at the age of thirty.[118]

Except in São Paulo province, the republicans remained an urban-based party, but one commanding the allegiance of relatively few voters. Republican candidates received only five percent of the vote in the September 1889 general elections in Recife.[119] In Rio's April 1888 congressional elections Quintino Bocaiúva polled only 108 votes, while Antônio Ferreira Vianna, a Conservative supported by the Abolitionist Confederation, received 1,347 votes.[120] The number of republican sympathizers beyond the limited electorate is more difficult to judge. Silva Jardim's public addresses, like Lopes Trovão's street meetings, attracted large audiences, and Silva Jardim no doubt raised hopes for a better life under the republic.

Some army officers, like republicans, issued declarations of sympathy for the urban workers. They mingled vague promises of protection and support for labor with vehement attacks on the government for neglecting the army.[121] After the Paraguayan War many Brazilian officers were not content to return to the old pattern of a smaller, less conspicuous army. They felt victimized by civilian politicians both during and after the war, and became more willing to question orders. Officers resented the continual reduction of army size as well as their relatively low salaries and the meager appropriations granted the army.

Younger officers not only attacked politicians they considered hostile to perceived army interests but also demonstrated impatience with the government's failure to resolve the slavery question. Military pride and the officers' personal and professional grievances joined with abolitionist sentiments. Throughout the 1880s, students at the military school in Rio de Janeiro supported abolitionist activities. Some officers and cadets joined abolitionist societies, although their frequent transfers generally kept them from becoming active members. Army officers could express their growing irritation with the imperial government through the abolition issue, and civilian abolitionists, like some republicans, supported military demands and insubordination.[122]

For most advocates of abolition, slavery was an evil corrupting the nation's moral character, as well as an obstacle to material progress and national self-respect. Liberation somehow would advance industry and agriculture and stimulate immigration, besides raising Brazil's status in the international community. Many abolitionists believed abolition meant merely replacing slavery with a free labor system; freedmen would continue to work for their former masters. In a society with severely limited educational opportunities, restricted political participation, and large landholdings, few individuals envisioned a different kind of world for the ex-slaves or for themselves. However, some of the movement's leaders saw the extinction of slavery as the beginning of a series of basic reforms ending the dominance of the slave-holding class. For Joaquim Nabuco, brilliant orator and well-educated patrician planter from Pernambuco, "slavery" signified not just the "relationship of the slave to the master," but "the sum of the power, influence, capital, and patronage of all the masters; the feudalism established in the interior," and the dependence of "commerce, religion, the poor, industry, Parliament, the Crown" and the state upon the aristocratic slave-holding minority.[123] Leading abolitionists like André Rebouças, mulatto engineer and teacher, denounced "territorial monopoly and landlordism" and called for the "subdivision of the latifundia and the creation of small property holdings."[124] The establishment of compulsory education, broader political representation, the separation of church and state, and readjustment programs for ex-slaves were all envisioned.

While a few abolitionists, like Rebouças, dreaming of "rural democracy," stressed rural reforms, others demonstrated their awareness of the dismal and "corrupting" living conditions of the urban poor and railed against the *cortiços*. Several, apparently reflecting beliefs in the superiority and necessity of agriculture in Brazil, as well as of small property holdings, proposed that some of Rio's slum dwellers be settled on small plots of land near the "overpopulated" city. There they could "be transformed from proletarians to proprietors and agricultural producers within a short time."[125] But until the actual achievement of their principal goal, liberation of all slaves, the collateral reforms abolitionists advocated would claim only a small part of their energies. Even those reform proposals, like most abolitionist propaganda and activities, were aimed at the governing groups. Abolitionists generally addressed the free, not the slaves.

During the 1880s abolitionists, particularly in São Paulo and Rio de Janeiro, grew increasingly radical. They frequently faced physical dangers and attacks by pro-slavery forces in the cities as in the countryside. Especially during the ministry of the Baron of Cotegipe (1885–1888), which temporarily banned abolition meetings in Rio de Janeiro, vendors of abolitionist newspapers were assaulted, newspaper offices attacked and even destroyed, meetings interrupted, and assassinations or beatings of anti-slavery leaders attempted. To these dangers were added frustrations over the pace of their work. Since legal methods, parades, meetings, emancipation funds, and parliamentary oratory produced only slow results, some radical abolitionists abandoned them for "direct action." In São Paulo, under the leadership of the mulatto Luís Gama and especially under his successor Antônio Bento de Souza e Castro, they directed their efforts toward the slaves, not just toward the free. As a laywer, Luís Gama specialized in liberating persons illegally held in captivity, as he once had been. Antônio Bento, a well-born zealot and the deeply religious head of the provincial abolition movement following the death of Luís Gama in 1882, organized the best underground movement in Brazil, with headquarters in the sacristy of the black lay brotherhood of Nossa Senhora dos Remédios. His agents conducted dangerous forays onto plantations and into slave quarters to foster slave flights and then assist the fugitives to urban sanctuary. The daring men who joined Antônio Bento came from all classes and political parties, including the black members of the brotherhood—who were largely day laborers—cigar makers, railroad workers, typographers, and the carriage drivers. The latter, who provided both information and transportation, were later praised by Bento as the group which best served the cause. [126]

While blacks and mulattoes played important roles in the abolitionist struggles, few, such as André Rebouças, Luís Gama, or the Rio journalists José do Patrocínio and José Ferreira de Menezes achieved important leadership positions. For those posts, formal education and social connections were needed, and generally unavailable to poor people of color. Most blacks and mulattoes, like whites, shunned the anti-slavery movement. And some avowed enemies of abolition, like the Baron of Cotegipe, were said to be light mulattoes. Whether poor blacks with no time or energy for anything beyond immediate personal or familial concerns, or upwardly striving mulattoes, most dark-skinned Brazilians did not participate in the formal abolition movement.

An undercurrent of hostility between lower-class blacks and the multi-hued urban middle sectors, who provided support and leadership for reform movements, could be detected. Blacks especially resented those mulattoes seeking to "pass" for whites. Unlike some mulattoes, the radical abolitionist Luís Gama remembered his past—in his case, the years he spent in captivity—and identified with his African mother, not with the white father who illegally sold him into slavery. In his satirical poetry, published under the pseudonym Getulino, Luís Gama expressed the resentments blacks felt toward those who denied their African ancestry:

> If the puffed-up aristocrats of this land
> Have relatives buried in Guinea,
> And, giving in to vainglory or mean weaknesses
> Forget their black fellow-countrymen:
> If mulattoes of a whitish shade
> Now deem themselves of polite origins,
> And warped by the mania possessing them,
> Reject and despise the grandmother who comes from the Sudan;
> Don't be astonished by this, dear Reader,
> Because everything in Brazil is extraordinary.[127]

Although the role of radical abolitionists like Antônio Bento, Luís Gama's successor as head of the *paulista* abolition movement, in aiding slaves to escape seems reasonably clear, questions may be raised as to whether they counseled violence or armed uprisings. Certainly such unquiet souls as Raul Pompéia, citing Luís Gama's admonition that "before the law the crime of homicide is justifiable when committed by a slave against his master," wrote that insurrection was consistent with human nature and justified by violations of liberty.[128] But did they actually urge slaves to act on such statements? Not only slave owners fearful of rebellion and massacres by vengeful slaves accused abolitionists of plotting acts of destruction.[129] One foreigner working in Brazil, admitting to an anti-abolitionist bias, reported meetings of radical abolitionists "who proclaim war against all masters, and counsel their murder and the dishonoring of their wives and daughters. . . . These abolitionists, according to all I hear, are the Socialists and Nihilists of Brazil, and their influence among the slave population is great."[130] A journalist from Rio Grande do Sul accused Rio de Janeiro abolitionists of directing "revolutionary propaganda" toward *capoeiras* and attempting to cause uprisings among blacks.[131] Abolitionist newspapers indicated that nocturnal agents not only counseled flight from *fazendas* but sometimes also supplied arms to the slaves. To be sure, slave revolts in Brazil date back to the colonial period. In the nineteenth century such provinces as Minas Gerais, Rio de Janeiro, São Paulo, and especially Bahia witnessed serious slave uprisings, often involving recent arrivals from Africa or urban slaves. During the last years of slavery in Brazil the incidence of revolts seemed highest in the southern coffee and sugar regions of São Paulo and Rio de Janeiro, and slave owners often blamed abolitionists for instigating the uprisings.

The Confederação Abolitionista in Rio de Janeiro emphasized propaganda and political mobilization, not illegal action, while also demonstrating concern for the welfare of runaway slaves and other poor black and racially mixed Brazilians. Formed in 1883 from a number of diverse anti-slavery groups organized along predominately occupational lines, the confederation included many members of the urban middle sectors and even some skilled workers. School teachers, journalists, commercial employees and shopkeepers, officials of the D. Pedro II Railway, engineering students, and military cadets all established separate abolitionist societies, as did printers with their Club Abolicionista Gutenberg. Members of most of these urban groups depended directly upon the government for employment, promotion, and prestige, and often expressed frustration with what they viewed as inadequate pay, job security, and recognition. Their professional interests complemented abolitionism as a political stance. As urban consumers, they suffered the burdens of economic policies geared to export agriculture, including high import duties levied on essentials such as foodstuffs, at a time when planters were reducing food production in favor of export crops. Abolitionist businessmen objected to what they perceived as privileges granted to agriculture and especially to the coffee sectors. In its efforts to stabilize the exchange rate, the government lowered export taxes and provided agricultural credit, while at the same time it raised import duties and reduced public programs and employment in an attempt to balance the budget hurt by falling agricultural prices. Thus the imperial government antagonized large segments of the urban population and facilitated abolitionist efforts to wed these people's aspirations and grievances to anti-slavery enthusiasm.[132]

The leaders of Rio's Abolitionist Confederation lacked the social positions and prestige and the nationwide prominence of leaders of the Brazilian Anti-Slavery Society. That society, headed by Joaquim Nabuco, included distinguished reformers with ready personal access to the national political structure. In contrast, the middle-sector leadership of the confederation came primarily from Rio's small businesses. João Clapp, the confederation's president, established a small investment company and later opened a china shop. The confederation's founders included journalists, a publisher, an accountant, a bookkeeper, an engineer, and government bureaucrats, not members of Parliament. Rather than commit themselves to working within the established political system, they sought to restructure it. While national leaders such as Nabuco produced the movement's ideological statements and prepared reform proposals, Rio activists mobilized popular opinion and worked directly with the slaves.[133]

Like radical abolitionists in São Paulo, but on a smaller scale, the Rio abolitionists probably constructed clandestine machinery with secret agents, passwords, and falsified manumission papers, to help slaves to freedom. Within the city of Rio, they attempted to provide safe havens and some jobs for fugitive slaves. The Abolitionist Confederation's middle sector leadership also stressed education. João Clapp directed a night school at the Freedman's Club of Niterói, across the bay from Rio, as had Luís Gama in São Paulo. This and other clubs also raised funds to liberate slaves and provided free legal services. While these abolitionists never neglected their own perceived interests, their view of abolition was not limited to mere legal emancipation. Nor did they merely denounce rising taxes and prices, of concern to the urban poor as well as to the middle sectors. The small contingent of radical abolitionists called for the incorporation of freedmen as well as racially mixed lower-class elements into a reformed Brazil.[134]

During the final months preceding the unconditional, uncompensated abolition of slavery in Brazil on 13 May 1888, republicans and abolitionists drew apart. Membership in these two movements had overlapped; for example, Joaquim Saldanha Marinho, long-term leader of the Republican Party, was a founding member of the Brazilian Anti-Slavery Society. But most activists gave priority to one or the other movement. Although Quintino Bocaiúva and Silva Jardim called themselves abolitionists, they devoted their major energies to the republican cause. José do Patrocínio and João Clapp placed abolition first. Even though Rio abolitionists at times supported anti-slavery Liberal and Conservative Party candidates, no irreparable split between abolitionists and republicans occurred until 1888.

A few abolitionists now drew closer to the throne. Once a severe critic of the Princess Imperial Isabel, Rio journalist José do Patrocínio became her grateful admirer. She had actively supported abolition while ruling in the stead of the ailing emperor, in Europe for medical treatment. Republicans accused Patrocínio, a mulatto who had signed the 1870 Republican Manifesto, of supporting a "Black Guard" which disrupted republican meetings. Patrocínio claimed that the "original" Black Guard was a spontaneous association of freedmen, "upright, hardworking men worthy of respect for the noble sentiments which united them," not "levies of *capangas*," who "always opposed" the abolitionists; "the mission of the Black Guard was to defend with their lives the Redeemer of their Race [Princess Isabel]" from vengeful planters who threatened her life and throne.[135] The involvement of abolitionists such as José do Patrocínio with the Black Guard offers a rare example of a direct liaison between middle-class activists, both black and white, and lower-class blacks.

The exact nature and activities of the Black Guard, the subject of endless polemics, remain unclear. Its composition may well have changed. Perhaps insufficient freedmen were attracted to the guard. Some politicians defending the throne probably reverted to the traditional use of *capoeiras* to harass opponents. *Capoeiras*, called Black Guards by the republican press, disrupted public meetings held by Silva Jardim in attacks resembling earlier officially condoned *capoeira* assaults against both abolitionists and republicans. Republican charges that the Black Guard was just a band of paid *capoeiras* were met with countercharges of republican provocations against blacks. Periodic clashes occurred between republicans and black groups in various areas of the country. Many republicans thought elements within the Conservative ministry were mobilizing black masses in support of the monarchy, not that blacks were mobilizing themselves politically through racially-based organizations.[136] Could both views be partially true? Traditional politicians apparently attempted to use José do Patrocínio's leadership role among dark-skinned groups in Rio de Janeiro to pit lower-class blacks against republicans. And many republicans appeared eager to turn planter desperation following abolition to their political advantage. Their party gained adherents among former slave owners. Not only personal gratitude—the motivation so often attributed to the abolitionists—but a belief that the monarchy represented Brazil's best hopes for social reform moved radical abolitinists like José do Patrocínio temporarily to support the crown.

Radical abolitionists had become increasingly disenchanted with a growing republican movement that generally ignored the freedmen. Abolition without reform would mean continued misery for the ex-slaves and for Brazil's poor. Radical abolitionists did not deny republicanism but rather a republican policy apparently beholden to large agricultural interests.

In Rio de Janeiro, the long-awaited final abolition of slavery led to days of celebrations, with parades, speeches, music, banquets, and public demonstrations of rejoicing in a city decorated with flowers and banners. The multitudes literally filled the vast expanses of the Campo de São Cristóvão for a solemn high mass attended by the Princess Regent and her husband, the cabinet, and most of the diplomatic corps.[137] On

20 May members of different sectors of the urban population, including skilled workers, participated in a grand victory parade lasting for hours organized by Rio's press; the printers' Club Abolitionista Gutenberg, one of the oldest abolitionist societies in Rio, had three carriages, one with a young woman and their standard, an open book, the second with "[club] members dressed in workers' blouses and caps," and the third with a bust of Gutenberg.[138] That day over a hundred thousand people filled Rio's streets. During the whole week following the signing of the "golden law" on 13 May there was nothing but "enthusiastic joy, good temper, and good order."[139] In contrast, no widespread popular emotion was displayed following the unexpected declaration of a republic on 15 November 1889. People remained "unconcerned, and in the midst of official salutes and celebrations, you could not hear a single firecracker, the inseparable signal of displays of noisy festivity by the people of Rio de Janeiro."[140]

Some would-be reformers and dissident political elements, primarily abolitionists and republicans, attempted to gain support among elements of the urban poor, generally ignored by the elite. In their efforts to undermine existing policies and structures, they echoed certain lower-class grievances, especially the high cost of living. A few radical abolitionists went beyond words to "direct action" to benefit slaves and other poor Brazilians. Abolitionists fought a battle of far greater importance to more people, rousing stronger emotions among larger numbers of Brazilians, than did the republicans. More than members of the two major monarchical parties, with ties to marginal elements, dissidents sought to fan lower-class resentments into acts of open hostility. But the poor were not mere passive recipients of upper-class attentions. Nor did political agitation alone lead to urban upheaval. An immense social and economic gap separated would-be reformers from the objects of their attention. Through violent disturbances, frequently tied to their precarious economic status, the lower classes demonstrated their distress and applied pressure to the political system. At ame time, a smaller sector of the urban working classes attempted to protect itself through means which proved less alarming to the nation's rulers than violent protests by the poor, organizing their own associations for mutual aid and defense.

3 / Organizing Urban Workers: *From Empire to Republic*

Beginning in the midnineteenth century, various groups of skilled workers in Brazil's growing cities organized mutual benefit societies to aid and protect themselves in an often hostile environment. By the 1870s some of these laborers displayed pride in their skills as well as expressing resentment of their poor economic position and of the disdain shown them by the elite. The abolitionist campaign of the 1880s helped stimulate their self-confidence and assertiveness, while the advent of the republic in 1889 provided the possibility of more rapid change. Although mutual benefit societies persisted in their activities during the final years of the century, a variety of recently formed labor associations pressed demands both for the amelioration of working conditions and for changes in society in the early 1890s. The initial years of the republican regime witnessed a flurry of labor activity as both workers and nonworkers tried to unify and mobilize urban laborers.

By the late nineteenth century, disparities in development between the northern and southern sections of the nation had increased, with south-central Brazil attracting larger quantities of European immigrants and capital. Bahia, especially Salvador and its surroundings, had been the first center of textile production in Brazil, and possessed approximately half the country's cotton mills is the 1860s.[1] But by the end of the century, Rio de Janeiro and São Paulo had pulled ahead. These cities offered larger regional markets for industrial products, as well as capital, labor, transportation facilities, and government connections. The *paulista* coffee economy helped provide capital for local industrialization. At the same time, the decadence of Paraíba Valley coffee cultivation by the 1880s perhaps impeded Rio's development. Although Rio long remained Brazil's biggest city and internal market, São Paulo would replace it as the nation's most important industrial center by 1920.[2]

Despite protective tariffs, expanded credit facilities, and the abolition of slavery, industrialization progressed slowly during the late empire without creating numerous new jobs. Many so-called factories long remained small shops, relying on muscle, not steam power. In Rio de Janeiro in the early 1880s, only a handful of hat, furniture, leather, and metal plants employed more than fifty workers apiece, and factories with fewer than twenty or even ten employees were far more common.[3]

Did available unskilled labor exceed steady employment possibilities? Many European immigrants imported to cultivate coffee moved to the cities in search of a better life, as did some freedmen and other Brazilians, thus augmenting the urban labor pool. Few alternatives existed. Opportunities to become small freeholders in settled or frontier areas remained remote for most Brazilians.[4] The lack of primary or technical schools also limited possibilities for improving individual situations. In 1878 the empire had only 5,661 primary schools, public and private, with a total of 175,714 pupils, leaving over a million-and-a-half school-age children without instruction.[5] While some textile factory owners complained of labor scarcity and of worker reluctance to submit to constant supervised toil, others presented evidence to the contrary. The proprietor of a wool cloth factory in Rio Grande do Sul employing sixty men, thirty women, and thirty children in the early 1880s stated categorically that they "never . . . had any trouble obtaining labor," although obtaining capital proved very difficult.[6] Only millowners offering wages as low as those paid by landowners encountered difficulties in attracting a permanent labor force.

Although workers might leave one factory for another in search of better wages and living conditions, they rarely found them. Whether laboring in mills, shops, or government installations, they suffered from long hours, poor pay, callous treatment, and paternalistic regulation. Not only were wages low by the standards of northern Europe, but food, housing, and clothing costs were also much higher. Like domestic servants, the young male immigrants employed in Portuguese retail stores were under constant surveillance, working, eating, and sleeping in their employers' establishments. Factory workers often lived in company housing, with some even receiving food and clothing from the proprietors;

they were subject to much the same treatment as that meted out to field hands by patriarchal coffee or sugar planters. Heavy fines diminished factory workers' already meager wages—a technique also employed by plantation owners. Even somewhat better paid skilled laborers in government installations complained of arbitrary and capricious treatment and unjust regulations. In Rio de Janeiro, workers at the naval arsenal often waited hours after work for their pay without always receiving it, while those at the war arsenal went without wages for weeks. Although workers felt more consideration should be shown them, the elite believed otherwise, viewing them as ignorant, lazy, and in need of close supervision. Under such conditions, some skilled craftsmen banded together for mutual support.[7]

By the midnineteenth century, mutual benefit societies, the oldest form of labor organization under the empire, appeared in Brazilian cities.[8] These secular associations partially paralleled a more venerable type of voluntary society, the religious brotherhoods, or *irmandades* and *ordens terceiras*. Brotherhoods such as the powerful Santa Casa da Misericórdia, brought to Bahia in 1550 and to Rio de Janeiro in 1532, provided their members with medical and financial aid as well as with proper funerals.[9] Although religious brotherhoods survived the colonial period, few new ones arose under the empire, in contrast to the increasing numbers of mutual benefit societies founded as the century progressed.

The development of one of the oldest mutual aid organizations in Brazil suggests one form of transition from religious brotherhood to mutual benefit society. Founded in Recife in 1841 as the Imperial Sociedade Auxiliadora da Indústria em Pernambuco, this organization drew most of its original members from the *irmandade* of São José do Ribamar. The society even met on church property. In 1851, it broadened its membership, accepting skilled craftsmen from all trades, not just carpenters and masons, and changed its name to the Imperial Sociedade dos Artistas Mecânicos e Liberais de Pernambuco, reflecting this general artisan orientation. In 1865 membership was extended to all skilled craftsmen regardless of nationality, not just Brazilian-born artisans. Besides performing mutual benefit functions, the society held classes in reading, mathematics, design, and French, and by the 1880s in trade skills like tailoring. This organization of artisans, who extolled civic and religious virtues, even secured some government subsidies.[10]

By the third quarter of the nineteenth century, there was a variety of social welfare institutions in Brazil's cities. A survey of such organizations undertaken in Rio de Janeiro in 1878 for presentation at an international conference in Paris detailed their variety and demonstrated that the city not only had brotherhoods and mutual aid societies but also pension funds, savings banks, and insurance companies.[11] These private organizations attempted to supplement the inadequate welfare work of both state and church. Some mutual benefit societies cut across nationality, class, or professional divisions, while others drew their membership from one occupational or immigrant group. In Rio, the members of the leading Portuguese societies—the Sociedade Portuguesa de Benificência, with some 20,000 members in 1877, and the Caixa de Socorros de D. Pedro V, with a membership of 40,000—far outnumbered those of other nationalities, which could scarcely muster several hundred members apiece.[12]

Like more prosperous urban dwellers, free skilled workers banded together for mutual aid and for the protection of their trades in a rural-oriented society based on slave labor. From Pará in the north to Rio Grande do Sul on Brazil's southern border, typographers, naval construction workers, carpenters, shoemakers, tailors, barbers, cashiers, masons, and machinists formed local protective associations. Some organizations, especially older ones like the Imperial Sociedade dos Artistas Mecânicos de Pernambuco, and societies formed in smaller cities with fewer artisans, included men from more than one trade. But, as the 1878 survey of Rio's social institutions indicates, most of the later workers' associations were organized by specific trade. Membership fees and monthly dues varied, generally reflecting the relative economic position of different craft groups, with monthly contributions equivalent to one day's salary or less. Compositors and typographers could afford to pay larger membership fees, for which they received greater financial benefits, than could naval construction workers (see Table 11).

Although skilled workers might achieve sufficient job security and income to support associations, mutual benefit societies often found themselves in a precarious economic situation. Many did not survive long enough to be included in surveys such as that carried out in Rio de Janeiro in 1878. They suffered great financial pressures, especially during periods of inflation, requiring them to expand membership and sometimes indulge in financial speculation. Payment of sickness and survivor's benefits could prove too costly for many associations. It was difficult to strike the delicate balance between payments and members' contributions.

The rapid rise and decline of the Associação de Socorros Mutuos Liga Operária illustrates some of these problems. Proposed by Octávio Hudson, a typographer and republican, and founded in Rio de Janeiro in 1872, this mutual benefit society sought to unite members of different trades, both Brazilian and foreign-born, in a more active defense of their rights than that pursued by other organizations. But its exceptionally low fees and dues, perhaps necessary to attract a wide variety of work-

Table 11. Workers' Mutual Benefit Societies in Rio de Janeiro, 1877

Name	Founded	Number of Members	Stated Goals	Membership Fee (in milreis)	Monthly Dues	Benefits
Imperial Sociedade Auxiliadora das Artes Mecânicas e Liberaes e Beneficente (Imperial Aid and Beneficient Society of Mechanical and Liberal Arts)	1835	741	Improve skills / Aid deceased members' families / Aid invalid members / Funeral aid	—	—	Funeral expense aid / Aid to families of deceased members
Sociedade Animadora da Corporação dos Ourives (Animating Society of the Goldsmiths' Corporation)	1838	21	Improve skills / Library / Aid invalid members and their families	—	—	Aid to invalid members and their families
Associação Nacional dos Artistas Brasileiros—Trabalho, União e Moralidade (National Association of Brazilian Artisans—Work Union & Morality)	1852	102	Promote love of work for sake of country, technical progress and artisans' reputation / Instruction / Unite workers for mutual aid / Aid deceased members' families	10$	1$	Illness or imprisonment—16$ monthly
Imperial Associação Tipografica Fluminense (Imperial Typographical Association of Rio de Janeiro)	1853	346	Develop craft / Professional instruction / Aid sick members / Aid deceased members' families	20$	1$	Death—100$ / Illness—30$ monthly

Table 11. *(continued)*

Name	Founded	Number of Members	Stated Goals	Membership Fee (*in milreis*)	Monthly Dues	Benefits
Sociedade Beneficente dos Artistas do Arsenal da Marinha (Beneficent Society of Marine Arsenal Artisans)	1856	394	Aid sick members Aid deceased members' families	20$ to 50$ (depending on member's age)	—	Funeral—50$ Illness—20$ monthly Invalid—8$ monthly Widow's pension—6$ monthly
Sociedade de Beneficência dos Artistas de Construção Naval (Beneficent Society of Naval Construction Artisans)	1858	406	Aid naval construction workers	6$ to 11$ (depending on member's age)	1$	Fourth class funeral Illness—20$ monthly Invalid—12$ monthly
Sociedade Filantrópica dos Artistas (Artisans' Philanthropic Society)	1858	728	Aid needy members and their families	—	—	Aid to needy members
Real Associação Beneficente dos Artistas Portuguesas (Royal Beneficent Association of Portuguese Artisans)	1863	1,300	Aid sick and invalid members Aid deceased members' families	20$ to 30$ (depending on member's age)	1$	Funeral aid Illness—20$ monthly Invalid—15$ monthly Survivors' pension—10$ monthly
Associação Beneficente dos Compositores do 'Jornal do Comércio' (Beneficent Society of the Compositors of the Jornal do Comercio)	1869	165	Aid sick and invalid members Funeral aid Pensions to deceased members' families Loans	30$	1$	Funeral—100$ Illness—60$ monthly Invalid—20$ monthly Survivors' pension—3$530 monthly Loans up to 100$

Table 11. *(continued)*

Name	Founded	Number of Members	Stated Goals	Membership Fee	Monthly Dues	Benefits
				(in milreis)		
Sociedade Protectora dos Barbeiros e Cabeleiros (Protective Society of Barbers and Hairdressers)	1869	200	Aid sick members Aid deceased members' families Funeral aid	—	1$	Funeral—32$ Illness—20$ monthly Survivors' pension—20 to 30$ monthly Jailed but not condemned—10$ monthly
Sociedade Beneficente dos Artistas de São Cristóvão (Beneficente Society of the Artisans of São Cristóvão District)	1870	1,020	Aid members and their families, who must live in district of São Cristóvão Pensions to sick and invalid members	10$ to 50$ (depending on member's age)	1$	Funeral—20$ Illness—10$ monthly Invalid—8$ monthly
Associação de Socorros Mutuos Liga Operária (Workers' League Mutual Aid Association)	1872	c. 200	Improve lot of working class Aid members Improve skills and education Classes	5$	$500	Night classes
Sociedade Beneficente de Marcineiros, Carpinteiros e Artes Correlativas (Beneficent Society of Joiners, Carpenters and Related Arts)	1875	224	Aid invalid members Aid families of indigent members Funerals for indigent members	15$	1$	Funeral—60$ Illness—10$ monthly Survivors' pension—10$ monthly Convalescence outside Rio—50$

Table 11. *(continued)*

Name	Founded	Number of Members	Stated Goals	Membership Fee *(in milreis)*	Monthly Dues *(in milreis)*	Benefits
Sociedade de Socorros Mutuos Protectora dos Artistas Sapateiros e Classes Correlativas (Mutual Aid Protective Society of Shoemakers and Related Groups)	1875	420	Aid members temporarily or permanently without means of sustenance	5$ to 10$ (depending on member's age)	1$	Aid to indigent members Medicines
Sociedade Auxiliadora dos Artistas Alfaiates (Aid Society of Tailors)	1876	600	Aid sick, invalid and imprisoned members Survivors' pensions	—	—	Funeral—38$ Illness—20$ to 80$ monthly Survivors' pensions— 10$ t0 40$ monthly Convalescence outside Rio—up to 3 months

Source: Joaquim da Silva Mello Guimarães, *Instituições de previdência fundadas no Rio de Janeiro* (1883), pp. 40–45, 48–50, 52–54, 57–59, 69, 77, 179, 205–6.

ers, placed the society in a precarious financial position and it encountered administrative and apparently political difficulties as well. The society's general committee, composed of a representative from each constituency— a machinist, typographer, shoemaker, stone mason, blacksmith, tailor, boiler maker, naval construction worker, tinsmith, calker, foundryman, wood turner, locksmith, sculptor, painter, musician, architect, and a fireworks maker—must have proved unwieldy. Even the desire for worker education articulated by the league's leaders met with frustration, for night classes were poorly attended. From a membership of 2,500—which made it by far the largest artisan society in Rio— the Liga Operária sank to less than a tenth of that peak figure by 1878, with only limited mutual bene-fit aims.[13]

Large, well-established, conservative immigrant societies, especially the Portuguese ones in Rio de Janeiro, survived best. No doubt many poor Portuguese laborers preferred to join such broadly based associa-tions, heavily subsidized by wealthy members of the "colony" who en-joyed prestige as "benefactors" and philanthropists, rather than contribute to craft organizations, although some must have belonged to both types. In 1872, Rio's skilled workers and artisans officially numbered 13,476 foreigners and 8,777 free Brazilians. The 1878 survey of the city's wel-fare institutions indicated that 6,867—one out of four—were members in fifteen workers' societies. Of these, the largest was the Real Associação Beneficente dos Artistas Portuguesas, the Portuguese artisans' associa-tion, with 1,300 members. Some crafts proved more highly organized than others. The carpenters' beneficent society claimed only 225 mem-bers in 1877, even though the 1872 census listed 4,620 carpenters, ex-cluding slaves. In contrast, the shoemakers' protective association enrolled 420 members, while the census recorded only 1,249 foreign and 563 free Brazilian shoemakers. Although the Italian, French, and Spanish beneficent societies claimed as members only one-tenth to one-fifth of their countries' nationals residing in Rio, the huge Portuguese colony, officially numbering 55,933 in 1872, supported two large organizations and one small general association totaling over 60,000 members in 1877. The two principal Portuguese organizations were by far the largest secu-lar beneficent societies in the city (Tables 3, 9, and 11). Of course, sons of immigrants, considered Brazilian citizens by the census, could and did join these associations. Still, a large contingent of the Portuguese colony in Rio de Janeiro, including many impoverished immigrants, must have belonged to the Portuguese societies, and some joined more than one. In this city of apparent "joiners," with a population of almost 275,000 in 1872, memberships in mutual benefit societies in 1877 totaled 103,794 while the less numerous religious associations claimed 84,058 members, and the Masons, 30,000.[14]

The statutes and regulations of the workers' mutual benefit societies reveal some of the fears, perceived problems, needs, and desires of
these groups. Reflecting their members' basic wishes, all societies provided payments toward funeral expenses as well as some income in time
of illness. Workers hoped to receive either a fourth class funeral or return passage to Europe (in the case of dying immigrants). Besides sickness and unemployment, these urban laborers feared the police, unjust
imprisonment, and forcible recruitment into the armed forces. The mutual benefit societies provided a way of saving against such potential disasters and dangers and "calamities of life." Some of the more skilled
workers, such as typographers and goldsmiths, proclaimed goals of improved skills and education and attempted to hold night classes or build
libraries.[15] As the statutes as well as the name of one of the oldest organizations, the National Association of Brazilian Artisans: Work, Union
and Morality (Associação Nacional dos Artistas Brasileiros: Trabalho, União e Moralidade), indicate, these Brazilian skilled workers hoped for
unity, to strengthen them, and desired instruction so that they would
have "the reputation and social importance that their brothers in enlightened nations enjoyed."[16] Elsewhere in Brazil also, such men resented being considered an inferior class in Brazilian society, without
any prestige, when they "know they are equal to other classes and just as
capable of fulfilling social responsibilities."[17]

Sales clerks and employees in retail establishments, who often labored from 6 A.M. to 10 P.M., comprised another low paid urban group
attempting to organize itself, but one far more eager and able to rise socially. Many had arrived from Portugal as fresh-faced boys of twelve and
thirteen, and, especially if literate, found positions in the Portuguese-
dominated retail trade of Brazil's major cities, toiling under unsanitary
conditions and sleeping on store counters.[18] However, unlike many other
workers, they did not envision themselves as remaining poor and lowly
employees forever, for they were "future honorable merchants."[19] But
few actually achieved the prosperity of the greedy Portuguese shopkeeper
in Aluísio Azevedo's novel, O Cortiço.

Like skilled workers, store clerks formed mutual benefit associations
to provide medical aid, funeral assistance, and some educational opportunities. Shopclerks constantly called for shorter hours, and especially
for Sunday business closings, or at least noon closings. But they generally declined to draw sharp distinctions between themselves and their
employers, to whose positions they aspired. The small group of clerks in
Rio de Janeiro who formed the Associação dos Empregados no Comércio do Rio de Janeiro in 1880, with forty-three members, willingly included a few liberal-minded store owners who supported Sunday closings.

Over the years, this combined mutual benefit society and commercial association grew larger—in excess of 12,000 members by the turn of the century—and more prosperous, and, as more businessmen joined, increasingly conservative.[20] Storeowners encouraged their clerks to believe that both were "commercial employees" and that "merchant and commercial employees differ only in degree, like first and second cashier or like the bookkeeper from his assistant."[21] Clerks resisted calls by skilled laborers to join their struggle.[22]

Of all urban workers, typographers exhibited one of the strongest traditions of organization during the empire. Skilled and literate, unlike the vast majority of Brazilian labor, they formed a highly self-conscious urban group. Everything published in the nation, including political debates, passed through their hands. Newspapers issued by typographers, abounding in literary and classical references and historical allusions, proclaimed pride in their work and skills.[23] Such journals not only demonstrated organizational capabilities but also provided instruments of struggle that workers in other fields lacked. Though never numerous, typographers formed some of Brazil's oldest and most enduring mutual benefit societies, fought several of the nation's earliest strikes, and, by the turn of the twentieth century, would contribute decisively to both socialist and anarchist labor leadership.

In December 1853 typographers in Rio de Janeiro founded the Imperial Associação Tipográfica Fluminense, "not only dedicated to mutual self-help but also to aid in perfecting their craft."[24] Similar associations appeared in other cities, such as the Associação Tipográfica Pernambucana in Recife in 1856.[25] These organizations endeavored to foster an image of printers as underpaid "poor artisans devoted to learning and progress," performing essential tasks for society.[26] They wished to enhance members' self-confidence and protect printers' interests while also appearing moderate and respectable in the eyes of the powerful upper classes. Some felt obliged to demonstrate that they were neither "illiterate" nor "troublemakers." Like other mutual aid societies, typographers' associations could invite the patronage of leading statesmen.[27]

During the typographers' strike of 1858 in Rio de Janeiro, the fledgling Imperial Associação Tipográfica Fluminense ventured upon more sensitive and dangerous ground. War with Uruguay and the invasion of Argentina (1851–1852) not only interfered with dried meat and wheat supplies destined for the Rio market, but also led to budgetary deficits; monetary emissions increased in the mid-1850s, stimulating inflation. The prices of such basic foodstuffs as beans, manioc flour, wheat, rice, sugar, and dried meat and cod reached new heights.[28] Workers complained that "their regular salaries no longer sufficed to feed them and their families," even though they worked on Sunday. In January 1858, typographers employed by three leading Rio newspapers, the *Jornal do Comércio, Correio Mercantil,* and *Diário do Rio de Janeiro,* struck for a salary increase, declaring that "the high cost of all primary necessities and the sharp increase in rents forced them into the dire predicament of either suffering hunger and misery" or stopping publication of the papers.[29]

Anxious to gain support during the first major strike in Rio de Janeiro, typographers founded their own newspaper, "as evidence of their love for work, as proof of the genuineness of their needs, and as a way of earning, in common, the means to secure the necessities of life."[30] For almost two months *O Jornal dos Tipógrafos* appeared daily, following the regular format of papers of the period, with shipping news, assorted foreign and domestic items, government decrees, and a serialized novel. Until the newspaper owners mounted their own strike paper, *O Jornal dos Tipógrafos* secured needed advertisements.

Although the Imperial Associação Tipográfica Fluminense had been established as a mutual benefit society, it lent support to the strike. First the association attempted to ensure "public opinion" of the strike's justice and necessity, stressing the moderate nature of the strikers' demands, and sent the emperor a letter of explanation. Then the association granted financial support to the strike journal and assumed responsibility for it.[31]

The typographers' strike finally collapsed after the imperial government placed printers of the National Press at the publishers' disposal. A few months later, one newspaper, boasting of its resistance to the workers' "irregular demands," "spontaneously" increased typographers' salaries, citing the rising cost of food and rents.[32]

The defeat of this long strike left the Imperial Associação Tipográfica Fluminense divided and in dire straits and inhibited vigorous defensive measures by printers for years to come. The association had donated nearly all its funds to support the strike, almost bankrupting itself. Attempts to strengthen the association or change its orientation, or to organize other, more venturesome societies in Rio, or even to hold a nationwide congress of typographers all failed. Only in the late 1880s did Rio's printers form a more assertive organization, amidst the upsurge of popular enthusiasm accompanying the conclusion of the abolitionist campaign.[33]

Achieving the unity some typographers postulated as the "basic condition for any group's progress"[34] proved difficult if not impossible for skilled craftsmen, let alone for the mass of the Brazilian workers. Existing divisions within the urban lower classes, as within the whole sprawling nation, did not fade as the empire drew to a close, while growing European immigration added large new elements to the population of

southern Brazil.[35] Nor did the abolition of slavery eliminate many barriers between components of Brazilian society.

The nation's major urban centers, where abolitionist sentiment
proved strongest, had long provided relatively safe hiding places for escaped slaves, as well as furnishing them with some employment. For
decades, police officials in Rio de Janeiro complained of fugitive slaves
hiding in the city's *cortiços*.[36] During the last years of the abolitionist
campaign, crowds formed quickly in cities like Rio de Janeiro and Santos to impede the work of slave catchers. But, after final emancipation,
how many ex-slaves joined other migrants to the cities? In southern Brazil the number may well have exceeded that in Pernambuco, where the
relatively few freedmen remained on the plantations.[37]

Precise answers to questions concerning the movement of former
slaves to all Brazil's cities can only be answered by archival research, for
printed census data present many problems. Such manuscript materials should also help resolve questions concerning competition between
freedmen and immigrants in the cities. According to Florestan Fernandes,
the immigrants swelling São Paulo's population were better prepared for
life in industrial society and better able to compete for jobs than former
slaves—or perhaps many other Brazilian migrants—due to their European experiences.[38] This argument tends to ignore the overwhelmingly
rural origins of the immigrants, although their values and expectations,
including work habits and propensity to save, may well have been different. Prejudice, as Fernandes demonstrates, should not be underestimated.

While the final abolition of slavery in Brazil in 1888 supposedly
substituted wage labor for unpaid servile labor, working conditions and
jobs performed by blacks and mulattoes in the cities remained largely
unaltered. Even in the days of slavery, few freedmen experienced a marked
change in their material condition because of manumission.[39] After 1888,
most urban black men still served as porters, garbage collectors, and street
vendors, performed various menial and odd jobs, or, if more fortunate,
toiled on the docks. Black women continued to work as maids, cooks,
nursemaids, laundresses, street vendors, and sometimes prostitutes. Many
black women labored far from their homes, departing early in the morning and returning late in the day. They had to leave their children with
relatives or friends, or to their own devices. Weak marital bonds and the
frequent absence of husbands or fathers among this struggling, unstable, disorganized group increased the burden upon black women. Perhaps they suffered less than black men from competition with European
immigrants in urban service and craft occupations, as Florestan Fernandes
suggests[40] however, even though black women maintained their position in domestic service, they did not rise into better paying and more

prestigious occupations in stores and offices, except in periods of great economic expansion. In a society of rigid class lines, blacks remained on the lowest rung of the social ladder. The movement to abolish slavery in Brazil may well have had a greater immediate impact on the organizational and political activities of some skilled urban workers than on the basic life structure of many former slaves.

The abolitionist campaign generated great enthusiasm in the cities and helped stimulate the self-confidence and assertiveness of skilled urban laborers like the typographers, introducing some to political action. Salaried workers performed many of the same tasks as skilled slaves and might see that slavery depressed their wages and status. Some compared the "moral captivity" and the "torments" endured by free workers to that of slaves. When the founders of the Imperial Associação Tipográfica Fluminense learned that a slave was among their number, they immediately attempted to free him. In 1870 Rio's typographers celebrated the successful termination of the Paraguayan War by freeing two slaves. A few years later they founded their own abolitionist organization, the Club Abolicionista Gutenberg. In groups and as individuals, typographers contributed to the abolitionist campaign. Alberto Victor Gonçalves da Fonseca, long time president of the Imperial Associação Tipográfica Fluminense, served as representative to the major abolitionist society in Rio de Janeiro, the Confederação Abolicionista.[41]

The victorious conclusion of the abolitionist struggle on 13 May 1888 further encouraged the hopes of some skilled workers and spurred the formation of new associations. As one Rio typographer, long an advocate of more vigorous labor organizations, declared, this was the time for a "new abolition for the *free slaves!*"[42] The Club Abolicionista Gutenberg resolved to turn itself into a mutual self-protection club. The participation eight hundred strong of Rio's typographers in the abolitionist victory parade led directly to the formation of another organization when the committee responsible for their part in the general festivities helped form the Centro Tipográfico Treze de Maio. This soon proved a more vigorous and popular association than the old Imperial Associação Tipográfica Fluminense, for it dealt with wages and hours, and supported a strike at the *Diário de Notícias* when that newspaper lowered wages. Within a few months of its founding, the center claimed almost a thousand members among the approximately 1,500 typographers in Rio de Janeiro. However, no direct conflict arose between the two organizations, and some officers of the Imperial Associação Tipográfica Fluminense also joined the Centro Tipográfico.[43]

Typographers in other cities also created new societies or reorganized existing ones. In the north, Recife's printers formed the Monte-Pio dos Tipográfos. Typographers in Juiz de Fora, Minas Gerais, established a Centro Tipográfico affiliated with the Rio center. In the state of São Paulo centers were organized in Campinas and in the capital, where typographers felt their conditions were especially unfortunate and humiliating. They bewailed the "discredit into which typographers are sinking" and their "sterile state of disunity," and saw the establishment of an active labor center as the "only remedy for so many evils."[44]

The abolition of slavery gave these skilled urban laborers a sense of strength, for they had participated vigorously and enthusiastically in a successful movement, always a rare occurrence for Brazil's workers. Some saw a new age dawning for the nation and for themselves. Not only were the slaves free, but their own lives would also improve.

Although the republican movement stirred less excitement among skilled workers than the abolitionist campaign, the fall of the empire in 1889 encouraged additional labor activity. The advent of the republic in theory gave all literate males the vote, providing the possibility of a slightly more open, fluid political structure at first. The cities offered greater, though still very limited, access to education than did the countryside. During the late nineteenth century, literacy among the urban population increased far more rapidly than among Brazil's entire population, and literacy rates in the capital surpassed those in other major urban centers like São Paulo (see Tables 12, 13, and 14). In rural areas votes were more easily controlled or manipulated through violence and fraud. By increasing the number of elective positions at all levels of government, the republic augmented the number of prizes to be sought.

The new republic's severe economic problems, particularly manifest in the cities, also contributed to worker dissatisfaction and activity. The swiftly mounting price levels of the 1890s contrasted sharply with the stable prices of the 1880s, a decade of scarce paper money. To remedy that shortage and to meet the agricultural crisis of the late empire, aggravated by prolonged droughts and by the abolition of slavery, the new republican government expanded credit to agriculture. This credit increase together with banking reforms establishing banks of emission led to an expansion in the paper money supply greatly in excess of the nation's needs. From 1889 to 1894, the money supply more than tripled, resulting in an annual increase in prices averaging some twenty percent and the rapid deterioration of the exchange rate. Between 1889 and 1898 internal prices would triple. The reduction in food production for the domestic market stemming from the agricultural crisis and the preference given coffee plantings only worsened matters for consumers. The unfavorable exchange rate led to higher prices for ever-increasing numbers of imported foodstuffs, led by rice, a dietary staple. In Bahia,

Table 12. Literacy in Brazil, 1872–1920

	Literate		Illiterate		Percentage of Literates Among Total Male Population	Percentage of Literates Among Total Female Population
	Men	Women	Men	Women		
1872	1,013,055	551,426	4,110,814	4,255,183	19.8	11.5
1890	1,385,854	734,705	5,852,078	6,361,278	19.1	10.4
1920	4,470,068	3,023,289	10,973,750	12,168,498	28.9	19.9

Sources: Brazil, Directoria Geral de Estatistica, *Recenseamento da população do Imperio do Brazil a que se procedeu no dia 1º de agosto de 1872*, XXI (Municipio Neutro), 1–2; Brazil, Directoria Geral de Estatistica, *Recenseamento do Brazil realizado em 1 de setembro de 1920*, IV, 4ª parte, xii, xvi.

Table 13. Literacy in Rio de Janeiro, 1872–1920

	Literate		Illiterate		Percentage of Literates Among Total Male Population	Percentage of Literates Among Total Female Population
	Men	Women	Men	Women		
1872	65,384	34,101	93,382	82,105	41.2	29.3
1890	169,960	100,370	123,697	128,624	57.9	43.8
1906	260,941	160,131	202,512	187,859	56.3	46.0
1920	398,144	312,108	200,163	247,458	66.5	55.8

Sources: *Recenseamento do Brazil . . . 1920*, II, 1ª parte, cvi, 414–415; IV, 4ª parte, xiii; Brazil, Directoria Geral de Estatistica, *Recenseamento do Rio de Janeiro (Districto Federal) realizado em 20 de setembro de 1906*, I, 108–9.

Table 14. Literacy in São Paulo (City), 1872–1920

	Literate		Illiterate		Percentage of Literates Among Total Male Population	Percentage of Literates Among Total Female Population
	Men	Women	Men	Women		
1872	5,055	2,673	10,672	12,984	32.1	17.1
1890	12,040	6,774	22,196	23,924	35.2	22.1
1920	189,097	148,605	104,910	136,421	64.3	52.1

Source: *Recenseamento do Brazil . . . 1920*, IV, 4ª parte, xxvi–xxvii.

prices of manioc, sugar, meat, oil, and coffee reached abrupt highs from 1889 to 1898. Among major food products in Rio de Janeiro, the cost of beans rose most steeply from 1888 to 1889, rice and sugar from 1890 to 1893, dried meat, 1889 to 1894, and manioc flour, 1893 to 1896.[45]

An 1893 Rio labor journal claimed that basic food prices had tripled within a few years' time, until fresh meat cost one *milreis* a kilo and beans 400 *reis* a kilo.[46] Wages did not keep pace with prices in the 1890s. Inflation cut deeply into salaries and profit margins. Small houses that had rented for ten or fifteen *milreis* rose to 30$ or 40$. Hence, due to inflation, a worker and his family, who some four or five years earlier had been able to manage on a 4$ or 5$ daily wage, now found themselves in dire straits with wages of 6$ or 8$. (For an explanation of the notation for *milreis*, see page xv.) With virtually no exceptions, living standards for people in all occupations declined.[47] Their deteriorating economic conditions propelled some workers onto the political scene.

In Brazil, disputes between various sectors, groups, and individuals tend to be seen as requiring political resolution. And Rio de Janeiro provided the nation with its prime political arena as well as its major center of influence. If any workers in Brazil might find themselves in a position to exercise political influence, it was those in Rio. They had long attracted the attention of ambitious or dissident politicians, who attempted to establish links with skilled labor. In 1872 Joaquim Saldanha Marinho, Aristides Lobo, and Salvador de Mendonça, leaders of the newly formed Republican Party, offered their services to the Liga Operária.[48] Some labor labor organizations invited participation by political figures. In the early 1880s the União Operária, composed of skilled workers like those at the Marine Arsenal as well as men of higher social rank, supported non-worker candidates for local office.[49] Many workers in Rio labored directly for the government and might look to political figures for protection. Neither anarcho-syndicalism, whose followers rejected political participation, nor marxist socialism had penetrated Rio's labor movement by the late nineteenth century. The nation's capital promised improvement through politics, not revolution.

Rio de Janeiro served as a pole of attraction for people from across the nation as well as from abroad. In 1890, only 44.2% of the city's inhabitants, or 62.9% of the Brazilian-born, were Rio natives (*cariocas*) (Table 15). Just as the Portuguese dominated the foreign-born component of Rio's population, comprising 68.6% of all foreigners in 1890, so did migrants from the city's hinterland in the state of Rio de Janeiro predominate among those Brazilians born beyond the limits of the Federal District.[50] According to the national census of 1890, *fluminenses* (natives of the state of Rio de Janeiro) contributed 49.6% of the internal

Table 15. Population of Rio de Janeiro By Place of Origin, 1872–1920

	Total City Population	Total Brazilian-Born	Brazilian-Born (Percentage of Total City Population)						Foreign-Born
			City of Rio	Province of Rio	North[a]	Northeast[a]	Central-West[c]	South[d]	
1872	274,972	190,242 (69.2)	164,857[e] (60.0)	—[f]	2,460 (1.0)	7,237 (2.6)	9,311 (3.4)	6,377 (2.3)	84,730[g] (30.8)
1890	522,651	367,449 (70.3)	230,976 (44.2)	67,752 (13.0)	4,813 (1.0)	24,856 (4.8)	22,973 (4.4)	16,079 (3.1)	155,202[h] (29.7)
1920	1,157,873	913,652[i] (78.9)	605,732 (52.3)	128,687 (11.1)	8,407 (0.7)	44,703 (3.9)	65,388 (5.6)	39,000 (3.4)	244,211[j] (21.1)

Adapted from: Brazil, *Recenseamento da população . . . 1872*, XXI (Município Neutro), 60–61. Brazil, *Recenseamento . . . do Brazil . . . 1890. Districto Federal*, 164–169, 177. Brazil, *Recenseamento do Brazil . . . 1920*, II, 1[a], 16–21, 29.

[a] Amazonas, Pará, Maranhão.
[b] Paiuí, Ceará, Rio Grande do Norte, Paraíba, Pernambuco, Alagoas, Sergipe.
[c] Bahia, Espírito Santo, Minas Gerais, Goiás, Mato Grosso.
[d] São Paulo, Paraná, Santa Catarina, Rio Grande do Sul.
[e] Population of city and province of Rio de Janeiro combined.
[f] Included in 1872 figure for city of Rio.
[g] Includes 18,070 Africans and 225 Chinese as well as 451 naturalized Brazilians.
[h] Includes 5,402 Africans and 358 Asians.
[i] Includes 25,566 of unknown state of origin; excludes 3,829 foreign-born who adopted Brazilian nationality.
[j] Includes 366 Africans and 1,177 Asians, as well as 1,263 of unknown nationality and 3,829 foreign-born who adopted Brazilian nationality.

migrants to the city of Rio de Janeiro.[51] They comprised 18.4% of the capital's Brazilian-born inhabitants, or 13% of the total city population. Unfortunately, the 1872 census did not distinguish between the city and the province of Rio de Janeiro as place of origin, hindering linkage of data. However, a comparison of the combined figures for city and province (86.7% of the native-born Brazilians in 1872, and 81.3% in 1890) suggests that no mass migration occurred following the abolition of slavery.[52] While some former slaves may have abandoned the exhausted soils and dwindling coffee groves of the Paraíba Valley for the capital as well as for more prosperous agricultural areas, as Stanley J. Stein indicates, they do not seem to have markedly altered the composition of the city's population.[53]

In 1890 no other state supplied the capital with even one-sixth as many people as did the state of Rio de Janeiro (67,752). Next came Bahia (10,633), Minas Gerais (9,598), Pernambuco (7,213), Ceará (6,974), São Paulo (6,813), and Rio Grande do Sul (5,457).[54] This same order existed in 1872, except that Ceará followed São Paulo, Rio Grande do Sul, and Maranhão.[55] Distance from the capital as well as the relative size of the different states appear to be obvious factors affecting migration to Rio de Janeiro. Specific events also played a part, such as severe drought in the *sertão* during the late 1870s, which helps to account for the far larger proportion of migrants from the Northeast among the capital's inhabitants in 1890 than in 1872. The percentage of *nordestinos* jumped from 2.6% of the city's total population, or 3.8% of the native-born, in 1872 to 4.8% of Rio's entire population, or 6.8% of the Brazilian-born in 1890. By 1920 those figures declined somewhat (Table 15).

In the late nineteenth century, Rio de Janeiro seemed the most attractive city in the country to those Brazilians migrating over large distances. Certainly, São Paulo's population included a far smaller proportion of such people. In 1893 only 3.2% of that city's Brazilian-born inhabitants, or 1.5% of the total urban population, came from the far north, the Northeast, and Bahia combined, while in 1890, 11% of the native-born in Rio de Janeiro, or 7.7% of this far larger city's total population originated in those areas.[56] From 1872 to 1920 Rio recorded more internal migration, both in relative and absolute terms, than did the entire state of São Paulo.[57]

Among Rio's Brazilian-born inhabitants in 1890 the sex ratio was fifty men to fifty women, in contrast to the foreign-born sector, in which men outnumbered women seventy-one to twenty-nine. The female component of the population was larger among *cariocas*, (forty-nine men to fifty-one women) and *fluminenses*, (forty-seven men to fifty-three women) than among those born further from the capital, with the imbalance greatest for *nordestinos* and those from the far north and west.[58] No doubt young women from nearby areas could migrate more easily to the capital, where large numbers found employment as domestic servants, than could women living much further from Rio.

Of all the lower-class occupations distinguished by the 1890 census, domestic service, an overwhelmingly female field, contained by far the highest proportion of blacks and mulattoes. In 1890, 66.2% of Brazilian domestics in Rio de Janeiro were non-white. In comparison, the census listed only 18.9% of the Brazilians in commerce, 49.6% of those in manufacturing, and 54.4% of those in land transportation as blacks, *caboclos* (translated by the census as Indians) or of mixed race (Table 16). Domestic service continued as the major field of employment for urban lower-class women of various shades, with lower status than factory work. Although the 1890 census did not distinguish domestics by sex, there is no reason to believe that the proportion of women fell below that of 1872, when 70% of all domestic servants in Rio were female, since the 1906 census listed 80.3% of the city's domestics as women. In contrast, almost all those engaged in commerce were male, and a very high proportion appear to have been young, single Portuguese. Women comprised only 1.9% of those employed in this area in 1872, and 1.7% in 1906. Transportation, an entirely male field in 1872, included only 0.5% women in 1906.[59] The proportion of foreigners in transportation was higher than in any other occupation listed by the 1890 census, no doubt due to the fact that almost all the teamsters in Rio were Portuguese.[60]

These figures raise some puzzling questions. What were the occupations pursued by men of the families or groups from which those female Brazilian domestic servants came? The sex ratio among Brazilians living in Rio de Janeiro was equal, unlike that of foreigners. Few poor adult males could survive without any income of their own. Although Florestan Fernandes contends that many black men were supported by women in São Paulo,[61] few women in Brazil could earn enough to sustain a man as well as dependent children—a lower-class man's earnings alone could rarely supply the needs of a family, and women generally received much lower wages than men.[62] Were the activities these men pursued even listed in the 1890 census? Unlike the censuses of 1872 and 1906, that of 1890 did not list day laborers. Certainly relatively few of these dark-skinned men appear in the census count of workers in the somewhat more skilled and socially recognized lower-class positions. Was the "working class" in Rio de Janeiro really as "foreign" as the 1890 census and various writers seem to indicate? This census lists 70.3% of Rio's total population as Brazilian-born, and although this figure may well be too high, it does not differ markedly from that given by the preceding

Table 16. Workers in Selected Occupations in Rio de Janeiro By Race and Nationality, 1890

	Brazilians					Foreigners[b]	Foreigners as percentage of Total	Total
	White	Black	Caboclos[a]	Mixed	Total Brazilians			
Manufacturing	14,930	4,362	759	9,599	29,650	19,011	39.1	48,661
Artisans	1,741	326	106	1,321	3,494	2,365	40.4	5,859
Land Transportation	1,982	834	163	1,370	4,349	5,121	54.1	9,470
Commerce	19,119	1,457	253	2,742	23,571	24,477	50.1	48,048
Domestic Service	21,090	18,014	1,867	21,439	62,410	12,375	16.5	74,785

Source: Brazil, Recenseamento . . . do Brazil . . . 1890. Districto Federal, 418–21.
[a]The 1890 census translates caboclos as Indians.
[b]The overwhelming majority of foreigners in Rio de Janeiro (a total of 155,202 foreigners based on place of birth) were white. The 1890 census tallied only 5,402 Africans and 358 Asians in Rio. Criteria for nationality are not always clear.

census (69.2% in 1872) or the subsequent census (74.1% in 1906).[63] Of all the members of the urban lower classes, the relatively small group of skilled and semi-skilled male workers was the most vocal and politically active, receiving the most attention then as later. The mass of urban labor did not participate in the flurry of labor activity marking the first years of the Brazilian republic.

During those unsteady years of the new republican regime, punctuated by frequent armed challenges to military-dominated governments, various elements and individuals struggled for power. In this politically charged atmosphere, some men attempted to establish a political base among skilled workers or win their sympathies. Both workers and non-workers attempted to unify and mobilize sectors of urban labor. New organizations and political parties were established, some with pronounced ideological content. Under the empire, as we have seen, only skilled workers had formed associations, mutual benefit societies to provide minimal protection against some of the insecurities of life and burial. Although mutual benefit societies persisted in their activities, new forms of labor organizations emerged, and different groups pressed demands both for the amelioration of working conditions and for changes in society.

During the 1890s varieties of both anarchism and socialism slowly began to penetrate some circles in cities of southern Brazil with large immigrant contingents, as will be discussed in a subsequent chapter.

In contrast, labor organizations in the north generally reflected the artisan tradition of self-help and self-improvement. As under the empire, their expressed concerns focused on the need for unity and, especially, for education.[64] In this more traditional or patriarchal region of Brazil even mildly reformist labor organizers encountered major obstacles to unionization, complaining bitterly of the excessive humility shown by workers to their "superiors." In Belém, according to a local labor newspaper, workers took off their shoes at the door "so as not to dirty the *white man's* floor," or removed a cigarette from their mouths when a "bourgeois" approached them, holding their hats humbly in their hands.[65] Little contact existed between workers in the north and south. Only some groups in Rio de Janeiro hoped to achieve nationwide status.

Within a few months of the establishment of the republic on 15 November 1889, calls went out for the formation of a workers' party in Rio de Janeiro which would elect representatives to the Constitutent Congress drafting the new regime's constitution. Following several preliminary gatherings in January 1890, two separate meetings were held on 9 February, at which some of the problems and divisions facing this incipient labor movement quickly surfaced. At least four major factions and contenders for labor leadership emerged from the confused and acrimonious events of that night. More than one labor party was created, with several would-be leaders later claiming credit for founding "the" Partido Operário.[66]

Some three thousand people attended the larger of the two meetings, held at the Recreio Dramático theater and chaired by naval lieutenant José Augusto Vinhais. Here dissension prevailed, although Vinhais later asserted that this meeting resulted in the formation of his labor party. A native of Maranhão and the son of a Portuguese merchant, Vinhais had entered the navy in 1875, rising to first lieutenant in 1887. Following the overthrow of the monarchy, his political predilections took precedence over his naval career. A republican known to such leading participants in the events of 15 November 1889 as Lieutenant Colonel Benjamin Constant Botelho de Magalhães and Quintino Bocaiúva, Vinhais was placed in charge of the bureau of telegraphs on that very day.[67] But he soon turned his attention to the labor movement. As an outsider attempting to build a political base for himself among the workers, Vinhais aroused the suspicion and hostility of some labor leaders. But he also attempted to dig more deeply into the mass of urban labor than had elitist workers such as the typographers.

A smaller faction at this meeting on 9 February 1890 supported Luís da França e Silva, editor of the *Revista Tipográfica*, who would become Vinhais's major rival for labor leadership in Rio de Janeiro during the first years of the republic. A young mulatto typographer from Rio Grande do Norte who had come to Rio at the age of ten, França e Silva remained distrustful of traditional parties and politicians.[68] Never a fervent republican nor a monarchist, he merely accepted the republic as an established fact, and prepard to lead larger numbers of workers in a "new party drawn exclusively from the nation's working class."[69]

The third, and perhaps the largest, faction at the major meeting on 9 February 1890 favored Francisco Joaquim Bethencourt da Silva, the oldest of the contenders for Rio labor leadership. An architect and founder of the Liceo de Artes e Ofícios, a school for workers, Bethencourt had been involved in their education for over thirty years. Like José Augusto Vinhais, he hoped for government aid in organizing workers and sought to reach more than just skilled craftsmen. Bethencourt's Federação Proletária das Classes Operárias actually requested the provisional republican regime to conduct a detailed working-class census and let it employ the results to issue a diploma, "Título Operário," for use in both federal and shop elections. But Bethencourt lacked political connections and the provisional government, unlike some later administrations in Brazil, demonstrated no interest in such schemes for controlling labor.[70]

At the second and smaller of the two meetings held on 9 February

1890—only fifty people apparently attended the one at the Fênix Dramático theater—another shortlived Partido Operário emerged, headed by Gustavo de Lacerda. A mulatto like Luís da França e Silva, but from the south, Gustavo de Lacerda was born in Florianópolis in 1853. He attended military school, but was dismissed for his republican and liberal ideas. After serving in the army ranks, he became a bookkeeper in Santos, a typographer, and then a reporter in Rio de Janeiro. Unlike José Augusto Vinhais's Partido Operário of 1890, that of Gustavo de Lacerda admitted workers only—but skilled workers—and advocated the establishment of cooperative workers' institutions, especially schools. This tall, thin journalist later wrote one of the first books of socialist propaganda in Brazil, albeit lacking in doctrinal vigor, published in 1901, and founded an association of newspapermen in 1908.[71]

During the first years of the republic, the contenders for labor leadership in Rio de Janeiro interspersed their calls for worker unity with denunciations of their rivals. Both França e Silva and Gustavo de Lacerda opposed José Augusto Vinhais as "a foreign element" in labor's ranks, and reserved their harshest words for him.[72] Lacerda claimed it was "absurd" that an officer should "claim to be the leader of workers," while França e Silva derided Vinhais's recent interest in the workers' plight, calling him "ambitious, conceited, and disloyal."[73] They resented newcomers like Lieutenent Vinhais who invaded their domain and contested their efforts to direct the incipient labor movement, especially since Vinhais's less exclusivistic and more freewheeling—and apparently better funded—approach proved popular in Rio de Janeiro. The new electoral potential of literate male workers attracted the attention of established political figures as well as would-be labor leaders. As França e Silva acidly remarked, "the Workers' Party nowadays is a political 'California' where everyone tries to find gold and diamonds."[74]

In May 1890 Lieutenant Vinhais resigned from the navy due to "physical incapacity," according to naval records. During the next few months, prior to the congressional elections in September, he devoted himself to labor activities, with the support of elements within the republican power structure. Through government connections Vinhais obtained the names of workers at federal installations. He maintained good relations with Quintino Bocaiúva, member of the provisional government and director of O País, Rio's major newspaper. O País backed Vinhais strongly, declaring him a major labor leader, and published his column on the "social question," in which he reiterated promises of loyalty and aid to the workers, if elected to congress. Vinhais lost no opportunity to address workers' meetings, such as those of cigar makers, and railroad workers. He expressed sympathy with their hardships rather than proposing specific measures or programs.[75]

Vinhais's views would not alarm the elite, some of whom might see him as a calming influence on the workers. Contending that Brazilians could always find work or receive private charity when ill, injured, or hungry, Vinhais declared that Brazil should not follow the European road of class warfare or of anarchism and hatred—the Brazilian proletariat did not suffer the "same indignities" as in Europe or the United States.[76]

Vinhais largely limited his activities to Rio de Janeiro, although he sent messages and emissaries to several states urging the formation of affiliated labor parties. In Rio he sought support from employees, or would-be employees, at government installations. Some of his followers even publicly thanked President Deodoro da Fonseca for giving them jobs. Vinhais concentrated on workers of the government-owned Estrada de Ferro Central do Brasil, the most important railroad in the nation. These men might be manipulated through rewards bestowed by a favorably inclined regime. Prior to the declaration of the republic, they had not been considered public functionaries, but the provisional republican regime of Marshal Deodoro da Fonseca, anxious for support, granted them retirement rights, annual vacations, and some salary increases. Workers on the Central do Brasil soon became involved in political questions.[77]

Lieutenant Vinhais succeeded in his quest for election to the Constituent Congress from the Federal District of Rio de Janeiro, unlike either Luís da França e Silva or Gustavo de Lacerda, who never achieved national or municipal office. While Vinhais received 5,401 votes in the 1890 congressional elections, França e Silva garnered only 689, and Gustavo de Lacerda just five votes. In Congress, Vinhais delivered a few speeches in favor of the workers, praising their patience and resoluteness in the face of the rising cost of basic necessities, deteriorating living conditions, and government neglect, and he called for equal justice for all. He also talked of forming a "Workers' Bank." Although a modification of the section of the 1890 Penal Code defining work stoppages as crimes has been attributed to him, he seems to have accomplished little.[78]

After President Deodoro da Fonseca unconstitutionally dissolved the largely civilian and hostile congress on 3 November 1891, José Augusto Vinhais joined the opposition. He used his influence among the railroad workers to organize a key strike on the Central do Brasil. Perhaps as a reward for his aid in Deodoro's ouster, Vinhais was nominated to a commission charged with investigating accidents on the Central attributed to railroad personnel. But strikes and accidents continued, as did constant complaints of bad service and of political activities among employees of the Central do Brasil.[79]

With the outbreak of the Naval Revolt in September 1893, Lieutenant Vinhais again attempted to employ railroad workers for political ends. During the early years of the republic, the traditional rivalry and jealousy between the army and the navy was exacerbated, and these contentions culminated in the Naval Revolt of 1893–94, the last and most serious military uprising against the regime of Marshal Floriano Peixoto, Deodoro da Fonseca's successor. Vinhais sided with his former comrades-in-arms against Marshal Floriano. On the night of 5 September 1893 he joined the naval insurgents who took possession of vessels in Rio's harbor and called on Floriano to resign. Vinhais conceived the idea of immobilizing the Central do Brasil, a strategic transportation link, by dynamiting one of the major tunnels, but the plan bore no results. Neither did Vinhais succeed in disrupting service on the Central through destruction of a key section of track or through strikes.[80] Like Admiral Custódio José de Melo, leader of the revolt, Vinhais mistakenly assumed he could repeat his assault on the Deodoro government of two years earlier, underestimating the ability and tenacity of Floriano Peixoto.

Following the collapse of the Naval Revolt in March 1894 and his temporary exile abroad, Vinhais demonstrated decreasing concern with the labor movement. His support of the losing side in the naval struggle had cost him his friends in power. For a few years Vinhais wrote occasional articles in labor newspapers, even claiming that he had begun the socialist movement in Rio in 1890. At the turn of the century he participated in an abortive monarchist conspiracy against the government, for which he was briefly imprisoned. Although Vinhais finally abandoned active politics, he still demonstrated a keen desire to secure government employment. For thirty years he served on the staff of the navy's *Revista Marítima Brasileira* while petitioning for better positions. After enjoying a long career in government employ and fathering a large family, Vinhais died on 29 December 1941, a few days before his eighty-fourth birthday. He had survived Luís da França e Silva, his chief rival for labor leadership in Rio de Janeiro during the early years of the republic, by almost half a century.[81]

Luís da França e Silva emerged from the narrow craft orientation of a single group of skilled workers, the typographers, to attempt to organize larger numbers of such workers on a nationwide basis. Neither a populist leader nor a political opportunist, he endeavored to establish the widely desired "labor party" more slowly, without links to major political figures. While he never achieved a position equal to Vinhais's in Rio de Janeiro, he secured a greater following elsewhere in the nation, particularly in the north.

França e Silva began his work by sponsoring a Partido Operário in Niterói and inviting Gustavo de Lacerda's participation. While Lacerda declined to join the party's leadership, the old typographers' leader Alberto Victor Gonçalves da Fonseca accepted election to the directorate. In April 1890, two months after the creation of the Niterói party, França e Silva formed his Partido Operário in Rio de Janeiro, assuming the vice-presidency. The president, J. Roberto Kinsmann Benjamin, a musician and the Brazilian representative of the New York Life Insurance Company, a heavy advertiser in França e Silva's newspaper, could be considered an outsider, something França e Silva claimed to oppose. Or perhaps Kinsmann Benjamin represented an effort to broaden the party's base of support. In any case, the following year, França e Silva assumed the party's presidency.[82]

The program of França e Silva's labor party emphasized concerns long voiced by skilled workers: cheaper housing and foodstuffs, support for the aged and infirm, and better education. Its constitution contained provisions for mutual benefit activities, as well as food cooperatives. The party manifesto called for efforts to "straighten out and settle the important question of salaries and length of work day," without specifying hour or wage demands. Rather than advocate radical change, the party promised to "avoid anything which could lead to anarchy or sedition,"[83] and did not support strikes. Perhaps only such a moderate position could command support and agreement among workers in northern states where European ideologies and immigrants rarely penetrated. As under the empire, those skilled workers still publicly placed their main hopes for the future in education.[84]

While his party claimed these mild views, França e Silva turned toward reformist democratic socialism. As editor of the *Revista Tipográfica* from 1888 to 1889, he had concentrated on the needs of his fellow typographers and had favored neither a monarchy nor a republic for Brazil. Shortly after the declaration of the republic, he envisioned "turning Brazil's inhabitants into a truly fraternal social and political community modeled on the Swiss Confederation."[85] After the Partido Operário's formation in 1890, he praised and publicized the manifesto of the Portuguese Socialist Workers' Party. But he considered their program— which included nationalization of the soil and its exploitation by workers' societies, replacement of all taxes by a progressive income tax, minimum salaries determined by workers' commissions, and the abolition of permanent armies—too advanced for Brazilian workers.[86] Continuing to advocate "real, positive, and practical" socialism, this well-read and testy typographer admitted in 1891 that "the socialist spirit had not yet deeply penetrated our land, perhaps due to the innumerable natural resources of our miraculous soil"[87]—an argument used by wealthier Brazilians to deny the need for socialism or any radical social changes in Brazil. But in cities the length of the nation, a few Brazilians as well as European immigrants stood ready to work for "socialism."

França e Silva's Partido Operário aspired to national status. According to its constitution, the party would be a federation of state parties, electing to office representatives who would secure laws benefitting workers. Under the empire, only Rio Grande do Sul had a labor party, founded in 1888, which succeeded in winning any provincial elections. But by early 1891 labor parties had been constituted in Ceará, Bahia, Paraná, São Paulo, and the state of Rio de Janeiro, and by the following year in Amazonas.[88]

The party in Ceará, founded in June 1890 with branches throughout the state, published its own newspaper, O Combate, for over five years. This party not only called for the eight-hour day and improved housing and education, but also backed major strikes, such as the Baturité Railroad strike in 1891. Originally affiliated with Lieutenant José Augusto Vinhais's organization in Rio de Janeiro, the Ceará party had switched its allegiance to that of Luís da França e Silva by the time of the 1892 labor congress in Rio, and would continue to revere his name, not that of Vinhais.[89]

Labor activities in Salvador, Brazil's second largest city, had long included a political dimension. Promised protection and support from political figures often proved appealing to groups of skilled workers, like those in the building trades, who directly benefitted from public works projects. In 1876 carpenters, stonemasons, smiths, painters, and other construction workers, some operating small-scale enterprises, formed the Sociedade Liga Operária Bahiana, hoping to receive government contracts and jobs—they complained bitterly that contractors sometimes used less skilled labor. The Liga Operária Bahiana prospered during the provincial presidency of Conservative Party leader Henrique Pereira de Lucena, who authorized repairs on the normal school and other public buildings, receiving "aid and protection" not continued by his Liberal Party successor.[90]

As in Rio de Janeiro, the advent of the republic stimulated political activities among skilled workers. Rising food prices joined the list of worker complaints long headed by low wages and unsteady employment. The first attempt to create a workers' party to elect representatives to the Constituent Congress ended in discord, with members of the old imperial parties endeavoring to secure artisans' support by giving them token representation on their slates. From Rio de Janeiro, Lieutenant José Augusto Vinhais designated Victorino José Pereira Júnior, brother of a leading Bahian politician, Manuel Victorino Pereira, to establish an affiliated organization, apparently short-lived. Dissidence rivalries, and multiple workers' parties and centers were not unknown in Salvador either. Upwardly striving, or at least upwardly oriented, some of Salvador's skilled workers and artisans wondered what their relationship with existing parties and political networks should be.[91]

Among the most vocal Bahianos seeking solutions to these problems was Manoel Raimundo Querino, long-time participant in Bahian labor affairs and chief organizer of the 1891 labor party. Although he opposed "accepting the direct or indirect protection of public authorities," which would cost workers their "liberty," Manoel Querino advocated active political involvement. Workers should "save their votes for those who provide them with laws covering salaries and work-related accidents" and who aid "educational institutions and carry out other helpful measures."[92] Elected in 1891 to a single term on Salvador's municipal council, his pro-labor activities cost him future office. A black proud of his African heritage and a survivor of forced recruitment into the army during the Paraguayan War, Manoel Querino had supported the abolition and republican movements as well. He looked to education as the remedy for the inferior social position of both skilled workers and blacks. Like other labor spokesmen in Bahia, he stressed the need to educate workers' children and redress past injustices. One of the founders of the Liceo de Artes e Ofícios, a school for workers, Manoel Querino pointed with pride to individuals who had risen through education and ability. Endlessly studying and writing, Querino himself progressed from "decorative painter" to minor public functionary; he remained in a low-level position, for he lacked powerful supporters and met with racial prejudices and political hostility. In 1892 the União Operária Bahiana responded to Luís da França e Silva's invitation to participate in the Rio labor congress by sending Manoel Querino. The skilled workers he represented placed their hopes for personal improvement in education, jobs, and proper politics.[93]

In the state of São Paulo a variety of politically oriented labor organizations, ranging from militant socialist associations of European-born workers to native Brazilian groups closely affiliated with dominant political elements, quickly took shape during the first years of the republic. The Centro do Partido Operário in the state capital acknowledged ties to supporters of Américo Brasiliense, a leading Paulista statesman. Seeking their votes, this political faction included one worker on their slate of candidates for the state legislature. The center's endorsement of this slate provoked criticism from other groups of skilled workers. Some "humble soldiers of the socialist vanguard" in Santos, as they termed themselves, appealed to the center to be more aggressive as well as socialist. At the same time, German workers in São Paulo not only espoused a more rigorous socialism, but also maintained relations with European socialists, to whom they reported the results of the first Brazilian labor congress, held in Rio de Janeiro in 1892.[94]

Representatives of different labor organizations throughout the country but especially from the north met in Rio de Janeiro from 1 August to 6 September 1892. Perhaps four hundred workers assembled for this meeting, sponsored by Luís da França e Silva's Partido Operário no Brasil and Gustavo de Lacerda's Centro Operário. These organizations envisioned political remedies for the ills workers suffered, and they wished to form the necessary nationwide structure to carry out the task. According to the constitution of the new Partido Operário Brasileiro, created by this congress, the state branches of the party would endeavor to elect members to government office as well as organize cooperatives and employment agencies and provide mutual benefits for members. The party's program combined civil liberties—"complete freedom of conscience, assembly, association, movement, and of the press"—with calls for universal suffrage, direct elections, land and tax reforms, local autonomy, and the abolition of permanent armies, as well as with demands for the eight-hour day, free medical aid, minimum salaries, factory inspections, abolition of child labor, and "free, obligatory, secular primary and technical education." These demands exceeded those proclaimed in França e Silva's 1890 party manifesto.[95]

The Argentine General Confederation of Workers found the new Brazilian party's position insufficiently advanced. In a letter to the Brazilian party's newspaper, they expressed surprise at the absence of a statement on the principle of property and on the class struggle.[96] Compared with the labor movement in Argentina, that in Brazil seemed weak and hesitant. But São Paulo's German social democrats felt that the Brazilian labor party represented the country's socialists well, as they informed the 1893 International Socialist Congress in Zurich.[97]

The 1892 manifesto of the Partido Operário Brasileiro also justified peaceful strikes when collective bargaining failed. For decades, skilled workers had sought to picture themselves as "peaceful warriors," not "revolutionaries" or enemies of industry, and as men who resorted to strikes only when they could not subsist on their wages.[98] Although the right to strike proved troublesome to some would-be labor leaders, actual strikes were mounted during the first inflationary years of the republic. In 1890 and 1891 printers, cartmen, shoemakers, and textile workers in Rio de Janeiro all struck, as did employees at the customs house, naval yard, and on the Central do Brasil railroad. Similar strikes occurred elsewhere in the nation. All too frequently, the frustrated workers were met by armed police, arrests were made, strikes suppressed, and labor associations destroyed.[99]

Disillusionment with the new republican government increased. As editor of O Socialista, the newspaper of the Partido Operário Brasileiro,

Luís da França e Silva still advocated reform, not destruction of the old system. But he became ever more critical. Relying on facts and logic rather than on verbage and bombast, he attacked the government on specific issues ranging from educational policies, elections, prices, and wages to army size. This admirer of English political freedoms complained bitterly that "the republic, like the monarchy, deludes the populace . . . and deceives with hope," and he called on Brazilians to march under the red flag of socialism. [100]

Luís da França e Silva had traveled beyond the mutual benefit concerns of the typographers into a world of reformist socialism and opposition to, rather than collaboration with, government. This dark-skinned, native-born Brazilian might well be termed a pioneer of socialist labor organization in Brazil, a movement not dominated by foreign-born workers during its earliest years. [101] But the contributions of this energetic and pugnacious social democrat were cut short by his death in April 1894 at the age of thirty-three. Although França e Silva left no heirs (unlike his long-lived rival, Lieutenant José Augusto Vinhais), in coming years some socialist workers would honor his memory and claim him as the precursor of the socialist labor movement in Brazil and as the organizer of the nation's first socialist labor congress. In contrast, Vinhais's name would awaken no fond memories among those involved in the labor movement.

The many issues dividing the young, tentative labor movement could not be resolved with the departure of Luís da França e Silva and José Augusto Vinhais from the labor scene. In Rio de Janeiro as elsewhere in Brazil, the question of worker versus non-worker involvement in labor organization would continue to be debated, as would that of a movement of skilled workers versus one incorporating broader sectors of the lower classes. Should workers concentrate on daily needs or search for political advantage? Should they attempt to establish nationwide organizations or local associations? Regional emphases varied, as did the interests of native-born and immigrant workers. Tactics and ideologies differed. Conscious of internal divisions and discord and of worker indifference, labor organizations repeatedly appealed for unity, but without success.

The mass of Brazilian labor, including the organized minority, would not attempt to force changes in the economy or society, much to the disgust of the handful of European-born socialists and anarchists. Many workers looked to the government for redress, and political or populist programs proved attractive, especially in Rio de Janeiro. While workers displayed little class consciousness or solidarity, small groups demonstrated increasing awareness of their own interests and sought specific improvements in their lives, particularly in the areas of wages, housing, and education. More and more, protests took the form of organized strikes, rather than popular outbursts or riots.

Especially in Rio de Janeiro, much of the urban population became more politicized during the early republic. But the Brazilian elite could repress, exploit, co-opt, or ignore the urban poor according to its perception of immediate circumstances. Ultranationalists, who sought labor as well as urban middle-sector support, posed a serious threat to conservative governments in the 1890s; the disunited workers did not.

Panoramic view of Rio de Janeiro from Guanabara Bay, ca. 1860. (Lithograph from photograph by Victor Frond in Charles Ribeyrolles, *O Brasil pittoresco*)

The Largo do Paço (now Praca 15 de Novembro) and Rua Direita (now Rua 1º de Março) in the center of Rio de Janeiro, ca. 1855. (Daniel Parish Kidder and J. C. Fletcher, *Brazil and the Brazilians*)

Poor people lining up for water during a water shortage in Rio de Janeiro, as depicted by the satirical review *Revista Ilustrada* in 1884.

View of Salvador, Bahia, with its upper and lower cities, and the Bay of All the Saints, ca. 1855, with one of the sedan chairs used by the wealthy to make the steep climb from the lower to the upper city. (Daniel Parish Kidder and J. C. Fletcher, *Brazil and the Brazilians*)

Downtown Recife, capital of Pernambuco. Mule-drawn streetcars on Rua Barão da Vitória, ca. 1900. (Courtesy of the Biblioteca Nacional do Rio de Janeiro)

Pedro II Bridge connecting the Santo Antonio district with central Recife, ca. 1900. (Courtesy of the Biblioteca Nacional do Rio de Janeiro)

Laundresses, ca. 1850. (Daniel Parish Kidder and J. C. Fletcher, *Brazil and the Brazilians*)

VAN-INGN-SNYDER

Market woman and customer, ca. 1850. (Daniel Parish Kidder and J. C. Fletcher, *Brazil and the Brazilians*)

Portuguese porters waiting for work in Rio de Janeiro, ca. 1880. (Herbert H. Smith, *Brazil: The Amazons and the Coast*)

Broom vendor, Rio de Janeiro, 1885. (Photograph by Marc Ferrez, courtesy of Gilberto Ferrez)

Immigrant workers harvesting coffee on a plantation in São Paulo, ca. 1905. (Photograph by Guilherme William Gaensly, courtesy of the Biblioteca Nacional do Rio de Janeiro)

Members of the Benjamin Constant Battalion, one of the "patriotic battalions" formed during the Naval Revolt (1893–94) to defend the Floriano Peixoto government and reassembled following the 1897 defeat of a government expedition against Canudos in the backlands of Bahia.

Nativist attack on the Portuguese in Brazil. *O Jacobino*, the most vituperative of Brazil's ultranationalistic newspapers, depicts a poor, lean immigrant arriving from Portugal, who, crude and greedy, becomes the owner of a retail food store, and finally returns fat and wealthy to Portugal. The Lusophobe cartoon also mocks his Portuguese accent. (*O Jacobino* [Rio de Janeiro], 8 August 1896)

Rua 15 de Novembro in the "triangle," the heart of downtown São Paulo, 1904. (Photograph by Guilherme Gaensly, courtesy of the Biblioteca Nacional do Rio de Janeiro)

An electric streetcar on Rua São José, São Paulo, ca. 1905. (Photograph by Guilherme Gaensly, courtesy of the Biblioteca Nacional do Rio de Janeiro)

Rio's Avenida Central (now called Avenida Rio Branco) in 1904, prior to its official inauguration. The west side between 7 de Septembro and São José streets, with the *País* building. (Photograph by Marc Ferrez, courtesy of the Biblioteca Nacional do Rio de Janeiro)

Avenida Central, Rio de Janeiro, 1911. By this time the wealthy could enjoy their promenades in automobiles along the city's most fashionable avenue. (Photograph by Augusto César Malta, courtesy of the Biblioteca Nacional do Rio de Janeiro)

Kiosque in Largo de Santa Rita, at the head of Avenida Marechal Floriano Peixoto, a prosperous commercial street near the Avenida Central in Rio de Janeiro, 1911. (Photograph by Augusto Malta, courtesy of the Biblioteca Nacional do Rio de Janeiro)

Kiosque, with more poorly dressed customers, in Largo do Depósito (now called Praça dos Estivadores) in the Saúde port area in the municipal district of Santa Rita, Rio de Janeiro, 1911. Kiosques like this one sold coffee, brandy, cigarettes, and other small items. (Photograph by Augusto Malta, courtesy of the Biblioteca Nacional do Rio de Janeiro).

Inhabitants of an *estalagem* in Rio de Janeiro, ca. 1905. *Estalagens* were far from the worst form of lower-class collective housing. Units of *estalagens* like this one are grouped around an internal patio where women tenants toiled as laundresses. (Everardo Backheuser, *Habitações populares*)

Workers and their children in front of company housing at the Santa Marta glass factory in São Paulo, 1915. The building in the background is a school. (Courtesy of the Biblioteca Nacional do Rio de Janeiro)

Opposite: A winding street, Travessa do Largo do Castelo, on Castelo Hill, Rio de Janeiro, 1922. (Photograph by Augusto Malta, courtesy of the Biblioteca Nacional do Rio de Janeiro)

Inhabitants of the run-down Castelo district, the oldest in Rio de Janeiro, 1922, shortly before the demolition of Castelo Hill. The old homes of the well-to-do, like these in the Largo de Misericórdia, had been turned into lower-class dwellings. (Photograph by Augusto Malta, courtesy of the Biblioteca Nacional do Rio de Janeiro)

Glassblowers and furnaces of the Fábrica de Vidros e Cristaes do Brasil in Rio de Janeiro, 1920. (Brazil, *Recenseamento do Brazil realizado em 1 de septembro de 1920*, II, 2ª parte)

Young apprentices learning shoemaking in Vitória, Espirito Santo, 1910. (Courtesy of the Arquivo Nacional)

Delegates to the 1906 anarcho-syndicalist-dominated "Second Brazilian Labor Congress." On formal occasions workers dressed in suits and ties. (Edgar Rodrigues, *Socialismo e sindicalismo no Brasil, 1675–1913*)

Striking workers marching down Ladeira do Carmo in São Paulo during the 1917 general strike. (*A Cigarra* [São Paulo], 26 July 1917)

Equally large demonstration by affluent Brazilians on Rua 15 de Novembro in downtown São Paulo after meeting held by the nationalistic Congresso da Mocidade (Youth Congress) in 1917. The legend on the banner, "Brazil expects every man to do his duty," must have been retouched, as it could not have photographed clearly. (*A Cigarra*, 29 November 1917)

Striking maritime workers, mostly black and mulatto, posed in their best clothes shortly before going to the Naval Ministry in 1917. (*A Carreta* [Rio de Janeiro], 24 March 1917)

4 / Workers, Presidents, and Ultranationalists in the 1890s

During the decade following the establishment of a republic in 1889, various civilian and military groups contended for power in Brazil, while rapidly rising prices aggravated urban unrest. Heightened nationalistic feeling fed the political and economic turbulence. Army officers, admirals, *paulista* planters, and ultranationalists all jockeyed for political advantage, and some sought worker support.

Like the imperial government, the military-dominated regimes of the first five years of the republic demonstrated little interest in aiding urban workers. Whether the predominant voices in the central government were those of conservative sugar planters from the north, *paulista* coffee growers, or middle-sector army officers, the government treated lower-class urban groups primarily as sources of disorder and dangerous diseases or as suppliers of muscle power and as potential cannon fodder. Even the government of Marshal Floriano Peixoto (1891–1894), generally considered the most sympathetic toward the workers as well as the most middle-class regime, did little to benefit them.

Those in command of the new republic devoted their main energies to preserving themselves in power. False fears of monarchist plots and actual revolts by dissident military elements together with military-civilian friction claimed the attention of government leaders. Urban workers were permitted to organize and to establish political parties. Although

131

some men sought to mobilize skilled workers and to gain their support, the provisional republican regime headed by Marshal Manuel Deodoro da Fonseca took little legal action on the workers' behalf. It modified the section in the 1890 Penal Code (Articles 205 and 206) which defined as crimes any attempt to "seduce or entice" workers into "abandoning their workplaces" or suspending work in order to obtain better wages or working conditions; such actions would now be illegal only when threats or violence were employed. The provisional government also passed a law regulating child labor in industry in the Federal District of Rio de Janeiro.[1] But this law, the only piece of federal labor legislation for the next two decades, was not enforced, and child labor in factories continued. Despite the changes in the penal code, strikes continued to be suppressed, strikers punished, and labor associations destroyed.

Only in the field of urban housing did Brazil's governments undertake consistent if minor programs to benefit the urban poor. And these were basically designed to meet the problems that unsanitary worker accommodations caused the elite. Proposed solutions to housing problems did not differ markedly from empire to republic. As imperial officials had long acknowledged, high housing costs spawned the *cortiços* in whose "small rooms live a large population composed of the poorer groups" of Rio de Janeiro, and which in turn became "centers of depravity" and "permanent havens for contagions endangering public health."[2] By law, the imperial government could require sanitary improvements in *cortiços*, and it did carry out some inspections and impose fines in the capital. An 1855 decree even ordered the demolition of *cortiços* under certain limited conditions. When fears of infectious disease led to sporatic campaigns of unannounced expulsions of *cortiço* dwellers by the police, hundreds of people suddenly found themselves homeless on the streets.[3]

In the 1860s, the imperial government considered granting various tax concessions and favors to companies petitioning to construct reasonably priced, sanitary worker housing in Rio de Janeiro.[4] Américo de Castro, one of the first and most persistent seekers of such concessions, presented his detailed proposals for houses called "Evoneas, destined to comfortably accommodate workers and poor families" in terms of their "highly humanitarian and philanthropic aims," for these houses would "take the place of existing *cortiços* which are so injurious to public health." In his 1880 petition to emperor Pedro II, Castro also played upon the Brazilian desire to conform to the latest European fashions, stressing that his company "proposed to endow the capital of the empire with improvements which would be coveted by Europe's most important cities." The Brazilian workers' housing would have "all the most modern improvements adopted in England, Belgium, and France," including "laundry rooms and hot and cold public baths." Américo de Castro envisioned filling in land, "opening great avenues," extending streets, and turning the capital into "one of the most beautiful cities in the world."[5] While Castro's company would never build any houses, let alone modernize Rio de Janeiro, such hopes and plans reflected the Brazilian elite's aspiration to emulate the civilized appearance and standards of European cities. Although the imperial government approved proposals by Américo de Castro and others in the 1870s and 1880s, and granted concessions, no projects were completed during the empire. Capital could not easily be raised for such enterprises, certainly not when *cortiços* yielded annual rents amounting to as much as half of their original cost.[6]

The provisional republican regime expanded the imperial policies of granting tax concessions to facilitate construction of appropriate housing and demolition of *cortiços*. It decreed the closing within forty-eight hours of *cortiços* judged a danger to public health. During this period of economic euphoria and speculation, government incentives led enterprising businessmen to petition for concessions to erect hygienic, low-rent worker accommodations. Perhaps twice as many petitions were filed with Rio's municipal government during late 1890 and 1891 as during the entire previous decade. Some petitioners sought to include low-ranking public funcionaries and small businessmen among the beneficiaries of this new housing for the poor. Among the concessionaries was the Banco dos Operários, headed by José Augusto Vinhais. Although the bank began preparations for its first project, nothing was ever completed. The sudden end of the speculation boom toppled this bank and many other concerns, ending the rush to make money with low-cost worker housing.[7]

Under Marshal Floriano Peixoto, Deodoro da Fonseca's successor, the municipal government of Rio de Janeiro pursued the same course of action, only on a larger scale, closing and tearing down *cortiços*, as well as subsidizing "worker housing." For these acts, Floriano received praise never accorded Deodoro da Fonseca.

In command of the nation from 1891 to 1894, Floriano proved a strong ruler whom few contemporaries regarded with dispassion or disinterest. Among his more loquacious countrymen he stood out as a man of epigrammatic utterances, silences, and silent smiles, all open to various interpretations. Unlike many other would-be conspirators in the various movements of the early republic, Floriano could keep his own counsel. A consummate politician, vehemently attacked as a military dictator by his opponents and glorified as the savior of the republic by his supporters, Floriano remained the focus of fierce emotions during his lifetime and for some years afterwards.

More than any other chief executive of the Old Republic, Floriano has been held up as a friend of the "people." Both contemporaries and later observers praised him for helping the middle and lower classes, including the urban workers. For example, Francisco Rangel Pestana, one of Floriano's principal *paulista* supporters, who edited a strongly progovernment newspaper in Rio de Janeiro during the Naval Revolt (1893–1894), the most serious of the military uprisings besetting the new republic, later asserted that Floriano had not only stimulated Brazilian industry and commercial development, but that he had "heightened national sentiments and awakened patriotism," and had "employed every effort to improve the lot of the people, opposing abuses of speculators in the markets who monopolized items of prime necessity, and had maintained workers' salaries, guaranteeing them their positions and work in the factories."[8] In a modern appraisal of Floriano's regime, Afonso Arinos de Melo Franco, a distinguished *mineiro* statesman and historian, makes similar claims: "the government decreed the establishment of fixed prices for foodstuffs, put an end to the monopoly in fresh meat, ordered the demolition of the *Cabeça de Porco* ["Pig's Head," a tenement] belonging to the Conde d' Eu who was accused of exploiting the humble tenants, while also proposing to construct houses for workers and poor families."[9] Afonso Arinos contends that Floriano, "as a man, as a politician, and as a soldier represented the Brazilian masses in their confused egalitarian and nationalist aspirations."[10]

Such statements require careful examination. It is necessary to question which "people"—urban workers, middle sector nationalists, or army officers—were actually aided by the Floriano government. Perhaps much of his help to the "people" can be seen as acts of political wisdom designed to secure support or as the application of some psychic balm, rather than as substantial assistance.

Floriano Peixoto's government did aid industry more than would his immediate successors. A definite expansion in economic activities and industrial production marked the early years of the republic. For example, textile enterprises increased in number from approximately 636 during the last year of the empire to 1,088 in 1895.[11] While imperial governments had sporadically granted indirect import exemptions, subsidies, and concessions to some companies, they still opposed state support for private enterprise. In 1892 a group of Brazilian industrialists appealed for and obtained direct financial assistance from the Floriano government. Like various other elements in the country, they couched their arguments in nationalistic terms. They contended that helping industry, which they identified with national progress, was an act of patriotism. Without such aid, they asserted, sound enterprises would be forced into bankruptcy and their workers left jobless. Not only would such arguments carry weight with a government anxious to prevent additional unrest, but the regime would be strengthened by the support of a group not closely tied to conservative agriculture interests with deep roots in the empire. First by presidential decree and then through congressional action, the credit-short industrialists received government assistance, mainly in the form of loans from the Banco da República. Brazilian industries also benefited from protective tariff increases and customs exemptions for machinery and raw materials. With *Paulistas* dominating the presidency following Floriano's departure from office, government patronage in times of crisis would once again be extended only to agricultural enterprise.[12]

During the Floriano administration military officers' salaries, numbers, and political influence increased markedly, as they had since the declaration of the republic in 1889. Within a few months of the overthrow of the empire, officers' salaries improved by forty or fifty percent, and more "fringe benefits" were later provided. Army strength rose from 13,500 in 1889 to 18,000 in early 1893, before the outbreak of the Naval Revolt, and the proportion of officers within the army increased. Officers now held government positions never occupied by military men under the empire, and they wielded crucial power. In 1893, eleven of the twenty state governors were officers on active duty. Entitled to hold more than one civilian position at a time, some army officers on active duty were both legislators and state governors. Moreover, they received salaries from all their different positions, including those as commissioned officers. The war department budget rose continuously, and "extraordinary" credits were frequent in these strife-ridden years. During the Floriano administration, the armed forces' share of the federal budget increased even more than it had in the initial stage of the republic, almost doubling between 1892 and 1894.[13]

Army officers and industrialists benefited far more from measures taken by the Floriano government than did workers, despite claims by the Marshal's non-lower-class admirers. Even agriculturalists did not suffer, for Floriano continued the policy of large loans to agriculture and federal aid for immigration. As articulate labor leaders of the 1890s recognized, the poor did not benefit greatly from such well-publicized acts of the Floriano government as the demolition of *cortiços*, the sponsorship of new housing few could afford, or attempts to hold down the cost of fresh meat, which was not a staple item in the diet of the urban laborers.

Under Marshal Floriano Peixoto, inspections and fines of *cortiços* increased, and the most famous *cortiço* of Rio de Janeiro, the *Cabeça de Porco* (Pig's Head), was destroyed in a surprise night attack. One of the largest *cortiços* in the capital, this collection of dilapidated buildings housed some 4,000 people, plus assorted animals.[14] However, some municipal officials had questioned the wisdom of demolishing cortiços in a city with a severe housing shortage and little new construction, for evicted tenants had no place to go. One official called for more care in condemning existing *cortiços*, "due mainly to the almost absolute scarcity" of housing, which brings "the most praiseworthy zeal to a crashing halt." He had not understood why the chief city health officer had "laconically" requested the demolition of Rio's largest *cortiço*, since he found some buildings in this *cortiço* to be "truly buildings, where we would live willingly with our family," and "all these are inhabited by respectable families." Instead, he advocated the renovation of *cortiços*, although this ran contrary to existing policies.[15]

The lack of decent housing urban workers could afford continued a problem—one not solved by government-sponsored construction or by demolitions. While many of Floriano's supporters applauded such acts, claiming these demonstrated his great concern for the workers, labor leaders did not. Certainly, workers wanted improved housing, and some early workers' parties hoped to receive benefits from the government and make the government attend to their needs. In major cities like Rio de Janeiro, São Paulo, and Santos, labor organizations and newspapers continued to call for government construction of hygienic, reasonably priced housing.[16] But labor leaders were aware that most tenants in these projects were not workers.[17] They denounced subsidized housing construction companies in Rio de Janeiro for charging rents far above legal amounts and for leasing apartments not to workers but to more prosperous elements. One company, in reply to such charges, published lists of tenants and their occupations, which merely confirmed a high proportion of public functionaires, employees in commerce, students, and military officers in the company's largest two "villas." Only in one of the smallest, built near a textile factory, were the tenants overwhelmingly factory workers.[18]

Urban laborers also resented such dramatic government acts as the demolition of the *Cabeça de Porco*. *O Socialista*, one of Brazil's first socialist newspapers, angrily denounced the Prefect of Rio de Janeiro who, "stimulated by the *calculating* praises of the bourgeois press, has placed himself above the law in the matter of demolishing buildings and tenements, thereby reducing to a grievous uncertain state the poor families whose lack of funds forces them to live in the least sanitary places of the large cities." In the "barbarous" case of the *Cabeça de Porco*, this journal charged, families were evicted at night—"in a city like this where a family searches for a home for one to two months without finding anything."[19] For urban workers, this *cortiço* was not the "fortress of crime" whose destruction Floriano's biographers celebrated.[20]

Throughout the early republic, skilled workers in different Brazilian cities complained that the new regime did nothing to help them.[21] Like some of the disappointed politicians of the period, they claimed that "this was not the republic promised us, but instead this is the republic of illusions."[22] All the republic brought them was "misery" and empty stomachs.[23] Food price increases in Rio led to continued complaints that "the lives of the poor and of those without privileges who do not live off the public treasury have become impossible."[24] Dramatic gestures glorified by Floriano's supporters, such as the Marshal's surprise visit to a market and reduction of food prices charged by a Portuguese shopkeeper, had little real effect.[25] Nor did measures taken by Cândido Barata Ribeiro, Floriano's energetic Prefect of Rio de Janeiro who had personally led the attack on the *Cabeça de Porco*, solve food and price problems. While Barata Ribeiro attempted to end fresh meat shortages and monopolies, most workers could still afford only dried meat. Only some 6,000 kilos of fresh beef were sold each day to Rio's population of over half a million.[26]

The question of war and the necessity of armies proved one of the basic issues dividing the urban workers from the government of Marshal Floriano Peixoto. Floriano's was a military regime, which could not be expected to sympathize with those claiming that "Brazil does not need a permanent army."[27] Labor manifestos called for the replacement of armies by civilian militias to maintain order and to further peace and stability.[28] Urban working and lower-class groups had long opposed forced recruitment into the army or the National Guard. This opposition not only appeared in labor newspapers, but also burst forth in popular riots and attacks on recruiting officers. A Rio labor journal denounced bloody acts and tyranny by both sides in Rio Grande do Sul's Federalist Revolt, as well as intervention by the federal government, for that caused sacrifices and losses to soldiers' families.[29] Instead of automatically condemning the insurgents and praising Floriano during the Naval Revolt, another labor newspaper regretted "this inexplicable struggle between brothers," which "occasions incalculable injury to the life of the nation."[30]

From the north as from the south came protests by skilled workers. In Belém, a labor journal criticized the Floriano regime not only for "hunting men like animals for active service in the National Guard, but also because the Marshal built up the National Guard" and the "so-called patriotic battalions" as a "second army" to keep himself in power.[31] This newspaper complained that under Floriano the people suffered from illegal imprisonments, police invasions of their homes, and increased taxation, including taxes on artisans working at home or in the streets, as well as from the rising cost of living. When members of the Partido O-perário Socialista in Belém prepared for May Day celebrations, the police arrested them. In 1894, several months before the end of the Floriano regime, the editors of this journal were jailed, and shortly afterward the newspaper ceased publication.[32]

The Rio labor leader Luís da França e Silva maintained a critical attitude toward the Floriano government. Not only did he accuse the regime of indifference toward the extremely steep increases in food prices and rent, but also of apathy toward legislative proposals for the eight-hour day, which was never approved. His labor organization sent a pro-test message to congress detailing the suffering inflicted on more and more workers by active service in the National Guard. França e Silva bitterly complained that under the empire Republicans had promised the vote to all literate men, but the Floriano government hypocritically attempted to limit the size of the electorate in order to facilitate corrup-tion at the polls. While the government was quick to move against strik-ing workers and enforce "the draconic articles of the penal code," the electoral law remained a "dead letter." Since the Floriano regime was a "dictatorship, rending the Constitution and the laws with impunity," França e Silva contended that only a "spirit of perversity" prevented it from "accomplishing the happiness of the people"; if it had used its power constructively, "we would not be suffering the horrors of hunger and misery."[33]

Floriano Peixoto proved no more sympathetic to radical labor move-ments or to foreign elements than his more "conservative" predecessors or successors. He remained suspicious of foreigners and fearful of anar-chists. Under his regime, methods customarily employed by the Brazil-ian oligarchy to deal with "foreign agitators" continued to be used, as in other countries during the period. His government expelled "anarchists" who tried to establish unions or "propagandize" factory workers, as well as other foreigners including a naturalist, presumably for political rea-sons. The government considered expelling the independent-minded, outspoken editor of the English language *Rio News*, which it closed down during the Naval Revolt, and in fact ousted the editor of a French paper.[34]

While Floriano was no mere "*caboclo* from the north," he well may have represented a more indigenous Brazil than that of commercially minded Rio de Janeiro, full of foreigners, and the rapidly modernizing southern section of the nation centered on São Paulo.[35] Floriano indi-cated no liking for the growing, turbulent cities of south-central Brazil. In calling for patriotism during the Naval Revolt, he opposed "cosmopolitanism"—a vague concept often connected with the Portuguese, advocated by them and denounced by the nativists—as weakening national unity. Floriano received the praises of fellow northerners, like Alexandre José Barbosa Lima of Pernambuco, distrustful of immigrants and proud of the Indian—and to him truly Brazilian—component of the population of the north. This positivist army officer-politician claimed that Floriano performed his "greatest service" to the nation by standing up to the foreigners and "proving that Brazil is an independent and soveriegn country which does not continually defer to other materially stronger nations."[36] Many military men responded to strong government and strong executive rule and to a regime which refused to seek European approval for its acts or behavior, as did the educated urban elite.

Floriano's appeal was greatest among middle-sector nationalists and army officers, ambitious for power. They, rather than urban workers, received his support and glorified his name. Both middle sector nativists and urban workers were outside the traditional power structure, but the workers remained even further removed from potential power. Efforts at cooperation between the two groups proved largely unsuccessful. While many urban workers responded to the rising nationalism of the 1890s, few joined the ranks of the *Jacobinos*, the virulent ultranationalists who mounted the most violent verbal and physical assaults on foreigners in Brazil.

In this period of rising republican passions and urban economic stress diverse forms of Brazilian nationalism flourished. The country's major cities provided opportunities for increased contact and communication between people, which contributed to growing nationalism. With the republic came a renaissance of literary nationalism.[37] One critic of the period, Tristão de Alencar Araipe Júnior, argued that the change of political institutions created an intense atmosphere which yielded fruitful results for Brazilian literature, although he personally did not approve of the demogogic tone and aggressions of the *Jacobinos*.[38] Out of this milieu came Rodrigo Octávio's 1893 schoolbook on national holidays, *Festas nacionaes*, with a violent introduction by the young novelist and poet Raúl Pompéia bitterly attacking foreign economic interests and foreign capital. An ardent supporter of Floriano Peixoto, who had just as enthusiastically followed the *paulista* abolitionist Antônio Bento a decade earlier, Pompéia provided a link between literati and activist *Jacobinos*; he served as official "agitator" (this was the actual title of the position) of the Club dos Jacobinos in Rio de Janeiro.[39] Milder forms of literary nationalism appeared in the work of writers like Alexandre José de Melo Morais Filho, who proudly gave the title *Mitos e poemas: Nacionalismo* to his first collection of folklore and folk poetry.[40] But no form of economic, political, or literary nationalism matched the virulent nativism and strident republicanism of the *Jacobinos*, who directed their most vehement attacks against the Portuguese in Rio de Janeiro in the 1890s.

The Portuguese have often been considered a tradition-bound people, and since colonial times Brazil was the major destination for Portuguese emigration, as we saw in Chapter 2. Historic, ethnic, linguistic, religious, and family ties helped lead some ninety percent of those emigrating from Portugal in the late nineteenth and early twentieth centuries along the well-traveled route to Brazil. Unlike subsidized immigrants such as the Italians, the Portuguese generally settled in the cities, where economic opportunities were the greatest. More Portuguese chose Rio de Janeiro, the best known place within Brazil, than any other city. In 1890 Rio de Janeiro's population of 522,651 included 106,461 Portuguese, two-thirds of the city's 155,202 foreign-born inhabitants.[41] The old, established Portuguese colony in Rio, with its wealthy merchants and property owners, including slumlords, its petty shopkeepers and clerks, its craftsmen and poor factory workers, street vendors, and porters, comprised by far the largest and most important foreign colony in the nation's capital. These Portuguese elements became targets of the severest ultranationalist attacks in the 1890s.

Those were not the first manifestations of Lusophobia in Brazil, for its roots go back to the early eighteenth century.[42] Even after Brazil secured political independence from Portugal, the Portuguese continued to predominate as merchants and financiers. During an earlier time of both political and economic unrest, the 1820s and 1830s, they were frequent victims during civil wars resulting partly from creditor-debtor disputes, as in Bahia and Pará.[43] Throughout the nineteenth century the Portuguese were blamed for the high prices of basic foodstuffs and imported goods in the cities, and demands were made for the restriction of retail trade to Brazilians.

Following the overthrow of the monarchy in 1889, radical republicans, fearing efforts to restore the old regime, often equated the existence of the Portuguese colony in Brazil with a supposed monarchist threat. Republicans like Júlio da Silveira Lobo attempted to expose the alleged evils of the previous regime, including the prominent places occupied by Portuguese in government and commerce, as had radical republicans of the late empire such as Antônio da Silva Jardim, and re-echoed the call for the nationalization of retail commerce.[44]

Steeply rising living costs heightened discontent. Coffee prices and the foreign exchange rate declined in the 1890s. The high duties levied on many imported goods consumed in the cities, including increasing quantities of foodstuffs, fed inflation, and inflation hit the urban population hardest. While some people accused speculators within Brazil of raising prices unmercifully, others faulted the government for failing to control inflation. As politicians of different persuasions recognized, people would place the blame somewhere.[45] A popular refrain from the north connected the high cost of living with the republic's leaders and their laws:

> This law of Deodoro
> This law of Floriano
> This republican law
> No one cares for any more.
> Shoddy cotton cloth
> That once cost a pittance,
> Today is so expensive
> That no one can buy it.[46]

In Rio de Janeiro, the favorite targets of popular ire were the merchants, a large proportion of whom were foreign-born, particularly Portuguese, and therefore highly visible.[47] Various foreign observers over the years commented both on the predominance of the Portuguese in commerce, especially in Rio's retail trade, and on the ill feelings caused by this preponderance.[48]

Portuguese merchants openly boasted of their dominant role in Rio's commerce, but denied responsibility for rapidly advancing prices.[49] On the contrary, they asserted that they too suffered because of inflation which, they insisted, resulted from a decline in food production following the abolition of slavery, from urban population growth, and from political turbulence; high prices simply reflected decreased supply and increased demand. But they combined these assurances with assertions of Portuguese pride and, as if to bolster the common stereotype of the Portuguese, they maintained that any appearance of their greater prosperity resulted from greater care and hard work.[50] The Portuguese would provide the best scapegoat for rising food costs in the 1890s.

Although the vast majority of Rio's large Portuguese colony possessed no great wealth, they were not immune from rising anti-Portuguese feelings. In fact, poor Portuguese had their own complaints about yellow fever–ridden Rio de Janeiro where they labored long and hard for little reward. Reality rarely matched the Lusophobe image of the Portuguese country boy who arrived in Rio with only the cotton shirt on his back and an empty box which he subsequently filled with ill-gotten profits and carried home to his native land. For many Portuguese immigrants, this popular refrain more closely described the reality of their lives, and death:

Oh Brazil, land of deceptions,
How many people are betrayed there;
So many go there for three years,
And remain there in their graves.[51]

Attacks on Portuguese residents in Brazil increased during the 1890s. The Portuguese press in Rio long complained of poor police protection accorded foreigners and of police arbitrariness. While Rio's population grew rapidly in the 1890s, the size of the police force did not keep pace.[52] After the navy revolted against the government of Marshal Foriano Peixoto in September 1893, attacks on Portuguese increased. The special circumstances of this insurrection, economic stress, and fears of a monarchist reaction when combined with a temporary toleration of nativist agitation by some of those in power, all facilitated the rise of the *Jacobinos*, the culmination of traditional Lusophobia in Brazil and the most extreme manifestation of the surge of nationalism of the early republic.

Under different circumstance, the *Jacobinos* might have caused no greater political impact than had the publication of *A Gallegada*, an anonymously edited anti-Portuguese newspaper a decade earlier. This Rio paper applauded "our good friend" yellow fever, the "true, perhaps only patriot of the empire," for killing so many Portuguese, those thieving "donkeys without tails." But *A Gallegada*'s insults, attacks, and crude anti-Portuguese jokes, such as "A Portuguese only takes a bath when it rains," provoked no anti-Portuguese reactions.[53] Not only did this newspaper fail to develop a political program like the later *Jacobinos*, but it also lacked support from highly-placed government officials. In fact, the imperial government seems to have listened to the demands of outraged Portuguese to close down the paper." But Floriano would behave in a contrary manner.

Marshal Floriano Peixoto's government proclaimed the Naval Revolt, the reaction of a jealous navy against an army-dominated regime, to be a monarchist threat. This enabled him to utilize the traditional antipathy to the Portuguese to strengthen his own position. In their attempts to whip up patriotic sentiments during the revolt, Floriano's supporters encouraged the widely voiced belief that the basically conservative Portuguese colony, allegedly the enemy of Brazil's democratic institutions, was financing the rebellion of the fleet. After their defeat, the naval insurgents would seek refuge on two small Portuguese ships in Rio's harbor, and when the Portuguese commander refused to surrender the refugees, Floriano would break diplomatic relations with Portugal.[55]

With rising republican passions and fears, urban economic stresses, and the Naval Revolt itself, other groups linked to the rise of the *Jacobinos,* such as the "patriotic battalions," made their appearance. Among these were members of the republican clubs. Such clubs had been formed during the late empire, and remained active in the first turbulent years of the republic. These clubs were linked with some of the "patriotic battalions" created at the time of the Naval Revolt, although a few battalions had been formed soon after the fall of the empire and during the early days of the Floriano regime as a kind of citizens' militia to protect the republic in case of danger, and they received government arms and military instruction. According to their detractors, they also attacked suspected monarchists. With the outbreak of the Naval Revolt, over a dozen "patriotic battalions" appeared, mainly in Rio de Janeiro. While the formation of a number of the battalions might be "spontaneous," and some sprang directly from certain republican clubs, the Floriano government no doubt sponsored the formation of others, such as the Republican Municipal Battalion composed of government employees, mostly manual workers, ranging in age from sixteen to seventy, with a heavy proportion in their fifties and sixties. These workers seem to have had little choice but to join. The Floriano government not only gave the battalions arms and official status and assigned regular military officers to them, but also placed several in positions of great danger during the Naval Revolt, where, led by regular army officers, they acquitted themselves well. Among their members were small businessmen, clerks, and bookkeepers, largely the same type of jobholders who would swell the ranks of those "fanatical republicans," the *Jacobinos.* [56]

Several months after the revolt's defeat but before Marshal Floriano Peixoto left office, the nativist contentions and demands of the *Jacobinos* crystalized into the program set forth by Deocleciano Martyr, the most vehement and extreme of the *Jacobinos,* in *O Jacobino,* the most vituperative of Brazil's nativist newspapers. While the pro-government press had continually found enemies of the republic lurking everywhere, and assailed foreigners for intervening in Brazil's affairs, no other newspaper matched *O Jacobino* in the virulence of its anti-Portuguese attacks. This paper, originally published twice, than once a week, claimed a printing of 15,000 to 30,000 copies.

Deocleciano Martyr, editor of *O Jacobino,* was born João Deocleciano Teixeira in Rio Grande do Sul in 1867. He began his political activities in the late empire, and opposed the reorganization of the National Guard as oppressive, demoralizing, and favoring the foreigner. Like Aníbal Mascarenhas, the editor of other nativist newspapers, *A Bomba* and *O Nacional,* Deocleciano had served in the Tiradentes "patriotic battalion." According to Deocleciano, a one-legged zealot who joined conflicts and attacks on Portuguese, hopping along wielding his crutch as a weapon, Floriano Peixoto had not only approved the launching of O *Jacobino* in September 1894, but had also contributed financially.[57]

During the late nineteenth century the Brazilian press, which included many ephemeral papers of differing political persuasions, often received subsidies. Just as the *Jacobinos* accused the major daily newspapers in Rio de Janeiro of accepting money from Portuguese commercial interests, so did their opponents claim that nativist newspapers benefitted from government favors under Floriano Peixoto. For example, a newspaper championing the rights of foreigners charged that A *Bomba* had been printed for some time at the national printing office on government-supplied paper.[58]

O *Jacobino* endlessly spewed forth highly colored versions of the traditional image of the Portuguese as a greedy, rough, but hard-working *burro* who returned home to Portugal laden with ill-gotten gains from Brazil. It gloated over such items as the "Portuguese run down by a Jacobin trolley," and printed crude, humorless anti-Portuguese jokes, perhaps the ancestors of some still current in Rio, such as this one about the creation of Adam and the animals: Adam had difficulty in regulating the animal world because his language differed from that of the animals, so he asked God to send him an interpreter; God obliged and created the Portuguese, since "the Portuguese is the animal who most resembles human beings."[59]

Jacobinos directed their demands against the Portuguese, reflecting their conviction that everything in Brazil would improve once these "reactionaries" were driven out. Echoing demands that had been made by Lusophobes during the 1830s and 1840s, *Jacobinos* urged the nationalization of commerce, the exclusion of Portuguese from the public service, and confiscation of the property of Portuguese slumlords. O *Jacobino* condemned the Portuguese not only for high prices and rents but also for having brought slavery to Brazil, for opposing Brazil's independence, for attempts to overthrow the republican government, for the low exchange rate, and for prostitution in Rio. The Portuguese were·alleged to be "the greatest obstacle" to Brazil's national development and prosperity.[60] To save the nation O *Jacobino* demanded laws which would not only reserve retail commerce for native-born Brazilians, confiscate Portuguese-owned buildings, prohibit foreigners from serving in the armed forces and in public administration, control immigration, and protect national industry and agriculture, but which would also provide for the immediate expulsion of any foreigner who dared criticize Brazilian acts or customs in the press and the expulsion of families who permitted their daughters to marry Portuguese. In their purifying zeal *Jacobinos* also demanded the prohibition of lotteries and games of chance, the removal of the federal capital from decadent Rio de Janeiro, and the institution of the death penalty.[61] Such laws were the "only measures capable of completely cleansing the nation and leading to its consequent inevitable prosperity."[62]

The ranks of the *Jacobinos* contained elements of what have been termed the urban middle sectors. For example, the important position of treasurer in a Jacobin club was held by a Brazilian shop owner who also advertised heavily in a nativist newspaper. In addition to petty businessmen and functionaries engaged in direct competition with the Portuguese, we find small proprietors, teachers, bookkeepers, journalists, some professionals like doctors, pharmacists, and engineers, students, some military men, and even a few sons of Portuguese immigrants.[63] According to the 1890 census, members of the liberal professions (jurists, lawyers, doctors, engineers, pharmacists, and dentists) in Rio de Janeiro totaled 3,453. Male schoolteachers, public and private, numbered 1,267; bookkeepers, 1,139; writers and journalists, 265; land surveyors, 67; and government officials, 5,967.[64] However, it is not possible to determine what percentage of each group were Jacobin activists or sympathizers.

Compared to their French revolutionary namesakes, the Brazilian *Jacobinos* and their action groups included far fewer artisans and no women. Neither were they composed to any major extent of the wage earners who, by the midnineteenth century, were replacing such social groupings as the urban poor of French revolutionary days as the main participants in urban social movements in Great Britain and France. The crowds associated with earlier outbursts in Brazil, such as the *Vintém* upheaval, had displayed no intentions of overthrowing the government or giving positive direction to the body politic, but the *Jacobinos* had a definite political program, which would benefit themselves.

Many *Jacobinos* were public functionaries or aspired to hold government position. Rio de Janeiro, the center of their agitation, had more public functionaries than any other city in Brazil. The percentage of bureaucrats among Rio's population was double that of São Paulo's, or in absolute numbers, 5,967 public functionaries in Rio in 1890 and 984 in São Paulo in 1894.[65] In varying numbers Portuguese had occupied positions in the civil bureaucracy from colonial days onward, which often resulted in friction with Brazilian-born office holders. Shortly after the proclamation of the republic, the provisional government promulgated the Law of the Great Naturalization, which granted Brazilian citizenship to all foreigners resident in the country on 15 November 1889 unless they publicly refused it. Government service then became more attractive to the Portuguese, who were competing for positions in the bureaucracy with the *Jacobinos* and their sympathizers in the tight job market of the economically depressed 1890s. Constant complaints about naturalized citizens invading public employment preceded the continual *Jacobino* demand for the revocation of the law of the Great Naturalization.

Relatively few *Jacobinos* came from the urban working classes. The *Jacobino* distrust and disdain for the *bacharéis*, the university-trained elite who had traditionally monopolized the best of everything, proved one of their few points of agreement with the urban workers. Besides *O Jacobino*, other nativist newspapers struck out against the "true troublemakers," the "degree-holding directors of the nation's affairs," or the "know-it-all *bachareis*" who "expect to cure the woes of the nation."[66]

Resentment of the position occupied by university graduates extended well beyond *Jacobino* ranks. In his novels and newspaper articles, the Rio-born mulatto writer Afonso Henriques de Lima Barreto (1881–1922) used ridicule and caricature to point out his country's foibles. And the *bacharéis* provided him with a prime target. A dark-skinned Brazilian for whom society offered limited opportunities, Lima Barreto never obtained a university degree and for most of his life earned his living as a public employee in the War Ministry. Claiming that most degree holders were conceited, ill-educated, and incompetent, this member of the dependent middle sectors mocked those who revered academic titleholders and believed that a university graduate "is more intelligent than any one else, and that he alone is intelligent; he is the wisest, although it may be recognized that sometimes he is illiterate; he is the most honest, despite everything; he is the most handsome, although a Quasimodo; he is white even if he is as black as night; . . . and he is, in some way, in communication with divinity."[67]

Unlike the *Jacobinos*, Lima Barreto attacked the bureaucracy as well as the *bacharéis*. His sympathies lay with Rio's working poor, who had long resented the easier life and shorter hours of public employees. Although both middle-sector nativists and urban workers suffered from rising food costs and rents in the 1890s, the former lived on daily wages, when work was available, and the latter sought safe salaried employment. Skilled workers in Rio de Janeiro during the early republic would agree with their predecessors who had bitterly complained that:

> A public employee, pensioner of the state, devourer of
> the taxes paid by the people, can show up at his office at
> 10 or 11 A.M.; he can even punch in and then go out to
> stroll along Ouvidor Street. A worker, the one who enriches
> the coffers of the nation, has to arrive at work at 5 o'clock
> in the morning, and if he shows up a minute late, he

unhappily find the door locked and thus misses a day's
work, which for him is a terrible loss.[68]

While public functionaries continued to call for salary increases during
the 1890s to meet inflation, many workers merely hoped that their wages
would not be decreased. *Jacobinos* advocated such measures as retirement benefits for government workers, while labor groups like Rio's early
socialists called for the extinction of all retirement funds for public
employees.[69]

Although few skilled workers seem to have joined the *Jacobino* ranks,
Deocleciano Martyr and his newspaper constantly appealed for labor support, championing many labor demands, such as obligatory primary education, the eight-hour day, and food cooperatives, while blaming all
the workers' problems on the Portuguese. During earlier periods of strife,
some native-born artisans had demanded the nationalization of commerce,
opposing the Portuguese monopolization of retail trade, and criticizing
the *galegos*, as the Portuguese were often derogatorily termed.[70] The *Jacobinos* could seek to reactivate and play upon such sentiments. Deocleciano Martyr also crusaded against the Portuguese as monopolizers of urban
real estate, who raised rents excessively. As the *Jacobinos* contended, the
Portuguese did control much of Rio's urban property, especially the *cortiços*.[71] For example, according to an 1895 census of such slum housing, the Portuguese owned 90 out of 163 *cortiços* in the densely populated
downtown São José District, and 117 out of 193 *cortiços* in the elegant
Glória district which comprised most of Rio's South Zone (Table 17).

Deocleciano Martyr, aware of the exploitation of workers living in
cortiços, appealed to them and to other members of the "national proletariat" when he ran for municipal office in December 1894 and again
in December 1896.[72] However, a large minority of Brazil's urban working class was foreign-born and not susceptible to nativist pleas (See Tables 10 and 13). In addition, the universalist appeals of the socialists and
anarchists were beginning to make limited headway among some urban
workers. Various labor associations proclaimed their membership open to
all workers, "without distinction of nationality." However, we should not
exaggerate the significance of the foreign component among the urban
workers in Rio de Janeiro, nor the extent to which European ideologies
had penetrated labor circles. More government jobs existed for workers as
well as for middle-sector bureaucrats in Rio than in cities like São Paulo.
Like public funcionaries, Brazilian laborers at government installations
in Rio sometimes protested the hiring of foreigners at their apparent expense. Certainly, *Jacobino* activities assumed a greater ferocity in the nation's capital.

Despite his appeals to urban workers and especially to nativists, De-

Table 17.   Nationality of Owners of *Cortiços* in São José and Glória Districts, Rio de Janeiro, 1895

| | São José | | | Glória | | |
	Male	Female	Total	Male	Female	Total
Brazilian	41	3	44	39	18	57
Portuguese	86	4	90	110	7	117
Italian	9	0	9	2	0	2
Spanish	8	0	8	2	1	3
English	1	0	1	1	0	1
French	4	1	5	7	5	12
German	0	0	0	0	1	1
Santa Casa da Misericórdia			6			
TOTALS	149	8	163	161	32	193

Source: Arquivo Geral da Cidade do Rio de Janeiro, 44–2–10.

ocleciano Martyr failed in his attempts to win municipal office. While he promised to do everything for the workers if elected, he simultaneously solemnly admonished them not to confide in non-workers or in those who would only temporarily champion their cause, citing the example of Lieutenent José Augusto Vinhais. However, Deocleciano attempted that which he accused Vinhais of having done, although Vinhais had been far more successful in carving out a political base among the workers before the Naval Revolt than was Deocleciano afterwards. In later years neither the name of Deocleciano nor Vinhais would awaken fond memories among labor groups.[73]

While the *Jacobinos* never won decisive support from urban labor, they increased in strength and ferocity in the years immediately following the Naval Revolt. Mobs chased individual Portuguese through the streets of downtown Rio to cries of *mata galego,* or "kill the Portuguese," while bystanders fled into nearby shops. *Jacobinos* attacked Portuguese cartment and laborers, as well as some Portuguese-owned stores, while the police stood by. In fact, soldiers and police frequently joined attacks on the Portuguese.[74] Such actions increased the difficulties faced by the Brazilian foreign ministry in relations with Portugal, for the Portuguese government continually insisted that the individual police soldiers be punished.[75] Foreign visitors registered surprise at the level of violence among Brazilians in Rio.[76] While other foreigners sometimes met with hostility in Rio, as in other cities, the most vicious verbal and physical assaults of the 1890s were reserved for the Portuguese.

After Marshal Floriano Peixoto left office in 1894, several urban groups found the central government, now controlled by different economic interests, unsympathetic to their needs. A group of civilians, composed principally of representatives from the economically powerful coffee-exporting state of São Paulo, had profited from the divisions among the armed forces and had managed to take direct political control out of the hands of officers like Floriano. The *Paulistas*, who had long favored the creation of a federal republican regime as in their own best interests, had opposed military predominance, for the resultant instability endangered economic growth and prosperity and state autonomy. They had seen that a successful military uprising would only encourage future revolts and would leave the government in military hands. During the Naval Revolt they gave decisive aid to the Floriano regime, mainly through their state militia, and were able to secure the election of one of their most anti-military colleagues, Prudente de Morais, as president.

The *Paulista* planters who dominated the national government for some years starting in 1894 emphasized agriculture, particularly coffee, and opposed attempts to protect nascent domestic industries, let alone protect Brazilians from Portuguese commercial competition. Perhaps in reaction to this, Floriano, especially after his death, became a symbol of resistance to the more conservative policies of the *Paulistas*, while remaining the idol of the nationalists. President Prudente de Morais, who helped ensure civilian rule, detested the *Jacobinos* and their agitation. Only a stable government would appeal to foreign bankers and investors. In fact, this dour *Paulista* came to regard all his enemies and all supporters of Floriano as *Jacobinos*.[77] However, at first Prudente lacked sufficient strength to control the *Jacobinos*, whose activities pleased some nationalist intellectuals, disaffected politicians, supporters of the previous regime, and disgruntled army officers who found themselves reduced in numbers, power, and salary.

The *Jacobinos*, virtual worshipers of Floriano's memory, engaged in ever more virulent and vicious attacks on Prudente and his government, claiming that Prudente had negated every act of Floriano's and had fired the Marshal's appointees and *Jacobino* sympathizers, besides favoring the Portuguese and proving weak and hesitant in the face of a monarchist threat and of territorial encroachments by Britain and France in the north. Prudente's enemies accused him of permitting those vanquished in the Naval Revolt to become the victors. *Jacobinos* also attacked his attempts to disarm the "patriotic battalions" and to reduce the size of the armed forces.[78]

Jacobino strength in Rio de Janeiro proved more difficult for the Prudente de Morais government to contain than did nativist outbreaks in cities like São Paulo. In August 1896 the Brazilian Chamber of Deputies seemed ready to approve the "Italian Protocols," which submitted to international arbitration Italian claims for damages sustained during the Federalist Revolt, until protest demonstrations were held in various cities. In São Paulo, anti-foreign sentiment already centered on the Italians, who comprised over one-third of the city's population (Table 10), and who seemed to be usurping Brazilians' position in petty retail commerce and manufacture. Even the few Italian volunteers in São Paulo's "patriotic battalions" could be forced out by their hostile comrades. On 22 August 1896 nationalistic and social tensions exploded into four days of turmoil in the state capital, with Brazilians and Italians fighting one another. Local police action finally ended the conflict. Since the *Paulista* planter elite wished to ensure the continued flow of foreign wage labor onto their estates, their state government sought to quiet nativist agitation. But these *Paulistas* did not enjoy the same degree of control in Rio de Janeiro, although later that year the federal government managed to sign a protocol with Italy.[79]

In this tense atmosphere, O *Jacobino*, under Deocleciano Martyr's editorship, advanced increasingly authoritarian proposals to save the nation. As the only way to purify and radicalize Brazil's republican institutions, O *Jacobino* first advocated a strong government with a powerful chief executive and virtually no interference from congress (a system resembling the positivist dictatorship proposed by some other Brazilians). Later O *Jacobino* denied the need for any form of congress, calling for a dictatorship of indeterminate length, and finally demanded a military dictatorship. For O *Jacobino*, civil or political liberties were just a fetish of the *bacharéis*. Civil liberties then were just an excuse for the protection of the Portuguese.[80]

Many reforms anticipated by both radical and moderate republicans in the years shortly before and after the overthrow of the monarchy had not been attained. Individuals occupying positions of power did not welcome basic changes. Energies of men like Floriano Peixoto, expected by some to produce major reforms, had been deflected into the Naval Revolt, which in turn contributed to growing Lusophobia. The vehemence and fury of *Jacobino* attacks on the Portuguese as the source of reaction would turn to rage against Prudente as well, when frustrated *Jacobinos* assailed him not only for blocking reform but also for negating acts of the Floriano regime.

Although the termination of the Federalist struggle in Rio Grande do Sul in 1896 and the consolidation of government control over the army strengthened the Prudente regime, the *Jacobinos* and other opponents came close to toppling it in the feverish days of the Canudos campaigns of 1896–97 in Bahia. In the backlands of that state, far from the concerns of the European-oriented governing elites, a dissident local movement had developed. That movement may have been the result of the religious fanaticism of a group isolated and alienated from the Brazilian society of the seaboard, or it may have been partially an outgrowth of local political rivalries and insubordination, but it was not a centrally controlled or subsidized monarchist uprising, as many of President Prudente de Morais's enemies charged. Not just fiery republicans but even many normally sensible Brazilians saw monarchists everywhere. Many thought that the religious fanatics at Canudos could not defeat regular troops without aid from the outside. An expedition sent by the state governor against Canudos, the base of Antônio "Conselheiro" and his followers, was easily defeated. Then the governor appealed for help to the central government, and two subsequent expeditions composed of federal and state troops were sent against the forces led by Antônio "Conselheiro." But these expeditions were poorly organized and their leaders were not familiar with the terrain, the nature of the enemy, or his mode of fighting, and they were repelled with great losses. In the distant southern cities many sincerely thought that this struggle posed a serious threat to republican institutions and involved prominent monarchists; others seized upon it for political gain.[81]

When the news of the defeat of the federal expedition commanded by Colonel Antônio Moreira César in the backlands of Bahia reached Rio de Janeiro, the growing fear that the republic was in mortal danger led to the mobbing and destruction of opposition newspapers and the assassination of a leading monarchist, as well as to the reassemblage of some "patriotic battalions." These had not disbanded with the termination of the Naval Revolt and had remained closely tied to some republican clubs and nativist newspapers. The *Jacobinos*, the extreme nativist wing of the opposition to Prudente and his policies, posed a very real threat.

In November 1897 the *Jacobino* challenge culminated in an unsuccessful attempt to assassinate the president. During the welcoming celebration for the victorious troops returning from Canudos, a soldier mounted the presidential reviewing stand and fired at Prudente. He missed, but in the struggle to disarm the would-be assassin the war minister was stabbed and killed. The widespread repugnance engendered by the assassination attempt enabled Prudente to move swiftly against his enemies. He proclaimed a state of siege and made some two dozen arrests. Crowds wrecked the offices of *O Jacobino*.[82]

Deocleciano Martyr had played a key role in the assassination plot, providing the necessary weapons and encouragement to the young soldier who killed the war minister. During the police investigations, this soldier, Marcelino Bispo, recalled that he "liked to read the newspaper *O Jacobino*," and that, since he was "fanatically devoted to the memory of Marshal Floriano Peixoto, Deocleciano's language delighted him." In their conversations, Deocleciano told him that "the Canudos affair was created by the government for the purpose of bringing back the monarchy," and that the way to avoid all the coming "evils" was "to assassinate the President of the Republic"; then "everything would improve."[83]

Deocleciano finally not only confessed his part, but he and others interrogated by the police also claimed that a number of prominent politicians were involved in the attempted assassination. However, despite the police report's accusation that the Vice President and several congressmen, in addition to a dozen army officers, bore some responsibility for the conspiracy, Prudente never arrested the most prominent of these fellow members of the political elite.[84] They were now discredited, and as long as they were not prosecuted, they would have no cause to seek revenge.

Deocleciano Martyr had gone further than other *Jacobinos* in word as well as in deed. Not all nativists, let alone devotees of Floriano Peixoto, engaged in the anti-Portuguese activities of the extreme *Jacobinos* or displayed the same depth of hostility toward the government of Prudente de Morais. While Prudente's supporters often used the terms *Jacobino* and *Florianista* interchangeably, some *Florianistas* resented the equation of the two. Others referred to themselves as radicals, *Jacobinos*, and devoted followers of Floriano all at the same time.[85] Still others changed their positions. Political power, or political appointments, soothed the anti-government feelings of some *Jacobinos*. In later life, Rodrigo Otávio, author of *Festas Nacionaes*, saw no contradiction between having been a "red Jacobin" during the Floriano regime and then accepting an appointment in Prudente's administration.[86]

Other *Jacobinos* who unsuccessfully sought political positions in the 1890s remained hostile to the Prudente government, but without necessarily resorting to Deocleciano's extremism. Aníbal Mascarenhas, the *mineiro* editor of Rio's *A Bomba*, which in January 1895 became *O Nacional*, also evoked Floriano's memory and spoke out against foreigners in government positions and in commerce, especially the "malign Portuguese influence" in Rio's commerce. But he admitted there were a few good foreigners, especially veterans of the "patriotic battalions." He claimed his newspaper was "sincerely republican and nativist, but not exclusivist."[87] Mascarenhas had been a clerk in a local bookstore who served in the Tirandentes battalion during the Naval Revolt and later acted as its secretary. Like Deocleciano Martyr, Mascarenhas was no *ba-*

charel, but he tried to associate with such men. More hopeful of attaining political power than Deocleciano, he demonstrated greater concern with candidates and elections. When defeated for municipal intendant in Rio, Mascarenhas like Deocleciano supported the Tiradentes Club's head, Manoel Timoteo de Costa, an engineer (and *bacharel*) in his successful bid for the Chamber of Deputies in 1895. Mascarenhas also served on the commission of the new opposition party, the Partido Republicano Nacional, along with various *bachareis* and with Júlio da Silveira Lobo, a radical republican from monarchical days.

These differences between Mascarenhas and Deocleciano, and no doubt their competition for the attention and support of nativists, led to exchanges of insults and attacks by their newspapers.[88] Although Mascarenhas expressed a strong desire to avoid "creating a schism between fellow believers," he denigrated Deocleciano's Jacobinism as "completely destitute of a political orientation" and Deocleciano himself as an ignorant, disorderly seeker of "notoriety" whose newspaper preached "disorder and obscurantism."[89] Deocleciano always remained further from seats of power and from those likely to attain them than did Mascarenhas and other nativists; he proved willing to resort to more extreme measures, leading to the repression of the whole movement.

The attempted assassination of Prudente de Morais had provided the president with the opportunity to overpower his opponents, especially the *Jacobinos*. They stood outside the perimeter of the politically accepted and did not enjoy the privileges of those opposition politicians and army officers who had helped channel blind *Jacobino* hatred into this direct political act. Deocleciano had been both a power and a pawn in the tangled political and social struggles of the 1890s. As disorderly as he appeared to many of Prudente's opponents, he had proved temporarily useful to them, until the attempted assassination failed. Deocleciano Martyr could claim no parliamentary immunities and received a thirty-year jail sentence. The protection he expected from men in high places failed to materialize.[90]

While urban workers would still face deplorable living and working conditions, the next few years would bring certain improvements to many of the *Jacobinos'* supporters. Under Prudente de Morais and especially under his successor and fellow *Paulista* Manoel de Campos Sales, president from 1898 to 1902, the federal government attempted to reduce budget deficits and to control the money supply. This rigid policy proved most effective between 1899 and 1902, years without extraordinary military expenses. The government decreased the amount of paper money emitted, eliminated budget deficits, and provoked steep deflation, which resulted in a virtually stable price level. At the same time, jobs available to Brazilians in the bureaucracy increased while Portuguese immigration declined. By 1906 the number of civilian functionaries in Rio de Janeiro climbed to 12,437, an increase of 108.4% from 1890, while the city's total population grew only 46.8%. During the late 1890s, the number of Portuguese entering Brazil dropped from over 32,000 a year (1891) to 15,105 (1898), and then to 8,250 (1900). Very likely the declining number of Portuguese arrivals was related to the spread of news concerning anti-Portuguese sentiments in Brazil. In 1906 only twenty-five percent of Rio's industrial workers were foreign-born as compared with thirty-nine percent in 1890.[91]

While here and there in the early years of the twentieth century a Jacobin Club might still occasionally meet and some individuals employ the term *Jacobino*, the movement itself had been effectively suppressed by the government. Even a newspaper called *O Jacobino* claimed to be "no enemy of foreigners but instead of monarchists," and praised the military politician Barbosa Lima and economic development, not Deocleciano Martyr or "war on foreigners."[92] The political and economic conditions that had fostered the rise of the *Jacobinos* in the 1890s had also changed by the turn of the century. Later radical groups would not be able to mount such a sharp challenge to the dominant elites. The resurgence of nationalist sentiments in the early twentieth century would differ in major respects, and even Deocleciano Martyr, following his release from prison in 1904, would practice another form of journalism, in which any attack on, or even mention of, the Portuguese was completely absent. Instead, he set himself up as the defender of public functionaries, while still ostensibly favoring the welfare of the proletariat and such causes as obligatory primary education and the end of monopolies, and even the emancipation of women—within the bounds of reason and morality, that is.[93] In later years he moved still further from his earlier positions, publishing a newspaper composed of virtually nothing but fulsome praise of Pereira Passos, prefect of the Federal District, whose demolition projects in the name of modernization and beautification left many of Rio's poorer classes homeless. Deocleciano himself became a petty bureaucrat in Rio's municipal government, and in atempting to build up a law practice, he even claimed a nonexistent title of nobility.[94]

During the 1890s much of Brazil's urban population, especially in Rio de Janeiro, became more politicized, and we can see changes in the more traditional forms of paternalistic politics and the beginnings of attempts at mass politics by would-be demagogues. But the *Jacobinos* were effectively repressed following the unsuccessful attempt to assassinate Prudente, and urban radicals of every kind and organized labor would be harassed for many years to come. The Brazilian republic was never pushed to its radical end, as desired by some nineteenth-century radical Republicans, who, similar to the *Jacobinos*, saw the Portuguese and the narrow monarchist structure as the major enemy. The extreme *Jacobinos'* aims represented an attempt by a minority of radical opponents of immigrants to move toward an authoritarian, closed society, disdaining parliamentarianism and its associated civil liberties, perhaps an early attempt at radicalism of the right, which received much sympathy in some military circles. Brazil would long remain a society with a relatively small, factious urban proletariat and middle-sector population and a strong, flexible elite capable of using its power to maintain its position. Public functionaries, not day laborers, would be permitted to make certain requests, but not demands, and to express less vehement nationalistic sentiments in the early twentieth century.

The *Paulistas* now controlling the federal government demonstrated far less concern for the problems of urban workers than had the *Jacobinos*. Rather than needing and seeking worker support, *Paulista* leaders desired only their labor, preferably in agriculture. Neither urban workers nor middle-sector nationalists received *Paulista* sympathy. But workers faced greater exploitation and repression in the twentieth century. When *Paulista* leaders turned their attention to urban problems, they focused on those of greatest concern to the elite, modernizing and sanitizing major urban centers for their own benefit.

5 / Boulevards and Tenements: *The Price of Progress*

In the early twentieth century Brazil's governing elite sought to sanitize, beautify, and modernize the nation's major cities. Responding to the demands of an export-oriented economy, they improved transportation and constructed new port works. They mounted campaigns against diseases like yellow fever which posed the greatest threat to their own health and to the nation's reputation abroad. Admirers of the latest European ideas, inventions, and trends, they remodeled city centers. First São Paulo, Brazil's fastest growing major city, received the benefits of this form of "progress."[1] Then other state capitals gained similar urban improvements. But the most money and attention was lavished on Rio de Janeiro, the nation's political center and principal port. For the elite, progress often meant ornate buildings and wide tree-lined avenues rather than adequate water supplies, lighting, or sewerage for all city districts. Public services did not keep pace with urban growth, and poor neighborhoods lagged furthest behind. The new thoroughfares which sliced through settled areas of Rio de Janeiro led to higher rents and housing shortages for the laboring poor. As under the empire, economic distress and frustrations, fanned by dissident politicians, helped generate outbursts of urban violence, disturbing the order dear to the Brazilian elite.

During the late nineteenth and early twentieth centuries, São Paulo expanded far more rapidly than all other major Brazilian cities, surpassing even its earlier growth rate. Between 1872 and 1890, the city's population doubled, increasing from 31,385 to 64,934. But in the next ten years it rose fourfold, reaching 239,820 in 1900. By 1920, according to the national census, the city had 579,093 inhabitants (Table 1). At the beginning of the twentieth century, São Paulo stood second in size only to Rio de Janeiro. Capital of the nation's leading coffee producing state, São Paulo served as regional center of commerce and credit and chief residence for the coffee *fazendeiros*. They spent part of their revenues in the city, adding to the amenities of urban life they enjoyed, while promoting their economic and political positions. Coffee exportation had increased markedly by the end of the nineteenth century, aided by the suitability of new western lands to production, massive European immigration, growing world markets for coffee, and a coffee blight in Ceylon which largely destroyed the plantations of São Paulo's chief rival. With the rapid expansion of export trade in the 1880s and 1890s, factories supplying cheap textiles or construction materials needed on the plantations increased in number. As Warren Dean has shown, São Paulo's merchant-importers pursued both importing and manufacturing as complimentary profit-making activities.[2]

Expanding in area as well as in population, São Paulo spread out in all directions. New trolley lines encouraged the construction of more distant residential districts. By 1887 seven lines carried a million-and-a-half passengers annually.[3] New residential districts appeared on the sides of Liberdade Avenue, which ascended southwest toward the outlying town of Santo Amaro. Farms were subdivided and marked into streets and house plots, creating the stylish residential districts of Campos Elísios and Higienópolis on rising terrain west of the city center. Unlike other segments of the urban populace, the upper classes were able to satisfy their preference for higher land, with its drier, more salubrious air. The poor occupied far less attractive or healthy areas. Railroad lines helped create an arc of lower-class districts on low-lying, dank lands east and north of the city center. In 1877 the railroad link joining the *paulista* capital with Rio de Janeiro was completed. Throughout the remainder of the century other lines cut deeper into the *paulista* hinterland, connecting the capital with the principal zones of the state, especially the leading coffee producing regions. Along those railroad lines, which followed the level river valleys into the city, workers' quarters and areas of small-scale commerce and industry arose. Brás, with its railway station (Rio–São Paulo Line) and its Immigrants' Hostel, and then Moóca accompanied the coastward growth of the Santos-Jundiaí line. Lands to the north, extending out from the Luz railway station, and served by the Santos-Jundiaí and Sorocabana lines, would also be settled by the poorer classes.[4]

Starting in the late nineteenth century, old thoroughfares were leveled and widened and new ones constructed. More streets were paved. Viaducts began to cross the valleys and link the city's central hill with other districts. The Chá Viaduct, completed in 1892, became a safety valve for the congested "triangle," the old city center. Brazilians from other states commented on the contrast between the city's old colonial nucleus, with its narrow winding streets, and the "modern aspect" of the spacious new districts, and noted the possibilities for future urban expansion.[5]

For the planters controlling the machinery of state government, urban improvements meant ornate buildings, parks, and wide, tree-lined avenues connecting the city center with their new residential districts, not the provision of adequate water, light, or sewerage for all urban neighborhoods. The elite would embellish the city rather than guide its growth. At the end of the nineteenth century, São Paulo's municipal government claimed as one of its most important accomplishments "the radical transformation . . . of our old, poorly illuminated squares, full of potholes, veritable seas of mud during the rains, which served as garbage dumps and often as refuges and centers of operations for criminals, now converted into tree-lined plazas bordered by cement walks, with paved thoroughfares and extensive lawns."[6] Even more attention was lavished on São Paulo's municipal theater, completed in 1911. This ostentatious structure, incorporating European materials and decorations, took a decade to construct and cost the equivalent of a year's municipal budget. The inauguration of the city's first electric trolley lines in 1900 also pleased residents of elite neighborhoods, which continued to receive improved municipal services first. The next year, a major hydroelectric plant began operation, providing electricity which could be used by future industries. In 1916 electric lights appeared on city streets, although gas illumination predominated throughout the 1920s. Although São Paulo's lighting and water supply improved, street cleaning and paving, sewerage and garbage disposal, and drainage of the lowlands did not keep pace with the city's swift growth. Municipal ordinances such as that requiring proper sewerage as well as ventilation and cleanliness of lower-class multiple dwellings were largely disregarded.[7]

Spurred by growth in raw material exports, other large state capitals soon acquired urban improvements similar to São Paulo's. In 1907, both Belém, a beneficiary of the brief Amazonian rubber boom, and Pôrto Alegre, a supplier of increasing quantities of tobacco, lard, beans, and manioc flour to the internal Brazilian market, received electric streetcar service. An elegant opera house, with external pillars finished in Italian marble and a gilded baroque interior, had already been constructed in Manaus, center of the rubber boom, at a reputed cost of two million

U.S. dollars. In Belém, officials also erected impressive new public buildings, boasted of the number of newly paved and tree-lined streets and
squares, inaugurated a municipal forest, and renovated the Teatro da
Paz. Falling sugar prices and the loss of foreign markets during much of
the late nineteenth and early twentieth centuries delayed some urban
improvements in Recife and Salvador. But the second decade of the twentieth century saw the restoration of Salvador's Government Palace and
other historic edifices and the construction of schools, hospitals, and a
government printing house. Broad, new avenues cut through the Bahian capital, linking growing suburbs with the old city center. In Recife
bridges were rebuilt and repaired and a new one opened in 1917. However, Recife's water system served only one-third of the city's houses in
1922. Water shortages limited the effectiveness of the sewerage system
inaugurated in 1915 and prevented its expansion, for houses lacking water could not be linked to this system.[8]

Rio de Janeiro, the nation's capital and principal port of entry, underwent the most striking transformation of all. In the first decade of the
twentieth century, the federal government "beautified and sanitized" Rio,
as Brazilian history textbooks proclaim, by installing the appurtenances
of a modern port city and national center and by eradicating yellow fever. Rio became a more attractive and healthy city both for the elite and
for their foreign guests. But the urban poor, less likely to promenade
along wide new avenues or enter elegant downtown buildings, suffered
from the resultant housing scarcities.

Endemic disease, especially that "dreadful scourge, yellow fever,
with which Rio has been so frightfully afflicted," scared away potential
European visitors, investors, and immigrants. Many bypassed Brazil in
favor of Argentina or Uruguay, where the disease seldom appeared. Late
nineteenth-century travelers found Rio, "one of the fairest cities in the
world [but] also one of the most fatal to health and even existence."[9]
While newly arrived foreigners faced the greatest threat from yellow fever, Brazilians from the interior, like the prosperous *paulista* coffee planter,
who lacked previous exposure to the disease frequently fell victim to this
scourge. In 1892 Francisco Rangel Pestana, a leading *paulista* statesman, related how he was "forced to leave Rio" because of yellow fever;
of the twenty-one persons in his household, only he and his wife "escaped the fever."[10] Foreign businessmen joined wealthy residents of coastal
cities like Rio de Janeiro and Santos in fleeing to higher altitudes during
the long hot summer. Although some of them commuted daily to their
places of employment, trade, commerce, and government still encountered constant interruptions, delays, and losses. During the empire, the
entire court summered in the mountains near Rio. The "hill towns" of

Petrópolis and Teresópolis remained comfortable retreats for the diplomatic corps and for wealthy Brazilians and foreigners alike. Not until the presidency of Francisco de Paula Rodrigues Alves (1902–1906), would the federal government muster the financial resources and newly developed scientific knowledge—the true manner through which yellow fever spread was not confirmed until the work of Walter Reed and his associates in Cuba in 1900—to cleanse and glamorize Rio de Janeiro.

Francisco Rodrigues Alves, who guided the transformation of Rio de Janeiro, was the third civilian president of the republic and the third *Paulista* to hold that office.[11] A statesman of the empire, not a "historic" republican like his predecessors Prudente Jóse de Morais Barros and Manuel Ferraz de Campos Sales, Rodrigues Alves had served as governor of São Paulo, the penultimate rung on the political ladder, before succeeding to the presidency in 1902. Unlike Prudente de Morais, who was obliged to devote his presidency to meeting threats to civilian government, and Campos Sales, who labored to reorganize the nation's financial apparatus, Rodrigues Alves inherited a stable state and treasury. Campos Sales had cut federal expenses, abandoned public works projects, and increased taxes in his struggle to balance the budget, strengthen the currency, and reestablish Brazil's international credit. Plantation agriculture, not industry, received the federal government's sympathy and support. Campos Sales's success in rehabilitating Brazil's finances enabled Rodrigues Alves to undertake the renovation of Rio de Janeiro and to carry out port and road construction, all designed to foster the economic progress which benefitted Brazil's coffee planters. As Rodrigues Alves's minister of industry declared, they must improve Brazil's "sanitary reputation" and its major cities, especially Rio, not only to help Brazilians but also to make the nation "attractive to foreigners who come here to work with us or invest their capital"; Rio demanded special attention since the "entire country inevitably shares in its good or bad name."[12] Like the *paulista* capital, the nation's capital would now receive some of the benefits of modern design, engineering, and sanitation.

The remodeling of downtown Rio de Janeiro, especially the creation of the Avenida Central (today named Rio Branco) would provide the elite with the European-looking city they craved. Although they hoped to emulate "the success of Hausmann's work in Paris," the "recent progress of Buenos Aires, our American rival," proved a sharper stimulus.[13] In the process of renovating Rio, several small hills would be demolished, land filled in, new avenues created, streets paved, extended, and widened, trees planted, and port facilities modernized, as well as old districts torn down, displacing many commercial establishments and members of the lower classes living in downtown *cortiços*. Rio de Janeiro, which possessed "not a single street worthy of showing to foreigners," according to one Brazilian writer, would now have a broad boulevard extending from "sea to sea."[14]

That ardently anticipated thoroughfare quickly became a reality. In 1903, the year after his inauguration, President Rodrigues Alves signed a series of decrees authorizing foreign loans, bonds, new taxes, and the expropriation of needed land. Actual construction of the Avenida Central proceeded rapidly under the direction of Francisco Pereira Passos, prefect of Rio de Janeiro. In February 1904 demolition began on the first of over six hundred buildings slated to be pulled down. In March the corner-stone of the first building on the Avenida Central was laid. Work proceeded twenty-four hours a day, as the avenue sliced through the densely populated central city for more than a mile, from the docks to the beginning of a new seaside promenade leading to the city's more expensive residential districts. For a Portuguese visitor, the pace of the demolitions and construction alone proved overwhelming, especially as compared with work in his own country; and so did the ever present, suffocating dust.[15] Soon ornate buildings appeared along the Avenida Central on sites designated by the government for leading organizations such as the Jockey, Derby, Engineering, Military, and Naval Clubs. The federal government itself constructed imposing buildings for Congress, the National Library, and the School of Fine Arts, as well as the most sumptuous structure of all, the Municipal Theater, modeled after the Paris Opera House. Along the avenue's edges Portuguese mosaic workers installed elegant sidewalks similar to those of Lisbon.[16] Now the Avenida Central "rivaled and even surpassed Buenos Aires' celebrated Avenida de Mayo," inaugurated in 1894. At 108 feet, it was also nine feet wider. The elite could gleefully proclaim that "it was Brazilians, sons of our legendarily indolent race, who projected, organized, and carried out this immense work!"[17]

On 15 November 1905, twenty months after work had begun, President Rodrigues Alves officially opened the Avenida Central to the public. Rio's newspapers reported a large popular turnout, despite the heat, the mud, and the rain marring the ceremony.[18] The *Jornal do Comércio*, the capital's leading paper, duly noted that "the Avenida Central provides foreigners who now visit our capital with a sublime example of the material progress which Rio de Janeiro is determined to achieve."[19] Like wealthy Brazilians, foreign visitors did exclaim over the "metamorphosis" of the metropolis, with its new "splendid" boulevard.[20] All of "society" promenaded along the city's "most fashionable thoroughfare."[21]

The renovation of Rio's port far surpassed the Avenida Central both in cost and in economic benefit, although it lacked that boulevard's ca-

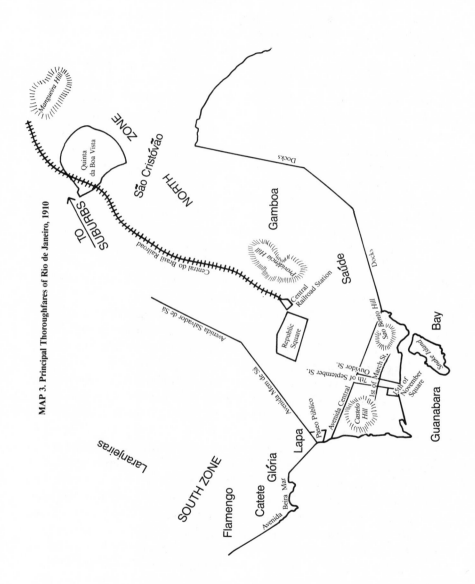

MAP 3. Principal Thoroughfares of Rio de Janeiro, 1910

chet. A loan from the Rothschilds facilitated the construction of an extensive seawall, new warehouses and piers, landfills, and dredging operations. Work began in March 1904, and in July 1910 the port of Rio de Janeiro was officially inaugurated. Through this re-built port flowed not only foreign trade but also goods from the states, including foodstuffs and raw materials such as cotton needed by local industries.[22]

Improved port works, essential to an export economy, received consistent national and local attention all along the Brazilian coast. First Santos, the port for São Paulo, gained modern facilities during the last decade of the nineteenth century. Then came the nation's capital. After modernizing Rio's port, the federal government aided construction in the states. Again, foreign loans and foreign construction companies played prominent roles. Port improvements began in Belém in 1907 and in Recife shortly afterwards. Economic difficulties sometimes prevented rapid completion of construction, as in Recife, whose new port was only officially inaugurated in 1918. Work on Salvador's port lasted from 1911 to 1928. Drainage of the access canal to Pôrto Alegre and dock construction continued from 1913 to 1920. Manaus, Vitória, Paranaguá, and other smaller ports also received improved facilities, designed to speed the shipment of Brazilian coffee, rubber, cotton, sugar, cacao, tobacco, hides, and yerba mate to the world's markets.[23]

To facilitate the movement of people and goods within Rio de Janeiro, the capital's reconstructed port was linked with the Avenida Central. Another new boulevard, the Avenida Beira Mar, stretched southward from the conclusion of the Avenida Central, past the stylish beaches of Glória and Flamengo, out to Botafogo Bay. Although some of Rio's lower-class suburbs still lacked gas illumination, this bayside extension of the Avenida Central, the longest avenue of all Rio's new roads, received electric light in September 1905.[24]

The construction of these avenues required the demolition of numerous buildings and forced the relocation of their inhabitants. In addition to the Avenida Central and the avenue paralleling the port, two more new thoroughfares, Avenida Mem de Sá, named after Rio's founder, and Avenida Salvador de Sá, honoring his successor, cut through downtown Rio de Janeiro. Over a dozen additional streets were widened or extended. A total of almost two thousand buildings had to be torn down. The small businessmen and the tenement dwellers dispossessed by these demolitions did not share the elite's enthusiasm for the elegant new thoroughfares. Even the owners of property condemned for Rio's reconstruction did not necessarily reap the benefits of rising real estate values. In 1903, for example, the government expropriated one hundred and thirty buildings in the process of widening Treze de Maio and Prainha streets and extending Sacramento street. Not only did the municipality acquire those properties "in a friendly fashion," at half the budgeted cost, but it then auctioned off unused land at a good price.[25]

While large companies and social clubs could afford to build impressive new headquarters along the Avenida Central and benefitted from the rising value of land they acquired along this promenade, less prosperous groups and individuals suffered financial losses. Owners of small and medium-size retail stores and small factories situated in the path of new avenues could not relocate their businesses easily. Many lacked funds to construct new installations. Vacant premises in the same area were almost impossible to find. Store owners complained that Rio's municipal government did not adequately compensate them. The Associação dos Empregados no Comércio do Rio de Janeiro, Rio's major retail commercial association, experienced difficulties in raising funds to purchase a plot of land on the Avenida Central so that they could extend their headquarters and construct a new entrance on that thoroughfare.[26]

Urban slum dwellers in downtown Rio de Janeiro were even less fortunate. Many were forced from their inadequate housing—sometimes with only forty-eight hours' notice—when they could not find equivalent shelter elsewhere. The municipal government not only demolished buildings for the construction of new avenues but also pulled down structures judged liable to collapse. *Cortiços* considered dangerous to public health were closed. In a two-and-a-half-year period, the federal Public Health Service in Rio alone closed over six hundred buildings housing more than 13,000 people, and the municipal government demolished as unsafe some seventy structures, sheltering over one thousand people.[27] While officials recognized the plight faced by the poor left homeless for the sake of Rio's beautification and sanitation, they did virtually nothing to help them. José Joaquim Seabra, Rodrigues Alves's Minister of Justice and Interior, merely echoed the phrases of previous administrations, acknowledging the need to "promote the construction of hygienic, low-rent houses, in which those people less favored by fortune can easily find safe shelter."[28] Rio's prefect, Pereira Passos, ordered the construction of some subsidized housing. But the total number of units actually built did not even equal the few hundred erected in the nineteenth century.[29]

Not only the Brazilian government but also private owners dispossessed poor tenants. In areas where Rio's renovation increased property values, landlords with plans for more profitable use of their real estate sometimes evicted all their tenants. A few protested. Fourteen "humble workers, earning very little," petitioned Pereira Passos to examine the condition of the tenement on Prainha street, near the port, where they had lived for five, ten, or more years, until ordered to vacate within a week. Although their landlord claimed to have a municipal order to demolish the building "as it was in ruins," the workers contended that their homes were in "perfect condition." Some of the units, they admitted, might not be "pretty," but even those were not about to collapse and certainly were better than others on the same street. These workers begged the prefect not to let the owner "throw us into the street; this is just a trick of his to make his property yield more profit."[30] Landlords' greed remained an article of faith with the urban poor.

In the early twentieth century Rio's laboring poor lived in a variety of housing types, a few better and others worse than lower-class dwellings of the late empire. But only collective habitations, not the small, damp one-story houses that had sheltered uncounted numbers of Brazilians for generations, received the attention of government officials or of observers advocating construction of sanitary low-cost housing.

The handful of government-subsidized *vilas*, with their frenchified names and separate family kitchens and bathrooms, ample bedrooms, and even occasional gardens, provided relatively comfortable, healthy housing. Between 1890 and 1896 yellow fever claimed only seven victims in the five solid and impressive *vilas operárias* erected by Arthur Sauer's Companhia Saneamento. But these *vilas*, the only ones actually constructed in Rio during the nineteenth century, housed only 5,102 people, less than a tenth of the projected population (61,060) for whose accommodation the company acquired land throughout the city. And, as we saw in the previous chapter, these *vilas* sheltered many more petty bureaucrats, clerks, and military officers than factory workers. Such relatively costly housing, lauded by government officials and outside observers alike, proved far too popular to meet the "enormous demand," as the officials acknowledged.[31]

Upper-class advocates of modern, modest-priced worker housing rhapsodized almost as enthusiastically over the *avenidas*, updated versions of the *estalagens*. One inspector termed the *avenida* "a perfected *estalagem*. Each *avenida* consists of a central alley paved and lined with small houses. Every unit is completely separate, with individual kitchens, baths, and latrines, all of which are nicely tiled, just as in the fanciest residences."[32]

The nineteenth-century term *cortiço* continued to be applied to some of the older tenements, "flimsy wooden structures consolidated by time through clandestine repairs." In these two-story buildings, generally erected around a cramped interior patio, the top floor, "surrounded by a small strange ramshackle veranda," was reached "with difficulty by steep stairs." Sanitation in *cortiços* compared unfavorably with that in *estalagens*. "The sleeping alcoves are hotter, smaller, and darker; there is far less separation of families; life, day or night, is therefore more promiscuous. You can only enter some *cortiços* with a hankerchief held to your nose, and you still leave nauseated."[33]

The *casas de cómodos*, which had appeared by the end of the nineteenth century, were even worse. Old multistoried mansions whose owners had moved from the city center to newer residential areas had been turned into warrens of rented rooms and cubicles. Landlords' efforts to "create the largest possible number of spaces which could be inhabited" resulted in rooms of any shape, even three feet wide and thirty feet long, carved from "underneath stairs, from storerooms, areaways, kitchens, and even from bathrooms, all to make sleeping areas." Such rooms received only "second-hand air and light," and basement quarters received neither. Each communal latrine generally served dozens of people, and bathing facilities were even scarcer. Families or groups of individuals of either sex slept, cooked their food on tiny gas or kerosene stoves, and washed their clothes all in the same room, which they sometimes shared with dogs, cats, parrots, rabbits, or chickens. In these crowded chambers, separated by flimsy wooden partitions or even burlap curtains, privacy was virtually nonexistent, day or night.[34]

Closely related to the *casas de cómodos* were the *dormidas* or *casas de dormidas*, *albergues*, *hospedarias*, *hotel-cortiços*, and the *zungas* (the designations reserved for the poorest and most crowded accommodations in Rio de Janeiro and São Paulo). Here male day laborers without families and poverty-stricken individuals of both sexes slept in beds rented by the night. Some *albergues*, open only at night, rented straw mats as well as beds. In Rio's *zungas*, beds lined the corridors as well as filling large and small rooms and the muddy cellars of fetid old buildings. Even the larger structures, with some fifty rooms, generally had only two or three water spigots and latrines.[35]

Infectious diseases spread rapidly among the inhabitants of dirty, malodorous, dimly lit tenements. Sanitary as well as safety regulations generally went unenforced. The records of Rio's sixth health district, comprising the old central city districts of Santo Antonio and Santa Ana, revealed that in 1905, sixty-one percent of that district's yellow fever cases, forty-seven percent of the incidents of plague, forty-eight percent of the cases of tuberculosis, and thirty-eight percent of the smallpox cases occurred in collective habitations.[36] While the sanitation campaign launched by Dr. Osvaldo Gonçalves Cruz, Rodrigues Alves's Director of Public Health, rapidly reduced the incidence of yellow fever in Rio, other diseases, especially tuberculosis, continued to claim numerous victims.

While the exact number of Rio's inhabitants living in different types of slum housing in the early twentieth century cannot be determined, we can roughly estimate how many lived in "collective dwellings." The terms for the different forms of urban housing are not always clear or comparable. Although government officials generally included hotels and boarding houses under the classification of "collective dwellings," they excluded buildings in which three or more families banded together to share expenses. Both the 1890 national census and the 1906 Rio census employed the term *estalagem*. But the 1890 census defined estalagens as collective habitations, while the 1906 census listed collective dwellings as a separate category from *estalgens*. Unlike the 1906 census, that of 1890 tallied the number of families in Rio's collective housing. In 1890 Rio had 1,449 collective dwellings accommodating 18,338 families or domiciles. The average domicile in Rio had 7.2 members, although more congested areas like the downtown São José district, with its heavy concentration of tenements, averaged 9.7 people per domicile.[37] Simple multiplication employing the city-wide average yields a total of 132,034 people living in Rio's collective dwellings, assuming, of course, that the number of individuals per domicile was not markedly lower in tenement units than in other city housing. Since the contrary is more likely, we might use the São José rather than the city average, which would yield a total of 177,878. Even based on the lower figure, we can estimate that at least one quarter of the population of the nation's capital lived in some form of collective housing.

Some questions concerning the capital's collective dwellings and their inhabitants, as well as changes wrought by the remodeling of Rio de Janeiro in the early twentieth century, can better be addressed if we concentrate on selected areas of the city. São José, a congested, old downtown commercial district, and Glória, one of Rio's "aristocratic" districts, provide a good contrast; moreover, there exists rare municipal manuscript material on their slum housing which can be used to supplement national census data. At the turn of the twentieth century, Glória comprised the present-day districts of Catete, Glória, Flamengo, and Laranjeiras. São José extended from Seventh of September Street and Fifteenth of November Square southwest to the beginning of present-day Lapa. It included Castelo hill, site of the city's oldest settlement, then covered with dilapidated housing as well as historic churches and monuments. One high-ranking government official called Castelo "a human anthill, with thousands of houses and hovels in which men, women, and children are piled up."[38] As in the midnineteenth century, the proportion of foreigners and males remained higher in the commercial district of São José than in predominantly residential Glória. In 1906, 40.3% of São José's population was foreign-born and 65% was male, as compared with 28.8% foreign-born and 55.9% male in Glória.[39]

Even in the late nineteenth century, São José contained worse slum housing than Glória. In Glória, more of the urban poor could find shelter in small, damp, individual houses rather than in tenements. Glória's collective housing included a far higher proportion of *avenidas* and *estalagens*, the best types, while in São José *casas de cómodos* predominated. In 1895 *estalagens* comprised over half of Glória's collective housing, but under ten percent of São José's. Furthermore, *avenidas* provided an additional fourteen percent of Glória's collective dwellings, while São José had not a single one.[40]

The new avenues driven through São José in the first decade of the twentieth century led to a decline both in numbers and quality of that district's total housing stock. Even part of the Morro do Castelo succumbed to the advancing avenues, although the entire hill would not be demolished until 1922. In contrast, sprawling Glória experienced a sixty-five percent increase in the total number of buildings from 1890 to 1906 (Table 18). But in both districts collective dwellings multiplied faster than did the population. By 1906—assuming a constant official use of the term *estalagem*—the proportion of *estalagens* and *avenidas* in São José had declined markedly, while *casas de cómodos* increased. In that year, only five *estalagens* remained, with a total of sixteen units, and one *avenida*, with eighteen units, as compared to a total of 319 units in the dozen *estalagens* of 1895. Yet the percentage of this district's buildings devoted to collective housing had tripled since 1890 (Table 18).

Housing conditions in São José had worsened, much more so than in Glória. By 1906, after the "modernization" of Rio de Janeiro, a larger proportion of this district's remaining inhabitants lived in increasingly crowded tenements. More unrelated or distantly related adults now shared the same "domicile," itself often just a single room. The number of people in an average "household" in São José more than doubled between 1890 and 1906, rising from 9.7 in 1890 to 19.2 in 1906, while the far lower mean for the entire city only increased from 7.2 to 9.6.[41]

Government officials acknowledged the deterioration in housing conditions following the massive remodeling of Rio de Janeiro. One physician claimed that for every *estalagem* destroyed, two or more *casas de cómodos* appeared.[42] Perhaps he exaggerated, but other municipal officials also found casas de cómodos more crowded. Those slum dwellers who could not afford to find housing elsewhere had to remain in the city center. Rents rose. According to a municipal engineer who studied Rio's lower-class housing in 1905, rooms in *casas de cómodos* now cost 20 to 25 *milreis* monthly, while rents in *cortiços* averaged 50$ to 60$, and in *avenidas* ranged from 80$ to 120$ per month.[43] Few skilled workers such as stonemasons earning 7$ daily could afford the better forms of lower-

Table 18. Inhabitants of Collective Dwellings in Rio de Janeiro
and Its Glória and São José Districts, 1890–1906

	Brazilian	Population Foreign	Total	Total Number of Buildings	Number of Collective Dwellings
1890					
Rio de Janeiro	398,299	124,352	522,651	48,576	1,449
Glória	33,123	10,982	44,105	3,327	147
São José	24,775	15,239	40,014	1,988	86
1906					
Rio de Janeiro	600,928	210,515	811,443	84,375	4,289[a]
Glória	41,079	16,398	57,477	5,486[b]	405[a]
São José	25,537	17,443	42,980	1,776	246[a]

Source: Brazil, Diretoria Geral de Estatistica, *Recenseamento geral da República dos Estados Unidos do Brazil em 31 de Dezembro de 1890. Districto Federal (Cidade do Rio de Janeiro)*, pp. 424–25; Brazil, Brazil, Directoria Geral de Estatistica; *Recenseamento do Rio de Janeiro (Districto Federal) realizado em 20 de setembro de 1906*, I, 32; 37; 118–19; 390–91.
[a]Unlike the 1890 census, the 1906 census counted the separate units of *estalagens* and *avenidas* as distinct buildings, as well as excluding them from the census category of collective habitations. The figures given here for 1906 have been adjusted so that *estalagens* and *avenidas* but not their separate units are included.
[b]There was a slight difference in the boundaries of the districts in 1890 and 1906, so this figure is slightly low.

class housing. Nor could textile workers, as men in those factories averaged just 3$ a day and women 2$500.[44] Housing costs absorbed a much higher proportion of the income of the laboring poor than that of other sectors of the population.

In heavily urbanized areas, few housing alternatives existed to ever more crowded *casas de cómodos*, *dormidas*, and *estalagens*. Rio's subsidized *vilas* accommodated only a few thousand people. The poor had to search elsewhere. Many of those forced from their homes during the remodeling of Rio joined the trek to the suburbs, while others took to hillsides and unoccupied land spaces within Rio and erected *favelas*.

In the early twentieth century increasing numbers of both rich and poor moved farther from the city center, but generally in opposite directions. Then as now, Rio's north zone contained far poorer and less prestigious residential areas than the city's south zone. Between 1890 and 1906 the north zone grew twice as fast as the south zone, while the central city's population scarcely changed. The number of people in the north zone districts of São Cristóvão, Engenho Velho, Engenho Novo, and Espírito Santo increased by 118.3%, while the south zone districts of Glória, Lagoa, and Gávea expanded by 55.5%, a figure virtually identical to the city average of 55.3%. Only sparsely populated Gávea, site of several large factories, demonstrated a much higher growth rate. Downtown Rio grew by only 5.1%, and some central districts experienced an absolute decline in population. Between 1890 and 1906, Candelária's population shrank by 54.1% and Sacramento's by 19.7% (Table 19).

Improved transportation facilitated suburban growth. Two tunnels pierced the hills that had isolated the sandy southern Atlantic beaches from Botafogo Bay. In 1892, the year that Rio received its first electric streetcars, the Botanical Garden Railroad Company completed a one-hundred-and-eighty-yard tunnel linking Copacabana with Botafogo. Within a few years vehicular traffic was also permitted to traverse this first tunnel of Copacabana (soon popularly called Tunel Velho or Old Tunnel). In 1906 the longer Leme Tunnel (termed Tunel Novo or New Tunnel) joined Botafogo with the juncture of Leme and Copacabana. Work then began on Avenida Atlántica, ringing Copacabana beach.[45] Less than a decade later foreign visitors described the pleasures of trolley rides along the "magnificent beaches" of Leme, Copacabana, and Ipanema. In those "pretty Atlantic suburbs," where "cool breezes always blow and excellent bathing may be had," the elite erected their elegant new homes.[46]

Northern districts like São Cristóvao, settled in the midnineteenth century, also benefitted from streetcar lines linking them to downtown Rio. No longer home to the imperial family, São Cristóvão attracted ever more industry, and its population increased by three times the city average between 1890 and 1906 (Table 19). Wealthy residents left for other districts. Smelly, dirty factories annoyed them. In their complaint to the municipal government, families living near a soap factory in São Cristóvão described how the "bad odors" hindered the hiring of domestic servants, and how the dirt soiled their laundry.[47] But factory workers and other poor laborers, in no position to protest conditions in São Cristóvão, continued to move there.

Unlike the privately owned streetcar lines, most of which were absorbed by the Canadian-based Rio de Janeiro Tramway, Light and Power Company in the early twentieth century, the suburban railroads belonged to the Brazilian government. During the latter half of the nineteenth century, the government extended the Estrada de Ferro Central do Brasil and built the Leopoldina, Auxiliar, and Rio d'Ouro lines, fostering the growth of the north zone and the outlying towns strung along these railway lines branching northward from Rio de Janeiro. The railroad suburbs, which lacked alternative trolley service, expanded even

Table 19.   Population of Rio de Janeiro By District, 1890–1906

District	Population[a] 1890	1906	Increase in Population Absolute	Percentage
Urban				
Candelária	9,701	4,454	− 5,247	− 54.09
São José	40,014	44,878	4,864	12.16
Santa Rita	43,805	45,929	2,124	4.85
Sacramento	30,663	24,612	− 6,051	− 19.73
Glória	44,105	59,102	14,997	34.00
Sant'Anna	67,533	79,315	11,782	17.45
Santo Antonio	37,660	42,009	4,349	11.55
Espírito Santo	31,389	59,117	27,728	88.34
Engenho Velho	36,988	91,494	54,506	147.36
Lagôa	28,741	47,992	19,251	66.98
São Cristóvão	22,202	45,098	22,896	103.13
Gávea	4,712	12,750	8,038	170.59
Engenho Novo	27,873	62,898	35,025	125.66
Suburban-Rural				
Irajá	13,130	27,410	14,280	108.76
Jacarépaguá	16,070	17,265	1,195	7.44
Inhaúma	17,448	68,557	51,109	292.92
Guaratiba	12,654	17,928	5,274	41.68
Campo Grande	15,950	31,248	15,298	95.91
Santa Cruz	10,954	15,380	4,426	40.41
Ilha do Governador	3,991	5,616	1,625	40.72
Ilha de Paquetá	2,709	2,283	− 426	− 15.73
Land population	518,292	805,335	287,043	55.38
Maritime population	4,359	6,108	1,749	40.12
Total population	522,651	811,443	288,792	55.26

Source: Brazil, *Recenseamento do Rio de Janeiro (Districto Federal) realizado em 20 de setembro de 1906*, I, 23.

[a]These figures are not completely accurate, as district boundaries were changed and new districts created between 1890 and 1906. But they represent an effort by the 1906 census authorities to make the best possible comparison over time, using the 1890 districts as a base.

faster than Rio's north zone. Inaúma, the closest suburb, experienced the city's most rapid population growth. Between 1890 and 1906 Inaúma's population rose six times faster than the city average. Irajá, the next suburb along the railway lines, expanded at three times the Rio average. Other distant suburban districts lacking railroad transportation grew more slowly (Table 19).

The "enormous" increase in passengers—the number of trips taken on the Estrada de Ferro Central do Brasil alone rose by 1,876,525 from 1904 to 1905—not only startled government officials, but also imposed a severe strain on services.[48] While the reliability, comfort, and speed of the extensive trolley system, especially in the south zone, might merit the praises of foreign visitors, poor Brazilians complained about the suburban trains.[49] Round trip second-class fares of 400 reis absorbed ten percent or more of many workers' daily wages. A popular song entitled "The Fare Increase" echoed many passengers' resentment not only of Perreira Passos's fare increase but also of poor service. Ticket windows were frequently closed, and rides slow, crowded, and uncomfortable. But what alternative to second class was there? "We are happy not to ride in the baggage car. . . . Thus you survive, if you can . . . If you can't, you must go on foot." As the song's refrain declared: "Every time it's the poor who get squeezed."[50]

Why endure the discomfort and cost of dependence on suburban trains? Why rise between 3:30 and 5:00 A.M. to arrive at a downtown place of employment by 6:00 or 7:00 A.M.? The same low land prices that attracted factories to the suburbs also enabled many settlers to rent less congested housing than in downtown Rio or even to purchase small plots of land on which to construct their homes. The "sad suburbs" scorned by wealthier Brazilians provided healthier housing than could be obtained for the same price downtown. While some *estalagens* and *casas de cómodos* existed in Rio's outlying districts, most suburban dwellers inhabited small, separate houses lining unpaved, treeless streets clustered about the railroad stations. In the backyards, chickens could be raised and fruit trees grown. The farther from the stations, however, the poorer the houses became and the emptier the streets. Families even spread out recently washed clothes in the streets to dry. Vast areas in the suburbs, between the railroad stations, stood empty.[51]

Unlike the south zone, the suburbs lacked decent roads linking them to one another or to the central city. Every rainfall transformed their dirt streets into muddy morasses and left enormous potholes. Cattle, horses, pigs, goats, dogs, and chickens roamed the nearly empty streets, adding to their semirural aspects. Only during the early morning and evening rush hours did the areas nearest the railroad stations show signs of intense activity. Although some suburban dwellers walked to nearby textile, soap, or match factories, many more workers commuted to their places of employment in the north zone or in downtown Rio. Many suburbs lacked urban suburbs services like sewerage and mail delivery. Water and gas supplies remained highly inadequate as did police and fire protection. Only at election time did government officials seem to remember suburbanites. But their complaints about arrogant bureaucrats and "abandonment" by the government demonstrated an ability to protest and an expectation of remedial action less often found among downtown tenement dwellers.[52]

Lima Barreto, the novelist of the suburbs who wrote of the limited horizons and circumscribed lives of their poor, racially mixed inhabitants, found emotional as well as physical stress and strain. Although close friendships and camaraderie developed in the suburbs, neighbors still squabbled and fought easily, "an effect of the constant trials and tribulations with which they are forced to live and their inability to find beyond their immediate and limited field of vision any reason that could explain their sorry plight." Housewives believed themselves "to be of the highest personal worth and descendants of the finest ancestry, but, in reality, they all are extremely poor and live in terrible poverty. An accidental difference in skin color is reason enough for someone to judge herself superior to her neighbor; the fact that one's husband earns more than another's is also a reason. . . . In general, however, these quarrels last only a short time. Along comes some disease and one of the women's children falls ill; her neighbor then immediately comes over to help with vials full of homeopathic cures."[53]

Moving to the suburbs required some initial capital to rent, buy, or construct a home. Skilled workers such as typographers or railroad and marine and war arsenal employees seemed best able to take advantage of suburban housing opportunities and to afford the transportation costs. Those without steady employment or those obliged to remain closer to the labor market were less likely to become suburbanites. The suburbs provided fewer opportunities for occasional employment. While some female factory workers and employees of the government printing house traveled long distances to their jobs, most commuters were male. In the outlying districts, married women might plant gardens or raise animals to help sustain their families. But they had less chance to earn a cash income by taking in laundry. Despite the long commutes and the lack of conveniences such as running water in many homes, the suburbs were generally perceived as healthy places, better for raising children.[54]

Other members of the urban poor displaced during the rebuilding of downtown Rio de Janeiro pursued a seemingly novel housing strategy. They erected their own shelters on unoccupied, undesirable land within the city. Though *favelas*, as these clusters of shacks were called, only caught the eye of the press and the authorities in the twentieth century, similar shanties had long dotted the outskirts of the city. In the nineteenth century small, improvised structures were built for sale or rent in urbanized areas. They appeared within the gardens and courtyards of large dwellings and at the rear of warehouses and stables in Rio and São Paulo. In lower-class neighborhoods, as on the edges of the cities, the laboring poor could buy shanties lacking water and all municipal services. Owners of land near factories rented shacks to the workers. Furthermore, some urban factory and property owners also rented plots of land to laborers who then constructed their own housing.[55]

Sudden influxes of people unable to pay rent led to larger encampments of rustic-appearing housing in urban areas. Escaped slaves fleeing to cities like Rio de Janeiro and Santos in the 1880s erected *quilombos* or communities of runaways. Jabaquara, the best known and organized, housed several thousand fugitives in zinc-roofed wooden, straw, and mud huts outside Santos. These people paid no rent for the land or their shacks.[56]

The remodeling of Rio de Janeiro forced more of the laboring poor to adopt a similar solution to the housing shortage. Rising rents and the demolition of many *casas de cómodos* drove them to join others already living in improvised structures on marginal land in Rio. Escalating land values and building costs had limited new tenement construction. The failure of the government, like private enterprise, to meet the demand for low-cost housing stimulated the growth of *favelas*. The shanties, lacking all urban services, represented the cheapest form of housing construction in Rio, in both labor and materials.

By the time the Avenida Central was inaugurated in 1905, Rio de Janeiro possessed a recognizable *favela*, on Providência Hill near the main railroad station, deemed worthy of inclusion in a glossy magazine article on lower-class housing. In the late 1890s returning soldiers from the Canudos campaign in the Northeast had erected improvised shelters on this hill, near the War Ministry, while awaiting settlement of their compensation and pension claims. Perhaps the veterans found some similarity between this site and that of their struggle in the backlands of Bahia, for they renamed the hill the Morro da Favela. More than likely this hill, like other areas of nineteenth-century Rio, already contained a few shanties. But the Canudos veterans' numbers and potential political impact gave their settlement visibility. When they decamped, they probably sold their shacks. The municipal engineer who climbed one of the two narrow, winding pathways up the Morro da Favela in 1905 encountered scattered structures "as high as a man, with floors of beaten earth and walls made of flattened kerosene cans and boards from crates, fastened with strips of wood chinked with mud; this same mixture of materials served as roofing, held down by large stones. . . ." Not only criminal elements feared by the elite lived in these shacks, but also "diligent workers cast by the shortage or high cost of accommodations upon these heights, where they enjoy a relative cheapness of abode and a continualy flowing gentle breeze."[57]

A few years later, Rio's municipal government indirectly contributed to the establishment of another *favela*, Mangueira, which subsequently became one of the city's most famous. Serzedelo Correia, Rio's prefect from 1909 to 1910, wished to install a tree nursery in the Quinta da Boa Vista and permitted soldiers of the ninth regiment, as well as a few civilians who had built shacks in that park, to move to nearby Mangueira Hill in the São Cristóvão district.[58]

In the north and south zones of Rio de Janeiro additional *favelas* arose on vacant land where regular construction was impossible without new technology or great investment of capital and equipment. Although hillside *favelas* remained the most visible, others appeared on marshes, mud flats, and dumps. All were free from the high fees and time-consuming government requirements and inspections which, according to a labor newspaper, hindered conventional housing construction by poor individuals.[59] While *favelas* lacked even the scanty urban services and sanitary facilities supplied the suburbs, they generally were situated nearer places of work. And they provided more air and sunshine than centrally located but more costly *casas de cómodos*. For a minority of the urban poor in the early twentieth century, *favelas* represented the best available housing option.

Favelas housed a far smaller proportion of São Paulo's inhabitants. Unlike Rio de Janeiro, with its constricted geographical setting, São Paulo expanded outward in concentric waves over land suitable for traditional housing construction. Nor did municipal improvements entail massive demolitions of existing housing. Profitable tenement rental units accompanied the outward movement of this city's frontier, as did urban transportation. European immigrants, who traditionally settled in *cortiços* and *casas de cómodos* rather than erecting Brazilian-style shacks, comprised a larger proportion of São Paulo's population. Even in 1961, when Rio's *favelados* clearly outnumbered the inhabitants of *barracos de quintal* (backyard *favela*-like rental units) and *cortiços* combined, São Paulo's *cortiços* sheltered ten times as many people as that city's *favelas*.

In the early twentieth century government authorities paid little attention to either *favelas* or *cortiços*. The massive sanitation campaign accompanying the renovation and beautification of Rio de Janeiro reduced the threat of infectious diseases such as yellow fever spreading from the slums to elite residences. Tuberculosis did not pose as serious a threat to the upper classes or to Rio's reputation. Government officials no longer demonstrated concern with conditions in Rio's *cortiços, casas de cómodos*, and other tenements. And *favelas* were not yet visible or numerous enough to claim their attention.[61]

As in the nineteenth century, economic distress fostered protests and violent disturbances in the cities. Specific resentments related to Rio's renovation added to lower-class discontent. Although strikes increasingly served as vehicles of political and social unrest during the first years of the twentieth century, major urban upheavals, especially the 1904 antivaccination uprising in Rio, continued to prove more alarming to the elite. That outburst far surpassed in intensity all others during the presidency of Rodrigues Alves or of his predecessor Campos Sales.

A native of Campinas, São Paulo, who had opened vast new coffee groves in the frontier area near Jaú, Manuel Ferraz de Campos Sales consolidated Brazil's external debt, raised the exchange rate, and stopped inflation at the expense of sizable segments of the population. They disliked the increased taxes, cuts in federal expenditure, and the abandonment of public works projects. A large man, as fond of good food as of good clothes, Campos Sales never sought or gained popular esteem. As he privately admitted, his government was viewed in a "better light abroad than at home."[62]

More than minor disturbances marked his presidency. On 15 June 1901 the São Cristóvão streetcar company in Rio de Janeiro raised its fares. To demonstrate their annoyance, some students paid their passage in small copper coins while other riders jeered or refused to pay. Later, stones and bottles flew, several trolley cars were overturned, and rails were pulled up. Before the rioting ended on 19 June, streetcars would be burned, commerce disrupted, and people killed by the police.[63]

As in the nineteenth century, police excesses and destructive acts by marginal groups in society intensified the disturbances and led to violence. An unsigned police report to Minister of Jutice Epitácio Pessoa blamed the destruction on "suspicious groups composed of the meanest elements of this capital's population: well-known ruffians, *capoeiras*, notorious individuals, outcasts of every kind and of the worst sort," and accused opposition journalists and monarchists of rousing these lawless elements.[64] Certainly Campos Sales's government had detractors as well as supporters among the press. Although other Brazilian politicians also subsidized newspapers, the president apparently raised payments to new levels and publicly defended these acts.[65] As governor of São Paulo, Campos Sales had done the same; he considered it a "great necessity" to pay for favorable editorials in respected journals rather than to support a party newspaper.[66] But during the June 1901 upheaval, even the pro-government, pro-property *Jornal do Comércio* faulted Rio's police for first remaining immobile when trolley cars were burned and for then overreacting and attacking "defenseless passersby."[67]

On 17 June, following two days of scattered incidents, growing crowds—some two to three thousand people according to the *Jornal do Comércio*—gathered in the Largo de São Francisco de Paula, where a few trolley cars still operated. Half a dozen streetcars were overturned and burned. General Hermes da Fonseca, commander of Rio's police brigade, arrived and ordered the crowds dispersed at saberpoint. Many were wounded. Bystanders panicked, as did local merchants, who closed their stores. Firemen, under personal orders from the Justice Minister, used jets of water to clear the square. Elsewhere in the city, police cavalry ran down rioters and passersby alike, sometimes causing more conflicts. Police infantry with naked swords beat pedestrians, including families awaiting heavily guarded trolleys. The next day crowds booed police still stationed in the Largo de São Francisco and, according to police officials, tore up paving stones and gas and drainage pipes to block the entrance to the Ouvidor, Rio's main shopping street. Police troops then fired, killing several people. Police cavalry swept down the Ouvidor, trampling men, women, and children, and forcing most stores to close.[68]

Although the police boasted of their own "conciliatory intervention" and "tolerance" when faced by jeering, stone-throwing crowds, they admitted that the cavalry charge through the Ouvidor was an "error, an excess, a mistake."[69] But, as the police chief informed the Justice Minister, they could not prevent "some lamentable acts" from occurring.[70] In his long report to the Minister of Justice, General Hermes da Fonseca denied that the police brigade "had overstepped itself in complying with orders . . . ; if some ordinary citizens had been wounded and killed, well, police also were wounded and killed," proving that "it would be ridiculous" to "capitulate to force" and be vanquished by "those who only make use of confusion and disorder to achieve their unpatriotic and criminal ends."[71]

Although ended by force, this outburst extracted immediate concessions from the authorities, as had the *Vintém* upheaval over twenty years earlier. President Campos Sales proposed a fare reduction, and the São Cristóvão streetcar company "spontaneously" rescinded its price increase.[72]

When Campos Sales left the presidential palace following the inauguration of his successor on 15 November 1902, he was greeted with eggs, boos, and whistles, and his carriage pelted with stones. Soldiers and security agents had to protect him at the railroad station when he departed for São Paulo. But neither the police cavalry nor the bands of music and organized supporters could stop or drown out the jeering crowds shouting "Get out" and "Death to the Peacock." Nor could anyone prevent the stoning and jeering of his train when mechanical difficulties forced it to stop briefly in Rio's suburbs.[73]

During the administration of Rodrigues Alves, who continued most of Campos Sales's economic policies, Rio de Janeiro experienced a far more serious urban upheaval than that of 1901. Rodrigues Alves's plans to sanitize the nation's capital led to a program of compulsory vaccination against smallpox which in turn precipitated a massive popular uprising as well as a military move against the government in November 1904.[74] In March 1903 Dr. Osvalo Gonçalves Cruz, a young physician and the first Brazilian to study at the Pasteur Institute of Paris, was chosen to head the Public Health Service in Rio. Rodriguez Alves endorsed and supported this young federal official's aggressive measures to combat yellow fever by adapting Walter Reed's techniques to Brazil. Teams of inspectors combed Rio and its surroundings, noting all pools, swamps, and gutters where mosquitos might breed. When a case of yellow fever was reported, as required by law, they isolated the victim and disinfected his house as well as those of his neighbors. The sanitary authorities also had the power to demolish buildings, with compensation determined by special courts. Critics questioned the scientific basis of the campaign. They denounced the measures employed by the health service, objecting to "unjustifiable" invasions of privacy by "mosquito swatters." But the government persevered, attacking smallpox and bubonic plague as well. Killing rats and fleas to prevent plague, however, proved far more acceptable than forcibly vaccinating people against smallpox. The antismallpox crusade generated even more resistance than that against yellow fever.

The federal government's sanitation campaign in Rio de Janeiro met with skepticism, hostility, political opposition, and finally open violence. Official efforts to justify a program of compulsory vaccination against smallpox proved inadequate. "Historic republicans," unhappy with a former monarchist's elevation to the presidency, monarchists hoping to restore the old regime, positivists defending the right of individual choice, and disaffected congressmen all attacked the government.

Through pamphlets and newspaper articles, the highly respected Brazilian Positivist Apostolate protested the vaccination program as an attempt to institute a form of social compulsion and coercion in personal matters. The positivist church stressed freedom of choice as the crucial issue. It also questioned the efficacy of the vaccine.[75] While the positivist church admonished members to avoid political activities and violence, some positivists embraced both.

In Congress, Major Alexandre José Barbosa Lima, Lieutenant Colonel Lauro Sodré, and Alfredo Varela, opposition leaders and positivists, denounced the government as unpatriotic and oligarchical and attacked the vaccination as endangering the populace. For years these frustrated followers of Marshal Floriano Peixoto had fought the *paulista* presidents. In 1901 Barbosa Lima headed the reorganized but short-lived opposition Partido Republicano Nacional and edited its newspaper, *O Nacional*, once again denouncing Portuguese domination of Rio's retail commerce. As Robert Nachman has pointed out, Barbosa Lima could not have favored the federal government's overthrow in 1904 simply because it sought compulsory vaccination.[76] While governor of his native Pernambuco in the late 1890s, Barbosa Lima had supported both smallpox vaccination and compulsory government projects like pension funds. Rather, like his fellow soldier-politician and "historic republican" Lauro Sodré of Pará, he had lost his power base in his home state when the old oligarchical families resumed control. Lauro Sodré secured election to the Senate from Rio de Janeiro following his service as governor and senator from Pará, and Barbosa Lima became a deputy from Rio Grande do Sul. Like their opponents in the federal government, they now focused their attention and aspirations on the nation's capital.[77]

As under the empire, opposition journalists played a major role in rousing Rio's populace to action. The antiadministration *Correio da Manhã*, the self-proclaimed "voice of the people," ceaselessly attacked the government and the vaccination campaign. So did Alfredo Varela's *Comércio do Brasil*, founded in May 1904 with monarchist funds. Once rabid *Jacobinos* like Deocleciano Martyr also assailed compulsory vaccination in A *Voz Pública*. They claimed that not only would "feminine delicacy" and the "sanctity of the home" be violated by the Rodrigues Alves regime, but tyranical government was also endangering people's lives with a vile vaccine, and should be resisted. The newspapers published cases of people refusing vaccination and helped create a climate of conflict and crisis.

Rio's laboring poor, suffering from rising rents, living costs, and unemployment, already had ample reason to be suspicious of government programs and activities. Many poor families were displaced by the renovation of Rio. Now public health officials invaded and threatened their homes. Sanitation teams protected by armed police—and police were never welcome in poor neighborhoods—forcibly entered slum dwellings and brutally performed their tasks. Once again, the lower classes were subjected to coercion, not persuasion. Opposition politicians could easily intensify and exploit lower-class fears and resentments.

Vicente de Souza's Centro das Classes Operárias served as the major point of contact between unhappy workers and leading opponents of the government. An ardent abolitionist and republican, a positivist from Bahia with a medical degree, a journalist and a professor of Latin and logic at the Colégio Dom Pedro II, Vicente de Souza had long supported reformist causes and moderate worker demands. Neither an orthodox positivist nor socialist—he wrote newspaper articles advocating a vague form of socialism—he established the Centro das Classes Operárias in 1902, with the collaboration of Gustavo de Lacerda. As president of this association composed mainly of maritime workers, Vicente de Souza raised money for their June 1903 strike against the Lloyd Brasileiro shipping line. Rio's socialists, however, denounced him as "bourgeois." In 1904 his Centro da Classes Operárias provided a podium for antivaccination leaders like Lauro Sodré and Barbosa Lima. And he encouraged protest against the Rodrigues Alves regime. Certainly, Vicente de Souza helped fan lower-class suspicions of government and tie these to the antivaccination movement. It is also possible that he attempted to foment riots in order to exhaust the government and ensure the success of a military revolt, a charge he later denied.[78] After all, early in 1900 monarchists and disgruntled officers including former naval lieutenant José Augusto Vinhais had conceived such a plot; they unsuccessfully sought to take advantage of a violent strike by Rio's teamsters, paralyze the Central do Brasil railroad, and proclaim a provisional government.[79]

On 31 October 1904, following months of heated debate, Congress approved the bill requiring vaccination against smallpox within six months. While this law mandated nationwide vaccination, the government could best concentrate its resources on the capital, as could the opposition. There the sharpest conflicts and worst upheavals occurred. On 5 November, at the Centro das Classes Operárias, Lauro Sodré founded the League Against Obligatory Vaccination, headed by himself, Vicente de Souza, and Barbosa Lima. In a fiery discourse, Sodré called on the people to oppose the "unconstitutional" and "arbitrary" vaccination law with force. Then an opposition newspaper published a draft sanitary code designed to enforce the law through heavy fines and job dismissals. Osvaldo Cruz, the code's author, was too politically inexperienced and absorbed in his work to make necessary modifications in the code's unpopular provisions, even though public health stations already registered a sharp decline in voluntary vaccinations.[80]

On 10 November, following the code's promulgation, disturbances broke out in Rio de Janeiro. That day saw only isolated clashes between police and demonstrators. Crowds gathered outside the Centro das Classes Operárias while the directorate of the League Against Obligatory Vaccination met. On 11 November police cavalry and infantry broke up a huge protest meeting in the Largo de São Francisco de Paula, arresting many people. As during previous upheavals, police cavalry with naked sabers ran down bystanders, causing panic and forcing stores to close. The evening of 12 November some three thousand people assembled for a mass meeting of the League Against Obligatory Vaccination. Barbosa Lima denounced the government but counseled prudence. Invoking the memory of Floriano Peixoto, Lauro Sodré condemned the *fazendeiro*-run regime. The next day huge crowds filled the principal downtown squares and jeered the government. More arrests, shooting, and cavalry charges followed. Using paving stones and construction materials, men erected barricades as protection against cavalry assaults. They broke gas lamps on the main streets and squares and overturned and burned trolley cars. Destruction was not indiscriminate; the São Cristóvão Line once again felt the brunt of popular ire, with some two dozen of its streetcars destroyed or damaged. Several police stations were overrun. Army and police troops had to guard the gas company's headquarters and those of streetcar concerns as well as the presidential palace. On 14 November rioters again successfully repulsed police attacks on barricades blocking major downtown streets and burned more trolley cars, using the debris to reinforce the barricades. The conflict spread to other districts and the number of dead and wounded mounted.[81] Soon the federal government would have to call in the army to regain control of the capital.

Late on November 14, the eve of the fifteenth anniversary of the proclamation of the republic, a military rebellion against Rodrigues Alves's government broke out. This conspiracy of officers and cadets had taken shape while congress debated the vaccination bill. But the popular uprising led them to advance their schedule. Their plan called for rebellions at the military prepatory and tactical school in suburban Realengo and at the military academy at Praia Vermelha. Columns from both schools would then march on the presidential palace and install a military dictatorship headed by Lauro Sodré. But forces loyal to the government arrested the rebellious officers in Realengo. At Praia Vermelha, Lieutenant Colonel Sodré and General Silvestre Rodrigues da Silva Travassos succeeded in leading several hundred cadets from the school toward the presidential palace in Catete. Even before reaching Botafogo beach, they clashed with almost two thousand troops loyal to the government. The surprised and confused cadets energetically returned their fire until the more numerous government troups withdrew in disarray. But with Lieutenant Colonel Sodré and General Travassos both wounded, the leaderless rebellious forces returned to the military school. The government regrouped its forces—those not guarding public installations against angry demonstrators—called in the navy, and suffocated the revolt the next day. An apparently related military conspiracy in Bahia was also snuffed out.[82]

The federal government now turned its full attention to the uprising in Rio, calling in the army. Remaining resistance centered on the Saúde district, the site of wholesale demolition near the new port works. Popularly called Port Arthur after the Russian port which withstood a long siege durig the recent Russo-Japanese War, this redoubt was protected by a barrier of paving blocks, telephone poles, trolley cars and rails, tree trunks, sandbags, and pieces of old buildings. Its predominantly black defenders, armed with rifles, pistols, and dynamite, fought on, led by "Black Foot," a well-known "ruffian." On 16 November army infantry took Port Arthur.[83]

Although President Rodrigues Alves blamed the military conspirators for provoking the "series of disorders" in Rio "as preparation for their criminal attempt" to overthrow him, he dealt less harshly with them than with the rioters and other lower-class elements.[84] General Travassos had died of his wounds. The government briefly arrested Lauro Sodré and several other officers. Deputy Varela fled and was never imprisoned. Barbosa Lima remained at large, keeping silent for months. With Vicente de Souza arrested and charged with conspiracy, the Centro das Classes Operárias disappeared. The government closed the military schools temporarily and sent the rebellious cadets to serve on the southern frontier. But some army supporters of the antivaccination campaign received promotions and positions of confidence.[85]

In contrast, hundreds of poor residents of Rio, whether or not implicated in the rioting, were imprisoned and shipped to the Amazon in the sealed holds of coastal vessels. Police employed an emergency state of siege to rid Rio of "vagabonds," "ruffians," and unemployed workers. In nightly raids they swept through poor neighborhoods, arresting suspected rioters, known troublemakers, and day laborers alike. In groups of some three hundred at a time, foreigners as well as Brazilians were herded into ships for the slow, suffocating voyage to Brazil's newly acquired Acre territory on the Bolivian frontier, where labor was needed for rubber gathering. If arrested foreigners could secure help from their governments' representatives in time, they might simply be expelled from Brazil. At the request of the Portuguese consul, the Brazilian government freed over 160 Portuguese subjects, most of them unjustly arrested. Forty Italians still ended up in Acre. Stevedores, servants, teamsters, and factory workers all endured Amazonian exile. While the military conspirators enjoyed a triumphant return to Rio the following year, most of the urban poor shipped to the Amazon were abandoned there.[86]

The "progress" promoted by the Brazilian governing elites in the early twentieth century heightened economic and social tensions in the cities. Discontent, fanned by dissident politicians, bred violence. But the opposition leaders who helped stimulate and channel popular resentments during the 1904 antivaccination upheaval in Rio de Janeir could not control them. In subsequent years, with the growth of industry and of labor organizations, urban protests would increasingly take the form of strikes and organized demonstrations rather than popular outbursts or riots. Even those riots that occurred would tend to incorporate elements of protest aimed against the nation and its political institutions rather than against specific abuses.

During the early years of the twentieth century Brazil's major cities gained a series of physical "improvements." Each received, in varying measure, new port works, avenues, ornate public buildings, and other appurtenances of modern urban centers. The governing elites congratulated themselves on the apparent transformation of the cities, especially Rio de Janeiro. But the progress they pursued brought few benefits to the laboring poor. The construction of Rio's Avenida Central left thousands of workers homeless. While some remained in ever more crowded downtown slums, others fled to the suburbs or to hilltop shantytowns in search of a better life. In future years, the *favelas,* rather than the Avenida Central would epitomize Rio de Janeiro for many visiting foreigners.

6 / The Dimensions of Urban Poverty: Lower-Class Life and Labor in the Early Twentieth Century

During the early twentieth century Brazil's working poor labored long and hard for petty returns at a seemingly unlimited variety of jobs. They endured not only crowded, unsanitary housing, but also job insecurity, miserable pay and working conditions, disease, and poor food and nourishment—problems ignored by Brazil's export-oriented governments. While some skilled workers maintained pride in their craft, other workers only performed tasks of brute force or endless repetition. In Brazil as in other countries of the Western Hemisphere, blacks, women, and children received some of the worst treatment. Diversions were few and life difficult for most urban laborers.

As in the nineteenth century, skilled craftsmen did not care to be confused with unskilled workers or those with uncertain, shifting occupations. Carpenters, plasterers, masons, cabinetmakers, printers, glassblowers, coopers, shoemakers, bakers, hat makers, and tailors still ranked well above street sellers, porters, dishwashers, and day laborers, as did streetcar conductors and teamsters, and even semiskilled mill hands. Some unskilled laborers found temporary employment in the industrial and service sectors. Poor women still took in laundry, girls sold sweets, and boys shined shoes and sold newspapers. For both skilled and unskilled workers, most fields of employment remained either overwhelmingly male or female.

Urban workers employed various strategies for survival. Household members pooled their limited resources and earnings. Those not bringing in cash income might serve as unpaid workers in home enterprises or perform necessary child care or homemaking functions. Even small children not only undertook household tasks but also labored as unremunerated helpers in home workshops producing goods for market, or at times earned wages in factories, especially textile factories, where employment of entire families was the norm. When unemployment, illness, or death struck, the composition of the family work force could be changed, with household tasks redistributed and more or different family members sent into the job market. But food consumption and health often suffered. All possible activities would be turned into revenue-producing ones. Even household members with recognized employment could perform odd jobs, generally in the service sector, to supplement salaries. Extending work time, not just the work day, remained a principal strategy for survival. Some members of the urban poor cut expenses by living in *favelas* rather than in rental housing. Others, in the suburbs, planted gardens or raised chickens to minimize cash outlays and help sustain their families. Or they might barter goods and services. Mutual favor networks also reduced expenditures. While the working poor had little free time for rest or recreation, they sought to enliven their labors in various ways, even through gossiping on the job, and bore long work days as best they could.

Some skilled workers, such as printers, hat makers, and cigar makers, felt threatened by technological advances. They did not want new machines to drive them from their jobs and into the ranks of the unskilled. A few called for the establishment of professional schools and for restrictions on admitting untrained individuals into factories and workshops, while others wanted the "menacing" machines outlawed. At times, the threat of loss of livelihood led to strikes. Craftsmen scorned workers who merely tended machines, producing supposedly inferior products, and sometimes even physically intimidated these competitors.[1]

With the introduction of typesetting machines, typographers suffered some of the sharpest blows to pride and pocketbook. At first, some typographers scoffed at linotype machines, although others expressed their "humiliation" at seeing machines produce several times the work of the most skilled typographer. Many simply feared the new machines. Linotypes "were launched into the typographers' midst like a grenade tossed into a defenseless crowd."[2] One machine did the work of five, six, or more men. When Rio's *Correio da Manhã* introduced linotypes in 1909, over three-quarters of the newspaper's typographers lost their jobs. By 1910, according to compositors' representatives, almost half their number in Rio de Janeiro lacked employment. Those still holding jobs had to work longer hours for less pay. In a tight job market, men who for years had dedicated themselves to the "art" of typography might have "to become street vendors or cashiers in beer halls."[3] In their fear and frustration, some typographers threatened to destroy composing machines or called on linotypers to refuse to work the new machines or to produce less. But their representatives, who had long proclaimed printers' support of "progress" and "science", could not condone such behavior, for progress could not be stopped and capitalists would only buy new machines. Nor did the short-lived Typographical Union of Resistance, founded in Rio in 1909 to oppose the imposition of typesetting machines, achieve any positive results. For a minority of typographers, however, the introduction of linotypes represented a personal advance. They became linotypers, at perhaps double their former colleagues' salaries. Rio's linotypers formed their own union in 1908. Animosities between typographers and linotypers were slow to be resolved. As industrial capitalism expanded in the early twentieth century, major differences in attitudes, wages, and working conditions among Brazil's skilled and unskilled laborers persisted and sometimes increased.[4]

In small workshops, where most skilled workers labored, relations between owners and workers appeared less impersonal and harsh than in large establishments. Owners of specialized shops with minimal capitalization and mechanization might work side by side with their employees, from whose ranks some had climbed, demonstrating the possibility, although not the probability, of social ascension. Skilled workers such as carpenters retained an artisan mentality, with more pride in their craft and no doubt greater job satisfaction than was possible in highly mechanized and less skilled manufactures such as textiles. Construction workers able to carve and decorate the facades of buildings concerned themselves with education and the improvement of their skills. However, even though skilled workers enjoyed relatively better working conditions and salaries, their wages remained low and hours long, in small shops as in large, and they were still subject to close supervision and control.

Unlike carpentry or construction, entirely male occupations, some skilled handwork remained women's work. Women not only toiled in "factories producing textiles, stockings, ties, pants, slippers, cord, string, oakum, etc.," but also in "innumerable workshops: dressmaking shops, shops producing embroideries, clasps, hats, and gloves."[5] They labored in repair shops and laundries. A dozen women might spend their days shut up in "dark, airless" rooms, "hunched over long tables," producing the luxury garments in which elite ladies promenaded on the Avenida Central, attended receptions, or frequented theaters and tea salons.[6] The few activists among São Paulo's seamstresses complained of toiling up to sixteen hours a day, "leaving for work at seven o'clock in the morning and returning home at eleven o'clock at night"; the remaining eight hours provided "insufficient time to recuperate our strength and to overcome our exhaustion through sleep."[7] Even when forced to work Sundays also, they earned only fifty to sixty *milreis* a month, or 1$500 to 2$000 a day, less than most female factory hands, let alone skilled male workers earning up to 10$000 daily.[8]

As in the nineteenth century, seamstresses with individual clients for their products still plied their needles at home. But the growth of the putting-out system increasingly turned tenement rooms into sweatshops, with women now performing piecework for industrial purposes up to eighteen hours a day. Thus industrialists cut costs and wages, while escaping some taxes and public notice. In Rio's early twentieth-century *cortiços*, outsiders observed "poor but modest girls" sewing heavy cloth goods for the arsenals in their tiny, clean rooms decorated with beloved family pictures. The "production of lingerie, canvas, slippers, and openwork fabric" lay in the hands of women laboring at home.[9]

Like other lower-class women, seamstresses remained in a weak position to resist the sexual advances of upper-class men. Some resorted to occasional prostitution to meet economic hardships. Prostitution never appears among occupational categories in Brazilian censuses, but one wonders how many of the seamstresses enumerated also followed this pursuit. Some dressmakers, particularly Frenchwomen, won renown as luxury prostitutes, or *cocotes*. The upper ranks of prostitution, but not the lower, provided an attractive alternative to sweatshop labor for some women.

Domestic service, another female field, continued to provide more employment for urban lower-class women than factories, workshops, or any other sector of the economy. According to the 1920 census, 80.7% of those employed in this sector were women, and these women comprised 19.3% of Brazil's total female population and 35.6% of nonagricultural women workers.[10] In Rio de Janeiro 50.2% of the female labor force was employed in domestic service (see Table 4). These women lacked much personal freedom or privacy. Almost all lived under close supervision in the homes of their employers, who regulated their working conditions. Day or night, domestic servants were on call, generally every day of the week. Although in theory they worked for pay, as well as receiving room and board, often their wages were merely symbolic. The prejudice against women working outside the home and the need for someone to perform domestic tasks helped keep women in these poorly paid, dreary jobs.

No government bureau ever investigated domestic service. Unlike factory inspections, inquiries into these traditional female tasks, considered proper work for women, would be viewed as an invasion of privacy. Not only the elite but also the amorphous middle classes, including bureaucrats, employed maids. Any inquiries into domestic service would constitute a violation of the sanctity of their homes. Industrialization, a modernizing intrusion, aroused more concern.

Brazil's factories received more official attention than any other area of lower-class employment. By 1920 both government and private bodies surveyed the nation's industrial productivity and proudly presented the results to both domestic and foreign audiences. The national census of that year examined Brazil's principal manufactures and found 275,512 workers employed in 13,336 "factories" of all sizes.[11] Textile workers totaled 46.9% of the industrial labor force in factories employing eight or more workers, followed by food processing with 16.1% of that labor force and apparel with 9.1%. Behind these came chemical products, ceramics, metalworking, woodworking, furniture, leather and skins, transportation equipment, and construction supplies (Table 20).

Industrial production centered in the south, especially the cities of São Paulo and Rio de Janeiro. Bahia had served as the nation's first center of textile manufacture in the midnineteenth century. But, as we have seen, south-central Brazil attracted greater quantities of European immigrants and capital than did the north. The cities of Rio de Janeiro and São Paulo offered larger regional markets for industrial products, as well as capital, labor, transportation facilities, and government connections. Nearly two-thirds of the 3,258 large and small, but predominately small, establishments employing 151,841 workers surveyed by a manufacturer's association in 1907 were concentrated in three areas of south-central Brazil: the Federal District of Rio de Janeiro (with 34,890 workers) and the states of São Paulo (24,816) and Rio Grande do Sul (15,426).[12] Industrial production expanded parallel to the rise in Brazilian exports, particularly coffee, or, as Warren Dean argues, because the export trade grew.[13] With its broadening market and growing coffee trade, the state of São Paulo in particular experienced rapid advances in industrialization. World War I marked the end of British predominance in Brazil and dealt the final blow to the country's century-old financial and commercial dependence on Great Britain. Whether or not the war accelerated Brazilian development as rapidly as writers other than Dean maintain, industry certainly became more visible and trade increased. With its newer machinery and growing market, São Paulo replaced Rio de Janeiro as the nation's most important industrial center by 1920.

In Brazil's large industrial enterprises, men, women, and children

Table 20. Distribution of Workers in Manufacturing, By Industry, 1920

Type of Industry[a]	Total Number of Workers	Adults		Minors[b]	
		Male	Female	Male	Female
Textiles	108,804	41,217	50,386	7,762	9,439
Leather, Skins	3,806	3,540	59	163	44
Wood Industries	9,614	9,137	62	395	20
Metal Working	12,031	9,634	510	1,706	181
Ceramics	12,281	9,840	748	1,515	178
Chemical Products	12,432	7,345	3,204	780	1,103
Food	37,356	25,991	8,267	2,077	1,021
Apparel	21,180	10,989	7,987	1,075	1,129
Furniture	6,631	5,313	632	632	54
Construction Supplies	2,571	2,424	18	129	—
Transportation Equipment	3,237	2,744	93	35	49
Production and Transmission of Physical Forces	1,012	995	2	15	—
Scientific, Literacy, and Luxury Industries	806	536	85	181	4
TOTAL	231,761	129,705	72,053	16,781	13,222

Source: *Recenseamento do Brazil . . . 1920*, V, 2a parte, x.
[a] Includes only enterprises with eight or more workers.
[b] Under fourteen years old.

190

exchanged long hours of weary work in unsanitary, often unsafe factories for meager wages. Many of the poorly lit and ventilated structures housing machinery had not been designed for manufacturing. With machines crowded together and gears and belts unshielded, accidents were frequent. As in other countries during initial stages of industrial capitalism, a general climate of job insecurity prevailed. In most industries job turnover was rapid. Some laborers, especially skilled male workers, even moved from city to city, searching for higher salaries, although generally without success. Accident or unemployment compensation was unknown. Government bureaucrats, not manual laborers, hoped to receive pensions. Reigning *laissez-faire* attitudes impeded passage of legislation regulating working conditions let alone salaries and hours. The only federal labor legislation enacted during the first two decades of the republic, the provisional republican regime's decree controlling child labor in Rio's factories, was not enforced.

Workers complained not only of long hours, miserable wages, irregular payments, inequitable piecework systems, unsanitary and unsafe working conditions, and arbitrary dismissals, but also of heavy fines imposed in the factories. These fines aroused deep anxieties, for they could reduce wages drastically. Management docked workers' wages for a wide variety of infractions, such as arrival at factories five minutes late or production of defective cloth. In the Central do Brasil railroad yards in suburban Rio de Janeiro, the minimum fine equaled five days' wages. Fines lowered industrial payrolls while serving as a major means of social control in factories and workshops.[14]

Textiles represented the main source of industrial employment in Brazil (Table 20). With the highest degree of mechanization, utilization of electricity, and concentration of workers per unit of machinery among Brazil's industries, major textile factories surpassed almost all others in size. While Salvador and its surroundings contained five of the nation's nine cotton mills in the 1860s, Rio de Janeiro acquired the greatest concentration of spindles and looms by the end of the empire. Between 1881 and 1895, the number of textile factories in Rio almost quadrupled while the total number of textile workers increased over tenfold, as did annual cloth production. By the late nineteenth century, Rio possessed half of Brazil's large textile mills. In 1895 the capital contained six cotton textile companies with over five hundred workers each (Table 21). Of these six companies, employing from 510 to 1,625 men, women, and children, four had been founded within the previous decade. The state of Rio de Janeiro had two additional large textile mills, one with 1,470 workers and the other with 935, both established in the early 1870s. In Bahia in 1895 one textile company employed 805 workers in three factories, and another, 620 workers. The states of São Paulo, Pernambuco, and Maranhão each had a large textile factory employing seven hundred, seven hundred, and six hundred workers respectively. In 1907 the Federal District of Rio de Janeiro was still the nation's major textile producer, but by 1920 textile manufacture in the state of São Paulo surpassed that in the Federal District. São Paulo now had twenty-four textile factories employing five hundred or more workers (out of a total of 247 mills with at least five workers) as compared with eight such factories (out of a total of 73) in the Federal District. In 1920 these large *paulista* factories employed 23,704, or 68.1% of the state's 34,825 textile workers, and the large Rio factories, 14,858, or 77.1% of the capital's 19,264 mill hands. Few other industries could match these textile factories in size. In Rio, textiles represented seven of the city's eight factories employing over a thousand workers in 1920 and seven out of nine such factories in the state of São Paulo.[15]

Textile manufacture demanded neither brute force nor slowly acquired skills, but rather vigilance and manual dexterity. Unskilled labor of both sexes and all ages could be "profitably" employed in the mills, and paid lower wages than in less mechanized industries. Nor was literacy essential. Only 5,061, or 51.1%, of the 9,896 largely foreign-born workers employed by the thirty textile factories in metropolitan São Paulo investigated by the state's department of labor in 1911 could read and write. In comparison, the 1920 census found 61.1% of the city's foreigners and 56.8% of the Brazilians to be literate. Child laborers were even less likely to be literate than were adult mill hands. The nation's capital enjoyed the highest literacy rates in Brazil. Yet of the 289 children between the ages of seven and fourteen employed by Rio's large Bangú textile factory in December 1899, only forty-seven could read and write. Since almost all of these children were born in Brazil, their education, or lack of it, did not directly reflect on European conditions. In 1920, when the Brazilian census first employed several age categories for education, 62.8% of Rio's children between the ages of seven and fourteen were literate. Children working in textile mills had little time or opportunity to acquire other than limited work skills.[16]

The proportion of child and female labor in textiles exceeded that in other manufactures. Only in this branch of industry did women outnumber men. According to the 1920 census, women comprised 55% of Brazil's adult textile workers. Minors under fourteen years of age formed 15.8% of the labor force in textile factories employing eight or more workers. These concentrations clearly exceed those in food processing and apparel, second and third in total number of industrial employees as well as in number of female and child laborers. In food-processing plants, women formed 24.1% of the adult labor force, while minors constituted 8.3% of the total labor force. Women comprised 42.1% of adult workers in the clothing industry, with minors totaling 10.4% of the total labor force (Table 21).

As in other industrializing countries, textile workers in Brazil were subject to speed-ups and fines. Child laborers might be struck or beaten if they did not fill production quotas or if they fell asleep on the job. Sometimes they cleaned machinery in motion. Even though occasional government investigations of larger, newer factories reported that sanitary and security regulations were obeyed, workers complained about terrible hygienic conditions in the textile factories. They cited closed windows, to prevent them from looking out, air choked with lint, rarely washed factory walls and floors, and a lack of toilets. In order to thread their looms, textile workers had to suck the shuttles, increasing the spread of infectious diseases like tuberculosis, a scourge of urban workers, in Brazil, as in other industrializing countries. The gruesome accidents workers witnessed heightened their distress. When two child "apprentices" fell into the machinery of one of Niterói's textile mills, their deaths, blamed on the foreman, led to a major strike in October 1907.[17]

The arbitrary and sometimes brutal behavior of factory foremen and supervisors figured prominently among worker complaints. Workers claimed that foremen humiliated, cursed, insulted, and capriciously dismissed them. Perhaps because foremen, unlike factory owners, directly controlled and punished workers, they felt the brunt of worker animosities. Foremen often rose out of the workers' ranks, which may account for their harshness as well as for the worker antipathy toward them. Minors and women, least able to defend themselves, received the worst treatment. While children suffered beatings, women were subject to sexual exploitation by foremen and supervisors. Women workers complained of the jokes, insults, and abuse they received when they had no lovers, and therefore no protectors, present. If they protested, they received no redress and were fired. Supervisors' conduct sometimes led to strikes, but factory owners supported their foremen, even the subjects of years of worker complaints.[18]

To increase profits, factory owners often prolonged the workday and increased the use of machinery by a largely unorganized labor force. In São Paulo, according to the state's labor department, textile workers toiled up to twelve hours a day in 1912, while hat workers, and some others, labored only nine hours.[19] As we shall see in the next chapter, textiles remained one of the most difficult sectors of industry to unionize.

For the efficient operation of the textile mills, some industrialists created a system of social services, assisting and regulating factory work-

Table 21. Largest Textile Factories in Rio de Janeiro, 1895 and 1908

Company	Name of Factory	Location	Date of Inauguration	Number of Workers 1895	Number of Workers 1908	Number of Looms 1895	Number of Looms 1908	Annual Production in Meters 1895	Annual Production in Meters 1908	Company Provisions (1900)
Cia. América Fabril	F. Cruzeiro F. Bonfim[a] F. Pau Grande	Andaraí S. Cristóvão Raiz da Serra (suburb)	1895 unknown 1885	450 165 530	1,320	440 62 100	1,100	5,280,000 unknown 1,440,000	10,000,000	
Cia. de Fiação, Tecelagem e Tinturaria Aliança	F.F. Aliança	Laranjeiras	1880	1,625	1,637	1,248	1,336	8,220,000	12,599,968	Company housing for most workers
Cia. de Fiação e Tecidos Carioca	F.F.T. Carioca	Jardim Botânico	1884	[c. 1,000 in 1900]	1,300	unknown	1,067	unknown	14,000,000	Doctor Company housing for almost all workers 124 company houses
Cia. de Fiação e Tecidos Confiança	F. Confiança Industrial	Vila Isabel	1887	557	1,354	600	1,500	7,000,000	17,000,000	
Cia. de Fiação e Tecidos Corcovado	F.F.T. Corcovado	Jardim Botânico	1889	480	794	500	806	7,000,000	10,000,000	Doctor three times a week Day care 24 company houses

Table 21. *(continued)*

Company	Name of Factory	Location	Date of Inauguration	Number of Workers 1895	1908	Number of Looms 1895	1908	Annual Production in Meters 1895	1908	Company Provisions (1900)
Cia. Progresso Industrial do Brasil	F.F.T. Bangú	Bangú (suburb)	1893	1,500	1,800	1,221	1,247	3,600,000	[11,000,000 in 1907]	Doctor Food stores 95 company houses Worker-constructed housing
Cia. União Industrial Sao Sebastião	F. São João	S. Cristóvão	1887	510	[450 in 1907]	274	unknown	6,400,000	[10,000,000 in 1907]	Primary schools

Sources: Brazil, Ministerio da Industria, Viação e Obras Publicas, *Relatorio*, 1896; Prefeitura do Districto Federal, *Noticia sobre o desenvolvimento da industria fabril no Districto Federal e sua situação actual* (1908), pp. 64–65; Ferreira da Rosa, *O Rio de Janeiro em 1900*, 69–73, 143–47, 333–55, 439–43; Centro Industrial do Brasil, *O Brasil. Suas riquezas naturaes. Suas industrias* (1909), III, 2ª parte, 23.

ªIn 1895 this factory belonged to Cia. União Industrial São Sebastião.

ers' lives (see Table 21). Implanted in the earliest textile mills, industrial paternalism persisted into the twentieth century, particularly in factories located beyond the city centers. In the midnineteenth century, cotton mill owners often furnished workers with food as well as housing, and sometimes provided clothing, too. As we saw in the previous chapter, some industrialists sold tiny plots of land to their factory workers or rented out housing units, often at a considerable profit to themselves. Company stores, owned and operated by the mills or leased to private entrepreneurs, continued to sell food to factory hands living far from other shops. High food prices at these general stores frequently figured among worker grievances, as did excessive rents for company housing. Some factories also provided medical care, schools, and even churches and sports fields. Few of these services were free, and some were granted in lieu of higher wages. They were apparently considered necessary, and sometimes profitable, arrangements for maintaining the work process and facilitating the close supervision of workers. If workers struck or demonstrated disrespect or disobedience, they could be summarily evicted from company housing. They remained dependent on mill owners and vulnerable to manipulation through paternalism.[20]

Large factories sometimes provided child care facilities, which enabled the mill owners to utilize lower-paid female labor more efficiently. According to various observers, textiles employed a larger proportion of married women than did other industries. In Bahia and Recife, as in the south, these observers found married women continuing to toil in the textile mills up to the last days of pregnancy and recommencing factory work shortly after childbirth. Most mothers could not afford to pay other women to take care of their younger offspring. Unless they could find willing friends or relatives to tend children too young for school or factory, they could not work a full day in the mills. Relatively few children began mill work before the age of ten, and not all the younger ones attended factory or outside schools. Thus nurseries and kindergartens enabled factory owners to extract larger quantities of low-cost female labor.[21]

Industrial wages varied throughout Brazil, from industry to industry, and between the sexes. In the more developed southern states, workers generally received higher salaries than in the north and the economically depressed Northeast. Average worker wages in the large but poorly paying textile industry illustrate this variation (Table 22). Wages in the two major industrial regions of São Paulo and the Federal District far exceeded those in Pernambuco and Bahia, two of Brazil's oldest textile manufacturing centers. Only the handful of textile workers in the rubber-exporting state of Pará, with its high consumer prices, earned salaries comparable to those in southern states. As the 1920 figures for different

Table 22. Salaries of Textile Workers, 1920

States and Federal District	Number of Workers[a]					Daily Average Wage			
		Adults		Minors[b]		Adults		Minors[b]	
	Total	Male	Female	Male	Female	Male	Female	Male	Female
Alagoas	5,287	1,577	2,695	408	607	3$011	2$643	$741	$953
Bahia	7,488	2,359	4,869	104	156	4$084	2$733	1$747	1$836
Ceará	2,195	967	1,137	59	32	2$735	1$090	$976	$756
Espírito Santo	446	85	139	71	151	4$086	2$522	1$762	1$894
Maranhão	2,833	928	1,762	39	104	3$497	2$196	1$633	1$370
Minas Gerais	9,157	2,626	4,256	1,095	1,180	4$134	2$302	1$262	1$150
Pará	53	12	41	—	—	6$417	3$000	—	—
Paraíba	1,433	858	489	46	40	3$331	2$270	1$267	$800
Paraná	232	94	96	15	27	3$513	4$222	2$233	1$926
Pernambuco	6,849	2,759	2,981	458	651	2$623	2$579	1$551	1$471
Piauí	26	26	—	—	—	2$834	—	—	—
Rio de Janeiro	9,832	4,281	3,553	1,314	684	5$759	4$089	2$253	2$052
Rio Grande do Norte	429	332	60	37	—	2$532	1$500	$978	—
Rio Grande do Sul	3,448	1,356	1,636	194	262	7$035	4$062	2$595	2$160
Santa Catarina	1,330	437	793	33	67	6$229	3$327	2$136	2$819
São Paulo	33,010	11,081	15,565	2,348	4,016	5$729	4$684	2$211	2$272
Sergipe	3,597	952	2,260	152	233	3$306	2$176	1$294	1$502
Federal District of Rio de Janeiro	21,140	10,468	8,054	1,387	1,231	6$720	5$165	2$479	2$825
BRAZIL	108,785	41,198	50,386	7,760	9,441	5$329	3$738	1$973	1$994

Source: *Recenseamento do Brazil . . . 1920*, V, 2ª parte, xi.
[a] Includes only enterprises with eight or more workers.
[b] Under fourteen years old.

Table 23.   Workers' Salaries in Rio de Janeiro, 1920

| Type of Industry[a] | Number of Workers | | | Daily Average Wage | | | |
| | | | | Adults | | Minors[b] | |
	Total	Male	Female	Male	Female	Male	Female
Textiles	19,264	11,053	8,211	6$720	5$170	2$480	2$830
Leather and Skins	631	626	5	5$850	3$170	2$170	—
Wood Industries	1,444	1,419	25	7$210	3$670	2$700	2$000
Metal Working	4,977	4,674	303	6$950	3$570	2$330	1$510
Ceramics	2,343	2,217	126	6$410	2$750	2$280	1$000
Chemical Products	3,454	2,392	1,062	5$930	2$830	2$150	1$980
Food	7,306	5,194	2,112	5$850	3$860	2$620	1$880
Apparel	10,639	5,838	4,801	7$580	4$220	2$380	2$050
Furniture	2,749	2,728	21	8$710	4$670	2$270	2$110
Construction Supplies	892	880	12	7$860	3$500	2$280	—
Transportation Equipment	1,944	1,940	4	7$200	8$000	2$060	1$380
Production and Transmission of Physical Forces	589	589	—	7$230	—	1$250	—
Scientific, Literary, and Luxury Industries	285	224	61	6$890	2$930	2$300	1$640
	56,517	39,774	16,743	6$900	4$600	2$380	2$460

Source: *Recenseamento do Brasil* . . . 1920, II, 2ª parte, lxiv, xcv.
[a] Includes only enterprises with eight or more workers.
[b] Under fourteen years old.

industries in Rio de Janeiro indicate, more highly skilled work such as furniture making generally paid better (Table 23). But salary disparities were not only based on the degree of mechanization or skill required in each industry; the sexual composition of the work force was at least as important.

Concentrated in a handful of industries, women labored at some of the most demanding and least desirable factory jobs for even lower wages than the pittance paid men. The textiles, food-processing, and clothing industries, which fabricated goods once produced by women in their own

Table 24.   Analysis of Salaries, Adult Workers in Rio de Janeiro, 1920

| Daily Wage | Number of Workers[a] | | | Percentage of Total Number of Workers | Percentage of Total Number of Male Workers | Percentage of Total Number of Female Workers |
	Total	Male	Female			
Up to 2$900	5,397	2,129	3,268	10.9	6.1	22.2
3$000 to 3$900	3,896	1,101	2,795	7.8	3.1	19.0
4$000 to 5$900	14,916	9,619	5,297	30.0	27.4	36.0
6$000 to 7$900	11,899	9,893	2,006	23.9	28.2	13.7
8$000 and over	13,670	12,339	1,331	27.4	35.2	9.1
TOTAL	49,778	35,081	14,697	100.0	100.0	100.0

Source: *Recenseamento do Brazil* . . . *1920*, II, 2ª parte, xciii.
[a]Includes only enterprises with eight or more workers.

homes, remained their major employers (see Table 20). According to the 1920 census, textiles employed an overwhelming majority of all female factory workers, 70%, as compared to 33.4% of male workers, in factories with eight or more laborers. While women may have clustered by chance in industries with low wage scales, it seems more likely that those industries paid such poor salaries because of the concentration of women; they could be seen as more appropriate for women, therefore justifying lower wages, even for men. Textiles ranked ninth in male industrial salary level, and food processing eleventh. In these, as in all major manufacturing fields, women's wages stayed well below men's, as the 1920 census shows (see Tables 22 and 23). While one-third of Brazil's male factory workers earned 4$000 to 8$000 daily, only one-tenth of the women were within this range.[22] In Rio de Janeiro, where approximately one-fourth of all Brazil's industrial workers found employment, adult women received an average wage of 4$600 while men earned 6$900, over fifty percent more (see Table 24). As in other countries, certain jobs were frequently known as men's jobs or women's jobs, the latter requiring less skill and providing lower pay and fewer chances for advancement. But even when women did the same work as men, they were paid less. According to Rio's textile workers' union, the Sindicato dos Trabalhadores em Fábricas de Tecidos do Rio de Janeiro, in 1913 men and women worked under equal conditions in the factories, but in the woolen textiles division men generally earned 3$000 daily and women

2$000. Men producing linen and cotton cloth received an average of 4$000 daily while women earned only 2$500. In burlap, men averaged 3$000 daily and women only 2$000.[23] Women's industrial wages would continue to lag far behind men's.

While Brazil's factories grew in size and numbers in the early twentieth century, as we saw in the case of textiles, relatively few workers in "manufacturing" found employment in them. Many more women and men apparently labored in smaller, less mechanized shops also producing finished goods, or in repair shops. Even so, employment opportunities in the entire sector failed to match national population growth. Censuses show scarcely twice as many people engaged in manufacturing, including crafts and handwork such as sewing, in 1920 as in 1872, yet Brazil's total population had tripled and that of many cities had risen even more rapidly between 1872 and 1920 (Tables 1 and 25).

We can question how industrialized even Brazil's major cities were in the early twentieth century. In Rio de Janeiro the total number of workers in "manufacturing" comprised barely thirty percent of the city's employed inhabitants in 1920, and factory workers apparently only some ten percent.[24] The city's 56,517 factory workers in establishments with at least eight workers were far outnumbered by domestic servants (71,752) and people in commerce (88,306). The combined ranks of government employees (25,563), police, and members of the armed forces stationed in Rio (24,835) almost equaled that of factory workers. Even the number of transportation workers (44,107) trailed not too far behind. Rio had half as many schoolteachers and other members of the rapidly growing liberal professions (26,041) as factory workers (Table 26). Industrial labor represented only a small proportion of Brazil's urban workers or "working class."

Outside of the nation's capital, there were even fewer industrial workers relative to the total number of people in manufacturing. In 1920, according to the national census, Brazilian factories with eight or more workers employed 231,961 men, women, and children scattered among a variety of industries (Table 20). But the same census recorded a total of 1,118,257 people employed in those manufactures—five times the number accounted for by the factories (Table 25). The discrepancy between the number of factory workers and the size of the entire work force is far greater in the largest manufacturing sector, clothing. The 1920 census recorded 21,080 laborers in clothing factories with over eight employees, as compared to 475,293 workers, or almost twenty-three times as many, in the entire sector. Were family enterprises or shops employing less than eight workers still the prevalent mode of "manufacturing" in Brazil, as these figures imply? No doubt handicraft production and repair work predominated among these enterprises.

Among female clothing workers, the discrepancy between indus-trial labor and total employment was even greater: 9,116 female factory workers as compared to 331,115 female workers, or over thirty-six times as many, in the entire clothing sector.[25] Were most of these women en-gaged in piecework for industrial purposes or were they seamstresses work-ing in small shops or for individual clients? The 1872 census recorded 506,450 seamstresses in Brazil (Table 2). Their numbers must have de-clined by 1920, when seamstresses no longer comprised a census cate-gory. As a feminist newspaper in Rio de Janeiro had accurately predicted in 1875, the introduction of sewing and weaving machines, while bene-ficial "to humanity," would cost "thousands of women" their jobs.[26] A drop in the number of seamstresses may also help explain the apparent absolute decline in the number of women in the total manufacturing sector between 1872 and 1920 (Table 25). Relatively few appear to have been absorbed into factory work, certainly as compared to men. Is this what occurs with the development of industrial capitalism and the de-cline of the family as a productive unit, as some writers on nonwestern nations maintain?[27]

According to Brazilian censuses, the percentage of women in the labor force declined markedly between 1872 and 1920 (see Table 25). In 1872 54.8% of the female population was employed, while in 1920 only 9.7% had occupations. The drop in male employment was far less se-vere, from 61.3% of the total male population in 1872 to 52.6% in 1920. It is very difficult, however, to believe that during the same half century in which Brazil's population more than tripled, the absolute number of women working could decline by over a million. Nor is it easy to under-stand how the proportion of women in agriculture and related activities, which according to the censuses declined from 29.4% of agricultural workers in 1872 to 9.4% in 1920, could then rise to the former figure by 1940 and remain at that level in subsequent decades.[28] Yet the Brazilian censuses show a marked decrease between 1872 and 1920 in both agri-cultural and nonagricultural employment for women, notably in the poorest paying fields.

How can we account for this apparent decline? One possibility in-volves a massive increase in the prosperity of the bulk of the population, which would permit large numbers of lower-class women to stay home and not contribute to family income. But we have seen little evidence of this. A more likely possibility is that women assumed less steady, or visi-ble, jobs. The 1920 census undercounted women working part time, irregularly, or as unpaid workers in family enterprises. Better paid work-ers in more prestigious fields were more accurately tallied. In the nine-teenth century, members of the elite expected the daughters as well as

Table 25. Occupations in Brazil, 1872–1920

Occupations	1872			1920		
	Men	Women	Male Component as a Percentage of Total	Men	Women	Male Component as a Percentage of Total
Agriculture (including pastoral, mining, fishing)	2,318,718	964,325	70.6	5,843,665	607,865	90.6
Manufacturing (including artisans and seamstresses)	180,948	653,970	21.7	758,757	429,600	63.8
Capitalists	23,140	9,723	70.4	27,384	13,406	67.1
Commerce	93,577	8,556	91.6	474,707	22,841	95.4
Transportation	—	—	—	249,879	3,708	98.5
Armed Forces and Police	27,716	—	100.0	88,363	—	100.0
Religious	2,332	286	89.1	6,059	2,944	67.3
Liberal Professions (including midwives and school teachers)	11,674	3,365	77.6	107,634	51,474	67.6

Table 25. *(continued)*

Occupations	1872			1920		
	Men	Women	Male Component as a Percentage of Total	Men	Women	Male Component as a Percentage of Total
Government Employment and Administration	10,710	—	100.0	94,487	3,225	96.7
Private Administration	—	—	—	37,303	2,864	92.9
Domestic Service	196,784	848,831	18.8	70,335	293,544	19.3
Day Laborers	274,217	90,162	75.3	—	—	—
Poorly Defined or Unknown	—	—	—	369,911	46,657	88.8
Without Profession[a]	1,984,053	2,171,663	47.7	7,314,334	13,713,659	34.8

Adapted from: *Recenseamento da População . . . 1872* (Quadros Gerais), XIX, 5; *Recenseamento do Brazil . . . 1920*, IV, 5ª parte, Tomo I, xii–xiii.
[a]Includes those who did not declare a profession and those under age.

the sons of the poor to work. But during the twentieth century, the view spread that employment outside the home was improper for women. Brazilian census-takers then classified people as working or inactive depending on what they considered their principal activity to be, and it was assumed that the principal activity of women was to run the home and socialize the children.

When we examine the situation in Rio de Janeiro, we do not see nearly as severe a decline in female employment figures. Perhaps it was easier for census takers to assess work roles in the nation's capital than in the hinterland. The percentage of employed women in Rio increased slightly, from 53.3% in 1872 to 59.3% in 1906, and then declined sharply to 22.1% in 1920. Yet that 1920 figure is still more than double the national average of 9.7%. Male employment in Rio declined far less— at approximately the same rate as in the nation as a whole—from 76.1% in 1872, to 70.3% in 1906, to 66% in 1920.[29] In Rio's "manufacturing" sector, we find no great drop in female employment between 1872 and 1920. On the contrary, at the same time as national census figures indicate an absolute decline in the number of female workers in this sector, a three-and-a half-fold increase occurred in Rio. Their ranks expanded almost as quickly as did the total population of this major industrial center and almost as rapidly as male employment in manufacturing, both of which quadrupled during this period (Tables 1, 25, and 26).

Even a high rate of female employment may denote large-scale relegation to low paying, unskilled, and dead-end positions, whose major social function is to supplement low family income or to support families without male heads of household. This certainly is the case with domestic service in Brazil.

While national census figures demonstrate a decline of almost two-thirds in the number of men and women engaged in domestic service— the major nonagricultural female employment category—between 1872 and 1920, data for Rio de Janeiro indicate an increase in female servants (see Tables 25 and 26). The absolute number of women in domestic service in Rio more than doubled from 1872 to 1906. While the 1920 figure represents a decline from 1906, it still exceeded that of 1872 by some thirty percent. Census officials claimed that the 1906 figures on domestic servants were far too high, since many women doing housework without remuneration were inadvertently included in this category. Yet the 1906 figure for men also exceeded that for either 1872 or 1920; presumably few Brazilian househusbands existed in 1906 who could be inadvertently included in the domestic service category. Moreover, the proportion of male to female domestic servants remained virtually unchanged in Rio from 1906 to 1920, as in the nation as a whole. Despite the difficulty of determining the exact number of domestic servants, it is clear that this sector, whose female component averaged eighty percent, was still the major source of jobs for women in urban areas, although declining somewhat in importance (Table 4).

Families could not survive without female and child labor. In 1913 Rio's major textile union calculated that a single male worker's average monthly expenses totaled 110$000, while a family with two children generally required 210$000. Even if he managed to obtain work every day but Sundays and holidays, an adult male factory worker earning 4$000 a day, the highest average wage among workers in different textile divisions, could only earn 90$000 a month. The adult male daily wage was not sufficient to purchase a kilo each of rice, beans, lard, sugar, and coffee.[30]

Brazilian labor leaders and representatives demonstrated an ambivalent attitude toward female remunerative labor not dissimilar to that seen in other industrializing countries. Male workers or their spokesmen lamented the need for the income female family members provided. Some even echoed the middle-class ideal of a male breadwinner and a female housekeeper, an arrangement which often did not correspond to traditional lower-class patterns. As one moderate socialist declared, "to remove a woman from the home where she comforts her children and watches over the household represents a frightful cruelty."[31] However, some female socialists complained not only about "companions," who, like bourgeois males, "consider women luxury objects," but also about those who "thought that women exist only to bear children and carry out household duties"; women workers were "enslaved and humiliated by men and by industry."[32]

Although many union leaders thought that women should be restricted to the domestic sphere, economic necessity, they admitted, forced women into the job market where they were miserably exploited. Male labor representatives at the anarcho-syndicalist-influenced 1906 labor congress blamed women for their own victimization, citing their lack of "cohesion and solidarity" as the "main cause of their exploitation," which in turn made them "terrible competitors with men."[33] At a 1912 congress of reformist labor unions, delegates concluded that ideally, "in the interests of humanity, it would be best if women did not pursue tasks other than those of the home and a few limited occupations appropriate to the female sex." But industrialization reduced men's salaries to the point where they could not support their families, and "forced women to leave home, compelling them to perform arduous labor for a ridiculously low salary that, none the less, is indispensable for meeting urgent family needs."[34] To end the exploitation of female and child labor, these

Table 26. Occupations in Rio de Janeiro, 1872–1920

Occupations	1872			1906			1920		
	Men	Women	Male Component as a percentage of Total	Men	Women	Male Component as a percentage of Total	Men	Women	Male Component as a percentage of Total
Agriculture (including pastoral, mining and fishing)	18,445	7,831	70.2	22,753	2,822	89.0	29,105	1,559	94.9
Manufacturing (including artisans and seamstresses)	28,108	11,825	70.4	93,503	22,276	80.8	112,962	41,435	73.2
Capitalists	984	1,023	49.0	2,183	1,339	62.0	3,593	2,317	60.8
Commerce	23,045	436	98.1	61,732	1,043	98.3	85,212	3,094	96.5
Transportation	—	—	—	22,702	105	99.5	43,053	1,054	97.6
Armed Forces and Police	5,474	—	100.0	16,484	—	100.0	24,835	—	100.0
Religious	214	50	81.1	346	280	55.3	616	562	52.3
Liberal Professions (including midwives and school teachers)	2,016	367	84.6	9,005	2,419	78.8	16,953	9,088	65.1

Table 26. (continued)

Occupations	1872 Men	1872 Women	1872 Male Component as a percentage of Total	1906 Men	1906 Women	1906 Male Component as a percentage of Total	1920 Men	1920 Women	1920 Male Component as a percentage of Total
Government Employment and Administration	2,351	—	100.0	12,350	87	99.3	24,466	1,097	95.7
Private Administration	—	—	—	—	—	—	—	—	—
Domestic Service	16,549	38,462	30.0	23,174	94,730	19.7	9,249	543	94.5
Day Laborers	23,696	1,990	92.3	29,514	419	98.6	12,857	58,895	17.9
Poorly Defined or Unknown	—	—	—	32,069	40,018	44.5	31,801	3,858	98.9
Without Profession[a]	37,884	54,222	41.1	137,638	182,452	43.0	203,605	436,064	31.8

Adapted from: *Recenseamento da População . . . 1872*, XXI (Munícipio Neutro), 61; *Recenseamento do Rio de Janeiro . . . 1906*, I, 104; *Recenseamento do Brazil . . . 1920*, IV, 5ª parte, Tomo I, 24–27.
[a]Includes those who did not declare a profession and those under age.

delegates demanded protective legislation, especially to stipulate minimum wages and maximum hours, but not equal pay for equal work. As we shall see in the next chapter, some unions did call for equal wages for women, but others proved ambivalent or even hostile in matters concerning female workers. Factory owners knew that they could pay women far less than men, particularly women supporting families without male heads of household who had no choice but to accept those pitiful wages.

Although the percentage of female-headed households among the urban lower classes cannot be accurately determined, available evidence indicates the existence of a number of families supported by women working as seamstresses or doing piecework. These households apparently greatly outnumbered those supported by female shop clerks or mill hands. Traditional female activities like sewing permitted women to work at home, put in longer hours, and no doubt also utilize the labor of their children. Factory employment required twelve or more hours a day away from home and apparently paid even less. A woman alone found it extremely difficult to support or care for her family by doing factory work. Female factory wages generally served to supplement male earnings.

Not untypical among steadily employed lower-income groups may be the high percentage of female-headed households found in the government-subsidized *vilas operárias* of the Companhia de Saneamento do Rio de Janeiro. In response to charges of rent gouging in the mid-1890s, the company published lists of tenants in their five projects in Rio. Not only laborers but also clerks, students, and low-level public functionaries and military officers lived in the biggest and best *vila*, the centrally located Vila Rui Barbosa. Of the eighty-one families there, twenty, or 24.7%, were headed by women: thirteen women doing piece work, five seamstresses, and two schoolteachers. In contrast, of the *vila's* 174 single inhabitants, only one, a schoolteacher, was female. Apparently respectable women rarely lived alone, unlike men. Perhaps too, child labor was often needed to supplement female earnings and pay rent. Of the thirty-two families living in Vila Sampaio, near the main railroad station, twelve, or 37.5%, were headed by women: eleven pieceworkers and one schoolteacher. Only in Vila Arthur Sauer in Jardim Botánico near the Carioca textile factory did any female factory workers support families. Two factory workers, a laundress, a nurse, and two pieceworkers paid the rent for 12.8% of the *vila's* forty-seven households. In addition, two widows, or 12.5% of the *vila's* sixteen single inhabitants, lived alone doing piecework. No women factory workers headed households in Vila Maxwell or Vila Senador Soares, both located in Rio's Vila Isabel district near the Confiança Industrial textile factory. Of Vila Maxwell's fifteen families, two were headed by women doing piece work and one by a seamstress. In Vila Senador Soares, 20.8%, or eleven out of fifty-three households, had female heads: eleven pieceworkers, two school-teachers, and one woman pensioner. No male head of household ever listed piecework as his employment. Opportunities for lower-class men, though very limited, generally exceeded those for women.[35]

Life for urban workers, never easy, could suddenly worsen. When illness, accidents, fines, or layoffs reduced wages, individual and family suffering increased. In some fields, like the construction trades, bad weather and shortages of materials further decreased the numbers of work days per month. Sometimes the deficit between income and necessary expenditures was met by reducing food consumption. As the representatives of Rio's textile workers union sadly recounted, "in order to pay their expenses, workers are obliged to deprive themselves of absolute necessities, . . . working more than their strength allows and eating less than their bodies require to function normally."[36] Female family members suffered most. Housewives deprived themselves of food to feed children and husbands. Female factory and shop workers living in Rio's suburbs who rose early to commute long distances by trolley or train to their work-places breakfasted on "a cup of coffee, a crust of bread." For women with special expenses, like ladies' hat makers, "obliged" by their employers to dress "elegantly, even sumptuously, . . . nothing remained" of their wages to purchase proper food.[37]

Few substantial changes had occurred in urban lower-class diets since the late empire, although mass immigration, especially the influx of Italians into São Paulo, introduced new staple foods such as pasta. Standard food combinations such as beans and dried beef, beans and manioc flour, rice and beans, or dried beef and manioc flour served as the basic diet in different urban areas, with dried beef less prevalent south of Rio de Janeiro. Except in Rio Grande do Sul and parts of Minas Gerais, workers generally found fresh meat expensive and often spoiled. Bread might be adulterated or sold below legal weight as well as at a high price. The daily fare of the working poor was limited and monotonous, deficient in animal proteins, fresh produce, and essential vitamins. They never experienced anything resembling the quantity, quality, or variety of food available to the upper classes. A government statistician calculated that in 1914 an "average" family of seven (with two servants) in Rio de Janeiro spent 279$045 a month on food alone—triple the monthly earnings of a male textile worker. Such a family consumed milk, tea, vegetables, eggs, butter, and fresh fish, in addition to salt cod, fresh meat, potatoes, and corn, and the ever-popular rice, beans, and manioc flour.[38] On special occasions the elite indulged in sumptuous feasts, comparable to those served their peers elsewhere in the Western world. Politicians honored one another and presented their platforms at elaborate banquets with ten courses and imported wines, accompanied by orchestral music as well as pompous oratory.[39]

Poor nutrition, like unsanitary housing and insufficient sleep, left the urban poor more susceptible to the ravages of disease, and medical care was difficult if not impossible for them to obtain when illness struck. Although charity hospitals such as Rio's Santa Casa da Misericórdia received indigent patients, shortages of medicine, space, and personnel limited the hospitals' effectiveness. Religious healers and practitioners of folk medicine (*feiticeiros* and *curandeiros*), mixing Indian, African, and Portuguese beliefs, provided alternative but illegal health care. While their understanding of herbal medicine made them popular with the lower classes, they could not cure the infectious and parasitic diseases which were responsible for most deaths in Rio. Tuberculosis, typhoid, paratyphoid, cholera, and diphtheria flourished in Rio. Despite vaccination campaigns, epidemics of smallpox still carried off numerous victims. Malaria also remained a public health problem in the early twentieth century. Even ordinarily nonlethal illnesses such as measles, whooping cough, gastroenteritis, and parasitic infections became killers, due largely to inadequate diet. In turn, the effects of bacterial infections such as cholera, typhoid, paratyphoid, diphtheria, and whooping cough, of viral and protozoal diseases like smallpox, mumps, and malaria, and of parasitic infections further exacerbated nutritional deficiencies in the population. Overworked and poorly fed, the urban poor were caught in a vicious circle of poor nutrition and infection.[40]

Babies suffered badly from disease, especially gastrointestinal afflictions. One doctor asserted that newborns accounted for sixty-five percent of the deaths from gastrointestinal diseases in Rio de Janeiro. Rather than receiving milk, many of the babies he examined were fed "water with wine, soup made of pasta, beans, bananas, and even dried beef."[41]

Children and adolescents seemed most vulnerable to tuberculosis, the deadliest killer in Rio de Janeiro. A 1907 examination of twelve-to-fourteen-year-old workers at the National Press found three-quarters of them to be suffering from this classic disease of sweatshops and tenements. In the mint, one or two workers died of tuberculosis each month. Hygienic conditions in such government installations generally surpassed those in private establishments. Even adult males healthy enough to be inducted into a not overly particular army—it accepted 78.6% of the recruits reporting for duty in 1922–1923—suffered extensively from tuberculosis. And half the nation's recruits rejected because of that disease came from the Federal District of Rio de Janeiro. In 1917 the leading cause of death in the army's Central Hospital in Rio was pulmonary tuberculosis. Government statistics show that between 1868 and 1908 more Brazilians died from tuberculosis than from typhoid, influenza, diphtheria, whooping cough, scarlet fever, mumps, bubonic plague, yellow fever, and smallpox combined. Between 1868 and 1914 tuberculosis claimed 111,000 known victims in the city of Rio de Janeiro alone. Public health officials admitted that tuberculosis mortality rates had not declined by 1920, as had yellow fever, smallpox, and plague mortality rates following the early twentieth-century sanitary campaigns. The capital's official mortality rates from this killer, which thrived amid poverty, surpassed those of leading European and American cities.[42]

Despite disease, overwork, and poor nutrition, urban workers did not live lives of relentless suffering. Some of their pleasures were simple and free, such as visiting relatives and friends. Birthdays and funerals provided occasions for large gatherings. Men might spend Sunday afternoons playing cards or dominoes. On the avenues of São Paulo's worker districts, young men and women promenaded and flirted in the evening. Children liked to play games like tag, blindman's bluff, and hide-and-seek. Boys also flew kites or spun tops, and girls jumped rope and sang songs. Other activities cost money. Better-paid workers might meet at neighborhood bars and drink soda, beer, or wine, and even purchase ice cream. Literate workers able to buy newspapers or secure access to them read not only political commentary but also stories and serialized novels. Like the general press, many labor newspapers printed tales of adventure, romance, and comedy, such as "Free Love," "The Nude Princess," "The Russian Underground," and "The Language of Animals."[43]

For some of the laboring poor, silent movies provided a new form of entertainment in major cities. Although Rio's workers were unlikely to purchase glossy illustrated magazines chronicling the activities of foreign movie stars like Mary Pickford, together with those of the *carioca* social elite, or to frequent first-class cinemas on the Avenida Central, they could attend lower-priced suburban theaters. The 1917–1918 season in Rio featured American cowboy movies. Admission to São Paulo's suburban movie "palaces" cost no more than a trolley ride. More expensive shows, lasting five hours, included a band playing marches, polkas, and *maxixes*, short subjects, and several feature-length foreign films. Entire families attended, bringing baskets full of sandwiches, sweets, and beverages. Even some church groups hastened to take advantage of the motion pictures' popularity and showed religious films.[44]

Soccer, introduced to Brazil by the British in the late nineteenth century, provided exercise as well as entertainment. Although limited at first to the foreign communities, the sport was taken up by the higher reaches of society, and then gained popularity among most social groups, spreading from the private clubs of the elite to the factory lots and city streets. In the early twentieth century, São Paulo's working-class districts, like the city's wealthier inhabitants, supported soccer clubs. But the workers played a rougher game. Players generally were chosen for strength rather than skill, and some even went armed to the matches. Factories and immigrants associations organized their own teams. Soccer required little equipment and could be enjoyed year-round. Soon barefoot boys were playing soccer with bundles of dirty rags in the streets of cities throughout much of southern Brazil.[45]

Although religious festivities had lost some of their nineteenth-century functions and importance in Rio de Janeiro and São Paulo—to a greater extent than in smaller cities to the north or in the interior—they still afforded free public displays. Church processions drew large crowds, which particularly admired the small girls dressed as angels, with their large wings and elaborate robes. Catholic pagentry had not yet been displaced by sports and movies. Fancy funerals also attracted numerous spectators. As the daughter of one *paulista* worker later recalled, children's funerals and "those of people who met with violent deaths, automobile accidents, disasters, or murders were the most prized."[46] In areas such as the Italian immigrant districts of Belènzinho and Bexiga in São Paulo, saints' days' festivities involved general and boisterous celebrations. Residents decorated the streets, held processions, and set off fireworks. Rio's Portuguese predominated among the enthusiastic pilgrims winding their way up the steep hill to the suburban church of Nossa Senhora da Penha and enjoying themselves at stands selling food and drink, although these European immigrants were increasingly joined by Rio's black and mulatto inhabitants with their own forms of music, dance, and food. But many poor Brazilians remained mere spectators on traditional holidays like Saint John's Day, watching others light bonfires and release hot-air balloons which slowly ascended to the skies.[47]

Carnaval also provided a temporary escape for the poor. In the early twentieth century the *entrudo* gave way to Carnaval. The old Portuguese institution of *entrudo*, in which all classes participated, had featured pelting everyone, friends, family, or passersby, with water-filled wax balls shaped like lemons or oranges. Syringes and even buckets of water ensured the enthusiastic participants that everyone they met would become thoroughly drenched. A German schoolteacher with a toothache, assaulted with multiple projectiles and streams of water on her way to the dentist's office, complained how "elegant ladies, dirty mulatto children, shop clerks, vagrants and even women on their balconies, seemingly transformed into devils," all enjoyed the sport.[48] During the second half of the nineteenth century, officials made repeated but unsuccessful efforts to prohibit the *entrudo* as uncivilized bahavior. As part of his efforts to modernize and Europeanize the capital at the beginning of the twentieth century, Rio's Prefect Pereira Passos also sought to outlaw the *entrudo*.[49]

Although the *entrudo* only slowly disappeared, new carnaval activities steadily gained greater popularity. Carnaval societies, established in the second half of the nineteenth century, held costume balls and built allegorical or satirical floats to parade through the streets. With the opening of Rio's Avenida Central in 1905, parades assumed a greater importance. Leading members of society cruised the boulevard in decorated automobiles or held confetti battles, considered refined and elegant forms of celebration. In poor neighborhoods, people held their own rougher versions of Carnaval. Groups of friends and neighbors formed associations called *cordões, ranchos, grupos,* or *blocos*, whose members paraded in costumes. Workers not only observed the frolicking of wealthier Brazilians but also participated in Carnaval societies like the "Flower of Gávea" (the Rio suburb noted for its textile factories), "Diamond of Gávea," "Golden Rainfall," and "Silver Bouquet."[50]

In Rio's old, largely black neighborhoods like Saúde and Gamboa, near the port, where the men worked as stevedores, and in the nearby congested Cidade Nova district directly north of the Praça da República and the terminus of the Central do Brasil railroad, Afro-Brazilian forms of music and dance prevailed. At Carnaval time, local groups paraded and danced through the streets, following in the tradition of the religious processions and celebrations associated with Nossa Senhora do Rosário, the patroness of slaves, and her black *irmandades*. Rio's Bahian minority, a cohesive group with its own Sudanese traditions, both religious and secular, gave these Carnaval activities clearer organization by the beginning of the twentieth century. At the same time, their Bahian music took on new *carioca* forms. Some of Rio's most durable lower-class Carnaval societies comprised stable working-class elements and were affiliated with unions or workplaces, such as the "Playground of Flowers," a *rancho* organized by the predominately black stevedores' union, the Sociedade de Resistência dos Trabalhadores em Trapiche e Café. A few of the more highly structured groups even secured police permission to parade. But Pereira Passos attempted to prohibit the boisterous *cordões* as well as the wild pranks of the *entrudo* as violent and barbaric customs. Masses of people dancing and shouting in the streets still met with elite disdain, and violent incidents provided excuses for police repression of both the celebrants and their Carnaval organizations.[51]

Rio's poor blacks and mulattoes saw the police as their deadly enemies, always maltreating and arresting them. A popular 1905 Carnaval song suggests the pervasiveness and persistence of lower-class practices which the upper classes sought to repress through police action:

> I'm going to drink
> I'm going to get drunk
> I'm going to make a racket
> So the police will nab me.
> The police don't want
> me to samba here
> or samba there
> or samba anywhere. [52]

In the various night spots of Cidade Nova and at the frequent house parties given by Bahian women such as "Aunt Ciata" (Hilária Batista de Almeida), different strands of the capital's black and mulatto musical traditions met and mingled. Black forms of social life, religious life, work, and consciousness, as well as recreation, grew stronger under the roofs of such leading community figures. The term *samba*, once applied to a gathering or party, now meant a new type of music, which spread beyond Cidade Nova and gained wide acceptance. In 1917 "Over the Telephone," a modern samba, became the first great Carnaval hit song. A nascent record industry and a developing theatrical world offered new possibilities of remuneration and prestige for the composers of successful songs, and the authorship of this *carioca* samba, registered by Ernesto dos Santos (Donga), remained in dispute. There was no question, however, that the once scorned samba had achieved acceptance among better-off sectors of society. [53]

By the 1920s the samba dominated Rio's Carnaval. At the same time, some of the neighborhood-based Carnaval societies, seeking to lend an air of legitimacy and seriousness to their activities, adopted the new title "samba school." But not until the Getúlo Vargas regime in the 1930s would concerted efforts be made to control and make use of these groups, as demonstrated by Alison Raphael. [54] The samba schools' need for acceptance and recognition, and for government services in their neighborhoods, meshed with the government's desire to integrate them into its web of institutions and ideologies. The schools would suffer an increasing loss of autonomy as they moved from neighborhood entertainment to competitive events in downtown Rio, subject to upper-class judgments and regulations. While they achieved recognition as part of popular Brazilian culture, the samba schools would also serve as mechanisms for social control, to co-opt black social movements for equality.

Music and dance remained general sources of pleasure for the laboring poor, not only at Carnaval time. In Rio's *estalagens*, tenement dwellers played guitars and accordians, sang, and danced lively *fandangos*. Numerous musical and recreational societies and clubs in Rio de Janeiro and São Paulo sponsored formal dances, as did some labor unions. No festive occasion seemed complete without the "inevitable ball," as one anarchist opponent of such frivolity termed it.[55] Rio's paternalistic textile factories maintained bands which played at church festivities. On special occasions, such as a mill's tenth anniversary, owners organized celebrations with music and comedies, as well as speeches and recitations by the owners' representatives. Other factories occasionally threw children's Christmas parties or even sponsored beauty contests for their employees. Such factories dominated workers' leisure time as well as their working hours.[56]

Amateur theatricals provided both social participation and entertainment for the laboring poor. In Rio's suburbs, drama clubs gave frequent performances of plays like "The Miracles of Santo Antonio," "Take Care with Women," and "Modern Children." Even the Roman Catholic Church sponsored theatricals; parish players put on sacred pieces and dramatized the lives of the saints. As we shall see in the next chapter, anarchist troups also presented their views through dramas such as "Workers on Strike," "May Day," "Disease," "The Dinner of the Poor," and "The Tenants' Strike," as well as organizing moral and healthy alternatives to the dances so popular among the laboring poor.[57]

Some forms of diversion and escape proved far more injurious to purse and health. Not only anarchists inveighed against drinking, gambling, and smoking. Innumerable denunciations of the "horrible vice" of alcohol attest to its popularity among the lower classes. Many urban workers chose to spend their free time in "taverns," the "ferocious and implacable enemy of workers," rather than following educational pursuits.[58] The use of alcohol gained wide acceptance among the poor, who believed it gave them extra strength to complete a day's labor. In numerous kiosks on city street corners in Rio de Janeiro, laborers could buy a cup of coffee, a strong cigarette, or a shot of *cachaça*, a rough sugarcane distillate. Alcoholism, the "fruit of excessive, brutalizing, exhaustive labor," remained deeply rooted in the working classes and "an obstacle to labor organization," according to delegates to the 1906 labor congress.[59] Cigarettes proved at least as popular as alcohol. Most men in Brazil smoked, regardless of social status, and young boys were frequently seen with cigarettes in their mouths. Workers also gambled. Even more popular than official lotteries was the "forbidden" *jogo do bicho*, invented, according to an English observer, "by Baron Drummond, the original proprietor of the local Zoo. To increase the revenue of this menagerie, he daily selected 25 animals, and apportioned 4 tickets to each, the lucky holder of the number corresponding to the *bicho* shown at the entrance getting 25$. Later, the prizes went to the numbers corresponding to the final of the lottery winner."[60] Both men and women played, and would interpret dreams to help them decide which animals to bet on. Despite complaints, warnings, occasional arrests, and the posting of police at buildings where gambling occurred, the *jogo do bicho* was never stamped out. In the early twentieth-century, lottery betting was still more of a working-class sport than soccer. Most poor workers felt that their only hope of marked material improvement in their lives lay in the lottery, rather than in organized protest or even individual efforts.[61]

Some pervasive lower-class activities and beliefs met with official hostility. Not only the *jogo do bicho* was subject to intermittant police crack downs, but also *candomblé, macumba,* and other Afro-Brazilian cults prevalent in such northeastern cities as Salvador and Recife as well as in Rio de Janeiro. Since the earliest days of slavery in Brazil not only had religious Africans used Roman Catholicism as a mask enabling them to maintain their own cults, but slaves also participated in and absorbed aspects of Catholic ritual and religion. While traditional *candomblé* kept the Catholic and black religions largely separated, the new syncretic cults like *macumba,* which appeared in Rio de Janeiro in the early twentieth century, contained mystic elements of diverse African and non-African origins. These cults provided solace and protection against life's hazards as well as opportunities for personal and collective self-expression, needs not met by the Roman Catholic Church. In 1920, when Rio de Janeiro had a population of 1,157,873, the overwhelming majority of whom were nominal Roman Catholics, the census recorded only 1,178 people as following a religious vocation. Of these, 562 were women, presumably nuns with little contact with the general public. Almost half the male clergy were foreign-born (291 out of 616).[62]

For years, foreign habits and values had been spreading among different social sectors. Some immigrant workers even brought to Brazil such recreational patterns as family picnics or excursions to the zoo on Sundays. But older Afro-Brazilian influences were not completely washed away by the flood of immigrants in the late nineteenth and early twentieth centuries, even in the south. As one experienced foreign observer noted, in Rio "all classes wear the clenched fist as a mascot."[63]

Just as the new republican government had sought to suppress the art of *capoeiragem* as well as individual *capoeiras* in the early 1890s, so did police often attempt to prohibit the celebration of Aftro-Catholic religious rites, as part of a broader move against customs of African origin. In Salvador and Rio, police raided the places where "barbarian and pagan" ceremonies were held, destroying property and injuring participants. Even more than "barbaric" Carnaval celebrations, those religious rites did not fit the national image which a Europeanized elite sought to project. In the racist world of the early twentieth century, the Brazilian government systematically denied its black heritage, even maintaining a carefully selected light-skinned diplomatic corps. The lower classes, whose ranks included the vast majority of dark-skinned Brazilians, endured more than political and economic domination and manipulation.[64]

Pessimism about the innate capacities of Afro-Brazilians prevailed in elite circles. When obliged to confront the concepts of scientific racism current in Europe, they advanced the doctrine of "whitening," based on the assumption of white superiority. In the introductory volume to the official 1920 census, Francisco José de Oliveira Vianna, who became one of the most widely read interpretors of Brazilian reality in the period prior to World War II, sought to offer empirical proof of Brazil's ascent toward whiteness, even though the 1920 census, like the 1900 census, did not include any breakdown by race. Brazil's population, he maintained, benefitted from a process which pointed toward the ultimate disappearance of the Negro as a distinct genetic component of Brazilian society.[65]

Rio de Janeiro's white population did grow more rapidly than nonwhites during the late nineteenth and early twentieth centuries, as demonstrated by Sam C. Adamo.[66] Whites, more than the poorer blacks, benefitted from the improvements in public health, sanitation, and disease control which lowered mortality levels in Rio in the early twentieth century. Socio-economic inequalities led to higher-than-average death rates for the capital's blacks and mulattoes. While infant mortality declined in the twentieth century, nonwhite infants continued to die in disproportionate numbers. Blacks and mulattoes remained less likely to enter into legal marriages, come from unbroken homes, or obtain education, contributing to their higher levels of mortality.

According to Carlos Alfredo Hasenbalg, Brazilian blacks experienced so little social mobility following the final abolition of slavery in 1888 that racial inequalities have been perpetuated up to the present day. Concentrated in the least developed sections of the nation at the time of abolition, they enjoyed fewer economic and educational opportunities than the whites concentrated in southeastern Brazil. European immigration to that region only reinforced those differences. A cycle of cumulative disadvantages limited social mobility for nonwhites, perpetuating severe racial inequalities. The ideal of "whitening," like the later myth of "racial democracy," limited both racial solidarity and potential social conflict. The range of skin color in Brazil fostered a fragmentation of racial identity among nonwhites, and transformed a potential for collective ac-

tion into hopes for individual social ascension. Rather than emphasizing the heritage of slavery, Hasenbalg points to racism and discrimination
as principal causes of the subordinate social and economic position of
blacks and mulattoes in Brazil.[67]

Even within the urban lower classes, racial discrimination existed.
Immigrant workers in São Paulo very rarely mixed socially or worked
with former slaves living in the same districts. Only blacks attended festive gatherings commemorating the "golden law" of 13 May 1888, which
abolished slavery in Brazil. Italian workers thought the sambas danced
on those occasions lascivious and the percussion instruments exotic.[68]
Even among Brazilians who worked together questions of skin color sometimes led to unpleasantness, such as that suffered by a young woman
worker denied entrance to a dance at a workers' club, the club das Ta-
rrachas, in Rio's Vila Isabel district, because she "was not light enough
to mingle with the others present."[69]

In his novels of early twentieth-century Rio de Janeiro, Lima Barreto depicts and protests discrimination against dark-skinned Brazilians
and the sexual exploitation of nonwhite women. The young mulatto narrator of *The Life and Death of M. J. Gonzaga de Sá* ponders the Brazilian disparagement of blacks and mulattoes and the prejudices they
encounter, among other faults and foibles of his society. The success-
oriented mulatto protagonist of the *Memoirs of the Clerk Isaías Caminha* not only descends to the corrupt moral level of the leaders of the
world of journalism, but also marries a white woman; thus his children
will be lighter and enjoy greater opportunities. The heroine of *Clara dos
Anjos* is an overprotected daydreamer with very sentimental and unreal-
istic ideas of love, a striking contrast to the stereotypical mulatta tempt-
ress or sexually promiscuous mixed-blood woman. In this tale of her
seduction and abandonment by a white ne'er-do-well of more elevated
social position, the narrator maintains that all girls of color and humble
origin are automatically judged to be immoral and inferior. As the naïve
Clara finally realizes, "she was not just a girl like all the others, but,
according to society's generally accepted beliefs, something much less."[70]
Although race and class were inextricably bound together in Brazil, Lima
Barreto considered race the critical factor.

The activities, attitudes, and aspirations of working poor varied from
one urban area and social or occupational group to another. Racial and
ethnic differences did not disappear. Along with poverty and police repression, this diversity would inhibit efforts at labor organization.

Brazil's workers suffered from poor health, nutrition, and consumption levels. They exchanged long hours of toil for miserable pay under

unsanitary and unsafe working conditions. But even if we could document all aspects of their lives, we should not attempt to judge the quality of those lives. Some workers no doubt were content with their lot. Perhaps they felt the satisfaction of a close communal life. Rather than uniting to oppose the existing economic and political systems, many urban workers pursued individual releases, such as drinking and gambling, or sought social advancement through individual efforts or through the purchase of lottery tickets. Some allied themselves with members of the dominant classes who could provide employment, charity, and protection. But others did seek to unite. During the first two decades of the twentieth century, more than ever before, some groups of urban workers formed labor organizations of diverse orientations and ideologies to improve their lives or to challenge the socio-economic structure.

7 / Unions and Disunity: *The Struggle to Create Effective Forms of Worker Resistance*

During the first two decades of the twentieth century, sectors of Brazil's working poor formed an increasing variety of generally short-lived labor organizations to protest their poverty. Mutual benefit societies, "workers' parties," Roman Catholic labor associations, and socialist and anarchist groups all sought to unite workers and defend their interests, although the majority of Brazil's urban poor remained beyond their reach. Craftsmen such as printers and shoemakers as well as construction and transportation workers, stevedores, and waiters, and eventually some textile workers—but never day laborers, piece workers, or domestic servants—organized separate local unions, reflecting the structure of the Brazilian economy. Although unions remained a means of resistance largely limited to the minority of skilled workers, it was these organizations which most concerned Brazil's dominant elites. But conflicts between ideologies and among labor leaders, hostilities between European and Brazilian-born workers, and racial and regional divisions weakened the incipient labor movement, leaving it more vulnerable to police repression.

As they had for decades, mutual benefit societies continued to attract skilled urban workers across the length and breadth of Brazil. Even in cities like São Paulo where militant European ideologies had their greatest impact, new mutual aid associations still appeared regularly during the first decades of the twentieth century. Although their numbers

diminished slowly over time, with the formation of newer, more assertive types of labor organizations, many mutual benefit societies enjoyed
a longevity which those rivals might well envy.[1] Nine out of the fifteen
workers' mutual benefit societies surveyed in Rio de Janeiro in 1877 still
functioned in 1912 (Tables 11 and 27).

Some labor associations drew close to sources of political power and
government or ecclesiastical authority. Such organizations advocated collaboration among members of different classes and demonstrated reluctance to strike. They often supported the election to office of reformist
candidates. Although bitterly denounced as *pelegos* or yellow unions by
militant anarchists and scorned or ignored by those militants' later sympathizers, some such associations attracted numerous followers.

In the early twentieth century, the Roman Catholic Church demonstrated increasing interest in urban workers. Faced with severe organizational and financial problems following its disestablishment in 1889, the
Brazilian Church drew closer to Rome. Even before it received reinforce-
ments of foreign priests and monies in the 1920s, the Brazilian Church
employed new ideas from Rome in meeting competitive value systems
ranging from Protestantism and Masonry to anarchism and socialism.
Moderate Catholic labor associations could be used to instill religious
values and beliefs while promoting harmony between labor and capital and
improving the lot of the poor. "Justice and charity" was the stated theme
of much of this church effort, which included the construction of subsidized worker housing and the establishment of food cooperatives.

Catholic workers' associations like the Corporação Operária Cristão de Pernambuco and its affiliated Federação do Operariado Cristão,
organized by a local Pernambucan manufacturer inspired by Leo XIII's
1896 encyclical *Rerum novarum*, gained adherents in many parts of Brazil. In 1904 fifteen affiliated associations, which set up food cooperatives, primary schools, and kindrgartens, claimed a total membership of
six thousand workers.[2] In 1908, Friar Inocêncio Reidick founded the
União Popular do Brasil, modeled on the German *Volksverein*. Within
a few years its branches stretched from Bahia to Santa Catarina. São Paulo
saw the creation of a Centro Operário Católico Metropolitano in 1907;
by 1920 Catholic workers' centers functioned in each of the city's major
working-class districts.[3] The size and attractiveness of such Catholic leagues
and centers, even in south-central Brazil, and the local clergy's "active
organizational campaign" worried anarchist leaders who warned workers against such "instruments of deception and blindness" which, they
said, "constituted the biggest school of strike-breaking and passivity."[4]

Especially in Rio de Janeiro and cities north of the capital, politically oriented and generally short-lived "workers' parties" persisted into the twentieth century. Like similar parties which had contended for labor leadership during the first years of the republic, they were frequently led by intellectuals sympathetic to worker needs. Sometimes such men called themselves socialists, a term often loosely employed in Brazil. In Rio de Janeiro, Vicente de Souza and Gustavo de Lacerda founded the short-lived Partido Socialista Colectiva as well as the Centro das Classes Operários in 1902. Vicente de Souza also contributed articles on "socialism" to the local press. But he ceased most of his labor activities following the government's closure of the Centro das Classes Operárias in the aftermath of the 1904 antivaccination uprising. Even less worker-oriented was the Partido Operário Progressista, headed by Major Tancredo Leal. This party, linked to leaders of the anticompulsory vaccination campaign, claimed to show workers how to fight for their rights, while also promoting education and mutual aid activities. A related organization, the Federação Operária e Artistica do Brazil, whose sponsors included Tancredo Leal and opposition congressman Ireneu Machado, survived the 1904 antivaccination upheaval. Like the Centro das Classes Operária, the federation drew heavily on maritime workers for its membership. It also claimed affiliates in northern states such as Paraíba. The federation counseled calm and moderation, and achieved such good relations with the government that a police band accompanied its expensive 1905 May Day celebrations.[5]

Even labor organizations run by workers often sought political support, especially in Rio de Janeiro. Reformist unions led by native-born skilled workers and inclined toward political compromise predominated among organized labor in the nation's capital. For example, the Círculo dos Operários da União, led by Francisco Sadock de Sá, a printer and supporter of Lieutenant José Augusto Vinhais in the early 1890s, sought favors from Rio's prefect Inocêncio Serzedelo Correia in the following decade. Sadock de Sá praised Lloyd George's efforts to secure social security legislation in England, no doubt hoping that some Brazilian politician would follow suit. Anarcho-syndicalists, who opposed political participation, controlled some of Rio's labor unions. But they remained far more visible in São Paulo, with its heavily foreign-born labor force, than in other large Brazilian cities. Socialists too admitted how much weaker they were in Rio than in São Paulo, despite the capital's larger working class population. The nation's capital offered more sources of government employment and patronage—and more aspiring politicians willing to sponsor limited labor demands—thus providing greater, though still very limited, opportunities for a few workers to secure concessions.

Popular protests and political pursuits, rather than industry-wide strikes, remained more characteristic of Rio's workers.[6]

Perhaps the most important reformist labor leader of the early twentieth century, at least in the nation's capital, was Antônio Augusto Pinto Machado. A native-born Brazilian, like most such leaders, and a former store clerk, Pinto Machado helped organize some of Rio's textile workers in 1902. In July 1903 he became president of the Union of Workers in Engenho de Dentro, established in that northern suburb of Rio de Janeiro in 1899. This same suburb had long supported clubs of railroad workers from the Central do Brasil, the labor sector which had provided José Augusto Vinhais with his strongest support in the early 1890s. Pinto Machado followed Vinhais's lead. Within a year after Pinto Machado assumed the presidency of the União dos Operários em Engenho de Dentro, he increased its membership, or so he later claimed, from eighty-two to some six thousand members, largely railroad workers.[7]

Pinto Machado opposed class conflict and expressed strong reservations concerning strikes. Workers should secure their goals by forming cooperatives and by electing candidates and exerting pressure on the government. But his efforts to create a strong nationwide labor organization proved unsuccessful, despite the formation of associated unions in the states of Rio de Janeiro and Minas Gerais. Although Pinto Machado helped organize the 1906 First Workers' Congress, his proposals, notably his advocacy of political involvement by unions, met with defeat. He and the newly formed, anarcho-syndicalist-controlled Confederação Operária Brasileira then engaged in mutual denunciations. Despite Pinto Machado's opposition to "foreign" doctrines of anarchism and socialism, and to their supporters, his efforts to win laws improving workers' status and his support of some strikes led to his occasional imprisonment. In later years, Pinto Machado drew closer to sources of political power, especially during the presidency of Marshal Hermes da Fonseca (1910–1914).[8]

For workers on government-owned railroads or other government installations, Pinto Machado's type of unionization promised the greatest immediate benefits. Generally Brazilian-born and literate, these skilled workers were a voting constituency of interest to politicians. In Rio de Janeiro 56.3% of the male population, more than twice the national average, could read and write in 1906 (Tables 12 and 13). According to one of the capital's leading newspapers in 1906, "even candidates for seats in the National Congress have gone, one by one, in turn to the União dos Operários em Engenho de Dentro," with its eight thousand members, seeking "to win the favor and enter into the good graces of this large body of electors."[9] The União dos Operários em Engenho de Dentro would decline markedly in strength a few years later, but Rio's railroad and port workers, among the largest groups of organized laborers in Brazil, would retain political links for decades to come. Other skilled workers, however, responded to advocates of socialism or anarchism.

"Socialist" ideas entered Brazil in the midnineteenth century, publicized by a handful of intellectuals. Influences of the Fourier School appeared in an 1846 newspaper, *O Socialista da Provincia do Rio de Janeiro*, dedicated to "all the improvement of which society is capable."[10] Saint Simon's ideas also secured adherents, and then some of Karl Marx's found an audience. By the end of the century, a few Brazilian intellectuals formed centers of "socialist propaganda" in major cities, notably the Centro Socialista de Santos, founded by Silvério Fontes, Sóter de Araujo, and Carlos Escobar in 1895, following an unsuccessful effort in 1889. They hoped to promote cooperatives, organize a labor party, and spread socialist ideas. The center's official journal, *A Questão Social*, stressed an evolutionary socialism which rejected "revolutionary agitation" and violence while praising Karl Marx as the *primus inter pares* of socialist thinkers.[11] "Socialists" such as Vicente de Souza contributed articles.

Like many other Brazilian intellectuals, Silvério Fontes was drawn to a series of causes and doctrines. A medical doctor born in Sergipe in 1858 but practicing in Santos, Fontes became a positivist, as well as a republican and abolitionist. Later attracted to anarchism, he also turned to the works of Karl Marx. Fontes not only led the short-lived Centro Socialista de Santos, but also helped draft the 1902 socialist party manifesto. Late in life he became a member of the Communist Party, whose founder, Astrojildo Pereira, perhaps for that reason called him the "pioneer of Marxism in Brazil."[12]

Some immigrant intellectuals also espoused socialist ideas. In *O Socialismo no Brasil*, first published in 1908, Antônio Piccarolo, the recipient of a doctorate from the University of Turin and one of the best known socialists in Brazil, expounded a historical materialism with Spencerian echoes. Piccarolo attempted to account for the insignificant inroads of socialism into Brazil by stressing the country's underdeveloped socio-economic status and by demonstrating the difficulties attendant in transplanting rigid European socialist programs and tactics to the New World. Although he contended that Brazil was only then entering the feudal period and would have to pass through other stages of European evolution before socialism could be achieved, he incorporated distinctive features of the Brazilian experience, such as European immigration, into his argument.[13]

As we saw in Chapter 3, not only intellectuals advocated a socialist solution to Brazil's, and workers', problems. Nor was socialist activity confined to the state of São Paulo, although the *paulista* contributions remain the best known. In the 1890s, socialist groups formed among both Brazilian-born and immigrant workers. In 1892 the first socialist congress took place in Rio de Janeiro under the leadership of Luís da França e Silva. While some affiliated labor organizations employed the term socialist very loosely, others, such as São Paulo's militant German social democrats, maintained close ties with the Second International.

Ten years later, in 1902, a second socialist congress met in São Paulo. Brazilian and immigrant skilled workers, such as the Spanish-born printer Valentim Diego, as well as Brazilian intellectuals like Silvério Fontes participated. By then socialist circles had turned into leagues of resistence and workers' federations, supporting strikes and consumer cooperatives. In São Paulo, according to Alceste De Ambris, editor of the Italian-language socialist newspaper *Avanti!*, the socialist movement comprised principally Italians, with some Brazilians and fewer Spanish.[14] Of the forty-five delegates attending the Second Socialist Congress, organized by *Avanti!*, twenty-eight were Italian, thirteen Brazilian, two Spanish and two German. Thirty-two of the forty organizations represented at the congress came from the state of São Paulo, with the remainder from Minas Gerais, Rio Grande do Sul, Pará, Pernambuco, Paraíba, and Bahia. None came from Rio de Janeiro. Communications among labor organizations from distant states remained difficult, and transportation problems limited attendance at such meetings. Nevertheless, the Partido Socialista Brasileira, a product of this congress, received support from federations of socialist parties in northeastern states such as Pernambuco, Bahia, and Paraíba, as well as from the Federal District of Rio de Janeiro.[15]

The program adopted at this Second Socialist Congress in 1902 combined the rhetoric of the Communist Manifesto—the proletariat must organize a party to gain power and transform capitalist society—with a desire for class conciliation and a willingness to accommodate all right-thinking people within the party. These socialists sought both improved working conditions and institutional changes. Demands included the eight-hour day, prohibition of child labor, universal suffrage, free secular education, and divorce laws.[16] Like other socialist organizations in Brazil, the Partido Socialista Brasileira which emerged from the 1902 congress was short-lived. No enduring national socialist party took form in Brazil.

As believers in political participation, socialists encountered problems in areas of high immigrant concentration like São Paulo, for European-born workers showed little inclination to acquire Brazilian citizenship and participate in electoral politics. They preferred the protection of their home governments. Many also demonstrated a lack of interest in the affairs of a country which they hoped to leave after accumulating a "nest egg." In other areas of Brazil, reformist unions of skilled workers following traditions of political patronage and compromise might gain more adherents than proponents of what still appeared to be a foreign doctrine. The nature of oligarchical politics encouraged indifference among the lower classes. Most of the population, Brazilian as well as foreign-born, did not participate directly in political affairs.

Like socialism, anarchism was an imported ideology. Immigrant intellectuals and workers introduced anarchism to Brazil during the late nineteenth century. In 1890 an Italian veterinary surgeon and utopian visionary, Giovanni Rossi, together with a group of Italian working-class immigrants founded the Cecília Colony, the best-known anarchist agricultural community, in the southern state of Paraná.[17] Members of these short-lived colonies moved to the cities and joined in the propaganda work of recently arrived Italian and Spanish militants who published ephemeral newspapers and attempted to organize urban workers.

Anarchists sought fundamental changes in the structure of society. They rejected the authority of the state as the ultimate regulator of relations among free individuals. Through direct economic action and ideological struggle—not political struggle—anarchists strove to modify the structure of society so that some form of association and cooperation between free individuals could be substituted for the authority of the state.[18]

Advocates of anarcho-syndicalism, which emphasized unions not only as instruments of struggle for working-class rights but also as basic nuclei of future society, sought to create syndicates in Brazil. They attempted to gather the workers in each trade into unions concentrating on economic struggle while eschewing partisan political activities. Unlike mutual aid societies, their unions refused to fill social service functions. Anarchists and anarcho-syndicalisms opposed mutual benefit associations as generating false expectations among workers which would divert them from economic issues and weaken their resolve. Instead, they emphasized solidarity and "direct action" through strikes, boycotts, sabotage, and public demonstrations. The true purpose of a union was "resistance."[19] Anarchists also helped organize "leagues" to protest food shortages, high prices, avaricious landlords, compulsory military service, and press censorship. Their concentration on economic issues and their refusal to participate in partisan political struggles may have appealed to some immigrants, unable and unwilling to take part in elections. But far more immigrants avoided anarchist activities as well as Brazilian politics.

According to anarchist theory, no distinction should be made between leaders and members, for that would instill the germ of authoritarianism. Anarchist federations should function on the basis of the sovereignty of individual members. An insistence on local autonomy and spontaneity accompanied anarchist internationalism. But relationships between the world of the "vanguard" and that of the "masses" were not always easy. Too often a rigid line was drawn, in both word and deed, between the "self-conscious" and "aware" and the unaware. Not unlike Brazil's political and economic elites, anarchist militants tended to view the working classes as backward.

Like other radical and labor organizations, anarchist circles suffered from internal dissension and divisions. Doctrinal questions, such as the relative value and effectiveness of general versus partial strikes and of propaganda versus organization, and even the importance of unions, provoked continual discussion. Anarchists criticized the more popular anarcho-syndicalists, intent on strikes to raise salaries, for concentrating on economic questions and losing sight of anarchist goals: bureaucratic unions might substitute their own power for that of bourgeois bosses, creating a labor aristocracy and forgetting to liberate the rest of humanity.

While "anarchism" attained greater resonance among organized labor in São Paulo during the second decade of the twentieth century than did "socialism," it never acquired a constituency among Brazilian-born workers in other cities equal to that of reformist labor organizations. In 1909 an Italian government police agent in São Paulo, perhaps inclined to exaggerate their number and menace, reported the Italian anarchists in Brazil as totaling one thousand.[20] However, anarchists viewed mere numbers as immaterial. They considered minority leadership of a movement preferable to mass groupings of workers lacking class consciousness or a willingness to fight. Brazil's courageous, hard-working anarchist adepts earned the respect of many contemporary urban workers, besides capturing the imagination of later investigators who emphasize their importance among organized labor.

Dedicated militants attempting to propagandize and organize urban workers in Brazil encountered deceptions and disappointments while also confronting the hardships of daily life. Frequently frustrated in their efforts, militant anarchists, like socialists, blamed their difficulties on Brazil's mass illiteracy, recent emergence from slavery, poverty, and relative lack of industrialization, as well as on police repression, ethnic rivalries and animosities, and individualistic attempts at economic gain. They bemoaned the fact that organized workers preferred to found cooperatives or gather strike funds rather than follow anarchist principles. European immigrants too often seemed intent only on personal social advancement, whether attainable or not. They generally remained oblivious to the call of class solidarity, while native-born Brazilians appeared merely apathetic.[21]

The presence of heavy concentrations of immigrants in many sectors of the working classes bears further examination. As we saw in Chapter 3, Rio's "working class" was not really as "foreign" as some writers indicate. But in São Paulo, 54.7% of the city's population was foreign-born in 1893, and 35.4% in 1920 (see Table 10), and certain industrial sectors, such as textiles, employed mostly immigrants. Boris Fausto argues that immigrants found the anarchist refusal to engage in political struggle and the implicit economics of anarchism appealing, since they were searching for social status in a new land, not for a new political world.[22] However, mutual benefit societies also avoided politics while aiding individual workers' attempts to lead more secure and comfortable lives. These far more numerous and popular societies carried out specific functions which anarchist organizations refused to undertake. As both Michael Hall and Sheldon Maram point out, most European immigrants lacked contact with organized labor in their European homelands. They were new to industry as well as to urban life, which compounded the problems of labor organization.[23]

These immigrants lacked the class consciousness which anarchists and socialists demanded. Many apparently believed in individual social advancement through individual efforts. According to Thomas Holloway, the possibility of upward social mobility did exist, as Brazil's industrial system was still largely an artisan system.[24] Geographical mobility in a state like São Paulo could also retard the development of class consciousness. Immigrants who perceived problems in terms of the personalities and policies of individual employers often sought solutions by moving from one job or region to another, or even returning to Europe, rather than through collective action.

Many Italian, Portuguese, and Spanish immigrants viewed Brazil as just a temporary home. Anarchists accused them of having only "one purpose: to amass a nest egg in order to return to their homeland."[25] This lack of interest and concern for Brazilian affairs easily extended to unionization and revolutionary struggle. As the anarchist newspaper *O Amigo do Povo* acknowledged, immigrants "shrug their shoulders at what happens" because they say "they are not from here."[26] According to the 1920 census only 3,829 out of Rio de Janeiro's total foreign-born population of 239,129, and 2,612 of the 205,245 foreigners in the city of São Paulo, had taken Brazilian citizenship, even though the majority met the requirements under Brazilian law.[27]

Few immigrants wished to cut ties with "home." When possible, they sent money back to relatives in Europe.[28] Portuguese officials, who admitted how essential emigration to Brazil was to the weak Portuguese economy, sought to sustain the flow of remittances, in part by discouraging the emigration of entire families to Brazil. Immigrants celebrated their homeland's national holidays, joined welfare associations based on nationality, and expected their government's representatives to protect them in time of trouble. To the dismay of the Portuguese consul in Rio de Janeiro in the late nineteenth century, Portuguese subjects kept running to him for aid, even over the most trivial matters: dealing with them gave him "more work, consumed more time, and caused more trouble and grief" than any of his other duties.[29] Italians in São Paulo flocked to "patriotic festivities" sponsored by the Italian consulate and beneficent societies despite socialist and anarchist efforts to persuade them of the "worthlessness of these celebrations because their harsh motherland forced them to seek their daily bread on foreign shores."[30] At the beginning of the twentieth century, the majority of the city's Italians belonged to associations loyal to the Italian monarchy, not to the Lega Democratica Italiana, which attempted to unite all antimonarchists: anarchists, socialists, and republicans. The large Portuguese beneficent societies in Rio loyally supported the monarchy. Only a handful of local Portuguese, and some Brazilians, joined the Portuguese republican movement in the 1890s, and that movement virtually disappeared from the Brazilian scene long before the overthrow of the Portuguese monarchy in 1910. For years after the establishment of a republic in Portugal, many Portuguese immigrants remained loyal to the fallen regime.[31]

Brazil's anarchists and socialists often found it necessary to attempt to calm the nationalistic feelings of both European immigrants and Brazilians. During the 1896 "Italian Protocols" dispute over the indemnification to be given Italian subjects for losses suffered in the Federalist Revolt, many lower-class immigrants in São Paulo publicly supported the Italian consul, clashing with Brazilians on the city streets. Decades later, the Brazilian-born anarchist militant and lawyer Benjamin Mota recalled how this incident caused lingering "hatreds" between Brazilians and Italians which the socialists and anarchists had unsuccessfully sought to quench.[32]

Ethnic rivalries and animosities, not only between Brazilians and foreigners but also among immigrant communities, weakened the labor movement in Brazil. Questions of language and culture, like mutual resentments and suspicions, separated the different nationalities in Brazil's major industrial centers. When members of different groups struggled for the same jobs, as when immigrants invaded a sector previously controlled by Brazilians, resentments could break out into open hostilities. In São Paulo, Italian labor militants accused the less well-established Portuguese, reluctant to join Italian-language unions, of being strikebreakers. When the Portuguese entered the glassmaking trade in São

Paulo, the Italian workers called them *krumiros*, strikebreakers willing to work for any salary. Rivalries between Italian and Portuguese boatmen sometimes led to bloodshed, for the Italians sought to keep control of the more profitable trade in transporting tiles, leaving the sand trade to the Portuguese.[33]

Brazilians resented the tendency of many European immigrants to consider them culturally and even racially inferior. Although the ultranationalism of the 1890s had subsided, Brazilians of all classes objected to immigrants' viewing them as lazy or undisciplined. Immigrant prejudices could hinder labor organization. As Everardo Dias, an anarchist and free thinker, recalled years later, some anarchist "globe-trotters" continually "disparaged" everything Brazilian; through his "intolerable insults to Brazil" one such anarchist propagandist "drove a great number of people from our ranks."[34]

Dark-skinned Brazilian workers, suffering from competition with European immigrants in urban service and craft occupations, generally resisted appeals by immigrant labor organizers.[35] Perhaps foreign-born labor militants, who registered dismay at the disinclination of the overwhelming majority of Brazilian urban workers to join unions, did not realize that economic necessity drove many Brazilians to take all available jobs, including those as strikebreakers.

Labor organizers in Rio de Janeiro or São Paulo generally lacked contact with individuals or events in northern Brazil. Although some labor militants moved back and forth between Rio, São Paulo, and Santos, and anarchists, like socialist leaders, in those three cities kept in close touch, communications between organizations or individuals in northern and southern Brazil remained very poor. Perhaps the tendency of some anarchist militants to view native-born Brazilians as apathetic and difficult to organize contributed to this division. Yet, the occasional experience in the Northeast of a *Paulista* like Everardo Dias suggests that they might sometimes be mistaken and their view of Brazilian reality too narrow. Following an unsuccessful government deportation attempt, the ship carrying this Spanish-born printer and journalist home to Brazil in 1920 stopped in Recife, where local labor leaders celebrated his victory. Dias expressed his utter surprise at finding an energetic native-born working class: "The labor associations are well established and have suitable headquarters. The foreign element is non-existent. Well then, this very Brazilian working class demonstrates more class consciousness and more enthusiasm than São Paulo's 'foreign' proletariat. This, for me, was a revelation."[36]

Labor leadership was largely composed of skilled workers, both Brazilian and European-born. As under the empire, printers contributed to the labor movement far out of proportion to their numbers. They formed a significant segment of socialist and anarchist leadership alike. Of the thirty-three key anarchist figures in Rio de Janeiro and São Paulo examined by Boris Fausto, twenty-two were skilled workers, and of these, ten were printers. The remainder were mostly Brazilian-born middle-sector intellectuals. Prior to World War I, none of the far more numerous but poorer paid and less skilled textile workers formed part of this nucleus of anarchist militants and propagandists. [37]

Using somewhat different criteria from Fausto's in analyzing labor leadership, Sheldon Maram demonstrates the magnitude of the foreign-born component among union officers and organizers in Rio, Santos, and São Paulo. His exclusion of radical intellectuals with little influence among the rank and file increases the relative size of this immigrant component. Of Maram's list of one hundred and nineteen anarchist, socialist, and moderate leaders in those three cities, seventy-one were known to be foreign-born, including twenty-four Italians, twenty-three Portuguese, and twenty-two Spanish. Eighty-two percent of São Paulo's labor leaders and eighty-eight percent of Santos's were born in Europe, as compared with forty-six percent of Rio's generally more moderate unionists. [38] Although not all militants in those cities were immigrants, hardly any moderate leaders were born abroad. In northern cities the immigrant component of labor leadership declined sharply, as did anarchist and socialist influences.

The labor leadership studied by both Fausto and Maram was entirely male. In fact, the world of organized labor in early twentieth-century Brazil, like the world of elite politics, remained overwhelmingly male. As in other industrializing countries, union activity among women was never as extensive or as successful as among men. Most of the trades organized into unions, such as printing, carpentry, shoemaking, and construction, generally employed men only. Women worked at traditionally hard to organize semi-skilled jobs in textiles, food processing, and apparel, or labored as pieceworkers in their own homes or as domestic servants in others' homes. Women's dual roles of work and family limited their participation in union activity. The great turnover in many women's jobs also hindered the establishment of a sense of collective membership or grievance. As in Rio's América Fabril factory, women textile workers tended to be concentrated in spinning, not weaving, where they were paid by the hour, with even less security than day laborers. [39] Furthermore, not all unions or labor leaders welcomed women into their midst or sought equal rights, and wages, for women.

Both anarchists and socialists called for the equality of women. The program of the Second Socialist Congress in 1902, for example, demanded equal wages for women, together with political and judicial equality, including the vote.[40] But problems arose in the pursuit of some socialist and anarchist ideals. For instance, when the "companion" of one member of the first anarchist circle in Rio de Janeiro in the 1890s put the doctrine of "free love" into practice by switching her affections to another member of the circle, her action caused the disintegration of the group.[41] On other occasions, this doctrine did not appeal to women, leading some anarchists, such as Giovanni Rossi, founder of the Cecília Colony, to suggest measures not in keeping with their stated beliefs. In a confidential letter proposing a new colony in Mato Grosso, Rossi admitted that the main problem with such ventures was that few women accepted the anarchist principles of free love. He proposed buying Indian girls from tribes in the interior and initiating them into these principles, free from the corrupting influence of bourgeois society.[42]

A few women workers, responding to anarchist or socialist doctrines, published urgent, often despairing appeals in labor newspapers for others to join their struggle for better wages and working conditions.[43] Seamstresses in São Paulo chastized their coworkers for their "apathy" and for not joining unions although they had "to work up to sixteen hours a day, double that of the stronger sex!"[44] In 1907, the year after three seamstresses issued this anguished plea for "solidarity," both among their mistreated colleagues and between seamstresses and other workers, that "most ignorant and backward group among the working classes" struck their employees. The strike was broken, according to the city's labor federation, by pressures brought against many strikers by male members of their families anxious to receive the women's pitiful wages.[45]

The ambivalent attitude of male labor leadership toward female workers is evident in the report of Rio's syndicalist-oriented União dos Alfaiates (Tailors' Union), sent to the 1913 Second Brazilian Labor Congress. Demonstrating both pity for female suffering and fear of female competition, the leaders of a union losing members maintained that "women are by far the most exploited people in our profession, and, although we regret saying so, at this time they are our most dangerous competitors, contributing mightly to our distress."[46] The anarcho-syndicalist-dominated 1906 labor congress also termed women "terrible competitors with men," and blamed them for their own victimization, claiming that the exploitation of women was largely due to their "lack of cohesion and solidarity."[47] When Rio's printers suffered massive unemployment following the introduction of linotype machines, their representatives opposed the hiring of women.[48] Certainly, labor organizations were far more inclined to advocate the "protection" of female labor than to demand equal pay for women. Such "protection," in the form of restrictions on female workers and the prohibition of night work, reinforced stereotypes of women as weak and dependent and of men as breadwinners. Furthermore, should "protection" be combined with "equal wages," as some urged, female workers would be placed at a marked disadvantage when seeking employment. Catholic jurist August Olympio Viveiros de Castro accused unions of "masculine hypocrisy" when they advocated equal salaries for women, claiming this was just a maneuver to get lower-paid women out of the job market; if owners were ever obliged to grant women equal wages, they would employ men only. Of course he wished women to remain at home as wives and mothers.[49] Among urban workers values and attitudes as to women's "place" persisted which often resembled, and perhaps reflected, those found among the dominant classes. Relationships within lower-class families need to be studied at length.

While many unions did accept women as members, they almost never chose them for leadership positions. As demonstrated by available lists of participants and from photographs of participants, delegates to labor conferences of various ideological hues were all male.[50] A perusal of dozens of labor newspapers from Rio de Janeiro and São Paulo in the late nineteenth and early twentieth centuries, all edited by men, reveals no female labor leaders among anarchists and socialists. While a few women contributed articles to these periodicals or signed manifestos, generally directed toward other women, they did not participate in decision making. In 1920, however, Rio's anarchist-oriented União dos Operários em Fabricas de Tecidos (Textile Factory Workers' Union) honored the recently deceased Elisa Gonçalves as "the greatest orator in the union."[51] She had achieved prominence if not power. Only in several reformist unions did a few women fill leadership roles, and their actual influence remains unclear. Elisa Schneid became vice-president of Rio's União Operária do Engenho de Dentro, giving newspaper interviews about the 8,000-member union's political position, and also headed the union's short-lived Partido Operário Independente. However, she was no manual laborer, but an educated office worker employed by the Central do Brasil railroad.[52] Perhaps Elisa Schneid served as an intermediary between her union and the larger world of elite concerns reflected in the general press, projecting the image of an articulate and intelligent labor representative.[53]

Far more than reformist labor organizations, Brazil's anarchist and socialist leadership depended upon their own newspapers to organize workers and propagate ideas.[54] Besides disseminating their theoretical positions, often in highly simplified versions, the journals provided news of labor activities and documented workers' oppression. Although the vast majority of labor newspapers were ephemeral, some anarchist journals in São Paulo survived for several years. Notable among these were *O Amigo do Povo* (1902–1904), edited by the lucid and shy Portuguese law graduate Neno Vasco (Gregório Nazanzeno de Vasconcelos); *A Terra Livre* (São Paulo, 1905–1907, 1910; Rio de Janeiro, 1907–1908), headed by the Brazilian-born typographer and journalist Edgard Leuenroth; and the Italian-language *La Battaglia* (1904–1912), edited by Oreste Ristori and then by Luigi Damiani. In contrast, the only anarchist newspaper in Rio de Janeiro to endure for more than a year was *A Voz do Trabalhador* (1908–1909, 1913–1915), originally the organ of the anarcho-syndicalist-dominated Confederação Operária Brasileira. None of the semisocialist papers (*Alvorado*, 1890; *Jornal dos Operarios*, 1891; *O Operario*, 1895; *Semana Operaria*, 1907; and *A Tribuna do Povo*, 1909) edited in Rio by Mariano Garcia, a former cigar maker and associate at times of Luís da França e Silva, Vincente de Souza, and Estevem Estrela, a Bahian socialist working in São Paulo, even lasted a full year. No other socialist, or anarchist, newspaper in Brazil achieved the longevity of São Paulo's leading socialist journal, *Avanti!* (1900–1915), published in Italian with sections in Portuguese. The problems labor newspapers encountered, such as high costs, police repression, and employer pressures, were not unique to Brazil. Most of Argentina's late nineteenth-century socialist newspapers also had brief lives, and all experienced financial difficulties.[55] And the Argentine working class was generally considered better organized and more militant than Brazil's. In Brazil some labor journals endured far longer than individual trade unions. Their persistence may be related to a gap between "vanguard" and "masses." Newspapers remained an essential element in socialist and anarchist organization, and not merely an arm of propaganda.

Judging the influence exercised by any newspaper is never easy. Even when available, circulation figures of labor journals give us no exact indication of their readership or the response to their message. The *paulista* anticlerical newspaper *A Laterna* achieved a circulation of 24,000 within two months of its appearance in 1902. In comparison, editions of the *paulista* anarchist journal *A Plebe* ranged from 3,000 to 4,000 in the second decade of the twentieth century. Rio's *Gazeta Operaria* sold 3,000 copies of its first issue in September 1902. *A Voz do Trabalhador* reappeared in 1913 with an edition of 3,000 and increased its circulation to 4,000 by the middle of that year. However, actual readership of such journals may well have surpassed these figures, since newspapers could circulate from hand to hand and be read aloud to illiterate workers.[56]

Labor newspapers expended much of their energy attacking rival ideologies and organizations, demonstrating the dissension and factionalism which hindered labor organization in Brazil. The world of small distinctions and big differences familiar to radical circles in other countries was not unknown in Brazil. Not only did reformist labor leaders attack both anarchists and socialists for their "foreign" ideologies and violent proclivities, but those radicals also sniped at each other. Socialists taunted anarchists as outsiders while the "more advanced" anarchists accused socialists of lacking sincerity, theoretical rigor, and revolutionary fervor, and even of worshiping their "martyrs." During the first years of the twentieth century, it is true, Rio's socialists honored the memory of Luís da França e Silva; they paid annual visits to that mulatto typographer's grave, marked by a modest memorial erected through local workers' contributions several years after his death in 1894. In turn, anarchists took considerable pains to point out occasions when Brazilians, especially blacks, participated in their debates. However, despite taunts and insults, anarchist-socialist exchanges never matched the bitterness of those between anarchists and Antônio Augusto Pinto Machado. Perhaps the potential popularity of Pintô Machado's form of unionization even in São Paulo led anarchists to send speakers to challenge him in meetings as well as to combat him in the press.[57] Despite the doctrinal differences separating socialists and anarchists, some claimed that in São Paulo and Rio de Janeiro they "almost always cooperated in strikes, commemorations, and demonstrations."[58] But they, like reformist leaders, found no common organizational ground. They seldom participated in the same labor congresses or federations. Those congresses only demonstrated their divergent positions and activities.

In their quest for unity and strength, Brazilian labor organizations formed federations and held a series of congresses during the first two decades of the twentieth century. Truly national labor congresses could facilitate interregional exchange and dispel some stereotypes and also serve as coordinating bodies for labor unions. But most delegates to labor congresses held in Rio de Janeiro or São Paulo came from nearby areas. In a huge, diverse, and poor nation with inadequate transportation, communication remained difficult. Many unions proved reluctant to send representatives to meetings controlled by men of divergent views. However, even though labor congresses led to no truly national federations, several regional and state labor federations emerged.

In 1905 São Paulo's hat makers', stone masons', shoemakers', and wood workers' unions founded the Federação Operária de São Paulo. Although this federation played an active role in the 1906 railroad workers' strike against the Companhia Paulista, it slid into decline well before its demise prior to the outbreak of World War I.[59] The first major labor federation in Rio de Janeiro, the Federação das Associações de Classes, was founded in 1903 in an attempt to coordinate the activities of local labor unions. Two years later the Federação Operária Regional Brasileira appeared. In 1906 that federation sponsored a labor congress in Rio called the "First Brazilian Labor Congress" by its adherents and their later admirers.

The First Brazilian Labor Congress demonstrated the growing influence of anarcho-syndicalism within Brazil's small, tentative labor movement. Not only anarchists and anarcho-syndicalists but also socialists and reformist labor leaders like Antônio Augusto Pinto Machado had joined in planning the week-long congress, which opened in Rio de Janeiro on 15 April 1906. Almost all the delegates came from Rio de Janeiro and São Paulo; only one labor organization from Pernambuco and one from Ceará were represented. Although outnumbered, the determined and disciplined anarcho-syndicalists maneuvered skillfully and blocked Pinto Machado's resolution supporting political participation by unions. Besides criticizing parties and political involvement, the delegates endorsed direct action and syndicates composed of militant minorities to serve as organs of economic resistance. However, unlike European revolutionary syndicalists, they did not debate the destruction of the state or the construction of a future society, and they almost never mentioned general strikes. Specific abuses affecting workers' daily lives, including payment of wages, long hours, accidents on the job, fines and piece work in factories, and high rents, aroused greater concern. Their orientation appeared far more syndicalist than revolutionary, perhaps as that approach would be more likely to attract a following in Brazil.[60]

The Confederação Operária Brasileira (C.O.B.) proposed at the 1906 First Brazilian Labor Congress only took shape in March 1908. With most of its activities limited to the nation's capital, the C.O.B. was often confused with Rio's regional federation, now reorganized into the anarcho-syndicalist Federação Operária do Rio de Janeiro. After publishing several issues of *A Voz do Trabalhador* and holding large public demonstrations protesting compulsory military service and the Spanish government's execution of the internationally respected educator Francisco Ferrer, the C.O.B. practically ceased operation until its revival in 1913 by the Federação Operária do Rio de Janeiro to hold the Second Brazilian Labor Congress.[61]

From 7 to 15 November 1912 a different type of labor congress, sponsored by President Hermes da Fonseca, met in Rio de Janeiro. This congress was officially called by the Liga do Operariado do Districto Federal, founded the previous year with the aid of Marshal Hermes and headed by Antônio Augusto Pinto Machado. However, Pinto Machado left the league with a depleted treasury before the congress met; aside from union officials' salaries and the rent for their headquarters, the league's only expenditure in 1912 was the cost of one funeral.[62] By calling the 1912 congress the "Fourth Brazilian Labor Congress," its sponsors made implicit claims for its legitimacy and descent from the 1892 labor congress in Rio de Janeiro, the 1902 São Paulo socialist congress, and the 1906 anarcho-syndicalist-dominated congress. Like some nineteenth-century manifestos, the resolutions of this 1912 congress stressed the need for worker unity to achieve a "public image of dignity" as well as to create organizations to "defend workers' interests and resist capitalism." A specific request for retirement benefits for government employees illustrates the continued support of such workers for this form of labor organization. Besides voicing old worker grievances concerning high food and housing costs, delegates demanded the eight-hour day, accident compensation, and obligatory primary education, as had labor militants. But the congress' final resolutions sought to refute anarchist and socialist positions, resolving to ignore "internationalist, anti-military, and anti-government doctrines," and to "leave to the future" the solution to questions of property organization. As the conference leaders contended, "the great majority of the Brazilian proletariat" showed slight interest in these matters.[63]

The 1912 congress reinforced differences between "reformists" and "militants," who disagreed on immediate tactics as well as on ultimate objectives. No unions from the city of São Paulo attended, and the delegation from Rio Grande do Sul's state labor federation walked out, denouncing the meeting as a tool of the politicians. The Centro Cosmopólita, Rio's restaurant and hotel workers' union, the only prominent anarchist-oriented association in attendance, also withdrew. However, even though this congress clearly demonstrated its official character, most of the sixty-eight participating associations were not paper or government-sponsored organizations. They included beneficent societies, "workers' parties," associations of workers at government installations, and organizations of skilled workers, principally from Rio de Janeiro and from the less industrialized states of Minas Gerais, Bahia, Pernambuco, and Rio Grande do Sul. Although the federal government showed little additional interest in labor leaders like Pinto Machado at this time, their path of labor legislation and government patronage, not that of labor militants eschewing politics, would be followed by Brazil in the 1930s.[64]

Less than a year after the conclusion of the government-sponsored "Fourth Brazilian Labor Congress," the newly revived anarcho-syndicalist-oriented C.O.B. responded by holding the "Second Brazilian Labor Congress." Fifty-nine workers associations sent representatives to the six-day meeting held in Rio de Janeiro in September 1913: nineteen organizations from the nation's capital, sixteen from the state of São Paulo, six from Minas Gerais, five from Rio Grande do Sul, including that state's labor federation representing nineteen unions, five from the state of Rio de Janeiro, and one each from Amazonas and Pará. None of Rio's transportation workers' associations and only one of the local maritime workers' unions attended. While the resolutions passed by this congress concerning the role of labor associations and their internal organization, working conditions, economic grievances, strikes, property relations, and education sometimes contained more militant language than those of the 1906 congress, the same basic anarcho-syndicalist orientation prevailed. This 1913 congress occurred at a high point in the early Brazilian labor movement, before a decline which only ended with the severe economic tensions and strikes accompanying World War I.[65]

With the Second Brazilian Labor Congress, the anarcho-syndicalist movement sought to spread its influence beyond south-central Brazil. Few unions in the north or Northeast had sent delegates to Rio de Janeiro for the congress. Following the conclusion of the meeting, the Confederação Operária Brasileira dispatched representatives to states with which it had little contact. José Elias da Silva, a former sailor, textile mill hand, shoemaker, and dock worker organizer, who represented the Federação Operária do Rio de Janeiro at the congress, was sent to his natal state of Pernambuco. There labor organization had not proceeded as rapidly as in the south. Beneficient societies remained the most common form of association, although stevedores, printers, and transportation workers formed active unions. But few labor organizations had a clear, consistent ideological position.[66]

Pernambuco produced men like João Ezequiel de Oliveira Luz, a printer and president of the União Tipográfico in the 1890s and early 1900s, who praised Marx and secured election to the state legislature. João Ezequiel worked through the Centro Protector dos Operários, founded in 1901 and linked to the local socialist party. Organized much like labor sectors in Rio de Janeiro in the 1890s, this center had branches in cities in the interior of Pernambuco and in nearby states. It even honored the memory of typographer and early Rio labor leader Luís da França e Silva, by naming its school after him. Pernambuco lacked the variety and vehemence of labor polemics in the south, although the Centro Protector dos Operários and the Federação Operária Cristã continually sniped at each other.[67]

In 1914, shortly after his arrival from Rio, José Elias da Silva helped found the Federação dos Trabalhadores de Pernambuco. But its growth was limited, and the number of anarcho-syndicalists within the federation remained very small. Pedro Alexandrino de Melo, editor of *O Lu-*

tador, the federation's official newspaper, had previously managed João Ezequiel's journal, *Aurora Social*; he also served as secretary of the local socialist party. Although the federation gained more support after World War I, despite splits and mergers, most members still favored participation in electoral politics. Residual nativist sentiment in Pernambuco could easily be directed against anarchists just as it was employed against the British-owned Great Western Railway during some of the state's biggest strikes.[68]

A full determination of the relative strength of different forms of labor organization in all Brazil's major cities over the decades remains a problem for future researchers. Even membership figures of labor organizations, which, as anarchists rightly recognized, do not necessarily denote determination or power, are most difficult to obtain. And those figures are very rarely broken down by nationality. Both labor leaders and their enemies had reasons for distorting or not reporting membership figures. Police repression only added to the loss of labor documentation, as did the lack of continuity among labor organizations.

Even in the same city, trade and union membership fluctuated greatly over the years. In 1904 São Paulo's União dos Trabalhadores Gráficos arose out of a merger between two other printers' associations. Soon it achieved, so printers a decade later claimed, a membership of 800 of the city's 1,000 graphics workers. Dissolved in 1907 after the loss of a key strike, police persecution, and competition from a "company" union, this labor association succeeded in reorganizing itself in 1912. Although it claimed 350 enlisted members by the following year, the number of dues payers dropped rapidly to twenty-five. However, a printers' mutual benefit society, created half a century earlier, continued to function. Refounded again in 1919, the União dos Trabalhadores Gráficos soon boasted a membership of over 1,000 of the city's some 4,000 printers.[69]

The years 1912 and 1913 marked the height of the pre–World War I union membership in Brazil. It is possible, and useful, to survey labor organizations at one point in one city, Rio de Janeiro. In 1913, the Second Labor Congress, dominated by anarcho-syndicalists, met in Rio, and that same year Rio's municipal government undertook a survey of several hundred voluntary and social welfare associations in the capital. Even some anarchist-oriented unions responded to the questionnaire, as did far more reformist unions and mutual benefit societies. Several newspapers also published information on unions and their membership. Although none of these sources is complete, together they provide an overview of labor organization in the nation's capital.[70]

In 1906 Rio's population totaled 811,433, of whom 554,109 were over the age of 15.[71] Rio's municipal government found more than

280,000 people enrolled in over 400 voluntary associations in 1912. Mutual benefit societies, religious brotherhoods, labor unions, professional groups, savings associations, charities, fraternal organizations, and other societies all coexisted in the capital. Although no claims of completeness can be made for this survey, it is likely that eighty percent of the viable groups are included.[72] No doubt some individuals, especially in the more prosperous sectors of society, joined more than one organization. And some associations, like the Portuguese benevolent societies, cut across class lines. As in the nineteenth century, many poor immigrants saw advantages to belonging to associations heavily subsidized by wealthy compatriots. Still, the percentage of worker-initiated mutual benefit or labor organizations surveyed is low, only ten percent. Excluding savings and funeral associations and societies organized by employers, such as the Corcovado textile factory or the Jardim Botânico tramway company, we find, based on the organizations's stated goals, only thirty workers' beneficent societies and fourteen unions with more activist aims, totaling almost 37,000 members (Table 27). In 1912 the largest labor organization, the Associação Geral de Auxilios Mutuos da Estrada de Ferro Central do Brasil, founded in 1884, enrolled 6,385 workers from the city's major railroad, and the Associação Beneficente dos Empregados da Leopoldina Railway claimed 2,165 members. Of the other workers' associations surveyed, only the seamen's Associação de Marinheiros e Remadores, the teamsters' Associação de Resistencia dos Cocheiros, Carroceiros e Classes Anexas, the motormen's Centro dos Empregados em Ferro-Vias, and the hotel and restaurant workers' Centro Cosmopólita, the only large anarchist-influenced union in Rio, had more than 2,000 members each. Most had fewer than 500 workers.

Only two labor associations enrolled women: the fifty-six-member textile workers' Sociedade Beneficente e Progressiva dos Operários em Fábricas de Tecidos, and the shop clerks' Fênix Caixeral, 1,673 strong. Each had two women members apiece. In contrast, the more numerous and often far larger religious brotherhoods generally enrolled women as well as men. Together the 31 *irmandades* and 7 *ordens terceiras* surveyed claimed over 65,000 members. The city-wide average for female enrollment in voluntary associations exceeded ten percent.[73]

No other voluntary organization in Rio even approached the size of the leading Portuguese beneficent society, the Real e Benmerita Sociedade Portuguesa de Beneficência, with its 40,384 male members. In comparison, the venerable Associação dos Empregados no Comércio do Rio de Janeiro enrolled 13,748 sales slerks and businessmen. As in the nineteenth century, the Portuguese societies, most of which also enrolled the sons of immigrants, far outnumbered those of other nationalities,

Table 27. Workers' Associations in Rio de Janeiro, 1912

Name	Founded	Number of Members			Stated Aims	Remarks
		Total	Brazilian	Foreign		
Associação Beneficente Amparo Económico dos Calafates (Beneficent Association of Economic Aid for Caulkers)	1890	1,103	464	639	Mutual aid	
Real Associação Beneficente dos Artistas Portuguesas (Royal Beneficent Association of Portuguese Artisans)	1863	422	0	422	Mutual aid	1,300 members in 1877
Associação Beneficente dos Empregados da Compagnie du Port do Rio de Janeiro (Beneficent Association of the Workers of the Compagnie du Port du Rio de Janeiro)	1911	297	193	104	Mutual aid	
Associação Beneficente dos Empregados do Jornal do Comércio (Beneficent Association of the Workers of the Jornal do Comércio)	1869	206	195	11	Mutual aid	165 members in 1877

Table 27. *(continued)*

Name	Founded	Number of Members			Stated Aims	Remarks
		Total	Brazilian	Foreign		
Associação Beneficente dos Empregados Jornaleiros da Estação Marítima (Beneficent Association of Day Laborers at the Maritime Station)	1903	293	175	118	Mutual aid	Exclusively for day laborers on the Central do Brasil Railroad
Associação Beneficente dos Empregados da Leopoldina Railway (Beneficent Association of Workers of the Leopoldina Railway	1907	2,165	—	—	Mutual aid	Did not record nationality of members
Associação Beneficente dos Empregados do Lloyd Brasileiro (Beneficent Association of Workers of Lloyd Brasileiro Lines)	1901	349	349	0	Mutual aid	
Associação Beneficente dos Operários da Imprensa Nacional (Beneficent Association of Workers of the National Press)	1905	52	52	0	Mutual aid	

Table 27. *(continued)*

Name	Founded	Number of Members			Stated Aims	Remarks
		Total	*Brazilian*	*Foreign*		
Associação dos Empregados Barbeiros e Cabeleireiros (Association of Barbers and Hairdressers)	1903	137	83	54	Mutual aid	
Associação Geral de Auxilios Mutuos da Estrada de Ferro Central do Brasil (General Mutual Aid Association of the Central do Brasil Railroad)	1884	6,385	6,385	0	Mutual aid	
Associação de Marinheiros e Remadores (Association of Seamen and Boatmen)	1904	2,563	1,945	618	Improvement of working conditions; mutual aid	
Associação Nacional dos Artistas Brasileiros Trabalho, União e Moralidade (National Association of Brazilian Artisans Work, Union, and Morality)	1855	180	180	0	Mutual aid	102 members in 1877

Table 27. *(continued)*

| Name | Founded | Number of Members | | | Stated Aims | Remarks |
		Total	Brazilian	Foreign		
Associação de Resistência dos Cocheiros, Carroceiros e Classes Anexas (Resistance Association of Teamsters, Cart Drivers and Associated Groups)	1906	2,333	625	1,708	Unity and defense; Better salaries and working conditions; mutual aid	
Associação dos Trabalhadores em Carvão Mineral (Association of Coal Workers)	1905	850	431	419	Better salaries and working conditions; mutual aid	
Associação União dos Operários do Districto Federal (Union Society of Workers in the Federal District)	1912	189	99	90	Funeral aid	
Centro dos Chauffeurs do Rio de Janeiro (Chauffeurs' Center of Rio de Janeiro)	1910	829	612	217	Aid when arrested or ill	
Centro Cosmopólita (Cosmopolitan Center)	1903	2,458	738	1,720	Mutual aid; defense	For hotel and restaurant workers
Centro dos Empregados em Ferro-vias (Streetcar Workers' Center)	1903	2,152	455	1,697	Mutual aid	For motormen and fare collectors

245

Table 27. *(continued)*

Name	Founded	Number of Members			Stated Aims	Remarks
		Total	*Brazilian*	*Foreign*		
Centro Protetor dos Fundidores e Classes Anexas (Protective Center of Foundry Workers and Associated Groups)	1912	86	86	0	Mutual aid	
Centro Internacional de Conferentes de Estiva (International Center of Cargo Checkers)	1912	56	40	19	Mutual aid	
Centro dos Operários Marmoristas (Marble Workers' Center)	1903	85	—	—	Resistance more than mutual aid	Center did not record nationality of members
Círculo dos Operários da União (Society of Federal Government Workers)	1883	750	—	—	Mutual aid	
Congregação dos Artistas Portuguesas (Society of Portuguese Artisans)	1883	316	0	316	Mutual aid	Restricted to Portuguese nationals
Grémio de Machinistas da Marinha Civil (Guild of Machinists of the Merchant Marine)	1911	307	307	0	Unity and defense; mutual aid	Restricted to Brazilians and naturalized foreigners

Table 27. *(continued)*

| Name | Founded | Number of Members | | | Stated Aims | Remarks |
		Total	Brazilian	Foreign		
Liga Federal dos Empregados em Padaria no Rio de Janeiro (Federal League of Bakery Workers in Rio de Janeiro)	1902	494	109	385	Unity and mutual aid	
Liga Operário do Distrito Federal (Workers' League of the Federal District)	1911	69	36	33	Mutual aid	
Fênix Caixeral do Rio de Janeiro (Shop Clerks' Phoenix of Rio de Janeiro)	1911	1,637	629	1,008	Improvement of working conditions; mutual aid	Two women members
Sociedade Animadora da Corporação dos Ourives (Animating Society of the Goldsmiths' Corporation)	1838	305	118	187	Mutual aid	21 members in 1877
Sociedade Auxiliadora dos Artistas Alfaiates (Aid Society of Tailors)	1876	197	19	178	Mutual aid	600 members in 1877

Table 27. *(continued)*

| Name | Founded | Number of Members | | | Stated Aims | Remarks |
		Total	Brazilian	Foreign		
Sociedade de Beneficência dos Artistas de Construcção Naval (Beneficent Society of Naval Construction Artisans)	1858	373	372	1	Mutual aid	406 members in 1877
Sociedade Beneficente dos Artistas em São Cristóvão (Beneficent Society of Artisans of São Cristóvão District)	1875	275	146	129	Mutual aid	1,020 members in 1877
Sociedade Beneficente Auxiliadora dos Artes Mecânicas e Liberaes (Aid and Beneficent Society of Mechanical and Liberal Arts)	1835	493	325	168	Mutual aid	741 members in 1877
Sociedade Beneficente dos Maquinistas da E.F. Central do Brasil (Beneficent Society of Machinists of the Central do Brasil Railroad)	1899	301	301	0	Solidarity and mutual aid	

Table 27. *(continued)*

| Name | Founded | Number of Members | | | Stated Aims | Remarks |
		Total	*Brazilian*	*Foreign*		
Sociedade Beneficente e Progressiva dos Operários em Fábricas de Tecidos (Beneficent and Progressive Society of Textile Factory Workers)	1912	56	48	8	Defense and mutual aid	Two women members
Sociedade Beneficente União dos Carteiros e Classes Anexas (Beneficent Society of Letter Carriers)	1912	287	287	0	Unity and mutual aid	
Sociedade Protetora dos Barbeiros e Cabeleireiros (Protective Society of Barbers and Hairdressers)	1869	364	50	314	Mutual aid	200 members in 1877
Sociedade de Resistência dos Trabalhadores em Trapiches e Café (Resistance Society of Coffee Warehouse Workers)	1905	1,131	—	—	Defense and mutual aid	
Sociedade União Beneficente Protetora dos Cocheiros (Beneficent Society and Protective Union of Teamsters)	1884	1,339	371	968	Mutual aid	

Table 27. *(continued)*

Name	Founded	Number of Members			Stated Aims	Remarks
		Total	Brazilian	Foreign		
Sociedade União dos Foguistas (Union Society of Stokers)	1903	2,426	1,833	593	Defense and mutual aid	
União Beneficente dos Operários das Obras Públicas (Beneficent Union of Workers on Public Projects)	1912	70	58	12	Mutual aid	
União dos Chapeleiros do Rio de Janeiro (Hatmakers' Union of Rio de Janeiro)	1910	51	21	30	Mutual aid and defense	
União Operário do Engenho de Dentro (Workers' Union of Engenho de Dentro District)	1899	205	205	0	Mutual aid and unity	
União dos Operários Estivadores (Stevedores' Union)	1903	1,942	1,269	673	Defense; improvement of working conditions; mutual aid	
União Protetora dos Catraeiros (Protective Union of Boatmen)	1912	293	293	0	Defense and mutual aid	

Source: Rio de Janeiro, *Assistencia publica e privada no Rio de Janeiro* (1922). Some additional information from Joaquim da Silva Mello Guimarães, *Instituições de previdencia fundadas no Rio de Janeiro* (1883).

scarcely able to muster several hundred members apiece.[74] Even though the nationality- and religion-based groups had declined markedly in size and importance since the nineteenth century, with the growth of civil servants', employers', and professional associations as well as labor unions, they still enrolled many more members than did labor organizations.

The most common workers' associations, the beneficent societies, demonstrated greater stability than other forms of labor organization. Of the fifteen such societies surveyed in Rio de Janeiro in 1877, nine still functioned in 1912 (Tables 11 and 27). But these were small artisans' organizations, most of which enrolled fewer members in 1912 than in 1877. Except for the railroad brotherhoods, the larger labor organizations of 1912 proclaimed more assertive goals. They embraced less skilled men, such as transportation and port workers, who lacked associations in 1877. Not until World War I would unions make substantial inroads among semiskilled textile mill hands. And, except for some employees of the Central do Brasil railroad, day laborers did not organize.

By 1912 Rio's largely black and mulatto port and maritime workers comprised one of the most unionized labor sectors in the capital. Dock work provided a large range and number of jobs, some of the best employment opportunities open to dark-skinned members of urban lower classes. Largely limited to menial labor, blacks and mulattoes generally did hard, unskilled work, serving as street porters or construction workers as well as stevedores, found employment in domestic service, worked as street vendors, or pursued odd jobs and marginal activities. A few found employment in factories, more in the army; for the lighter-skinned ones, there were jobs with the police. Although classified as reformist unions by anarchists and their sympathizers, some of the predominantly black and mulatto labor associations in Rio de Janeiro could be quite militant. Rio's police chief considered the União dos Estivadores (stevedores), Sociedade de Resistencia dos Trabalhadores em Trapiches e Café (coffee warehouse workers), Associão dos Trabalhadores em Carvão Mineral (coal workers), União dos Forguistas (stokers), and Associação de Marinheiros e Remadores (seamen) to be among the city's most violent and rebellious unions. Anarchists viewed the stevedores' union in particular as "very strongly organized," but deplored its political orientation.[75] None of these unions were affiliated with the C.O.B., and only the Sociedade de Resistência dos Trabalhadores em Trapiches e Café attended the C.O.B.'s Second Brazilian Labor Congress. Instead, these five maritime workers' unions, together with the Grêmio dos Maquinistas da Marinha Civil and several very small groups, created their own maritime federation at the time of the 1913 labor congress. Their combined membership totaled well over 9,000 men—predominantly Brazilian and heavily black—while the 1906 city census counted 6,648 maritime workers and the 1920 census 17,098.[76] In comparison, the C.O.B. may have included 5,000 workers in sixteen Rio unions in 1912, less than half that of its São Paulo city membership and less than a quarter of the Santos adherents.[77]

Little precise information is available on the nationality of union members, but available evidence indicates that the proportion of foreigners in Rio's labor organizations varied by sector, generally reflecting the ethnic make-up of that sector. Of the C.O.B. affiliates in Rio, only the shop clerks' Fênix Caixeral and the marble workers' Centro dos Operários Marmoristas replied to the 1912 municipal survey, which inquired as to members' nationalities. However, the 185-member marble workers' center, like several other unions including the coffee warehouse workers', refused to record membership by nationality. Perhaps this was one way to muffle or ease ethnic revalries and hostilities. Certainly harmony was needed in the union, which proclaimed its membership rolls open to all warehouse workers, regardless of race as well as nationality; this association had suffered from severe racial and ethnic antagonisms after foreigners entered port work, a field dominated by Brazilians of African descent since the days of slavery. Membership in the store clerks' Fênix Caixeral (1,008 foreigners and 629 Brazilians), as in the far larger and older owner-dominated Associação dos Empregados no Comércio do Rio de Janeiro (6,859 foreigners, 6,380 Brazilians, 509 unknown) reflected the makeup of Rio's commercial sector in 1906 (36,202 foreigners and 25,760 Brazilians).[78] In contrast, most railway men, like maritime workers, were Brazilian-born and their politically-oriented or mutual benefit associations reveal a largely Brazilian enrollment (Table 27). Membership in Rio's unions reflected the ethnic diversity and divisions found among the capital's skilled workers.

Even more than labor federations or labor parties, individual unions tended to be fragile and short-lived. Many existed largely on paper. Police and employer pressures destroyed unions, as did economic depression. Worker interest and commitment fluctuated. Organizations founded after a successful strike might die when a subsequent walkout failed. Rival unions within the same trade in the same city often weakened one another, as happened to Rio's stonecutters during the first decade of the twentieth century. The technological innovations which fostered unemployment also widened distinctions between workers in the same industrial sector, weakening their capacity for united action. Skilled craftsmen and workers tending machines in the same manufacture generally formed separate unions, as did São Paulo's hat makers in the early twentieth century. Even unions surviving several years often suffered from a rapid turnover in both membership and leadership. When the leaders of Rio's anarcho-syndicalist Federação Operária do Rio de Janeiro, first organized in 1905, sought to reconstruct the federation's history for presentation to the 1913 Second Brazilian Labor Congress, their only source of information was an incomplete book of minutes.[79]

Unions engaged in numerous activities which varied according to those organizations' orientation, ideology, and individual circumstances. Although all types of labor organizations favored worker education, only a few unions managed to establish schools or libraries for members and their children. Reformist unions carried out mutual assistance functions. Socialist associations often organized cooperatives also. Many groups sponsored festivities and raffles whose profit helped support them. Their May Day celebrations, which sometimes included picnics and dances in addition to bands and parades, could reinforce solidarity while providing recreation and amusement.[80]

For anarcho-syndicalists, in contrast, unions served as instruments of struggle which should also prefigure the society of the future. Rather than fill social service functions, their unions favored boycotts, public demonstrations, sabotage, and strikes. Through these means, worker syndicates would develop solidarity while taking "direct action" to gain minimum working-class rights. Anarchists sponsored libertarian schools designed to give children a modern, rational, moral education untainted by clericalism or nationalism. Rather than organize parades, they sponsored lectures on the arts and sciences, gave concerts, and presented plays illustrating the ravages of alcohol, the cruelties of capitalists, and the heroism of workers. Through such performances they could collect funds to aid sick, imprisoned, or deported workers and their families. Anarchists not only inveighed against alcohol, tobacco, gambling, and soccer, but also against dancing; however, to assure the success of their festivities, anarchists sometimes felt obliged to compromise and to include dances among their educational or propaganda activities.[81]

Of all labor activities, strikes remained the most dramatic, generating the greatest opposition from Brazil's ruling classes.[82] Although few unions carefully planned or organized strikes, they often helped channel worker discontent, voice grievances, clarify strike objectives, and negotiate with owners. The same discontent which led to the formation of a union might involve it in a strike soon afterwards. Fines, dismissals, and nonpayment of wages, and arbitrary acts by foremen precipitated strikes. Rather than seek to win improvements in wages, hours, and working conditions, let alone force changes in the economy or society, strikers often attempted simply to halt reductions in wages or to prevent poor working conditions from deteriorating further. Strikes were often badly planned and timed. Few lasted longer than several days or involved more than one trade or one or two factories.

The relative power positions and degree of organization of both workers and capitalists in a particular industry at a specific time, and, of course, government attitudes and actions, partly determined strike results. If owners in a struck industry could unite and present a common front before their workers, gain political support, or secure police aid in suppressing labor activities, they might achieve a quick victory. When workers were well-organized, possessed relatively rare skills, or confronted small businessmen themselves facing contract deadlines and payment problems, as in the construction trade, they might win some of their demands. Control of a key sector of the economy, as enjoyed by well-organized transportation or port workers, could permit those men to take effective action against their bosses. They might paralyze internal commerce or interrupt the flow of taxes and foreign exchange. A disruption of coffee export in Brazil, like interference with wheat in Argentina or nitrates in Chile, could threaten the national economy. However, threats to a strategic activity linked to the export sector were more likely to lead to government intervention and the use of force.

In northern as in southern Brazil, railroad workers with access to facilities for rapid communications staged numerous strikes. They wielded some of the most effective strike power. In 1910 alone, Bahia experienced several major railway strikes. Three times workers of the Companhia de Viação da Bahia went on strike, the last one enduring over a month: workers on the state-owned Estrada de Ferro de Nazareth struck over wages, and managed temporarily to sabotage locomotives by removing key pieces. A battery of outbreaks occurred on the British-owned Great Western Railway in Pernambuco. The federally-owned Estrada de Ferro Central in the south also experienced numerous strikes, especially during the first years of the republic.[83]

Salary reductions and worker dismissals led to the major railroad strike of the period, the 1906 paralyzation of the Companhia Paulista, involving 3,800 workers. Although the strikers received support from fellow workers on several local lines, those on the São Paulo Railway refused to join them. Therefore, traffic from Santos to the interior of São Paulo could not be cut off and the state's coffee economy disrupted. However, the threat of disruption led the governor of São Paulo to request federal aid, which arrived in the form of a cruiser and two army battalions, as well as to increase arrests and other repressive measures. Capitalists and government officials worked closely together. Antônio Prado, president of the Companhia Paulista, was also mayor of the state capital with control over the city's police force. São Paulo's Federação Operária called a solidarity strike in the state capital. But, slowly, various groups of sympathy strikers and then railroad workers returned to their jobs. Following violent clashes between police and strikers, more dismissals and arrests, and the destruction of labor newspapers and union headquarters, the employees of the Companhia Paulista returned to work, some two weeks after the strike began.[84]

Strikes by skilled workers in less essential industries might lead to specific gains, especially if the workers remained more united than their adversaries. In 1906, the same year in which São Paulo railroad workers met defeat, Rio's shoemakers succeeded in winning union recognition and wage concessions—rather, they forced shop owners to respect earlier agreements dating from a 1903 strike and stop lowering wages. Shoe production still centered in small shops rather than in large factories. To meet foreign competition and capital shortages, shop owners had attempted to reduce wages. Rather than confronting powerful industrialists with close state ties, Rio's shoemakers faced a number of small-scale producers who lacked a trade association when the strike began. These artisans, long organized into the reformist União Auxiliadora dos Artistas Sapateiros, which included some ninety percent of the city's shoemakers according to one labor newspaper, demonstrated more unity than their bosses. For over two months, the strikers stood firm, supported by a number of Rio's labor unions until, gradually, smaller proprietors broke ranks and agreed to a compromise solution, finally forcing the larger manufacturers to follow suit. Yet even this union, considered one of the most militant and violent in Rio by the city's police chief right after the strike, became virtually "inactive" less than three years later.[85]

Brazil's textile industry witnessed the greatest number of recorded strikes in the early decades of the twentieth century. But although textile workers were the most numerous, concentrated industrial workers in the nation, their walkouts proved far less likely to achieve specific results than did strikes by skilled workers long involved in union activities. Mill hands formed no part of Brazil's early labor leadership. The few small textile unions suffered a more precarious existence than did other labor associations. Not until World War I did unions make significant inroads into the nation's textile mills. The high percentage of female and child laborers in this industry made labor organization more difficult. Although mill hands frequently went on strike, their relative disunion when facing factory owners controlling large manufacturing plants placed them at a great disadvantage and their demands were rarely met. With their large capital assets and well-organized trade associations, textile factory owners could withstand long strikes. They easily secured police aid in intimidating workers and readily replaced strikers with other semi-skilled laborers. Following a strike, activists would be fired to enforce obedience. Dismissed textile workers encountered great difficulties in securing jobs in other mills, since textile manufacturers were able to institute industry-wide blacklists; nor could they easily find other employment, due to their limited occupational skills. Each strike failure led to a temporary decline in union activity.

In August 1903, following a series of brief, slightly successful walkouts, thousands of textile workers struck Rio de Janeiro's mills, precipitating Brazil's greatest pre-World War I stoppage. Operatives at the Bomfim factory briefly walked out in early June when their wages were reduced. Then workers at the huge Carioca mill struck after a foreman fired a woman who resisted his advances, but management proved willing to talk. So, the workers' commission said, the conflict ended "honorably for both sides." In their search for "justice," Brazil's textile workers continually demonstrated very respectful attitudes toward authority, never seeking to embarrass management. When the Mattoso mill dismissed women workers protesting a new payment schedule which reduced their wages, another walkout followed. In July, a broader conflict erupted at the Carioca textile factory over the arbitrary hiring of temporary workers, ending three weeks later amid labor organizations' claims of success.[86]

The precise role played by labor unions in such disputes remains unclear. Police agents blamed them for stirring up naïve workers. But no union declared the July 1903 textile mill strikes, nor the general strike of August 1903, although various labor organizations supported the walkouts. Union members and nonmembers alike participated in deliberations over the course of the strike at the Carioca mill. Both the reformist Federação de Operários das Fábricas de Tecidos, Rio's first major textile union, founded in February 1903 with help from Antônio Augusto Pinto Machado, and the Sociedade Operária do Jardim Botânico, based in the same neighborhood as the Carioca factory, lent support to the strike, just as they would the August walkout, and formed negotiating committees. Representatives of other unions attended their strike meetings. Perhaps the presence of a textile union, operatives' contacts with other trade associations, and the mill hands' "success" in several disputes increased their confidence and willingness to strike.[87]

In mid-August 1903 thousands of textile operatives struck Rio's mills, leading to Brazil's first general strike. At the time anarchists admitted that this was a spontaneous movement, which did not proceed entirely to their liking. However, a decade later, the anarcho-syndicalist Sindicato dos Trabalhadores em Fábricas de Tecidos do Rio de Janeiro claimed otherwise. Perhaps with wishful hindsight, or seeking to demonstrate strength and continuity, that union contended that the Federação dos Operários em Fábricas de Tecidos, uniting almost all Rio's textile workers along the lines of French syndicalism, launched the strike on 15 August 1903, for the eight-hour day and a forty percent wage increase.[88]

In fact, specific grievances had once again caused a work stoppage. But this time, operatives from most of Rio's mills quickly joined the strike, followed by workers in various trades. Operatives at the Aliança mill in Laranjeiras—considered one of the most "tyrannical"—walked out on 15 August, when managers refused to reinstate several dismissed workers, including, according to an anarchist newspaper, a woman fired by a factory foreman after she gave birth to his child. Commissions created to present the operatives' position to bosses, the press, and other workers requested colleagues to join the strike. At the same time, workers at the Cruzeiro factory walked out, demanding the reinstatement of operatives dismissed for protesting the broken promise of a small wage increase, and appealed for support from other workers.[89]

Although the arbitrary and sometimes brutal behavior of factory foremen and supervisors frequently led to walkouts, industrial paternalism could help prevent or limit strikes. Textile operatives frequently demonstrated unconscious attitudes of dependence, remaining more vulnerable to manipulation through paternalism than through impersonal regulation. Operatives at the huge, isolated, virtually self-contained Bangú mill did not join the August 1903 walkout. Even more striking was the attitude of those workers at the Corcovado factory who not only refused to leave their jobs but also supported their bosses. Except for shorter Saturday hours, they received no special "benefits," but their bosses listened to complaints. Early in 1903 a socialist newspaper described the mill's manager, José da Cruz, as "the only industrialist who shows workers a little consideration."[90] When this mill, like the rest, closed its doors during the strike, management provided workers with basic foodstuffs on credit. A reporter from the *Correio da Manhã* found the factory guarded not by the police, like other mils, but by workers who spent the night there. In his conversations with these operatives, the reporter found them "extremely content witth their bosses," especially José da Cruz, "who treats us like a true father."[91]

Shortly after the August 1903 walkout began, strikers broadened their demands to include the eight-hour day and a major salary increase. The attraction of the eight-hour day, first demanded by operatives from the Carioca factory meeting on 17 August at the headquarters of the Sociedade dos Operários do Jardim Botánico, no doubt helped them win support in other textile mills and from workers in various trades. Although streetcar and railway workers' unions declared their "neutrality," hat makers, tailors, stonemasons, painters, shoemakers, cabinetmakers, and stevedores struck for the eight-hour day and a wage increase. Within a week, over 20,000 workers had joined the strike. The sympathetic response to the textile operatives' "just demands" by several leading Rio newspapers, especially the *Correio da Manhã* and *O País*, provided strikers with favorable publicity, thus helping to spread and perhaps also prolong the walkout. Rather than discovering the hand of anarchists plotting violence, these journals depicted an unplanned strike by overworked, underpaid laborers.[92]

Rio's textile mill owners moved vigorously to defeat the strike. Organized into the Centro Industrial de Fiação e Tecelagem de Algodão, they maintained a united front, publicized their position, employed potent weapons such as lockouts, and secured police support. The owners closed down factories, contending that their workers faced physical threats from strikers. However, overstock and lagging demand had already led to layoffs in Rio's mills. Further reductions in output and payroll benefitted owners, not workers.[93]

With police cavalry and infantry stationed not only at textile mills but also at other factories, violence mounted. Police raided union headquarters, intimidated workers in their homes, and beat up or arrested scores of strikers. Some workers exchanged shots with the police, or strung wire across streets to impede police cavalry. Stories spread about strikers using dynamite. Trolley cars were attacked and streetlamps broken, but generally not by strikers. As in the past, continuing conflict increased the level of destruction, especially when the police employed gangs of armed toughs against strikers.[94] In this as in other labor disputes, Rio's police chief Antonio Augusto Cardoso de Castro occupied a powerful if sometimes ambiguous position. While textile mill owners praised him for guaranteeing the "right to work" and settling disputes "in a friendly fashion," many workers sought his support. Not only textile operatives but committees of striking hat makers and tailors also endeavored to convince him of their peaceful intentions and respectfully requested police arbitration. Although Cardoso de Castro refused to serve as an "intermediary," he did release some imprisoned tailors and requested hat company representatives to meet with strikers. He suggested that factory owners reopen factories. But he never ended police violence or arrests. Labor militants claimed that police agents, as well as company spies, undermined the strike.[95] In his published report on the events of 1903, Cardoso de Castro recognized the economic basis of such strikes: "Whenever capital begins to acquire great profits, labor necessarily will start demanding its share"; as long as this inevitable struggle between two forces equally worthy of respect" remained peaceful, the "state should not intervene directly."[96] But in his correspondence with his superior, the Minister of Justice, Cardoso de Castro claimed that the police had "suffocated the strike," keeping factories open and arresting strikers, without harming "even one citizen."[97]

Pressures exerted by police and millowners forced strikers back to work. As Rio's police chief suggested, the millowners' association resolved to reopen the factories. Management met with workers and made minor concessions. Although many operatives stayed away on 24 August, the next day large numbers of mill hands returned to work. At the same time as workers in several other trades finally adhered to their movement, textile operatives found themselves obliged to return to the factories or lose their livelihood. Although workers in other industries secured some benefits from the 1903 general strike, textile operatives obtained only a small increase in wages and a slight reduction in hours. With massive firings of the most militant textile workers, the Federação dos Operários em Fábricas de Tecidos soon collapsed. Only in 1908 would another attempt be made to unionize the mills, but that effort failed the following year after an unsuccessful strike. Rio's textile workers would not form a strong union until World War I.[98]

Effective labor organization proved very difficult during the first decades of the republic. Only a small proportion of the nation's urban workers ever joined any type of labor association. The relative lack of both industry in Brazil and of literacy among workers in this vast country hindered communications and organizational efforts. A crowded labor market, chronic unemployment, and government and employer hostility, along with ethnic, racial, and regional divisions among the lower classes and the barriers separating skilled and unskilled workers severely limited unionization. To the consternation of both anarchists and socialists, few lower-class laborers, Brazilian or European-born, were imbued with a sense of "worker solidarity." Brazilian workers hoping for individual advancement and immigrants seeking a successful return to Europe proved reluctant to join unions, and the unions were often themselves rent by dissension and factionalism or engaged in ideological disputes. Rather than suffering from "apathy," these workers might have been rationally and realistically evaluating the limitations of unions and the general political and economic situation in Brazil. Certainly strikes achieved few permanent gains for workers. Most of the urban poor toiled in areas difficult to organize or lacked steady jobs. They cold be dissatisfied or angry and still not form unions.

Even those sectors of the urban poor able to create organized forms of resistance had conflicting approaches to political activity. Anarchists, who rejected political struggle, remained far more independent and stead-fast than did reformist labor leaders, never seeking the safety of govern-ment patronage, with its concomittant control. However, these largely foreign-born militants underestimated the extent of government might in Brazil, and they placed too much reliance on strikes, often poorly timed and organized. More moderate and even "tame" unions under-stood the need to write minimum labor demands into law, but they could not achieve those goals. Socialists not only sought to form parties and to pressure the government into granting their minimum demands but also to integrate immigrant workers into Brazilian society. However, they met with immigrant indifference and official obstacles. The governing elites demonstrated no desire to incorporate immigrant or native-born workers into the electoral process.

In Brazil, unlike neighboring Argentina, urban workers could not find effective political allies within the nation's closed and narrow politi-cal process. Few alliances with Brazilian middle-class elements, them-selves lacking political strength, were possible. Following the failure of the *Jacobinos* and other middle-class radicals in the 1890s, no similar movement emerged in the early twentieth century seeking worker sup-port in a struggle for power with the dominant elites. Before 1930, few upper-class Brazilians saw any benefits to be derived from working-class participation in elections. Rather, the government often sought to silence the voices which labor militants helped give some urban workers. Those workers' attempts to protest their poverty through organized resistance met with increasing repression during the second decade of the twenti-eth century.

8 / The Urban Poor and the Elite: *Upheaval, Reaction, and Repression*

By the second decade of the twentieth century, Brazil's governing elite demonstrated growing concern with lower-class challenges to the existing economic and political structures. No longer did protests by the poor generally take the form of spontaneous outbursts or unplanned uprisings, as under the empire. Organized resistance and demonstrations increasingly replaced violent disturbances. Lower-class resentments often erupted in strikes rather than in riots, culminating in the general strikes of the World War I years.

In the late nineteenth century, the government had treated the urban poor primarily as sources of disorder, dangerous diseases, muscle power, and cannon fodder. Although the need for laborers and soldiers continued unabated into the twentieth century, the fear of contagion eased. The massive sanitation campaign of the first decade of the century reduced the threat of infectious diseases spreading from the slums to elite residences. Urban unrest, however, remained worrisome, even as it took new forms, such as mass demonstrations against compulsory military service or the soaring prices of basic necessities. Although the danger of "anarchism" preoccupied conservative politicians, certain members of the elite expressed concern with integrating the lower class into the existing social and political structure. For years, a few ambitious politicians had sought worker support. But in the second decade of the twentieth century, those concerned with workers' welfare secured a broader audience.

Although organized, sustained agitation, often in the form of strikes or mass demonstrations, became the dominant form of popular protest in urban Brazil, older and very different types of disturbances still broke out sporadically. But none of those traditional riots and spontaneous outbursts, which continued to erupt periodically as the twentieth century progressed, proved as frightening to the dominant elites as the antivaccination outbreak of 1904. Even after World War II, explosions of *quebra-quebras* ("break-break") marred the urban scene. As in the first decade of the century, surging masses of angry people periodically set trolley cars or buses on fire, smashed coaches on commuter trains, and looted businesses when fares were raised, taxes imposed, or other hardships and burdens seemed too great to bear. In the mid-1970s Brazil's rapidly expanding industrial centers witnessed a wave of popular protests against transportation conditions. With other means of political expression denied the urban lower classes following the military coup d'etat of 1964, they demonstrated their growing discontent with their living conditions through a series of riots directed against the suburban railways of Rio de Janeiro and São Paulo.[1] Even when strikes again became possible by the early 1980s, riots could still erupt, and masses of people sacked stores, as in São Paulo in 1983. But strikes and other organized forms of sustained agitation overshadowed such riots during the course of the twentieth century.

By the early years of the century the major cities of south-central Brazil had labor unions capable of organizing protest movements such as strikes or antiwar demonstrations. With wages falling far behind inflation during the first two decades of the twentieth century, unions grew in apparent strength and numbers, and some of the workers' demands got a sympathetic hearing. A few politicians advocated social legislation. Strikes, rather than riots, caused the greatest concern for the governing elites.

With lower-class urban discontent assuming more visible and alarming forms by World War I, the "social question" could no longer be ignored. The dominant elites sought new ways to deal with urban unrest, not just more elaborate and effective forms of repression. Two different but complementary approaches would be used: not only direct physical repression but also more subtle forms of control. The Brazilian government took a few tentative steps toward the paternalistic and protective policies elaborated after 1930, attempting to control urban discontent and channel class conflicts by guiding or forcing them into institutional forms administered by the state.

During the first decades of the twentieth century, Brazil's governing elites refined and expanded traditional means of social control. They responded to protests and manifestations of discontent principally with force, and applied that force more effectively than in the past. State armies, as well as local police, were employed in breaking major strikes, such as the 1906 Companhia Paulista railroad strike. Jorge Tibiriçá, governor of São Paulo at the time of that strike, vastly strengthened the state police force, as well as establishing a career civil police force. Between 1900 and 1920 expenditures for the São Paulo state military police far outpaced inflation. Like state forces, federal troops often guarded textile factories or railroad stations and patrolled streets during strikes and disturbances. But local police served as the major means of intimidating and harassing workers and labor militants. In Rio de Janeiro, the tie between local police and the top level of government remained especially close, since the president of the republic, not the municipal administration, appointed Rio's police chief.[2]

Police still displayed the arbitrary and violent behavior which generated unending lower-class resentment and hostility. As in past decades, they searched slum dwellings for "disorderly elements," assaulting the inhabitants, and attacked bystanders during demonstrations and disturbances. Poorly paid, trained and regarded, the police displayed very low professional standards. In the early twentieth century, as in the nineteenth century, able citizens demonstrated almost as much reluctance to join the police force as to enter army ranks. Rio's newspapers not only levied numerous charges of incompetence, corruption, and brutality against the police, but also accused them of recruiting "well-known vagabonds and disorderly characters" into the force.[3] Few credited the police with enthusiastically pursuing known criminals. The police often behaved brutally toward suspects, and subjected inmates to harsh treatment in overcrowded, unsanitary penal institutions.[4]

In the early twentieth century, the police focused more specifically on repression, reinforcing the power that employers exercised over their workers. Policemen attacked demonstrators, beat workers, broke up rallies, destroyed union headquarters, and arrested strikers. Whether involved in specific strike activities or not, known labor leaders were hauled before police officials, threatened, or imprisoned. Police chiefs like Antônio Augusto Cardoso de Castro, who played a key role in defeating the 1903 general strike in Rio de Janeiro, maintained a network of police agents to attend labor meetings, spy on workers, and sometimes serve as agents provocateurs. Police surveillance in the twentieth century far surpassed that of the late nineteenth century.[5]

Not only did the police play an even larger role in breaking strikes, but their analysis of those strikers also grew more sophisticated. Although some police officials blamed strikes on "foreign agitators," others, like Cardoso de Castro, acknowledged the economic basis of strikes. He drew a distinction between strikes by factory workers and strikes by workers in essential public services. Certainly the police in major Brazilian cities responded more rapidly and roughly to strikes by railroad workers, teamsters, gas company employees, and especially stevedores interrupting coffee exports, than to walkouts in small factories and workshops. Despite some police claims of attempts at conciliation, repression remained their major response to expressions of worker grievances.[6]

By the end of the nineteenth century the authorities demonstrated a stronger interest in crime in general, not just in breaking strikes. Numerous government reports and projects as well as newspaper accounts focused on the dangers posed by criminal elements, largely ignoring the poverty that characterized the depressed urban areas where most violent and property crimes occurred. In Rio de Janeiro, as Sam Adamo has shown, nonwhites were overrepresented in those crimes, which correlate highly with such problems as unemployment, low income, and crowding.[7] The inmates of Rio's jails tended to be young, nonwhite males who had migrated to the capital, often single people with unstable family backgrounds. As Rio's newspapers reported, criminals frequently found havens from the police in the capital's "celebrated" *favelas*.[8] The concentration of crime in poor neighborhoods contributed to the formation of stereotypes associating criminal behavior with nonwhites.

Public order offenses also preoccupied the police. In São Paulo, as Boris Fausto has demonstrated, public order offenses such as drunkenness, disorderly conduct, and vagrancy greatly predominated over crimes against persons and property during the late nineteenth and early twentieth centuries. In São Paulo, a city experiencing massive European immigration and explosive urban growth, those victimless crimes accounted for 75.5% of arrests in the period from 1892 to 1896 and 85.6% from 1912 to 1916.[9] Such a disparity, reflecting deep police preoccupation with people's public behavior, denotes efforts to control that behavior rather than to control crime. Although available data do not permit a direct, year-by-year comparison between Rio de Janeiro and São Paulo, especially since information on the total number of arrests, as opposed to convictions, in Rio is lacking during this period, São Paulo's police appear to have been more concerned with public order offenses. In Rio, public order infractions averaged forty-four percent of all the capital's criminal behavior between 1908 and 1915, declining in that period from a peak of 53% in 1908 to 32% in 1915. Furthermore, in Rio, unlike São Paulo, violent crimes far outnumbered crimes against property.[10] Only after 1920, according to available evidence, would there be a sharp decline in public order offenses in Rio, as co-optation came increasingly to supplement other methods of controlling the poor.

Expulsions of foreigners served as another major means of social control, one given new legal forms and substance during the early twentieth century in Brazil as in Argentina, Chile, Uruguay, and Cuba. With deportation laws, the Brazilian government could not only remove European "troublemakers" but also intimidate other immigrants. For years, anyone thought to be disturbing the social order or threatening elite control had been called an "anarchist." But by the late nineteenth century, government correspondence and police reports reflected fears of foreign conspiracies and of terrorists' "dynamite bombs." Such fears helped generate and justify harsh government measures. Like neighboring Argentina, though not on a systematic basis, Brazil expelled "anarchists" who tried to establish unions or "propagandize" factory workers. However, the 1890 Penal Code provided only for the deportation of foreign vagrants and *capoeiras*, and the Constitution of 1891 granted foreigners equality under the law without mention of possible expulsion. The government of Floriano Peixoto, an army officer who demonstrated little tolerance of dissent, not only expelled foreign labor organizers but also the editor of a French-language newspaper in Rio de Janeiro. Although bills to limit the rights of foreigners were introduced into Congress during the nationalistic ferment of the 1890s, no legislation was passed until the early twentieth century.[11]

Deportation laws would provide the government with a quick, legal method of dealing with undesirable foreigners, not subject to the constitutional objections raised over expulsions in the 1890s. Thus the government could rid the country of "foreign agitators" stirring up "naïve" Brazilian workers in this "new land" of opportunity. Labor unrest, politicians loudly proclaimed, was simply the work of antisocial elements intent on disrupting the nation. Rio's police chief, Alfredo Cinto Vieira de Mello, contended that "foreign anarchists" were exploiting the unions, "protected by the mildness of our laws which leave Brazilian authorities without the means to defend society from such malefactors."[12]

In 1903 the Chamber of Deputies quietly approved a deportation law, the year after Argentina's congress passed such legislation. But the bill came to a standstill in the Brazilian Senate, opposed on constitutional grounds by a group led by elder statesman Augusto Olympio Gomes de Castro, a member of the imperial parliament for two decades. However, a series of strikes in 1906 convinced Congress of the immediate need for such legislation, and the bill was reconsidered and approved. Despite continued legal objections raised by political liberals like Rui

Barbosa, that 1907 law remained in effect, with some modifications, until 1921 when Congress passed a new deportation act widening the basis for expulsion and imposing restrictions on immigration. Under the 1907 law foreigners who "endanger national security or public peace" could be expelled without lengthy court procedures. A denunciation usually sufficed.[13]

Although the number of foreigners expelled from Brazil during the first two decades of the twentieth century ranged in the hundreds, not the thousands, the perceived threat to immigrant workers was great.[14] Deportation laws served as an instrument for intimidating immigrant workers, not just as a means of expelling labor leaders. The anarchist journalist and freethinker Everardo Dias, himself once expelled from Brazil, later recalled how the deportation law remained "a constant threat to everyone, a means of intimidation and punishment, a sword suspended above the heads of the irreverent or nonconformist"; workers could "either submit to any or all injustices, accepting distressful and deleterious conditions, or be denounced as endangering public tranquility."[15]

No group fought harder for expulsion laws than did the leaders of coffee-rich São Paulo. That state had not only the highest concentration of immigrants and of foreign-born labor activists in Brazil but also some of the country's most forceful industrialists. In the 1890s the governor of São Paulo pressed the federal government to deport foreign "anarchists" arrested in São Paulo for planning to "subvert" public order or bomb buildings.[16] Arch-conservative *paulista* businessman Adolfo Afonso da Silva Gordo led the successful congressional campaign for the 1907 deportation law. Under that law, popularly called the "Adolfo Gordo Law," state governments would send their deportation requests, accompanied by a police report, to the federal ministry of justice in the expectation of quick approval. But São Paulo sought to short-circuit the law and secure the expulsion of foreign "anarchist agitators" and strike organizers even before the establishment of procedures for enforcing the law. São Paulo's minister of justice, Washington Luís Pereira de Sousa, wrote directly to the president of Brazil, Afonso Augusto Moreira Pena, asking the president to "speak with" his justice minister and rush their deportation request since "we are overrun with strikes." Like most politicians, Washington Luís denied the existence of social conditions which could cause labor unrest. In Brazil, he maintained, "workers are well paid and there is a shortage of labor as well as insufficient capital; this means that there is no reason for all these *strikes*."[17] President Afonso Pena not only informed his justice minister, Augusto Tavares de Lyra, of the "urgency" of this request but also advised him to help the *paulistas* file the necessary papers.[18] Although Tavares de Lyra had opposed "acting precipitously, especially when dealing with the first deportation case" under the still unregulated new law, he hastened to do the president's bidding.[19] In Congress the *paulistas* then campaigned to eliminate the exemptions from deportation granted foreigners with two years' continuous residence in Brazil, those married to Brazilians, or widowers with Brazilian-born children. But not until 1921 did Congress revoke the exemptions to the law.

On all levels of government, national to municipal, industrialists and government representatives cooperated to maintain "order." Not only did the federal government pass repressive legislation like the Adolfo Gordo Law and local police react harshly to strikes, but state governments also responded with force to manifestations of discontent. This was especially true of the leading industrial state of São Paulo. As Warren Dean has shown, the leadership of the Center for Spinning and Weaving Manufacturers of São Paulo established a "harmonious relationship" with the police. This employers' association not only used the police as strikebreakers but also had them jail troublemakers.[20] Although some of the old landed elite might demonstrate disdain for São Paulo's immigrant entrepreneurs and even consider them undeserving of their new wealth, both groups favored stability, order, and an obedient working class. Neither thought in terms of expanding the domestic market by raising workers' consumption of additional goods. Workers, they felt, were unproductive and unprofessional, apt to waste higher wages. Industrialists, large landowners, and merchants alike generally referred to themselves as the "conservative classes," a designation reflecting their admiration for hierarchy and the established order and their desire to keep the subordinate classes subordinate.

Other comfortably situated Brazilians expressed a new concern with workers' welfare. Without wishing to overturn the structure of Brazilian society, they sought solutions to the "social question." That phrase was widely used in Europe and Latin America to describe problems of poverty, illiteracy, illness, and discontent among the urban populace. In late nineteenth-century Europe concern with the social question prompted Leo XIII's encyclical *Rerum novarum*, Bismark's social security system, and other efforts to improve the living and working conditions of the lower classes. Brazilians followed suit, discussing, if not attempting to "solve," the social question.

Articles in glossy fashionable reviews and magazines like *Kosmos*, always quick to report trends abroad, characterized the "worker question" as "without a doubt one of the questions currently most worrisome to politicians, philosophers, publicists, and philanthropists throughout the entire world." However, the magazine's wealthy Brazilian readers

could rest assured that they bore no personal responsibility for this problem, since, as a 1904 article argued, in uncrowded New World countries like Brazil, "the proletarian problem still does not exist except in
the imagination of a few . . . known agitators who seek to extract political or personal advantages from the movements they instigate."[21]

Alarmed by the possibility of conflict between labor and capital and
fearful of anarchism and socialism, some serious writers lamented the
low salaries paid workers during a period of rising living costs, and condemned the exploitation of women and children. Disparate individuals
lacking decisive political power—a few journalists and politicians, Roman Catholic thinkers, positivists, and even monarchists—proffered their
opinions on the "worker question." And some sought solutions in social
legislation. To help "incorporate the proletariat into modern society,"
Raimundo Teixeira Mendes, a leader of the Brazilian Positivist Apostolate, advocated wage and hour regulations, pensions, and accident insurance. D. Luís of Bragança, pretender to the Brazilian throne, criticized
the republican government's neglect of the workers' well-being and proposed social welfare legislation in his 1913 manifesto setting forth the
program to be pursued by a restored empire. Like his political adversaries, this grandson of Pedro II saw the specter of anarchism as threatening
Brazil.[22] Roman Catholic thinkers such as Augusto Olympio Viveiros
de Castro also wished to secure "social peace" and avoid dangerous conflicts between labor and capital through the intervention of the state.
Thus, according to this Rio law professor, Brazil might become a harmonious society, with "neither oppressive capitalism nor a revolutionary proletariat."[23] But not until World War I would major proposals for
protective legislation be introduced into Congress.

The social question surfaced as a political issue during Brazil's first
seriously contested presidential election in 1910. Under the Old Republic (1889–1930) coalitions of political leaders from major states like São
Paulo and Minas Gerais, backed by the army, controlled national political affairs and chose the president. Rarely were those elections disputed.
National politics in Brazil remained largely a game of patronage and economic privilege, with the president of the republic dispensing the major
prizes. Elections were little more than a formality. With the vote limited to literate male citizens over the age of twenty-one, less than three
percent of the nation's population participated in presidential elections.[24]

In 1910 the narrow circle of dominant elites experienced difficulties in chosing a concensus candidate. Their succession maneuvers, especially the disputes among *mineiros* and *paulistas*, produced the official
candidacy of Marshal Hermes da Fonseca, nephew of former President
Deodoro da Fonseca and War Minister under Afonso Pena (1906–1909).

But Rui Barbosa of Bahia, backed by São Paulo's leaders fearful that "militarism" might threaten Brazil's foreign credit, disputed the presidency. A small man with an imposing head filled with encyclopedic and almost pedantic knowledge, Rui stood in strong contrast to Hermes, a hearty career officer of undistinguished intelligence. Rui, an eminent jurist and statesman who, according to Brazilian legend, had dazzled European diplomats with his erudition and multilingual eloquence at the Second Hague Peace Conference in 1907, stirred up enthusiastic crowds during the country's first major electoral campaign.

Although Rui's oratory focused on the issue of civilian versus military authority in Brazil, it included appeals to urban voters. By amending the constitution to strengthen the federal government, reforming the judiciary, revising legal codes, promoting public education, and instituting the secret ballot, Rui would weaken the rural-based state oligarchies.[25] Even though some of his followers sought to link the antimilitarist campaign to labor grievances, stressing workers' hatred of war, this staunch defender of civil liberties ignored the "social question." Marshal Hermes did not.

The Marshal's more conservative electoral platform—he called for a balanced budget and a stable currency and rejected any revision of the constitution—proclaimed that the "proletariat merits the benevolent attention" of the government. Although Hermes denied that Brazil faced the same kinds of conflicts between labor and capital as those agitating the Old World, he recognized that high food prices and low wages caused "hardships and suffering for those disfavored by fortune." However, rather than propose specific remedies for the "worker problem," he merely declared it "difficult" to solve.[26] Nor did Hermes's supporters, some of whom carried the campaign directly into Rio's suburban working-class districts, descend from pompous generalities. João Coelho Gonçalves Lisboa, an opposition politician from Paraíba, dispensed a mixture of sympathy and flattery—workers were "the primary agents of progress" in Brazil—reminiscent of republican campaigns of the 1880s in which he had participated.[27]

During his four-year presidential term, Marshal Hermes da Fonseca, well-meaning but indecisive and susceptible to flattery, accomplished little.[28] Army "salvationists," including members of Hermes's family, sought to save the nation from "oligarchical rule" by violently overthrowing several state governments. And the foreign debt mounted. The Marshal did build token worker housing, *vilas operárias*, in suburban Rio de Janeiro, a mere some two hundred units. While supporters praised this aid to "humble workers," opponents waged a congressional campaign against the exorbitant costs and corruption involved in the construction.

Hermes also granted a request tha May Day be observed in government installations.[29]

The 1912 Fourth Brazilian Labor Congress constituted the major labor initiative of the Hermes da Fonseca government. None of the Marshal's predecessors or immediate successors attempted to build up or control a labor constituency in this, or other, ways. Lieutenant Mário Hermes, the Marshal's eldest son and a federal deputy for Bahia, suggested holding the labor congress, which met in Rio's Monroe Palace, an ornate structure erected at the southern terminus of the Avenida Central for the 1906 Pan American Conference. The federal government even supplied accredited delegates with free transportation on the ships of Lloyd Brasileiro or paid their train fare. Not only did the government invite "reformist" labor associations likely to accept official leadership, and create other organizations especially for the occasion, but it also sought to undermine independent unions. In Rio de Janeiro, Mário Hermes tried to break up the Cabinetmakers' Union, the Sindicato dos Marceneiros e Artes Correlativas, affiliated with the C.O.B., and organize a new association willing to participate in his labor congress. Nevertheless, many of the delegates vehemently opposed a motion of praise and support for the Hermes government. Delegates demanded the eight-hour day, accident compensation, and obligatory primary education, as had labor militants. Although Mário Hermes conveyed all resolutions to the Chamber of Deputies, no legislation followed. Nor did anything positive result from the Confederacão Brasileira de Trabalho, the short-lived political party created by the congress with Mário Hermes as honorary president and Antônio Augusto Pinto Machado as secretary. However, despite its lack of immediate impact, the 1912 Fourth Brazilian Labor Congress suggested a future path for government-labor relations.[30]

What Marshal Hermes da Fonseca cared about most was the army. As war minister under Afonso Pena, Hermes not only sent officers to Europe for advanced training, but he also visited imperial Germany, where he was awed by the Kaiser's efficient army. Hermes sought to modernize the Brazilian army by providing better instruction, equipment, and barracks, by expanding periodic exercises and field maneuvers, and especially by instituting obligatory military service.[31] Earlier attempts at replacing forced recruitment with a draft had failed, and press gangs continued to prey upon poor Brazilians. The harsh life of a soldier, badly paid, fed, and housed, attracted no more men in the early twentieth century than it had in the nineteenth. As one reform-minded young officer complained, the major sources of volunteers were the "unemployed in the large cities," northeasterners fleeing periodic droughts, "those incompatible with civilian life, and incorrigibles of every sort ordered into the army by the police."[32] Only the most desperate remained in the disease-ridden ranks, enduring corporal punishments capriciously applied, for fifteen or more years.[33]

Like Brazil's soldiers, the nation's sailors lived hard lives. Impressment, fifteen-year terms of enlistment, and harsh punishments like the frequent use of the *chibata*, a lash studded with iron nails, characterized the far smaller navy. As the minister of the navy admitted in 1911, "police jails provided the largest source of enlistments" for the navy, and naval regulations limiting corporal punishments went largely unenforced."[34] An immense social, cultural, and racial gap—even greater than in the army—separated sailors from their white officers in this traditionally more aristocratic branch of the armed forces. The navy lacked the intimate contact between officers and troops which reduced some tensions within the army. According to one naval officer, some fifty percent of the ships' crews were black, with thirty percent mulatto, and only ten percent white or near white. He maintained that the "fear of punishment" served to control the "disagreeable-looking Negroes," who demonstrated "all the depressing signs of the most backward African tribes"; until conditions improved within the navy, the *chibata* remained "literally indispensable," for to abolish it would be "to endanger the officers' lives and open the door to indiscipline."[35] It proved far easier for the navy to acquire modern war material than to modify attitudes or behavior inherited from the days of slavery.

Late on 22 November 1910 ships' crews in Rio's harbor rebelled against bad treatment and frequent floggings. The seamen on the *Minas Gerais* and the *São Paulo*, two dreadnoughts recently purchased in England, seized control of the ships and expelled their officers, killing several in the process. While in England preparing to take possession of the new battleships, Brazilian soldiers had had the opportunity to observe the better treatment accorded English seamen. What previously were flareups in the Brazilian navy over harsh treatment would now become a rebellion against corporal punishment, a protest against the legacy of slavery, but not, however, a political insurrection envisioning changes in government. The apparently well-planned revolt was precipitated by the punishment of 250 lashes meted out to a sailor on the *Minas Gerais* in front of the entire ship's crew, as was the custom. Led by João Cândido, a black sailor from Rio Grande do Sul described as "a big man of energy and resolution" by Lord James Bryce, then visiting Rio, the seamen easily gained control of the warships in Guanabara Bay.[36] Training the battleships' powerful guns on the virtually defenseless capital, they demanded an end to the use of the *chibata*. In their neatly written but poorly spelled message to President Hermes da Fonseca, the crew of the

São Paulo insisted on the abolition of corporal punishment, as well as improved salaries, better training, and the removal of incompetent officers, firmly declaring that as "Brazilian citizens and republicans" they could "no longer bear slavery in the Brazilian navy."[37] In a telegram to the president, the crew of the other dreadnought, the *Minas Gerais*, further insisted that "the guilty ones in our rebellion are the good naval officers who make us their slaves."[38]

Although the mutineers only fired a few warning shots, this revolt deeply frightened the governing elite, as had slave revolts in the past. Fear of the lower classes, who now had guns and the capacity to use them, mingled with race prejudice. The revolt was not only a physical threat but also a blow to elite pride. The rebellious sailors were holding for ransom the recently modernized capital of the nation, and using as their weapon the newest European-built ships, which the elite had viewed as symbols of national strength.

After Congress voted an amnesty and promised to improve conditions in the navy, the sailors surrendered and allowed their officers back on board on 26 November 1910. But the government moved quickly to revoke the amnesty, which the naval officer corps had vehemently opposed, disarming the ships and preparing to discharge sailors implicated in the revolt. Then, in early December, several hundred marines stationed on the Ilha das Cobras, just off Rio's waterfront, also mutinied, thereby providing the federal government with an excuse to punish the naval insurgents. Since the marine base lacked powerful guns, it posed no real threat, and was quickly bombarded into surrender by shore artillery. The crews on the *São Paulo* and *Minas Gerais* refused to aid the rebellious marines. But the government arrested and maltreated the leaders of the previous revolt (only two out of eighteen men imprisoned in one stifling cell survived), and sent the others in chains to Acre. On that slow, suffocating voyage, more perished and others were shot. As after the 1904 antivaccination uprising, the authorities took advantage of the "Revolt of the *Chibata*" to ship troublemakers and unemployed workers to the Amazon where labor was needed for rubber gathering. Such an insurrection in the nation's recently rebuilt capital, carried out in full view of a distinguished visitor like Lord Bryce, not only frightened and humiliated Brazil's governing elites, but also threatened the nation's financial credit and reputation abroad. Rebellious or recalcitrant members of the lower classes who directly threatened elite interests received harsh and certain punishment.[39]

Just as civilian politicians, spurred by Buenos Aires's progress, sought to modernize and embellish Rio de Janeiro, so did the officer corps crave armed forces equal to Argentina's. Growing rivalry with that neighboring republic prompted not only the purchase of new warships and modern European armaments, but also the enactment of measures designed to provide the army with properly trained soldiers. Brazilian army officers privately recognized Argentine military superiority and complained about their own undisciplined troops. What most impressed Brazil's able military attaché in Buenos Aires, Lieutenant Colonel Augusto Tasso Fragosso, "and demonstrated the progress of Argentina was the *extraordinary order which reigns in everything,* whether in the bivouacs or whether on the marches and countermarches. There is no shouting, scurrying, or disorder. The troops appear well under the control of their officers, who know their job." The Argentine army proved that "forcibly recruited troops must be vastly inferior to conscripts, who temporarily leave their homes for the sole purpose of fulfilling a patriotic duty," and that Brazil needed a conscription law.[40] Like the civilian elites, Brazil's military leaders turned to European models. As General José Bernardino Bormann wrote Hermes de Fonseca from Paris, once Brazil has "an obligatory service law which improves the moral conditions of our army, we will no longer have to be envious of European armies."[41]

In 1908 Congress approved a new draft law, the centerpiece of the army reform program.[42] According to Marshal Hermes da Fonseca, this "essentially democratic" law would make the "army an eminently national institution, equalizing . . . all citizens, without distinction of class or race," called upon to "uphold the greatness of our Brazil."[43] The law provided for an obligatory service lottery of all twenty-one-year-old males. Those selected would serve two years and then enter the new army reserves.[44] However, membership in government-sponsored shooting clubs (*linhas de tiro*), voluntary participation in army maneuvers, or attendance at a school offering military training qualified a man as a reservist immediately, exempting him from active duty.[45] Thus the sons of the middle and upper classes who greeted the idea of military service with patriotic enthusiasm could avoid serving in the ranks. Without mixing with the lower classes, they could play soldier, practicing their marksmanship in the *linhas de tiro* and parading down Rio's avenues. Their skills and training surpassed those of the regular troops, whom a United States military attache found "physically unfitted for military service; only a very small portion would pass any recruiting surgeon in our service. When they shoot their rifles they shut their eyes to avoid the flash and will not aim from the shoulder for fear of recoil." In his jaundiced view, the Brazilian armed forces remained far inferior to those of Argentina or Chile.[46] Even after Brazil's first draft lottery finally took place in December 1916, the social composition of the army rank and file underwent no serious change. As the army commander in São Paulo sadly admitted, the obligatory service law proved a "fiasco." The only men reporting for duty, "with few exceptions," were "poor youths, those without luck, those lacking a tie, and the barefoot."[47]

The major reason for the long delay in instituting a draft was public opposition. Introduced into Congress in October 1906, the obligatory service law only gained final approval in January 1908. Congressional leaders like the positivist soldier-politician Major Alexandre José Barbosa Lima obstructed the bill, and orthodox positivists such as Raimundo Teixeira Mendes condemned it as fostering the militarization of Brazil. Leading newspapers such as the anti-administration *Correio da Manhã*, *O Século*, and *A Gazeta de Notícias*, edited by Rui Barbosa, attacked the measure as "warlike and a destroyer of individualism."[48]

Although the law's supporters claimed that it would strengthen the army's ties to the "people," many Brazilians thought otherwise. They knew who would pay the price for patriotic rhetoric and be forced to serve in an enlarged army. A leading popular poet from the Northeast, Leandro Gomes de Barros, mocked the draft's rapacity:

Wake up men!
These are not favorable times,
Young, old, blind, lame
Everyone now becomes a soldier,
Bishop and sexton bound together
Everyone marches to the tune of a gun.

The new draft law only added to the sufferings of the Brazilian people:

Brazilians are wrenched and twisted
More than screws,
Drought grips you in the north,
From the south come abuses,
Taxes place you in a vise
And the draft clamps it shut.[49]

Lower-class Brazilians demonstrated what President Afonso Pena described as their "repugnance" for the draft law.[50] As in the nineteenth century, angry crowds of men and women invaded government offices in different towns and destroyed registration records. Those acts, designed to damage the authorities' capacity for future recruitment and harassment, resembled lower-class resistance during the Paraguayan War, when the Brazilian government first sought to impose a national system of military registration and enlistment. No doubt poor Brazilians still suspected that a better organized system of recruitment would make them more likely to be seized for military service.[51]

Some members of the political elite feared that an uprising could occur in the capital. Feliciano Augusto de Oliveira Pena, a *mineiro* political chieftain and Afonso Pena's brother-in-law, warned the president that "odious laws" like the draft bill "incite the populace to commit the greatest excesses"; in Rio a revolution was possible. He rightly advised delay in enforcing the new law to avoid a "catastrophy."[52]

Rio now had labor unions capable of organizing protest movements. For years, socialist and anarchist groups had called for the abolition of permanent armies. Anarchist internationalists attacked the very idea of war as well as the notion of a "fatherland." According to the recently formed anarcho-syndicalist oriented C.O.B., patriotism was just a mask for oppressing the proletariat.[53] Anarcho-syndicalist labor organizers could draw on deep popular feelings in their campaign against the draft law.

Early in 1908 the Confederação Operária Brasileira founded the Liga Anti-Militarista, which distributed antiwar material, held rallies, and organized protest demonstrations. This Anti-Militarist League termed the obligatory military service law the equivalent of the "restoration of slavery in Brazil," destroying the family and national progress.[54] On 1 December 1908, the C.O.B. held its first big antiwar demonstration in Rio de Janeiro. Almost 3,000 people, so *A Voz do Trabalhador*, the confederation's newspaper claimed, marched through downtown Rio behind the red flag of the C.O.B. and the insignia of various unions. Besides C.O.B. affiliates, the maritime unions, gas company employees, and even members of the Positivist Apostolate participated. The marchers carried banners proclaiming "Peace between Peoples," "War on War," "Long Live Friendship between the Brazilian and Argentine Proletariats," "Long Live South American Brotherhood," and, in English, "Peace on Earth," as they moved toward the Largo de São Francisco, where some 5,000 people assembled for a rally.[55] The Rio demonstrations and the C.O.B.'s antimilitarist campaign evoked sympathetic responses from distant labor organizations with very different orientations. In São Luís de Maranhão, the reformist Centro Artístico Operário Maranhense, comprised of artisans favoring electoral participation, applauded the C.O.B.'s activities.[56]

With widespread opposition, both planned and unplanned, to the obligatory service law, the Brazilian government's efforts to register potential draftees proved a fiasco. The government lacked the manpower to enforce such an unpopular law. Even when open resistance ceased, passive resistance continued. Relatively few men registered with their draft boards. Not until 1916, amidst the patriotic fervor induced by World

War I, would the government begin holding draft lotteries, only to find that many of those selected failed to report for duty. Of the 7,137 men selected in the first drawing, only 3,709 presented themselves to the authorities. And, as in past years, desertion was common.[57]

Like compulsory military service, rising food prices provoked lower-class resentment and organized protests. Buffeted by the high cost of living in 1912 and 1913, workers sought salary increases. But most factory owners, fearful that recession abroad would spread to Brazil, refused to raise salaries, and some even reduced wages. In Rio de Janeiro, the anarcho-syndicalist-oriented Federação Operária reappeared and organized a series of demonstrations protesting exorbitant food prices.[58] Following the 16 March 1913 rally in the Largo de São Francisco de Paula, "over 10,000 people marched through the main streets" of downtown Rio, so the Federação Operária do Rio de Janeiro claimed. But, as the federation admitted, these protests produced no "practical" results.[59]

In mid-1913 the Brazilian economy entered into recession. The international crisis of 1913 sharply reduced prices for Brazil's leading exports, producing large trade deficits. The outbreak of World War I and the loss of coffee markets in Germany and Austria only exacerbated the balance of payments problem, since foreign investments virtually ceased while Brazil had to service its foreign debt in hard currency. As the recession spread, urban unemployment rose. Factories shortened the workweek and laid off up to half their workers, construction stagnated, and many public works projects ground to a halt. Those laborers still employed often toiled longer hours for lower wages. Within six months, according to the São Paulo state department of labor, salaries in the city of São Paulo fell some twenty percent. Fewer workers could pay union dues, many labor organizations disappeared or ceased activity, and the incidence of strikes declined sharply.[60]

During World War I, the cost of living in Brazil soared. To maintain coffee export prices and finance budget deficits, the federal government increased the money supply, feeding inflation. Food shortages drove prices higher. High world market prices stimulated agricultural exports, including basic foodstuffs such as beans and rice once imported in large quantities. Although the Allies reduced their intake of nonessentials like coffee, they purchased increasing quantities of sugar and meat as well as beans and rice (see Table 28). Since domestic production did not rise markedly, exports reduced the supply available to Brazil's urban population. At the same time, imports of wheat and dried codfish declined as their prices rose. According to a Treasury Ministry study, retail food prices in Rio de Janeiro climbed by almost fifty percent from 1914 to 1919,[61] while some key items showed sharper increases (see Table 29). The cost

Table 28. Importation and Exportation of Basic Foodstuffs, 1913–1920

Food Item	1913 (in kilos)		1915[a] (in kilos)		1916 (in kilos)		1917 (in kilos)	
	Import	Export	Import	Export	Import	Export	Import	Export
Rice	7,777,361	51,322	6,947,602	14,952	714,353	1,315,372	35,412	44,638,866
Beans	8,544,594	6,590	1,317,590	305,252	994,918	45,816,581	134,168	93,536,449
Dried codfish	49,469,328	0	33,031,779	0	23,830,675	0	20,569,448	0
Wheat	438,425,582	0	370,745,399	0	423,872,436	0	191,935,320	0
Wheat flour	170,160,288	0	128,812,132	0	118,121,133	0	109,959,519	0
Manioc flour	0	4,876,133	0	4,628,632	0	5,369,922	0	18,745,298
Chilled and frozen meat			0	8,513,970	0	33,660,930	0	66,451,967
Dried beef	14,371,413	20,554	2,053,940	2,265,080	782,076	7,121,603	1,570,931	8,728,015
Lard	432,155	25,345	85,293	3,606	81,714	3,724	27,937	10,234,701

Food Item	1918 (in kilos)		1919 (in kilos)		1920 (in kilos)	
	Import	Export	Import	Export	Import	Export
Rice	850	27,915,768	0	28,422,957	0	134,533,686
Beans	29,081	70,913,518	0	58,607,395	0	23,101,357
Dried codfish	21,762,216	0	17,876,107	0	29,538,005	0
Wheat	297,605,078	0	311,734,524	0	281,478,468	0
Wheat flour	149,439,381	0	216,333,723	0	109,379,048	0
Manioc flour	0	65,321,637	0	21,833,597	0	8,659,597
Chilled and frozen meat	0	60,508,678	0	54,094,223	0	63,599,965
Dried beef	1,339,479	4,809,316	952,224	5,556,389	4,455,821	7,889,072
Lard	15	13,269,680	0	20,028,204	0	11,165,866

Source: Brazil, Ministério da Fazenda, Diretoria de Estatística Comercial, *Comercio exterior do Brasil*, 1913–1920.
[a]No statistics are available for 1914.

Table 29.   Retail Food Prices in Rio de Janeiro, 1914 and 1919

Food Item	Price per kilo in *milreis* 1914	1919	Index 1914	1919
Rice	$747	1$060	100	129
Black beans	$380	$380[a]	100	100[a]
Dried codfish	$906	2$700	100	278
Manioc flour	$330	$420	100	127
Wheat flour	$492	$800	100	163
Fresh beef	$900	1$200	100	133
Dried beef	1$525	2$400	100	158
Bread	$600	$900	100	150
Potatoes	$316	$560	100	177
Corn	$180	$280	100	156
Lard	1$400	2$000	100	143
Oil	2$541	7$000	100	275
Coffee	1$200	2$000	100	167
Salt	$100	$200	100	200

Source: Léo de Affonseca Junior, *O custo da vida na cidade do Rio de Janeiro* (1920), p. 13.
[a] Apparently incorrect. Contemporary newspaper accounts indicate higher prices.

of housing, clothing, kerosene, and other necessities also rose steeply. Yet, as available data indicates, wages remained stationary or even fell.[62] Leandro Gomes de Barros, the most widely read popular poet in the Northeast, summarized the situation:

The War arrived,
Dried cod became tainted,
Meat ran out,
Everything got worse . . .

. . . .
Besides paying higher prices
For goods,
You get short weight;
How can anyone survive?
Only government people
Can say: I'm getting on fine.[63]

By mid-1915, Brazilian industry began to climb out of the depression. Without entering into the debate over the significance of World War I for Brazilian industrialization, we can say that production had advanced by the end of the war. Industrialists extended the workday and utilized idle capacity in the factories. But wages kept pace neither with profits nor with food prices during the war years. Lagging wage levels, food shortages caused by World War I, and the government's inflationary policy produced hardship and unrest.[64]

When wages fell far behind spiraling living costs, workers had to reduce expenses. But how? Unlike the "average" Rio family in a 1919 Treasury Ministry study, the working poor did not live in comfortable houses with electricity, drink tea, or eat fresh vegetables.[65] When forced to reduce an already low standard of living they confronted difficult choices. Some managed to cut housing costs, their single largest expense. Artur de Souza Lima, a streetcar dispatcher with five children, told a reporter for *O Correio da Manhã*, a leading Rio daily, in December 1916 that his fixed salary no longer covered his expenses, up some thirty percent in the last few years; to "economize," his family moved to a "zinc-roofed, wattle-and-daub shanty without a street number" in a *favela* on the Morro da Babilônia. An unemployed painter, Rodolpho dos Santos, living in a *casa de cômodos* in Laranjeiras described ever more crowded conditions in the old tenements; to pay the rent, two families now frequently shared the same room, divided by "flimsy curtains hung from cords," Maria Marques, a widowed laundress, lived with her three children in one room renting for 35$000 a month. She could neither reduce her housing costs nor earn higher wages to meet her rising expenses. As she told the *Correio da Manhã* correspondent, "I am a laundress, and I cannot ask my customers to give me more money for washing clothes. Before I charged 200 *reis* to wash and starch a pair of cuffs, and today no one wants to pay more than this. Yet bluing which before cost me 300 *reis* today costs 500; starch has gone from 400 to 800 *reis* a box." One expense Maria Marques would not reduce: education, so that her boys "could learn to read." And to attend public school "it is necessary that they show up clean and neat." Therefore she had to purchase cloth, which had more than doubled in price, to make clothing for them. How could she then afford her old diet of dried meat and black beans?[66] Reduced food consumption, like more congested housing, left the poor more vulnerable to disease. As the minister of justice admitted in 1918, "the high cost of living caused an increase in tuberculosis" in Rio de Janeiro.[67]

In 1917 a wave of major strikes rolled across Brazil.[68] Not only skilled workers but also groups never before effectively unionized, particularly textile operatives, participated in these walkouts. The years from 1917 to 1920 marked the most active period in the history of organized labor during the Old Republic, before that labor movement was crushed by the government.

The first and most important of this series of confrontations was the São Paulo general strike. More a protest movement against hunger than a modern industrial dispute, it erupted in the state capital early in July 1917. Beginning with a cotton textile factory conflict over wages, the strike spread through the city's service and manufacturing sectors. Moribund labor organizations sprang to life and new ones were formed in working-class neighborhoods rather than in workplaces. By the second week in July the strike encompassed more than thirty-five companies and involved over 15,000 workers. The vast dimensions of the general strike and the rapid mobilization of thousands of previously unorganized workers frightened the state government. Police violence mounted as police broke up meetings, invaded workers' homes, and arrested more strikers. Police infantry and cavalry sent into the working-class district of Brás charged a crowd in front of a textile factory, killing an anarchist shoemaker. Almost 10,000 people accompanied his coffin through the streets of São Paulo. The strikers, now some 40,000 strong, paralyzed the city for several days. Streetcars ceased to run, stores stayed shut, and factories stood empty.[69]

Although the strikers demonstrated worker consciousness and militance, this strike did not portend rebellion or revolution. The *paulista* workers' demands, presented by a hastily formed Committee of Proletarian Defense, did not even demonstrate much obvious anarcho-syndicalist influence. The workers called on the state government to free imprisoned strikers, recognize their right to unionize, and take steps to reduce rents and lower the cost of essential foodstuffs. In addition to salary increases of twenty-five to thirty-five percent, they demanded the eight-hour day, a shorter workweek, an end to child labor and night work for women, and the punctual payment of wages.[70]

The strike committee refused to negotiate directly with either the government or the industrialists. Nor did the industrialists demonstrate a willingness or ability to deal directly with the strikers. Few channels of communication existed between the workers' world and that of the industrial and commercial elites. But, through the mediation of a committee of journalists, an accord was reached and the strike ended. Most industrialists agreed to grant a twenty percent wage increase and to rehire strikers. The state government promised to free those arrested, recognize the right of assembly, and seek social legislation. However, the state government soon violated the accord and mounted an extensive campaign of reprisals against organized labor. Police raided union halls and padlocked their doors, destroyed labor newspaper offices, jailed strike leaders and labor representatives, and deported foreign-born militants. But São Paulo's workers remained restive, especially when some owners refused to grant agreed-upon wage increases.[71]

As in São Paulo, demonstrations against high food prices and textile walkouts preceded the massive 1917 strikes in Rio de Janeiro. In mid-July groups of skilled workers, beginning with cabinetmakers, struck for higher wages. Within a week over 50,000 workers left their jobs. However, unlike the *paulistas*, the Rio unions did not coordinate their walkouts and major associations refused to participate. The anarcho-syndicalist-oriented Federação Operária do Rio de Janeiro sought to generalize the strike but could not obtain aid from the larger Federação Marítima or from the Associação Gráfica do Rio de Janeiro. Textile operatives kept working until the strike was nearly over. The Rio unions negotiated separate settlements and some even sought police mediation. None received more than a ten percent wage increase, while others gained only a slight reduction in hours, if that. Meanwhile, the police carried out widespread arrests and closed down militant labor associations such as the Federação Operária do Rio de Janeiro and the Centro Cosmopólita.[72]

The 1917 São Paulo general strike reverberated more strongly in south-central Brazil than in the Northeast. Not only did strikes erupt in Rio de Janeiro and throughout the interior of that state of São Paulo, but massive strikes also paralyzed commerce and transportation in Curitíba and Pôrto Alegre. However, events in Recife were marked by meetings and manifestos, not strikes. In early August, several thousand people marched on the government palace in Salvador, where the palace guard received them with bullets. Only in Rio Grande do Sul did the state government, influenced by positivist paternalism, move quickly to meet workers' demands. In August, workers in Pôrto Alegre struck for higher wages, and the local labor federation formed a Popular Defense League to coordinate the general strike. The state government consciously avoided repeating the repressive policies followed in São Paulo, promising to limit food exports and raise salaries of state workers, as well as to intercede with the private sector.[74]

The 1917 strikes forced the "social question" into the halls of Congress. No longer could the nation's elected representatives ignore lower-class suffering and resentments. Through labor legislation, such as that proposed for years by certain socially minded congressmen, some segments of the laboring poor might be aided, pacified, and controlled.

Although several congressmen introduced social legislation, only two federal deputies persistently criticized repressive government labor policies during the second decade of the twentieth century. These two dissident politicians, Nicanor do Nascimento and Maurício Paiva de Lacerda, both secured election from the Federal District of Rio de Janeiro where an opposition press flourished and voters proved harder to control than in rural areas or other urban centers. Nicanor do Nascimento represented Rio, his birthplace, in the Chamber of Deputies from 1911 until 1921, when he was denied his seat on a flimsy pretext. Besides sponsoring maximum hours regulations and the creation of a congressional commission on social legislation, Nascimento also investigated working conditions and police violence, denouncing abuses on the floor of the legislature. Even though Nascimento never claimed to represent the working class in Congress, his general moderation, and especially his involvement with various conservative politicians and unions, infuriated anarchists and anarcho-syndicalists.[74]

Maurício de Lacerda received less personal abuse. A member of a landowning family from the old coffee-growing region of Vassouras in the state of Rio de Janeiro, Lacerda entered the Chamber of Deputies in 1912. Unlike most intellectuals of his day, he had supported Hermes da Fonseca's candidacy in 1910. But Lacerda broke with the Marshal and remained an opponent of all presidents until the end of the Old Republic in 1930, participating in the military revolts of 1922 and 1924. More vocal and flamboyant than Nascimento, this noted orator gave a record number of speeches in the Chamber of Deputies prior to his supposed defeat by a government candidate in 1921.[75] Although Lacerda claimed to speak in the name of Brazil's workers until they could elect their own representatives, he disavowed class warfare, envisioning, instead, harmony between all the divergent forces in society. He contended that the varied activities of his "embattled life" all stemmed from his "love of liberty" and "hatred of injustice."[76] His defense of the workers won the praise and lasting admiration of men such as anarchist journalist Everardo Dias, against whose deportation in 1919 Lacerda and Nascimento successfully campaigned.[77]

Another leading defender of the working class, Antônio Evaristo de Morais, pursued a different path. He fought for the workers not in Congress but in the courts. Unlike Lacerda or Nascimento, this well-known criminal lawyer and moderate socialist only obtained his law degree, the traditional passport to a political career, after practicing law for almost three decades. A mulatto from Rio's northern suburbs, Evaristo de Morais enlisted in the republican movement, following Silva Jardim, as a youth, and then served as official orator of Luís da França e Silva's Labor Party in 1890. For decades he participated in the formation of short-lived socialist parties. Evaristo de Morais published widely on criminal and legal matters, including a series of newspaper articles advocating the enactment of protective labor legislation, which was published as a book in 1905.[78] In 1910, as in 1919, he aided Rui Barbosa's campaign for the presidency. Morais served as a lawyer, and mentor, for numerous labor organizations. He was deeply involved in the 1906 Rio shoemakers' strike as well as closely tied to the capital's predominantly black and mulatto port and maritime workers. In the courts he undertook the defense of João Cândido and other leaders of the "Revolt of the *Chibata*," as well as the defense of anarchists and anarcho-syndicalists, whose ideas he opposed and who sometimes attacked him in their newspapers. Following the 1917 strikes, he fought the deportation of foreign-born militants and secured the acquittal of anarchist Edgard Leuenroth, accused of being the "psychological-intellectual author" of an assault on a food warehouse during the São Paulo general strike. Although Evaristo de Morais accepted a high post in President Getúlio Vargas's newly created Labor Ministry following the 1930 revolution, he left the ministry in 1932 and later broke with Vargas over the president's increasingly authoritarian policies.[79]

During the strike-ridden World War I years, government forces responded to the social question not only by intensifying repressive measures against independent-minded labor organizations but also by approving a few minor pieces of social legislation. In 1917 Maurício de Lacerda alone introduced bills to establish the eight-hour day, regulate working conditions for women, create child care centers in factories, institute a minimum working age of fourteen, and revoke the controversial articles in the 1890 Penal Code which had been used to stop strikes. However, only in 1919, following more strikes and government repression, would the first federal welfare legislation be enacted, a workers' compensation plan for accidental injury and death, similar to the systems proposed since 1904 by several congressmen.[80] Even this limited law remained largely unenforced. Issues of vital importance to the workers, such as the legal recognition of unions or union contracts, continued to be ignored. It proved far easier to win sympathy for injured workers, or for defenseless women and children, than for strikers supposedly stirred up by "foreign agitators." One of Maurício de Lacerda and Nicanor do Nascimento's most significant proposals, the creation of a National Labor Department to study working conditions and implement labor legislation, gained congressional approval but was not put into practice. The task of drafting a labor code incorporating proposed legislation, urged by Lacerda, fell to a congressional committee whose project died quietly in the Chamber of Deputies. Contrary to the intentions of Lacerda, a "champion of labor" who supported an autonomous, active workers' movement, a national labor code would be used in coming years to regulate labor activities, with the state considered the ultimate arbitrator of relations between labor and capital.

Even economic liberals like Rui Barbosa, running for president again in 1919, advocated social legislation. This erudite and combative seventy-year-old took up the social question during his last major political campaign. Displaying an energy beyond the capacities of many far younger men, Rui traveled across Brazil seeking electoral support. He concentrated on two issues: greater authority for the federal government and social welfare legislation for Brazil's workers. In a major campaign address on the social question delivered in Rio de Janeiro on 20 March 1919 Rui denounced past government inaction and recent congressional maneuvering crippling the 1919 workers' compensation bill; he proposed a system of labor legislation including the eight-hour day, restrictions on child labor and night work, maternity leaves, and "equal pay for equal work."[81] Years later, Evaristo de Morais recalled how he, José Agostinho dos Reis, and Caio Monteiro de Barros had talked with Rui, providing him with the detailed information needed for that address: "He was aghast at the evidence we presented concerning the hardships, distress, abuses, and exploitation workers suffered. . . , and to him the situation we described seemed unbearable. Heaven knows how very much it cost him to abandon the principles of his old economic liberalism and publicly advocate interventionist legislative measures."[82]

By stressing the plight of the workers, Rui appealed to his middle-class supporters' humanitarian sentiments. Limited labor legislation could aid such unfortunates without upsetting the social order. Some members of the amorphous urban middle sectors might even see advantages for themselves in the passage of welfare legislation whose implementation required the creation of additional middle-class jobs in the bureaucracy. Rui rejected violence and advocated class collaboration, advising workers to achieve their goals through the franchise. In essence, his solution to the social question was a paternalistic state which would arbitrate between labor and capital. Rui brought out the first significant urban vote in Brazil's history.[83] He amassed the largest vote of any opposition candidate during the Old Republic, almost thirty percent, carrying the Federal District of Rio de Janeiro as well as the states of Pará and Rio de Janeiro. Urban voters were beginning to play an independent role in Brazilian politics, but these included few workers. In the Federal District the total vote in the 1919 presidential elections amounted to less than 22,000 votes: 12,954 for Rui to 8,588 for the official candidate, Epitácio da Silva Pessoa of Paraíba, who remained at his diplomatic post in Europe while being duly elected president of Brazil.[84]

President Epitácio Pessoa continued the use of repressive measures to counter lower-class unrest, supplemented by minor concessions to "cooperative" unions. In 1919, when the greatest wave of strikes to pound the Old Republic reached its peak, federal and state government increased the level of force and physical violence employed against workers. The May 1919 general strike in São Paulo, which encompassed over 45,000 workers, resembled the 1917 movement. Strikers even made many of the same demands, since inflation had far outpaced wage gains obtained during the 1917 general strike, and the state mounted a similar campaign of reprisals. General strikes paralyzed Salvador and Recife. Rio's maritime workers, shoemakers, tailors, barbers, and other groups of skilled workers struck for the eight-hour day. In June 1919 Rio's textile operatives demanded higher wages, the eight-hour day, union recognition, and the rehiring of workers fired following their November 1918 walkout. But this costly, six-week-long strike proved no more successful than their 1918 walkout in the midst of an economic slump producing huge stockpiles in the factories. When workers on the English-owned Leopoldina Railway in Rio de Janeiro struck for higher wages and a union contract in March 1920, the government sent not only police troops but also army cavalry and infantry against the strikers, and attempted to use government employees to keep trains running. Alarmed by a spreading general strike, as Rio's construction workers, bakers, tailors, and metalworkers walked off their jobs in sympathy with the railroad men, the government practiced more acts of violence and carried out massive arrests to destroy the strikers' resistance.[85]

The Brazilian government took advantage of the heightened nationalistic feelings engendered by World War I in its repression of autonomous labor organizations. Charges that strikes were the result of foreign conspiracies increased as did efforts to divide workers along national lines. Only with firm government action against "foreign agitators" who "denied the sanctity of the Fatherland" and sought to destroy "the State, the family, and property" could the country be saved.[86] Brazil's declaration of war against Germany on 26 October 1917 served as a justification not only for continuing economic policies which hurt the urban poor but also for disbanding labor organizations promoting work stoppages. In November 1917 the federal government placed Rio de Janeiro, São Paulo, and the southern states of Paraná, Santa Catarina, and Rio Grande do Sul—with their large German populations but only a hypothetical danger of German aggression—under a state of seige and used those emergency powers to suppress labor unrest. Early in January 1921 Congress gave final approval to a new, stiffer deportation law revoking previous exemptions; any foreigner who had resided in Brazil for less than five years could be expelled should "his conduct be considered a danger to public order or national security."[87] A few days later President Epitácio Pessoa signed another major bill, intended to "regulate the repression of anarchism." It prescribed jail sentences for crimes intended to "subvert the present social order," as well as authorizing the government to close down labor unions and organizations engaging in "acts injurious to the public welfare."[88]

Unions responsive to government or employer direction might receive better treatment as long as they continued to be "cooperative" and "responsible." The government paid particular attention to workers in such strategic sectors of the export-oriented economy as transportation and shipping. When a general strike loomed in Rio in 1918, the police sought to dissuade the leaders of the city's transportation and port workers from adhering. Rio's trolley car workers received a twenty-five percent wage increase to keep them from joining the strike. Nor did the streetcars stop running during the 1920 strikes. The leaders of Rio's port and maritime workers generally maintained cordial relations with the police, keeping their unions out of general strikes, although they conducted their own walkouts. During the Leopoldina Railway strike of 1920 they sought the "good offices" of President Epitácio Pessoa to help mediate the strike, requesting the rehiring of strikers and the releasing of imprisoned workers. But late in 1921, as the great strike wave subsided, Rio's major maritime union launched another work stoppage. Although some strikers held on for several months, the strike proved a failure and the police temporarily closed the union's headquarters.[89]

Labor organizations crumbled under the government onslaught. In São Paulo and other southern cities, police not only shut down labor newspapers, destroyed union halls, and arrested and beat strikers, but also deported foreign-born militants, devastating labor leadership. Early in 1921 the government closed Rio's construction workers' union, the most powerful anarcho-syndicalist association left in the capital, as well as other autonomous labor organizations. By then Rio's anarchist-oriented Centro Cosmopólito had reverted to its original functions as a mere mutual aid society. Fewer workers were willing to pay the painful price for labor militancy and for strikes which brought increased suffering rather than even minimal gains. The 1921 May Day celebrations in Rio de Janeiro attracted less than a thousand participants, in contrast to the tens of thousands who had attended the 1919 rallies.[90]

Brazil's ruling elites reacted harshly to perceived challenges to their power and position. By the second decade of the twentieth century, they found themselves facing organized resistance, demonstrations, and strikes, rather than the unplanned uprisings and outbursts more characteristic of the empire. To preserve "order," the government not only refined and expanded traditional means of social control, but also created new legal mechanisms for intimidating workers and decimating labor leadership, such as the 1907 deportation law. In contrast, some writers and dissident politicians sought solutions to the "worker question" in social legislation. They wished to avoid dangerous conflicts between labor and capital through the intervention of the state. But the Brazilian government was slow to see how such legislation could help pacify and control segments of the laboring poor. Only when lower-class urban discontent assumed highly visible and threatening forms during the World War I years did the "social question" become a major political issue, but one settled primarily by force.

With the suppression of a fragile but independent labor movement following the 1917–1921 strike wave, Brazil's ruling elites ended any serious lower-class challenges to the existing political and economic structure for decades to come. During the 1920s few major strikes would trouble government or industry. Nor would displays of violence by less articulate or organized segments of the urban poor pose a serious threat. Although they granted minor concessions to "cooperative" and "responsible" labor associations, Brazil's governing elites remained intent upon a policy of repression toward organized labor and would pursue that policy to the end of the Old Republic in 1930. Some politicians favored conciliation, not confrontation, but the government devoted far greater energy to constructing more elaborate and effective forms of repression than to developing new ways to deal with popular discontent. Until the rise to power of Getúlio Vargas (1930–1945) the federal government largely ignored the plight of the workers. His administration would mix inducements with constraints in an attempt to control urban unrest and establish a new system of labor relations for Brazil. Such policies and measures, however, supplemented rather than eliminated the violence and repression which has marked much of Brazil's history.

Conclusion

Between 1870 and 1920 urban society in Brazil became more complex and diversified. The balance of income and population shifted more decisively from the Northeast to the south, whose rapidly expanding urban centers were swelled by waves of European immigrants as well as by internal migrants. Increasing industrialization and commercial activity, improved communications and transportation, and rising literacy in major cities facilitated the appearance of new groups, ideas, and ideologies, contributing to an intensification of political life. Although the "social question" was commonly considered just a "police issue," in the notorious Brazilian phrase of the Old Republic, more subtle means of social control slowly came to supplement the use of force. But many aspects of workers' lives remained largely unchanged.

Before as after 1920, Brazil's urban workers labored long and hard for petty returns, enduring not only miserable pay and working conditions, job insecurity, and chronic unemployment, but also congested, unsanitary housing, poor food and nourishment, and disease. In the early twentieth century, the quality of lower-class urban housing deteriorated markedly, especially in Rio de Janeiro, as new avenues, beloved by the progress-minded elite, sliced through slum neighborhoods, destroying tenements; *favelas*, which would become a symbol of Brazil's cities by the late twentieth century, experienced their first pronounced growth.

Articulate workers constantly complained of high rents and rising food costs, which stimulated popular protests ranging from the unplanned uprisings and outbreaks characteristic of the nineteenth century to twentieth-century mass demonstrations and strikes. Forced recruitment into the army proved another long-term source of popular resentment and resistance. Although this book has examined most closely events and conditions in Rio de Janeiro, then the nation's capital and largest city, enough examples have been provided to show that similar patterns existed in other major urban centers.

Despite the development of a larger urban middle sector, whose members filled positions in expanding public and private bureaucracies as well as in the professions, the social and economic distance separating rich from poor remained at least as great during the Old Republic as under the empire. The wealthy sought the outward appearance of a stable, Europeanized civilization without the so-called problems of Europe, such as class conflict, although the "progress" they promoted heightened social and economic tensions in the cities. Export-oriented political leaders like *paulista* president Manuel de Campos Sales clearly manifested disdain for the poor. They expected immigrants, often seen as mere slave substitutes, and native Brazilians alike to be docile, obedient, and hard-working. Only when contagions such as yellow fever spread from the slums to elite residences, protestors overturned streetcars and broke gas lamps along the new avenues, or strikers impeded exports and disrupted key sectors of the economy did wealthy Brazilians respond to working-class demands. And then they generally replied with force or repressive measures. Few sought peaceful solutions to the "social question."

Not only did an immense gulf separate the ruling elites from the mass of the population, but the urban poor also remained divided among themselves. They could not act as one, as the dominant elites well knew. Split along lines of race and ethnicity and separated by levels of employment and education, the urban lower classes demonstrated a diversity of attitudes, aspirations, and activities. Skilled craftsmen did not care to be confused with unskilled workers or those who hired out their labor on a casual basis. Immigrants often sought just a successful return to Europe. Labor leaders demonstrated ambivalent attitudes toward women workers, who were clustered in traditional female occupations, marginally productive and even more poorly paid and regarded than male workers. But the greatest division in the lower classes was between the wage-earning stable poor and the large mass of shifting, unskilled, illiterate, marginalized poor.

Like members of the elite, urban laborers tended to see society as divided into rich and poor rather than into working class versus capitalists. They demonstrated class feeling rather than class consciousness. When workers found themselves in a position to organize—and few did—most turned to reformist labor organizations and politicians full of vague promises rather than to militant associations.

Under the empire only select groups of skilled workers banded together for protection, their mutual benefit societies ignored by the elite since these were perceived as neither threatening nor disruptive. Protests by the poor generally took the form of unplanned uprisings and outbursts. But with the development of a tenuous labor movement in the early twentieth century, lower-class resentments tended to be expressed by strikes rather than riots, culminating in the general strikes of the World War I years. Like employers, the state then sought to regulate and control the behavior of the working poor and subjected the fragile labor movement to severe repression while continuing to employ force and violence against marginal elements of society.

Although the vast majority of the working poor remained beyond the reach of organized labor, it was that sector which most concerned Brazil's dominant elites. And it was this same minority, comprised of more articulate skilled and semi-skilled workers, which most interested those politicians willing to support certain limited labor demands. Like the government, opposition forces concentrated their attention on those workers capable of striking or voting.

The swift government response to the strikes of 1917 to 1921, which frightened politicians and employers alike, demonstrated the elite's awareness of the potential force of the urban working classes as well as the effectiveness of the use of repression. All but smothered by police violence, organized labor remained weak and on the defensive throughout the 1920s. Brazil possessed a strong, flexible elite, capable of using its power to maintain its position and keep the subordinate classes subordinate. As compared with Argentina's, Brazil's ruling classes demonstrated a far greater degree of cohesion and homogeneity. Quarrels within this small, unified elite, with its regional alliances cemented by control of a rural-based clientele, never degenerated into bloody fights which might have encouraged some politicians to seek worker support to counterbalance rivals. The vaunted Brazilian spirit of compromise did exist, but only among the elites, not between them and their "inferiors." With the suppression of an independent labor movement following the 1917–1921 strike wave, the governing elites could more easily implement a policy of co-optation, creating the framework for a system of labor relations which would continue into our own day.

By 1920 so-called enlightened industrialists had already created a set of social services to assist and regulate factory workers' lives without abandoning recourse to force and threats. The government followed suit, developing new ways to deal with urban unrest, not just more elaborate and effective forms of repression. Under Getúlio Vargas, the state became a more efficient agency of social control, appearing to bestow benefits on some urban laborers while destroying autonomous working-class organizations. The powerful Brazilian institution of patronage, which had long pervaded society, would now be employed by the state in its dealings with some groups of urban poor. For years, through paternalism and clientelism, vertical ties extending across class lines had been established, conflicts muted, and the formation of autonomous lower-class organizations inhibited. In the nineteenth and early twentieth centuries, some members of the urban poor sought alliances with individuals from the upper classes who could protect them from police persecution or from forced recruitment into the armed forces. Under the empire, some bands of *capoeiras* served as political shock troops in exchange for protection and favors. By incorporating these black and mulatto *capoeiras* into the lowest levels of the political system, politicians stifled whatever potential threat they may have posed to that system. Co-optation continued to function as an effective control mechanism.

Under Getúlio Vargas, not only did the state's role in labor matters grow, but the state also became a more efficient agency of social control, appearing to bestow benefits on some urban laborers while destroying autonomous working-class organizations. Rio's samba schools, for example, would suffer an increasing loss of autonomy as they were incorporated into the government's web of institutions and ideologies, becoming mechanisms for ensuring effective state control over large numbers of nonwhites in the capital. The paternalistic and protective policies elaborated after 1930 were designed to control urban discontent and channel class conflicts by guiding or forcing them into institutional forms administered by the state. Nevertheless, without elements within the labor movement open to collaboration with the government and willing to accept a system of state tutelage and control, Getúlio-style populism could not have succeeded. Like members of the middle classes, some labor leaders responded to the lure of bureaucratic employment.

In Brazil, unlike neighboring Argentina, urban workers could not find effective allies within the nation's generally closed and narrow political process. Few alliances with Brazilian middle-class groups, themselves lacking political strength, were available. Under the empire, dissident politicians, especially abolitionists and republicans, at times attempted to utilize lower-class discontent in their own challenges to the existing order, and in the process helped to raise political aspirations among some skilled workers. But they fled before any possibility of political upheaval or mass violence in the cities. And their interest in these urban workers declined abruptly once slavery was abolished and a republic declared. Following the failure of the *Jacobinos* and other middle-class radicals in the 1890s, no similar movement emerged in the early twentieth century seeking worker support in a struggle for power with the dominant elites. Only some disgruntled politicians attempted to stir up lower-class resentments. But by World War I a small group of social democrats, led and typified by Maurício de Lacerda and Nicanor do Nascimento, emerged to fight for the recognition of workers' rights. Brazil, however, lacked a socialist party like Argentina's to mediate between the middle classes and radical labor elements. The rebellious young military officers who took up arms against oligarchical government in the 1920s offered no clearly articulated position on the role of the working class. And the states of seige imposed from 1922 to 1927 to combat military rebellions also served to suppress workers. Until 1930 and the end of the Old Republic, the governing elites remained united in their repressive approach to labor relations, employing force tempered by occasional pieces of welfare legislation. Only under the aegis of Getúlio Vargas was a new government consensus formed, combining conciliation and co-optation with repression and control, and a system of labor relations created which has now survived for a half a century.

Through their policies, government leaders helped to widen the gap between the more skilled, organized, and articulate workers and the unskilled, precariously employed mass of the urban poor. They sought to incorporate the former, not the latter, into existing social and political structures, creating new legal distinctions between the two and increasing the distance separating them. Only the urban working poor, especially potential voters, benefitted from Vargas's system of social legislation, not the marginalized poor, always subject to extra-legal means of control. The urban laboring poor remained the focus of twentieth-century programs designed to benefit the "Brazilian people."

Various sectors of the urban poor had their own identity and participated actively in shaping their own destiny. Rather than acquiesce passively to elite decisions and activities troubling their lives, they might employ direct action to demonstrate their distress. Nineteenth-century popular protests and displays of violence sometimes achieved immediate objectives such as the end of forced recruitment into the army in a specific town or the rescinding of trolley fare increases in the capital. Instead of suffering from the apathy often attributed to them, many skilled workers who proved reluctant to join unions or who sought individual advancement may have been rationally and realistically evaluating the limitations of unions and the general political and economic situation in early twentieth-century Brazil. They had good reasons to expect the ruling elites to react violently to any perceived challenges to their power and position. But some workers still resisted the authority of both industrialists and the state, as during World War I. The independence and defiance shown by sectors of organized labor in the early 1980s, as Brazil experienced a renewal of political discourse and activity, is not surprising when compared to the pre-1920 labor movement rather than to post-1930 patterns. With a redemocratization process underway, the demands, needs, and desires of poor Brazilians received renewed attention from members of comfortably situated sectors of society. But as under the Old Republic, the "social question" still awaits an effective solution.

Notes

Preface

1. See Donald E. Worcester, *Brazil: From Colony to World Power* (New York: Charles Scribner's Sons, 1973); Rollie E. Poppino, *Brazil: The Land and the People* (New York: Oxford University Press, 1968); Richard P. Momsen, *Brazil: A Giant Stirs* (Princeton: D. Van Nostrand, 1968); Robert A. Hayes, *The Brazilian World* (St. Louis: Forum Press, 1982); and José Maria Bello, *A History of Modern Brazil, 1889–1964*), trans. James L. Taylor (Stanford: Stanford University Press, 1966). E. Bradford Burns, *A History of Brazil*, 2d ed. (New York: Columbia University Press, 1980), gives the fullest picture of Brazil's distinct social groups, although he largely ignores the urban poor.

2. Robert J. Alexander, *Labor Relations in Argentina, Brazil, and Chile* (New York: McGraw-Hill, 1962) and *Organized Labor in Latin America* (New York: Free Press, 1965). Alexander always made his anti-communism and ideological assumptions very clear. See also the other early hemispheric overviews by Moisés Poblete Troncoso and Ben G. Burnett, *The Rise of the Latin American Labor Movement* (New York: Bookman Associates, 1960), and Victor Alba, *Politics and the Labor Movement in Latin America* (Stanford: Stanford University Press, 1968).

3. Compare the essay on "Research on the Urban Working Class and Organized Labor in Argentina, Brazil, and Chile: What is Left to Be Done," *Latin American Research Review* 9 (Summer 1974), 115–42, by Kenneth Paul Erickson, Patrick V. Peppe, and Hobart A. Spalding, Jr., with the more recent

reviews by Eugene F. Sofer, "Recent Trends in Latin American Labor Histor-iography," *Latin American Research Review* 15, No. 1 (1980), 167–76, and Charles Bergquist, "What is Being Done? Some Recent Studies on the Urban Working Class and Organized Labor in Latin America," *Latin American Research Review* 16, No. 2, (1981), 203–23. Thomas E. Skidmore carefully ana-lyzes trends and developments in the field in the first section of his essay, "Workers and Soldiers: Urban Labor Movements and Elite Responses in Twentieth-Century Latin America," in Virginia Bernhard, ed., *Elites, Masses, and Mo-dernization in Latin America, 1850–1930* (Austin and London: University of Texas Press, 1979), pp. 79–126. Hobart A. Spalding, Jr., *Organized Labor in Latin America. Historical Case Studies of Urban Workers in Dependent So-cieties* (New York: Harper 1977), which incorporates primary research into its synthesis of available secondary works, provides the best analytical survey of the history of organized labor in Latin America yet published.

4. Suggestive discussions of the new labor history and the new social his-tory include: James A. Henretta, "Social History as Lived and Written," *American Historical Review* 84 (December 1979), 1293–1322; David Brody, "The Old Labor History and the New: In Search of An American Working Class," *Labor History* 20 (Winter 1979), 111–26; David Montgomery, "To Study the People: The American Working Class, *Labor History* 21 (Fall 1980), 485–512; and Robert Ozanne, "Trends in American Labor History," *Labor History* 21 (Fall 1980), 513–21.

5. The impact of E. P. Thompson, *The Making of the English Working Class* (New York: Pantheon Books, 1964), was great; he spurred a generation of scholars in the United States to seek to recreate an earlier world of working peo-ple. The work of *Annalistes* like Fernand Braudel, with his monumental trea-tise on *The Mediterranean and the Mediterranean World in the Age of Philip II*, trans. Siân Reynolds, 2 vols. (New York: Harper & Row, 1972–73), had a less direct impact in the United States.

6. Herbert G. Gutman, *Work, Culture, and Society in Industrializing America. Essays in American Working-Class and Social History* (New York: Al-fred A. Knopf, 1976). In his earlier work, Gutman pioneered the community study approach exemplified in later studies like that of Daniel J. Walkowitz on the iron molders of Troy, New York, *Worker City, Company Town: Iron and Cotton-Worker Protest in Troy and Cohoes, New York 1855–84* (Urbana: Uni-versity of Illinois Press, 1978).

7. Edward Shorter and Charles Tilly, *Strikes in France, 1830–1968* (Lon-don and New York: Cambridge University Press, 1974).

8. *Latin American Research Review* 15, No. 1 (1980), 167–82.

9. Skidmore, "Workers and Soldiers," in Bernhard, ed., *Elites, Masses, and Modernization in Latin America*.

Chapter 1

1. General works on Brazilian urban history include: Richard M. Morse, *From Community to Metropolis. A Biography of São Paulo* (Gainesville: Uni-

versity of Florida Press, 1958) and "Brazil's Urban Development: Colony and Empire," in A. J. R. Russell-Wood, ed., *From Colony to Nation: Essays on the Independence of Brazil* (Baltimore and London: Johns Hopkins); Pedro Pinchas Geiger, *Evolução de rêde urbana brasileira (Rio de Janeiro: Instituto Nacional de Estudos Pedagógicos, Ministério da Educação e Cultura, 1963); Paul Singer, Desenvolvimento econômico e evolução urbana (Análise da evolução econômica de São Paulo, Blumenau, Pôrto Alegre, Belo Horizonte e Recife* (São Paulo: Companhia Editôra Nacional, 1968); Michael L. Conniff, Melvin K. Hendrix, and Stephen Nohlgren, "Brazil," pp. 36–52 in Richard M. Morse, ed., *The Urban Development of Latin America, 1750–1920* (Stanford: Stanford University, 1971).

2. Singer, *Desenvolvimento econômico e evolução urbana*, p. 272.

3. Morse, *From Community to Metropolis*, p. 11.

4. Morse, "Brazil's Urban Development," p. 173. Illustrations and maps of both Rio de Janeiro and Salvador in the eighteenth century are found in Gilberto Ferrez, *As cidades do Salvador e Rio de Janeiro no Século XVIII* (Rio de Janeiro: Instituto Histórico e Geográfico Brasileiro, 1963).

5. For general studies of the empire see: Sérgio Buarque de Hollanda, ed., *História geral da civilização brasileira*, vols. III–VII, *O Brasil monárquico* (São Paulo: Difusão Européia do Livro, 1962–1972); Manoel de Oliveira Lima, *O Império Brasileiro (1821–1889)*, 4th ed. (São Paulo: Edições Melhoramentos, 1962); João Camillo de Oliveira Torres, *A democracia coroada. Teoria política do Império do Brasil*, 2d ed. (Petrópolis: Editôra Vozes, 1964).

6. For discussions of social and economic changes during the last decades of the empire see: Richard Graham, *Britain and the Onset of Modernization in Brazil, 1850–1914* (Cambridge: Cambridge University Press: 1968), pp. 23–50; Octávio Ianni, *Industrialização e desenvolvimento social no Brasil* (Rio de Janeiro: Editôra Civilização Brasileira, 1963), pp. 75–114; Emília Viotti da Costa, *Da senzala à colônia* (São Paulo: Difusão Européia do Livro, 1966), pp. 428–41.

7. Detailed studies of specific railroad ventures include Edmundo Siqueira, *Resumo histórico de The Leopoldina Railway Company, Limited* (Rio de Janeiro: Gráfico Editôra Carioca, 1938), and Robert H. Mattoon, Jr., "The Companhia Paulista de Estradas de Ferro, 1868–1900: A Local Railway Enterprise in São Paulo, Brazil" (unpublished Ph.D. dissertation, Yale University, 1971). Still useful older general studies include: Adolpho Augusto Pinto, *História da viação pública de S.Paulo (Brasil)* (São Paulo: Type. e Pap. de Vanorden & Cia., 1903); Clodomiro Pereira da Silva, *A evolução de transporte mundial (Enciclopédia dos transportes)*, 6 vols., V (São Paulo: Imprensa Oficial do Estado, 1940–1946); and Julian Smith Duncan, *Public and Private Operation of Railways in Brazil* (New York: Columbia University Press, 1932). See also Graham, *Britain and the Onset of Modernization in Brazil*, especially pp. 51–72.

8. Antonio Rocha Penteado, *Belém do Pará (Estudo de geografia urbana)* 2 vols. (Belém: Universidade Federal do Pará, 1968); Herbert H. Smith, *Brazil:*

298   NOTES TO CHAPTER 1

The Amazons and the Coast (New York: Charles Scribner's Sons, 1879), pp. 37–77; William Scully, *Brazil: Its Provinces and Chief Cities* (London: Murray and Co., 1866), pp. 278–79; Geiger, *Evolução do rede urbana brasileira*, pp. 407–15; Ernesto Cruz, *Belém. Aspectos eco-sociais do município* (Rio de Janeiro: José Olympio, 1945).

9. *Falla recitado na abertura de Assembléa Legislativa Provincial de Pernambuco pelo sr. Diogo Velho Cavalcanti de Albuquerque no 1° de março de 1871* (Recife: Typ. de M. Figueiroa de F. & Filhos, 1871), p. 56. See also *Fallas*, 1871–1878.

10. Geiger, *Evolução da rede urbana brasileira*, pp. 351–406; Singer, *Desenvolvimento econômico e evolução urbana*, pp. 271–357; Smith, *Brazil*, pp. 439–43; Scully, *Brazil*, pp. 200–204; James C. Fletcher and Daniel Parish Kidder, *Brazil and the Brazilians Portrayed in Historical and Descriptive Sketches*, 7th ed. (Boston: Little, Brown, & Co., 1867), pp. 513–18. For a history of the drought of 1877–1880 see Rodolpho Theophilo, *História da sêcca do Ceará, 1877–1880* (Rio de Janeiro: Imprensa Ingleza, 1922) and Roger L. Cunniff, "The Great Drought: Northeast Brazil, 1877–1888" (unpublished Ph.D. dissertation, University of Texas, 1971). An invaluable firsthand account is furnished by the United States naturalist Herbert H. Smith, *Brazil*, pp. 398–435. See also Bainbridge Cowell, Jr., "Cityward Migration in the Nineteenth Century: The Case of Recife, Brazil," *Journal of Interamerican Studies and World Affairs* 17 (February 1975), 43–63.

11. Milton Santos, *O centro da cidade de Salvador* (Salvador: Universidade da Bahia, 1959); Geiger, *Evolução da rede urbana brasileira*, pp. 322–50; Smith, *Brazil*, pp. 448–50; Scully, *Brazil*, pp. 346–52; Fletcher and Kidder, *Brazil and the Brazilians*, pp. 474–78; Charles Hastings Dent, *A Year in Brazil* (London: Kegan, Paul, Trench, and Co., 1886), pp. 242–43. Affonso Ruy, *História política e administrativa da cidade de Salvador* (Salvador: Tip. Beneditina, 1949).

12. Singer, *Desenvolvimento econômico e evolução urbana*, pp. 141–91; Geiger, Evolução de rêde urbana brasileira, pp. 284–321; Francisco Riopardense de Macedo, *Pôrto Alegre, origem e crescimento* (Pôrto Alegre: Liv. Sulina, 1968); Oscar Canstatt, *Brasil. Terra e gente (1871)*, trans. Eduardo de Lima Castro (Rio de Janeiro: Conquista, 1975) pp. 273–78.

13. Among the numerous works on São Paulo are: Morse, *From Community to Metropolis*; Ernani Silva Bruno, *História e tradições da cidade de São Paulo*, 3 vols., 2d ed. (Rio de Janeiro: José Olympio, 1954); Afonso d'Escragnolle Taunay, *Historia da cidade de São Paulo* (São Paulo: Edições Melhoramentos, 1953); Gilberto Leite de Barros, *A cidade e o planalto. Processo de dominancia da cidade de São Paulo* (São Paulo: Edições Melhoramentos, 1953); Arnoldo de Azevedo, ed., *A cidade de São Paulo. Estudos de geografia urbana*, 4 vols. (São Paulo: Companhia Editôra Nacional, 1958); Maria Luiza Marcílio, *La ville de São Paulo. Peuplement et population, 1750–1850* (Rouen: Université de Rouen 1968); Paulo Cursino de Moura, *São Paulo do Outrora (Evocações de metrópole)* (São Paulo: Companhia Editôra Nacional, 1941); Caio

Prado Júnior, "Contribuição para a geografia urbana da cidade de São Paulo," pp. 97–146 in *Evolução política do Brazil e outros estudos*, 4th ed. (São Paulo, 1963).

14. Among the numerous works on Rio de Janeiro are: Associação dos Geógrafos Brasileiros (Secção do Rio de Janeiro), *Aspectos da geografia carioca* (Rio de Janeiro: Conselho Nacional de Geografia, 1962); Alberto Ribeiro Lamego, *O homem e a Guanabara* (Rio de Janeiro: Conselho Nacional de Georgrafia, 1948); Adolfo Morales de los Rios Filho, *O Rio de Janeiro Imperial* (Rio de Janeiro: Editôra A Noite, 1946); Francisco Agenor Noronha Santos, *Meios de transporte no Rio de Janeiro*, 2 vols. (Rio de Janeiro: Typ. do Jornal do Commércio, 1934); Gastão Cruls, *Aparência do Rio de Janeiro*, 2 vols. (Rio de Janeiro: José Olympio, 1956); and Nelson Costa, *O Rio através dos séculos. A história da cidade e seu IV centenário* (Rio de Janeiro: Edições O Cruzeiro, 1965).

15. A detailed discussion of the increasing commerce from Minas Gerais and the growing political projection of the *mineiro* landowners in the first half of the nineteenth century is found in Alcir Lenharo, *As tropas da Moderação (O abastecimento da Corte na formação política do Brasil. 1808–1842)* (São Paulo: Edições Símbolo, 1979). See also Maria Yedda Leite Linhares, *História do abastecimento. Uma problemática em questão (1530–1918)* (Brasília: BINAGRI Edições, 1979). Some traders from São Paulo, such as Antônio da Silva Prado, the future Barão de Iguape, also furnished cattle to the Rio market in the early nineteenth century, as shown by Maria Thereza Schorer Petrone, *O Barão de Iguape. Um empresário da época da independência* (São Paulo: Companhia Editôra Nacional, 1976).

16. See Joseph Earl Sweigart, "Financing and Marketing Export Agriculture. The Coffee Factors of Rio de Janeiro, 1850–1888" (Unpublished Ph.D. dissertation, University of Texas at Austin, 1980), and Stanley J. Stein, *Vassouras: A Brazilian Coffee County, 1850–1900* (Cambridge, Mass.: Harvard University Press, 1957).

17. Christopher Columbus Andrews, *Brazil: Its Condition and Prospects* (New York: D. Appleton and Company, 1887), p. 22; Smith, *Brazil*, pp. 453, 457.

18. Fletcher and Kidder, *Brazil and the Brazilians*, pp. 30–31.

19. Andrews, *Brazil*, pp. 28–29.

20. Fletcher and Kidder, *Brazil and the Brazilians*, pp. 22–36; Andrews, *Brazil*, pp. 22–23; Smith, *Brazil*, pp. 450–60; Scully, *Brazil*, pp. 151–57; William Hadfield, *Brazil and the River Plate in 1868. Showing the Progress of Those Countries Since His Former Visit in 1853* (London: Bates, Hendy and Co., 1869), pp. 31–37; Frank Vincent, *Around and About South America. Twenty Months of Quest and Query*, 5th ed. (New York: D. Appleton and Company, 1895), pp. 215, 225.

21. Lamego, *O homem e a Guanabara*, pp. 322–23; Morales de los Rios, *O Rio de Janeiro Imperial*, pp. 83–95; Hadfield, *Brazil and the River Plate in 1868*, pp. 34–37; Geiger, *Evolução da rêde urbana brasileira*, p. 151; Antonio Martins de Azevedo Pimentel, *Subsidios para o estudo de hygiene do Rio de*

Janeiro (Rio de Janeiro: Typ. e Lith. de Carlos Gaspar da Silva, 1890), pp. 76–77, 226–36; Ferreira da Rosa, *Rio de Janeiro. Notícia histórica e descritiva da Capital do Brasil* (Rio de Janeiro: Typ. do Annuario do Brasil, 1924), p. 7; Alfred Agache, *Cidade do Rio de Janeiro. Extensão, remodelação, embellezamento* (Paris: Foyer Bresilien, 1930), pp. 64–65. See also Charles J. Dunlop, *Subsídios para a história do Rio de Janeiro* (Rio de Janeiro: Editôra Rio Antigo, 1957).

22. Brazil, Directoria Geral de Estatistica, *Recenseamento do Brazil realizado em 1 de setembro de 1920* (Rio de Janeiro: Typ. da Estatistica, 1922–1930, II, 3ª parte, vii).

23. See maps reproduced in *Album cartográfico do Rio de Janeiro (séculos XVIII e XIX)*, organized and with a text by Lygia da Fonseca Fernandes da Cunha (Rio de Janeiro: Biblioteca Nacional, 1971). See also: Geiger, *Evolução da rede urbana brasileira*, pp. 142–89; Morales de los Rios, *O Rio de Janeiro Imperial*, pp. 17–23; Doxiadis Associates, *Guanabara: A Plan for Urban Development* (Athens: K. Papadimitropulos, [1966]), pp. 23–25.

24. For a concise discussion of urbanization in U.S. history, stressing the importance of the means of transportation in governing the shape of the city, see Richard C. Wade, "Urbanization," pp. 187–205 in C. Vann Woodward, ed., *The Comparative Approach to American History* (New York and London: Basic Books, Inc., 1968).

25. Petition of Residents of the Streets of Gamboa, Livramento, Harmonia, and Other Nearby Streets to Câmara Municipal, Rio de Janeiro, 6 February 1884, Arquivo Geral da Cidade do Rio de Janeiro (hereafter AGCRJ), 43-2-95.

26. Fletcher and Kidder, *Brazil and the Brazilians*, p. 27.

27. Andrews, *Brazil*, p. 26; Smith, *Brazil*, pp. 459–60.

28. João Chagas, *De bond. Alguns aspectos da civilização brasileira* (Lisbon: Parceira A. M. Pereira, 1897), p. 156.

29. Andrews, *Brazil*, pp. 30, 32.

30. See Graham, *Britain and the Onset of Modernization in Brazil*.

31. Scully, *Brazil*, p. 11.

32. Smith, *Brazil*, pp. 467, 501.

33. Joseph Earl Sweigart, "Financing and Marketing Export Agriculture. The Coffee Factors of Rio de Janeiro, 1850–1888" (unpublished Ph.D. dissertation, University of Texas at Austin, 1980).

34. Brazil, Directoria Geral de Estatistica, *Recenseamento da população do Império do Brazil a que se procedeu no dia 1° de agosto de 1872* (Rio de Janeiro: Typ. Leuzinger, 1873–1876), XIX (Quadros gerais), 1–2, 61.

35. The problem of defining and treating historically the middle class, especially the lower middle class, extends well beyond the boundaries of Brazilian studies. For a stimulating discussion of the relative lack of scholarly attention accorded this complex and changeable sector of society and its role in European history, see Arno J. Mayer, "The Lower Middle Class as Historical Problem," *Journal of Modern History* 47 (September 1975), 409–36.

Although far less studied than the Brazilian elite, or even urban labor, the urban middle classes have been viewed as major historical opponents of regional oligarchies and elite policies by such writers as Nelson Werneck Sodré, *Formação histórica do Brasil* (São Paulo: Editôra Brasiliense, 1964), Virgínio Santa Rosa, *Que foi o tenentismo* (Rio de Janeiro: Civilização Brasileira, 1964), and Hélio Jaguaribe, *Desenvolvimento econômico e político* (Rio de Janeiro: Paz e Terra, 1969). Actual historical studies are rare; they include Décio Saes, *Classe média e política na Primeira República Brasileira (1889–1930)* (Petrópolis: Vozes, 1975); Nícia Villela Luz, "O papel das classes médias no movimento republicano," *Revista de História* No. 57 (January-March, 1964), 13–27, who argues that the middle class lacked political strength as well as social and ideological cohesion at the time of the fall of the empire in 1889; and Michael M. Hall's case study of one group of middle-class reformers, "Reformadores de classe média no Império Brasileiro: A *Sociedade Central de Imigração*," *Revista de História* 53, No. 105 (1976), 147–71. Even sociological analyses of the contemporary middle classes, such as J. A. Guilhon Albuquerque, ed., *Classes médias e política no Brasil* (Rio de Janeiro: Paz e Terra, 1977), are not common. The question of social mobility in the midtwentieth century has been studied by Bertram Hutchinson, *Mobilidade e trabalho. Um estudo na cidade de São Paulo* (Rio de Janeiro: Ministério da Educação e Cultura, Centro Brasileiro de Pesquisas Educacionais, 1960).

Information concerning certain sectors of the middle classes in nineteenth-century Brazil is greater than for others. Available evidence indicates that members of liberal professions such as law and medicine, sometimes termed the upper middle classes, were frequently the sons or impoverished relatives of large landowners. Through access to higher education, which remained extremely limited in Brazil, they achieved secure, prestigious positions in society.

Army officers comprised another major sector of the urban middle classes. During the late empire, as demonstrated by John Henry Schulz, "The Brazilian Army and Politics, 1850–1894" (unpublished Ph.D. dissertation, Princeton University, 1973), the average army officer came from a family of small landholders. But such "men of middle-class origins" (p. 4) often received the assistance of well-placed relatives or friends in preparing for their careers. As Schulz correctly states, the urban poor had virtually no chance of becoming army officers, but, like their contemporaries, he still refers to many officers as poor men, and says that "many poor men became army officers." (p. 60).

Various officers and civilians of the period contended that students at the army academy were poor, ambitious boys who had chosen a military career in order to obtain a free education. The positivist leader Raymundo Teixeira Mendes, in his biography of his fellow positivist and republican, Lieutenant Colonel Benjamin Constant Botelho de Magalhães, a popular instructor at the Military School during the last years of the Empire, (*Benjamin Constant. Esbôço de uma apreciação sintetica da vida e da obra do fundador da república braziliera* [Rio de Janeiro: Imprensa Nacional, 1936]), stressed the fact that the Military School was an accessible avenue of education for poor boys. Vicente Licínio Cardoso, one of Benjamin's pupils, described the Military School as a haven for "poor boys," unlike the navy ("Benjamin Constant," in *A margem da história da re-*

pública (Ideas, crenças, e affirmações) [Rio de Janeiro: Edição do Annuario do Brasil, 1924], p. 296). According to a civilian observer of the period, Felisbello Firmo de Oliveira Freire, the army officer corps included many "poor boys" of middle-class origins, and often of mixed races, who attended the Military School less from love of a military career than from a desire to distinguish and improve themselves (*História constitucional da República dos Estados Unidos do Brasil* [Rio de Janeiro: Typ. Moreira Maximino, Chagas & C., 1894], II, 219–20). However, entrance to the Military School remained limited to those with personal connections or preparatory education.

Evidently the gulf between middle-class groups such as army officers and the real urban poor was so great that the officers and their friends did not even think about those below them when evaluating their own status and financial position. Within the army itself, an immense social, educational, economic, and even racial gap separated the commissioned officers from the common soldiers, drawn from the lower classes and forced to serve in the poorly paid and treated ranks. Like other members of the middle classes, officers measured themselves in relation to the elite, not the poor.

But even if members of the working poor could rarely attain secure middle-class positions as army officers, could they achieve lower-middle-class status? How much class slippage, as well as social ascension, occurred? What were the principal channels of mobility? We lack studies of the composition, inner life, and boundaries of the middle classes. Our current information is too defective to allow us to say much, but it is clear that education served as a pathway to social mobility for certain exceptional men. Through endless study, Manoel Querino (1851–1923), a poor Bahian black who made notable contributions to Afro-Brazilian studies in the early twentieth century, progressed from painter to minor public functionary; but he remained in a low-level position since he lacked powerful supporters (Antonio Vianna, "Manoel Querino," *Revista do Instituto Geográfico e Histórico da Bahia* 54, Part II [1928], 305–16; Manoel Querino, *As artes na Bahia (Escorço de uma contribuição histórica [Bahia: Typ. do Lyceu de Artes e Ofícios, 1909], pp.* 95–96; Preface by Arthur Ramos in Manoel Querino, *Costumes africanos no Brasil* [Rio de Janeiro: Editôra Civilização Brasileira, 1938], pp. 9–12). Luck and diligence might permit a street vendor to acquire a fixed place of business or a petty shopkeeper to become a property owner and businessman, like the crude, ambitious, none-too-honest Portuguese store owner in Aluísio Azevedo's novel, *O cortiço* (São Paulo: Livraria Martins, 1965), first published in 1890.

36. Smith, *Brazil*, p. 463.

37. Historical occupational classifications such as that undertaken for Argentina by Mark D. Szuchman and Eugene F. Sofer, "The State of Occupational Stratification Studies in Argentina: A Classificatory Scheme," *Latin American Research Review* 11, No. 1 (1976), 159–71, are lacking for Brazil. However, attempts at historical surveys of social classes have been made, notably by João Camillo de Oliveira Torres, *Estratificação social no Brasil. Suas origens históricas e suas relações com a organização política do país* (São Paulo:

Difusão Européia do Livro, 1965), who focuses on political organization and activities of the upper classes. A brief, general description of social structure during the monarchy is found in Leoncio Basbaum, *História sincera de República*, I, *Das origens até 1889*, 2d ed. (São Paulo: Edições LB, 1962), pp. 200–227. In *A República Velha (Instituições e classes sociais)* (São Paulo: Difusão Européia do Livro, 1970), pp. 145–245, Edgard Carone discusses social classes and class actions at the end of the empire through the Old Republic, although he hardly touches on the lower middle class. The accounts of perceptive foreigners, such as Smith, *Brazil*, are most useful in understanding occupational and social distinctions. The variety of such marginals as beggars, thieves, and swindlers is described in Alexandre José de Mello Filho, *Factos e memorias* (Rio de Janeiro and Paris: H. Garnier, 1903), pp. 1–93; and Paulo Barreto (pseud. João do Rio), *A alma encantadora da ruas* (Rio de Janeiro and Paris: H. Garnier, 1908), pp. 35–44; 193–210. For an investigation into perceived relative status and prestige of occupations in Brazil in the midtwentieth century, see Bertram Hutchins, "The Social Grading of Occupations in Brazil," *British Journal of Sociology* 8 (June 1957), 176–89.

   38. Smith, *Brazil*, p. 464.

   39. Brazil, *Recenseamento da população . . . 1872*, XIX (Quadros Gerais), 1; XXI (Município Neutro), 61; XIX (São Paulo), 427–29; III (Bahia), 508–10; XIII (Pernambuco), 214–15; X (Pará), 211–12; XVII (São Pedro do Rio Grande do Sul), 205–6.

   40. Thomas Ewbank, *Life in Brazil; or, a Journal of a Visit to the Land of the Cocoa and the Palm* (New York: Harper and Brothers, 1856), pp. 74–75, 92–94, 113–15; Robert Walsh, *Notices of Brazil in 1828 and 1829* (London: A. H. Davis, 1830), I, 137–38, 391–92, 501–2; II, 18–19; Daniel P. Kidder, *Sketches of Residence and Travel in Brazil* (Philadelphia: Sorin & Ball, 1848), I, 125–26; Maria Dundas Graham (Lady Maria Calcott), *Journal of a Voyage to Brazil and Residence There During Part of the Years 1821, 1822, 1823* (Rpt. New York: Praeger, 1969); Antonio Corrêa de Sousa Costa, *Qual a alimentação de que usa a classe pobre do Rio de Janeiro e sua influencia sobre a mesma classe* (Rio de Janeiro: Typ. Perseverança, 1865), p. 30; Mary Karash, "From Porterage to Proprietorship: African Occupations in Rio de Janeiro, 1808–1850," pp. 369–93 in Stanley L. Engerman and Eugene D. Genovese, eds., *Race and Slavery in the Western Hemisphere: Quantitative Studies* (Princeton, N.J.: Princeton University Press, 1975).

   41. Brazil, *Recenseamento da população . . . 1872*, XXI (Município Neutro), 61; XIX (São Paulo), 429.

   42. Smith, *Brazil*, pp. 465, 486–87; Andrews, *Brazil*, pp. 36–37.

   43. Cf. Stanley J. Stein, *The Brazilian Cotton Manufacture: Textile Enterprise in an Underdeveloped Area, 1850–1950* (Cambridge, Mass.: Harvard University Press, 1957), especially pp. 20–21, 191.

   44. Brazil, *Recenseamento da população . . . 1872*, XXI (Município Neutro), 61; Brazil, Directoria Geral de Estatistica, *Recenseamento do Rio de Janeiro (Districto Federal) realizada em 20 de setembro de 1906* (Rio de Janeiro:

Officina da Estatistica, 1907), I, 104; Brazil, *Recenseamento do Brazil . . . 1920*, IV, 5ª parte, Tomo I, 24–27.

45. Andrews, *Brazil*, pp. 32–33; Gilberto Amado, *História da minha infancia* (Rio de Janeiro: José Olympio, 1954), p. 40; Chagas, *De bond*, pp. 89–90; Smith, *Brazil*, p. 50.

46. Andrews, *Brazil*, pp. 39–40; Amado, *História da minha infancia* p. 40; Corrêa de Sousa Costa, *Qual a alimentação*, p. 32; *Revista Typographica* (Rio de Janeiro), 26 May 1888, p. 5; Chagas, *De bond*, p. 156; Kidder, *Sketches of Residence and Travel in Brazil*, I, 161–62.

47. Corrêa de Sousa Costa, *Qual a alimentação*, p. 31.

Scholarly works on English lower-class housing include Enid Gauldie, *Cruel Habitations: A History of Working-Class Housing, 1780–1918* (New York: Harper and Row, 1974), and S. D. Chapman, ed., *The History of Working-Class Housing: A Symposium* (London: Newton Abbot, 1971). Among the best-known contemporary accounts of conditions in tenements in New York City at the turn of the twentieth century are those by Jacob A. Riis, especially *The Battle with the Slum* (New York: The Macmillan Company, 1902) and *How the Other Half Lives: Studies Among the Tenements of New York* (New York: Charles Scriber's Sons, 1917). In *Buenos Aires: Plaza to Suburb, 1870–1910* (New York: Oxford University Press, 1974), James R. Scobie deals with the *conventillos* of Buenos Aires.

48. José Francisco de Paula e Silva to Municipal Council of Rio de Janeiro, Rio de Janeiro, 1 August 1855, AGCRJ, 44-2-7.

49. Brazil, Ministério da Justiça, *Relatório*, 1877, p. 258.

50. Joaquim Polycarpo Lopes de Sousa to João d'Almeida Pereira Filho, Rio de Janeiro, 13 March 1860, AGCRJ, 41-3-36.

51. Andrews, *Brazil*, p. 38.

52. "Parecer da Commissão de Privilegiados sobre a proposição relativa a construcção de casas demoninadas 'Evoneas,' " Rio de Janeiro, 1880, AGCRJ, 40-4-45.

53. Brazil, Ministério da Justiça, *Relatório*, 1866, Report of the Chief of Police, p. 7; 1870, p. 29; 1875, p. 214; 1877, p. 258; 1878, pp. 59–60.

54. Brazil, Ministério da Justiça, *Relatório*, 1867, p. 69; 1895, p. 214; "Estatistica Municipal. Recenseamento das habitações collectivas. Setembro 1895" (Glória), AGCRJ, 44-2-11; Brazil, Directoria Geral de Estatistica, *Recenseamento geral da Republica dos Estados Unidos do Brazil em 31 de dezembro de 1890. Districto Federal (Cidade do Rio de Janeiro) Capital da Republica dos Estados Unidos do Brazil* (Rio de Janeiro: Typ. Leuzinger, 1895), xii–xiii; *O Nacional* (Rio de Janeiro), 27 July 1895, p. 3.

55. São Paulo [city], *Relatorio apresentado à Câmara Municipal*, July 1894, pp. 65, 70–72; "Relatório apresentado à Câmara Municipal de São Paulo pelo Intendente Municipal Cesario Ramalho da Silva," 1893, Arquivo do Estado de São Paulo, Livros No. 972.

56. Andrews, *Brazil*, pp. 38–39.

57. This novel, first published in 1890, proved very popular, going through

several editions in a few years. A recent edition was published by Livraria Martins of São Paulo in 1968. For an English-language edition see *A Brazilian Tenement*, trans. Harry W. Brown (New York: R. M. McBride, 1926).

58. Paulo Barreto, *A alma encantadore das ruas*, pp. 184–91; Antonio Martins de Azevedo Pimental, *Subsidios para o estudo de hygiene do Rio de Janeiro* (Rio de Janeiro: Typ. e Lith. Carlos Gaspar da Silva, 1890), p. 189.

59. Corrêa de Sousa Costa, *Qual a alimentação*, pp. 30–31.

60. *Gazeta dos operarios*, (Rio de Janeiro), 20 December 1875, p. 1; 21 December 1875, p. 1; *Revista Typographica*, 31 March 1882, p. 2; Azevedo Pimentel, *Subsidios para o estudo de hygiene*, p. 189; Corrêa de Sousa Costa, *Qual a alimentação*, p. 31; Américo de Castro to D. Pedro II, Rio de Janeiro, 18 December 1884, AGCRJ, 40-4-45; *Gazeta da Tarde* (Rio de Janeiro), 21 February 1884, p. 21.

61. Minutes of 22 November 1885 session of Conselho do Estado, Arquivo Nacional, Codice 277 (I am indebted to John H. Hann who kindly called my attention to this document); Corrêa de Sousa Costa, *Qual alimentação*, pp. 33–42; John Mawe, *Travels in the Interior of Brazil, Particularly in the Gold and Diamond Districts of that Country* (Philadelphia: M. Carey, 1816), pp. 160, 203–5; Antonio Martins de Azevedo Pimentel, *Quaes os melhoramentos hygienicos que devem ser introduzidos no Rio de Janeiro para tornar esta cidade mais saudavel* (Rio de Janeiro: Typ. e. Lith. de Moreira Maximino & Co., 1884), pp. 128–37; Azevedo Pimentel, *Subsidios para o estudo de hygiene*, pp. 191, 237–46; *Gazeta dos Operarios*, 15 Dec. 1875, p. 1; Louis Agassiz and Elizabeth C. Agassiz, *A Journey in Brazil* (Boston: Ticknor and Fields, 1868), p. 73; Harold B. Johnson, "A Preliminary Inquiry into Money, Prices, and Wages in Rio de Janeiro, 1763–1823," pp. 248–50 in Dauril Alden, ed., *Colonial Roots of Modern Brazil* (Berkeley and Los Angeles: Univeristy of California Press, 1973); *Collecção dos trabalhos do Conselho Geral de Salubridade Pública da Provincia de Pernambuco, 1849*, quoted on pp. 235–36 in E. Bradford Burns, ed., *A Documentary History of Brazil* (New York: Alfred A. Knopf, 1966). For meat production and supply problems and concessions in Rio see Aureliano Restier Gonçalves, "Carnes verdes em São Sebastião do Rio de Janeiro, 1500–1900," *Arquivo do Distrito Federal. Revista de documentos para a história da cidade do Rio de Janeiro* (Rio de Janeiro: Prefeitura do Districto Federal, 1952), III, 281–358.

Histories of diet are rare, as are attempts to set the food habits of people in a wider historical context. Some readings in this area are found in Elborg Forster and Robert Forster, eds., *European Diet from Pre-Industrial to Modern Times* (New York: Harper and Row, 1975).

62. Smith, *Brazil*, pp. 486–87; 500–501.

63. Minutes of 22 November 1855 session of Conselho do Estado, Arquivo Nacional, Codice 277; Eulália Maria Lahmeyer Lobo, Octávio Canavarros, Zakia Feres Elias, Sonia Gonçalves, and Lucena Barbosa Madureira, "Evolução dos preços e do padrão de vida no Rio de Janeiro, 1820–1930— resultados preliminares," *Revista Brasileira de Economia* 25 (October-December 1971), 241, 247–48, 251, 257; Eulália Maria Lahmeyer Lobo, Octávio Canavarros,

Zakia Feres Elias, Simone Novais, and Lucena Barbosa Madureira, "Estudo das categorias socioprofissionais, dos salários e do custo da alimentação no Rio de Janeiro de 1820 à 1930," *Revista Brasileira de Economia* 27 (October-December 1973), 153–56, 169; and Eulália Maria Lahmeyer Lobo et al., "Evolution des prix e du cout de la vie a Rio de Janeiro (1820–1930), in Colloques Internationaux du C.N.R.S., *L'histoire quantitative du Brésil de 1800 à 1930*, pp. 206–7; Johnson "A Preliminary Inquiry into Money, Prices and Wages in Rio de Janeiro, 1763–1823," in Alden, ed., *Colonial Roots of Modern Brazil*, pp. 248–50; Kátia de Queirós Mattoso, "Os preços na Bahia de 1750 à 1930," in Colloques Internationaux du C.N.R.S., *L'historie quantitative du Brésil de 1800 à 1930*, pp. 171, 182; Smith, *Brazil*, p. 487; Stein *The Brazilian Cotton Manufacture*, pp. 50–65.

64. Brazil, Ministério da Justiça, *Relatório*, 1875, p. 214; Azevedo Pimentel, *Quaes os melhoramentos hygienicos*, pp. 67, 84–94, and *Subsidios para o estudo de hygiene*, p. 319; Corrêa de Sousa Costa, *Qual a alimentação*, pp. 41–42; Joaquim da Silva Mello Guimarães, *Instituições de previdencia fundadas no Rio de Janeiro* (Rio de Janeiro: Typographia Nacional, 1883), pp. 193–94; Kátia de Queirós Mattoso and Johildo de Athayde, "Epidemias e flutuações de preços na Bahia no século XIX," in Colloques Internationaux du C.N.R.S., *L'histoire quantitative du Brésil de 1800 à 1930*, pp. 185–87.

65. Raphael Archanjo Galvão Filho, *Abastecimento d'agua a cidade do Rio de Janeiro* (Rio de Janeiro: Typ. Laemmert, 1873), pp. 12–13, 40–41, 78–70; Azevedo Pimentel, *Subsidios para o estado de hygiene*, pp. 179, 264, 270, 275; São Paulo [province], *Relatorio apresentado á assemblea legislativa provincial de São Paulo pelo presidente de provincia exm. sr. dr. Sebasião José Pereira, 2 de Fevereiro de 1876* (São Paulo: Typ. do 'Diario,' 1876), p. 11; Corrêa de Sousa Costa, *Qual a alimentação*, p. 42.

66. *Revista Typographica*, 12 March 1888, p. 14; 12 May 1888, p. 13; Smith, *Brazil*, pp. 39–41; 454–55; *Andrews, Brazil*, pp. 39–41; Francisco Rangel Pestana (pseud. Thomas Jefferson), *Notas republicanas. I. A reacção e os novos partidos. II. A politica do marechal Floriano Peixoto* (Rio de Janeiro: n.p., 1898), p. 127; Corrêa de Sousa Costa, *Qual a alimentação*, pp. 35–36; Azevedo Pimentel, *Quaes os melhoramentos hygienicos*, pp. 132–37; *Kosmos* (Rio de Janeiro), October 1905 (unpaged).

67. Smith, *Brazil*, p. 454.

68. Corrêa de Sousa Costa, *Qual a alimentação*, p. 32; Azevedo Pimental, *Subsidios para o estudo de hygiene*, p. 302.

Chapter 2

1. For the political reprocussions of this clientelism in rural areas, see the classic analyses of Victor Nunes Leal, *Coronelismo, enxada e voto. O município e o regime representativo no Brasil (Da colônia à primeira República)* (Rio de Janeiro and São Paulo: Forense, 1948), and Maria Isaura Pereira de

Queiroz, *O mandonismo local na vida política brasileira* (São Paulo: Instituto de Estudos Brasileiros, 1969).

2. Numerous works have been written describing the political system of the Brazilian empire, ranging from the Marxist, such as Leoncio Basbaum, *História sincera da República*, II, *Das origens até 1889*, 2d ed. (São Paulo: Edições LB, 1962), to the monarchist, such as João Camillo de Oliveira Torres, *A democracia coroada. Teoria política do Império do Brasil*, 2d ed. (Petrópolis: Editôra Vozes, 1964). Like an older work, José Maria dos Santos, *A política geral do Brasil* (São Paulo: J. Magalhães, 1930), Oliveira Torres pictures the monarchy as a democracy, preferable to its republican successor. Newer studies concentrating on particular aspects of imperial politics, particularly the elite, include: Thomas Flory, "Judicial Politics in Nineteenth-Century Brazil," *Hispanic American Historical Review* 55 (November 1975), 664–92; Eul Soo Pang and Ron L. Seckinger, "The Mandarins of Imperial Brazil," *Comparative Studies in Society and History* 14 (March 1972), 215–44; and Roderick and Jean Barman, "The Role of the Law Graduate in the Political Elite of Imperial Brazil," *Journal of Interamerican Studies and World Affairs* 18 (November 1976), 423–50, part of their extensive and quantitative project on imperial politics utilizing the papers of leading statesmen of the empire. Also of interest are: Joseph L. Love, "Political Participation in Brazil, 1881–1969," *Luso-Brazilian Review* 7 (December 1970), 3–24, an analytical overview of political participation in Brazil; and Raymundo Faoro, *Os donos do poder. Formação do patronato político brasileiro* (Pôrto Alegre: Editôra Globo, 1958).

3. Writings on Pedro II range from the antagonistic to the eulogistic, with the latter continuing to outnumber critical accounts of him, both as man and as emperor. Among the lauditory biographies, old and new are: Mary Wilhelmine Williams, *Dom Pedro the Magnanimous: Second Emperor of Brazil* (Chapel Hill: University of North Carolina Press, 1937), a synthesis of imperial panegyrics; and the extensive study by Pedro Calmon, *História de D. Pedro II*, 4 vols. (Rio de Janeiro: José Olympio, 1975). In sharp contrast stand the writings of some of D. Pedro's republican antagonists, such as Anfriso Fialho, *História da fundação da República* (Rio de Janeiro: Typ. Laemmert & C., 1891), pp. 17–22, 33–35. Few take a more balanced approach, as did another republican, Cristiano Benedito Ottoni, in his essay *D. Pedro de Alcântara* (Rio de Janeiro: Typ. Jornal do Commercio, 1893), written shortly after the emperor's death, or Heitor Lyra, in his multivolume highly favorable biography, *História de Dom Pedro II*, 3 vols. (São Paulo: Companhia Editôra Nacional, 1940).

4. D. G. Nogueira Santos, Portuguese Minister to Brazil to Henrique de Barros Gomes, Foreign Minister, Petrópolis, 15 November 1887, Legação de Portugal no Rio de Janeiro, Arquivo do Ministério dos Negocios Estrangeiros (Lisbon), Cx. 222.

5. This brief discussion of elite composition is based on Barman and Barman, "The Role of the Law Graduate in the Political Elite of Imperial Brazil."

6. Alberto Salles, "Catecismo Republicano," in Luís Washington Vita,

Alberto Sales. Ideólogo da República (São Paulo: Companhia Editôra Nacional, 1965), p. 193.

7. Alberto Salles, *A patria paulista* (Campinas: Typ. Gazeta de Campinas, 1887), pp. 148–49, 184. See also Vita, *Alberto Sales.*

8. Studies of different aspects of the republican movement in Brazil include: George C. A. Boehrer, *Da monarquia à república. História do Partido Republicano do Brasil (1870–1889),* trans. Bernice Xavier (Rio de Janeiro: Ministério da Educação e Cultura, 1954); José Maria dos Santos, *Os republicanos paulistas e a abolição* (São Paulo: Livraria Martins, 1942) and *Bernardino de Campos e o Partido Republicano Paulista. Subsídios para a história da República* (Rio de Janeiro: José Olympio, 1960); Marc Jay Hoffnagel, "O movimento republicano em Pernambuco, 1870–1889," *Revista do Instituto Arquelógico, Histórico e Geográfico Pernambucano* 49 (January 1977), 31–60.

9. The two major studies of the abolition of slavery in Brazil are Robert Conrad, *The Destruction of Brazilian Slavery, 1850–1888* (Berkeley and Los Angeles: University of California Press, 1972) and Robert Brent Toplin, *The Abolition of Slavery in Brazil* (New York: Atheneum, 1971). Unlike Richard Graham, in his earlier, perceptive essay, "Causes for the Abolition of Negro Slavery in Brazil: An Interpretive Essay," (*Hispanic American Historical Review* 46 [May 1966], 123–37), Conrad argues that until 1886 *Paulista* coffee planters were strong defenders, not opponents, of slavery. Emília Viotti da Costa's thorough and provocative study of slavery, the coffee economy, and abolition, *Da senzala à colônia* (São Paulo: Difusão Européia do Livro, 1966), deals extensively with São Paulo. The final years of slavery and abolition in the Northeast are analyzed by Peter L. Eisenberg, "Abolishing Slavery: The Process on Pernambuco's Sugar Plantations," *Hispanic American Historical Review* 52 (November 1972), 580–97, and J. H. Galloway, "The Last Years of Slavery on the Sugar Plantations of Northeastern Brazil," *Hispanic American Historical Review* 51 (November 1971), 586–605. For the abolition movement in the city of Rio de Janeiro, see Rebecca Baird Bergstresser, "The Movement for the Abolition of Slavery in Rio de Janeiro, Brazil, 1880–1889" (unpublished Ph.D. dissertation, Stanford University, 1973); for the Campos region of the province of Rio de Janeiro see Cleveland Donald, Jr., "Slave Resistance and Abolitionism in Brazil: The Campista Case, 1879–1888," *Luso–Brazilian Review* 13 (Winter 1976), 182–93. Also of value is the older account by Evaristo de Moraes, *A campanha abolicionista (1879–1888)* (Rio de Janeiro: Freitas Bastos, 1924). Carolina Nabuco has written a biography of her father, the celebrated abolitionist and patrician planter from Pernambuco, *The Life of Joaquim Nabuco,* trans. Ronald Hilton (Stanford: Stanford University Press, 1950).

10. Brazil, Directoria Geral de Estatistica, *Recenseamento da população do Imperio do Brazil a que se procedue no dia 1° de agosto de 1872* (Rio de Janeiro: Typ. Leuzinger, 1873–1876), XIX (Quadros gerais), 1; Perdigão Malheiro, *A escravidão no Brasil,* 3rd ed. (Petrópolis: Editôra Vozes, 1976), II, 150–51. While the 1819 estimate is based on fairly reliable church data, the 1864 figures are only rough estimates. Even the later government figures present problems, for

numbers of slaves could be exaggerated or undercounted depending on particular political and economic circumstances.

The relative importance of the interregional slave trade in supplying the labor needs of the expanding coffee economy is open to debate. Herbert S. Klein questions the degree to which this traffic ever reached high levels, especially after 1870, and suggests that needed fieldhands were supplied by declining areas within the south-central provinces, in "The Internal Slave Trade in Nineteenth-Century Brazil: A Study of Slave Importations into Rio de Janeiro in 1852," *Hispanic American Historical Review* 51 (November 1971), 580–83.

11. Brazil, Ministério da Agricultura, *Relatório*, 14 May 1888, p. 24; Brazil, Directoria Geral de Estatistica, *Recenseamento do Brazil realizado em 1 de setembro de 1920* (Rio de Janeiro: Typ. da Estatistica, 1922–1930), IV, ix.

12. Baron of Cotegipe to Rodrigues Alves, Rio de Janeiro, 12 December 1887, Rodrigues Alves Papers (Rio de Janeiro).

13. See Thomas H. Holloway, *Immigrants on the Land: Coffee and Society in São Paulo, 1886–1934* (Chapel Hill: University of North Carolina Press, 1980), and Michael M. Hall, "The Origins of Mass Immigration in Brazil, 1871–1914" (unpublished Ph.D. dissertation, Columbia University, 1969).

14. Viotti da Costa, *Da senzala à colônia*, pp. 65–123; Eisenberg, "Abolishing Slavery: The Process on Pernambuco's Sugar Plantations"; Holloway, *Immigrants on the Land*; Hall, "The Origins of Mass Immigration in Brazil"; Robert Conrad, "The Planter Class and the Debate over Chinese Immigration to Brazil, 1850–1893," *International Migration Review* 9 (Spring 1975), 41–55; Conrad, *The Destruction of Brazilian Slavery*, pp. 30–40; Toplin, *The Abolition of Slavery in Brazil*, pp. 145–74.

15. Sérgio Buarque de Holanda, "As colônias de parceria," in Holanda, ed., *História geral da civilização brasileira* (São Paulo: Difusão Européia do Livro, 1960–1978), V, 245–60.

16. A valuable general study of immigration and urbanization in Brazil is Manuel Diéges Júnior, *Imigração, urbanização e industrialização (Estudos sôbre alguns aspectos da contribuição cultural do imigrante no Brasil)* (Rio de Janeiro: Centro Brasileiro de Pesquisas Educacionaes, Instituto Nacional de Estudos Pedagógicos, Ministério da Educação e Cultura, 1964). Also useful as brief introductions are Octavio Alexandre Moraes, "Immigration into Brazil: A Statistical Statement and Related Aspects," pp. 49–73 in Margaret Bates, ed., *The Migration of Peoples to Latin America* (Washington, D.C.: Catholic University of America Press, 1957); and José Fernando Carneiro, *Imigração e colonização no Brasil* (Rio de Janeiro: Universidade do Brasil, 1950).

17. The standard account of Italian immigration is Robert F. Forester, *The Italian Emigration of Our Times* (Cambridge, Mass.: Harvard University Press, 1924). See also José Arthur Rios, *Aspectos políticos da assimilação do italiano no Brasil* (São Paulo: Fundação Escola de Sociologia e Política de São Paulo, 1959).

18. Michael M. Hall, "Immigration and the Early São Paulo Working Class," *Jahrbuch für Geschichte von Staat, Wirtschaft und Gesellschaft Latein-*

310   NOTES TO CHAPTER 2

amerikas 12 (1975), 400. Cf. Douglas H. Graham and Sérgio Buarque de Hollanda Filho, *Migration, Regional and Urban Growth, and Development in Brazil. A Selective Analysis of the Historical Record, 1872–1970* (São Paulo: Instituto de Pesquisas Econômicas, Universidade de São Paulo, 1971), pp. 35–36.

19. According to São Paulo state reports, many immigrants stayed in the city rather than entering agriculture, and this included many who had declared themselves to be agriculturalists. For example, the 1894 statistical report stated that 74,478 immigrants entered the state in 1893 through the port of Santos, with 59,429 subsidized by the state, 13,253 subsidized by the federal government, and 2,296 entering on their own account. Of these, 41,150 gave agriculture as their profession, while 4,971 were artisans and 28,857 declared no profession. Not only did most of those in the latter two categories remain in the cities, but of the 41,150 who declared themselves farm workers, only 37,327 actually entered agriculture (São Paulo [State], Repartição de Estatistica e Arquivo, *Relatório*, 1894, p. 121). Similarly, statistics for 1895 indicate that of the 104,124 immigrants who passed through the state-run hostel for immigrants that year, 68,040 went to the *fazendas* while 36,084 stayed in the cities (São Paulo, Repartição de Estatistica, *Relatório*, 1895, p. 73).

20. Cf. Holloway, *Immigrants on the Land*, and Hall, "Immigration and the Early São Paulo Working Class."

21. For the imperial government's laws and landholding policies, see Warren Dean, "Latifundia and Land Policy in Nineteenth-Century Brazil," *Hispanic American Historical Review* 51 (November 1971), 606–25.

22. São Paulo (state), Repartição de Estatistica e Arquivo, *Relatório apresentado ao presidente do Estado de São Paulo Cesario Motta Junior pelo director da Repartição da Estatistica e Arquivo Antonio de Toledo Piza em 31 de julho de 1894* (Rio de Janeiro: Typ. Leuzinger, 1894), unpaged; Argentina, Censo, Comisión Directiva, *Segundo censo de la República Argentina. Mayo 10 de 1895*, 3 vols. (Buenos Aires: Taller Tipográfico de la Penitenciaría Nacional, 1898), II, 17; United States, Department of the Interior, Census Office, *Report on the Population of the United States at the Eleventh Census: 1890*, 15 vols. in 25 (Washington, D.C.: Government Printing Office, 1892–97), I, Part I, pp. lxvii, 672.

23. The problems relating to the use of immigration statistics of the period are numerous. Data are sometimes fragmentary or unreliable. Moreover, the Brazilian government generally and rather arbitrarily defined immigrants as all those and only those arriving in third class.

The problems of evaluating Portuguese emigration are complicated by the fact that Portuguese officials only recorded authorized emigrants, and many Portuguese emigrated illegally through Spain. Although the exact numbers of such clandestine emigrants are unknown, they must have comprised a sizeable proportion of the so-called Spanish emigrants to Brazil, arriving with Spanish passports, as some Portuguese had lamented for years (see, for example, Augusto de Carvalho, *Questões internacionaes*. [Oporto: Typ. Central, 1875]; p. 32).

Taking the years 1891 and 1892, for example, we can note that the Portuguese government recorded 29,630 emigrants destined for Brazil in 1891 (far behind, in second place, was "North America," basically the United States, with only 1,929, followed by West Africa with 1,524, despite years of government efforts to direct emigration toward the Portuguese territories in Africa); and 15,102 emigrants for Brazil in 1892 (compared with 825 for West Africa, in second place, and only twelve for "North America") (Portugal, Ministério da Fazenda, *Annuario estatistico de Portugal, 1892,* [Lisbon: Imprensa Nacional, 1899, pp. 26–27). The Brazilian government's statistics for those years recorded 32,349 Portuguese immigrants in 1891, and 17,797 in 1892. In addition, 22,146 "Spanish" immigrants were recorded as having arrived in 1891, and 10,471 in 1892. For the period 1884–1893 a total of 510,533 Italian, 170,621 Portuguese, and 103,116 Spanish emigrants are recorded; for 1894–1903, 537,784 Italians, 157,542 Portuguese, and 102,142 Spanish; for 1904–1913, 196,521 Italians, 384,672 Portuguese, and 224, 672 Spanish (*Revista de Imigração e Colonização* 1 [October, 1940], 617–26).

The overwhelming preference of Portuguese emigrants for Brazil continued until the mid-twentieth century. In 1956, 19,931 Portuguese officially emigrated to Brazil, followed, in second place, by just 4,321 to Venezuela, and 4,158 to the United States, with France in fourth place with 3,102 (José Fernando Nunes Barata, *Estudos sobre a economia do Ultramar* [Lisbon: Companhia Nacional Editôra, 1963], p. 29).

24. *União Lusitana* (Rio de Janeiro), 16 July 1892, p. 1.

25. Portugal, *Ministério das Obras Públicas, Comércio e Indústria, Movimento da População. Estado Civil. Emigração. Estatistica Especial. Anno 1887* (Lisbon: Imprensa Nacional, 1890), i, xiv.

26. C. de Sampayo Garrido, *Emigração portuguesa. Relatório consular* (Rio de Janeiro: Typ. Júlio Costa & C., 1920), p. 25.

27. João Chagas, *De bond. Alguns aspectos da civilização brazileira* (Lisbon: Livraria Moderna, 1897), p. 128.

28. Maurício Lamberg, *O Brazil,* trans. Luiz de Castro (Rio de Janeiro: Typ. Nunes, 1896), pp. 84, 99.

29. Manuel Duarte Moreira de Azevedo, *Pequeno panorama ou descripção dos principaes efidicios da cidade do Rio de Janeiro* (Rio de Janeiro: Typ. do Apostolo, 1867), p. 62.

> Que a carne secca está cara,
> Que a pobreza se amofina
> Não brada a imprensa, só diz
> A gaz virou lamparina!

30. Published studies of popular uprisings in Brazil have concentrated on rural movements and especially on their social deviant and millenarian aspects. See, for example, Maria Isaura Pereira de Queiroz, "Messiahs in Brazil," *Past and Present* 31 (July 1965), 62–86, and *O messianismo no Brasil e no mundo* (São Paulo: Dominus, 1965). Studies of particular "messianic" move-

ments include: Maurício Vinhas de Querioz, *Messianismo e conflito social no Brasil (A guerra sertaneja do Contestado, 1912–1916)* (Rio de Janeiro: Editôra Civilização Brasileira, 1966), on the Contestado; Leopoldo Petry, *O episódio do Ferrabraz (Os Muckers). Documentos para o estudo da história dos "muckers" do Ferrabraz* (São Leopoldo, Rio Grando do Sul: Ed. Rotermund, 1957), and Ambrosio Schupp, *Os Muckers. Episódio histórico extrahido da vida contemporanea nas colonias allemãs do Rio Grande do Sul*, trans. Alfredo A. Pinto, 2d ed. (Pôrto Alegre: Selback & Mayer, [1900]), on the Muckers. The classic account of Canudos and Antônio Conselheiro is Euclydes da Cunha, *Rebellion in the Backlands*, trans. Samuel Putnam (Chicago: University of Chicago Press, 1944). However, Roderick Barman's excellent study of the Quebra-Quilo revolt clearly demonstrates that rural uprising's political character: "The Brazilian Peasantry Reexamined: The Implications of the Quebra-Quilo Revolt, 1874–1875," *Hispanic American Historical Review* 57 (August 1977), 401–24.

31. Pernambuco, *Falla com que o excellentissimo senhor desembarcador Henrique Pereira de Lucena abrio a assemblêa legislativa provincial de Pernambuco em 1° de marco de 1875* (Recife: Typ. de M. Figueiroa de F. & Filhos, 1875), p. 35.

32. Thomas Ewbank, *Life in Brazil; or, a Journal of a Visit to the Land of the Cocoa and the Palm* (New York: Harper and Brothers, 1856), pp. 277–78.

33. For a discussion of the enlistment and treatment of Brazilian soldiers during the First Empire, see Michael C. McBeth, "The Brazilian Recruit during the First Empire: Slave or Soldier?" pp. 71–86 in Dauril Alden and Warren Dean, eds., *Essays Concerning the Socioeconomic History of Brazil and Portuguese India* (Gainesville: University Presses of Florida, 1977).

34. Joaquim José Gonçalves Fontes to Manoel António Durate de Azevedo, Minister of Justice, Rio de Janeiro, 16 January 1874, Arquivo Nacional, (Rio de Janeiro), IJ;6 433; João Batista Magalhães, *A evolução militar do Brasil (Anotações para a história)* (Rio de Janeiro: Biblioteca do Exercito, 1958), pp. 274, 289–90; *Revista Typographica* (Rio de Janeiro), 9 Feb. 1889, p. 2.

35. *O Typographo* (Rio de Janeiro), 20 June 1868, p. 1.

36. Charles Greenough, President of the Botanical Garden Rail Road Company, to D. Pedro II, Rio de Janeiro, Jan. 18, 1868, Museu Imperial (Petrópolis), Maço CXLI, Doc. 6950.

37. *Revista Typographica*, 11 Aug. 1888, p. 4; 26 Jan. 1889, p. 3; *Rio News*, (Rio de Janeiro), 29 Sept. 1893, p. 5; 3 March 1897, p. 4; *O Paiz*, (Rio de Janeiro), 20 Jan. 1889, p. 3; Louis Agassiz and Elizabeth C. Agassiz, *A Journey in Brazil* (Boston: Tichnor and Fields, 1868), pp. 269; Magalhães, *A evolução militar do Brasil*, p. 290.

38. *O Paiz*, 20 Jan. 1889, p. 3.

39. Brazil, Ministério da Justiça, *Relatório*, 1869, p. 7.

40. José Joaquim de Medeiros e Albuquerque, *Minha vida. Memórias*, 2 vols., 2d ed. (Rio de Janeiro: Calvino Filho, 1933–1934), I, 210.

41. *Tribuna Artistica* (Rio de Janeiro), 26 Nov. 1871, p. 1.

42. Brazil, Directoria Geral de Estatistica, *Recenseamento do Rio de Ja-*

neiro (Districto Federal) realizado em 20 de setembro de 1906, 2 vols. (Rio de Janeiro: Officina da Estatistica, 1907), I, 164, 169.

43. Pedro Vicente de Azevedo, President of Pará, to Manoel Antonio Duarte de Azevedo, Minister of Justice, Pará, 22 Aug. 1874, Arquivo Nacional, IJ¹ 212.

44. Ewbank, *Life in Brazil*, p. 278; *Revista Typographica*, 9 Feb. 1889, p. 2; *Rio News*, 24 Nov. 1888, p. 4.

45. President of the Province of São Paulo to José Martiniano d'Oliveira Borges, Delegado of Guaratingueta, São Paulo, 17 Sept. 1868, Museu Imperial. Maço CXLII, Doc. 7014.

46. Baron of Itabapoana to Eduardo Pindahyba de Mattos, Vice President of the Province of Rio de Janeiro, July 16, 1867 and July 27, 1867 (copy), Museu Imperial, Maço CXXIX, Doc. 6823; Pernambuco, *Falla . . . 1° de marco de 1875*, p. 35.

47. See: Maria Isaura Pereira de Queiroz, *O mandonismo local na vida política brasileira*; Victor Nunes Leal, *Coronelismo, enxada e voto*; Eul-Soo Pang, "Coronelismo in Northeast Brazil," pp. 65–88 in Robert Kern, ed., *The Caciques, Oligarchical Politics, and the System of Caciquismo in the Luso-Hispanic World* (Albuquerque: University of New Mexico Press, 1973); and Jeanne Berrace de Castro, "A Guarda Nacional," pp. 274–98 in Sérgio Buarque de Hollanda, ed., *História geral da civilização brasileira*, VI.

48. Ewbank. *Life in Brazil*, p. 277.

49. Brazil, Ministério da Justiça, *Relatório*, 1869, pp. 8–9; Pernambuco, *Relatório apresentado á assembléa legislativa provincial de pelo exm. Barão de Villa-Bella na sessão do 1° de março de 1868* (Recife: Typ. do Jornal do Recife, 1868), pp. 3–4; *Rio News*, 15 Dec. 1888, p. 3.

50. The ministry's program, that is, the decrees and laws, is found in Ministério da Justiça e Negócios Interiores, Arquivo Nacional, *Organizações e programas minsterios. Regime parlamentar no Império*, 2d ed. (Rio de Janeiro: Imprensa Nacional, 1962), pp. 162–70.

51. Brazil, Ministério da Guerra, *Relatório apresentado a assembléa geral legislativa na quarta sessão da décima quinta legislatura pelo ministro e seretario de estado dos negócios da Guerra João José de Oliveira Junqueira* (Rio de Janeiro: Typ. Carioca, 1875), p. 8.

52. Pernambuco, *Falla com que o exm. sr. João Pedro Carvalho de Moraes abrio a assembléa legislativa provincial de Pernambuco em 1° de março de 1876* (Pernambuco: Typ. de M. Figueiroa de F. & Filhos, 1876), p. 26; Pernambuco, *Falla com que o exm. sr. desembarcador Manoel Clementino Carneiro da Cunha abrio a assembléa legislativa provincial de Pernambuco em 2° de março de 1877* (Recife: Typ. de M. Figueiroa de F. & Filhos, 1877), pp. 26–27; Brazil, Ministério da Guerra, *Relatório*, 1875, p. 8.

53. As part of its modernization program, the Rio Branco ministry sought to substitute the new metric system for the old Portuguese weights and measures. Late in 1874, peasants in market towns across the interior of the Northeast rioted and smashed the "kilos." They refused to pay taxes, demonstrated open

314   NOTES TO CHAPTER 2

hostility toward government officials, and burned tax and judicial records. Once they achieved their immediate aims, the rioters disbanded and the uprising ended. See Barman, "The Brazilian Peasantry Reexamined: The Implications of the Quebra-Quilo Revolt."

54. "Relatório do commandante das forças imperiaes estacionadas na Província da Parahyba do Norte," Areia, 8 Jan. 1874, *Publicações do Arquivo Nacional 34* (1937), p. 115; *O Jornal da Parahyba*, 19 Nov. 1874, and 9 Dec. 1874, quoted in Geraldo Irinêo Joffily, "O Quebra-Quilo. A revolta dos matutos contra os doutores (1874)," *Revista de História* 54 (July-Sept. 1976), 93, 96.

55. Minutes of the enlistment junta of Moritiba, Bahia, 2 Oct. 1875 [copy], Arquivo Nacional, IJ¹ 424; Luíz Antônio da Silva Nunes, President of Bahia, to Minister of Justice, Salvador, 1 Sept. and 15 Sept. 1875, Arquivo Nacional, IJ¹ 424; Pernambuco, *Falla*, 1876, p. 27.

56. Minas Gerais, *Relatório apresentado á assemblêa legislativa provincial de Minas Gerais na sessão ordinario de 1876 pelo presidente da mesma província Barão da Villa da Barra* (Ouro Preto: Typ. de J. F. de Paula Castro, 1876), p. 52.

57. Minutes of enlistment junta of Moritiba, Bahia, 2 Oct. 1875 [copy], President of Bahia to Minister of Justice, Salvador, 1 Sept. 1875, Arquivo Nacional, IJ¹ 424; São Paulo, *Relatório apresentado á assemblêa legislativa provincial de S. Paulo pelo presidente da provincia o exm. Dr. Sebastião José Pereira em Febeiro de 1877* (São Paulo: Typ. do 'Diario,' 1877, pp. 26–27); São Paulo, *Relatório com que Sebastião José Pereira passou a administração da provincia ao 5° vice-presidente Monsenhor Joaquim Manoel Gonçalves de Andrade* (São Paulo: Typ. do 'Diario,' 1878), p. 51.

58. President of Bahia to Minister of Justice, Salvador, 19 July 1875, Arquivo Nacional, IJ¹ 424; João Baptista de Nora Lima, Police Delegado, to Miguel Calmon du Pin e Almeida, Police Chief of Rio de Janeiro, Leopoldina, Minas Gerais, 13 Dec. 1876 [copy], IJ⁶ 519; President of Bahia to Minister of Justice, Salvador, 15 Sept. 1875, IJ¹ 424.

59. Bahia, *Documentos annexos ao Relatório com que o exm. sr. presidente da Provincia Dr. Luíz Antônio da Silva Nunes abriu à assemblêa legislativa provincial da Bahia no dia 1° de Maio de 1876* (Bahia: Typ. do 'Correio da Bahia,' 1876), Police Report, 18 March 1876, p. 3; President of Bahia to Minister of Justice, Salvador, 19 July 1875, Arquivo Nacional, IJ¹ 424.

60. Pernambuco, *Falla com que o exm. sr. desembarcador Manoel Clementino Carneiro da Cunha abrio à assemblêa legislativa provincial de Pernambuco em 2° de março de 1877* (Pernambuco: Typ. de M. Figueiroa de F. & Filhos, 1877), p. 15; *Relatório que o exm. sr. Dr. José Antônio de Souza Lima presidente de Pernambuco apresento ao exm. 1° vice presidente António Epaminondas de Barros Correa ao entregou a administração da provincia em 17 de dezembro de 1881* (Pernambuco: Typ. de M. Figueiroa de F. & Filhos, 1882), p. 24; *Relatório com que José Manoel de Freitas entregou a administração . . . em 20 de setembro de 1884* (Pernambuco: Typ. de M. Figueiroa de F. & Filhos, 1884), p. 15; *Falla com que o presidente da provincia José Fernandes da Costa*

Pereira Junior dirigio á assemblêa legislativa de Pernambuco no dia de sua instalação, a 6 de março de 1886 (Recife: Typ. de M. Figueiroa de F. & Filhos, 1886), p. 9.

61. See: George Rudé, *The Crowd in History. A Study of Popular Disturbances in France and England, 1730–1848* (New York: John Wiley and Sons, 1964) and *The Crowd in the French Revolution* (Oxford: Oxford University Press, 1959); Albert Soboul, *The Parisian Sans-Culottes and the French Revolution, 1793–1794*, trans. Gwynne Lewis (Oxford: Oxford University Press, 1964).

62. See Torcuato S. Di Tella, "The Dangerous Classes in Early Nineteenth-Century Mexico," *Journal of Latin American Studies* 5 (May 1973), 79–108.

63. Unlike the first half of the nineteenth century, the second half did not produce major rebellions involving conflicts between urban lower and middle classes and the dominant political elite, such as the Pernambuco revolts of 1817 and 1823, the uprisings in Bahia culminating in the Sabinada of 1837–1838, or the Praieira rebellion of 1847–1848 in Pernambuco. For these movements see: Sérgio Buarque de Hollanda, ed., *História geral da civilização brasileira,* IV, 193–241; Carlos Guilherme Mota, *Nordeste 1817* (São Paulo: Perspectiva, 1972); Amaro Quintas, *O sentido social da revolução praieira* (Rio de Janeiro: Editôra Civilização Brasileira, 1967); Norman Holub, "The Brazilian Sabinada (1837–1838): Revolt of the Negro Masses," *Journal of Negro History* 54 (July 1969), 275–83.

64. Kátia M. de Queirós Mattoso, *Bahia: A cidade do Salvador e seu mercado no século XIX* (Salvador: Editôra Hucitec, 1978), pp. 236–37, 301, 339–47, 367–70; John Morgan, British Consul, to Earl of Clarendon, Bahia, 16 March 1858, Foreign Office, Public Record Office (London), F. O. 13/365. Roderick Barman kindly called my attention to the existence of this report.

65. Morgan to Earl of Clarendon, Bahia, 16 March 1858, Public Record Office, F. O. 13/365.

66. Morgan to Earl of Clarendon, Bahia, 16 March 1858, F. O. 13/365; Bahia, *Relatório feito ao exm. 1° vice-presidente da provincia da Bahia, a dezembargador Manoel Messias de Leão pelo presidente dezembargador João Lins Vieira Cansansão de Sinimbú por occasião de passar-lhe a administração da mesma provincia em 11 de maio de 1858* (Bahia: Typ. de Antônio Olavo da França Guerra, 1858), pp. 2–5, and Report of the Chief of Police, pp. 3–5; Affonso Ruy, *História da Câmara Municipal da cidade do Salvador* (Salvador: Câmara Municipal de Salvador, 1953), p. 221.

67. Bahia, *Relatório . . . Sinimbú . . . 11 d maio de 1858,* Report of the Chief of Police, p. 2.

68. Morgan to Earl of Clarendon, Bahia, 16 March 1858.

69. Morgan to Earl of Clarendon, 16 March 1858; Report of Chief of Police, p. 5.

70. Report of Chief of Police, pp. 2, 4.

71. Report of Chief of Police, p. 2; Morgan to Clarendon, 16 March 1858.

72. Bahia, *Relatório . . . Sinimbú . . . 11 de maio de 1858*, p. 5; Report of the Chief of Police, pp. 5–6.
73. Bahia, *Relatório . . . Sinimbú . . . 11 de maio de 1858*; Queirós Mattoso, *Bahia*, p. 339.
74. Mello Barreto Filho and Hermeto Lima, *História da polícia do Rio de Janeiro. Aspectos da cidade e da vida carioca* (Rio de Janeiro: Editôra A Noite, 1939–1944), III, 37–38.
75. *Gazeta de Notícias* (Rio de Janeiro), 10 Nov. 1882, pp. 1–2; 11 Nov. 1882, p. 1; 12 Nov. 1882, p. 1; 13 Nov. 1882, p. 1.
76. Carl von Koseritz, *Imagens do Brasil*, trans. Afonso Arinos de Melo Franco (São Paulo: Livraria Martins Editôra, 1943), pp. 233–35, 238–40; *Gazeta de Notícias*, 26 Oct. 1883, *p. 1*; 27 Oct. 1883, *p. 1*; Edwin Corbell, British Minister to Brazil, to Earl Granville, Rio de Janeiro, 7 Nov. 1883, Public Record Office, F. O. 13/588; Antônio de Tovar de Lemos, Portuguese Minister to Brazil, to Antônio de Serpa Pimentel, Foreign Minister, Rio de Janeiro, 31 Oct. 1883, Arquivo do Ministério dos Negócios Estrangeiros, Cx. 220; Brazil, *Relatório apresentado ao exm. sr. conselheiro Francisco Presco de Souza Paraiso ministro e secretário de estado dos negocios da justiça pelo conselheiro desembargador Tito Augusto Pereira de Mattos* (Rio de Janeiro: Typ. Nacional, 1884), pp. 3–5.
77. Koseritz, *Imagens do Brasil*, pp. 233–34; Corbet to Granville, Rio de Janeiro, 7 Nov. 1883, Public Record Office, F. O. 13/588.
78. Kosertiz, *Imagens do Brasil*, p. 239; Mello Barreto Filho and Hermeto Lima, *História da polícia do Rio de Janeiro*, II, 120–21.
79. Antônio de Tovar de Lemos to Antônio de Serpa Pimentel, Rio de Janeiro, 31 Oct. 1883, Arquivo do Ministério dos Negócios Estrangeiros, Cx. 220; D. G. Nogueira Soares to Henrique de Barros Gomes, Rio de Janeiro, 15 Nov. 1887, Cx. 222.
80. Luiz Carlos de Paiva Teixeira, Chief of Police, to Martim Francisco Ribeiro de Andrada, Minister of Justice, Rio de Janeiro, 26 Oct. 1867, Arquivo Nacional, IJ[6] 517; Secretary of Rio police to Manuel Antônio Duarte de Azevedo, Minister of Justice, Rio de Janeiro, 30 Dec. 1874, AN, IJ[6] 519.
81. Brazil, Ministry of Justice, *Relatório*, 1875, p. 214.
82. *O Typographo*, 21 Jan. 1868, p. 4.
83. Dario Raphael Callado, Chief of Police, to Nabuco de Araujo, Rio de Janeiro, 30 July 1866, Museu Imperial, Maço CXXVIII, Doc. 6786.
84. José Basson de Miranda, President of Paraíba, to José Lustosa de Cunha Paranaguá, Viscount of Paranaguá, Prime Minister, Paraíba, 12 Jan. 1883, Museu Imperial, ID PP 12.1.883 Oso. cl-2.
85. Joaquim Nabuco to Baron of Homem de Mello, n.p., c. 1880, Museu David Carneiro (Curitiba).
86. Joaquim Serra, *A capangada, parodia muito seria pelo Amigo Ausente* (Rio de Janeiro: Typ. da Reforma, 1872).
Several decades earlier, another writer from Maranhão, João Francisco Lisboa, contributed a graphic description of electoral fraud, violence, and vote manipulation at the provincial level in the 1840s, which was reprinted in *Obras de*

João Francisco Lisboa, 2 vols. (Lisbon: Typ. Mattos Moreira & Pinheiro, 1901) I, 79–196.

87. For readers who relish such details and can appreciate the satire in Portuguese, here are several stanzas of Serra, A *capangada* (pp. 10–11, 13):

Chegou o dia grande. O ministerio
Vai consultar o voto da . . . policia,
A senha dada foi a todo o imperio.
As ordens expedidas com pericia:
Não fez a circular nenhum mysterio
E disse claramente e sem malicia,
Que convinha voltar firme e unida
Aquella rabadilha dissolvida.

Pelo que delegados, e inspectores,
E guarda nacional, corpo de urbanos,
Mestrança do arsenal e mandadores,
E fiscaes, e mezarios soberanos
Seriam todos elles os tutores
Da nossa opinião, pobres humanos!
Grantia do voto essa quadrilha,
Que o voto livre opprime, arranca, e pilha!
. . . .
Vamos a Gloria. N'essa freguezia
O barulho é cruel, da nossa morte!
A soldadesca murcha alli não pia
E leva trambulhão bonito e forte
Não pode o cidadão votar, que a iia
Decide do seu voto, de sua sorte:
Si a tropa em S. José faz bandalheiras
Fazem na Gloria os feros capoeiras.
. . . . . .
Depois de procellosa tempestade,
Muita trapaça e sangue derramado,
Proclamaram as urnas da cidade
Do governo o triumpho assignalado!
D'essa eleição, de tal monstruosidade
Foi a policia o pai desnaturado;
O monstrengo ahi está, póde ir á
fava, Que de tal pai tal filho se
esperava.

88. Manoel Garcia da Rosa, Portuguese Minister to Brazil, to Anselmo José Braamcamp, Foreign Minister, Petrópolis, 20 July 1880, Arquivo do Ministério dos Negócios Estrangeiros, Cx. 219.

89. The best general study of *capoeira* is Waldeloir Rego, *Capoeira angola. Ensaio socio-etnográfico* (Salvador: Editôra Itapuã, 1968).

The Argentine *compadrito*, famed in the folklore of Buenos Aires, and his role in politics and popular culture, would be an excellent subject for comparison with the Brazilian *capoeira*.

90. Euzebio de Queiroz Coutinho, Police Chief of Rio de Janeiro, to Judge of 1st District of Candelaria, Rio de Janeiro, 18 June 1836 [copy]; João Jacinto de Mello, Administrado dos Africanos, to João de Oliveira Fausto, President of the Municipal Council, Rio de Janeiro, 23 Nov. 1858, Rio de Janeiro; José João do Cunha Telles, Fiscal in Candelaria, to José João do Cunha Telles, President of the Municipal council, Rio de Janeiro, 20 Aug. 1861, Arquivo Municipal da Cidade do Rio de Janeiro, 40-3-78; James C. Fletcher and Daniel Parish Kidder, *Brazil and the Brazilians Portrayed in Historical and Descriptive Sketches*, 7th ed. (Boston: Little, Brown, & Co., 1867), p. 137; Mello Barreto Filho and Hermeto Lima, *História da polícia do Rio de Janeiro*, I, 202–8.

91. Brazil, Ministério da Justiça, *Relatório*, 1878, p. 31; Ministério da Justiça, *Relatório*, Report of Police Chief of Rio de Janeiro, 31 Dec. 1881, pp. 5–6; Ministério da Justiça, *Relatório*, 1889, p. 5; Antônio de Tovar de Lemos, Minister to Brazil, to Antônio de Serpa Pimentel, Foreign Minister, Rio de Janeiro, 31 Oct. 1883, Arquivo do Ministério dos Negocios Estangeiros, Cx. 220; *Jornal do Comércio* (Rio de Janeiro), 4 July 1871, p. 5; 11 Dec. 1872, p. 3; Alexandre José de Melo Morais Filho, *Festas e tradições populares do Brasil*, 3rd ed. (Rio de Janeiro: F. Briguiet & Cia., 1946), pp. 444–50; Coelho Neto, *Bazar* (Oporto: Livraria Chadron, 1928), pp. 134–37; Adolfo Morales de los Rios Filho, *O Rio de Janeiro Imperial* (Rio de Janeiro: Editôra A Noite, 1946), p. 52; João Dunshee de Abranches Moura, *Actas e actos do governo provisório. Cópias authénticas dos protocollos das sessões secretas do conselho de ministros desde a proclamação da república até o organização do gabinete Lucena, acompanhadas de importantes revelações e documentos*, 3rd ed. (Rio de Janeiro: Officinas Gráficas do 'Jornal do Brasil,' 1953), p. 361; Mello Barreto Filho and Hermeto Lima, *História da polícia do Rio de Janeiro*, II, 255–56.

92. Melo Morais Filho, *Festas e tradições populares do Brasil*, pp. 452–55.

93. Franciso de Faria Lemos, Police Chief of Rio de Janeiro, to Francisco de Paula de Negreiros Sayão Lobato, Rio de Janeiro, 8 July 1871, Arquivo Nacional, IJ[6] 518; Tovar de Lemos to Serpa Pimentel, Rio de Janeiro, 31 Oct. 1883, Arquivo do Ministério dos Negocios Estrangeiros, Cx. 220; *Jornal do Comércio*, 4 July 1871, p. 4; 9 July 1871, p. 5; Brazil, Ministério da Justiça, Relatório, 1873, p. 184; *Relatório*, 1878, p. 32; Melo Morais Filho, *Festas e tradições populares do Brasil*, pp. 450–51; Dunshee de Abranches, *Actas e actos do governo provisório*, pp. 362–66; Mello Barreto Filho and Hermeto Lima, *História da polícia do Rio de Janeiro*, II, 99.

94. Rio News, 13 Jan. 1891, p. 3; Dunshee de Abranches, *Actas e actos do governo provisório*, pp. 167–77, 361–66; Lamberg, *O Brazil*, p. 308.
95. Rego, *Capoeira angola*, p. 292; Rio News, 16 Sept. 1889, p. 3; *Gazeta de Notícias*, 30 Nov. 1902, p. 1.
96. *Gazeta da Tarde* (Rio de Janeiro), 5 Jan. 1885, p. 1; 8 Aug. 1887, pp. 1–2; *Rio News*, 15 Aug. 1887, p. 2; Mello Barreto Filho and Hermeto Lima, *História da polícia do Rio de Janeiro*, III, 51–52; Alexandre José de Mello Morais Filho, *Factos e memorias* (Rio de Janeiro and Paris: H. Garnier, 1904), pp. 329–33; Toplin, *The Abolition of Slavery in Brazil*, p. 191.
97. *Tribuna Artistica* (Rio de Janeiro), 25 Feb. 1872, p. 1.
98. Marc Jay Hoffnagel, "O movimento republicano em Pernambuco, 1870–1889," *Revista do Instituto Arquelógico, Histórico e Geográfico Pernambucano* 49 (January 1977), 38–39.
99. *O Grito dos Pobres* (São Paulo), 30 May 1889, p. 1.
100. Arquivo Nacional, *Organizações e programas ministeriais*, pp. 180–82; *Gazeta de Notícias*, 13 Dec. 1879, p. 1; 28 Dec. 1879, p. 1.
101. Christopher Columbus Andrews, *Brazil: Its Condition and Prospects* (New York: D. Appleton and Company, 1887), pp. 30–32, 38; *Gazeta de Notícias*, 15 Dec. 1879, p. 1; 17 Dec. 1879, p. 1.
102. *Gazeta de Notícias*, 22 Dec. 1879, p. 1; 23 Dec. 1879, p. 1; 24 Dec. 1879, p. 1; 28 Dec. 1879, p. 1; 29 Dec. 1879, p. 1; *Rio News*, 5 Jan. 1880, p. 2; *Revista Illustrada* (Rio de Janeiro), 27 Dec. 1879, pp. 1–4.
103. Pedro II to Countess of Barral, Rio de Janeiro, 1–3 Jan. 1880, in Raimundo Magalhães Júnior, ed., *D. Pedro II e a Condessa de Barral através da correspondência íntima do imperador, anotada e comentada* (Rio de Janeiro: Editôra Civilização Brasileira, 1956), p. 303.
104. *Rio News*, 5 Jan. 1880, p. 2; *Jornal do Comércio*, 2 Jan. 1880, p. 2; *Revista Illustrada*, 9 Jan. 1880, p. 8; Melo Morais Filho, *Factos e memorias*, pp. 219–24, 333–34; Brazil, Ministério da Justiça, *Relatório*, 1880, p. 4.
105. *Rio News*, 5 Jan. 1880, p. 2.
106. *Revista Illustrada*, 27 Dec. 1879, p. 2.
107. *Rio News*, 5 Jan. 1880, p. 2; *Revista Illustrada*, 7 Jan. 1880, p. 2; 17 Jan. 1880, pp. 4–5.
108. *Rio News*, 5 Jan. 1880, p. 2; *Jornal do Comércio*, 2 Jan. 1880, p. 1; 3 Jan. 1880, p. 1; 4 Jan. 1880, p. 1; 5 Jan. 1880, p. 1; *Revista Illustrada*, 7 Jan. 1880, p. 2; 9 Jan. 1880, pp. 2, 5.
109. *Revista Illustrada*, 7 Jan. 1880, p. 1.
110. Melo Morais Filho, *Factos e memorias*, pp. 220–24.

> Quando houve o pega-pega,
> Nessas gentes pequeninas,
> O Dr. Lopes Trovão
> Correu com as pernas finas,
> Foi ter mão na Praia Grande
> Sem não molhar as botinas.

111. Pedro II to Countess of Barral, Rio de Janeiro, 1–3 Jan. 1880, in Magalhães Júnior, ed., *D. Pedro II e a Condessa de Barral*, p. 303.

112. *Journal do Comércio*, 4 Jan. 1880, p. 1.

113. *Gazeta de Notícias*, 31 Oct. 1881, *p. 1; 11 March 1889, p. 1; 12 March 1889, p. 1; 13 March 1889, p. 1; 15 March 1889, p. 1; 16 March 1889, p. 1; 17 March 1889, p. 1; 25 March 1889, p. 1; 26 March 1889, p. 1; Ernesto Senna, Rascunhos e perfis (Notas de um reporter)* (Rio de Janeiro: Typ. do Jornal do Commercio, 1909), pp. 393–97; Mello Barreto Filho and Hermeto Lima, *História da polícia do Rio de Janeiro*, III, 112–14, 170–72; Luíz Dodsworth Martins, *Presença de Paulo de Frontin* (Rio de Janeiro and São Paulo: Livraria Freitas Bastos, 1966), pp. 38–39, 46–55.

114. Works on Silva Jardim include: José Leão, *Silva Jardim. Apontamentos para a biographia do illustre propagandista hauridos nas informações paternas e dados particulares e officiaes* (Rio de Janeiro: Imprensa Nacional, 1895); João Dornas Filho, *Silva Jardim* (São Paulo: Companhia Editôra Nacional, 1936); Maurício Vinhas de Queiroz, *Paixão e morte de Silva Jardim* (Rio de Janeiro: Editôra Civilização Brasileira, 1967).

115. Antônio da Silva Jardim, *Salvação da patria (Governo republicano). Conferencia realizado no Clube Republicano de São Paulo, em noite de 7 de abril de 1888* (Santos: Typ. do Diario, 1888), p. 371. See also Silva Jardim, A *patria em perigo (Braganças e Orleans). Conferencia-meeting sobre a actual situação brasileira, realizada na cidade de Santos, em noite de 28 de janeiro de 1888* (São Paulo: Typ. da Provincia, 1888).

116. Silva Jardim, *Fechamento das portas (A questão do descanso para os empregados no commercio realisada a convite da Associação dos Empregados no Commercio do Rio de Janeiro a 27 de outubro de 1888* (Rio de Janeiro: Typ. Mont'Alverne 1888), p. 5.

117. Silva Jardim, *Fechamento das portas*, pp. 14–16.

118. Silva Jardim, A *situação republicana (Questão do chefia do partido) Manifesto e artigos* (Rio de Janeiro: Typ. da Gazeta de Notícias, 1889); Joaquim Saldanha Marinho to Francisco Glicério, Rio de Janeiro, 31 Oct. 1888, Arquivo Municipal da Cidade do Rio de Janeiro, 41-1-61; Boehrer, *Da monarquia à república*, pp. 193–211; Queiroz, *Paixão e morte de Silva Jardim*, pp. 57–93.

119. Marc Jay Hoffnagel, "O movimento republicano em Pernambuco, 1870–1889," *Revista do Instituto Arquelógico, Histórico e Geográfico Pernambucano* 47 (January 1977), 52.

120. Boehrer, *Da monarquia à república*, p. 61.

121. *O Soldado* (Rio de Janeiro), 18 March 1881, p. 1; 22 March 1881, p. 1; 29 March 1881, p. 1; 6 May 1881, p. 1; 28 June 1881, p. 1; *Tribuna Militar* (Rio de Janeiro), 10 July 1881, p. 1; *O Nihilista* (Rio de Janeiro), 13 Dec. 1882, p. 3.

122. *Tribuna Militar*, 10 July 1881, p. 1; 28 July 1881, p. 1; Bergstresser, "The Movement for the Abolition of Slavery in Rio de Janeiro," pp. 51, 66–71; Santos, *Os republicanos paulistas e a abolição*, p. 30.

On the army, see June E. Hahner, "The Brazilian Armed Forces and the

Overthrow of the Monarchy: Another Perspective," *The Americas* 26 (October 1969), 171–82; William S. Dudley, "Institutional Sources of Officer Discontent in the Brazilian Army, 1870–1889," *Hispanic American Historical Review* 55 (February 1975), 44–65; Heitor Lyra, *História da queda do império*, 2 vols. (São Paulo: Companhia Editôra Nacional, 1964); Magalhães, A *evolução militar* do Brasil; and Raimundo Magalhães Júnior, *Deodoro. A espada contra o Império*, 2 vols. (São Paulo: Companhia Editôra Nacional, 1967).

123. Joaquim Nabuco, *Abolitionism. The Brazilian Antislavery Struggle* trans. Robert Conrad (Urbana: University of Illinois Press, 1977), p. 11.

124. André Reboucas to Domingos Jaguaribe, Rio de Janeiro, 11 Feb. 1882, in A *Redempção* (São Paulo), 13 May 1899, p. 2.

125. *Gazeta da Tarde* (Rio de Janeiro), 14 Feb. 1884, p. 1; 16 Feb. 1884, p. 1; 21 Feb. 1884, p. 1.

126. *Gazeta da Tarde*, 8 Jan. 1881, p. 2; 5 Jan. 1885, p. 1; 14 May 1886, p. 1; 7 May 1887, p. 2; 9 Aug. 1887, p. 2; *Cidade do Rio* (Rio de Janeiro), 10 Nov. 1887, p. 1; Moraes, A *campanha abolicionista*, pp. 241, 251–74; Santos, *Os republicanos paulistas e a abolição*, pp. 177–79; 310–11; Conrad, *The Destruction of Brazilian Slavery*, pp. 154–55; Toplin, *The Abolition of Slavery in Brazil*, pp. 75–76, 242–45.

127. Luís Gama, *Trocas burlescas* (São Paulo: Editora Três, 1974), p. 30.

> Se os nobres desta terra empanturrados,
> Em Guiné têm parentes enterrados;
> E, cedendo à prosápia, ou duros vícios,
> Esquecem os negrinhos seus patrícios;
> Se mulatos de cor esbranquiçada,
> Já se julgam de origem refinada,
> E, curvos à mania que os domina,
> Desprezam a vovó, que é preta mina;
> Não te espantes, ó Leitor, da novidade,
> Porque tudo no Brasil é raridade!

128. Moraes, A *campanha abolicionista*, pp. 263–64.

129. For an example of slavocrat accusations, see the 13 September 1887 Senate speech by the Baron of Cotegipe in Barão de Cotegipe (João Maurício Wanderley), *Fuga de escravos em Campinas. Discursos pronunciados no Senado* (Rio de Janeiro: Imprensa Nacional, 1887), pp. 3–8.

130. Charles Hastings Dent, A *Year in Brazil* (London: Kegan, Paul, Trench, and Co., 1886), pp. 285–87.

131. Koseritz, *Imagens do Brasil*, p. 239.

132. Bergstresser, "The Movement for the Abolition of Slavery in Rio," pp. 49–98.

133. Bergstresser, "The Movement for the Abolition of Slavery in Rio," pp. 98–136.

134. *Gazeta da Tarde*, 1 Aug. 1881, p. 1; 17 April 1883, p. 1; 21 May

1883, p. 1; Moraes, *A campanha abolicionista*, pp. 36–39; Dent, *A Year in Brazil*, p. 282; Bergstresser, "The Movement for the Abolition of Slavery in Rio de Janeiro," pp. 99–136; Conrad, *The Destruction of Brazilian Slavery*, pp. 158–59.

135. *Cidade do Rio*, 20 July 1889, p. 1.

136. *O Paiz*, 5 Jan. 1889, p. 2; 6 Jan. 1889, p. 3; *Cidade do Rio*, 20 July 1889, p. 1; Medeiros e Albuquerque, *Minha vida*, pp. 123–28; Moraes, *A campanha abolicionista*, pp. 372–76; D. G. Nogueira Soares, Portuguese Minister to Brazil, to Henrique de Barros Gomes, Foreign Minister, Petrópolis, 12 Jan. 1889, Arquivo do Ministério dos Negocios Estrangeiros, Cx. 222; Bergstresser, "The Movement for the Abolition of Slavery in Rio," pp. 137–88; Boehrer, *Da monarquia à república*, p. 49; Mello Barreto Filho and Hermeto Lima, *História da polícia do Rio de Janeiro*, III, 160–61.

137. See photograph reproduced in Gilberto Ferrez, "A fotografia no Brasil e um de seus mais dedicados servidores: Marc Ferrez (1843–1923)," *Revista do Patrimônio Histórico e Artístico Nacional* 10 (1946), Plate 18.

138. *Revista Typographica*, 26 May 1888, p. 5; 2 June 1888, p. 5.

139. *Rio News*, 24 May 1888, p. 3.

140. A. Coelho Rodrigues, *A república na América do Sul ou um pouco de história e crítica offerecido aos Latino-Americanos*, 2d ed. (Einsiedeln, Switzerland: Typ. dos Estabelecimentos Benzinger & Co., 1906), p. 16.

Chapter 3

1. Stanley J. Stein, *The Brazilian Cotton Manufacture: Textile Enterprise in an Underdeveloped Area, 1850–1950*. (Cambridge, Mass.: Harvard University Press, 1957), p. 21.

2. Some of the most valuable historical studies concerning industrialization in Brazil are: Warren Dean, *The Industrialization of São Paulo, 1880–1945* (Austin and London: University of Texas Press, 1969); Stein, *The Brazilian Cotton Manufacture*; Nícia Villela Luz, *A luta pela industrialização do Brasil 1808 a 1930* (São Paulo: Difusão Européia do Livro, 1961); Annibal Villanova Villela and Wilson Suzigan, *Polítical do governo e crescimento da economia brasileira, 1889–1945* (Rio de Janeiro: IPEA/INPES, 1973).

3. *Relatório apresentado a sr. ex. o Ministro de Fazenda pela Commissão de Inquerito Industrial* (Rio de Janeiro: Typ. Nacional, 1882). This incomplete survey was based on companies' replies to a government inquiry. Responding metal industries in Rio de Janeiro listed a total of 453 workers, while the 1872 census enumerated 2,987 metal workers. No doubt the smallest establishments, with only a handful of craftsmen, were the least likely to be included in this 1882 government survey and report.

4. For better opportunities for immigrants in prosperous São Paulo province, see Thomas H. Holloway, *Immigrants on the Land: Coffee and Society in São Paulo, 1886–1934* (Chapel Hill: University of North Carolina Press, 1980).

5. Rui Barbosa, *Reforma do ensino primário e varias instituições complementares da instrução pública*, Vol. X, Tomo I of *Obras completas de Rui Barbosa* (Rio de Janeiro: Ministério da Educação e Saúde, 1947) pp. 9–11; Brazil, Directoria Geral de Estatistica, *Recenseamento da população do Imperio do Brazil a que se procedeu no dia 1° de agosto de 1872* (Rio de Janeiro: Typ. Leuzinger, 1873–1876), XIX (Quadros gerais), 1.

6. *Informações apresentadas pela Commissão Parlamentar de Inquerito ao Corpo Legislativo no terceira sessão da decima oitava legislatura* (Rio de Janeiro: Typ. Nacional, 1883), pp. 366–67.

7. *Gazeta dos Operários* (Rio de Janeiro), 8 Dec. 1875, p. 1; 10 Dec. 1875, p. 1; 20–21 Dec. 1875, p. 1; *Tribuna Artistica* (Rio de Janeiro), 31 Dec. 1871, p. 1; Stein, *The Brazilian Cotton Manufacture*, pp. 50–65; Eulália Maria Lahmeyer Lobo, Octávio Canavarros, Zakia Feres Elias, Sonia Gonçalves, Lucena Barbosa Madureira, "Evolução dos preços e do padrão de vida no Rio de Janeiro, 1820–1930—resultados preliminares," *Revista Brasileira de Economia* 25 (October-December 1971), 225; Aluízio de Azevedo, *O cortiço*.

8. Older accounts of the Brazilian labor movement, which deal only briefly with pre-1900 developments, include: Hermínio Linhares, *Contribuição a história das lutas operarias no Brasil* (Rio de Janeiro: Baptista de Souza & Cia., 1955); Edgar Rodrigues, *Socialismo e sindicalismo no Brasil, 1675–1913* (Rio de Janeiro: Laemmert, 1969); José Albertino Rodrigues, *Sindicato e desenvolvimento no Brasil* (São Paulo: Difusão Européia do Livro, 1968); Azis Simão, *Sindicato e estado. Suas relações na formação do proletariado de São Paulo* (São Paulo: Dominus Editôra, 1966); and Jover Telles, *O movimento sindical no Brasil* (Rio de Janeiro: Vitória, 1962). A succinct account of the late nineteenth-century labor movement in Rio de Janeiro is found in Boris Fausto's excellent *Trabalho urbano e conflito social (1890–1920)* (São Paulo: Difel/Difusão Editorial, 1976). Valuable articles by Sheldon L. Maram concentrate on Rio and São Paulo in the early twentieth century: "Labor and the Left in Brazil, 1890–1921: A Movement Aborted," *Hispanic American Historical Review* 57 (May 1977), 254–72; "The Immigrant and the Brazilian Labor Movement, 1890–1920," pp. 178–210, in Dauril Alden and Warren Dean, eds., *Essays Concerning the Socioeconomic History of Brazil and Portuguese India* (Gainesville: University Presses of Florida, 1977); and "Anarcho-Syndicalism in Brazil," *Proceedings of the Pacific Coast Council on Latin American Studies* IV (1975), 101–16. None of these studies deals with labor under the empire in any detail.

9. A. J. R. Russell-Wood, *Fidalgos and Philanthropists: The Santa Casa da Misericordia of Bahia, 1550–1775* (Berkeley and Los Angeles: University of California Press, 1968).

A pioneering study of voluntary associations in Brazil is provided by Michael L. Conniff, "Voluntary Associations in Rio, 1870–1945: A New Approach to Urban Social Dynamics," *Journal of Interamerican Studies and World Affairs* 17 (February 1975), 64–81.

10. *União Operaria* (Recife), 5 Nov. 1905, p. 3; 26 Nov. 1905, pp. 1–3.

11. Joaquim da Silva Mello Guimarães, *Instituições de previdência fundadas no Rio de Janeiro* (Rio de Janeiro: Typographia Nacional, 1883).

12. Guimarães, *Instituições de previdência*, pp. 60–81.

13. *Tribuna Artistica*, 19 Nov. 1871, *pp. 1–4; 3 Dec. 1871, p. 2; 25 Feb. 1872, p. 1; Guimarães, Instituições de previdência*, pp. 54, 77; *O Alvorado* (Rio de Janeiro), 24 Aug. 1890, p. 2; *O País* (Rio de Janeiro), 12 Feb. 1890, p. 2; "Rapport de la Commission Executive du Parti Ouvrier du Brésil a Presenter au Congres Socialiste International de Zurich, 1893," p. 52 in "Militants sociaxdémocrates allemands au Brésil (1893–1896), présentation par Georges Haupt," *Le Mouvement Social* 84 (July-September 1973) (I am indebted to Professor Michael M. Hall of the Universidade de Campinas for calling this article to my attention); George C. A. Boehrer, *Da Monarquia à República. História do Partido Republicano do Brasil (1870–1889)*, trans. Berenice Xavier (Rio de Janeiro: Ministério da Educação e Cultura, 1954), p. 35.

14. Guimarães, *Instituições de previdência*, Table 8.

15. Guimarães, *Instituições de previdência, pp. 45, 53, 58, 69, 77, 81, 194; Tribuna Artistica*, 19 Nov. 1871, p. 2; 25 Feb. 1872, p. 1; *Revista Typographica* (Rio de Janeiro), 21 July 1888, p. 6.

16. Guimarães, *Instituições de previdência*, p. 69.

17. *Liga Operaria* (Recife), 24 May 1877, p. 2.

18. *Boletim da Sociedade de Geografia de Lisboa*, 3ª serie, n. 1, 1882, 23–25, 238; Negocios Exteriores, *Documentos apresentados ás Cortes na sessão legislativa de 1877 pelo Ministro e Secretario d'Estado dos Negocios Extrangeiros. Emigração portuguesa* (Lisbon: Imprensa Nacional, 1875), pp. 5, 53; Sociedade de Geografia de Lisboa, *Colonias portuguesas em paises estrangeiros* (Lisbon: Tipografia Universal, 1915), pp. 46–47; Azevedo, *O cortiço*.

19. *O Caixeiro* (Rio de Janeiro), 15 Nov. 1881, p. 2.

20. Ferreira da Rosa, *Associação dos Empregados no Comércio do Rio de Janeiro. Meio século. Narrativa histórica.* (Rio de Janeiro: Paulo, Pongetti & Cia. 1930); "Associação dos Empregados no Commercio do Rio de Janeiro, Relatorio do anno de 1880," Arquivo da Associação dos Empregados no Comércio do Rio de Janeiro, Rio de Janeiro; *Relatório da Associação dos Empregados no Commercio do Rio de Janeiro relativo ao anno administrativo de 1898* (Rio de Janeiro: Typ. do *Jornal do Commercio* 1899), p. 163.

21. Speech by Thomaz da Costa, president of the Associação dos Empregados no Comércio do Rio de Janeiro, on laying the cornerstone for the construction of the association's own building in Ferreira da Rosa, 8 July 1899, *Meio século*, p. 166.

22. *O Socialista* (Rio de Janeiro), 18 Feb. 1893, p. 4.

23. The Imperial Associação Tipográfica Fluminense of Rio de Janeiro had as its organ during the empire a series of short-lived newspapers: *O Echo da Imprensa*, in 1856, *Revista Typographica*, 1864; and *O Artista*, 1883. Typographer's associations in other cities across the nation often had their own journals also, as in the case of the Associação Tipográfica Alagoana de Soccorros Mutuos of Maceió, which published the *Guttemberg*, 1881–1883. An association of

typographers in São Paulo published *O Trabalho* in 1876. Other typographers' newspapers during the empire include *O Typographo* of Paraíba do Norte, 1876; *Revista Typographica* in Rio de Janeiro, 1888–1889; and the most out-spoken, *O Typographo,* in Rio, 1867–1868.

24. *Revista Typographica* (Rio de Janeiro), 1 March 1864, p. 1. See also *Estatuto da Imperial Associação Typographica Fluminense* (Rio de Janeiro: Typ. de Domingos Luiz dos Santos, 1860), p. 3.

25. *O Echo da Imprensa* (Rio de Janeiro), 7 Sept. 1856, p. 3.

26. *Revista Typographica,* 1 Feb. 1864, p. 2.

27. *O Echo da Imprensa,* 7 Sept. 1856, pp. 2–3; 14 Sept. 1856, p. 2; 19 Oct. 1856, p. 3; 26 Oct. 1856, pp. 1–2.

28. Eulália Maria Lahmeyer Lobo, Otávio Canavarros, Zakia Feres Elias, Simone Novias, and Lucena Barbosa Madureira, "Estudo das categorias socio-profissionais, dos salários e do custo da alimentação no Rio de Janeiro de 1820 á 1930," *Revista Brasileira de Economia* 27 (October-December 1973), 153–54; Eulália Maria Lahmeyer et al., "Evolução dos preços e do padrão de vida no Rio de Janeiro, 1820–1930," *Revista Brasileira de Economia* 25 (October-December 1971), 247; minutes of 22 November 1855, session of Conselho do Estado, Arquivo Nacional, Códice 277.

29. *O Jornal dos Typographos* (Rio de Janeiro), 13 Jan. 1858, p. 1; 20 Jan. 1858, p. 1; 22 Jan. 1858, p. 1; Imperial Associação Typographica Flumi-nense, *Relatório apresentado á Imperial Associação Typographica Fluminense em assemblea geral pelo Conselho Administrativo a 13 de dezembro de 1863* (Rio de Janeiro: Typ. Laemmert, 1863), vii.

30. *O Jornal dos Typographos,* 20 Jan. 1858, p. 1.

31. *O Jornal dos Typographos,* 13 Jan. 1858, p. 1; 16 Feb. 1858, p. 1; *O Typographo* (Rio de Janeiro), 4 Nov. 1867, p. 1.

32. *O Correio Mercantil* (Rio de Janeiro), 18 May 1858, p. 1.

33. Imperial Associação Typographica Fluminense, *Relatório,* 1863, vi–vii; *O Typographo,* 4 Nov. 1867, p. 1; 30 Aug. 1868, p. 1; *O Artista* (Rio de Ja-neiro), 14 April 1883, p. 3.

34. *O Typographo,* 30 Aug. 1868, p. 1.

35. Some of the best existing studies of the Brazilian working classes in-clude Boris Fausto, *Trabalho urbano e conflito social (1890–1920),* Sheldon L. Maram, "Labor and the Left in Brazil, 1890–1921" and "The Immigrant and the Brazilian Labor Movement, 1890–1920," and Azis Simão, *Sindicato e es-tado.* Such studies tend to focus on São Paulo, as well as on unions, industrial workers, and immigrants. Far fewer questions are raised concerning the origins of native-born laborers even in that city. Everardo Dias, an anarchist printer and prominent journalist living in São Paulo in the early twentieth century, once went so far as to deny the existence of a Brazilian-born proletariat (*His-tória das lutas sociais no Brasil* [São Paulo: Editôra Edaglit, 1962], p. 18).

As demonstrated by Douglas H. Graham and Sérgio Buarque de Hollanda Filho (*Migration, Regional and Urban Growth, and Development in Brazil: A Selected Analysis of the Historical Record, 1872–1970* [São Paulo: Instituto de

Pesquisas Economicas, Universidade de São Paulo, 1971]), printed census data permit the study of interregional migrations, but shed much less light on rural-urban migration. These statistics generally do not distinguish urban dwellers by color, let alone previous condition of servitude. However, the 1893 municipal census of the city of São Paulo does indicate place of origin, although, unfortunately, it does not distinguish between those born in the state or in the city of São Paulo. Of the city's Brazilian-born inhabitants (forty-five percent of the total city population), eighty-five percent came from "São Paulo," followed by only five percent from the state of Rio de Janeiro, less than three percent from Minas Gerais, and three percent from Bahia and all the states to its north combined. (São Paulo [state], Repartição de Estatistica e Arquivo, *Relatório apresentado . . . pelo diretor . . . Antonio de Toledo Piza, 31 de julho de 1894* [Rio de Janeiro: Typ. Leuzinger, 1895], unpaged). Certainly there was no large-scale migration from the Northeast, as would occur in the midtwentieth century.

The lower classes in the northern cities, which have received far less scholarly attention than those in São Paulo, included a much smaller proportion of foreigners, as relatively few immigrants went there in the late nineteenth century. Only some five percent of Recife's population was foreign born, compared to over half of São Paulo's (Bainbridge Cowell, Jr., "Cityward Migration in the Nineteenth Century: The Case of Recife, Brazil," *Journal of Interamerican Studies and World Affairs* 17 [February 1975], 49). By the end of the century, the northeastern sugar industry, beset by competition from European sugar beet producers, entered a slow decline, in sharp contrast to the vigorous state, and high profitability, of the south-central coffee economy. In their attempts to meet foreign competition, some urban capitalists in Pernambuco, the principal sugar producing state, began a process of concentration and modernization, through more capital-intensive technology. As Peter L. Eisenberg demonstrates (*The Sugar Industry in Pernambuco: Modernization Without Change, 1840–1910* [Berkeley and Los Angeles: University of California Press, 1974]), neither masses of immigrants nor larger numbers of Brazilian workers were necessary to maintain or expand local sugar production.

36. Brazil, Ministério da Justiça, *Relatórios,* Report of the Chief of Police of Rio de Janeiro, 1866, p. 7; 1874, p. 206; 1878, p. 60.

37. Florestan Fernandes, *The Negro in Brazilian Society,* ed. Phyllis B. Eveleth, trans. Jacqueline D. Skiles, A. Brunel, and Arthur Rothwell (New York: Columbia University Press, 1969), pp. 29–39, 69–71; Emília Viotti da Costa, *Da senzala à colônia* (São Paulo: Difusão Européia do Livro, 1966), p. 488; Robert Conrad, *The Destruction of Brazilian Slavery, 1850–1888* (Berkeley and Los Angeles: University of California Press, 1972), p. 269; Eisenberg, *The Sugar Industry in Pernambuco,* pp. 180–94; Cowell, "Cityward Migration in the Nineteenth Century," p. 55.

Free labor had become dominant in Pernambuco by the 1870s. Both the subsistence sector to the west and the state capital already had "surplus" populations (Celso Furtado, *The Economic Growth of Brazil: A Survey from Colonial to Modern Times,* trans. Ricardo W. de Aguiar and Eric Charles Drysdale [Berkeley and Los Angeles: University of California Press, 1963], p. 151). Peter Eisenberg (*The Sugar Industry in Pernambuco*, pp. 181–82) notes that the percentage of colored persons among Recife's inhabitants remained virtually constant from 1872 to 1890, comprising slightly over half the population. However, urban migration did occur, and the city grew more rapidly than did the surrounding rural areas. But what was the precise nature of that migration? Bainbridge Cowell, Jr.'s painstaking research in parish marriage records in Recife indicates that twenty-five percent of the city's habitants were born elsewhere in Pernambuco, especially in the sugar zone, in the 1890s, as compared to fifteen percent in the 1870s. At the same time, the percentage of those born in Recife decreased from sixty-one percent in the 1870s to fifty-four percent in the 1890s, while the proportion of those born abroad declined from five to three percent ("Cityward Migration in the Nineteenth Century," pp. 50–54). But Cowell's published tables do not indicate sex or color. According to national census figures, Recife grew more slowly in the second half of the nineteenth century than other large Brazilian cities, notably São Paulo and Rio de Janeiro, but apparently Salvador as well. (Table 1).

38. Fernandes, *The Negro in Brazilian Society*, pp. 1–54.

39. Mary Catherine Karasch, "Slave Life in Rio de Janeiro, 1808–1850" (unpublished Ph.D. dissertation, University of Wisconsin, 1972), p. 538.

40. Fernandes, *The Negro in Brazilian Society*, pp. 96–117.

41. *O Typographo*, 4 Nov. 1867, p. 2; *O Artista*, 14 April 1883, p. 1; *Revista Typographica*, 12 March 1888, p. 4; 19 May 1888, p. 4; 2 June 1888, p. 5; Maurício Vinhas de Queiroz, "Notas sobre o processo de modernização no Brasil," *Revista do Instituto de Ciências Socais* III (Jan.-Dec. 1966), 150–51.

42. *Revista Typographica*, 26 May 1888, p. 8.

43. *Revista Typographica*, 26 May 1888, p. 3; 9 June 1888, p. 3; 23 June 1888, p. 4; 21 July 1888, p. 6; 8 Sept. 1888, p. 2; 27 Oct. 1888, pp. 1–4; 7 Nov. 1888, pp. 1–3; 17 Nov. 1888, pp. 1–2; 26 Jan. 1889, p. 3; 2 Feb. 1889, pp. 3, 4, 7.

44. *Revista Typographica*, 18 Aug. 1888, p. 2; 25 Aug. 1888, pp. 1–2; 1 Dec. 1888, p. 3; 22 Dec. 1888, p. 6; 9 Feb. 1889, p. 5.

45. Villela and Suzigan, *Política do governo e crescimento da economia brasileira*, pp. 30–37; 99–104; 111–12; Mircea Buescu, *300 anos de inflação* (Rio de Janeiro: APEC, 1973), pp. 213–21; Lobo et al., "Evolução dos preços e do padrão de vida no Rio de Janeiro, 1820–1930," *Revista Brasileira de Economia* 25 (October-December 1971), 248–51; Kátia de Queirós Mattoso, "Os preços na Bahia de 1750 a 1930," in Colloques Internationaux du Centre National de la Recherche Scientifique No. 543, *L'histoire quantitative du Brésil de 1800 a 1930* (Paris: Editions du Centre National de la Recherche Scientifique, 1973), pp. 177, 182; Oliver Onody, *A inflação brasileira (1820–1958)* (Rio de Janeiro: n.p., 1960), passim.

46. *O Socialista*, 18 Feb. 1893, p. 3.

47. Lobo et al., "Estudo das categorias socioprofissionais, dos salários e do custo da alimentação no Rio de Janeiro de 1820 a 1930," *Revista Brasileira*

de Economia 27 (October-December 1973), 169; Lobo et al., "Evolution des prix e du cout de la vie a Rio de Janeiro (1820–1930)," p. 211 in *L'histoire quantitiative du Brésil de 1800 a 1930*; A. P. Monteiro Manso to Floriano Peixoto, Rio de Janeiro, 16 Dec. 1893, Arquivo Nacional, Cx 1209; *Rio News* (Rio de Janeiro), 3 Feb. 1891, p. 3.

48. *Tribuna Artistica*, 25 Feb. 1892, p. 1.

49. *Jornal do Comércio* (Rio de Janeiro), 14 June 1880, p. 1; 30 June 1880 p. 1; 27 Jan. 1881, p. 1.

50. Brazil, Directoria Geral de Estatistica, *Recenseamento geral da República dos Estados Unidos do Brazil em 31 de dezembro de 1890. Districto Federal (Cidade do Rio de Janeiro) Capital da República dos Estados Unidos do Brazil* (Rio de Janeiro: Typ. Leuzinger, 1895), pp. 164–69, 172–77.

The 1890 census undercounted foreigners, but the size of this error is extremely difficult to determine. However, the relative proportions of different foreign-born groups one to another may not have been seriously distorted.

This census has other problems as well. Two different criteria were used for determining nationality: place of birth and citizenship. It cannot be determined whether the former—which would indicate a foreign-born population of 29.7 percent of Rio de Janeiro's inhabitants—rather than the latter—which shows 23.7 percent of Rio's population as foreign—was used in the occupational data. Furthermore, the 1890 census did not distinguish between owners and workers in different fields of activity. Nor did it utilize a criterion of principal employment—an individual was listed under as many professions as he declared, although the majority of the population declared but one. Sex, race, and nationality were only tabulated for some occupations. However, the 1872 national census and the 1906 Rio de Janeiro census did not correlate race and occupation at all. Of course, racial categories and classifications were never precise.

51. Brazil, *Recenseamento geral . . . 1890. Districto Federal*, pp. 164–69.

52. Brazil, *Recenseamento da populacão . . . 1872*, XXI (Município Neutro), 60; Brazil, *Recenseamento geral . . . 1890. Districto Federal*, pp. 164–69.

53. Stanley J. Stein, *Vassouras: A Brazilian Coffee County, 1850–1890* (Cambridge, Mass.: Harvard University Press, 1957), pp. 287–88.

54. Brazil, *Recenseamento geral . . . 1890. Districto Federal*, pp. 164–69.

55. Brazil, *Recenseamento da população . . . 1872*, XXI (Município Neutro), 60.

56. São Paulo (State), Repartição de Estatistica e Arquivo, *Relatório*, 1894, unpaged; Brazil, *Recenseamento geral . . . 1890. Districto Federal*, pp. 164–69.

57. Graham and Buarque de Hollanda Filho, *Migration, Regional and Urban Growth, and Development in Brazil*, p. 25.

58. Brazil, *Recenseamento geral . . . 1890. Districto Federal*, pp. 164–70, 177.

59. Brazil, *Recenseamento da população . . . 1872*, XXI (Município Neutro), 61; Brazil, Directoria Geral de Estatistica, *Recenseamento do Rio de*

Janeiro (Districto Federal) realizado em 20 de setembro de 1906 (Rio de Janeiro: Officina da Estatistica, 1907), I, 104.

60. Brazil, *Recenseamento do Rio de Janeiro* . . . 1906, I, 408–21; Manoel Garcia da Rosa, Portuguese Minister to Brazil, to José Vicente Barboza du Bocage, Foreign Minister, Petrópolis, Dec. 5, 1890, Legação de Portugal no Rio de Janeiro, Arquivo do Ministério dos Negócios Exteriores (Lisbon), Cx. 223.

61. Fernandes, *The Negro in Brazilian Society*, pp. 40–41.

62. See June E. Hahner, "Women and Work in Brazil, 1850–1920: A Preliminary Investigation," pp. 87–117 in Dauril Alden and Warren Dean, eds., *Essays Concerning the Socioeconomic History of Brazil and Portuguese India* (Gainesville: University Presses of Florida, 1977).

63. Brazil, *Recenseamento da população* . . . 1872, XXI (Município Neutro), 60–61; Brasil, *Recenseamento geral* . . . 1890. *Districto Federal*, pp. 164, 177; Brazil, *Recenseamento do Rio de Janeiro* . . . 1906, I, 122.

64. *O Operário* (Recife), 28 May 1879, p. 1; *Guttemberg* (Maceió, 27 June 1881, p. 1; *A Voz do Operário* (Salvador), 19 Sept. 1891, p. 1.

65. *Tribuna Operária* (Belém), 26 June 1893, p. 1.

66. *Voz do Povo* (Rio de Janeiro), 6 Jan. 1890, pp. 1–2; 7 Jan. 1890, p. 1; *Diário de Comércio* (Rio de Janeiro), 7 Feb. 1890, p. 1; 10 Feb. 1890, p. 1; 18 Feb. 1890, p. 1; 20 Feb. 1890, p. 3; 24 Feb. 1890, p. 1; *O País*, 27 Jan. 1890, p. 1; 30 Jan. 1890, p. 1; 10 Feb. 1890, p. 1; 12 Feb. 1890, p. 3; *Gazeta de Tarde* (Rio de Janeiro), 10 Feb. 1890, p. 1; *Echo Popular* (Rio de Janeiro), 11 March 1890, p. 1; 13 May 1890, p. 1.

67. Bellarmino Carneiro to Quintino Bocaiúva, Ceará, 3 Dec. 1889, and Benjamin Constant Botelho de Magalhães to Quntino Bocaiúva, Rio de Janeiro, 29 Nov. 1889, Quintino Bocaiúva Papers (Rio de Janeiro); Arquivo do Ministério da Marinha, Fés de Ofício, Vol. 48262, p. 236; João Dunshee de Abranches Moura, *Governors e congressos da República dos Estados Unidos do Brazil, 1889–1917* (São Paulo: M. V. Abranches, 1918), I, 342; *O País*, 23 Jan. 1890, p. 2; 5 Feb. 1890, p. 2.

68. *O Combate* (Fortaleza), 8 March 1896, p. 3. See also *Echo Operário* (Rio Grande do Sul), 18 Aug. 1901, p. 1; *Gazeta Operário* (Rio de Janeiro), 11 Jan. 1903, p. 2.

69. *Voz do Povo* (Rio de Janeiro), 6 Jan. 1890, p. 2.

70. *Diário do Comércio*, 15 Feb. 1890, p. 1; 24 Feb. 1890, p. 2; *Echo Popular* (Rio de Janeiro), 10 June 1890, pp. 2, 3.

71. *Echo Popular*, 11 March 1890, p. 1; *O País*, 10 Feb. 1890, p. 1; Nelson Werneck Sodré, *A história da imprensa no Brasil* (Rio de Janeiro: Editôra Civilização Brasileira, 1966), pp. 352–55; Gustavo de Lacerda, *O problema operário no Brasil. Propaganda socialista* (Rio de Janeiro: n.p., 1901).

72. *O País*, 12 Feb. 1890, p. 3; 18 Feb. 1890, p. 2.

73. *Echo Popular*, 11 March 1890, p. 1; 10 April 1890, p. 1; *Diário do Comércio*, 17 Feb. 1890, p. 2.

74. *Echo Popular*, 6 Aug. 1890, p. 1.

75. Arquivo do Ministério da Marinha, Fés de Ofício, Vol. 48262, p.

237; *O País*, 23 Feb. 1890, p. 2; 24 Feb. 1890, p. 3; 8 March 1890, p. 3; 17 March 1890, p. 3; *Echo Popular*, 13 March 1890, p. 1; *O Socialista*, 31 March 1893, p. 3.

76. *O País*, 10 Feb. 1890, p. 1.

77. *O País*, 15 Feb. 1890, p. 2; 10 March 1890, p. 1; 20 March 1890, p. 2; *O Socialista*, 31 March 1893, p. 3; Roberto Macedo, A *administração de Floriano*, Vol. V of *Floriano. Memórias e documentos* (Rio de Janeiro: Ministério da Educação, 1939), p. 198; Manuel Fernandes Figueira, *Memória histórica da Estrada de Ferro Central do Brazil* (Rio de Janeiro: Imprensa Nacional, 1908), p. 319.

78. *Echo Popular*, 23 Oct. 1890, p. 1; 7 Nov. 1890, p. 1; *A União Lusitana* (Rio de Janeiro), 26 July 1892, p. 1; Evaristo de Morais *Apontamentos de direito operário* (Rio de Janeiro: Imprensa Nacional, 1905), p. 59; Brazil, Câmara dos Deputados, *Annaes do Congresso Constituinte da República*, 3 vols., 2 ed. (Rio de Janeiro: Imprensa Nacional, 1924–26), II, 26–29, session of 4 Feb. 1891; III, 253–54, session of 23 Feb. 1891.

79. Floriano Peixoto to Campos Sales, Rio de Janeiro, Nov. 1891, p. 412 in Antonio Joaquim Ribas, *Perfil biographico do dr. Manoel Ferraz de Campos Salles, ministro da justiça do governo provisório, senador federal pelo Estado de São Paulo* (Rio de Janeiro: Typ. Leuzinger, 1896); Custódio José de Mello, *O governo provisório e a revolução de 1893* (São Paulo: Companhia Editôra Nacional, 1938), I, 95; Macedo, A *administração de Floriano*, p. 200; *A União Lusitana*, 26 Oct. 1892, p. 3; 16 Nov. 1892, p. 1; *O Socialista*, 31 March 1893, p. 3.

80. *Notas de um revoltoso. (Diário de bordo). Documentos authenticos publicados pelo "Commercio de São Paulo"* (Rio de Janeiro: Typ. Moraes, 1895), pp. 14–93; Alcindo de Guanabara, *História da revolta de 6 de septembro de 1893* (Rio de Janeiro: Typ. e Papelaria Mont'Alverne, 1894), pp. 48–49; Macedo, A *administração de Floriano*, p. 204; Figueira, *Memória histórica da Estrada de Ferro Central do Brazil*, p. 378. For a fuller discussion of army-navy rivalries and the Naval Revolt, see June E. Hahner, *Civilian-Military Relations in Brazil 1889–1898* (Columbia, S.C.: University of South Carolina Press, 1969), pp. 47–72.

81. Arquivo do Ministério da Marinha, Fés de Ofício, Vol. 48262, p. 237; *O Socialista* (São Paulo), 14 June 1896, p. 1; *O Operário* (Rio de Janeiro), 16 Nov. 1895, p. 2; Reis Júnior and Costa Mendes to Rui Barbosa, Ilha das Cobras, 4 Aug. 1900; José Augusto Vinhais, Costa Mendes, and Reis Júnior to Rui Barbosa, Ilha das Cobras, 21 Aug. 1900, 27 Aug. 1900, 2 Sept. 1900, Casa de Rui Barbosa, Pasta Reis Júnior; José Augusto Vinhais to President Epitácio Pessoa, Rio de Janeiro, 1 Feb. 1922, Arquivo do Instituto Histórico e Geográfico Brasileiro, Epitácio Pessoa Papers, Pasta 15; *Revista Marítima Brasileira* LIII (July-August 1933), 111–15; Bricio de Abreu, *Esses populares tão desconhecidos* (Rio de Janeiro: E. Raposo Carneiro, 1963), p. 71.

82. *Echo Popular*, 6 March 1890, p. 2; 12 April 1890, p. 1; 29 April 1890, p. 1; *O Combate* (Fortaleza), 17 July 1891, p. 2.

83. *Echo Popular*, 29 April 1890, p. 1.

84. *O Operario* (Recife), 28 May 1879, p. 1; *Guttemberg* (Maceió), 27 June 1881, p. 1; *A Voz do Operário* (Salvador), 19 Sept. 1891, p. 1.

85. *Echo Popular*, 29 April 1890, p. 1.

86. *Echo Popular*, 25 March 1890, p. 1.
For the contemporary Portuguese labor movement, see: Alexandre Vieira, *Para a história do sindicalismo em Portugal* 2d ed. (Lisbon: Seara Nova, 1974); J. M. Gonçalves Viana, *A evolução anarquista em Portugal* (Lisbon: Seara Nova, 1975); Cesar Oliveira, *O operariado e a república democrática (1910–1914)*, 2d ed. (Lisbon: Seara Nova, 1974); David de Carvalho, *Os sindicales operarios e a república burguesa (1910–1928)* (Lisbon: Seara Nova, 1977); César Nogueira, *Notas para a história do socialismo em Portugal*, 2 vols. (Lisbon: Portugália Editôra, 1966).

87. *O Combate*, 16 May 1891, p. 1.

88. *O Combate*, 9 April 1891, p. 1; 17 April 1891, p. 2; *Voz do Povo*, 6 Jan. 1890, p. 2; *Echo Popular*, 21 March 1890, p. 2; 22 April 1890, pp. 1–2; 29 April 1890, p. 1; 10 June 1890, p. 1; 12 June 1890, p. 1; 17 June 1890, p. 1; 21 June 1890, p. 1; 2 July 1890, p. 1; 12 July 1890, p. 1; *Jornal dos Operários*, 1 May 1891, p. 2; *Voz do Operário*, 19 Sept. 1891, p. 1; *Tribuna Operária* (Belém), 10 July 1892, p. 1.

89. *O Combate*, 4 April 1891, p. 1; 9 April 1891, p. 1; 19 April 1891, p. 1; 22 April 1891, p. 1; 6 July 1891, p. 1; 24 July 1891, p. 1; 15 Oct. 1891, p. 1; 17 Jan. 1892, p. 1; 1 May 1896, p. 1; Abelardo F. Monteiro, *História dos partidos políticos cearenses* (Fortaleza: n.p., 1965), pp. 35–36.

90. Manoel Querino, *As artes na Bahia (Escorço de uma contribuição histórica)* (Bahia: Typ. do Lyceu de Artes e Ofícios, 1909), pp. 70–85; Kátia de Queirós Mattoso, "Os preços na Bahia de 1750 a 1930," pp. 177, 182 in *L'histoire quantitiative du Brésil de 1800 a 1930*.

91. Querino, *As artes na Bahia*, pp. 86–94.

92. Querino, *As artes na Bahia*, pp. 80, 96.

93. Antonio Vianna, "Manoel Querino," *Revista do Instituto Geográfico e Histórico da Bahia* 54, Part II (1928), 305–16; Querino, *As artes na Bahia*, pp. 95–96; preface by Arthur Ramos to Manoel Querino, *Costumes africanos no Brasil* (Rio de Janeiro: Editôra Civilização Brasileira, 1938), pp. 9–12; *A Voz do Operário*, 19 Sept. 1891, p. 1. For Manoel Querino's contributions to Afro-Brazilian studies, see E. Bradford Burns, "Manuel Querino's Interpretation of the African Contribution to Brazil," *Journal of Negro History* 54 (January 1974), 78–86.

94. *O Operário* (São Paulo), 28 April 1891, pp. 1–4; 26 July 1891, p. 1; *Jornal dos Operários* (Rio de Janeiro), 1 May 1891, p. 1; *O Operário* (Santos), 30 Oct. 1891, p. 1; "Rapport de la Commission Executive du Parti Ouvrier du Brésil a Presenter au Congres Socialiste International de Zurich, 1893," *Le Mouvement Social* (July-September 1973), 52–57.

95. *A União Lusitana*, 7 May 1892, p. 2; *O Socialista*, 18 Feb. 1893, p. 4; 25 Feb. 1893, pp. 3–4; 4 March 1893, p. 3; "Rapport de la Commission

Executive du Parti Ouvrier du Brésil a Presenter au Congres Socialiste International de Zurich, 1893," *Le Mouvement Social* (July-September 1973), 52–57.

96. *O Socialista*, 18 Feb. 1893, p. 4.

97. "Rapport de la Commission Executive du Parti Ouvrier du Brésil a Presenter au Congres Socialiste International de Zurich, 1893," *Le Mouvement Social* (July-September 1973), 52–57.

98. *O Socialista*, 25 Feb. 1893, p. 4; *Gazeta dos Operários*, 11 Dec. 1875, p. 4; 15 Dec. 1875, p. 4; *Revista Typographica*, 31 March 1888, p. 2; 5 May 1888, p. 3; *Echo Popular*, 15 April, 1890, p. 1; 23 July 1890, p. 1; *O Alvorado*, 24 Aug. 1890, p. 2.

99. Brazil, Ministério da Justiça, *Relatório*, June 1891, p. 6; 1892, p. 10; Manoel Garcia da Rosa, Portuguese Minister to Brazil, to José Vicente Barboza du Bocage, Foreign Minister, Petrópolis, 5 Dec. 1890, Arquivo do Ministério dos Negócios Exteriores (Lisbon), Cx. 223; A *União Lusitana*, 15 June 1892, p. 1; 26 Oct. 1892, p. 3; Morais, *Apontamentos direito operário*, pp. 58–63; Azis Simão, *Sindicato e estado*, pp. 102–3; Brazil, *Annaes do Congresso Constituinte*, III, 253–54.

100. *O Socialista*, 18 Feb. 1893, p. 1.

101. Although socialist labor tendencies did not emerge in Brazil until the beginning of the republic, socialist ideas in one vague form or another had been uttered by various Brazilian intellectuals since the midnineteenth century. Influence of the Fourier school appeared in an 1846 newspaper, *O Socialista da Provincia do Rio de Janeiro*, dedicated "to all the improvement of which society is capable" (9 Jan. 1846, p. 1). During the second half of the nineteenth century, some intellectuals read Marx, and a few well-intentioned ones would address themselves to the workers.

For the development of socialist ideas in Brazil, see Vamireh Chacon, *História das idéias socialistas no Brasil* (Rio de Janeiro: Editôra Civilização Brasileira, 1965). In *Socialismo e sindicalismo no Brasil*, Edgar Rodrigues deals with some early socialist views (pp. 23–33).

Chapter 4

1. Evaristo de Morais, *Apontamentos de direito operário* (Rio de Janeiro: Imprensa Nacional, 1905), pp. 31–33, 58–59; *O Socialista* (Rio de Janeiro) 11 March 1893, p. 2; Brazil, Ministério da Justiça, *Relatório*, 1891, pp. 6, 12.

2. José Francisco de Paula e Silva to Municipal Council of Rio de Janeiro, 1 Aug. 1855, Arquivo Geral da Cidade do Rio de Janeiro, 44-2-7 (hereafter AGCRJ).

3. *Gazeta da Tarde* (Rio de Janeiro), 14 Feb. 1884, p. 1; 16 Feb. 1884, p. 1.

4. See documents in AGCRJ, 41-3-36 and 40-4-47.

5. Américo de Castro to D. Pedro II, Rio de Janeiro, 8 Nov. 1877, and 26 May 1880, AGCRJ, 40-4-45.

6. "Parecer da Commissão de Privilegiados sobre a proposição relativa a

construcção de cases denominadas 'Evoneas,' " Rio de Janeiro, 1880, AGCRJ, 40-4-45.

7. Guilherme A. Moreira Guimarães to Inspector General of Hygiene, Rio de Janeiro, 8 June 1891, 43-1-37 [copy]; José Augusto Vinhais to Minister of Interior, Rio de Janeiro, 28 July 1890, AGCRJ, 46-4-56; Vinhais to Deodoro da Fonseca, Rio de Janeiro, 10 Jan. 1891, AGCRJ, 40-4-56; *O País* (Rio de Janeiro), 18 April 1890, p. 2.

8. Francisco Rangel Pestana (pseud. Thomas Jefferson), *Notas republicanas. I. A reacção e os novos partidos. II. A política do marechal Floriano Peixoto* (Rio de Janeiro, n.p., 1898), pp. 129, 180.

9. Afonso Arinos de Melo Franco, Chapter 2, A *República, as oligarquias estaduais* Vol. V of *História do povo brasileiro*, Jânio Quadros, Afonso Arinos de Melo Franco, and others, 2d ed. (São Paulo: J. Quadros Editôres Culturais, 1968), pp. 31, 51.

10. Afonso Arinos, Chapter 2, *História do povo brasileiro*, V, 32.

11. Manuel Diégues Júnior, *Imigração, urbanização e industrialização (Estudo sobre alguns aspectos da contribuição cultural do imigrante no Brasil)* (Rio de Janeiro: Centro Brasileiro de Pesquisas Educacionaes, Instituto Nacional de Estudos Pedagógicos, Ministério da Educação e Cultura, 1964), p. 227.

12. Stanley J. Stein, *The Brazilian Cotton Manufacture: Textile Enterprise in an Underdeveloped Area, 1850–1950* (Cambridge, Mass.: Harvard University Press, 1957), pp. 81–97; Nícia Vilela Luz, A *luta pela industrialização do Brasil (1808–1930)* (São Paulo, Difusão Européia do Livro), pp. 169–72.

13. Brazil, Ministério da Guerra, *Relatório*, 1889, *Annexos*, p. 12; *Relatório*, 1893, p. 62; *Jornal do Comércio* (Rio de Janeiro), 25 June 1893, p. 1; Richard Graham, "Government Expenditures and Political Change in Brazil, 1880–1899: Who Got What," *Journal of Interamerican Studies and World Affairs* 19 (August 1977), 344, 368; Felisbello Firmo de Oliveira Freire, *História da revolta de 6 de setembro de 1893* (Rio de Janeiro: Cunha & Irmãos, 1896), p. 75; Theodorico Lopes and Gentil Torres, *Ministros da guerra do Brasil (1808–1950)*, 4th ed. (Rio de Janeiro: Borsoi, 1950), p. 30; Gustavo Barroso, *História militar do Brasil* (São Paulo: Companhia Editôra Nacional, 1935), p. 83; Roberto Macedo, *A administração de Floriano*, Vol. V of *Floriano. Memórias e documentos* (Rio de Janeiro: Serviço Gráfico do Ministério da Educação, 1939), p. 246; Amador Pereira Gomes Nogueira Cobra, *Brios de gente armada (Páginas republicanas na história do Brazil)* (São Paulo: Beccari, Jannini & Cia., [1924?]), p. 180.

14. Macedo, *A administração de Floriano*, pp. 171–172.

15. Miguel Guimarães to Director of Works, Rio de Janeiro, 18 Feb. 1893, AGCRJ, 44-2-9.

16. *Echo Popular* (Rio de Janeiro), 21 June 1891, p. 1; *O Operário* (Santos), 30 Oct. 1892, p. 3; *O País* (Rio de Janeiro), 19 Feb. 1893, p. 1: *O Socialista*, 25 Feb. 1893, p. 4.

17. *O Socialista*, 25 Feb. 1893, p. 3.

18. *O País*, 19 Feb. 1893, p. 1.

19. *O Socialista*, 18 Feb. 1893, p. 2.

20. Macedo, A *administração de Floriano*, p. 172.

21. *Jornal dos Operários* (Rio de Janeiro), 1 May 1891, p. 1.

22. *A Voz do Operário* (Salvador), 19 Sept. 1891, p. 2.

23. *Tribuna Operária* (Belém), 26 June 1893, p. 1.

24. *O Socialista*, 18 Feb. 1893, p. 3; 11 March 1893, pp. 1–2.

25. Francolino Câmeu and Arthur Vieira Peixoto, *Floriano Peixoto. Vida e governo* (Rio de Janeiro: Officinas Gráficas da A Norte, 1925), p. 77.

26. Aureliano Restier Gonçalves, "Carnes verdes em São Sebastião do Rio de Janeiro, 1500–1900," in Arquivo do Districto Federal, *Revista de documentos para a história da cidade do Rio de Janeiro* (Rio de Janeiro: Secretaria Geral da Educação e Cultura, 1952), III, 308.

27. *O Socialista*, 18 Feb. 1893, p. 2.

28. *Echo Popular*, 24 May 1890, p. 1: *A União Lusitana* (Rio de Janeiro), 17 Sept. 1892, p. 3; *O Socialista*, 25 Feb. 1892, p. 4; *O Operário* (Rio de Janeiro), 12 Oct. 1895, p. 2.

29. *O Socialista*, 31 March 1893, p. 2; 25 Feb. 1893, p. 1.

30. *Gazeta Operária* (Rio de Janeiro), 7 Dec. 1893, p. 1.

31. *Tribuna Operária*, 10 July 1892, p. 1.

32. *Tribuna Operária*, 26 June 1893, p. 2; 1 May 1894, pp. 2–3.

33. *O Socialista*, 18 Feb. 1893, p. 3; 25 March 1893, p. 3; 31 March 1893, p. 3; 14 April 1893, p. 1; *Tribuna Operária*, 10 July 1892, p. 1.

34. Brazil, Ministério da Justiça, *Relatório* April 1893, Relatório of Police Chief of Federal Capital, p. 22; Ministério da Justiça, *Relatório, March 1894, p. 59*; Cassiano do Nascimento to Fernando Lobo, Rio de Janeiro, 29 Nov. 1893, and 4 Dec. 1893, Arquivo Histórico do Ministério das Relações Exteriores, 302-3-7; *Rio News* (Rio de Janeiro), 5 Dec. 1893, pp. 3, 5; 2 Jan. 1895, p. 3; 15 Jan. 1895, p. 5.

35. The term *caboclo* is traditionally used to describe someone of mixed Indian-European ancestry, or even a "civilized" Indian. However, the term is also applied to an individual from the interior, especially the *sertão*, a backwoodsman.

36. Barbosa Lima, "Floriano Peixoto, Nacionalista," p. 47 in *Commemoração cívica do Marechal Floriano Peixoto* (Rio de Janeiro: Typ. Pacheco, Silva & C., 1899).

37. A valuable study of nationalism in Latin America is Arthur P. Whitaker and David C. Jordan, *Nationalism in Contemporary Latin America* (New York, 1966). See also the earlier Arthur P. Whitaker, *Nationalism in Latin America* (Gainesville: University of Florida Press, 1962). The published, brief histories of nationalism in Brazil are Barbosa Lima Sobrinho, *Desde quando somos nacionalistas?* (Rio de Janeiro: Editôra Civilização Brasileira, 1963) and E. Bradford Burns, *Nationalism in Brazil: A Historical Survey* (New York: Praeger, 1968). See also Hélio Jaguaribe, *Burguesía y proletariado en el nacionalismo brasileno* (Buenos Aires: Ediciones Coyoacán, 1961); Antônio Cândido Mendes de Almeida, *Nacionalismo e desenvolvimento* (Rio de Janeiro: Instituto Brasileiro de Estudos Brasileiros, 1963); and Thomas E. Skidmore, *Black into*

White: Race and Nationality in Brazilian Thought (New York: Oxford University Press, 1974).

38. Tristão de Alencar Araipe Júnior, *Literatura brasileira: Movimento de 1893* (Rio de Janeiro: Typographica da Empreza Democratica Editôra, 1896), pp. 3–23.

39. Rodrigo Octavio de Langgaard Menezes, *Festas nacionaes* (Rio de Janeiro: F. Briguiet & C., 1893). For a biography of Pompéia, see Eloy Pontes, *A vida inquieta de Raul Pompéia (Rio de Janeiro: José Olympio, 1936)*.

40. Alexandre José Mello Moraes Filho, *Mythos e poemas*. Nacionalismo (Rio de Janeiro: G. Leuzinger & Filhos, 1884).

41. Brazil, Directoria Geral de Estatistica, *Recenseamento geral da República dos Estados Unidos do Brazil em 31 de dezembro de 1890. Districto Federal (Cidade do Rio de Janeiro) Capital da República dos Estados Unidos do Brazil* (Rio de Janeiro: Typ. Leuzinger, 1895), xii, xxiii, xxvii.

42. For information about the War of the Mascates, see C. R. Boxer, *The Golden Age of Brazil, 1695–1750: Growing Pains of a Colonial Society* (Berkeley and Los Angeles: University of California Press, 1962), pp. 106–25.

43. Luiz Vianna Filho, A *Sabinada. A república bahiana de 1837* (Rio de Janeiro; José Olympio, 1938).

44. Júlio da Silveira Lobo, *Apontamentos para a história do Segundo Reinado*, n.p., 1895; Antônio da Silva Jardim, *A patria em perigo (Bragança e Orleans)* (São Paulo: Typ. da Provincia, 1888); *Salvação da patria (Governo republicano)* Santos: Typ. Diário de Santos, 1888).

45. *Jornal dos Operários*, 1 May 1891, p. 2; *O País*, 29 Jan. 1891, p. 1; *O Socialista*, 18 Feb. 1893, p. 3: Américo Werneck, *O Brazil. Seu presente e seu futuro* (Petrópolis: Typ. da Gazeta de Petrópolis, 1892), pp. 37–39; Azis Simão, *Sindicato e estado. Suas relações na formação do proletariado de São Paulo* (São Paulo: Dominus Editôra, 1966), p. 18; Rangel Pestana, *Notas republicanas*, p. 126; João Severiano da Fonseca to Deodoro da Fonseca, n.d., Clodoaldo da Fonseca Papers, Rio de Janeiro; Celso Furtado, *The Economic Growth of Brazil. A Survey from Colonial to Modern Times*, trans. Ricardo W. de Aguiar and Eric Charles Drysdale (Berkeley and Los Angeles: University of California Press, 1965), pp. 182–94.

46. Mario Sette, *Anquinhas e Bernardas* (São Paulo: Livraria Martins, 1940), p. 199.

> Essa lei de Deodoro
> Essa lei de Floriano
> Essa lei republicana
> Ninguém pode mais ama.
> Covo de chita
> Que custava uma pataca
> Hoje e tanto dinheiro
> Que ninguém pode compra.

47. According to the 1890 census, the foreign-born working in commerce

in Rio de Janeiro slightly outnumbered Brazilians by 24,477 to 23,571 (Table 13). Unfortunately, the percentage of Portuguese among these foreign-born cannot be determined. By the 1890s the Almanak Laemmert had ceased to record that distinction.

48. Maurício Lamberg, *O Brazil*, trans. Luiz de Castro (Rio de Janeiro: Typ. Nunes, 1896), pp. 84–85; Pierre Denis, *Brazil*, trans. Bernard Miall (New York: Charles Scribner's Sons, 1911), pp. 24–25; Alured Gray Bell, *The Beautiful Rio de Janeiro* (London: William Heinenmann, 1914), p. 44.

49. *A União Lusitana*, 14 May 1892, p. 1.

50. *Correio Portuguez* (Rio de Janeiro), 23 March 1892, p. 1; *A União Lusitana*, 14 May 1892, p. 1.

51. Joel Serrão, *A emigração portuguesa. Sondagem histórica*, 2d ed. (Lisbon: Livros Horizonte, 1974), p. 179.

> O Brasil, terra de enganos,
> Quantos lá vão enganados;
> Tantos lá vão por três anos,
> E ficam lá sepultados.

52. *A União Lusitana*, 8 June 1892, p. 1; *Correio Portuguez*, 30 March 1892, p. 1; Luiz Edmundo da Costa, *De um livro de memórias*, 5 vols. (Rio de Janeiro: Imprensa Nacional, 1958), II, 424; Richard Graham, "Government Expenditures and Political Change in Brazil, 1880–1899: Who Got What," *Journal of Interamerican Studies and World Affairs* 19 (August 1977), 356.

53. *A Gallegada* (Rio de Janeiro), 8 May 1883, pp. 1–4.

54. *O Portuguez* (Rio de Janeiro), Bulletin, n.d.; 13 May 1883, p. 1; 19 May 1883, p. 1; 26 May 1883, p. 1; *A Gallegada*, 15 May 1883, p. 2; 5 June 1883, p. 3; 5 Aug. 1886, p. 1.

55. Brazil, Department of Foreign Affairs, *Correspondence Exchanged with the Legation of Portugal and the Legation of Brazil at Lisbon in Regard to the Surrender of the Insurgent Refugees on Board the Portuguese Corvettes "Mindello" and "Affonso de Albuquerque"* (Rio de Janeiro: Typ. Leuzinger, 1894).

56. *Diário Popular* (Rio de Janeiro), 25 Nov. 1889, p. 1; Macedo, *A administração de Floriano*, pp. 246–47; "Ordem do dia no. 1, Batalhão Republicano Municipal," Rio de Janeiro, December 1893, AGCRJ, 40-2-12; "Relação do pessoal da Estação Central Desinfecção que espontaneamente faz franca adhesão ao patriotico Batalhão Republicano Municipal," AGCRJ, 40-2-11; Conde de Paço de Arcos, Portuguese Minister to Brazil, to Conde de Valbom, Foreign Minister, Rio de Janeiro, 23 Dec. 1891, Legação de Portugal no Rio de Janeiro, Arquivo do Ministério dos Negócios Estangeiros, Cx. 223; Brazil, Ministério da Guerra, *Relatório*, 1894, p. 4; *Rio News*, 11 Oct. 1893, p. 5; *A Bomba* (Rio de Janeiro), 2 Nov. 1894, p. 1; *O Nacional* (Rio de Janeiro), 29 June 1895, p. 2; 31 Aug. 1895, p. 2.

57. João de Deos Teixeira to Rui Barbosa, Rio de Janeiro, 8 March 1904, Casa de Rui Barbosa, Pasta Teixeira; *O Jacobino* (Rio de Janeiro), 29 June 1901, p. 3; *Cidade do Rio* (Rio de Janeiro), 22 Sept. 1889, p. 1; *A Bomba*, 16 Oct. 1894, p. 2; *O Nacional*, 7 July 1895, p. 2; Luiz Edmundo da Costa, *O Rio de Janeiro do meu tempo*, 3 vols. (Rio de Janeiro: Imprensa Nacional, 1938), III, 1027; Costa, *De um livro de memórias*, II, 426; *O Jacobino* (Rio de Janeiro), 12 Sept. 1896, p. 1.

58. *O Estrangeiro* (Rio de Janeiro), 29 Oct. 1894, pp. 1–2; *A Bomba*, 30 Oct. 1894, p. 1.

59. *O Jacobino*, 13 Sept. 1894, p. 1; 30 April 1895, p. 1.

60. *O Jacobino*, 26 Sept. 1894, p. 3; 20 Oct. 1894, p. 1; 7 Nov. 1894, p. 3; 10 Nov. 1894, p. 1; 1 Nov. 1894, p. 1; 26 Dec. 1896, p. 1.

61. *O Jacobino*, 13 Sept. 1894, p. 1; 26 Sept. 1894, p. 3; 24 Oct. 1894, p. 1; 10 Oct. 1896, p. 1; 17 April 1897, p. 1; 15 May 1897, p. 1. See also: *O Nativista* (Rio de Janeiro), 4 June 1895, p. 2; 27 Aug. 1895, p. 3; *A Bomba*, 1 Sept. 1894, p. 1.

62. *O Jacobino*, 15 May 1897, p. 1.

63. *O Nativista*, 19 Oct. 1895, p. 3; *A Bomba*, 1 Sept. 1894, p. 1; *O Jacobino*, 13 Sept. 1894, p. 1; 26 Sept. 1894, p. 3; 15 May 1897, p. 1; 7 Nov. 1894, p. 2; 14 Nov. 1894, p. 4; *Rio News*, 30 July 1895, p. 5; João Chagas, *De bond. Alguns aspectos da civilização brazileira* (Lisbon: Livraria Moderna, 1897), p. 142; Conde de Paço de Arcos to Hintze Ribeiro, Foreign Minister, Petrópolis, 6 May 1894, Arquivo do Ministério dos Negócios Estrangeiros, Cx. 224.

64. Brazil, Directoria Geral de Estatística, *Recenseamento . . . 1890. Districto Federal*, pp. 408–15.

65. Brazil, Directoria Geral de Estatística, *Recenseamento . . . 1890. Districto Federal*, pp. 45, 413; São Paulo [state], Repartição de Estatística e Arquivo, *Relatório apresentado a . . . Cezario Motta Junior pelo director da repartição da Estatística e Arquivo Antonio de Toledo Piza, 31 de julho de 1894* (Rio de Janeiro: Typ. Leuzinger, 1894), unpaged.

66. *O Nativista*, 14 June 1895, p. 1; *O Nacional*, 17 July 1895, p. 1.

67. Afonso Henriques de Lima Barreto, *Bagatelas*, 2d ed. (São Paulo: Editôra Brasiliense, 1961), pp. 42–43.

68. *Gazeta dos Operários* (Rio de Janeiro), 8 Dec. 1875, p. 1.

69. *O País*, 17 Feb. 1890, p. 1; *O Socialista*, 25 Feb. 1893, p. 4; *O Jacobino*, 10 Nov. 1894, p. 1.

70. *O Artista Pernambucano* (Recife), 25 Jan. 1853, p. 1.

71. *O Jacobino*, 13 Sept. 1894, p. 4; 26 Sept. 1894, p. 1; 20 Oct. 1894, p. 1; 7 Nov. 1894, p. 2; 10 Nov. 1894, p. 1; 18 Nov. 1894, p. 1; 15 Dec. 1894, p. 3; 26 Dec. 1896, p. 1.

72. *O Jacobino*, 15 Dec. 1894, p. 3.

73. *O Jacobino*, 1 Dec. 1894, p. 2; 15 Dec. 1894, p. 3; 19 Jan. 1895, p. 1; 21 Nov. 1896, p. 1; 2 Jan. 1897, p. 1; Everardo Dias, *História das lutas sociais no Brasil* (São Paulo: Editôra Edaglit, 1962), p. 67.

74. *Rio News*, 29 Jan. 1895, p. 5; 1 Oct. 1895, p. 8; 14 July 1896, p. 8;

Corriere Italiano (São Paulo), 30 Sept. 1894, p. 2; Costa, *De um livro de memórias*, II, 424–25; Costa, *O Rio de Janeiro do meu tempo*, III, 1026.

75. Carlos de Carvalho, Minister of Foreign Affairs to Ministry of Justice, 30 Dec. 1895; Ministry of Foreign Affairs to Ministry of Justice, 15 Jan. 1896, 7 Nov. 1896, 24 Nov. 1896, Arquivo Histórico do Ministério das Relações Exteriores, 302-3-11.

76. Chagas, *De bond*, p. 177.

77. Prudente de Morais to Bernardino de Campos, Rio de Janeiro, 10 Jan. 1896, p. 272 in Cândido Mota Filho, *Uma grande vida. Biografia de Bernardino de Campos* (São Paulo: Editôra Companhia Nacional, 1941).

78. *O Jacobino*, 21 Nov. 1894, p. 2; 22 Dec. 1894, p. 3; *A Bomba*, 30 Nov. 1894, p. 1; *O Corsário* (Rio de Janeiro), 29 Jan. 1896, p. 3.

79. Campos Sales to Augusto Costa, São Paulo, 27 Feb. 1894, Instituto Histórico e Geográfico de São Paulo, 920 S163c AI; Campos Sales to Prudente de Morais, São Paulo, 22 Aug. 1896, Prudente de Morais Papers, Instituto Histórico e Geográfico Brasileiro; *Estado de São Paulo* (São Paulo), 24 Aug. 1896, p. 1; 25 Aug. 1896, p. 1; 28 Aug. 1896, p. 1; *Rio News*, 11 Aug. 1896, p. 7; 25 Aug. 1896, p. 6–8; Elysio de Araujo, *Atravez de meio seculo. Notas históricas* (São Paulo: São Paulo Editôra, 1932), pp. 98–100.

80. *O Jacobino*, 13 Sept. 1894, p. 1; 22 Sept. 1894, p. 1; 21 Nov. 1894, p. 1; 10 Oct. 1896, p. 1; 5 June 1897, p. 1.

81. See June E. Hahner, *Civilian-Military Relations in Brazil, 1889–1898* (Columbia, S.C.: University of South Carolina Press, 1969), pp. 148–78.

82. Brazil, Ministério da Justiça, *Relatório*, pp. 39–57; *Jornal do Comércio*, 6 Nov. 1897, p. 1; 7 Nov. 1897, p. 1; *Rio News*, 9 Nov. 1897, p. 4; 16 Nov. 1896, p. 5.

83. "Depoimento de Marcellino Bispo," 13 Nov. 1897, pp. 56–61 in Vicente Neiva, *Attentado de cinco de novembro. Relatorio de dr. Vicente Neiva, 1° delegado auxiliar, e diversas peças do inquerito* (Rio de Janeiro: Imprensa Nacional, 1898).

84. Neiva, *Attentado de cinco de novembro.*

85. Eduardo A. Socrates, Raiz de Serra, Estado do Rio, 21 March 1896, to Quintino Bocaiúva, Quintino Bocaiúva Papers, Rio de Janeiro; *Commemoração civica do Marechal Floriano Peixoto*, p. 31; *A Bomba*, 7 Dec. 1894, p. 1. *O Nativista*, 19 Oct. 1895, p. 1; *Rio News*, 9 March 1897, p. 6.

86. Rodrigo Otavio de Langgaard Menezes, *Minhas memórias dos outros*, 2 vols. (Rio de Janeiro: José Olympio, 1934–36), I, 39, 138.

87. *A Bomba*, 1 Sept. 1894, p. 3; 7 Sept. 1894, p. 1; 7 Dec. 1894, p. 1; *O Nacional*, 27 July 1895, p. 2; 10 Aug. 1895, p. 1.

88. *A Bomba*, 29 Sept. 1894, p. 3; 30 Oct. 1894, p. 1; 7 Dec. 1894, p. 1; 21 Dec. 1894, p. 1; *O Nacional*, 24 July 1895, p. 1; 27 July 1895, p. 2; 5 Dec. 1896, p. 3; *O Jacobino*, 10 Oct. 1896, p. 1.

89. *A Bomba*, 29 Sept. 1894, p. 1.

90. Neiva, *Attentado de cinco de novembro*, pp. 56–61, 72–79; Cancea, *Attentado de cinco de novembro. Artigos de Caneca publicados na "Gazeta de*

Noticias" sobre o "Despacho" do juiz Affonso de Miranda (Rio de Janeiro; Imprensa Nacional, 1898), pp. 61, 116–18; *Rio News*, 18 Jan. 1898, p. 7.

91. Annibal Villanova Villela and Wilson Suzigan, *Política do governo e crescimento da economia brasileira, 1889–1945* (Rio de Janeiro: Instituto de Planejamento Econômico e Social Institito de Pesquisas, 1973), pp. 35–39, 81, 100, 105–7; Brazil, Directoria Geral de Estatística, *Recenseamento . . . 1890. Districto Federal*, pp. 412–21; Brazil, Directoria Geral de Estatística, *Recenseamento do Rio de Janeiro (Districto Federal) realizado em 20 de setembro de 1906* (Rio de Janeiro: Officina da Estatística, 1907), I, 104; *Revista de Imigração e colonização 1* (Oct. 1940), 617–22.

92. *O Jacobino*, 29 June 1901, pp. 1–3.

93. *A Voz Pública* (Rio de Janeiro), 19 Oct. 1904, p. 1.

94. *Districto Federal [Rio de Janeiro]*, 1 July 1905, *p. 1*; *Aurora* (Rio de Janeiro), 23 Jan. 1909, p. 1; *O Operário* (Rio de Janeiro), 3 Feb. 1909, p. 3; "Processo de Deocleciano Martyr," Arquivo Nacional, Secão do Poder Judicial, 1ª Vara Criminal 1926, Processo 1717, Cx. 1949, Maço 446.

Chapter 5

1. General themes of progress and cultural conflict, the elite, and the "folk" in nineteenth-century Latin America, are discussed by E. Bradford Burns in his significant essay *The Poverty of Progress: Latin America in the Nineteenth Century* (Berkeley and Los Angeles: University of California Press, 1980). Progress, or as it is termed in the twentieth century, modernization, in Brazil is analyzed by Richard Graham in *Britain and the Onset of Modernization in Brazil, 1850–1914* (Cambridge University Press, 1968).

2. Warren Dean, *The Industrialization of São Paulo, 1880–1945* (Austin and London: University of Texas Press, 1969), pp. 19–35.

3. Richard M. Morse, *From Community to Metropolis: A Biography of São Paulo, Brazil* (Gainesville: University of Florida Press, 1958), p. 181. On public transportation in late nineteenth-century São Paulo see Gerald Michael Greenfield, "Algumas notas sobre a história da viação urbana no velho São Paulo," *Revista de História* 49 (July-September 1974), 117–43.

4. São Paulo [city], *Relatorio apresentado á Camara Municipal de São Paulo pelo Intendente Municipal Cesario Ramalho da Silva*, 1893 (São Paulo: Typ. de Espinola, Siqueira & Comp., 1894), p. 4; São Paulo [city], *Relatorio apresentado á Camara Municipal . . . 1897*, p. 5; "Relatorio da Commissão de exame e inspecção das habitações operarias e cortiços no districto de Santa Ephigenia, apresentado ao cidadão Dr. Cezario Motto Junior, M.D., Secretario dos Negocios do Interior do Estado de São Paulo," 19 Oct. 1893, Arquivo do Estado de São Paulo, Livro No. 972; Pasquale Petrone, "São Paulo no século XX," in Arnoldo de Azevedo, ed., *A cidade de São Paulo. Estudos de Geografia urbana*, 3 vols. (São Paulo: Companhia Editôra Nacional, 1958), II, 104–5; Pedro Pinchas Geiger, *Evolução de rêde urbana brasileira* (Rio de Janeiro: Instituto Nacional de Estudos Pedagógicos, Ministério da Educação e Cultura, 1963), pp. 204–10; Morse, *From Community to Metropolis*, pp. 179–83.

5. Carl von Koseritz, *Imagens do Brasil*, trans. Afonso Arinos de Melo Franco (São Paulo: Livraria Martins Editôra, 1943), pp. 294–96.

6. São Paulo [city], *Relatorio apresentado á Camara Municipal de São Paulo pelo Intendente de Obras Dr. Pedro Augusto Gomes Cardim, 1897* (São Paulo: Escola Typographica Salesiana, 1898), p. 4.

7. São Paulo [city], *Relatorio apresentado á Camara Municipal . . . 1897*, pp. 4–5; *Relatorio* 1898, pp. 4–10, *Relatorio* 1899, p. 19; Relatorio 1901, p. 14; *Relatorio* 1903, pp. 30–31; *Relatorio* 1904, pp. 41–45; *Relatorio* 1905, pp. 38–39; *Relatorio* 1906, pp. 41–45; *Relatorio* 1907, pp. 41–53; *Relatorio* 1909, pp. 27–32; *Relatorio* 1910, pp. 31–32; Geiger, *Evolução da rêde urbana brasileira*, p. 205; Manuel Diégues Júnior, *Imigração, urbanização e industrialiazação (Estudos sôbre alguns aspectos da contribuição cultural do imigrante no Brasil* (Rio de Janeiro: Centro Brasileiro de Pesquisas Educacionaes, Instituto Nacional de Estudos Pedagógicos, Ministério da Educação e Cultura, 1964), p. 181; Morse, *From Community to Metropolis*, pp. 178-80; Petrone, "São Paulo no século XX," in Azevedo, *A cidade de São Paulo*, II, 132–35.

8. Pará, *Mensagem dirigido ao congresso legislativo pelo governador do estado . . . 1897*, pp. 18–19; 1900, pp. 18–19; 1904, pp. 84–101; 1905, pp. 63–75; 1909, pp. 102–3; Bahia, *Mensagem apresentada á assembléa geral legislativa . . . pelo governador do estado . . . 1904*, pp. 78–79; 1912, pp. 60–61; 1913, pp. 15–17; 49–53; 1914, pp. 71–74; 1915, pp. 105–10; Pernambuco, *Mensagem do . . . governador do estado*, 1906, pp. 5–6; 1907, p. 4; 1909, p. 6; 1910, pp. 5–7; 1911, pp. 5–;9 1912, pp. 6–8; 1913, pp. 10–14; 1915, p. 7; 1916, pp. 6–19; 1917, pp. 8–25; 1918, pp. 17–18; 29–31; 1919, pp. 68–69; 1922, pp. 11–12; 1923, pp. 32–36; Paul Singer, *Desenvolvimento econômico e evolução urbana (Analise da evolução econômica de São Paulo, Blumenau, Pôrto Alegre, Belo Horizonte e Recife* (São Paulo: Companhia Editôra Nacional, 1968), pp. 157–83; 299–314; Geiger, *Evolução da rêde urbana brasileira*, pp. 290–93; 324–29; 355–417; Ernesto Cruz, *Belém. Aspectos eco-sociais do município* (Rio de Janeiro: José Olympio, 1945), pp. 266–71; Graham, *Britain and the Onset of Modernization in Brazil*, pp. 93–94.

9. Frank Vincent, *Around and About South America: Twenty Months of Quest and Query* (New York: D. Appleton and Company, 1890), p. 224.

10. Francisco Rangel Pestana to Quntino Bocaiúva, Petrópolis, 6 March 1892, Quintino Bocaiúva Papers, Rio de Janeiro.

11. The best biography of Rodrigues Alves is Afonso Arinos de Melo Franco, *Rodrigues Alves. Apogeu e declínio do presidencialismo*, 2 vols. (Rio de Janeiro and São Paulo: José Olympio and Editôra da Universidade de São Paulo), 1973.

12. Brazil, Ministério da Indústria, Viação, e Obras Públicas, *Relatorio*, 1904, iii–iv.

13. *Renascença*, July 1904, p. 181.

14. Luiz Edmundo da Costa, *O Rio de Janeiro do meu tempo*, 3 vols. (Rio de Janeiro: Imprensa Nacional, 1930), I, 26.

15. Manoel de Sousa Pinto, *Terra moça. Impressões brasileiras* (Porto: Livraria Chardron, 1910), pp. 81–88.

16. Brazil, Ministério da Indústria, Viãção, e Obras Públicas, *Relatorio* 1903, pp. 506–7; *Relatorio* 1904, pp. 651–81; *Relatorio* 1905, pp. 679–84; *Relatorio* 1906, pp. 666–68; *Renascença*, Aug. 1904, pp. 32–35; Sept. 1904, pp. 75–80; Oct. 1904, pp. .131–34; Ferreira da Rosa, *Rio de Janeiro. Notícia histórica e discritiva da capital do Brasil* (Rio de Janeiro: Typ. do Annuario do Brasil, 1924), pp. 4̇1–44; Clayton Sedgwick Cooper, *The Brazilians and Their Country* (New York: Frederick A. Stokes Co., 1917), pp. 272–76; Sousa Pinto, *Terra moça*, pp. 73–90; Nevin Otto Winter, *Brazil and Her People of To-Day; An Account of the Customs, Characteristics, Amusements, History and Advancement of the Brazilians, and the Development and Resources of Their Country* (Boston: L. C. Page and Co., 1910), pp. 53–69; Melo Franco, *Rodrigues Alves*, I, 312.

17. *Renascença*, Oct. 1904, p. 131.

18. *O País* (Rio de Janeiro), 16 Nov. 1905, p. 1; *Jornal do Comércio* (Rio de Janeiro), 16 Nov. 1905, p. 1.

19. *Jornal do Comércio*, 16 Nov. 1905, p. 1.

20. Winter, *Brazil and Her People of To-Day*, p. 51; Cooper, *The Brazilians and Their Country*, p. 272.

21. Alured Gray Bell, *The Beautiful Rio de Janeiro* (London: William Heinenmann, 1914), p. 22.

22. Brazil, Ministério da Industria, Viação, e Obras Públicas, *Relatorio*, 1904, pp. 524–32; 1905, pp. 586–610; 1906, pp. 563–601; *Renascença*, August 1904, p. 32; Melo Franco, *Rodrigues Alves*, I, 328–44.

23. Bahia, *Mensagem apresentada á assembléa geral legislativa . . . pelo governador, 1904*, pp. 75–76; 1905, p. 84; 1910, pp. 20–23; 1911, p. 49; 1912, pp. 58–61; Pernambuco, *Mensagem do . . . governador, 1915*, p. 18; 1919, pp. 68–69; 1920, p. 22; 1922, p. 11; 1923, p. 37; Pará, *Mensagem dirigido ao congresso legislativo pelo governador, 1898*, p. 27; 1907, pp. 93–95.

24. Brazil, Ministério da Indústria, Viação e Obras Públicas, *Relatorio*, 1904, pp. 113–21; 1905, pp. 114–22; 1906, pp. 114–18; *Renascença*, August 1904, p. 33; December 1904, pp. 250–52.

25. *Renascença*, August 1904, p. 34.

26. *União Portugueza* (Rio de Janeiro), 13 April 1905, p. 1; *Renascença*, September 1904, p. 76; Ferreira da Rosa, *Associação dos Empregados no Comércio do Rio de Janeiro. Meio seculo. Narrativa histórica* (Rio de Janeiro: Paulo, Pongetti & Cia., 1930), pp. 213, 218, 225–30.

27. *Semana Operária* (Rio de Janeiro), 20 May 1907, p. 3; Everardo Backheuser, *Habitações populares. Relatório apresentado ao exm. sr. dr. J. J. Seabra Ministro da Justiça e Negocios Interiores* (Rio de Janeiro: Imprensa Nacional, 1906), pp. 106, 113.

28. Brazil, Ministério da Justiça e Negócios Interiores, *Relatorio* 1906, II, 300.

29. F. M. de Souza Aguira, *Mensagem do Prefeito do Districto Federal lido na sessão do Conselho Municipal de 2 de abril de 1909* (Rio de Janeiro: Officinas Graphicas do Paiz, 1909), p. 8; Innocencio Serzedello Correa, *Men-*

sagem do Prefeito do Districto Federal lido na sessão do Conselho Municipal de 1 de setembro de 1909 (Rio de Janeiro: Typ. do Jornal do Commercio, 1909), pp. 14–15; Backheuser, *Habitações populares*, pp. 112–13.

30. Manoel Monteiro da Motta and others to Francisco Perreira Passos, Prefect of Rio de Janeiro, Rio de Janeiro, 29 May 1905, Arquivo Geral da Cidade do Rio de Janeiro, 43-1-38 (hereafter AGCRJ).

31. Backheuser, *Habitações populares*, p. 90; *Renascença*, May 1905, pp. 188–89; Serzedello Correa, *Mensagem do Prefeito do Districto Federal*, pp. 14–15; Brazil, Ministério da Justiça, *Relatorio*, 1898, pp. 455–58; Honório Souto to Minister of Interior, Rio de Janeiro, 7 Nov. 1892, AGCRJ, 40-4-55; Arthur Sauer to Nascimento e Silva, Rio de Janeiro, 10 Feb. 1893, AGCRJ, 40-4-46.

32. *Renascença*, March 1905, p. 92.

33. Ibid.

34. *A Noite* (Rio de Janeiro), 3 Feb. 1919, p. 1.

35. "Relatorio apresentado á Câmara Municipal de São Paulo pelo Intendente Municipal Cesario Ramalho da Silva," 1893, Arquivo do Estado de São Paulo, Livros No. 972; AGCRJ, 44-2-11; Backheuser, *Habitações populares*, p. 106; *Renascença*, March 1905, p. 90; Paulo Barreto (pseud. João do Rio), *A alma encantadora das ruas* (Paris and Rio de Janeiro: Tip. Garnier, 1908), p. 191.

36. *Jornal de Comércio*, 30 Jan. 1910, p. 4.

37. Brazil, Directoria Geral de Estatística, *Recenseamento geral da República dos Estados Unidos do Brazil em 31 de dezembro de 1890, Districto Federal (Cidade do Rio de Janeiro) Capital da República dos Estados Unidos do Brazil* (Rio de Janeiro: Typ. Leuzinger, 1895), xlii; 424–25.

38. Brazil, Ministério da Justiça e Negócios Interiores, *Relatorio* 1906, II, 302.

39. Brazil, Directoria Geral de Estatística, *Recenseamento do Rio de Janeiro (Districto Federal) realizada em 20 de setembro de 1906* (Rio de Janeiro: Officina da Estatística, 1907), I, 44, 123.

40. "Estatistica Municipal. Recenseamento das habitações collectivas. Setembro 1895" [Glória], AGCRJ, 44-2-11; "Recenseamento das habitações collectivas. 1 á 10 de setembro 1895," [São José], AGCRJ, 44-2-10.

41. Brazil, Ministério da Justiça e Negócios Interiores, *Relatorio* 1906, I, 36–37.

42. *Jornal do Comércio*, 30 Jan. 1910, *p. 4*.

43. *Backheuser, Habitações populares, p. 107.*

44. *Brazil Opérario (Rio de Janeiro), 16 June 1903, p. 1*; Backheuser, *Habitações populares*, p. 107.

45. Pedro Pinchas Geiger, *Evolução da rêde urbana brasileira* (Rio de Janeiro: Instituto Nacional de Estudos Pedagógicos, Ministério da Educação e Cultura, 1963), p. 152; Charles Julius Dunlop, *Apontamentos para a história dos bondes no Rio de Janeiro* (Rio de Janeiro: Gráfica Laemmert, 1953), pp. 187–95; Luiz Dodsworth Martins, *Presença de Paulo de Frontin* (Rio de Janeiro and São Paulo: Livraria Freitas Bastos, 1966), pp. 147–48.

46. Bell, *The Beautiful Rio de Janeiro*, p. 49.

47. A. C. de Chaves Faria and others to Prefect of Rio de Janeiro, Rio de Janeiro, 18 Oct. 1895, AGCRJ, 43-3-4.

48. Brazil, *Recenseamento do Rio de Janeiro (Districto Federal) realizada em 20 de setembro de 1906*, I, 25.

49. João Chagas, *De bond. Alguns aspectos de civilização brasileira* (Lisbon: Livraria Moderna, 1897), pp. 86, 112–13.

50. Alexandre José Melo Morais Filho, *Serenatas e saráos* (Rio de Janeiro and Paris: H. Garnier, 1901–1902), III, 107–8.

51. *O País (Rio de Janeiro)*, 22 Feb. 1890, *p.* 2; 24 Feb. 1890, *p.* 3; *O Echo Suburbano* (Rio de Janeiro), 3 Aug. 1901, p. 1; 10 Aug. 1901, p. 2; 16 Oct. 1901, p. 1; *Commercio Suburbano* (Rio de Janeiro), 6 July 1901, p. 1; *Progresso Suburbano* (Piedade, Rio de Janeiro), 6 Aug. 1902, p. 1; 23 Aug. 1902, p. 1.

52. *O Suburbio* (Méier, Rio de Janeiro), 2 July 1904, p. 1; 16 July 1904, p. 1; 16 July 1904, p. 1; *O Suburbio (Rio de Janeiro)*, 16 *July* 1908, *p.* 1; 3 *Aug. 1907, p. 3; A Noite*, 22 March 1919, p. 1; Donat Alfred Agache, *Cidade do Rio de Janeiro. Extensão, remodelação, embellezamento* (Paris: Foyer Brésilien, 1930), p. 188.

53. Afonso Henriques de Lima Barreto, *Clara dos Anjos*, 2d ed. (São Paulo: Editora Brasiliense, 1961), pp. 116–17.

54. *Tribuna do Povo* (Rio de Janeiro), 18 March 1909, p. 2; *O Echo Suburbano*, 3 Aug. 1901, p. 1; 10 Aug. 1901, p. 1; *Gazeta Operaria* (Rio de Janeiro), 28 Dec. 1902, p. 2.

55. Luis Barreto Correa de Menezes, Police Chief, to Barão Homen de Mello, Ministro dos Negócios do Império, Rio de Janeiro, 25 June 1881, Arquivo Nacional, IJJ[1] 783; Arquivo do Estado de São Paulo, Livro No. 972; Antonio Corrêa de Sousa Costa, *Qual a alimentação de que usa a classe pobre do Rio de Janeiro e sua influencia sobre a mesma classe* (Rio de Janeiro: Typ. Perseverança, 1865), p. 31; *Gazeta Operária*. 28 Sept. 1902, p. 3; *Semana Operária*, 20 May 1907, p. 3; *A Voz do Trabalhador* (Rio de Janeiro), 9 Dec. 1909, p. 2; Augusto Olympio Viveiros de Castro, *A questão social* (Rio de Janeiro: Livraria Editora Conselheiro Candido de Oliveira, 1920), p. 276.

56. Corrêa de Sousa Costa, *Qual a alimentação*, pp. 31–32; José Maria dos Santos, *Os republicanos paulistas e a abolição* (São Paulo: Livraria Martins, 1942), pp. 182–83; Robert Brent Toplin, *The Abolition of Slavery in Brazil* (New York: Atheneum 1975), p. 208; Emília Viotti da Costa, *Da senzala à colônia* (São Paulo: Difusão Européia do Livro, 1966), pp. 315–16; Fernando Bastos Ribeiro, *Cronicas da polícia e da vida no Rio de Janeiro* (Rio de Janeiro: Imprensa Nacional, 1958), p. 71.

57. *Renascença*, March 1905, pp. 92–94; Andrew Pearse, "Some Characteristics of Urbanization in the City of Rio de Janeiro," p. 191 in Philip M. Hauser, ed., *Urbanization in Latin America* New York: International Documents Service, 1961).

58. Gastão Cruls, *Aparência do Rio de Janeiro*, 2 vols. (Rio de Janeiro: Livraria José Olympio, 1965), II, 787.

59. *Semana Operária*, 20 May 1907, p. 3.

60. H. D. Barruel de Lagenest, "Os cortiços de São Paulo," *Anhembi* 12 (June 1962), 6.

61. *Jornal do Comércio*, 30 Jan. 1910, p. 4; A *Noite*, 6 Feb. 1919, p. 1; 7 March 1919, p. 1.

62. Campos Sales to José Carlos Rodrigues, editor, *Jornal do Comércio*, Rio de Janeiro, 23 May 1899, Biblioteca Nacional, Secção de Manuscritos, I, 3, 4, 85.

63. *Jornal do Comércio*, 10 June 1901, p. 10; 16 June 1901, p. 2; 17 June 1901, p. 1; 18 June 1901, p. 1; 19 June 1901, p. 1; 20 June 1901, p. 2. *Correio da Manhã* (Rio de Janeiro), 18 June 1901, p. 1; 19 June 1901, p. 1; 20 June 1901, p. 1; Eneas Galvão, Chief of Police, to Epitácio Pessoa, Justice Minister, Rio de Janeiro, 30 June 1901, Arquivo Nacional, IJ⁶ 375.

64. Unsigned, undated police report, Instituto Histórico e Geográfico Brasileiro, Epitácio Pessoa Papers, Pasta 20.

65. João Lampreia, Portuguese Minister to Brazil, to Francisco Antonio da Veiga Beira, Foreign Minister, Petrópolis, 6 March 1900, Arquivo do Ministério dos Negócios Estrangeiros (Lisbon), Cx. 226; Manuel Ferraz de Campos Salles, *Da propaganda á presidencia* (São Paulo: n.p., 1908), pp. 357–59.

66. Campos Sales to Francisco Glicério, São Paulo, 28 May 1896, Francisco Glicério Papers (São Paulo and Campinas).

67. *Jornal do Comércio*, 19 June 1901, p. 1; *Correio do Manhã*, 16 Nov. 1902, p. 1; A *Nação* (São Paulo), 12 Dec. 1915, p. 1.

68. Eneas Galvão to Epitácio Pessoa, Rio de Janeiro, 30 June 1901, Arquivo Nacional, IJ⁶ 375; Souza Aguiar, Commander of Corps of Firemen, to Epitácio Pessoa, Rio de Janeiro, 2 July 1901, Instituto Histórico e Geográfico Brasileiro, Epitácio Pessoa Papers, Pasta 20; Hermes Rodrigues da Fonseca, Commander of Police Brigade, to Epitácio Pessoa, Rio de Janeiro, June 1901, Arquivo Nacional, IJ⁶ 375; *Correio da Manhã*, 19 June 1901, p. 1; *Jornal do Comércio*, 18 June 1901, p. 1; 19 June 1901, p. 1.

69. Unsigned, undated police report, Instituto Histórico e Geográfico Brasileiro, Epitácio Pessoa Papers, Pasta 20.

70. Eneas Galvão to Epitácio Pessoa, Rio de Janeiro, 30 June 1901, Arquivo Nacional, IJ⁶ 375.

71. Hermes da Fonseca to Espitácio Pessoa, Rio de Janeiro, June 1901, Arquivo Nacional, IJ⁶ 375.

72. *Jornal do Comércio*, 20 June 1901, p. 2; *Correio da Manhã*, 20 June 1901, p. 1.

73. *Correio da Manhã*, 16 Nov. 1902, p. 1; 19 Nov. 1902, pp. 1–2; *Jornal do Comércio*, 19 Nov. 1902, p. 1; *Gazeta de Notícias* (Rio de Janeiro), 20 Nov. 1902, p. 1; Raimundo de Menezes, *Vida e obra de Campos Sales* (São Paulo: Prefeitura Municipal de Campinas/Livraria Martins, 1974), pp. 210–11.

74. Accounts of some of these events, focusing on political aspects, are

given by Melo Franco, *Rodrigues Alves*, I, 361–436; Edgard Carone, A *República Velha*, II *(Evolução política)* (São Paulo: Difusão Européia do Livro, 1971), pp. 198–214; and Robert G. Nachman, "Positivism and Revolution in Brazil's First Republic: The 1904 Revolt," *The Americas* 34 (July 1977), 20–39.

75. The position of Raimundo Teixeira Mendes, a leader of and spokesman for the Brazilian Positivist Apostolate, is developed in: Raimundo Teixeira Mendes, A *liberdade espiritual e a vacinção obligatória* (Rio de Janeiro: Igreja Pozitivista do Brazil, 1902); *Contra a vaccinação obligatória* (A *propózito do projéto do Governo*) (Rio de Janeiro: Igreja Pozitivista do Brazil, 1904); O *depotismo sanitário* (Rio de Janeiro: Igreja e Apostolado Pozitivista do Brazil, 1907); A *política republicana e a tirania vacinista* (Rio de Janeiro: Igreja Pozitivista do Brazil, 1908); and A*inda a questão da varíola e da vacina* (Rio de Janeiro: Igreja a Apostolado Pozitivista do Brazil, 1908). For a good history of research science in Brazil focusing on the Oswaldo Cruz Institute, which includes an account of the yellow fever campaign, see Nancy Stepan, *Beginnings of Brazilian Science* (New York: Science History Publications, 1976).

76. Robert G. Nachman, "Positivism and Revolution in Brazil's First Republic: The 1904 Revolt," *The Americas* 34 (July 1977), 32–33.

77. Examples of speeches opposing compulsory vaccination are found in *Contra a obrigatoriedade da vaccina. Resumo dos discursos pronunciados pelos Senadores Lauro Sodré e Barata Ribeiro* (Rio de Janeiro: n.p., 1904). Lauro Sodré's son, an admiral, has provided a biography of his father: Benjamin Sodré, *Lauro Sodré. Vida, carater e sentimento a serviço de um povo* (Belém: Imprensa Official, 1955). A biographical sketch of Barbosa Lima by his grandson Barbosa Lima Sobrinho prefaces a collection of congressional speeches: Alexandre José Barbosa Lima, *Discursos parlamentares*, 2 vols. (Brasília: Câmara de Deputados, 1963).

78. Galeria Nacional, *Vultos proeminentes da história brasileira* (Rio de Janeiro: Officinas Graphicas do Jornal do Brasil, 1931), p. 146; *Jornal do Comércio*, 27 Jan. 1881, p. 1; *Democracia* (Rio de Janeiro), 4 March 1890, p. 2; 5 March 1890, p. 2; *Echo Popular* (Rio de Janeiro), 6 March 1890, p. 3.

79. Brazil, Ministério da Justiça, *Relatório* 1900, pp. 14–19; Antonio Ferreira Viana, A *conspiração policial* (Rio de Janeiro: Typ. do Jornal do Commércio, 1900, pp. 20–23; Campos Sales to Epitácio Pessoa, Petrópolis, 28 Feb. 1900, Instituto Histórico e Geográfico Brasileiro, Epitácio Pessoa Papers, Pasta 3; and unsigned, undated memorandum on the conspiracy, Pasta 20. For a summary of monarchist activities in the Old Republic see Edgard Carone, A *República Velha (Instituições e classes sociais)* (São Paulo: Difusão Européia do Livro, 1970), pp. 377–87.

80. *Correio da Manhã*, 11 Nov. 1904, p. 1; 12 Nov. 1904, p. 1; 13 Nov. 1904, p. 1; 14 Nov. 1904, p. 1; Melo Franco, *Rodrigues Alves* I, 399–402.

81. *Jornal do Comércio*, 13 Nov. 1904, p. 2; 14 Nov. 1904, p. 1; *Correio da Manhã*, 13 Nov. 1904, pp. 1–2; 14 Nov. 1904, pp. 1–2; A. A. Cardoso de Castro (Chief of Police), *Relatorio apresentado ao Dr. J. J. Seabra* (Rio de Janeiro: Imprensa Nacional, 1904), pp. 18–21.

82. *Jornal do Comércio*, 15 Nov. 1904, p. 1; Dantas Barreto, *Conspirações* (Rio de Janeiro: Livraria Francisco Alves, 1917), pp. 5–42; Castro, *Relatorio*, pp. 22–41; 58–78.

83. Henry Nevil Dering to Marquess of Landsdowne, Petrópolis, 18 Nov. 1904, Foreign Office, Public Record Office (London) F.O. 13/841; *Jornal do Comércio*, 17 Nov. 1904, p. 1. *Jornal do Brasil*, 17 Nov. 1904.

84. Brazil, Ministério da Justiça, *Relatorio* 1905, p. 6.

85. Melo Franco, *Rodrigues Alves*, I, 414–35.

86. João Lampreia, Portuguese Minister to Brazil, to Antonio Eduardo Villaça, Petropólis, 22 Nov. 1904; 26 Dec. 1904, Arquivo do Ministério dos Negócios Estrangeiros, Cx. 227; 22 April 1905, Cx. 228; Henry Nevill Dering to Marquess of Landsdowne, Petrópolis, 5 Dec. 1904, Public Record Office, F.O. 13/841; Rio Branco, Foreign Minister, to J. J. Seabra, Minister of Justice, Rio de Janeiro, 17 Aug. 1905, Arquivo Histórico do Ministério das Relações Exteriores, 302-4-3, and Alberto Fialho to Rio Branco, Lisbon, 9 June 1905, 214-4-1; Castro, *Relatorio*, p. 63.

Chapter 6

1. *O País* (Rio de Janeiro), 25 March 1890, p. 3; *Democracia* (Rio de Janeiro), 27 March 1890, p. 3; *Gazeta Operaria* (Rio de Janeiro), 28 Sept. 1902, pp. 1, 3; 4 Oct. 1902, p. 3; 15 Feb. 1903, p. 1; *O Chapeleiro* (São Paulo), 1 May 1904, p. 4; *O Trabalhador Graphico* (São Paulo), 5 May 1904, pp. 1–4; Aug. 1904, pp. 2, 3; Baron of Rio Branco, Minister of Foreign Affairs, to Minister of Justice, 11 Oct. 1906, Arquivo Histórico do Ministério das Relações Exteriores, 302-4-4.

2. A *Voz do Trabalhador* (Rio de Janeiro), 1 June 1909, p. 1.

3. *O Componedor* (Rio de Janeiro), May 1909, p. 2.

4. *Tribuna Operaria* (Rio de Janeiro), April 1901, p. 4; *O Trabalhador Graphico*, April 1905, p. 4; 5 Aug. 1905, pp. 1, 4; March 1906, p. 2; *O Componedor*, May 1909, pp. 1–3; June 1909, p. 1; July 1909, p. 1; Aug. 1909, p. 3. Sept. 1909, p. 1; 12 Oct. 1909, pp. 1–2; A *Voz do Trabalhador*, 6 Dec. 1908, p. 3; 1 June 1909, pp. 1–2; 15 June 1909, pp. 1, 2, 4; 15 Nov. 1909, p. 2; 9 Dec. 1909, p. 1; J. C. Oakenfull, *Brazil in 1912* (London: Robert Atkinson Ltd., 1913), p. 439.

5. *O Imperial* (Rio de Janeiro), 18 Jan. 1923, p. 1.

6. "These apresentada pelo União dos Empregados no Commercio do Rio de Janeiro á 1ª Conferencia pelo Progresso Feminino, realisada no Rio de Janeiro sob auspices da Federação Brasileira das Ligas pelo Progresso Feminino," 21 Dec. 1922, Arquivo Nacional, Arquivo Particular no. 46, Arquivo da Federação Brasileira pelo Progresso Feminino (uncatalogued).

7. A *Terra Livra* (São Paulo), 29 July 1906, p. 2.

8. A *Terra Livre*, 17 Feb. 1906, p. 4; J. C. Oakenfull, *Brazil in 1911* (London: Butler and Tanner, 1912), p. 355.

9. *Renascença* (Rio de Janeiro), March 1905, pp. 89–90; *O Imparcial*,

18 Jan. 1923, p. 1; "Condições do trabalho na industria de chapeus," São Paulo [state], *Boletim do Departamento Estadual do Trabalho* I, no. 3 (2d trimester 1912), 226–27; "O trabalho domiciliar," São Paulo, *Boletim* IV, no. 17 (4th trimester 1915), 613–20; "O trabalho domiciliar," São Paulo, *Boletim* VI, no. 25 (4th trimester 1917), 617–20; "Hygiene e segurança do trabalho e a industria em domicilio," Brazil, Congress, Câmara dos Deputados, *Documentos Parlamentares. Legislação social*, 3 vols. (Rio de Janeiro: Typ. do Jornal do Commercio, 1919–1922), III, 7–125.

10. Brazil, Directoria Geral de Estatistica, *Recenseamento do Brazil realizado em 1 de setembro de 1920* (Rio de Janeiro: Typ. da Estatistica, 1922–1930), IV, 5ª parte, tomo 1, xii–xiii, xv, xxii.

11. Brazil, *Recenseamento do Brazil . . . 1920*, V, 2ª parte, v.

12. Centro Industrial do Brazil, *O Brasil. Suas riquezas naturaes. Suas industrias* (Rio de Janeiro: M. Orosco & C., 1909), III, 2ª parte, 37, 99, 130, 150.

For a history of this center, see Edgar Carone, *O Centro Industrial do Rio de Janeiro e sua importante participação na economia nacional (1827–1977)* (Rio de Janeiro: Centro Industrial do Rio de Janeiro/Editora Cátedra, 1978).

13. Warren Dean, *The Industralization of São Paulo, 1880–1945* (Austin and London: University of Texas Press, 1969), pp. 83–104.

14. *O Operario* (Rio de Janeiro), 12 Oct. 1895, p. 1; *O Echo Suburbano* (Engenho de Dentro, Rio de Janeiro), 3 Aug. 1901, p. 1; 24 Aug. 1901, p. 1; *Gazeta Operaria*, 11 Jan. 1903, pp. 2–3; *O Trabalhador Graphico*, April 1905, p. 1; *O Marmorista* (Rio de Janeiro), 1 Dec. 1906, pp. 1–2; *A Terra Livre* (Rio de Janeiro), 22 June 1907, p. 3; *A Voz do Trabalhador*, 17 May 1909, p. 3; *O Operario* (Sorocaba), 18 Dec. 1910, p. 1; *O Operario* (Tatuhy, São Paulo), 1 April 1911, p. 2; "Documentos do movimento operário. Resoluções do Primeiro Congresso Operário Brasileiro," 1906 *Estudos Sociais* 4 (March 1963), 393.

15. Stanley J. Stein, *The Brazilian Cotton Manufacture: Textile Enterprise in an Underdeveloped Area, 1850–1950* (Cambridge, Mass. Harvard University Press, 1957), pp. 20–21; Eulália Maria Lahmeyer Lobo, *História do Rio de Janeiro (Do capital comerical ao capital industrial e financeiro)* (Rio de Janeiro: Instituto Brasileiro de Mercado de Capitais, 1978), II, 477; Brazil, Ministério de Indústria, Viação e Obras Públicas, *Relatorio* 1895, unpaginated; Brazil, *Recenseamento do Brazil . . . 1920*, V, 1ª parte, 278–79, 294–95.

16. "Condições do trabalho na industria textil no Estado de S. Paulo," São Paulo (state), *Boletim do Departamento Estadual do Trabalho*, I, nos. 1 and 4 (4th trimester 1911 and 1st trimester 1912), 74; Brazil, *Recenseamento do Brazil . . . 1920*, IV, 4ª parte, x–xi, xxi; "Relação de operarios com 16 annos ou menos que, no dia 1° de dezembro de 1899, trabalharam em Bangú, na fabrica tecelegem, branqueação e estamparia da Companhia Progresso Industrial do Brasil, fornecido a pedido do agente da Prefeitura do 2° districto da frequesia do Campo Grande da Capital Federal," Arquivo Geral de Cidade do Rio de Janeiro, 43-3-3.

17. "Relatorio do Sindicato dos Trabalhadores em Fabricas de Tecidos

Para o 2° Congresso operario Brazilerio," 1913, Arquivo Geral da Cidade do Rio de Janeiro, Cx. 5, Doc. 154; "Federação Operaria do Rio de Janeiro," A Voz do Trabalhador, 15 Oct. 1913, reprinted in Paulo Sérgio Pinheiro and Michael M. Hall, eds., A classe operária no Brasil. Documentos (1889 a 1930), 2 vols. (São Paulo: Editora Alfa Omega, 1979–1981), I, 164; A Terra Livre 24 March 1906, p. 2; O Operario, 2 Jan. 1910, p. 1; A Noite (Rio de Janeiro), 22 June 1917, p. 4; "Condições do trabalho na industria textil no Estado de S. Paulo," São Paulo [state], Boletim do Departamento Estadual do Trabalho, I, nos. 1 and 4 (4th trimester 1911 and 1st trimester 1912), 36.

18. Gazeta Operaria, 28 Nov. 1902, p. 3; A Tribuna do Povo (Rio de Janeiro), 18 March 1909, pp. 1–2, 18 April 1909, p. 3; A Voz do Trabalhador, 22 Nov. 1908, p. 1; 1 June 1909, p. 2; O Operario, 9 Jan. 1910, p. 2; 3 April 1910, p. 2.

19. "Condições do trabalho na industria textil no Estado de S. Paulo," São Paulo (state), Boletim do Departamento Estadual do Trabalho, I, nos. 1 and 4 (4th trimester 1911 and 1st trimester 1912), 37; "Condições do trabalho na industria de chapeus," São Paulo, Boletim, I, no. 3 (2nd trimester 1912), p. 227.

20. Gazeta Operaria 2 Nov. 1902, p. 1; 9 Nov. 1902, p. 2; A Terra Livre, 30 Dec. 1905, p. 3; 24 March 1906, p. 2; Tribuna do Povo, 18 March 1909, p. 2; 18 April 1909, p. 3.

21. União Operario (Recife), 4 June 1905, p. 4; 5 Nov. 1905, p. 3; O Imparcial, 18 Jan. 1923, p. 1; Diário da Bahia (Salvador), 11 Nov. 1931; Ferreira da Rosa, O Rio de Janeiro em 1900. Visitas e excursões, 2d ed. (n.p., n.p.), p. 73; "Condições do trabalho na industria textil no Estado de S. Paulo, São Paulo [state], Boletim do Departamento Estadual do Trabalho, I, nos. 1 and 4 (4th trimester 1911 and 1st trimester 1912), pp. 46, 57, 60.

22. Brazil, Recenseamento do Brazil . . . 1920, V 2ª parte, vi–vii, ix, xiv.

23. "Relatorio do Sindicato dos Trabalhadores em Fabricas de Tecidos para o 2° Congresso operario Brazileiro," 1913, Arquivo Geral de Cidade do Rio de Janeiro, Cx. 5, Doc. 154.

24. Brazil, Recenseamento do Brazil . . . 1920, II, 2ª parte, lxiv, IV, 5ª parte, tomo 1, 24–27.

25. Ibid., IV, 5ª parte, tomo 1, xii–xiii.

26. O Sexo Feminino (Rio de Janeiro), 29 July 1875, p. 2.

27. See Esther Bosserup, Women's Role in Economic Development (New York: St. Martin's Press, 1970); and Nadia Haggag Youssef, Women and Work in Developing Societies (Berkeley: Institute of International Studies, University of California, 1974).

28. See Felicia R. Madeira and Paulo I. Singer, Estrutura do emprego e trabalho feminino no Brasil, 1920–1970, Cadernos CEBRAP 13 (São Paulo: CEBRAP, 1973), p. 25.

29. Brazil, Directoria Geral de Estatistica, Recenseamento da populção do Imperio do Brazil a que se procedeu no dia 1° de agosto de 1872 (Rio de Janeiro: Typ. Leuzinger, 1873–1876), XXI (Municipio Neutro), xxi, 61; Brazil, Directoria Geral de Estatistica, Recenseamento do Rio de Janeiro (Districto Fed-

eral) realizado em 20 de setembro de 1906 (Rio de Janeiro: Officina da Estatistica, 1907), 1, 100, 104; Brazil, *Recenseamento do Brazil . . . 1 de setembro de 1920*, IV, 5ª parte, tomo 1, 24–27.

30. "Relatorio do Sindicato dos Trabalhadores em Fabricas de Tecidos para o 2° Congresso operario Brazileiro," 1913, AGCRJ, Cx. 5, Doc. 154; Leo de Affonseca Junior, *O custo da vida na cidade do Rio de Janeiro* (Rio de Janeiro: Imprensa Nacional, 1920), p. 13; J. C. Oakenfull, *Brazil* [1913] (London: Butler and Tanner [1914]), pp. 571–74.

31. *A Tribuna do Povo*, 18 March 1904, p. 4.

32. *Brazil Operario* (Rio de Janeiro), August (first fortnight), 1903, p. 4.

33. "Documentos do movimento operário. Resoluções do Primeiro Congress Operário Brasileiro," 1906, *Estudos Sociais* 4 (March 1963), 396.

34. "Documentos do movimento operário. Congress Operário de 1912," *Estudos Sociais* 5 (June 1963), 77.

35. *O País*, 19 Feb. 1893, p. 3; 20 Feb. 1893, p. 3; 21 Feb. 1893, p. 3; *Renascença*, May 1905, pp. 185–89.

36. "Relatorio do Sindicato dos Trabalhadores em Fabricas de Tecidos para o 2° Congresso operario Brazileiro," 1913, AGCRJ, Cx. 5, Doc. 154. See also *O Imparcial*, 18 Jan. 1923, p. 1.

37. "These apresentada pela União dos Empregados no Commercio do Rio de Janeiro á 1ª Conferencia pelo Progresso Feminino, realisada no Rio de Janeiro sob auspices da Federação Brasileira das Ligas pelo Progresso Feminino," 21 Dec. 1922, Arquivo Nacional, Arquivo Particular no. 46, Arquivo da F.B.P.F. (uncatalogued).

38. *O País*, 22 Feb. 1890, p. 2; *O Operario* (Fortaleza), 6 March 1892, p. 1; 27 March 1892, p. 1; 2 Oct. 1892, p. 1; *O Jornal do Brasil* (Rio de Janeiro), 2 April 1899, pp. 2, 6; *Gazeta Operaria*, 8 Feb. 1903, p. 1; *O Amigo do Povo* (São Paulo), 20 Aug. 1904, p. 1; *A Voz do Trabalhador*, 1 Aug. 1908, p. 2; *A Tribuna do Povo*, 18 March 1909, p. 4; *O Componedor*, May 1909, p. 1; *Correio da Manhã* (Rio de Janeiro), 12 Nov. 1916, p. 2; Affonseca Junior, *O custo da vida na cidade do Rio de Janeiro*, p. 15; Oakenfull, *Brazil* [1913], pp. 568–75.

39. The menu for a banquet honoring Ex-President Campos Sales shortly after he left office in November 1902 read as follows:

Potages; A la Edouard VII. Consomme de Madrid.
Poisson: Turbans de robalo á la Diarios.
Relevé: Petites bouchèes Présidence.
Entrées: Train de Côtes á la Diplomate, Quartiers de chapon á la Orleans.
Coup du milieu: Punch á la Republique.
Légumes: Fonds d'artichauds á la molle, petits-pois ála crême.
Roti: Dindonneau á la bresilienne, jambon d'York, salade japponnaise.
Entremets: Millesfeuilles, moka praliné.
Glaces: Vanille, abaxti, fraises, petit fours assortis.
Fruits confits, marrons glacés, croquents bouche d'orange.
Piecés nougat, fruits, fromages.

Vins: Yérez, Chateau Yquem 1882, Chateau Pougeaux
1881, Chambertin 1884, Pommery, Porto vieux.
Café: Liquers.

Gazeta de Notícias *(Rio de Janeiro)*, 18 Nov. 1902, *p. 1.*
   40.   Sam C. Adamo, "The Broken Promise: Race, Health, and Justice in
Rio de Janeiro, 1890–1940" (unpublished Ph.D. dissertation, Univerity of New
Mexico, 1983), pp. 112–83.
   41.   Brazil, *Documentos parlamentares. Legislação social*, I, 519.
   42.   *Assistencia publica e privada no Rio de Janeiro (Brasil). Historia e
estatistica* (Rio de Janeiro: Typ. do "Annuario do Brasil," 1922), pp. 36–37;
Jornal Operario (São Paulo), 29 Oct. 1905, p. 1; *A Terra Livre*, 18 Aug. 1907,
p. 2; *A Noite*, 26 March 1917, p. 4; 22 June 1917, p. 4; Arthur Lobo da Silva,
"A anthropologia no Exercito Brasileiro," *Archivos do Museu Nacional* 30 (1928),
38–40, unpaged tables; Frank D. McCann, "The Nation in Arms: Obligatory
Military Service during the Old Republic," p. 223 in Dauril Alden and Warren
Dean, eds., *Essays Concerning the Socioeconomic History of Brazil and Portuguese India* (Gainesville: University Presses of Florida, 1977); Ferreira d'Almeida
Carvalho to Bernardino de Machado, Foreign Minister, Rio de Janeiro, 17 March
1914, Arquivo do Ministério dos Negócios Estrangeiros, Cx. 231; São Paulo
(state), *Boletim do Departamento Estadual do Trabalho*, IV, no. 17 (4th trimester 1915), 614–17.
   43.   *Gazeta Operaria*, 28 Sept. 1902, p. 4; *Brazil Operario*, 13 May 1903,
p. 2; August (first fortnight) 1903, p. 4; October (first fortnight), 1903, p. 4;
Renascença, March 1905, p. 91; Everardo Dias, *História das lutas sociais no
Brasil* (São Paulo: Editôra Edaglit, 1962), p. 220; Jacob Penteado, *Belènzinho,
1910 (Retrato de uma época)* (São Paulo: Livraria Martins, 1962), pp. 51–52,
256–59.
   44.   J. C. Oakenfull, *Brazil: Past, Present, and Future* (London: John Bale,
Sons, and Danielsson, Ltd., 1919), pp. 662–63; Penteado, *Belènzinho*, pp. 52,
59–60; José Joaquim de Campos da Costa Medeiros e Albuquerque, *O perigo
americano* (Rio de Janeiro: Leite Ribeiro & Maurtillo, 1919), p. 9.
   45.   Oakenfull, *Brazil: Past, Present, and Future*, p. 669; Penteado,
Belènzinho, pp. 60–61; 136; 220–25; Richard Graham, *Britain and the Onset
of Modernization in Brazil, 1850–1914* (Cambridge: Cambridge University Press,
1968), p. 122. For a brief discussion of Brazil's national sport, see Robert M.
Levine, "The Burden of Success: *Futebol* and Brazilian Society through the
1970's," *Journal of Popular Culture* 14 (Winter 1980), pp. 453–64.
   46.   Zélia Gattai, *Anarquistas, graças a Deus* (Rio de Janeiro: Editora Record, 1979), p. 45.
   47.   Penteado, *Belènzinho*, pp. 58; 61, 251–55; Gattai, *Anarquistas, graças
a Deus*, pp. 44–47; 86–87; Alexandre José de Mello Morais Filho, *Festas e
tradições populares do Brasil*, 3rd ed. (Rio de Janeiro: F. Briguiet & Cia., 1946),
pp. 153–65; Roberto Moura, *Tia Ciata e a pequena Africa no Rio de Janeiro*
(Rio de Janeiro: FUNARTE, 1983), pp. 71–75.

48. Binzer, Ina von, *Os meus romanos. Alegrias e tristezas de uma educadora alemã no Brasil*, trans. Alice Rossi and Luisita de Gama Cerqueira (Rio de Janeiro: Paz e Terra, 1980), p. 68.

49. Mello Morais Filho, *Festas e tradições populares do Brasil*, pp. 135–43; Daniel Parish Kidder and James C. Fletcher, *Brazil and the Brazilians Portrayed in Historical and Descriptive Sketches*, 7th ed. (Boston: Little Brown and Co., 1867), pp. 148–50.

50. Eneida de Morais, *História do carnaval carioca* (Rio de Janeiro: Editôra Civlização Brasileira, 1955), pp. 17–65; Melo Morais Filho, *Festas e tradições populares do Brasil*, pp. 27–45; Gattai, *Anarquistas, graças a Deus*, pp. 184–85; *Gazeta Operaria*, 28 Sept. 1902, pp. 3–4; 4 Jan. 1903, p. 3.

51. Moura, *Tia Ciata*, pp. 42–70; Paulo Barreto (pseud. João do Rio), *A alma encantadora das ruas* (Paris and Rio de Janeiro: Tip. Garnier, 1908), pp. 141–53; Luiz Edmundo da Costa, *O Rio de Janeiro do meu tempo*, 2nd ed. (Rio de Janeiro: Conquista, 1957), IV, 767–828.

52. Edigar de Alencar, "O carnaval do Rio em 1900 e na década seguinte," p. 152 in Luiz Antônio Severo da Costa et al., *Brasil 1900–1910* (Rio de Janeiro: Biblioteca Nacional, 1980), III.

53. Eneida de Morais, *História do carnaval carioca*, pp. 173–82; Moura, *Tia Ciata*, pp. 76–82.

54. Alison Raphael, "Samba and Social Control: Popular Culture and Racial Democracy in Rio de Janeiro" (unpublished Ph.D. dissertation, Columbia University, 1980).

55. *O Amigo do Povo*, 9 July 1904, p. 4.

56. *Gazeta Operaria*, 4 Jan. 1903, p. 3; *O Suburbio* (Meier, Rio de Janeiro), 16 July 1904, p. 1; *Operario* (Rio de Janeiro), 24 Jan. 1909, p. 2; *A Voz do Trabalhador*, 30 Oct. 1909, p. 3; 9 Dec. 1909, p. 2.

57. *O Echo Suburbano*, 24 Aug. 1901, p. 2; *Progresso Suburbano* (Piedade, Rio de Janeiro), 6 Aug. 1901, p. 2; *Gazeta Operaria*, 28 Sept. 1902, p. 4; *O Amigo do Povo*, 9 July 1904, p. 4; *O Suburbio*, 16 July 1904, p. 1; *Portugal Moderno* (Rio de Janeiro), 29 Jan. 1910, p. 3; Edgard Rodrigues, *Nacionalismo e cultura social, 1913–1922* (Rio de Janeiro: Laemmert, 1972), pp. 77–81, 446–47.

58. *O Operario* (Tatuhy, São Paulo), 3 Dec. 1910, p. 3.

59. "Documentos do movimento operário. Resoluções do Primeiro Congresso Operário Brasileiro," 1906, *Estudos Sociais* 4 (March 1963), 392, 396.

60. Oakenfull, *Brazil: Past, Present, and Future*, p. 666.

61. *O Despertar* (Rio de Janeiro), 3 Dec. 1892, p. 2; *O Echo Suburbano*, 17 Aug. 1901, p. 1; *Gazeta Operaria*, 11 Jan. 1903, p. 2; *O Amigo do Povo*, 17 Sept. 1904, p. 3; *O Operario* (São Paulo), 27 Oct. 1905, p. 3; *Semana Operaria* (Rio de Janeiro), 20 May 1907, p. 1; *A Tribuna do Povo*, 14 April 1907, p. 1; *O Luctador* (Rio de Janeiro), 1 Dec. 1908, p. 1; 2 Jan. 1909, p. 1; *O Baluarte* (Rio de Janeiro), May 1910, p. 1; *O Operario* (Tatuhy, São Paulo), 1 April 1911, p. 1; *A Noite*, 27 March 1917, p. 1; Herbert H. Smith, *Brazil: The Ama-*

zons and the Coast (New York: Charles Scribner's Sons, 1879), p. 454; Gattai, *Anarquistas, graças a Deus*, pp. 52–54, 60–66.

62. Brazil, *Recenseamento do Brazil . . . 1920*, II, 1ª parte, tomo 2, 514, 515.

In 1890, when the census broke down this occupational category into Roman Catholic and non-Catholic, only seventeen out of a total of 230 religious were non-Catholics: Rio also had just seven nuns and twenty-three monks (Brazil, Directoria Geral de Estatistica, *Recenseamento geral da Republica dos Estados Unidos do Brazil em 31 de dezembro de 1890. Districto Federal (Cidade do Rio de Janeiro), Capital da Republica dos Estados Unidos do Brazil* (Rio de Janeiro: Typ. Leuzinger, 1895), pp. 408–9).

63. Oakenfull, *Brazil, Past, Present, and Future*, pp. 668–69; Everardo Dias, *História das lutas sociais no Brazil* (São Paulo: Editôra Edaglit, 1962), p. 220; E. Bradford Burns, "Manuel Querino's Interpretation of the African Contribution to Brazil," *The Journal of Negro History* 59 (January 1974), 83.

Among the detailed studies of various cults are: Ruth Landes, *The City of Women* (New York: Macmillan, 1947), on Bahia; Seth and Ruth Leacock, *Spirits of the Deep: A Study of an Afro-Brazilian Cult* (New York: Natural History Press, 1972), on the batuque of Pará; Nina Rodrigues, *O animismo fetichista dos negros bahianos* (Rio de Janeiro: Civilização Brasileira, 1935; René Ribeiro, *Cultos africanos do Recife. Um estudo de ajustamento social* (Recife: Instituto Joaquim Nabuco, 1952); and Edison Carneiro, *Candomblés da Bahia*, 3rd ed. (Rio de Janeiro: Conquista, 1961).

65. Francisco José de Oliveira Vianna, "O povo brasileiro e sua evolução," in Brazil, *Recenseamento do Brazil . . . 1920*, I, 279–344.

66. Adamo, "The Broken Promise," pp. 81–111.

67. Carlos Hasenbalg, *Discriminação e desigualdades racias no Brasil*, trans. Patric Burgin (Rio de Janeiro: Edições Graal, 1979).

68. Penteado, *Belènzinho*, pp. 215–18.

69. *A Voz do Trabalhador*, 30 Oct. 1909, p. 3.

70. Afonso Henriques de Lima Barreto, *Clara dos Anjos*, 2d ed. (São Paulo: Editôra Brasiliense, 1962), p. 196.

Chapter 7

1. Lists of twentieth-century worker associations in the state of São Paulo are given in: Azis Simão, *Sindicato e estado. Suas relações na formação do proletariado de São Paulo* (São Paulo: Dominus Editôra, 1966), pp. 203–17.

2. Brazil, Congress, Câmara dos Deputados, *Documentos parlamentares. Legislação social* (Rio de Janeiro: Typ. do Jornal do Commercio, 1919–1922), II, 381–82; 427; *União Operaria* (Recife), 13 May 1905, p. 2; 28 Feb. 1907, p. 2; 10 May 1907, p. 2; 24 June 1907, p. 2.

3. *A Terra Livre* (Rio de Janeiro), 27 July 1907, p. 1; *A Voz do Povo* (Rio

de Janeiro), 8 Oct. 1911, p. 1; 15 Oct. 1911, pp. 2–3; 19 Nov. 1911, p. 1; Simão, *Sindicato e estado*, p. 207.

Among the Brazilian writers addressing the "social question" during this period, some, including A. de Sampaio Doria (*A questão social. Quaes os principios scientificos a adoptar na formação de legislação social do Brasil?* [São Paulo: Monteiro Lobato & C., 1922]), advocated a Roman Catholic solution.

4. Theme 19, "Resoluções do Segundo Congresso Operário Brasileiro," pp. 189–99 in Paulo Sérgio Pinheiro and Michael M. Hall, eds., *A classe operária no Brazil. Documentos (1889 a 1930)*, Vol. I, *O movimento operário* (São Paulo: Editora Alfa Omega, 1979).

5. *Tribuna Operaria* (Rio de Janeiro), 15 Oct. 1900, pp. 1, 3; 1 Nov. 1900, pp. 1–3; *Gazeta Operaria* (Rio de Janeiro), 21 Dec. 1902, p. 3; *Correio da Manhã* (Rio de Janeiro), 7 July 1903, p. 4; 8 July 1903, p. 3; *O Artista* (Rio de Janeiro), June 1905, pp. 1–4, *O Amigo do Povo* (São Paulo), 14 May 1904, p. 1.

6. *O País* (Rio de Janeiro), 7 Feb. 1890, p. 2; 9 Feb. 1890, p. 3; *Gazeta Operaria*, 28 Nov. 1902, p. 1; 14 Dec. 1902, p. 1; *Kultur* (Rio de Janeiro], March 1904, p. 2; *O Amigo do Povo*, 26 Nov. 1904, p. 1; *A Terra Livre*, (São Paulo), 30 Dec. 1905, p. 2; *Correio Operario* (Rio de Janeiro), 1 Sept. 1910, p. 1; "Do seguro contra a molestia e contra a falta de trabalho," presented to Círculo Operario Fluminese, Niterói, by Francisco Sadock de Sá, 9 May 1911, and written and sent to "Segundo Congresso Operario" 5 Sept. 1913, Arquivo Geral da Cidade do Rio de Janeiro (hereafter AGCRJ), Cx. 5, Doc. 151.

7. *O País*, 15 Feb. 1890, p. 2; *Gazeta Operaria*, 2 Nov. 1902, p. 2; 15 Feb. 1903, p. 3; *União Caixeiral* (Rio de Janeiro), 1 May 1903, p. 2; *Correio da Manhã*, 26 Aug. 1903, p. 4; *A União Operaria* (Rio de Janeiro), 1 May 1904, pp. 1, 6; *Gazeta de Notícias* (Rio de Janeiro), 5 Jan. 1906, p. 2.

8. *O Tres de Abril* (Rio de Janeiro), 16 April 1905, p. 1; 3 Sept. 1905, p. 2; *O Jornal do Brasil* (Rio de Janeiro), 14 Nov. 1906, p. 5; 21 Nov. 1906, p. 3; *A Terra Livre*, 24 March 1906, pp. 3–4; 13 July 1906, p. 2.

9. *Gazeta de Notícias*, 5 Jan. 1906, p. 2; see also *A Terra Livre*, 17 Feb. 1906, p. 3.

10. *O Socialista da Provincia do Rio de Janeiro* (Niterói), 9 Jan. 1846, p. 1.

Vamireh Chacon traces the development of socilist ideas in Brazil in *História das idéias socialistas no Brasil* (Rio de Janeiro: Editôra Civilização Brasileira, 1965).

11. *A Questão Social* (Santos), I, 1, [1 Oct. 1895], pp. 1–5.

12. Astrojildo Pereira, "Silvério Fontes, pioneiro do marxismo no Brasil," *Estudos Sociais* 3 (April 1962), 404–19.

13. Antonio Piccarolo, *O socialismo no Brasil*, 3rd ed. (São Paulo: Editôra Piratininga, [1932]), pp. 30–57.

14. Pinheiro and Hall, eds., *A classe operária no Brasil*, I, 35–41.

15. *Gazeta Operaria*, 28 Sept. 1902, p. 2; 2 Nov. 1902, p. 3; 14 Dec. 1902, p. 1; 11 Jan. 1903, p. 3; 28 Feb. 1903, p. 1; *O Estado de São Paulo* (São Paulo), 28 Aug. 1902, p. 3; Pinheiro and Hall, eds., *A classe operária no Bra-*

sil, I, 35–41; Everardo Dias, *História das lutas sociais no Brasil* (São Paulo: Editôra Edaglit, 1962), pp. 244–45.

16. *O Estado de São Paulo*, 28 Aug. 1902, p. 3; *Gazeta Operaria*, 28 Sept. 1902, pp. 1–3; *O Operario* (Rio de Janeiro), 3 Feb. 1909, p. 1.

17. On Colônia Cecília, see: Newton Stadler da Sousa, *O anarquismo da Colônia Cecília* (Rio de Janeiro: Editôra Civilização Brasileira, 1970); Edgar Rodrigues, *Nacionalismo e cultura social, 1913–1922* (Rio de Janeiro: Laemmert, 1969), pp. 34–48; and the somewhat fictionalized account of Afonso Schmidt, *Colônia Cecília. Uma adventura anarquista na América, 1889 a 1893* (São Paulo: Editôra Anchieta, 1942).

18. One of the best summaries in English of anarchism and the international libertarian movement remains George Woodcock, *Anarchism: A History of Libertarian Ideas and Movements* (Cleveland: World Publishing Company, 1962).

19. *A Terra Livre*, 24 March 1906, p. 4.

20. Report of Ceasare Alliate-Bronner to Luigi Bruno, Italian Minister to Brazil, 30 June 1909, reproduced on page 2 of Pinheiro and Hall, eds., *A classe operária no Brasil*, I.

21. *Gazeta Operaria*, 11 Jan. 1903, p. 2; *El Grito del Pueblo* (São Paulo), 20 Aug. 1889, p. 2; *A Voz do Trahalhador* (Rio de Janeiro), 1 June 1909, p. 1.

22. Boris Fausto, *Trabalho urbano e conflito social (1890–1920)* (São Paulo: Difel/Disfusão Editorial, 1976), p. 69.

23. Michael M. Hall, "Immigration and the Early São Paulo Working Class," *Jahrbuck für Geschichte von Staat, Wirtschaft und Gesellschaft Lateinamericakas* 12 (1975), 395; Sheldon L. Maram, "The Immigrant and the Brazilian Labor Movement, 1890–1920," p. 189 in Dauril Alden and Warren Dean, eds., *Essays Concerning the Socioeconomic History of Brazil and Portuguese India* (Gainesville: University Presses of Florida, 1977).

24. Thomas H. Holloway, *Immigrants on the Land: Coffee and Society in São Paulo, 1886–1934* (Chapel Hill: University of North Carolina Press, 1980). See also the study of social mobility in São Paulo by Bertram Hutchinson, *Mobilidade e trabalho. Um estudo na cidade de São Paulo* (Rio de Janeiro: Centro Brasileiro de Pesquisas Educacionais. Instituto Nacional de Estudos. Ministério da Educação e Cultura, 1960).

25. Neno Vasco quoted in Edgard Leuenroth, *Anarquismo. Roteiro da libertação social. Antologia de doutrina, critica, história, informações* (Rio de Janeiro: Editôra Mundo Livre, 1963), p. 103.

26. *O Amigo do Povo*, 6 Dec. 1903, p. 2.

27. Brazil, Directoria Geral de Estatistica, *Recenseamento do Brazil realizado em 1 de setembro de 1920* (Rio de Janeiro: Typ. da Estatistica, 1922–1930), II, 1ª parte, 11; IV, 1ª parte, 545.

28. C. de Sampayo Garrido, *Emigração portuguesa. Relatorio consular* (São Paulo: Typ. Julio Costa & C., 1920), pp. 27–28. For a brief discussion of remittances by Italians, see Warren Dean, "Remittances of Italian Immigrants:

From Brazil, Argentina, Uruguay and U.S.A., 1884–1914," New York University Occasional Papers No. 14, 1974.

29. D. G. Nogueira Soares, Portuguese Minister to Brazil, to Henrique de Barros Gomes, Portuguese Minister, Rio de Janeiro, 15 Nov. 1887, Arquivo do Ministério dos Negócios Estrangeiros (Lisbon), Cx. 222.

30. Statement of Benjamin Mota read by deputy Nicanor Naxcimento in Chamber of Deputies, 22 May 1919, Brazil, Congress, *Documentos parlamentares. Legislação social*, II, 713.

31. Alceste de Ambris, "Il movimento operario nello Stato de São Paulo," p. 37 in Pinheiro and Hall, eds. *A classe operária no Brasil*, I; Conde de Paço d'Arcos, Portuguese Minister to Brazil, to Conde de Valbom, Foreign Minister, Petrópolis, 12 Oct. 1891, and 20 Oct. 1891, Arquivo do Ministério dos Negócios Estrangeiros, Cx. 223; Antonio Luiz Gomes, Portuguese Minister to Brazil, to Bernardino Machado, Foreign Minister, Rio de Janeiro, 13 Feb. 1911, and 18 June 1911, AMNE, Cx. 230; Domingos Lopes Fidalgo, Portuguese Minister to Brazil, to Augusto de Vasconcelos, Foreign Minister, Rio de Janeiro, 13 May 1912, AMNE, Cx. 231.

32. Benjamin Mota, in Brazil, *Documentos parlamentares*, II, 713.

33. Jacob Penteado. *Belénzinho, 1910 (Retrato de uma época)* (São Paulo: Livraria Martins, 1962).

34. Everardo Dias, *História das lutas sociais no Brasil* (São Paulo: Editôra Edaglit, 1962), pp. 209–10.

35. For such competition see Florestan Fernandes, *The Negro in Brazilian Society*, trans. Jacqueline D. Skiles, A Brunel, and Arthur Rothwell (New York: Columbia University Press, 1969), pp. 96–117.

36. Everardo Dias, *Memorias de um exiliado. Episodio de uma deportação* (São Paulo, n.p., 1920), p. 86.

37. Fausto, *Trabalho urbano e conflito social*, pp. 95–97.

38. Maram, "The Immigrant and the Brazilian Labor Movement," pp. 182–86 in Alden and Dean, eds., *Essays*.

39. Eulália Maria Lahmeyer Lobo, *História do Rio de Janeiro (Do capital comercial ao capital industrial e financeiro)* (Rio de Janeiro: Instituto Brasileiro de Mercado de Capitais, 1978), II, 523.

40. *O Estado de São Paulo*, 28 Aug. 1902, p. 3.

41. *O Amigo do Povo*, 28 May 1904, p. 3.

42. Giovanni Rossi to Alfred G. Sanftleben, Taquary, 29 Nov. 1896, cited in Eric Gordon, Michael M. Hall, and Hobart A. Spalding, Jr., "A Survey of Brazilian and Argentine Materials at the International Instituut voor Sociale Geschiedenis in Amsterdam," *Latin American Research Review* 8 (Fall 1973), 39.

43. *Brazil Operario* (Rio de Janeiro), August (first fortnight), 1903, p. 4; *A Terra Livre*, 17 Feb. 1906, p. 4; 29 July 1906, p. 2; 15 Aug. 1906, p. 4.

44. *A Terra Livre*, 29 July 1906, p. 2.

45. Ibid.; Hall, "Immigration and the Early São Paulo Working Class,"

Jahrbuch für Geschichte von Staat, Wirtschaft und Gesellschaft Lateinamerikas 12 (1975), 402.

46. "Relatorio tranzitorio que a União dos Alfaiates apresenta ao Segundo Congresso Operario reunido nesta capital nos dias 8, 9, 10, 11, 12, 13, 14 de setembro de 1913 na séde do Centro Cosmopolita á Rua do Senado 273," AGCRJ, Cx. 5, Doc. 153.

47. "Documentos do movimento operário. Resoluções do Primeiro Congresso Operário Brasileiro," *Estudos Sociais* 4, no. 16 (March 1963), 396.

48. *O Componedor* (Rio de Janeiro) 1 May 1909, p. 3.

49. Augusto Olympio Viveiros de Castro, *A questão social* (Rio de Janeiro: Livraria Editôra Conselheiro Candido de Oliveira, 1920), pp. 193–201.

50. See manuscript list of delegates to the 1913 "Second Brazilian Labor Congress" AGCRJ, Cx. 5, Doc. 178. Delegates to the 1906 "First Labor Congress" as well as to the 1913 congress are listed in PInheiro and Hall, eds., *A classe operária no Brasil*, I, 44–45, 182–85. Edgar Rodrigues, *Socialismo e sindicalismo no Brasil, 1675–1922* (Rio de Janeiro: Laemmert, 1969), pp. 180, 239–40, gives delegates to the "First São Paulo State Labor Congress" in 1906 and the "Second São Paulo Labor Congress" of 1908. See also photograph of delegates to the 1906 "First Labor Congress" in this book, as well as photographs in Pinheiro and Hall, eds., *A classe operária no Brasil*, I.

51. *A Voz do Povo*, 7 March 1920, p. 2.

52. *A União Operaria*, 1 May 1904, pp. 1, 3, 5–6; *Gazeta de Notícias*, 5 Jan. 1906, p. 2; *O Tres de Abril*, 10 Sept. 1905, p. 1; *Jornal Operario*, 29 Oct. 1905, p. 2.

53. Various female intellectuals such as the socialist Ernestina Lesina and Maria Lacerda de Moura supported radical or labor causes. The somewhat disorganized views of Maria Lacerda de Moura, who opposed the church, capitalism, and militarism, are found in numerous publications, including *Religião do amor e da belleza*, 2d ed. (São Paulo: Editora O Pensamento, 1929). Teresa Maria Carini, born into a provincial, aristocratic Italian family near Parma, became a passionate socialist and able public speaker in Brazil, supporting strikes and workers' schools. Antonio Candido paints an appealing portrait of her in *Teresina etc.* (Rio de Janeiro: Editora Paz e Terra, 1980). These women also held strong women's rights positions.

54. The best study of Brazil's labor press is Maria Nazareth Ferreira, *A imprensa operária no Brasil, 1880–1920* (Petrópolis: Editora Vozes, 1978), which also lists newspapers in the large Edgard Leuenroth collection, the best organized archive of labor and militant newspapers in Brazil. In *Nacionalismo e cultura social*, pp. 425–44, Edgar Rodgrigues lists labor newspapers, giving dates and directors. Boris Fausto, *Trabalho urbano e conflito social*, pp. 91–94, gives a brief analysis of the anarchist press. For the development of the general press in Brazil, see Nelson Werneck Sodré, *A história da imprensa no Brasil* (Rio de Janeiro: Editôra Civilização Brasileira, 1966).

The Biblioteca Nacional do Rio de Janeiro possesses the largest collection of newspapers in Brazil, including labor newspapers from across the nation. In this collection is a copy of the anarchist journal *A Terra Livre* (17 Feb. 1906) addressed to Hermes de Olinda, a bookbinder working at the Biblioteca Nacional. Perhaps this socialist, once attacked by another anarchist newspaper, *A Voz do Trabalhador* (22 Nov. 1908, p. 3), served as the channel through which the Biblioteca Nacional obtained its collection of *A Terra Livre*.

55. Richard J. Walter, "The Socialist Press in Turn-of-the-Century Argentina," *The Americas* 37 (July 1980), 1–24.

56. *O Livre Pensador* (São Paulo), 20 Aug. 1905, p. 1; *Gazeta Operaria*, 5 Oct. 1902, p. 1; "Relatório da Confederação Operária Brasileira apresentado ao Segundo Congresso," 1913, *Estudos Sociais* 5, no. 18 (Nov. 1963) 203.

57. *O Operario* (Rio de Janeiro), 23 Nov. 1895, p. 2; *O Combate* (Fortaleza), 8 March 1896, p. 4; *Echo Operario* (Rio Grande do Sul), 18 Aug. 1901, p. 1; *Kultur*, March 1904, p. 2; *O Amigo do Povo*, 9 April 1904, p. 2; 28 May 1904, p. 3; *Semana Operaria* (Rio de Janeiro), 20 May 1907, p. 2; *A Terra Livre*, 30 Dec. 1905, p. 2; 13 Jan. 1906, p. 3; 17 Feb. 1906, p. 3; *Jornal do Brasil*, 14 Nov. 1906, p. 5; *A Voz do Trabalhador*, 15 Aug. 1908, p. 1; 22 Nov. 1908, p. 3; 29 Nov. 1908, p. 2; 8 July 1909, p. 3; 22 July 1909, p. 1.

58. Benjamin Mota, in Brazil, *Documentos parlamentares*, II, 712.

59. *Jornal Operario* (São Paulo), 29 Oct. 1905, p. 2.

60. *Jornal do Brasil*, 21 Nov. 1906, p. 3; *A Terra Livre*, 12 April 1906, p. 1; 13 July 1906, p. 4; "Documentos do movimento operária. Resoluções do Primeiro Congresso Operário Brasileiro," *Estudos Sociais* 4, no. 16 (March 1963), 387–98.

61. *A Voz do Trabalhador*, 15 Oct. 1910 and 15 Nov. 1910, pp. 161–72 in Pinheiro and Hall, eds., *A classe operária no Brasil*, I.

62. Rio de Janeiro, *Assistencia publica e privada no Rio de Janeiro (Brasil). Historia e estatistica* (Rio de Janeiro: Typographia do "Annuario do Brasil," 1922), p. 320.

63. "Documentos do movimento operário. Congresso operário de 1912," *Estudos Sociais* 5, no. 17 (July 1963), 69–87.

64. *Correio da Manhã*, 20 Oct. 1912, p. 5; 5 Nov. 1912, p. 5; 7 Nov. 1912, p. 5; 8 Nov. 1912, p. 5; 9 Nov. 1912, p. 4; 10 Nov. 1912, p. 7; 11 Nov. 1912, p. 4; 14 Nov. 1912, p. 3; *A Noite* (Rio de Janeiro), 7 Nov. 1912, p. 3; 8 Nov. 1912, p. 3; 18 Nov. 1912, p. 1; "Documentos do movimento operário. Congresso operário de 1912," *Estudos Sociais* 5, no. 17 (July 1963), 70–71; Everardo Dias, *Histórica das lutas sociais no Brasil*, pp. 277–81.

65. "Documentos do movimento operário. Um relatório datado de 1913," *Estudos Sociais* 5, no. 18 (November 1963), 194–206.

66. Manuscript list of Delegates to Second Brazilian Labor Congress, 1913, AGCRJ, Cx. 5, Doc. 178; Joaquim Pimenta, *Retalhos do passado*, 2d ed. (Rio de Janeiro: Imprensa Nacional, 1949), pp. 194–95; 202; John W. F. Dulles, *Anarchists and Communists in Brazil, 1900–1935* (Austin and London: University of Texas Press, 1973), pp. 29–30; *União Operaria*, 1 May 1905, p. 1; 10 April 1906, pp. 1–4; 1 May 1906, p. 6; *Correio Operario* (Rio de Janeiro), 1

Aug. 1910, pp. 1, 3; A *Lucta Social* (Manaus), 29 March 1914, pp. 1–3; *O Protesto* (Recife), 1 May 1910, p. 1.

67. A *União* (Recife), 27 Dec. 1897, p. 2; *União Operaria*, 13 May 1905, p. 2; 28 Feb. 1907, p. 2; *Aurora Social* (Recife), 1 May 1902, pp. 2, 4; 11 June 1906, p. 1; 26 June 1906, pp. 2, 3; 10 July 1906, pp. 2, 3; 31 Aug. 1906, p. 1; 30 Sept. 1906, pp. 1–4; 31 Oct. 1906, p. 1; 31 Dec. 1906, pp. 1, 3; 18 April 1907, p. 2; *Echo Operario* (Rio Grande do Sul), 15 June 1901, p. 3; Pimenta, *Retalhos do passado*, pp. 192–93.

68. *O Protesto*, 1 May 1910, p. 3; *Aurora Social*, 26 June 1906, pp. 2, 3; *O Luctador Social* (Recife), 20 June 1914, p. 1; *O Hora Social* (Recife), 10 Dec. 1919, p. 1; *Avanti!* (Recife), 9 June 1920, pp. 1, 2; 19 June 1920, p. 3; 4 Sept. 1920, p. 2; A *Vanguarda (Recife)*, 11 Sept. 1920, p. 1; Pimenta, Retalhos do passado, pp. 202–203.

69. "Alguns dados relativos do que tem sido a vida dos operarios Graphicos em São Paulo desde que se ha memoría de sua movimentação em sentido economico, que a União Graphica de São Paulo apresenta ao 2° Congresso Operario Brazileiro a realizar-se no Rio de Janeiro nos dias 8 a 13 de Setembro presente," AGCRJ, Cx. 5, Doc. 166; A *Terra Livre*, 30 Dec. 1905, p. 4; 13 Jan. 1906, p. 4; *O Trabalhador Grafico* (São Paulo), Sept. 1922, 28 Feb. 1923.

70. These original documents from the 1913 "Second Labor Congress," some of the rarest original Brazilian labor union documentation preserved, are found in the Arquivo Geral de Cidade do Rio de Janeiro. Several of the *relatórios*, reports which labor associations were requested to sent to the congress, together with the final report and resolutions, are printed on pp. 132–233 in Pinheiro and Hall, eds., A *classe operária no Brasil*, I. The *relátorio* of the Confederação Operária Brasileira is also found in "Documentos do movimento operário. Um relatório datado de 1913," *Estudos Sociais* 5, no. 18 (November 1963), on pp. 194–206. The 1913 municipal survey data together with some additional information gathered in 1920 was published as: Rio de Janeiro, *Assistencia publica e privada no Rio de Janeiro (Brasil). Historia e estatistica* (Rio de Janeiro: Typographia do 'Annuario do Brasil,' 1922).

71. Brazil, Directoria Geral de Estatística, *Recenseamento do Rio de Janeiro (Districto Federal) realizada em 20 de setembro de 1906* (Rio de Janeiro: Officina da Estatística, 1907), I, 113.

72. Michael L. Conniff, "Voluntary Associations in Rio, 1870–1945: A New Approach to Urban Social Dynamics," *Journal of Interamerican Studies and World Affairs* 17 (February 1975), 67.

73. Rio de Janeiro, *Assistencia publica e privada no Rio de Janeiro*, pp. 257–305, 328–52, 356–67, 380–81, 748. A membership breakdown by sex is not available for the larger Sindicado dos Trabalhadores em Fabricas de Tecidos do Rio de Janeiro, part of the anarcho-syndicalist-dominated Confederação Operária Brasileira; the union did not give such information in its report to the 1913 "Second Labor Congress."

74. Rio de Janeiro, *Assistencia publica e privada no Rio de Janeiro*, pp. 81–83, 232–33, 393–99.

75. Alfredo Cinto Vieira de Mello to Augusto Tavares de Lyra, Rio de Janeiro, 4 Dec. 1906, Arquivo Nacional, IJ[6] 382; Marcel Verme, p. 107 in "Brésil," in Pinheiro and Hall, eds., *A classe operária no Brasil*, I.

76. Manuscript list of delegates to 1913 "Second Brazilian Labor Congress," AGCRJ, Cx. 5, Doc. 178; *A Noite* (Rio de Janeiro), 21 Nov. 1912, p. 1; Brazil, *Recenseamento do Rio de Janeiro (Districto Federal) realizada em 20 setembro de 1906*, I, 104; Brazil, *Recenseamento do Brazil realizado em 1 de setembre de 1920*, IV, 5ª parte, tomo I, 26–27. On nationality and race, see Paulo Barreto (pseud. João do Rio), *A alma encantadora das ruas* (Paris and Rio de Janeiro: Tip. Garnier, 1908), pp. 169–71; and Alured Gray Bell, *The Beautiful Rio de Janeiro* (London: William Heinenmann, 1914), p. 39; as well as photographs of striking maritime workers in *Fon-Fon* (Rio de Janeiro), 24 March 1917, and the picture of the strikers' meeting reproduced in this book.

77. *A Noite*, 19 Nov. 1912, p. 1. Some of these figures for C.O.B. membership given by *A Noite* seem exaggerated. For example, the Federação Operária de Santos, in its report to the "Second Labor Congress" in 1913, following several violent strikes, claimed 8,000 to 10,000 adherents, of whom only 400 were paid members, as compared to the 22,500 members reported by *A Noite* ("Relatorio Histórico da Federação Operaria Local de Santos ao 2° Congresso Operario Brasileiro," AGCRJ, Cx. 5, Doc. 164).

In 1913, the sixteen member unions of the C.O.B., comprised largely of artisans and construction workers, were:

Centro dos Operários Marmoristas
União dos Alfaiates
União Geral dos Pintores
Sindicato dos Sapateiros
Sindicato dos Carpinteiros
Sindicato Operário de Ofícios Vários
Sindicado dos Estucadores
Sindicato dos Operários das Pedreiras
Fênix Caixeiral
Sindicato dos Funileiros e Bombeiros Hidráulicos
Sindicato dos Pedreiros e Serventes
Sindicato Operário da Indústria Elétrica
Sindicato dos Marceneiros e Artes Correlativas
Sindicato Opérario dos Caldeireiros de Ferro
Sindicato dos Trabalhadores em Ladrilhos e Mosaicos
Sindicato dos Trabalhadores em Fábricas de Tecidos
("Relatório da Confederação Operaria Brazileira apresentado ao Segundo Congresso," *Estudos Sociais* 5, no. 18 [November 1963], 204)

Only five of these unions sent the requested reports of their history and activities to the 1913 congress, and of those five, only the tailors' (500 members) and the tile workers' (120 members) unions gave their membership figures

(AGCRJ, Cx. 5, Docs. 153 and 156). One major Rio union, the Federação das Artes Gráficas, neither appears in the 1912 Rio municipal survey nor formed part of the C.O.B.

78. Rio de Janeiro, *Assistencia publica e privada no Rio de Janeiro*, pp. 108–13; 356; Brazil, *Recensamento do Rio de Janeiro (Distrito Federal) realizada em 20 de setembro de 1906*, I, 388–89.

79. *A Terra Livre*, 7 Feb. 1906, p. 3; *Gazeta Operaria*, 30 Nov. 1902, p. 1; *O Chapeleiro*, 1 May 1904, p. 4; "A Federação Operaria do Rio de Janeiro," *A Voz do Trabalhador*, 15 Oct. 1913; 15 Nov. 1913; 1 Dec. 1913; 15 Dec. 1913, in Pinheiro and Hall, eds., *A classe operária no Brazil*, I, 161–72.

80. *Gazeta Operaria*, 9 Nov. 1902, pp. 1, 3; *O Chapeleiro*, 1 May 1904, pp. 1, 4; *Echo Operario*, 15 June 1901, p. 2; A União Operaria, 1 May 1904, p. 2; *O Operario (Sorocaba)*, 18 July 1910, *p.* 2; 31 July 1910, *p.* 1; 11 Dec. 1910, *p.* 1; *O Amigo do Povo*, 14 May 1904, p. 1; *Jornal do Brasil*, 25 May 1899, p. 1; *A Terra Livre*, 24 March 1906, p. 4; *Portugal Moderna* (Rio de Janeiro), 3 May 1913, p. 2; Jacob Penteado, *Belènzinho, 1910*, p. 149; Rodrigues, *Nacionalismo e cultura social, pp.* 447–51.

81. *A Voz do Trabalhador*, 15 Aug. 1908, p. 2; 6 Dec. 1908, p. 2; 12 Jan. 1909, p. 2; 22 July 1909, p. 1; 3 Aug. 1909, pp. 1, 2; 30 Aug. 1909, p. 2; 30 Oct. 1909, p. 2; *A Terra Livre*, 24 March 1906, p. 4; 9 Oct. 1906, p. 3; *O Amigo do Povo*, 26 Nov. 1904, p. 4; *O Libertario* (Rio de Janeiro), 8 Oct. 1904, p. 1; Rodrigues, *Nacionalismo e cultura social*, pp. 77–81, 178–83, 241–42, 446–48.

82. Although research conducted on Brazil's lower classes in recent years concentrates on labor organizations, especially ideologically oriented ones, and on strikes, studies of specific strikes are rare. In *Trabalho urbano e conflito social*, Boris Fausto examines several in São Paulo. Other specific studies include Maria Cecília Baeta Neves, "Greve dos sapateiros de 1906 no Rio de Janeiro: Notas de pesquisa," *Revista de Administração de Empresas* 13 (April-June 1973), 49–66, and Silvia I. L. Magnani, "A classe operária vai à luta: a greve de 1907 em São Paulo," *Cara a Cara* 1 (May 1978), 105–24. *Os companheiros de São Paulo* (São Paulo: Edições Símbolo, 1977), by Paula Beiguelman, a description of labor activities in São Paulo based on an examination of fifty years of local newspapers, contains abundant references to and information on strikes in the state capital and in Santos from 1891 to 1920.

Research on strikes in Brazil can never equal in precision that possible for a country like France, where police kept accurate strike statistics, including the number and kind of workers involved in each strike; such records permit studies like Edward Shorter and Charles Tilly, *Strikes in France, 1830–1968* (London and New York: Cambridge University Press, 1974). Even lists of strikes in one state in Brazil, São Paulo, in one year, 1917 (Azis Simão, *Sindicato e estado*, pp. 155–58), or in that state and in the city of Rio de Janeiro during the crisis years of 1917 to 1920 (Fausto, *Trabalho urbano e conflito social*, pp. 253–73), are incomplete. Those notable contributions rely heavily on newspaper accounts, the most widely used source of information on strikes and other labor activities in Brazil, even though newspapers ignored many brief strikes.

83. João Ferreira de Araujo Pinho, *Mensagem apresentada á legislativa do Estado na Bahia na abertura da 2ª sessão ordinaria de 10° legislativa* (Salvador: Officinas da Empreza 'A Bahia,' 1910), pp. 20–21.

84. Beiguelman, *Os companheiros de São Paulo*, pp. 34–31; Fausto, *Trabalho urbano e conflito social*, pp. 135–46.

85. Alfredo Cinto Vieira de Mello to Augusto Tavares de Lyra, Rio de Janeiro, 4 Dec. 1906, Arqhivo Nacional, IJ⁶ 382; *Gazeta Operaria*, 15 Feb. 1903, p. 2; *A Tribuna do Povo* (Rio de Janeiro), 18 March 1909, p. 2; Maria Cecília Baeta Neves, "Greve dos sapateiros de 1906 do Rio de Janeiro: Notas de pesquisa," *Revista de Administração de Empresas* 13 (April-June 1973), 49–66.

86. *Correio da Manhã*, 16 June 1903, p. 3; 11 July 1903, p. 3; 12 July 1903, p. 4; 14 July 1903, p. 2; 15 July 1903, p. 2; 16 July 1903, pp. 2–3; 18 July 1903, pp. 2–3; 19 July 1903, p. 4; 23 July 1903, p. 3; 25 Aug. 1903, p. 2; *Brazil Operario*, July (second fortnight), 1903, pp. 2–3.

87. Henrique Fernandes Porto to head of police agents, Rio de Janeiro, 3 July 1903 [copy], Arquivo Nacional, IJ⁶ 378, *Gazeta Operaria*, 15 Feb. 1903, p. 3; *Correio da Manhã*, 14 July 1903, p. 2; 16 July 1903, p. 3; 23 July 1903, p. 3.

88. *O Amigo do Povo*, 13 Sept. 1903, p. 2; "Relatorio do Sindicato dos Trabalhadores em Fabricas de Tecidos para o 2° Congresso Operario Brazileiro," 1913, AGCRJ, Cx. 5, Doc. 154.

89. *O Amigo do Povo*, 29 Aug. 1903, p. 1; *Correio da Manhã*, 17 Aug. 1903, p. 2; 20 Aug. 1903, p. 2; 21 Aug. 1903, p. 2; 22 Aug. 1903, p. 2; 23 Aug. 1903, p. 2.

90. *Gazeta Operaria*, 11 Jan. 1903, p. 2.

91. *Correio da Manhã*, 23 Aug. 1903, p. 2.

92. *Correio da Manhã*, 18 Aug. 1903, p. 2; 19 Aug. 1903, pp. 2–3; 21 Aug. 1903, p. 2; 22 Aug. 1903, p. 2; 25 Aug. 1903, p. 2; 26 Aug. 1903, p. 3; 27 Aug. 1903, p. 2; *O País*, 19 Aug. 1903, p. 1; *O Amigo do Povo*, 29 Aug. 1903, p. 1.

93. *Correio da Manhã*, 19 Aug. 1903, p. 2; 23 Aug. 1903, p. 2; 24 Aug. 1903, p. 2; 25 Aug. 1903, p. 2.

94. *Correio da Manhã*, 17 Aug. 1903, p. 2; 18 Aug. 1903, p. 2; 19 Aug. 1903, pp. 2–3; 21 Aug. 1903, p. 2; 22 Aug. 1903, p. 2; 23 Aug. 1903, p. 2; 25 Aug. 1903, p. 2; *O Amigo do Povo*, 29 Aug. 1903, p. 1; 13 Sept. 1903, p. 2.

95. *Correio da Manhã*, 22 Aug. 1903, p. 2; 23 Aug. 1903, pp. 2–3; 27 Aug. 1903, p. 2; 28 Aug. 1903, p. 2; *Brazil Operario*, July (second fortnight) 1903, pp. 2–3; *O Amigo do Povo*, 13 Sept. 1903, p. 2; "Relatorio do Sindicato dos Trabalhadores em Fabricas de Tecidos para o 2° Congresso Operario Brazileiro," 1913, AGCRJ, Cx. 5, Doc. 154.

96. *Relatorio apresentado no Exmo. Snr. Dr. J. J. Seabra, Ministro da Justiça e Negocios Interiores pelo chefe de Policia do Districto Federal A. A. Cardoso de Castro*, in *Relatorio apresentado ao Presidente da Republica dos Estados Unidos*

do Brasil pelo Dr. J. J. Seabra, Ministro de Estado da Justiça e Negocios Interiores em Março de 1904 (Rio de Janeiro: Imprensa Nacional, 1904), p. 29.
  97. A. A. Cardoso de Castro to José Joaquim Seabra, Rio dê Janeiro, 4 Sept. 1903, Arquivo Nacional, IJ[6] 378.
  98. *Correio da Manhã*, 26 Aug. 1903, p. 3; 27 Aug. 1903, p. 2; 28 Aug. 1903, pp. 2–3; *O Amigo do Povo*, 13 Sept. 1903, p. 1; *A Tribuna do Povo*, 18 March 1909, p. 2; 18 April 1909, p. 1; *A Voz do Trabalhador*, 13 Jan. 1909, p. 1; 1 May 1909, p. 3; "Relatorio do Sindicato dos Trabalhadores em Fabricas de Tecidos para o 2° Congresso Operario Brazileiro," 1913, AGCRJ, Cx. 5, Doc. 154.

Chapter 8

  1. See: José Álvaro Moisés and Verena Martinez-Alier, "A revolta dos suburbanos ou 'Patrão, o trem atrasou,' " in José Alvaro Moisés et al., *Contradições urbanas e movimentos sociais*, 2d ed. (Rio de Janeiro: Centro de Estudos de Cultura Contemporânea/Paz e Terra, 1978), pp. 13–63. See also José Alvaro Moisés, "Protesto urbano e política: O quebra-quebra de 1947," pp. 50–64; Lícia do Prado Valladares, "Quebra-quebras na construção civil: O caso dos operários do metrô do Rio de Janeiro," pp. 65–91; and "Inventário dos quebra-quebras nos trens e ônibus em São Paulo e Rio de Janeiro, 1977–1981," pp. 92–108, in José Alvaro Moisés et al., *Cidade, povo e poder* (Rio de Janeiro: Centro de Estudos de Cultura Contemporânea/Paz e Terra, 1982).
  2. São Paulo [state], *Relatorio apresentado ao Secretario dos Negocios da Justiça pelo chefe de policia do Estado de S. Paulo, Augusto Meirelles Reis, 1905* (São Paulo: Typographia do Diario, 1907), pp. 6–8; Brazil, Ministry of Justice, *Relatorio* March 1890, pp. 157–58; *O Protesto* (Rio de Janeiro), Dec. 24, 1899, p. 1; *A Terra Livre* (Rio de Janeiro), 8 June 1907, p. 3; Joseph L. Love, *São Paulo in the Brazilian Federation, 1889–1937* (Stanford: Stanford University Press, 1980), pp. 126–29, 302–6. See also Heloísa Rodrigues Fernandes, *Política e Seguranca. A força pública de São Paulo* (São Paulo: Editora Alfa e Ômega, 1974).
  3. *Rio News* (Rio de Janeiro), 19 March 1901, p. 5.
  4. See: Sam C. Adamo, "The Broken Promise: Race, Health, and Justice in Rio de Janeiro, 1890–1940" (unpublished Ph.D. dissertation, University of New Mexico, 1983), pp. 184–94; and *A polícia e a força policial no Rio de Janeiro*, Série Estudos PUC/RJ No. 4 (Rio de Janeiro: Pontifícia Universidade Católica do Rio de Janeiro, 1981.
  5. "Relatorio do Sindicato dos Trabalhadores em Fabricas de Tecidos para o 2° Congresso Operario Brazileiro," 1913, Arquivo Geral da Cidade do Rio de Janeiro, Cx. 5, Doc. 154; Henrique Fernandes Porto to head of police agents, Rio de Janeiro, July 3, 1903 [copy], Arquivo Nacional (hereafter AN), IJ[6] 378; São Paulo [state], *Relatorio apresentado . . . pelo chefe de policia de S. Paulo . . . 1905*, pp. 5–10. *Brasil Operario* (Rio de Janeiro), August (second fortnight), 1903, p. 1; *A Terra Livre* (São Paulo), 30 Dec. 1905, p. 2; 12 April

1906, p. 2 (Rio de Janeiro), 25 May 1907, p. 1; 1 June 1907, p. 3; *O Operario* (Sorocaba), 20 March 1910, p. 2; A *Voz do Trabalhador* (Rio de Janeiro), 13 Jan. 1909, p. 3.

6. Relatorio apresentado ao Exm. Snr. D. J. J. Seabra, *Ministro da Justiça e Negocios Interiores pelo chefe de policia do Districto Federal* A. A. Cardoso de Castro, in Brazil, Ministry of Justice, *Relatorio apresentado ao Presidente da Republica dos Estados Unidos do Brasil pelo Dr. J. J. Seabra, Ministro de Estado de Justiça e Negocios Interiores em Março de 1904* (Rio de Janeiro: Imprensa Nacional, 1904), pp. 29–30; Ministry of Justice, *Relatorio* March 1900, pp. 157–64; São Paulo [state], *Relatorio apresentado . . . pelo chefe de policia de S. Paulo . . . 1905*, pp. 5–10; Alfredo Cinto Vieira de Mello, police chief, to Augusto Tavares de Lyra, Minister of Justice, Rio de Janeiro, 4 Dec. 1906, AN, IJ⁶ 382; "Relatorio apresentado pelo snr. dr. Belisario Fernandes da Silva Tavares, chefe de policia do Districto Federal, as exm. sr. dr. Rivadavia da Cunha Corrêa, Ministro da Justiça e Negocios Interiores," Rio de Janeiro, 15 Feb. 1912, AN, IJ⁶ 391; "Relatorio da policia do Districto Federal apresentado ao exm. snr. dr. Esmeraldino Olympio de Torres Bandeira, Ministro da Justiça e Negocios Interiores pelo dr. Carolino de Leoni Ramos, chefe de policia," Rio de Janeiro, AN, IJ⁶ 386.

7. Adamo, "The Broken Promise," pp. 184–247.

8. A *Noite* (Rio de Janeiro), 15 March 1917, p. 4.

9. Boris Fausto, *Crime e cotidiano. A criminalidade em São Paulo (1880– 1924)* (São Paulo: Editora Brasiliense, 1984), p. 34.

10. Adamo, "The Broken Promise," pp. 238, 242; Fausto, *Crime e cotidiano*, p. 46. The valuable study by Martha Knisely Huggins, *From Slavery to Vagrancy in Brazil: Crime and Social Control in the Third World* (New Brunswick, N.J.: Rutgers University Press, 1984), focuses on the rural poor, emphasizing social control as a powerful force in labor mobilization in Pernambuco following the end of slavery, when the state tried to criminalize marginality and help large landowners obtain a labor force for the sugar plantations. Data are included on crime patterns and on the occupations, age, gender, race, and crimes of those held in Recife's House of Detention. Recent police violence and the larger question of violence in Brazil have aroused scholarly interest in Brazil, more than has past violence, as seen in such works as Maria Célia Paoli et al., *A violência brasileira* (São Paulo: Editora Brasilense, 1982).

11. Serzedello Corrêa, Foreign Minister, to Minister of Justice, Rio de Janeiro, 18 June 1892, Arquivo Histórico do Ministério das Relações Exteriores, Itamarati (hereafter AHI), 302-3-4; Cassiano do Nascimento, Foreign Minister, to Minister of Justice, Rio de Janeiro, 23 Dec. 1893, AHI, 302-3-7; Cassiano do Nascimento to Minister of Justice, 20 July 1894, and 2 Aug. 1894, AHI, 302-3-9; Carlos de Carvalho, Foreign Minister, to Minister of Justice, Rio de Janeiro, 6 Dec. 1894, AHI, 302-3-9; Olyntho de Magalhães, Foreign Minister, to Minister of Justice, Rio de Janeiro, 23 Nov. 1898, 1 Dec. 1898; 3 Dec. 1898; and 15 Dec. 1898, AHI, 302-3-13; Olyntho de Magalhaes to Foreign Minister, 25 Sept. 1902, AHI, 302-3-18; Baron of Rio Branco, Foreign Minister, to Min-

ister of Justice, Rio de Janeiro, 9 Dec. 1902, AHI, 302-3-18; Rio Branco to Minister of Justice, 30 April 1903; 31 Aug. 1903; and 30 Sept. 1903, AHI, 302-4-1; Brazil, Ministry of Justice, *Relatorio* April 1896, pp. 71–72; São Paulo (state); *Relatorio apresentado ao secretario dos Negocios da Justiça do Estado de S. Paulo pelo chefe de policia Bento Pereira Bueno em 31 de Janeiro 1896* (São Paulo: Typ. a Vap. Espinola, Siqueira & Comp., 1896), pp. 10–11; *Rio News* (Rio de Janeiro), 17 Oct. 1893, pp. 3, 5; 24 Oct. 1893, p. 4; 31 Oct. 1893, p. 3; 7 Nov. 1893, p. 3; 21 Nov. 1893, p. 3; 28 Nov. 1893, p. 5; 5 Dec. 1893, pp. 3, 5; 15 Jan. 1895, p. 5; 28 May 1895, p. 7; 16 July 1895, p. 3; 13 Aug. 1895, p. 7; 11 Aug. 1896, pp. 7–8; Anor Butler Maciel, *Expulsão de estrangeiros* (Rio de Janeiro: Imprensa Nacional, 1953), pp. 30–36.

12. Alfredo Cinto Vieira de Mello, police chief, to Augusto Tavares de Lyra, Minister of Justice, Rio de Janeiro, 4 Dec. 1906, AN IJ[6] 382.

13. *Gazeta Operaria* (Rio de Janeiro), 28 Dec. 1902, p. 1; João Dunshee de Abranches Moura, *Governos e congressos da República dos Estados Unidos do Brazil, 1889–1917* (São Paulo: M. V. Abranches, 1918), I, 486–88; Brazil, Ministry of Justice, *Relatorio* March 1908, pp. 108–21; *Portugal Moderno* (Rio de Janeiro), 19 March 1913, p. 1; Maciel, *Explusão de estrangeiros*, pp. 36–42; Carl E. Solberg, *Immigration and Nationalism in Argentina and Chile, 1890–1914* (Austin: University of Texas Press, 1970), pp. 109–10.

14. Sheldon L. Maram, "The Immigrant and the Brazilian Labor Movement, 1890–1920," pp. 198–200 in Dauril Alden and Warren Dean, eds., *Essays Concerning the Socioeconomic History of Brazil and Portuguese India* (Gainesville: University of Florida, 1977).

15. Everardo Dias, *História das lutas sociais no Brasil* (São Paulo: Editôra Edaglit 1962), p. 56.

16. Cassiano do Nascimento, Foreign Minister, to Minister of Justice, Rio de Janeiro, 20 July 1894, 26 July 1894, and 28 Aug. 1894, AHI, 302-3-9; Carlos de Carvalho, Foreign Minister, to Minister of Justice, Rio de Janeiro, Dec. 6, 1894, AHI, 302-3-9; São Paulo [state], *Relatorio apresentado . . . pelo chefe de policia de S. Paulo . . . 1896*, pp. 10–11; São Paulo [state], Repartição de Estatística e Arquivo, *Relatorio* 1894, p. 122; *O Socialista* (Rio de Janeiro), 18 March 1893, p. 3.

17. Washington Luís to Afonso Pena, São Paulo, 7 May 1907, Afonso Pena Papers, AN, L 11-1.2.1277.

18. Afonso Pena to Tavares de Lyra, Rio de Janeiro, 12 May 1907, and 13 May 1907, (Copies), Afonso Pena Papers, AN, L 2-1.2.533 and L 1-2.533C.

19. Tavares de Lyra to Afonso Pena, Rio de Janeiro, 12 May 1907, Afonso Pena Papers, AN, L 1-2.533B.

20. Warren Dean, *The Industrialization of São Paulo, 1880–1945* (Austin and London: University of Texas Press, 1969), pp. 165–67.

21. Demetrio de Toledo, "Operarios do Velho e do Novo Mundo," *Kosmos* (Rio de Janeiro), July 1904 (unpaged).

22. Raymundo Teixeira Mendes, *A verdadeira politica republicana e a incorporação do proletariado na sociedade moderna* (Rio de Janeiro: Tipografia

do Apostolado Pozitivista do Brazil, 1908); *O pozitivismo e a questão social* (Rio de Janeiro: Tiopografia do Apostolado Pozitivista do Brazil, 1915); *As greves, a órdem republicana, e a reorganização social* (Rio de Janeiro: Tipografia do Apostolado Pozitivista do Brazil, 1906): *O Imperio Brazileiro e a Republica Brazileira perante a regeneração social. A proposito do "Manifesto de S.A.I. D. Luiz de Bragança"* (Rio de Janeiro: Tipografia do Apostolado Pozitivista do Brazil, 1913).

23. Augusto Olympio Viveiros de Castro, *A questão social* (Rio de Janeiro: Livraria Editora Conselheiro Candido de Oliveira, 1920), pp. 5–8, 32–34, 116–49.

24. For the election figures and for an incisive study of political participation in Brazil, see Joseph L. Love, "Political Participation in Brazil, 1881–1969," *Luso-Brazilian Review* 7 (December 1970), 3–24. An excellent set of coordinated regional political studies is provided by Love, *São Paulo in the Brazilian Federation*, together with John D. Wirth, *Minas Gerais in the Brazilian Federation, 1889–1937* (Stanford: Stanford University Press, 1977), and Robert M. Levine, *Pernambuco in the Brazilian Federation, 1889–1937* (Stanford: Stanford University Press, 1978). See also: Joseph L. Love, *Rio Grande do Sul and Brazilian Regionalism, 1882–1930* (Stanford: Stanford University Press, 1971), and Eul-Soo Pang, *Bahia in the First Republic. Coronelismo and Oligarchies, 1889–1934* (Gainesville: University of Florida Presses, 1979).

25. Ruy Barbosa, *Plataforma*, 2nd ed. (Salvador: Empreza 'A Bahia,' 1910).

26. *Hermes-Wenceslau. O Sr. General Pinheiro Machado* (Rio de Janeiro: n.p., 1910), pp. 43–44.

27. João Coelho Gonçalves Lisboa, *Conferencias republicanas* (Rio de Janeiro: Typ. Luiz Miotto, 1910), pp. 3–4.

28. For biographies of Hermes da Fonseca, see: Nini Miranda, *A vida do Marechal Hermes Rodrigues da Fonseca. Sua ação no exército a na política* (Rio de Janeiro: n.p., 1942); and Hermes da Fonseca Filho, *Marechal Hermes. Dados para uma biografia* (Rio de Janeiro: n.p., 1961).

29. Umberto Peregrino, *Significação do Marechal Hermes* (Rio de Janeiro: Biblioteca do Exército, 1956), p. 45; José Maria dos Santos, *A política geral do Brasil* (São Paulo: J. Magalhães, 1930), p. 436; *A Noite* (Rio de Janeiro), 18 Nov. 1912, p. 3; Fonseca Filho, *Marechal Hermes*, pp. 206–9.

30. *Correio da Manhã* (Rio de Janeiro), 5 Nov. 1912, p. 5; 7 Nov. 1912, p. 5; 10 Nov. 1912, p. 7; 11 Nov. 1912, p. 4; 14 Nov. 1912, p. 3; *A Noite*, 7 Nov. 1912, p. 3; 9 Nov. 1912, p. 3; 18 Nov. 1912, p. 1; "Documentos do movimento operário. Congresso operário de 1912," *Estudos Sociais* 5, no. 17 (July 1963), 69–87; Dias, *História das lutas socias no Brasil*, pp. 277–81.

31. See Hermes's annual reports as war minister: Brazil, Ministério da Guerra, *Relatorio apresentado ao presidente da Republica do Brazil pelo Marechal Hermes Rodrigues da Fonseca, Ministro da Guerra, em Maio de 1907* (Rio de Janeiro: Imprensa Nacional, 1907), and *Relatorio apresentado ao Presidente da Republica dos Estados Unidos do Brazil pelo Marechal Hermes da Fonseca,*

Ministro da Guerra, em Junho de 1908 (Rio de Janeiro: Imprensa Nacional, 1908).

32. Lieutenant Estevão Leitão de Carvalho, in *Defeza Nacional* (Rio de Janeiro), 10 Nov. 1913, pp. 40–41.

33. A valuable firsthand account of life among the troops is found in the memoirs of Bertoldo Klinger, *Parade e desfile duma vida de voluntario do Brazil na primeira metade do século* (Rio de Janeiro: Emprêsa Gráfica O Cruzeiro, 1958).

34. Brazil, Ministério da Marinha, *Relatório* 1911, pp. 20, 25–28.

35. Um official da armada, *Politica versus marinha* (Paris: Imprimerio Français-Etrangere, n.d.), pp. 85–90.

36. James Bryce, *South America: Observations and Impressions* (New York: The Macmillan Co., 1912), p. 396.

37. Sailors on board the *São Paulo* to Hermes da Fonseca, President of the Republic, 22 Nov. 1910, Arquivo do Ministério da Marinha, Serviço de Documentação Geral da Marinha, Pasta 46.

38. Sailors on board the *Minas Gerais* to Hermes da Fonseca, 11:25 A.M., 25 Nov. 1910, Hermes da Fonseca Papers.

39. Un official da armada, *Política versus marinha*, pp. 45–47, 77–78, 85–90; Alvaro Bomilcar, *A política no Brasil ou o nacionalismo radical* (Rio de Janeiro: Leite Ribeiro & Maurillo, 1920), pp. 10–13, 27–29; José Carlos de Carvalho, *O livro da minha vida. Na guerra, na paz e nas revoluções (1847–1910)* (Rio de Janeiro: Typ. do Jornal do Comércio, de Rodrigues & C., 1912), pp. 320, 351–58, 365, 378–82; *O País* (Rio de Janeiro), 23 Nov. 1910, p. 1; 24 Nov. 1910, pp. 1, 4; 25 Nov. 1910, p. 1; 27 Nov. 1910, pp. 2–3; 10 Dec. 1910, pp. 1–2; 11 Dec. 1910, pp. 1–3; 12 Dec. 1910, p. 1; 13 Dec. 1910, pp. 1–2; 14 Dec. 1910, pp. 1–2; *Correio de Manhã*, 6 May 1911, pp. 1–2; 7 May 1911, pp. 2–3; 9 May 1911, p. 1; 12 May 1911, p. 1; 15 May 1911, p. 1; Brazil, Ministério da Marinha, *Relatorio* 1911, pp. 4–35. See also Edmar Morel, *A revolta da chibata*, 2d ed. (Rio de Janeiro: Editora Letras e Artes, 1963), a popular account of the insurrection.

40. Augusto Tasso Fragoso to Hermes da Fonseca, Buenos Aires, 22 Nov. 1909, Hermes da Fonseca Papers (Rio de Janeiro). For a biography of Tasso Fragoso, one of Brazil's most respected army officers, see General Tristão de Alencar Araipe, *Tasso Fragoso. Um pouco de história do nosso exército* (Rio de Janeiro: Biblioteca do Exército, 1960).

41. José Bernardino Bormann to Hermes da Fonseca, Paris, 19 June 1907, Hermes da Fonseca Papers.

42. On obligatory military service during the Old Republic see Frank D. McCann, "The Nation in Arms: Obligatory Military Service during the Old Republic," in Dauril Alden and Warren Dean, eds., *Essays Concerning the Socioeconomic History of Brazil and Portuguese India* (Gainesville: University Presses of Florida, 1977).

43. Brazil, Ministério da Guerra, *Relatorio* 1908, p. 4.

44. The full text of the law is found in *Lei N. 1.860 de 4 de Janeiro de*

1908. *Regula o alistamento e sorteio militar e reorganisa o exercito* (Rio de Janeiro: Imprensa Nacional, 1908).

45. On the development of the *linhas de tiros* see the account by the first director of the Confederaçaõ do Tiro: Elysio de Araujo, *As linhas de tiro* (Rio de Janeiro: Almanak Laemmert, 1940).

46. "Inefficiency and lack of morale of the Army and Navy of this country. From Capt. LeVert Coleman, Military Attaché, Petrópolis, Brazil. 17 Dec. 1912," Army War College Document Collection No. 7283-2, Records of the [U.S.] War Department General and Special Staffs, National Archives, Record Group No. 165.

47. Luis Barbedo, Commander of Second Military Region, to Frederico Vergueiro Steidl, President of the Liga Nacionalista de São Paulo, São Paulo, March 1920, Instituto Histórico e Geográfico de São Paulo, Estante no. 3-7, pacote 2.

48. Raymundo Teixeira Mendes, *Ainda o militarismo perante a política moderna* (Rio de Janeiro: Tipografia do Apostolado Positivista do Brazil, 1908): Edgard Carone, *A República Vaelha II (Evolução política)* (São Paulo: Difusão Européia do Livro, 1971), pp. 227–28.

49. Leandro Gomes de Barros, *O tempo de hoje. O sorteio militar* (Guarabira, Rio Grande do Norte: Editora Pedro Baptista, 1918), pp. 10, 15. This poem, "O sorteio militar," was first published in 1906. Some other poems by Leandro Gomes de Barros (1865–1918), Brazil's first great *folheto* writer, are reproduced in *Literatura popular em verso. Antologia, Tomo II* (Rio de Janeiro: Ministério da Educação e Cultura, Fundação Casa de Rui Barbosa, Fundação Universidade Regional do Nordeste, 1976); and *Literatura popular em verso. Antologia Tomo III. Leandro Gomes de Barros 2* (Rio de Janeiro: Ministério da Educação e Cultura, Fundação Casa de Rui Barbosa, Universidade Federal da Paraíba, 1977). His extensive works are listed in Sebastião Nunes Batista, *Bibliografia prévia de Leandro Gomes de Barros* (Rio de Janeiro: Biblioteca Nacional, 1971). Published in pamphlet form, such poems continue to be produced and circulated in the Northeast and, more recently, in other places in Brazil where *nordestinos* have migrated in large numbers. These works comprise the principal literature of the lower classes in the Northeast. For a recent study of this form of popular literature see Candace Slater, *Stories on a String: The Brazilian Literatura de Cordel* (Berkeley: University of California Press, 1982).

50. Afonso Pena to Hermes da Fonseca, Petrópolis, 21 Feb. 1908, in Hermes da Fonseca Filho, *Marechal Hermes*, p. 73.

51. *A Voz do Trabalhado*, 22 Nov. 1908, p. 1; *Não Matarás* (Rio de Janeiro), 3 Dec. 1908, p. 3.

52. Feliciano Augusto de Oliveira Pena to Afonso Pena, n.p., 22 Feb. 1908, Afonso Pena Papers, AN, L 9-1.2897.

53. *A Voz do Trabalhador*, 1 May 1909, p. 1.

54. *A Terra Livre*, 10 Feb. 1908, p. 2.

55. *A Voz do Trabalhador*, 29 Nov. 1908, p. 1; 6 Dec. 1908, pp. 1–3; 13

Jan. 1909, pp. 1–3; 13 Jan. 1909, p. 3; *A Gazeta de Notícias* (Rio de Janeiro), 2 Dec. 1908, p. 1.

56. *Jornal dos Artistas* (São Luís de Maranhão), 15 Nov. 1908, p. 1; 13 Dec. 1908, p. 1.

57. *A Voz do Trabalhador*, 13 Jan. 1909, p. 3; *Journal de Notícias* (Salvador), 16 May 1909, p. 3; Brazil, Ministério da Guerra, *Relatorio apresentado ao Presidente da Republica dos Estados Unidos do Brazil pelo Marechal Graduado José Caetano de Faria, Ministro de Estado da Guerra, em Maio de 1918* (Rio de Janeiro: Imprensa Militar, 1918), p. 12.

58. Dias, *História das lutas sociais no Brasil*, pp. 273–83; Paula Beiguelman, *Os companheiros de São Paulo* (São Paulo: Edições Símbolo, 1977), pp. 61–71; *Correio da Manhã*, 12 Oct. 1912, p. 4; 14 Oct. 1912, p. 3; *A Noite*, 11 March 1913, p. 1; 15 March 1913, p. 3; *Portugal Moderno*, 22 Feb. 1913, p. 2; 19 March 1913, p. 2.

59. "Documentos do movimento operario. Um relatório datado de 1913," *Estudos Sociais* 5, no. 18 (Nov. 1963), 202.

60. Annibal Villanova Villela and Wilson Suzigan, *Política do governo e crescimento da economia brasileira, 1889–1945* (Rio de Janeiro: Instituto de Planejamento Economico e Social/Instituto de Pesquisas, 1973), pp. 42–44, 135–37; "Salarios correntes no municipio da Capital," São Paulo [state], *Boletim do Departamento Estudual de Trabalho* 2, nos. 8 and 9 (3rd and 4th trimester, 1913), 571–75; Eulália Maria Lahmeyer Lobo, *História do Rio de Janeiro (Do capital comercial ao capital industrial e financeiro)* (Rio de Janeiro: Instituto Brasileiro de Mercado de Capitais, 1978), II, 521; Boris Fausto, *Trabalho urbano e conflito social 1890–1920)* (São Paulo: Difel/Difusão Editorial, 1976), pp. 157–58.

61. Leo de Affonseca Junior, *O custo da vida na cidade do Rio de Janeiro* (Rio de Janeiro: Imprensa Nacional, 1920), p. 17.

62. Villela and Suzigan, *Política do governo e crescimento da economia brasileira*, pp. 42–44, 110–13; Eulália Maria Lahmeyr Lobo et al., "Estudo das categorias socioprofissionais, dos salarios e do custo da alimentação no Rio de Janeiro de 1820 à 1930," *Revista Brasileira de Economia* 27 (October-December 1973), 169–72; Dean, *The Industrialization of São Paulo*, pp. 93–96; Affonseca, *O custo da vida na cidade do Rio de Janeiro*, pp. 6–17; *Correio da Manhã*, 20 Dec. 1916, p. 1; 21 May 1917, p. 1.

63. Barros, *O tempo de hoje*, pp. 3, 6.

A Guerra chegou,
Bacalhão damnou-se,
A Carne acabou-se
Tudo peiorou,

. . . .
Além do preço alterado
Que a mercadoria tem
Falta no kilo ou na cuia;
Como se salva ninguém?

Só o povo do governo
Pode dizer: Eu vou bem.

64. Neréu Rangel Pestana (pseud. Ivan Subiroff), A *oligarchia paulista* (São Paulo: O Estado de São Paulo, 1919), pp. 250–79; Lobo, "Estudo das categorias socioprofissionais dos salarios e do custo da alimentação no Rio de Janeiro de 1820 à 1930," pp. 171–72; Beiguelman, *Os companheiros de São Paulo*, pp. 79–83.

65. Affonseca, *O custo da vida na cidade do Rio de Janeiro*, pp. 15–16.

On working-class diet at this time, see: "Custo de vida. Alimentação. Custo provavel da alimentação na cidade de São Paulo," São Paulo [state], *Boletim do Departmento Estadual do Trabalho* 9, nos. 34 and 35 (1st and 2nd trimester 1920), 13–16; and Edgard Leuenroth and Antonio Duarte Candeias (pseud. Hélio Negro), *O que é o maximismo ou bolchevismo* (São Paulo: n.p., 1919), quoted on pp. 216–18 in Edgar Rodrigues, *Nacionalismo e cultura social, 1913–1922* (Rio de Janeiro: Laemmert, 1972).

66. *Correio da Manhã*, 27 Dec. 1916, p. 1.

67. Brazil, Ministério da Justiça, *Relatorio apresentado ao Presidente da Republica dos Estados Unidos do Brasil pelo Ministro da Justiça e Negocios Interiores Dr. Carlos Maximiliano Pereira dos Santos em Agosto de 1918* (Rio de Janeiro: Imprensa Nacional, 1918), pp. xiv–xv.

68. The events of 1917 to 1921, especially those in São Paulo, have received more attention than any others in the history of Brazil's early labor movement. John W. F. Dulles, *Anarchists and Communists in Brazil, 1900–1935* (Austin and London: University of Texas Press, 1973), pp. 44–150, provides a detailed account of the activities of anarchist militants. Boris Fausto, *Trabalho urbano e conflito social*, pp. 157–216, concentrates on events in São Paulo, and Paula Beiguelman, *Os companheiros de São Paulo*, pp. 79–111, summarizes newspaper accounts of the *paulista* strikes. Key documents from this period are found in Paulo Sérgio Pinheiro and Michael M. Hall, eds., *A classe operaria no Brasil. Documentos (1889 a 1930)*, 2 vols. (São Paulo: Editora Alfa Omega, 1979 and Editora Brasiliense, 1982). On the Brazilian reaction to the Russian Revolution, see Moniz Bandeira, Clovis Melo, and A. T. Andrade, *O ano vermelho. A revolução russa e seus reflexos no Brasil* (Rio de Janeiro: Editora Civilização Brasileira, 1967), which, like some other Brazilian marxist studies, portrays this period as one of great revolutionary ferment.

69. *O Estado de São Paulo* (São Paulo), 3 July 1917, p. 6; 9 July 1917, p. 5; 12 July pp. 4–5; 13 July 1917, pp. 5–6; Dias, *História das lutas sociais no Brasil*, pp. 294–98.

70. These demands are found in Pinheiro and Hall, eds., *A classe operaria no Brasil*, II, 232–34; and in Dias, *História das lutas sociais no Brasil*, pp. 229–31.

71. *O Estado de São Paulo*, 14 July 1917, pp. 1, 4; 16 July 1917, p. 2; 18 July 1917, pp. 2–5; 21 July 1917, pp. 5–6; 5 Sept. 1917, p. 6; 14 Sept. 1917, p. 7; 16 Sept. 1917, p. 6; Dias, *História das lutas sociais no Brasil*, pp. 231–32.

72. A *Noite*, 28 Jan. 1917, p. 3; 25 Feb. 1917, p. 3; 4 March 1917, p. 3; 18 March 1917, p. 3; 22 March 1917, p. 5; 26 March 1917, p. 5; 11 May 1917, p. 3; 13 May 1917, p. 1; *Correio da Manhã*, 2 May 1917, pp. 1, 3; 12 May 1917, p. 3; 13 May 1917, p. 2; 15 July 1917, p. 7; 18 July 1917, p. 2; 19 July 1917, p. 1; 22 July 1917, p. 2; 23 July 1917, pp. 1, 3; 26 July 1917, p. 3; 27 July 1917, pp. 1, 3; A Razão (Rio de Janeiro), 1 May 1919, p. 6; Aurelino de Araujo Leal, *Polícia e poder de polícia* (Rio de Janeiro: Imprensa Nacional, 1918), pp. 253–55.

73. *Diário de Pernambuco* (Recife), 1 Aug. 1917, p. 2; 2 Aug. 1917, p. 3; 11 Aug. 1917, p. 2; 12 Aug. 1917, p. 2; 15 Aug. 1917, p. 3; 18 Aug. 1917, p. 3; *Diário de Notícias* (Salvador), 7 Aug. 1917, p. 1; 8 Aug. 1917, p. 1; 10 Aug. 1917, p. 1; A *Federação* (Pôrto Alegre), 1 Aug. 1917, p. 3; 2 Aug. 1917, p. 1; 3 Aug. 1917, p. 1; 4 Aug. 1917, p. 1; 6 Aug. 1917, p. 1; 7 Aug. 1917, p. 5; 8 Aug. 1917, p. 5.

74. Abranches Moura, *Governos e congressos da República dos Estados Unidos do Brazil*, II, 310; A *Voz do Povo* (Rio de Janeiro), 4 March 1920, p. 2.

75. Abranches Moura, *Governos e congressos da República dos Estados Unidos do Brazil*, II, 400; Pinheiro and Hall, eds., A *classe operaria no Brasil*, II, 113–14; Maurício Caminha de Lacerda, "Maurício de Lacerda, meu pai," *Revista Brasiliense* 6 (September-October 1960), 195–217, a biographical sketch by his son.

76. Maurício de Lacerda, *Entre duas revoluções* (Rio de Janeiro: Editora Leite Ribeiro, 1927), pp. 7, 189–91.

77. Everardo Dias, *Memórias de um exilado. Episódio de uma deportação* (São Paulo: n.p., 1920), p. 10; Dias, *História das lutas sociais no Brasil*, p. 97.

78. Evaristo de Moraes, *Apontamentos de direito operario* (Rio de Janeiro: Imprensa Nacional, 1905).

79. Evaristo de Moraes, *Reminiscencias de um rabula criminalista* (Rio de Janeiro: Livraria Leite Ribeiro, 1922), pp. 14, 43, 221–30, 283; Evaristo de Moraes, *Minhas prisões e outros assumptos contemporaneos* (Rio de Janeiro: n.p., 1924), pp. 75–77; *Echo Popular* (Rio de Janeiro), 3 June 1890, p. 1; 3 Aug. 1890, p. 1; *Gazeta Operaria*, 19 Oct. 1902, p. 3; A *Terra Livre*, 15 June 1907, p. 1; 22 June 1907, p. 1; A *Voz do Trabalhador*, 29 Nov. 1908, p. 1; 6 Dec. 1908, p. 1; Rodrigues, *Nacionalismo e cultura social*, pp. 162–68; Evaristo de Moraes Filho prefaces the second edition of Moraes, *Apontamentos de direito operario* (São Paulo: LTr Editora, 1917), with a biographical study of his father.

80. Brazil, Congress, Câmara dos Deputados, *Documentos parlamentares, Legislação social* (Rio de Janeiro: Typ. do Jornal do Commercio, 1919–1922), I, 4–34, 111–38, 441–821; II, 527–52, 578–98.

81. A *Noite*, 20 March 1919, pp. 1–3.

82. Evaristo de Moraes Filho, preface to Moraes, *Apontamentos de direito operario*.

83. Joseph L. Love, "Political Participation in Brazil, 1888–1969," *Luso-Brazilian Review* 7 (December 1970), 13.

84. Brazil, Congress, *Diário do Congresso*, XXX, 54 (10 July 1919), 693.

85. *O Estado de São Paulo,* 3 May 1919, p. 5; 6 May 1919, p. 5; 8 May 1919, 9 May 1919, p. 5; 21 May 1919, p. 3; 22 May 1919, p. 5; *Jornal de Notícias* (Salvador), 3 June 1919, pp. 2–3; 4 June 1919, p. 2; 5 June 1919, p. 3; *A Razão,* 1 May 1919, p. 6; 1 June 1919, p. 5; 2 June 1919, p. 5; 3 June 1919, p. 5; 4 June 1919, pp. 1, 4; 7 June 1919, p. 1; 8 June 1919, pp. 1, 2; 20 June 1919, p. 2; 24 June 1919, p. 3; 27 June 1919, p. 1; 3 July 1919, p. 3; 18 March 1920, p. 1; 26 March 1920, pp. 1, 3, 5; 27 March 1920, pp. 2, 3.

86. Brazil, Ministerio da Justiça, *Relatorio apresentado ao Presidente da Republica dos Estados Unidos do Brazil pelo Ministro da Justiça e Negocios Interiores Dr. Alfredo Pinto Vieira de Mello em Junho de 1920* (Rio de Janeiro: Imprensa Nacional, 1920), v, viii.

87. Maciel, *Expulsão de estrangeiros,* pp. 43–45.

88. Brazil, Ministério da Justiça, *Relatorio* 1921, v.

89. *A Razão,* 1 May 1919, p. 6; 8 May 1919, p. 1; 29 May 1919, p. 3; 18 March 1920, p. 1; 26 March 1920, p. 5; 28 March 1920, p. 1; *A Noite,* 27 April 1917, p. 1; *Correio da Manhã,* 24 March 1920, p. 1; 25 March 1920, p. 1; 27 March 1920, p. 1; 10 Feb. 1921, p. 2.

90. Brazil, Ministério da Justica, *Relatorio,* 1921, pp. 3–4; *A Razão,* 3 May 1919, pp. 1, 3; 30 Jan. 1921, p. 6; 3 May 1921, p. 3; *Correio da Manhã,* 10 Feb. 1921, pp. 1, 2.

Bibliography

Archives and Private Papers

Arquivo do Estado de São Paulo, São Paulo
Arquivo da Fundação Casa de Rui Barbosa, Rio de Janeiro
Arquivo Histórico do Ministério das Relações Exteriores (Itamarati) (AHI), Rio de Janeiro
Arquivo do Instituto Histórico e Geográfico Brasileiro, Rio de Janeiro
Arquivo do Instituto Históico e Geográfico de São Paulo, São Paulo
Arquivo do Ministério da Marinha, Rio de Janeiro
Arquivo do Ministério dos Negócios Estrangeiros, Lisbon
Arquivo do Museu Imperial, Petrópolis
Arquivo Nacional (AN), Rio de Janeiro
Arquivo Geral da Cidade do Rio de Janeiro (AGCRJ), Rio de Janeiro
Biblioteca National do Rio de Janeiro, Seção de Manuscritos, Rio de Janeiro
Clodoaldo da Fonseca Papers, Rio de Janeiro
Foreign Office, Public Record Office, London
Francisco Glicério Papers, São Paulo and Campinas ·
Hermes da Fonseca Papers, Rio de Janeiro
Museu David Carneiro, Curitiba
National Archives, Washington, D.C.
Quintino Bocaiúva Papers, Rio de Janeiro

Rodrigues Alves Papers, Rio de Janeiro

Printed Material

Periodicals

Dates of publication are given for periodicals of limited duration and for the period in which they were consulted in their entirety.

O Alvorado, Rio de Janeiro (1890)
O Alvorado, Rio de Janeiro (1910)
O Amigo do Povo, São Paulo (1903–1904)
O Artista, Rio de Janeiro (1883)
O Artista, Rio de Janeiro (1905)
O Artista Pernambucano, Recife (1853)
Aurora, Rio de Janeiro (1909)
Aurora Social, Recife (1902, 1906–1907)
Avanti!, São Paulo
Avanti, Recife (1920)
O Baluarte, Rio de Janeiro (1910)
La Battaglia, São Paulo
A Bomba, Rio de Janeiro (1894)
Brazil Operario, Rio de Janeiro (1903–1904)
O Chapeleiro, São Paulo (1904)
O Caixeiro, Rio de Janeiro (1881)
Cidade do Rio, Rio de Janeiro
O Combate, Fortaleza (1891, 1896)
Commercio Suburbano, Rio de Janeiro (1902)
O Componedor, Rio de Janeiro (1909)
Correio da Manhã, Rio de Janeiro
Correio Mercantil, Rio de Janeiro
Correio Operario, Rio de Janeiro (1910)
Correio Paulistano, São Paulo
Correio Portuguez, Rio de Janeiro (1892)
Corriere Italiano, Rio de Janeiro (1894)
O Corsario, Rio de Janeiro (1896)
O Corsario, Rio de Janeiro (1900)
O Corsario, Rio de Janeiro (1910)
A Defesa Nacional, Rio de Janeiro (1913–1914)
Democracia, Rio de Janeiro (1890–1891)
O Despertar, Rio de Janeiro (1892)
Diário do Comércio, Rio de Janeiro
Diário do Congresso Nacional, Rio de Janeiro
Diário Official, Rio de Janeiro
O Districto Federal, Rio de Janeiro (1905)

O Echo da Imprensa, Rio de Janeiro (1856)
Echo Operario, Rio de Janeiro (1901)
O Echo Suburbano, Rio de Janeiro (1901)
Eco Popular, Rio de Janeiro (1890)
Eco Portuguez, Rio de Janeiro (1895)
O Estado de São Paulo, São Paulo
O Estrangeiro, Rio de Janeiro (1894)
A Federação, Porto Alegre
A Gallegada, Rio de Janeiro (1883, 1886)
Gazeta de Notícias, Rio de Janeiro
Gazeta dos Operarios, Rio de Janeiro (1875–1876)
Gazeta Operaria, Rio de Janeiro (1893)
Gazeta Operaria, Rio de Janeiro (1902–1903)
Gazeta da Tarde, Rio de Janeiro (1884)
El Grito del Pueblo, São Paulo (1899)
O Grito dos Pobres, São Paulo (1899)
Guttemberg, Maceió (1881)
A Hora Social, Recife (1919)
O Imparcial, Rio de Janeiro
O Internacional, Rio de Janeiro (1911)
O Jacobino, Rio de Janeiro (1894–1897)
Jornal do Brasil, Rio de Janeiro
Jornal do Comércio, Rio de Janeiro
Jornal dos Artistas, São Luís de Maranhão (1908–1909)
Jornal de Notícias, Salvador
Jornal dos Operarios, Rio de Janeiro (1891)
Jornal dos Typographos, Rio de Janeiro (1858)
Jornal Operario, São Paulo (1905)
Jornal Suburbano, Madureira [Rio de Janeiro] (1911)
Kosmos, Rio de Janeiro (1904–1908)
Kultur, Rio de Janeiro (1904)
O Libertario, Rio de Janeiro (1904)
Liga Operaria, Recife (1877)
A Lucta Social, Manaus (1914)
O Marmonista, Rio de Janeiro (1906)
A Nação, São Paulo (1915)
O Nacional, Rio de Janeiro (1895–1896)
Não Matarás, Rio de Janeiro (1908)
O Nativista, São Paulo (1895)
O Nihilista, Rio de Janeiro (1882–1883)
A Noite, Rio de Janeiro
O Operario, Recife (1879)
O Operario, São Paulo (1891)
O Operario, Fortaleza (1892)
O Operario, Santos (1892)

BIBLIOGRAPHY

O Operario, Rio de Janeiro (1895)
Operario, Florianópolis (1901)
O Operario, Rio de Janeiro (1908–1910)
O Operario, Sorocaba, São Paulo (1910)
O Operario Tatuhy, São Paulo (1910)
O País. Rio de Janeiro
Portugal Moderno, Rio de Janeiro
O Portuguez, Rio de Janeiro (1883)
Progresso Suburbano, Piedade [Rio de Janeiro] (1902)
O Protesto, Rio de Janeiro (1899–1900)
O Protesto, Recife (1910)
A Questão Social, Santos (1896)
A Razão, Rio de Janeiro (1919–1920)
A Redempção, São Paulo (1899)
Renascença, Rio de Janeiro (1904–1905)
Revista Illustrada, Rio de Janeiro
Revista Typographica, Rio de Janeiro (1864)
Revista Typographica, Rio de Janeiro (1888–1889)
Rio News, Rio de Janeiro
O Sexo Feminino, Campanha, Minas Gerais (1837– 1874); Rio de Janeiro (1875–1876)
Semana Operaria, Rio de Janeiro (1907)
O Socialista, Rio de Janeiro (1893)
O Socialista, São Paulo (1896)
O Socialista da Provincia do Rio de Janeiro, Niterói (1846)
O Soldado, Rio de Janeiro (1881)
O Suburbano, Ilha do Governador [Rio de Janeiro] (1900)
O Suburbio, Méier [Rio de Janeiro] (1904)
O Tempo, Rio de Janeiro
A Terra Livre, São Paulo (1905–1907, 1910); Rio de Janeiro (1907–1908)
O Trabalhador Graphico, São Paulo (1904–1906)
O Trabalho, São Paulo (1876)
O Tres de Abril, Rio de Janeiro (1905)
Tribuna Artistica, Rio de Janeiro (1871–1872)
Tribuna Militar, Rio de Janeiro (1881)
Tribuna Operaria, Belém (1892–1893)
Tribuna Operaria, Rio de Janeiro (1900, 1901)
A Tribuna do Povo, Rio de Janeiro (1909)
O Typographo, Rio de Janeiro (1867–1868)
O Typographo, Penedo, Alagoas (1897)
União Operaria, Recife (1905–1906)
União Caixeral, Rio de Janeiro (1903)
A União Lusitana, Rio de Janeiro (1892)
A União Operaria, Engenho de Dentro [Rio de Janeiro] (1904)
União Operaria, Recife (1905–1906)

União Portugueza, Rio de Janeiro (1896)
A *Vanguarda*, Recife (1920)
Vinte e Cinco de Março, Campos (1884)
A *Voz do Operario*, Salvador (1891, 1894)
Voz do Povo, Rio de Janeiro (1890)
A *Voz do Povo*, Bangú [Rio de Janeiro] (1911)
A *Voz do Povo*, Rio de Janeiro (1920)
A *Voz do Trabalhado*, Rio de Janeiro (1908–1909)

Public Documents

Album cartográfico do Rio de Janeiro (séculos XVIII e XIX). Organized and with a text by Lygia da Fonseca Fernandes da Cunha. Rio de Janeiro: Biblioteca Nacional, 1971.

Argentina, Censo, Comisión Directiva. *Segundo censo de la República Argentina. Mayo 10 de 1895*. 3 vols. Buenos Aires: Taller Tipográfico de la Penitenciaria Nacional, 1898.

Arquivo do Distrito Federal. *Revista de documentos para a história da cidade do Rio de Janeiro, 1500–1900*. Rio de Janeiro: Prefeitura do Districto Federal, 1952.

Arquivo Nacional. *Organizações e programas ministeriais. Regime parlamentar no Império*. 2d ed. Rio de Janeiro: Imprensa Nacional, .1962.

———. *Publicações do Arquivo Nacional*. 34 (1937).

Associação dos Empregados no Comércio do Rio de Janeiro. *Relatorio*. 1880–1915.

Bahia. *Mensagem do . . . governador do estado. . . .* 1904– 1923.

———. *Relatorio com que . . . abriu a assemblea legislativa provincial da Bahia. . . .* 1876–1878.

———. *Relatoria feito . . . pelo presidente . . . por occasião de passarlhe a administração. . . .* 1858, 1877.

Brazil. *Anuario Estatistica do Brasil*. 1939/1940.

———. Congress. Câmara dos Deputados. *Annaes do Congresso Constituinte da República*. 3 vols. 2d ed. Rio de Janeiro: Imprensa Nacional, 1924–1926.

———. Congress. Câmara dos Deputados. *Documentos Parlamentares. Legislação social*. 3 vols. Rio de Janeiro: Typ. do Jornal do Commercio, 1919–1922.

———. Department of Foreign Affairs. *Correspondence: Exchange with the Legation of Portugal and the Legation of Brazil at Lisbon in Regard to the Surrender of the Insurgent Refugees on board the Portuguese Corvettes "Mindello" and "Affonso de Albuquerque."* Rio de Janeiro: Typ. Leuzinger, 1894.

———. Directoria Geral de Estatística. *Recenseamento do Brazil realizado em 1 de setembro de 1920*. 5 vols. in 18. Rio de Janeiro: Typ. da Estatística, 1922–1930.

———. Directoria Geral de Estatística. *Recenseamento geral da Republica dos*

Estados Unidos do Brasil em 31 de dezembro de 1890. Districto Federal (Cidade do Rio de Janeiro), Capital da Republica dos Estados Unidos do Brazil. Rio de Janeiro: Typ. Leuzinger, 1895.

―――. Directoria Geral de Estatística. *Recenseamento da população do Império do Brazil a que se procedeu no dia 1° de agosto de 1872.* 22 vols. Rio de Janeiro: Typ. Leuzinger, 1873–1876.

―――. Directoria Geral de Estatística. *Recenseamento do Rio de Janeiro (Districto Federal) realizado em 20 de setembro de 1906.* 2 vols. Rio de Janeiro: Officina da Estatística, 1907.

―――. *Informações apresentadas pela Commissão Parlamentar de Inquerito ao Corpo Legislativo na terceira sessão da decima oitava legislatura.* Rio de Janeiro: Typ. Nacional, 1883.

―――. Ministério da Fazenda. Directoria de Estatística Commercial. *Commercio exterior do Brazil. Importação. Exportação. Annos 1913–1915–1916 1917–1918.* Rio de Janeiro: Officinas de Estatística Commercial 1919.

―――. Ministério da Fazenda. Directoria de Estatística Commercial. *Commercio exterior do Brasil. Movimento maritimo. Movimento bancario. Janeiro a dezembro 1916–1917–1918–1919–1920.* Rio de Janeiro: Officinas de Estatística Commercial, 1921.

―――. Ministério da Guerra. *Relatório.* 1875, 1889, 1893–1894, 1907–1908, 1917–1918.

―――. Ministério da Indústria, Viação e Obras Públicas. *Relatório. 1896, 1903–1906.*

―――. *Ministério da Justiça. Relatório.* 1866–1924.

―――. Ministério da Marinha. *Relatório.* 1911.

―――. *Relatorio apresentado a sr. ex. o Ministro da Fazenda pela Commissão de Inquerito Industrial.* Rio de Janeiro: Typ. Nacional, 1882.

Centro Industrial do Brasil. *O Brasil. Suas riquezas naturaes. Suas industrias.* Vol. III. Rio de Janeiro: M. Orosco & C., 1909.

"Documentos do movimento operário. Congresso operário de 1912," *Estudos Sociais,* 5 (June 1963), 69–87.

"Documentos do movimento operário. Pela Paz!", *Estudos Sociais,* 4 (December 1962), 285–93.

"Documentos do movimento operário. Um relatório datado de 1913," *Estudos Sociais,* 5 (November 1963), 195–206.

"Documentos do movimento operário. Resoluções do primeiro congresso operário brasiliero," *Estudos Sociais,* 4 (March 1963), 387–98.

Districto Federal. *Mensagem do Prefeito. . . .* 1909.

Imperial Associação Typographica Fluminese. *Estatuto da Imperial Associação Typographica Fluminese.* Rio de Janeiro: Typ. de Domingos Luiz dos Santos, 1860.

―――. *Relatorio apresentado á Imperial Associação Typographica Fluminense em assemblea geral pelo Conselho Administrativo a 13 dezembro de 1863.* Rio de Janeiro: Typ. Laemmert, 1863.

Liga da Defesa Nacional. *Estatutos da Liga da Defesa Nacional.* Rio de Janeiro: Typ. do Jornal do Commercio, 1916.

Minas Gerais. *Relatorio apresentado á assemblea legislativa provincial de Minas Gerais.* . . . 1876.

Pará. *Mensagem dirigido ao congresso legislativo pelo governador do estado.* . . . 1897–1909.

Pernambuco. *Falla com que* . . . *abrio a assemblêa legislativa provincial de Pernambuco.* . . . 1867–1885.

———. *Falla que o presidente da provincia* . . . *dirigio á assemblêa legislativa no dia de sua instalação.* . . . 1886–1888.

———. *Mensagem do* . . . *governador.* . . . 1915–1923.

———. *Relatorio que* . . . *ao passar a administração desta provincia.* . . . 1877, 1881, 1884.

Portugal, Ministério da Fazenda. *Annuario estatistico de Portugal.* 1891–1892.

———. Ministério dos Negócios Exteriores. *Documentos apresentados ás Cortes na sessão legislativa de 1877 pelo Ministro e Secretario d'Estado dos Negocios Extrangeiros. Emigração portuguesa.* Lisbon: Imprensa Nacional, 1875.

———. Ministério das Obras Públicas, Comércio e Indústria. *Movimento da população. Estado civil. Emigração. Estatistica especial. Anno 1887.* Lisbon: Imprensa Nacional, 1890.

Prefeitura do Districto Federal. *Noticia sobre o desenvolvimento da industria fabril no Districto Federal e sua situação actual publicada para ser distribuida durante a Exposição Nacional de 1908.* Milan: Tip. Treves, 1908.

Regula o alistamento e sorteio militar e reorganisa o exército. Rio de Janeiro: Impresa Nacional, 1908.

Revista do Instituto Histórico e Geográfico Brasileiro.

Rio de Janeiro [city]. *Assistencia publica e privada no Rio de Janeiro (Brasil). História e estatística.* (Rio de Janeiro: Typ. do "Annuario do Brasil," 1922.

São Paulo [city]. *Relatorio apresentado á Câmara Municipal.* 1893–1911.

São Paulo [province]. *Relatorio apresentado á assemblea legislativa provincial de São Paulo pelo presidente da provincia.* . . . 1876–1878.

São Paulo [state]. *Boletim do Departamento Estadual do Trabalho.* 1911–1920.

———. *Relatorio apresentado pelo chefe de policia do Estado de São Paulo.* . . . 1907.

———. Repartição de Estatistica e Arquivo. *Relatorio.* 1894–1895.

Sociedade da Georgrafica de Lisboa. *Boletim.* 1882.

———. *Colonias portuguesas em paises estrangeiros.* Lisbon: Tipografia Universal, 1915.

United States, Department of the Interior, Census Office. *Report on the Population of the United States at the Eleventh Census; 1890.* 15 vols. in 25. Washington, D.C.: U.S. Government Printing Office, 1892–1897.

Books, Articles, and Unpublished Dissertations

Abranches Moura, João Dunshee de. *Governos e congressos da República dos Estados Unidos do Brazil, 1889–1918.* 2 vols. São Paulo: M. V. Abranches, 1918.

Abreu, Bricio de. *Esses populares tão desconhecidos.* Rio de Janeiro: E. Raposa Carneiro, 1961.

Adamo, Sam C. "The Broken Promise: Race, Health and Justice in Rio de Janeiro, 1890–1940." Unpublished Ph.D. dissertation, University of New Mexico, 1983.

Affonseca Junior, Léo de. *O custo da vida na cidade do Rio de Janeiro.* Rio de Janeiro: Imprensa Nacional, 1920.

Agache, Donat Alfred. *Cidade do Rio de Janeiro. Estensão, remodelação, embellezamento.* Paris: Foyer Brésilien, 1930.

Agassiz, Louis and Elizabeth C. Agassiz. *A Journey in Brazil.* Boston: Ticknor and Fields, 1868.

Alba, Victor. *Politics and the Labor Movement in Latin America.* Stanford: Stanford University Press, 1968.

Albuquerque, J. A. Guilhon, ed. *Classes médias e política no Brasil.* Rio de Janeiro: Paz e Terra, 1977.

Alexander, Robert J. *Labor Relations in Argentina, Brazil, and Chile.* New York: McGraw-Hill, 1962.

———. *Organized Labor in Latin America.* New York: Free Press, 1965.

Amado, Gilberto. *História da minha infancia.* Rio de Janeiro: José Olympio, 1954.

Andrews, Christopher Columbus. *Brazil: Its Condition and Prospects.* New York: D. Appleton and Company, 1887.

Araipe, Tristão de Alencar. *Litteratura brasileira. Movimento de 1893.* Rio de Janeiro: Typographia da Empreza Democratica Editora, 1896.

———. *Tasso Fragoso. Um pouco de história do nosso exército.* Rio de Janeiro: Biblioteca do Exército, 1960.

Araújo, Elysio de. *As linhas de tiro.* Rio de Janeiro: Almanak Laemmert, 1940.

———. *Atravez de meio século. Notas Históricas.* São Paulo: São Paulo Editora Ltda., 1932.

Assis Brazil, José de. *O attentado de 5 novembro de 1897 contra o presidente da republica. Causa e effeitos.* São Paulo: Casa Vanordem, 1909.

Associação dos Geógrafos Brasileiros, (Secção do Rio de Janeiro). *Aspectos da geografia carioca.* Rio de Janeiro: Conselho Nacional de Geografia, 1962.

Avila, Fernando Bastos de. *Economic Impacts of Immigration. The Brazilian Immigration Problem.* The Hague: Martinus Nijhoff, 1954.

Azevedo, Aluízio. *O cortiço.* São Paulo: Livraria Martins, 1965.

Azevedo, Arnoldo ed. ed., *A cidade de São Paulo. Estudos de geografia urbana.* Vol. II. *A evolucão urbana.* São Paulo: Companhia Editôra Nacional, 1958.

Azevedo, Fernando de. *Brazilian Culture. An Introduction to the Study of Culture in Brazil.* Trans. William Rex Crawford. New York: The Macmillan Company, 1950.

Azevedo, Manuel Duarte Moreira de. *Pequeno panorama ou descripção dos principaes edificios da cidade do Rio de Janeiro.* Rio de Janeiro: Typ. do Apostolo, 1867.

Backheuser, Everardo. *Habitações populares. Relatorio apresentado ao exm. sr. dr. J. J. Seabra, Ministro da Justiça e Negocios Interiores.* Rio de Janeiro: Imprensa Nacional, 1906.

Baer, Werner. *The Brazilian Economy: Growth and Development.* 2d ed. New York: Praeger, 1983.

Bakota, Carlos Steven. "Crisis and the Middle Classes: The Ascendancy of Brazilian Nationalism: 1914–1922." Unpublished Ph.D. dissertation, Univeristy of California, Los Angeles, 1973.

Bandecchi, Pedro Brasil. *Problems de imigração na região sul.* São Paulo: Editôra Obelisco, 1967.

Bandeira, Moniz, Clovis Melo, and A. T. Andrade. *O ano vermelho. A revolução russa e seus reflexos no Brasil.* Rio de Janeiro: Editôra Civilização Brasileira, 1967.

Barbosa, Luiz, *Servicos de assistencia no Rio de Janeiro.* Rio de Janeiro: Typ. Ao Luzeiro, 1908.

Barbosa, Ruy. *Plataforma.* 2d ed. Salvador: Empreza 'A Bahia,' 1910.

Barbosa Lima Sobrinho, Alexandre José. *Desde quando somos nacionalistas?* Rio de Janeiro: Editôra Civilização Brasileira, 1963.

Barman, Roderick. "The Brazilian Peasantry Reexamined: The Implications of the Quebra-Quilo Revolt, 1874–1875." *Hispanic American Historical Review* 57 (August 1977), 401–24.

Barman, Roderick, and Jean Barman. "The Role of the Law Graduate in the Political Elite of Imperial Brazil." *Journal of Interamerican Studies and World Affairs* 18 (November 1976), 423–50.

Barreto, Dantas. *Conspiraçoes.* Rio de Janeiro: Livraria Francisco Alves, 1917.

Barreto Filho, João Paulo de Mello, and Lima, Hermeto. *Historia da polícia do Rio de Janeiro. (Aspectos da cidade e da vida carioca).* 3 vols. Rio de Janeiro: Editôra 'A Noite', 1939–1944.

Barreto, Paulo (pseud. João do Rio). *A alma encantadora das ruas.* Paris and Rio de Janeiro: Tip. Garnier, 1908.

Barros, Gilberto Leite de. *A cidade e o planalto. Processo de dominancia da cidade de São Paulo.* São Paulo: Edições Melhoramentos, 1953.

Barros, Leandro Gomes de. *Literatura popular em verso. Antologia.* Tomos I, II. Rio de Janeiro: Ministério da Educação e Cultura, Fundação Casa de Rui Barbosa, 1976 and 1977.

———. *O tempo de hoje. O sorteio militar.* Guarabira, Rio Grande do Norte: Editora Pedro Baptista, 1918.

Barrozo, Collatino. *Defesa nacional*. 2d ed. Rio de Janeiro: Typ. do 'Jornal do Commercio', 1915.

Bates, Margaret, ed. *The Migration of Peoples to Latin America*. Washington, D.C.: Catholic University of America Press, 1957.

Beiguelman, Paula. *Os companheiros de São Paulo*. São Paulo: Edições Símbolo, 1977.

Bell, Alured Gray. *The Beautiful Rio de Janeiro*. London: William Heinenmann, 1914.

Bello, José Maria. *A History of Modern Brazil, 1889–1964*. Trans. James L. Taylor. Stanford: Stanford University Press, 1966.

Bergstresser, Rebecca Baird. "The Movement for the Abolition of Slavery in Rio de Janeiro, Brazil, 1880–1889." Unpublished Ph.D. dissertation, Stanford University, 1973.

Bergquist, Charles. "What is Being Done? Some Recent Studies on the Urban Working Class and Organized Labor in Latin America." *Latin American Research Review* 16, No. 2 (1981), 203–23.

Bernhard, Virginia, ed. *Elites, Masses, and Modernization in Latin America, 1850–1930*. Austin and London: University of Texas Press, 1979.

Bilac, Olavo. *A defesa nacional (Discursos)*. Rio de Janeiro: Liga de Defesa Nacional, 1917.

Binzer, Ina von. *Os meus romanos. Alegrias e tristezas de uma educadora alemã no Brasil*. Trans. Alice Rossi and Luisita da Gama Cerqueira. Rio de Janeiro: Paz e Terra, 1980.

Boehrer, George C. A. *Da monarquia à república. História do Partido Republicano do Brasil (1870–1889)*. Trans. Berenice Xavier. Rio de Janeiro: Ministério da Educação e Cultura, 1954.

Bomilcar, Álvaro. *A política no Brasil ou o nacionalismo radical*. Rio de Janeiro: Leite Ribeiro & Maurillo, 1920.

———. *O preconceito de raça no Brasil*. Rio de Janeiro: n.p., 1916.

Bosch, Renato Raul, ed. *Violência e cidade*. Rio de Janeiro: Zahar Editores, 1962.

Brody, David. "The Old Labor History and the New: In Search of An American Working Class." *Labor History* 20 (Winter 1979), 111–26.

Boyer, Richard E. and Keith A. Davies, *Urbanization in 19th Century Latin America: Statistics and Sources*. Supplement to the *Statistical Abstract of Latin America*. Los Angeles: UCLA Latin American Center, 1973.

Bruno, Ernani Silva. *História e tradições da cidade de São Paulo*. 3 vols. 2d ed. Rio de Janeiro: José Olympio, 1954.

Bryce, James. *South America. Observations and Impressions*. New York: The Macmillan Co., 1912.

Burns, E. Bradford. *A History of Brazil*. 2d ed. New York: Columbia University Press, 1980.

Burns, E. Bradford. *Nationalism in Brazil. A Historical Survey*. New York: Frederick A. Praeger, 1968.

———. "Manaus, 1910: Portrait of a Boom Town." *Journal of Inter-American Studies* 7 (July 1965), 400–21.

————. "Manuel Querino's Interpretation of the African Contribution to Brazil." *Journal of Negro History* 54 (January 1974), 78–86.

————. *The Poverty of Progress: Latin America in the Nineteenth Century.* Berkeley and Los Angeles: University of California Press, 1980.

Buescu, Mircea. *300 annos de inflação.* Rio de Janeiro: APEC, 1973.

Caldas, Honorato Candido Ferreira. *A explosão da Escola Militar e as tradições d'O Paiz.* Rio de Janeiro: Comp. Litho-Typographia, 1905.

Calmon, Pedro. *História de D. Pedro II.* 4 vols. Rio de Janeiro: José Olympio, 1975.

————. *História do Brasil na poesia do povo.* Rio de Janeiro: Editôra Noite, 1949.

Camêu, Francolino, and Peixoto, Arthur Vieira. *Floriano Peixoto. Vida e governo.* Rio de Janeiro: Officinas Graficas da A. Noite, 1925.

Campos Salles, Manuel Ferraz de. *Da propaganda à presidencia.* São Paulo: Typ. A. Editora, 1908.

Candido, Antonio. *Teresina etc.* Rio de Janeiro: Editora Paz e Terra, 1980.

Caneca. *Attentado de cinco de novembro. Artigos de Caneca publicados na "Gazeta de Noticias" sobre o "Despacho" du juiz Affonso de Miranda.* Rio de Janeiro: Imprensa Nacional, 1898.

Cardoso, Vicente Licínio. *A margem da historia da republica (Ideas, crenças, e affirmações).* Rio de Janeiro: Edição do Annuario do Brasil, 1924.

Carneiro, José Fernando. *Imigração e colonização no Brasil.* Rio de Janeiro: Universidade do Brasil, 1950.

Carone, Edgard. *O Centro Industrial do Rio de Janeiro e a sua importante participação na economia nacional (1827–1977).* Rio de Janeiro: Centro Industrial do Rio de Janeiro/Editora Cátedra, 1978.

————. *O movimento operário no Brasil, 1877–1944.* São Paulo: Difel, 1979.

————. *A primeira república (1889–1930). Texto e contexto.* São Paulo: Difusão Européia do Livro, 1969.

————. *A República Velha (Instituições e classes sociais).* São Paulo: Difusão Européia do Livro, 1970.

————. *A República Velha II (Evolução política).* São Paulo: Difusão Européia do Livro, 1971.

Carvalho, Augusto de. *Questões internacionaes.* Porto: Typographia Central, 1875.

Carvalho, David de. *Os sindicales operarios e a república burguesa (1910–1928).* Lisbon: Seara Nova, 1977.

Carvalho, José Carlos de. *O livro da minha vida. Na guerra, na paz e nas revoluções (1847–1910).* Rio de Janeiro: Typ. do 'Jornal do Comércio', de Rodrigues & C., 1912.

Castro, Agostinho Raymundo Gomes de. *Os successos de 14 de novembro de 1904. Os Republicanos à nação brasileira. O major Gomes de Castro no plenario militar.* Rio de Janeiro: Typ. do 'Jornal do Commercio', 1905.

Castro, Augusto Olympio Viveiros de. *A questão social.* Rio de Janeiro: Livraria Editora Conselheiro Candido de Oliveira, 1920.

Chacon, Vamireh. *História das idéias socialistas no Brasil.* Rio de Janeiro: Editôra Civilização Brasileira, 1965.

Chagas, João. *De bond. Alguns aspectos da civilização brazileira.* Lisbon: Livraria Moderna, 1897.

Chapman, S. D., ed. *The History of Working-Class Housing: A Symposium.* London: Newton Abbot, 1971.

Coelho Netto, Henrique. *Bazar.* Oporto: Liv. Chardon, 1928.

Colson, Roger Frank. "The Destruction of a Revolution. Polity, Economy and Society in Brazil, 1750–1895." Unpublished Ph.D. dissertation, Princeton University, 1979.

Commemoração civica do Marechal Floriano Peixoto. Rio de Janeiro: Typ. Pacheco, Silva, & C., 1899.

Conniff, Michael L. *Urban Politics in Brazil: The Rise of Populism, 1925–1945.* Pittsburgh: University of Pittsburgh Press, 1981.

———. "Voluntary Associations in Rio, 1870–1945. A New Approach to Urban Social Dynamics." *Journal of Interamerican Studies and World Affairs* 17 (February 1975), 64–81.

Conrad, Robert. *The Destruction of Brazilian Slavery, 1850–1888.* Berkeley: University of California Press, 1972.

Constatt, Oscar. *Brasil. Terra e gente.* Trans. Eduardo de Lima Castro. Rio de Janeiro: Conquista, 1975.

Cooper, Clayton Sedgwick. *The Brazilians and Their Country.* New York: Frederick A. Stokes, Co., 1917.

Cooper, Donald B. "Oswaldo Cruz and the Impact of Yellow Fever on Brazilian History." *The Bulletin of the Tulane University Medical Faculty* 26 (1967), 49–52.

Corrêa, Inocêncio Serzedello. *Uma figura da república. Páginas do passado.* 2d ed. Rio de Janeiro: Freitas Bastos, 1959.

Costa, Antonio Corrêa de Sousa. *Qual a alimentação de que usa a classe pobre do Rio de Janeiro e sua influencia sobre a mesma classe.* Rio de Janeiro: Typ. Perseverança, 1865.

Costa, Emília Viotti da. *Da senzala à colônia.* São Paulo: Difusão Européia do Livro, 1966.

Costa, Luiz Edmundo da. *De um livro de memórias.* 5 vols. Rio de Janeiro: Imprensa Nacional, 1958.

———. *Recordações do Rio antigo.* Rio de Janeiro: Editôra 'A Noite', 1950.

———. *O Rio de Janeiro do meu tempo.* 3 vols. Rio de Janeiro: Imprensa Nacional, 1938.

Costa, Nelson. *O Rio através dos séculos. A história da cidade e seu IV centenário.* Rio de Janeiro: Edições O Cruzeiro, 1965.

Costa, Luiz Antônio Severa da., et al. *Brasil 1900–1910.* 3 vols. Rio de Janeiro: Biblioteca Nacional, 1980.

Cowell, Jr., Bainbridge, "Cityward Migration in the Nineteenth Century. The Case of Recife, Brazil." *Journal of Interamerican Studies and World Affairs* 17 (February 1975), 43–63.

Cruls, Gastão. *Aparencia do Rio de Janeiro.* 2 vols. Rio de Janeiro: José Olympio, 1965.

Cruz, Ernesto. *Belém. Aspectos eco-sociais do município.* Rio de Janeiro: José Olympio, 1945.

Cruz Costa, João. *Contribuição a história das idéias no Brasil (O desenvolvimento da filosofia no Brasil e a evolução histórica nacional).* Rio de Janeiro: José Olympio, 1956.

————. *O positivismo na república. Notas sobre a história do positivismo no Brasil.* São Paulo: Companhia Editôra Nacional, 1956.

Cunha, Euclides da. *Contrastes e confrontos.* São Paulo: Editôra Lello Brasileira, 1967.

Cunha, Lygia da Fonseca Fernandes da, org. *Album cartográfico do Rio de Janeiro (séculos VIII e XIX).* Rio de Janeiro: Biblioteca Nacional, 1971.

Cunha e Costa. *A colonia portugueza no Brazil. A lucta civil brazileira e o sebastianismo portuguez.* Porto: Typ. da Empreza Litteraria e typographica, 1894.

Cunniff, Roger L. "The Great Drought: Northeast Brazil, 1877–1888." Unpublished Ph.D. dissertation, University of Texas, 1971.

Dean, Warren. *The Industrialization of São Paulo, 1880–1945.* Austin and London: University of Texas Press, 1969.

————. "Latifundia and Land Policy in Nineteenth-Century Brazil." *Hispanic American Historical Review* 51 (November 1971), 606–25.

————. *Rio Claro: A Brazilian Plantation System, 1820–1920.* Stanford: Stanford University Press, 1976.

Deffontaines, Pierre. "The Origin and Growth of the Brazilian Network of Towns." *Geographic Review* 28 (1938), 379–99.

Denis, Pierre. *Brazil.* Trans. Bernard Miall. New York: Charles Scribner's Sons, 1911.

Dent, Charles Hastings. *A Year in Brazil.* London: Kegan, Paul, Trench, and Co., 1886.

Dias, Everardo. *História das lutas sociais no Brasil.* São Paulo, Editôra Edaglit, 1962.

————. *Memórias de um exilado. Episódio de uma deportação.* São Paulo: n.p., 1920.

Diégues Júnior, Manuel. *Imigração, urbanização e industrialização (Estudo sobre alguns aspectos da contribuição cultural do imigrante no Brasil).* Rio de Janeiro: Centro Brasileiro de Pesquisas Educacionaes, Instituto Nacional de Estudos Pedagógicos, Ministério da Educação e Cultura, 1964.

Di Tella, Torcuato S. "The Dangerous Classes in Early Nineteenth Century Mexico." *Journal of Latin American Studies* 5 (May 1973), 79–108.

Doria, A. de Sampaio. *A questão social. Quaes os principios scientificos a adoptar na formação da legislação social do Brasil?* São Paulo: Monteiro Lobato & C., 1922.

Donald, Jr., Cleveland. "Slave Resistance and Abolitionism in Brazil: The Campista Case, 1879–1888." *Luso-Brazilian Review* 13 (Winter 1976), 182–93.

Dornas Filho, João. *Silva Jardim.* São Paulo: Companhia Editôra Nacional, 1936.

Doxiadis Associates. *Guanabara: A Plan for Urban Development*. Athens: K. Papadimitropoulos, 1966.

Dudley, William S. "Institutional Sources of Officer Discontent in the Brazilian Army, 1870–1889." *Hispanic American Historical Review* 55 (February 1975), 44–65.

Dulles, John W. F. *Anarchists and Communists in Brazil, 1900–1935*. Austin and London: University of Texas Press, 1973.

Duncan, Julian Smith. *Public and Private Operation of Railways in Brazil*. New York: Columbia University Press, 1932.

Dunlop, Charles Julius. *Apontamentos para a história dos bondes no Rio de Janeiro*. Rio de Janeiro: Grafica Laemmert, 1953.

———. *Subsídios para e história do Rio de Janeiro*. Rio de Janeiro: Jornal A. Cruz, 1957.

Eisenberg, Peter L. "Abolishing Slavery: The Process on Pernambuco's Sugar Plantations." *Hispanic American Historical Review* 52 (November 1972), 586–605.

———. *The Sugar Industry in Pernambuco: Modernization without Change, 1840–1910*. Berkeley and Los Angeles: University of California Press, 1974.

Erickson, Kenneth Paul, Patrick V. Peppe, and Hobart A. Spalding, Jr. "Research on the Urban Working Class and Organized Labor in Argentina, Brazil, and Chile: What is Left to Be Done." *Latin American Research Review* 9 (Summer 1974), 115–42.

Ewbank, Thomas. *Life in Brazil or a Journal of a Visit to the Land of the Cocoa and the Palm*. New York: Harper and Brothers, 1856.

Faoro, Raymundo. *Os donos do poder. Formação do patronato político brasiliero*. Pôrto Alegre: Editôra Globo, 1958.

Fausto, Boris. *Crime e cotidiano. A criminalidade em São Paulo (1880–1924)*. São Paulo: Editora Brasiliense, 1984.

———. *História geral da civilização brasileira*. Vols. VIII, IX. *O Brasil republicano*. São Paulo: Difel/Difusão Editorial, 1975–1978.

———. *Trabalho urbano e conflito social (1890–1920)*. São Paulo: Difel/Difusão Editorial, 1976.

Fernandes, Florestan. *The Negro in Brazilian Society*. Trans. Jacqueline D. Skiles, A. Brunel, and Arthur Rothwell. New York: Columbia University Press, 1969.

Ferreira, Maria Nazareth. *A imprensa operária no Brasil, 1880–1920*. Petrópolis: Editôra Vozes, 1978.

Ferreira, Rosa Maria Fischer. *Meninos da rua. Valores e espectativas de menores marginalizados em São Paulo*. São Paulo: IBREX [1980].

Ferrez, Gilberto. *As cidades do Salvador e Rio de Janeiro no século XVIII*. Rio de Janeiro: Instituto Histórico e Geográfico Brasileiro.

Fialho, Anfriso. *Historia da fundação da Republica*. Rio de Janeiro: Typ. Laemmert & C., 1891.

Figueira, Manuel Fernandes. *Memoria histórica da Estrada de Ferro Central do Brazil*. Rio de Janeiro: Imprensa Nacional, 1908.

Flory, Thomas. "Judicial Politics in Nineteenth-Century Brazil." *Hispanic American Historical Review* 55 (November 1975), 664–92.

Foerster, Robert F. *The Italian Emigration of Our Times.* Cambridge, Mass.: Harvard University Press, 1924.

Fonseca Filho, Hermes da. *Marechal Hermes.* Rio de Janeiro: n.p., 1961.

Foot, Francisco. *Nem pátria nem patrão. Vida operária e cultura anarquista no Brasil.* São Paulo: Brasiliense, 1983.

Foot, Francisco, and Victor Leonardi. *História da indústria e do trabalho no Brasil. Das origens aos anos vinte.* São Paulo: Global Editora, 1982.

Forster, Elborg, and Robert Forster, eds. *European Diet from Pre-Industrial to Modern Times.* New York: Harper and Row, 1975.

Freire, Felisbello Firmo de Oliveira. *Historia constitucional da Republica dos Estados Unidos do Brasil.* Vols. I and III, Rio de Janeiro: Typ. Aldina, 1894–95; Vol. II, Rio de Janeiro: Cunha & Irmãos, 1896.

Furtado, Celso. *The Economic Growth of Brazil: A Survey from Colonial to Modern Times.* Trans. Ricardo W. de Aguiar and Eric Charles Drysdale. Berkeley and Los Angeles: University of California Press, 1965.

Gabaglia, Laurita Pessoa Raja. *Epitácio Pessoa.* 2 vols. Rio de Janeiro: José Olympio, 1951.

Galeria Nacional. *Vultos prominentes da história brasileira.* Rio de Janeiro: Officinas Graphicas do Jornal do Brasil, 1931.

Galvão Filho, Raphael Archanjo. *Abastecimento d'agua á cidade do Rio de Janeiro.* Rio de Janeiro: Typ. Laemmert, 1873.

Galloway, J. H. "The Last Years of Slavery on the Sugar Plantations of Northeastern Brazil." *Hispanic American Historical Review* 51 (November 1971), 586–605.

Gama, Luís. *Trovas burlescas.* São Paulo: Editôra Três, 1974.

Garrido, C. de Sampayo. *Emigração portuguêsa. Relatorio consular.* São Paulo: Typ. Julio Costa & C., 1920.

Gattai, Zélia. *Anarquistas, graças à Deus.* Rio de Janeiro: Editora Record, 1979.

Gauldie, Enid. *Cruel Habitations. A History of Working-Class Housing, 1780–1918.* New York: Harper and Row, 1974.

Geiger, Pedro Penchas. *Evolução da rêde urbana brasileira.* Rio de Janeiro: Instituto Nacional de Estudos Pedagógicos, Ministério de Educação e Cultura, 1963.

Gonçalves, Aureliano Restier. "Carnes verdes em São Sebastiao do Rio de Janeiro, 1500–1900." In Arquivo do Districto Federal, *Revista de documentos para a história da cidade do Rio de Janeiro.* Rio de Janeiro: Secretaria Geral da Educação e Cultura, 1952.

Graham, Douglas H. and Sérgio Buarque de Hollanda Filho. *Migration, Regional and Urban Growth, and Development in Brazil. A Selected Analysis of the Historical Record, 1872–1971.* São Paulo: Instituto de Pesquisas Economicas, Universadade de São Paulo, 1971.

Graham, Maria Dundas (Lady Maria Calcott). *Journal of a Voyage to Brazil and Residence There During Part of the Years 1821, 1822, 1823.* Rpr. New York: Praeger, 1969.

Graham, Richard. *Britain and the Onset of Modernization in Brazil, 1850–1914.* Cambridge: Cambridge University Press, 1968.

———. "Causes for the Abolition of Negro Slavery in Brazil: An Interpretive Essay." *Hispanic American Historical Review* 46 (May 1966), 123–37.

———. "Government Expenditures and Political Change in Brazil, 1880–1899. Who Got What." *Journal of Interamerican Studies and World Affairs* 19 (August 1977), 339–68.

Graham, Sandra Lauderdale. "The Vintém Riot and Political Culture: Rio de Janeiro, 1880." *Hispanic American Historical Review* 60 (August 1980), 431–49.

Guanabara, Alcindo. *Historia da revolta de 6 de setembro de 1893.* Rio de Janeiro: Typ. e Papelaria Mont'Alverne, 1894.

———. *A presidencia de Campos Salles. Politica e finanças, 1898–1902.* Rio de Janeiro: Laemmert & C., 1902.

———. *Serviço militar obrigatorio. Discurso pronunciado na sessão de 14 de november de 1907.* Rio de Janeiro: Imprensa Nacional, 1907.

Guimarães, Joaquim da Silva Mello. *Instituições de previdencia fundadas no Rio de Janeiro.* Rio de Janeiro: Typ. Nacional, 1883.

Gutman, Herbert G. *Work, Culture, and Society in Industrializing America. Essays in American Working-Class and Social History.* New York: Alfred A. Knopf, 1976.

Hadfield, William. *Brazil and the River Plate in 1868, Showing the Progress of Those Countries Since His Former Visit in 1853.* London: Bates, Hendy and Co., 1869.

Hahner, June E. "The Brazilian Armed Forces and the Overthrow of the Monarchy: Another Perspective." *The Americas* 26 (October 1969), 171–82.

———. *Civilian-Military Relations in Brazil, 1889–1898.* Columbia S.C.: University of South Carolina Press, 1969.

———. "Women and Work in Brazil, 1850–1920: A Preliminary Investigation." In *Essays Concerning the Socioeconomic History of Brazil and Portuguese India.* Dauril Alden and Warren Dean, eds. Gainesville: University Presses of Florida, 1977.

Hall, Michael M. "Immigration and the Early São Paulo Working Class." *Jahrbuch für Geschichte von Staat, Wirtschaft and Gesellschaft Lateinamerikas* 12 (1975), 393–407.

———. "The Origins of Mass Immigration in Brazil, 1871–1914." Unpublished Ph.D. dissertation, Columbia University, 1969.

———. "Reformadores de classe média no Império Brasileiro: A Sociedade Central de Imigração." *Revista de História* 53, no. 105 (1976), 147–71.

Hasenbalg, Carlos. *Discriminação e desigualdades raciais no Brasil.* Trans. Patrick Burgin. Rio de Janeiro: Edições Graal, 1979.

Hauser, Philip M., ed. *Urbanization in Latin America.* New York: International Documents Service, 1961.

Henretta, James A. "Social History as Lived and Written." *American Historical Review* 84 (December 1979), 1293–1322.

Hermes-Wenceslau. O sr. General Pinheiro Machado. (Rio de Janeiro: n.p., 1910)

História da policia militar do Districto Federal desde a época de sua fundação. 3 vols. Rio de Janeiro: Departamento de Imprensa Nacional, 1953.

Hoffnagel, Marc Jay. "O movimento republicano em Pernambuco, 1870–1889." *Revista do Instituto Arqueológico, Histórico, e Geográfico Pernambucano* 49 (January 1977), 31–59.

Hollanda, Sérgio Buarque de, ed. *História geral da civilização brasileira.* Vols. 3–7. *O Brasil monárquico.* São Paulo: Difusão Européia do Livro, 1962–1972.

Holloway, Thomas H. *Immigrants on the Land: Coffee and Society in São Paulo, 1886–1934.* Chapel Hill: University of North Carolina Press, 1980.

Holub, Norman. "The Brazilian Sabinada (1837–1838): Revolt of the Negro Masses." *Journal of Negro History* 54 (July 1969), 275–83.

Huggins, Martha Knisely. *From Slavery to Vagrancy in Brazil: Crime and Social Control in the Third World.* New Brunswick, N.J.: Rutgers University Press, 1984.

Hutchinson, Bertram. *Mobilidade e trabalho. Um estudo na cidade de São Paulo.* Rio de Janeiro: Ministério da Educação e Cultura, Centro Brasileiro de Pesquisas Educacionais, 1960.

Ianni, Octávio. *Industrialização e desenvolvimento social no Brasil.* Rio de Janeiro: Editôra Civilização Brasileira, 1963.

Jaguaribe, Helio. *Burguesía e proletariado en el nacionalismo brasileña.* Buenos Aires: Ediciones Coyoacán, 1966.

———. *Desenvolvimento econômico e político.* Rio de Janeiro: Paz e Terra, 1969.

Joffily, Geraldo Irinêo. "O Quebra-Quilo. A revolta dos matutos contra os doutores. (1874)." *Revista de História* 54 (July-September 1976), 69–145.

Johnson, Harold B., Jr. "A Preliminary Inquiry into Money, Prices, and Wages in Rio de Janeiro, 1763–1823," In *Colonial Roots of Modern Brazil.* Dauril Alden, ed. Berkeley and Los Angeles: University of California Press, 1973.

Karasch, Mary. "From Porterage to Proprietorship: African Occupations in Rio de Janeiro, 1808–1850," in Stanley L. Engerman and Eugene D. Genovese, eds. *Race and Slavery in the Western Hemisphere: Quantitative Studies.* Princeton, N.J.: Princeton University Press, 1975.

———. "Slave Life in Rio de Janeiro, 1808–1850." Unpublished Ph.D. dissertation, University of Wisconsin, 1972.

Kern, Robert, ed. *The Caciques: Oligarchical Politics and the System of Caciquismo in the Luso-Hispanic World.* Albuquerque: University of New Mexico Press, 1973.

Kidder, Daniel Parish and James C. Fletcher. *Brazil and the Brazilians Portrayed in Historical and Descriptive Sketches.* 7th ed. Boston: Little Brown and Co., 1867.

Klein, Herbert S. "The Internal Slave Trade in Nineteenth-Century Brazil: A

Study of Slave Importations into Rio de Janeiro in 1852." *Hispanic American Historical Review* 51 (November 1971), 567–85.

Klinger, Bertoldo. *Parade e desfile duma vida de voluntario do Brazil na primeira metade do século.* Rio de Janeiro: Emprêsa Gráfica O Cruzeiro, 1958.

Koseritz, Carl von. *Imagens do Brasil.* Trans. Afonso Arinos de Melo Franco. São Paulo: Livraria Martins Editora, 1943.

Lacerda, Gustavo de. *O problema operaria no Brasil. Propaganda socialista.* Rio de Janeiro: n.p., 1901.

Lacerda, Mauricio de. *Entre duas revoluções.* Rio de Janeiro: Editora Leite Ribeiro, 1927.

―――. *Evolução legislativa do direito social brasileiro.* Rio de Janeiro: Ministério do Trabalho, Indústria e Comérico, 1960.

―――. *História de uma covardia.* Rio de Janeiro: Livraria Editôra Freitas Bastos, 1931.

Lacerda, Maurício Caminha de. "Maurício de Lacerda, meu pai." *Revista Brasiliense* 6 (September-October 1960), 195–217.

Lagenest, H. D. Baruel de. "Os cortiços de São Paulo." *Anhembi* 12 (June 1962), 5–17.

Lamberg, Maurício. *O Brazil.* Trans. Luiz de Castro. Rio de Janeiro: Typografia Nunes, 1896.

Lamego, Alberto Ribeiro. *O homem e a Guanabara.* Rio de Janeiro: Editôra 'A Noite', 1946.

Landes, Ruth. *The City of Women.* New York: Macmillan, 1947.

Leacock, Seth and Ruth. *Spirits of the Deep: A Study of an Afro-Brazilian Cult.* New York: Natural History Press, 1972.

Leal, Aurelino de Araujo. *Policia e poder de policia.* Rio de Janeiro: Imprensa Nacional, 1918.

Leal, Joaquim Bagueira. *A questão da vacina.* Rio de Janeiro: Tipografia da Apostolado Pozitivista do Brazil, 1904.

Leal, Victor Nunes. *Coronelismo, enxada e voto. O município e o regime representativo no Brasil (Da colônia a Primeira Repúblic).* Rio de Janeiro and São Paulo: Forense, 1948.

Leão, José. *Silva Jardim. Apontamentos para a biographia do illustre propagandista hauridos nas informações paternas e dados particulares e officiaes.* Rio de Janeiro: Imprensa Nacional, 1895.

Leclerc, Max. *Cartas do Brasil.* Trans. Sérgio Milliet. São Paulo: Companhia Editôra Nacional, 1942.

Lenharo, Alcir. *As tropas da moderação (O abastecimento da Corte na formação política do Brasil. 1808–1842).* São Paulo: Edições Símbolo, 1979.

Leuenroth, Edgard. *Anarquismo. Roteiro da libertação social. Antologia de doutrina, crítica, história, informações.* Rio de Janeiro: Editôra Mundo Livre, 1963.

Levine, Robert M. *Pernambuco in the Brazilian Federation, 1889–1937.* Stanford: Stanford University Press, 1978.

Lima, Alexandre José Barbosa. *Discursos Parlamentares*. Brasília: Documentos Parlamentares, 1963.

Lima Barreto, Afonso Henriques de. *Bagatelas*. 2d ed. São Paulo: Editôra Brasiliense, 1961.

—————. *Clara dos Anjos*. 2d ed. São Paulo: Editôra Brasiliense, 1961.

—————. *Recordações do escrivão Isaías Caminha*. 2d ed. São Paulo: Editôra Brasiliense, 1961.

—————. *Vida e morte de M. J. Gonzaga de Sá*. 2d ed. São Paulo: Editôra Brasiliense, 1961.

Linhares, Hermínio. *Contribuição a história das lutas operárias no Brasil*. Rio de Janeiro: Baptista de Souza e Cia., 1955.

Linhares, Maria Yedda Leite. *História do abastecimento. Uma problemática em questão (1530–1919)*. Brasília: BINAGRI Edições, 1979.

Lins, Ivan. *História do positivismo no Brasil*. São Paulo: Companhia Editôra Nacional, 1964.

Lisboa, João Coelho Gonçalves. *Conferencias republicanas*. Rio de Janeiro: Typ. Luiz Miotto. 1910.

Lisboa, João Francisco. *Obras de João Francisco Lisboa*. 2 vols. Lisbon: Typ. Mattos Moreira & Pinheiro, 1901.

Lobo, Eulália Maria Lahmeyer. *História do Rio de Janeiro (Do capital comercial ao capital industrial e financeiro)*. 2 vols. Rio de Janeiro: Instituto Brasileiro de Mercado de Capitais, 1978.

Lobo, Eulália Maria Lahmeyer, Octávio Canavarros, Zakia Feres Elias, Sonia Gonçalves, and Lucena Barbosa Madureira. "Evolução dos preços e do padrão de vida no Rio de Janeiro, 1820–1930—resultados preliminares." *Revista Brasileira de Economia* 25 (October-December 1971), 235–65.

Lobo, Eulália Maria Lahmeyer, Lucena Barbosa Madureira, Octávio Canavarros, Simone Novaes, and Zakhia Feres Elias. "Evolution des prix e du cout de la vie a Rio de Janeiro (1820–1930)." In *L'histoire quantitative du Bresil de 1800 à 1930*. Colloques Internationaux du Centre National de la Recherche Scientifique No. 543. Paris: Editions du Centre National de la Recherche Scientifique, 1973.

—————. "Estudo das categorias socioprofissionais, dos salários e do custo da alimentação no Rio de Janeiro de 1820 à 1930." *Revista Brasileira de Economia* 27 (October-December 1973), 129–76);

Lobo, Julio da Silveira. *Apontamentos para a historia do Segundo Reinado*. n.p., 1895.

Love, Joseph L. "Political Participation in Brazil, 1881–1969." *Luso-Brazilian Review* 7 (December 1970), 3–24.

—————. *Rio Grande do Sul and Brazilian Regionalism, 1882–1930*. Stanford: Stanford University Press, 1971.

—————. *São Paulo in the Brazilian Federation, 1889–1937*. Stanford: Stanford University Press, 1970.

Luz, Nícia Vilela. A luta pela industrialização do Brasil (1808 à 1930). São Paulo: Difusão Européia do Livro, 1961.

————. "O papel das classes médias brasileiras no movimento republicano." Revista de História 57 (January-March 1964), 13–27.

Lyra, Heitor. História de Dom Pedro II. 3 vols. São Paulo: Companhia Editôra Nacional, 1940.

Lyra, João. As classes contribuintes. Operariado. O funccionalismo publico. A administração da Fazenda Federal. Instituto Brasileiro de Contabilidade. Discursos. Rio de Janeiro: Typ. do 'Jornal do Commercio', 1917.

McBeth, Michael C. "The Brazilian Recruit during the First Empire: Slave or Soldier?" In Essays Concerning the Socioeconomic History of Brazil and Portuguese India. Dauril Alden and Warren Dean, eds. Gainesville: University Presses of Florida, 1977.

McCann, Frank D. "The Nation in Arms: Obligatory Military Service during the Old Republic." In Essays Concerning the Socioeconomic History of Brazil and Portuguese India. Dauril Alden and Warren Dean, eds. Gainesville: University Presses of Florida, 1977.

Macedo, Francisco Riopardense. Pôrto Alegre: Origem e crescimento. Pôrto Alegre: Liv. Sulina, 1968.

Macedo, Roberto. A administração de Floriano. Vol. V of Floriano. Memórias e documentos. Rio de Janeiro: Serviço Gráfico do Ministério de Educação, 1939.

Maciel, Anor Butler. Expulsão de Estrangeiros. Rio de Janeiro: Imprensa Nacional, 1953.

Madeira, Felicia R., and Paulo I. Singer. Estrutura do emprego e trabalho feminino no Brasil, 1920–1970. Cadernos CEBRAP 13. São Paulo: CEBRAP, 1973.

Magalhães, Manoel Lourenço de. Gustavo de Lacerda e a fundação da A.B.I. Rio de Janeiro: 'Jornal do Comércio', 1954.

Magalhaes Junior, Raimundo. Deodoro. A espada contra o Império. 2 vols. São Paulo: Companhia Editôra Nacional, 1967.

Magalhães Júnior, Raimundo, ed. D. Pedro II e a Condessa de Barral através da correspondencia íntima do imperador, anotada e comentada. Rio de Janeiro: Editôra Civilização Brasileira, 1956.

Maram, Sheldon L., "Anarcho-Syndicalism in Brazil." In Latin America: Power and Poverty. Proceedings of the Pacific Coast Council on Latin American Studies, IV, 1975.

————. "Labor and the Left in Brazil, 1890–1921: A Movement Aborted." Hispanic American Historical Review 57 (May 1977), 254–72.

————. "The Immigrant and the Brazilian Labor Movement, 1890–1920." In Essays Concerning the Socioeconomic History of Brazil and Portuguese India. Dauril Alden and Warren Dean, eds. Gainesville: University Presses of Florida, 1977.

Marcílio, Maria Luiza. La ville de São Paulo. Peuplement et population, 1750–1850. Rouen: Université de Rouen, 1968.

Martins, J. P. Oliveira. *O Brazil e as colonias portuguezas*. Lisbon: Livraria Bertrand, 1880.

Martins, Luiz Dodsworth. *Presença de Paulo de Frontin*. Rio de Janeiro and São Paulo: Livraria Freitas Bastos, 1966.

Mattoon, Robert H., Jr. "The Companhia Paulista de Estradas de Ferro, 1868–1900: A Local Railway Enterprise in São Paulo, Brazil." Unpublished Ph.D. dissertation, Yale University, 1971.

Mattoso, Katia M. de Queirós. *Bahia: A cidade do Salvador e seu mercado no século XIX*. São Paulo: Editora Hucitec Ltda., 1978.

————. "Os preços na Bahia de 1750–1930." In *L'histoire quantitative du Bresil de 1800 à 1930*. Colloques Internationaux du Centre C.N.R.S. Paris: Editions du Centre National de la Recherche Scientifique, 1973.

———— and Johildo de Athayde. "Epidemias e fluctuações de preços na Bahia no século XIX." In *L'histoire quantitative du Bresil de 1800 à 1930*. Colloques Internationaux du C.N.R.S. Paris: Editions du Centre National de la Recherche Scientifique, 1973.

Mawe, John. *Travels in the Interior of Brazil, Particularly in the Gold and Diamond Districts of That Country*. Philadelphia: M. Carey, 1816.

Mayer, Arno J. "The Lower Middle Class as Historical Problem." *Journal of Modern History* 47 (September 1975), 409–36.

Medeiros e Albuquerque, José Joaquim de Campos da Costa. *Minha vida. Memórias*. 2 vols. Rio de Janeiro: Calvino Filho, 1933–1934.

————. *O perigo americano*. Rio de Janeiro: Leite Ribeiro & Maurillo, 1919.

Mello, Custódio José de. *O governo provisório e a revolução do 1893*. 2 vols. São Paulo: Companhia Editôra Nacional, 1938.

Mello Morais Filho, Alexandre José de. *Factos e memorias*. Rio de Janeiro and Paris: H. Garnier, 1903.

————. *Festas e tradições populares do Brasil*. 3rd ed. Rio de Janeiro: F. Briguiet & Cia., 1946.

————. *Mythos e poemas. Nacionalismo*. Rio de Janeiro: Typographia de G. Leuzinger e Filhos, 1884.

————. *Serenatas e Saráos*. 3 vols. Rio de Janeiro and Paris: H. Garnier, 1901–1902.

Melo Franco, Afonso Arinos de. *Rodrigues Alves. Apogeu e declínio do presidencialismo.* 2 vols. Rio de Janeiro and São Paulo: José Olympio/Editôra da Universidade de São Paulo, 1973.

Menezes, Raimundo de. *Vida e obra de Campos Sales*. São Paulo: Prefeitura Municipal de Campinas/Livraria Martins, 1974.

Menezes, Rodrigo Octavio de Langgaard. *Festas nacionaes, com una introducção de Raul Pompeia*. Rio de Janeiro: F. Briguiet & Co., 1893.

————. *Minhas memórias dos outros*. 3 vols. Rio de Janeiro: José Olympio, 1934–1936.

Merrick, Thomas W., and Douglas H. Graham. *Population and Economic Development in Brazil, 1800 to the Present*. Baltimore and London: Johns Hopkins, 1979.

Moisés, José Alvaro, et al. *Cidade, povo e poder*. Rio de Janeiro: Centro de Estudos de Cultura Contemporânea/Paz e Terra, 1982.

―――. *Contradições urbanas e movimentos sociais*. 2d ed. Rio de Janeiro: Centro de Estudos de Cultura Contemporânea/Paz e Terra, 1978.

Monteiro, Albelardo F. *História dos partidos políticos cearenses*. Fortaleza: n.p., 1965.

Montgomery, David. "To Study the People: The American Working Class." *Labor History* 21 (Fall 1980), 485–512.

Moraes, Evaristo de. *Crianças abandonadas e crianças criminosas*. Rio de Janeiro: n.p., 1901.

―――. *Os accidentes no trabalho e a sua reparação. (Ensaio de legislação comparada e commentario a Lei Brazileira)*. Rio de Janeiro: Livraria Leite Ribeiro & Maurillo, 1919.

―――. *Apontamentos de direito operario*. Rio de Janeiro: Imprensa Nacional, 1905.

―――. *A campanha abolicionista (1879–1888)*. Rio de Janeiro: Freitas Bastos, 1924.

―――. *Minhas prisões e outros assumptos contemporaneos*. Rio de Janeiro: n.p., 1924.

―――. *Reminiscencias de um rabula criminalista*. Rio de Janeiro: Livraria Leite Ribeiro, 1922.

Moraes, Octavio Alexander de. "Immigration into Brazil. A Statistical Statement and Related Aspects." In *The Migration of Peoples to Latin America*. Margaret Bates, ed. Washington, D.C.: The Catholic University of America Press, 1957.

Morais, Eneida de. *História do carnaval carioca*. Rio de Janeiro: Editôra Civilização Brasileira, 1955.

Morel, Edmar. *A revolta da chibata*. 2d ed. Rio de Janeiro: Editôra Letras e Artes, 1963.

Morse, Richard M. *From Community to Metropolis: A Biography of São Paulo, Brazil*. Gainesville: University of Florida Presses, 1958.

Morse, Richard M., ed. *The Urban Development of Latin America, 1750–1920*. Stanford: Center for Latin American Studies, Stanford University, 1971.

Mota, Carlos Guilherme. *Nordeste 1817*. São Paulo: Perspective, 1972.

Mota Filho, Cândido. *Uma grande vida. Biografia de Bernardino de Campos*. São Paulo: Campanhia Editôra Nacional, 1941.

Moura, Maria Lacerda de. *Religião do amor e da belleza*. 2d ed. São Paulo: Editora O Pensamento, 1929.

Moura, Paulo Cursino de. *São Paulo de Outrora (Evocações da metrópole)*. São Paulo: Companhia Editôra Nacional, 1941.

Moura, Roberto. *Tia Ciata e a pequena África no Rio de Janeiro*. Rio de Janeiro: FUNARTE, 1983.

Nabuco, Carolina. *The Life of Joaquim Nabuco*. Trans. Ronald Hilton. Stanford: Stanford University Press, 1950.

Nabuco, Joaquim. *Abolitionism: The Brazilian Antislavery Struggle*. Trans. Robert Conrad. Urbana: University of Illinois Press, 1977.

———. *Um estadista do Império*. *Nabuco de Araujo*. *Sua vida, suas opinões, sua época*. 2 vols. São Paulo: Companhia Editôra Nacional, 1936.

Nachman, Robert G. "Positivism and Revolution in Brazil's First Republic: The 1904 Revolt." *The Americas* 34 (July 1977), 20–39.

Neiva, Vicente. *Attentado de cinco de novembro. Relatorio do dr. Vicente Neiva 1° delegado auxiliar e diversas peças do inquerito*. Rio de Janeiro: Imprensa Nacional, 1898.

Neves, Maria Cecília Baeta. "Greve dos sapateiros de 1906 no Rio de Janeiro: Notas de pesquisa." *Revista de Administração de Empresas* 13 (April-June 1973), 49–66.

Nogueira, César. *Notas para a história do socialismo em Portugal*. 2 vols. Lisbon: Portugália, Editora, 1966.

Notas de um revoltoso. (Diário de bordo). Documentos authenticos publicados pelo "Commercio de São Paulo." Rio de Janeiro: Typ. Moraes, 1895.

Oakenfull, J. C. *Brazil in 1909*. Paris: Brazilian Government Commission of Propaganda and Economic Expansion, 1909.

———. *Brazil: A Century of Independence, 1822–1922*. Freiburg, Germany: C. A. Wagner, 1922.

———. *Brazil: Past, Present and Future*. London: John Bale, Sons, and Danvl.8ielsson, Ltd., 1919.

Um official da armada. *Política versus marinha*. Paris: Imprimerie Français-Etrangère, n.d.

Onody, Oliver. *A inflação brasileira (1820–1958)*. Rio de Janeiro: n.p., 1960.

Ottoni, Christiano Benedicto. *O advento da republica no Brazil*. Rio de Janeiro: Perseverança, 1890.

———. *D. Pedro de Alcântara*. Rio de Janeiro: Typ. 'Jornal do Commercio', 1893.

Ozanne, Robert. "Trends in American Labor History." *Labor History* 21 (Fall 1980), 513–21.

Pang, Eul-Soo. *Bahia in the First Republic: Coronelismo and Oligarchies, 1889–1934*. Gainesville: University of Florida Presses, 1979.

Paoli, Maria Célia, et al. *A violência brasileira*. São Paulo: Editora Brasiliense, 1982.

Pearse, Andrew. "Some Characteristics of Urbanization in the City of Rio de Janeiro." In *Urbanization in Latin America*. Philip M. Hauser ed. New York: International Documents Service, 1961.

Pena, Maria Valéria Junho. *Mulheres e trabalhadoras. Presença feminina na constituição do sistema fabril*. Rio de Janeiro: Paz e Terra, 1981.

Penteado, Antonio Rocha. *Belém do Pará (Estudo de geografia urbana)*. 2 vols. Belém: Universidade Federal do Pará, 1968.

Penteado, Jacob. *Belènzinho, 1910 (Retrato de uma época)*. São Paulo: Livraria Martins, 1962.

Peregrino, Umberto. *Significação do Marechal Hermes*. Rio de Janeiro: Biblioteca do Exército, 1956.

Pereira, Astrojildo. *Formação do PCB. 1922–1928. Notas e documentos*. Rio de Janeiro: Vitória, 1962.

————. "Silverio Fontes, Pioneiro do Marxismo no Brasil." *Estudos Sociais* 3 (April 1962), 404–12.

Pestana, Francisco Rangel (pseud. Thomas Jefferson). *Notas republicanas. I. A reacção e os novos partidos. II. A politica do marechal Floriano Peixoto*. Rio de Janeiro: n.p., 1898.

Pestana, Nereu Rangel (pseud. Ivan Subiroff). *A oligarchia paulista*. São Paulo: O Estado de São Paulo, 1919.

Petrone, Maria Thereza Schorer. *O Barão de Iguape. Um empresário da época da independência*. São Paulo: Companhia Editora Nacional, 1976.

Piccarolo, Antonio. *O socialismo no Brasil. Esboço de um programma de ação socialista*. São Paulo. Editora Pirantininga, 1932.

Pimenta, Joaquim. *Retalhos do passado*. 2nd ed. Rio de Janeiro: Imprensa Nacional, 1949.

Pimental, Antonio Martins de Azevedo. *Quaes os melhoramentos hygienicos que devem ser introduzidos no Rio de Janeiro para tornar esta cidade mais saudavel*. Rio de Janeiro: Typ. e Lith. de Moreira Maximino & Co., 1884.

————. *Subsidos para o estudo de hygiene do Rio de Janeiro*. Rio de Janeiro: Typ. e Lith. de Carlos Gaspar da Silva, 1890.

Pinheiro, Paulo Sérgio, and Michael M. Hall, eds. *A classe operaria no Brasil. Documentos (1889 a 1930)*. 2 vols. São Paulo: Editora Alfa Omega, 1979 and Editora Brasiliense, 1982.

Pinto, Manoel de Sousa. *Terra moça. Impressões brasileiras*. Oporto: Livraria Chardron, 1910.

Poblete Troncoso, Moisés, and Ben G. Burnett. *The Rise of the Latin American Labor Movement*. New York: Bookman Associates, 1960.

A polícia na Corte e no Distrito Federal, 1831–1930. Série Estudos PUC/RJ No. 3. Rio de Janeiro: Pontifícia Universidade Católica do Rio de Janeiro, 1981.

A polícia e a força policial no Rio de Janeiro. Série Estudos PUC/RJ No. 4. Rio de Janeiro: Pontifícia Universidade Católica do Rio de Janeiro, 1981.

Poppino, Rollie E. *Brazil: The Land and the People*. New York: Oxford University Press, 1968.

Querino, Manoel. *As artes na Bahia (Escorço de uma contribuição histórica)*. Salvador: Typ. do Lyceu de Artes e Oficios, 1909.

————. *Costumes africanos no Brasil*. Rio de Janeiro: Editôra Civilização Brasileira, 1938.

Queiroz, Maria Isaura Pereira de. *O mandonismo local na vida política brasileira*. São Paulo: Instituto de Estudos Brasileiros, 1969.

————. "Messiahs in Brazil." *Past and Present* 31 (July 1965), 62–86.

Queiroz, Maurício Vinhas de. "Notas sobre o processo de modernização no

Brasil." *Revista do Instituto de Ciências Sociais* 3 (January-December 1966), 139–62.

———. *Paixão e morte de Silva Jardim.* Rio de Janeiro: Editôra Civilização Brasileira, 1967.

Quintas, Amaro. *O sentido social da revolução praieira.* Rio de Janeiro: Editôra Civilização brasileira, 1967.

Raphael, Alison. "Samba and Social Control: Popular Culture and Racial Democracy in Rio de Janeiro." Unpublished Ph.D. dissertation, Columbia University, 1980.

Rego, Waldeloir. *Capoeira Angola. Ensaio sócio-etnográfico.* Salvador: Editôra Itapuã, 1968.

Ribas, Antonio Joaquim. *Perfil biographico do dr. Manoel Ferraz de Campos Salles, ministro da justiça do governo provisorio, senador federal pelo Estado de São Paulo.* Rio de Janeiro: Typ. Leuzinger, 1896.

Ribeiro, René. *Cultos africanos do Recife. Um estado de ajustamento social.* Recife: Instituto Joaquim Nabuco, 1952.

Rios, José Arhur. *Aspectos politicos da assimilação do italiano no Brasil.* São Paulo: Fundação Escola de Sociologia e Política de São Paulo, 1959.

Rios Filho, Adolfo Morales de los. *O Rio de Janeiro imperial.* Rio de Janeiro: Editôra 'A Noite', 1946.

Rodrigues, A. Coelho. *A Republica na America do Sul ou um pouco de historia e critica offerecido aos Latino-Americanos.* 2d ed. Einsiedeln, Switzerland: Typ. dos Establecimentos Benzinger & Co., 1906.

Rodrigues, Edgar. *Nacionalismo e cultura social, 1913–1922.* Rio de Janeiro: Laemmert, 1972.

———. *Socialismo e sindicalismo no Brasil, 1675–1913.* Rio de Janeiro: Laemmert, 1969.

Rodrigues, José Albertino. *Sindicato e desenvolvimento no Brasil.* São Paulo: Difusão Européia do Livro, 1968.

Rodrigues, Leônico. *Conflito industrial e sindicalismo no Brasil.* São Paulo: Difusão Européia do Livro, 1966.

Rodrigues, Nina. *O animismo fetichista dos negros bahianos.* Rio de Janeiro: Civilização Brasileira, 1935.

Rosa, Ferreira da. *Associação dos Empregados no Comercio do Rio de Janeiro. Meio Seculo. Narrativa histórica.* Rio de Janeiro: Paulo, Pongetti & Co., 1930.

———. *O Rio de Janeiro em 1900. Visitas e excursões.* 2d ed. n.p., n.d.

Rudé, George. *The Crowd in History: A Study of Popular Disturbances in France and England, 1703–1848.* New York: John Wiley and Sons, 1964.

Ruy, Affonso. *História política e administrativa da cidade de Salvador.* Salvador: Tip. Beneditina, 1949.

Saes, Décio. *Classe média e política na Primeira República Brasileira (1889–1930).* Petrópolis: Vozes, 1975.

Salles, Alberto [Alberto Sales]. *A patria paulista.* Campinas: Typ. da Gazeta de Campinas, 1887.

Santa Rosa, Virgínio. *Que foi o tenentismo*. Rio de Janeiro: Civilização Brasileira, 1964.

Santos, Francisco Agenor Noronha. *Barata Ribeiro. Administração do primeiro prefeito do Distrito Federal*. Rio de Janeiro: Departamento Administrativo do Serviço Público, 1955.

―――. *Meios de transporte no Rio de Janeiro*. 2 vols. Rio de Janeiro. José Olympio, 1956.

Santos, José Maria dos. *Bernardino de Campos e o Partido Republicano Paulista. Subsídios para a história da República*. Rio de Janeiro: Livraria José Olympio. Editôra, 1960.

―――. *A política geral do Brasil*. São Paulo: J. Magalhães, 1930.

―――. *Os republicanos paulistas e a abolição*. São Paulo: Livraria Martins, 1965.

Santos, Milton. *O centro da cidade de Salvador*. Salvador: Universidade da Bahia, 1959.

Schmidt, Afonso. *Colônia Cecília. Uma adventura anarquista na América, 1889 à 1893*. São Paulo: Editôra Anchieta, 1942.

Schulz, John Henry. "The Brazilian Army and Politics, 1850–1894." Unpublished Ph.D. dissertation, Princeton University, 1973.

Shorter, Edward, and Charles Tilly. *Strikes in France, 1830–1968*. London and New York: Cambridge University Press, 1974.

Scobie, James R. *Buenos Aires: Plaza to Suburb, 1870–1910*. New York: Oxford University Press, 1974.

Scully, William. *Brazil: Its Provinces and Chief Cities*. London: John Murray and Co., 1866.

Serra, Joaquim (pseud. Amigo ausente). *A capangada, parodia muito séria*. Rio de Janeiro: Typ. da Reforma, 1872.

Serrão, Joel. *A emigração portuguesa. Sondagem história*. 2d ed. Lisbon: Livros Horizonte, 1974.

Silva, Jardim, Antonio da. *Fechamento das portas (A questão do descanso para os empregados no commerico, realisada a convite da Associação dos Empregados no Commerico do Rio de Janeiro a 27 de outubro de 1888*. Rio de Janeiro: Typ. Mont'Alverne, 1888.

―――. *A patria em perigo (Braganças e Orleans). Conferencia-meeting sobre a actual situação brasileira, realizada na cidade de Santos, em noite de 28 de janeiro de 1888*. São Paulo: Typ. da Provincia, 1888.

―――. *Memoria e viagens. I. Campanha de um propagandista (1887–1890)*. Lisbon: Typ. da Comp. Nacional Editora, 1891.

―――. *Salvação de Patria (Governo republicano). Conferencia realizada no Club Republicano de São Paulo, em a noite de 7 de abril de 1888*. Santos: Typ. do Diario de Santos, 1888.

―――. *A situação republicano (Questão da chefia do Partido). Manifestos e artigos publicados no Gazeta de Noticias em maio e junho de 1889*. Rio de Janeiro: Typ. da Gazeta de Noticias, 1889.

Simão, Azis. *Sindicato e estado. Suas relações na formação do proletariado de São Paulo.* São Paulo: Dominus Editôra, 1966.

Singer, Paul. *Desenvolvimento econômico e evolução urbana (Análise da evolução econômica de São Paulo, Blumenau, Pôrto Alegre, Belo Horizonte e Recife).* 2d ed. São Paulo: Companhia Editôra Nacional, 1977.

Siqueira, Edmundo. *Resumo histórico de The Leopoldina Railway Company, Limited.* Rio de Janeiro: Gráfica Editôra Carioca, 1938.

Skidmore, Thomas E. *Black into White: Race and Nacionality in Brazilian Thought.* New York: Oxford University Press, 1974.

Slater, Candace. *Stories on a String: The Brazilian Literatura de Cordel.* Berkeley: University of California Press, 1982.

Smith, Herbert H. *Brazil. The Amazons and the Coast.* New York: Charles Scribner's Sons, 1879.

Soboul, Albert. *The Parisian Sans-Culottes and the French Revolution, 1793–1794.* Trans. Gwynne Lewis. Oxford: Oxford University Press, 1964.

Sodré, Lauro. *Crenças e opiniões.* Belém: Typ. do Diario Official, 1896.

———. *A evolução politica do Brasil.* Rio de Janeiro: n.p., 1906.

———. and Ribeiro, Barata. *Contra a obrigatoriedade de vaccina. Rezumo dos discursos pronunciados pelos Senadores Lauro Sodré e Barata Ribeiro.* Rio de Janeiro: 'Jornal do Brasil', 1904.

Sodré, Nelson Werneck. *Formação histórica do Brasil.* São Paulo: Brasiliense, 1964.

———. *A história da imprensa no Brasil.* Rio de Janeiro: Editôra Civilização Brasileira, 1966.

Sousa, Newton Stadler de. *O anarquismo da Colônia Cecília.* Rio de Janeiro: Editôra Civilização Brasileira, 1970.

Souza, Vicente de. *Processo crime motivado pelos acontecimentos occorridos na Capital Federal, a 14 e 15 de Novembro de 1904. Razões de defesa e recurso apresentadas pelo Dr. Vicente de Souza, accusado pelo crime de conspiração. Advogado Alberto de Carvalho.* Rio de Janeiro: Typ. do 'Jornal do Commercio', 1905.

Spalding, Hobart A., Jr. *Organized Labor in Latin America: Historical Case Studies of Urban Workers in Dependent Societies.* New York: Harper and Row, 1977.

Stein, Stanley J. *The Brazilian Cotton Manufacture: Textile Enterprise in an Underdeveloped Area, 1850–1950.* Cambridge, Mass: Harvard University Press, 1957.

———. *Vassouras: A Brazilian Coffee County, 1850–1900.* Cambridge, Mass.: Harvard University Press, 1957.

Stepan, Nancy. *Beginnings of Brazilian Science.* New York: Science History Publications, 1976.

Sweigart, Joseph Earl. "Financing and Marketing Export Agriculture: The Coffee Factors of Rio de Janeiro, 1850–1888." Unpublished Ph.D. dissertation, University of Texas at Austin, 1980.

Szuchman, Mark D., and Eugene F. Sofer. "The State of Occupational Stratification Studies in Argentina: A Classificatory Scheme." *Latin American Research Review* 11, No. 1 (1976), 159–71.

Taunay, Afonso d'Escragnolles. *História da Cidade de São Paulo*. São Paulo: Edições Melhoramentos, 1953.

Teixeira Mendes, Raymundo. *Ainda o militarismo perante a política moderna*. Rio de Janeiro: Tipografia do Apostolado Pozivitivsta do Brazil, 1908.

———. *Ainda pelos martyrizados descendentes dos indigenas e dos africanos*. Rio de Janeiro: Tipografia do Apostolado Pozitivista do Brazil, 1912.

———. *Ainda a vacinação obrigatoria e a politica republicana*. Rio de Janeiro: Tipografia do Apostolado Pozitivista do Brazil, 1908.

———. *Benjamin Constant. Esbôço de uma apreciação sintetica da vida e da obra do fundador da república brazileira*. Rio de Janeiro: Imprensa Nacional, 1936.

———. *Contra a vaccinção obrigatoria. (A proposito do parecer da Commissão de Instrucção e Saude Publica da Camara dos Deputados)*. Rio de Janeiro: Typ. do Jornal do Commercio, 1904.

———. *Contra a vacinação obrigatoria (A propózito do projéto de Governo)*. Rio de Janeiro: Tipografia do Apostolado Pozitivista do Brazil, 1904.

———. *O despotismo medico-legista e a dignidade humana, especialmente feminina*. Rio de Janeiro: Tipografia do Apostolado Pozitivista do Brazil, 1917.

———. *As greves, a órdem republicana, e a reorganização social*. Rio de Janeiro: Tipografia do Apostolado Pozitivista do Brazil, 1906.

———. *O Imperio Brazileiro e a Republica Brazileira perante a regeneração social. A proposito do "Manifesto de S.A.I. D. Luiz de Braganca."* (Rio de Janeiro: Tipografia do Apostolado Pozitivista do Brazil, 1913.

———. *A incorporação do proletariado na sociedade moderna e os ensinos de Augusto Comte*. Rio de Janeiro: Tipografia do Apostolado Pozitivista do Brazil, 1917.

———. *A liberdade espiritual e a vacinação obrigatoria*. 2d ed. Rio de Janeiro: Tipografia do Apostolado Pozitivista do Brazil, 1902.

———. *Mais uma vês as greves, a órdem republicana, e a reorganização social*. Rio de Janeiro: Tipografia do Apostolado Pozitivista do Brazil, 1908.

———. *A política republicana e a tirania vacinista*. Rio de Janeiro: Tipografia do Apostolado Pozitivista do Brazil, 1908.

———. *O pozitivismo e a questão social*. Rio de Janeiro: Tipografia do Apostolado Pozitivista do Brazil, 1915.

———. *O regimen republicano e o respeito a dignidade do proletariado, especialmente o culto pela mulher proletaria*. Rio de Janeiro: Tipografia do Apostolado Pozitivista do Brazil, 1917.

———. *A verdadeira política republicana e a incorporação do proletariado na sociedade moderna*. Rio de Janeiro: Tipografia do Apostolado Pozitivista do Brazil, 1908.

Telles, Jover. *O movimento sindical do Brasil*. Rio de Janeiro: Vitória, 1962.

Theophilo, Rodolpho. *História da sêcca do Ceará, 1877–1880.* Rio de Janeiro: Imprensa Ingleza, 1922.

Thompson, E. P. *The Making of the English Working Class.* New York: Pantheon Books, 1964.

Toplin, Robert Brent. *The Abolition of Slavery in Brazil.* New York: Atheneum, 1971.

Torres, João Camillo de Oliveira. *A democracia coronada. Teoria política do império do Brasil.* 2d ed. Petrópolis: Editôra Vozes, 1964.

―――. *Estratificação social no Brasil. Suas origens históricas e suas relações com a organização política do País.* São Paulo: Difusão Européia do Livro, 1965.

―――. *O positivismo no Brasil.* 2d ed. Petrópolis: Editôra Vozes, 1957.

Viana, Antonio. "Manoel Querino." *Revista do Instituto Geográfico e Histórico da Bahia* 54, Part II (1928), 305–16.

Viana, J. M. Gonçalves. *A evolução anarquista em Portugal.* Lisbon: Seara Nova, 1975.

Vieira, Alexandre. *Para a história do sindicalismo em Portugal.* 2d ed. Lisbon: Seara Nova, 1974.

Vieira, Celso. *Defesa social. Estudos juridicos.* Rio de Janeiro: Imprensa Nacional, 1920.

Villela, Annibal Villanova and Wilson Suzigan. *Política do governo e crescimento da economia brasileira, 1889–1945.* Rio de Janeiro: Instituto de Planejamento Economico e Social/Instituto de Pesquisas, 1973.

Vincent, Frank. *Around and About South America: Twenty Months of Quest and Query.* New York: D. Appleton and Company, 1890.

Vita, Washington Luis. *Alberto Sales. Ideólogo da República.* São Paulo: Companhia Editora Nacional, 1965.

Walkowitz, Daniel J. *Worker City, Company Town: Iron and Cotton-Worker Protest in Troy and Cohoes, New York, 1855–84.* Urbana: University of Illinois Press, 1978.

Walsh, Robert. *Notices of Brazil in 1828 and 1829.* 2 vols. London: A. H. Davis, 1830.

Walter, Richard J. "The Socialist Press in Turn-of-the-Century Argentina." *The Americas* 37 (July 1980), 1–24.

Wanderly, João Maurício (Barão de Cotegipe). *Fuga de escravos em Campinas. Discursos pronunciados no Senado.* Rio de Janeiro: Imprensa Nacional, 1887.

Werneck, Américo. *O Brazil. Seu presente e seu futuro.* Petrópolis: Typ. da Gazeta de Petrópolis, 1892.

Williams, Mary Wilhelmine. *Dom Pedro the Magnanimous. Second Emperor of Brazil.* Chapel Hill: University of North Carolina Press, 1937.

Winter, Nevin Otto. *Brazil and Her People of To-Day: An Account of the Customs, Characteristics, Amusements, History and Advancement of the Brazilians, and the Development and Resources of Their Country.* Boston: L. C. Page and Co., 1910.

Wirth, John D. *Minas Gerais in the Brazilian Federation, 1889–1937.* Stanford: Stanford University Press, 1977.

Wirth, John D., and Robert L. Jones, eds. *Manchester and São Paulo: Problems of Rapid Urban Growth.* Stanford: Stanford University Press, 1978.

Woodcock, George. *Anarchism: A History of Libertarian Ideas and Movements.* Cleveland: World Publishing Company, 1962.

Worcester, Donald E. *Brazil: From Colony to World Power.* New York: Charles Scribner's Sons, 1973.

Index